Monarch Notes

QUICK COURSE

Classics of American Literature

Macmillan General Reference
A Prentice Hall Macmillan Company
15 Columbus Circle
New York, NY 10023

An Arco Book
ARCO, Prentice Hall and colophons are registered trademarks of Simon & Schuster, Inc.

ISBN: 0-02-860016-9

Manufactured in the United States of America

10 9 8 7 6 5 4 3 2 1

Contents

Contributing Authors

A FAREWELL TO ARMS by Ernest Hemingway
Lawrence Klibbe
Professor of Romance Languages
New York University

THE AWAKENING by Kate Chopin
Nettie Litwak
Lecturer
New York University

DEATH OF A SALESMAN by Arthur Miller
Joan Thellusson Nourse
Department of English
St. John's University

MY ANTONIA by Willa Cather
Joan T. Nourse
Department of English
Seton Hall University

TO KILL A MOCKINGBIRD by Harper Lee
Donald F. Roden
Department of English
Seton Hall University

THE ADVENTURES OF HUCKLEBERRY FINN by Mark Twain
Alexander J. Butrym
Associate Professor of English
Seton Hall University

THE CATCHER IN THE RYE by J.D. Salinger
Charlotte A. Alexander
Department of English
St. John's University

THE CRUCIBLE by Arthur Miller
Joan Thellusson Nourse
Department of English
St. John's University

THE GRAPES OF WRATH by John Steinbeck
Charlotte Alexander
Department of English
New York University

THE GREAT GATSBY by F. Scott Fitzgerald
Stanley Cooperman
Department of English
Simon Fraser University

THE RED BADGE OF COURAGE by Stephen Crane
Joseph E. Grennen
Chairman, Department of English
Fordham University

THE SCARLET LETTER by Nathaniel Hawthorne
Charles Leavitt
Associate Professor of English
Montclair State University

Ernest Hemingway's A Farewell to Arms

Analysis and Comment

BOOK ONE

ANALYSIS

FREDERIC HENRY: Frederic Henry is the "hero" of the novel and the main character throughout the book. The story is narrated in the first person; with the exception of some use of "we" to denote his identity with other soldiers, the plot is developed from the point of view of "I." However, it must be kept in mind that Frederic Henry is a "Hemingway Hero." There is undoubtedly an autobiographical aspect to the literary creation of Frederic Henry. Hemingway, having volunteered and having been rejected because of an eye injury for the American Army, enlisted in early 1918 as an ambulance driver with the Italian forces. Shortly after his arrival in Milan, Hemingway experienced the hardships of war at first hand: the explosion of an ammunition plant in the city caused many casualties, and the young man of nineteen aided in the disaster. When he was sent to the front, Hemingway insisted upon being close to the trenches; he handed out Red Cross supplies to the Italian soldiers until he was wounded on July 8, 1918. His experiences resemble those of Frederic Henry in the first book of the novel. Hemingway, like his hero, also spent a long period in hospitals, where he underwent twelve operations. He returned to the war, fought with the infantry, and won two decorations from the Italian government. The battle scenes, so strikingly executed in *A Farewell to Arms*, are perhaps the best elements of the book; Hemingway is certainly writing from a sure and painfully gained knowledge.

FREDERIC HENRY AS AN IDEAL: It is impossible to separate the fictional from the factual in the literary analysis of Frederic Henry. He not only represents the young Hemingway but probably represents the youth of America who searched for idealism and objectives in a world torn by war.

FREDERIC HENRY'S SEARCH: The young man is searching for values in the war.

FREDERIC HENRY'S SPEECH: The style of speech of Frederic Henry is noteworthy. Indeed, the style of the entire novel is terse and economical, and the critics have had a field day praising and condemning the stylistic efforts of Ernest Hemingway. When Hemingway was awarded the Nobel Prize for literature in 1954, the citation called attention to his "forceful and style-making mastery of the art of modern narration." Frederic Henry is never unmasked in descriptions and this omission of physical and personality traits is one of the contributions of the Hemingway style. The characters are indicated through the dialogue; they are never shown in full light, only in shades and shadows. It is the responsibility of the reader to uncover the significance of the actors on the Hemingway stage. In the first book of *A Farewell to Arms*, Frederic Henry is characterized by an almost monosyllabic tone. Even in the crucial meeting with the priest in the hospital, he talks in short, concise sentences. Little is known of Henry's family; it is conveyed in Book One that he is estranged in some way from them by mention of the sight draft for money which will be honored by the family. Some critics have argued that the tone of the novel is set within the first book by Henry's laconic style: he has abandoned abstractions and noble phrases because of disillusionment with the war. Fearful of rhetorical devices which have served to lure youth into fighting for empty phrases, Henry only speaks with words he can clearly understand. He does not want to confuse or to be confused.

Henry's relations with Rinaldi are paralleled by his contact with the priest. The symbolism of these friendships has been established and is quite evident. The priest represents the effort to maintain religious and spiritual values in a world at war; he has hopes of instilling some of these attitudes in his companions, particularly Frederic Henry. Rinaldi is at the opposite end of the scale of values and it is no coincidence that Hemingway notes that the Italian officer is a surgeon. The contrast between priest and surgeon, religion and science, believer and nonbeliever, is very obvious. Despite a surface vulgarity, Rinaldi, like the priest, is fundamentally a good man, and Henry is cognizant of this goodness. Hemingway undoubtedly placed these chapters one after the other, ten and eleven, the visits of Rinaldi and the priest, in order to compare and contrast the two viewpoints. At the conclusion of the interviews, Frederic Henry is torn between the realistic, crude world of Rinaldi and the glimmer of hope that the priest expresses.

CATHERINE BARKLEY: Catherine Barkley plays a comparatively minor role in Book One of *A Farewell to Arms*. The few encounters with Catherine Barkley in Book One have not led to the creation of a strong character whose will struggles for expression. Edmund Wilson has pointed out Hemingway's tendency to portray obedient females who easily accept male domination, and Carlos Baker finds that the heroines, although stable, are abstract.

HELEN FERGUSON: Helen Ferguson, a minor character throughout the novel, is introduced briefly in this first book. In a sense, she might be considered the counterpart of Rinaldi although the latter has made an important contribution to the plot development so far.

COMMENT

In the first book of *A Farewell to Arms*, the war is the principal theme. There are the descriptions of the landscape, the towns, and the troops in general. In this first part, there are no lengthy descriptions of battles and military strategy because Hemingway concentrates on the very personal reactions of the hero to the campaigns. Thus, the war is depicted in terms of the comfort and suffering of Frederic Henry. This is not a selfish view, however, because the American lieutenant is attentive to the feelings of the common soldiers. He suffers along with them and Hemingway creates the total impression of war-weariness.

WAR: The war is nothing glorious; in fact, boredom and monotony are characteristics of the Italian front noted in the first twelve chapters. Until Chapter IX, the war is ever-present but not immediate. In Chapter IX, significantly a very long chapter, the meaning of war is brought sharply into focus. It is one of the major episodes of the novel and illustrates why the book is primarily a war book and not a love story. Frederic Henry no longer remains a somewhat detached observer; he is now intimately involved. Thus, the war, in Book One of *A Farewell to Arms*, is studied from an angle of detachment so that it is omnipresent but deadening in its stillness; from the direct participation of the hero in front-line action and the consequent wounding; and finally from the reaction to fighting, in the vision of the wounded and dying in hospitals. Hemingway has also prepared with outstanding mastery the deeper insight into war he will portray later in the novel. In short, the war has no glorious, heroic, and idealistic traits; the war is a cruel, incomprehensible, and disillusioning way of life.

LOVE: The love story is merely introduced in the first twelve chapters; the war so overpowers all other considerations that meetings between lovers are brief, subject to cancellation, and generally unplanned.

SYMBOLISM: One of the most frequent symbols in the novel is that of the mountain and the plain; the mountain signifies the good and the plain the bad, according to Carlos Baker. This critic states: "*A Farewell to Arms* is entirely and even exclusively acceptable as a naturalistic narrative of what happened. To read it only as such, however, is to miss the controlling symbolism: the deep central antithesis between the image of life and home (the mountain) and the image of war and death (the plain)."

During the Fascist regime of Benito Mussolini, the book was banned in Italy, not for any slights against the Italian people, but because the Fascists believed that the novel instilled pacifist feelings in the populace. It depicted military defeats instead of victories.

In Book One, the reader must keep his attention centered on the development of the hero. One critic, Earl Rovit, has affirmed that "the total effect of the story depends on the degree of Frederic's self-realization or acceptance of the implicit meanings in his experience; for, as we have seen with Hemingway, the identity of a man is measured by the progressive recognitions of his meaningful experience." In his search for manhood in the twelve chapters, Henry has come into contact with the cynical realism of Rinaldi, the subtle idealism of the priest, and the personal sufferings of war. Sex is an apparent palliative in this quest for maturity; love is the goal which the priest advocated. Thus, in Book One, the major characters have been presented, and the love affair, overshadowed by the war as the dominant motif, has entered to disrupt the existence of Frederic Henry and Catherine Barkley.

BOOK TWO

ANALYSIS

FREDERIC HENRY: Frederic Henry in the second book of *A Farewell to Arms* undergoes an important change in his personality and attitude toward life. Hemingway has received recognition in recent criticism as a very careful craftsman. It is said that he rewrote the book's conclusion seventeen times. Therefore, the differences and changes in Frederic Henry's character should be carefully noticed in the initial and final two chapters of Book Two.

CATHERINE BARKLEY: Catherine Barkley undergoes no fundamental change in character in the second book of *A Farewell to Arms*. Her prosaic personality has been severely ridiculed by critics, such as Edmund Wilson and Malcolm Cowley. Stewart Sanderson writes that "she is too highly idealised, the romantic vision of an adolescent's erotic daydream; the relationship between her and Frederic is altogether too smooth and perfect to be true." Although this critic modifies his judgment later in the text, the critique is quite typical of unacceptance of the Hemingway heroine. Nevertheless, Catherine Barkley forms an interesting comparison and contrast with the hero. It must be kept in mind, also, that Hemingway has centered his novelistic art on the development of Frederic Henry and not Catherine Barkley. He dominates each of the five books of the novel; he is in the vortex of the action during Book Three, and Catherine plays no part in the third section.

Keeping in mind, therefore, this intention of Hemingway and his known preoccupation with the male rather than the female protagonists of his novels, the balancing of Frederic and Catherine seems to be skillfully executed. Frederic is realistic, and Catherine is romantic. In many ways, the girl is in love with love itself.

CATHERINE'S PREGNANCY: In Chapter XIX, the symbol of the rain is used to convey her fright; she is unsure of herself in rainy, damp, and windy weather. Thus, when Hemingway notes the condition of the day, there is an indirect indication of Catherine's mood.

MINOR CHARACTERS: The three doctors, who are incompetent and dour individuals, contrast sharply with Valentini, the lively, skillful surgeon, Hemingway is probably indicating, as in other works, that those who are most human, sincere, and kind are also the most reliable in providing care and treatment.

Mr. and Mrs. Meyers, Ettore Moretti, and Ralph Simmons, as well as various other persons, some of them nameless, provide a light and frivolous side to the serious love story developed in Book Two. They are quite removed from the war and its consequences, except for Moretti, the braggart. These characters have not really lived and experienced; therefore, they contribute nothing to the unfolding of the personalities of Frederic and Catherine. It is a rather common device in Hemingway to introduce characters who are extraneous to the plot and characters; in other words, not every person must be judged as vital to a comprehension of the main drift of the story.

COMMENT

Hemingway has now inverted his themes in terms of importance and emphasis. In Book One, the war overshadowed the nascent love affair between Frederic and Catherine; in Book Two, the love story comes to the fore, and the war is never directly inserted in the text. The war is restricted to the scenes in the military hospital, comments on military progress, and the inevitable meetings with combat personnel, such as Moretti and the nameless British major. However, the war is an omnipresent motif as the summer yields to the fall and Frederic's convalescence is completed. It is part of Hemingway's technique to have the lovers omit from their frequent conversations mention of this separating force; it is also forceful technique for Hemingway to conclude this part with a scene on the train, so characteristic of the episodes in the first book. Hemingway thereby indicates clearly that the war is returning in the coming book to occupy the reader's main attention.

LOVE: Thus, the theme of love reaches its apex in Book Two. Both characters find that love unites against the blows of life, and the two, even at the departure, are prepared to accept the consequences of their commitment to this ideal. Slowly, as the second part comes to its conclusion, disaster looms more immediate. Part of the great interest in the developing love motif is in the dialogue between the two; there are no descriptions of the physical action and no psychological probing. The form is made highly dramatic by this use of dialogue; in fact, *A Farewell to Arms* was adapted to theatrical presentation in the early nineteen thirties. It is the only novel of Hemingway's to find its way to the stage.

STYLE: The conversations between the lovers are generally indicated by the concise, simple language usual in Hemingway and noted in Book One. Neither of the two speaks at great length; often one line represents the speech of each person. The language is indicative of the speaker and his attendant personality; for example, Catherine uses the word "darling" very frequently throughout the chapters. The language of Frederic tends to be less lively and exuberant than that of Catherine; it may also be the reflection of the stoic attitude which Hemingway gives his hero. Consequently, there are really no tensions built up between the lovers; indeed, this aspect is one of the criticisms of Edmund Wilson, Malcolm

Cowley, and others. Hemingway, these critics claim, never gets the relationship off the ground; the lovers are still living an idyllic existence and do not engage in the daily exchange of agreement and disagreement. Even in their agony and tragedy, brought to the surface as Book Two unfolds, they really do not partake in a meaningful dialogue.

SYMBOLISM: Hemingway continues to employ a repeated symbolism as in the first book. In this part, Hemingway employs the recurrent contrast of summer and autumn, and the rain. The love affair blossoms during the fateful summer in Milan, and the author inaugurates Chapter XVIII, the beginning of the idyll, with the statement that they had a wonderful experience during that summer. Since it is the summer, and so many of these enjoyable times take place out-of-doors, the weather is in favor of the lovers' trysts. Occasionally, the rain interferes with their pleasures, and it is significant that Catherine fears the rain. As the summer turns to fall and the rains increase, the symbolic use of the seasons and the weather is joined together. Then, the rain will take on added meaning: it will become synonymous with death, an inevitable thought as Frederic's leave expires.

Finally, in the last two chapters, there is an able employment of the symbols: the autumn with rainy weather becomes associated with the sadness of parting, the impending doom, and death. Also, illicit love is indicated by rain, and Catherine dwells upon this thought when rainy weather intervenes. She has more preoccupations about their immoral state in bad weather; in good weather, she believes that they are already sanctified except for the formal church bonds. In short, the rain denotes evil, war, and sin; whenever Hemingway wishes to convey these impressions, he conveniently gives the reader a spell of foul weather. Carlos Baker, who has studied in great detail the symbolism of Hemingway, insists upon this interpretation, but it is important to bear in mind that there is opposition to this opinion. E. M. Halliday is emphatic in opposing this viewpoint; he believes that Baker has overstated his case. He is pointed in his rebuttal: "What all this illustrates, it seems to me, is that Mr. Baker has allowed an excellent insight into Hemingway's imagery and acute sense of natural metonymy to turn into an interesting but greatly overelaborated critical gimmick." However, Carlos Baker is just as insistent on the importance of symbolism in *A Farewell to Arms*: "Once the reader has become aware of what Hemingway is doing in those parts of his work which lie below the surface, he is likely to find symbols operating elsewhere." These divergent points of view are important to remember and, during the reading of the novel, the reader should try to determine for himself the extent of symbolism in the book. The fact that two critics can disagree so visibly on this matter illustrates that *A Farewell to Arms* bears a very careful study.

BOOK THREE

ANALYSIS

THE RETREAT: Hemingway has certainly not exaggerated the extent of the Italian collapse, and the defeat at Caporetto represents a terrible military disaster for Italy and for the Allies.

Hemingway never states bluntly how Frederic Henry is changing; the variations in his hero come about subtly but surely. In other words, Hemingway indulges in understatement which allows the reader to grasp the meaning through the simple and repeated vocabulary. Harry Levin, analyzing Hemingway's style, concludes that "it remained for Hemingway—along with Anderson—to identify himself wholly with the lives he wrote about, not so much entering into them as allowing them to take possession of him, and accepting—along with their sensibilities and perceptions—the limitations of their point of view and the limits of their range of expression." Thus,

Hemingway identifies himself completely with the characters, particularly the "Hemingway Hero," so that the reader in turn accepts easily that he is closely associated with the adventures and trials of the protagonist. Harry Levin continues in his deductions about Hemingway's methods that "we need make no word-count to be sure that his literary vocabulary, with foreign and technical exceptions, consists of relatively few and short words. The corollary, of course, is that every word sees a good deal of hard use. Furthermore, his syntax is informal to the point of fluidity, simplifying as far as possible the already simple system of English inflections." Part of the ease of identification is consequently effected by this simple and repetitious use of words.

FREDERIC'S DESERTION: Malcolm Cowley asserts that "when Frederic Henry dives into the flooded Tagliamento, in *A Farewell to Arms*, he is performing a rite of baptism that prepares us for the new life he is about to lead as a deserter from the Italian army." Carlos Baker finds again the familiar symbol of the rain, this time in the form of water, as indicative of a change in Frederic's character. It is virtually impossible to say what Hemingway intended: whether or not a deliberately symbolic act is depicted or whether it happens as part of the realistic frame in which a river is Frederic's best means of escape.

HIS ANGUISH: In the two brief chapters concluding Book Three, there is one of the few extensive passages of stream-of-consciousness and lack of dialogue to convey mental impressions and psychological attitudes.

ESCAPE: In this concluding idea of Book Three, much of the Hemingway credo is to be understood. The decision of Frederic Henry has been built up gradually and logically but it has not been thought through to its full implications. Earl Rovit deduces that Hemingway "leaves the significant facts in the narrative structure; they are there because the narrator Frederic has abstracted them from the actor Frederic's experience. And these tell us that Frederic does not return to the Rinaldi position where there is nothing but emptiness and dryness underneath; nor does he embrace the faith of the priest. He accepts the reality of the naturalistic world in which death is a fact every bit as real as sex; but he also accepts the reality of a love which he helped to create, and this fact is also as real as death." The significance of the title, *A Farewell to Arms*, is probably due to this abandonment of a military career by Frederic Henry. Certainly in this section, he has passed through several interesting facets of spiritual growth and development.

OTHER CHARACTERS: In Book Three, Frederic Henry is the only character sketched in detail. Catherine Barkley, the heroine, does not appear at all. Rinaldi adds little or nothing to the portrait painted previously.

The various soldiers and civilians with whom the hero comes into contact are all caught up in a terrible tragedy. Good or bad, all of them struggle in various ways to save their lives. The main problem which all the minor characters face is that of immediate death. Even the fear of death, as observed when the word "Germans" is sounded, causes them to react abnormally. Hemingway is writing sharply and vividly of the little men and women enmeshed in the vortex of senseless and cruel war. In fact, most of the time Hemingway does not even bother to record the names of the soldiers. Piani, Aymo, Bonello are named because they are the ambulance helpers, and Henry has to address them separately. Otherwise, there is a vast anonymity cast over the characters in the great retreat from Caporetto; this anonymity adds to the pathos of these individuals caught in a net not of their own making.

COMMENT

The outstanding theme in *A Farewell to Arms* is war, which is brought to the fore in this third book. For that reason, it has been compared to Leo Tolstoy's *War and Peace*, particularly for the resemblance to the retreat from Moscow of Napoleon in 1812. The novel has achieved status with Erich Maria Remarque's *All Quiet on the Western Front* as one of the most important books dealing with World War I. Although the love story overshadows the war motif in the total framework of the novel, Book Three is devoted exclusively to the martial aspect. In fact, much of the fame Hemingway gained from this book is due to his masterly and accurate rendition of the sights and sounds of battle. Stewart Sanderson writes: "Hemingway's highly developed interest in military matters, which brought him back to Spain in the Civil War and to France at the head of an irregular fighting unit in the second World War, is mirrored in the accounts of the fighting on the Italian front. The descriptions of conditions in the lines, the troops and equipment and field dressing stations, are perfectly realised reportage, presented with a highly selective eye for telling detail. But there are other aspects of his writing about the war which concern us here. The emotional reactions to the facts of trench warfare, the attacks and retreats, the shelling and the casualties, the gap between the words and the realities of courage and victory and honor, are carefully analyzed and re-created." However, Hemingway never goes into the strategy of the overall campaign; there is no indication of the exact details of the Caporetto retreat in precise military terms. The reader is never told exactly when the attack started; at what sector the offensive was launched; and the effect produced for the Allied or Italian cause. The author does, nevertheless, give the small items of the debacle as it affected Frederic Henry and the common soldiers caught in the campaign. This emphasis upon the results of war as it involves the individual and the civilian is certainly one of the noteworthy contributions of Hemingway in *A Farewell to Arms*. In this regard, he has made the war seem very personal; the reader comprehends the plight of the soldier, who might very well be himself, in the detailed and selective manner of Hemingway. By choosing to depict not a victorious episode but a military defeat, and especially a disastrous retreat, Hemingway has shown the utter folly of war and the breakdown of men under its strains. The lieutenant-colonel, who is arrested and shot by the military police at the same time Frederic is arrested, is not a coward. In one vignette, Hemingway has summed up his doctrine of the "Hemingway Hero," that stoical, fundamentally courageous individual, as well as the idea of war's absurdity.

SYMBOLISM: Also in Book Three, the weather is emphasized as part and parcel of the elements acting against Frederic Henry. Although it is perilous to explore how deeply symbolic all this mention of "rain" and "water" is, it is probably no coincidence that Hemingway has employed this technical device in the Third Book.

THE "HEMINGWAY HERO": Finally, one must keep in mind how the "Hemingway Hero" is formed by adversity and hardship, although there is the inevitable breaking point. A critic said that "for Hemingway life is inseparable from death and is a fight at close quarters in which his heroes overcome not only the fear of death but the fear of life's intricacies and the disintegration threatening the individual. It is real life, work, and creative power that give him strength for the fight." This critic, Ivan Kashkeen, finds in this idea the pattern of being "alive in the midst of death," not only for the heroes of Hemingway but also in the life of the author.

BOOK FOUR

ANALYSIS

FREDERIC HENRY: Frederic Henry accepts his course of action in this book; there are no radical changes in his mood and personality but rather a deepening sense of obligation and appreciation. Thus, Earl Rovit writes: "in Book Four, Frederic's course is confirmed. Moved by circumstances beyond his control, he accepts the consequences of his forced actions, among them the obligations of *caring* for Catherine in the priest's sense."

FREDERIC'S STOICISM: Malcolm Cowley analyzes this power of Hemingway to evoke the hidden depths of man: "And it is this instinct for legends, for sacraments, for rituals, for symbols appealing to buried hopes and fears, that helps to explain the power of Hemingway's work and his vast superiority over his imitators. The imitators have learned all his mannerisms as a writer, and in some cases they can tell a story even better than Hemingway himself; but they tell only the story; they communicate with the reader on only one level of experience." Thus, there is a more profound aspect to Hemingway's work than the surface simplicity of vocabulary and syntax would indicate; Hemingway is really digging deep into the subconscious of his characters, and Cowley concludes that ". . . most of us are also primitive in a sense, for all the machinery that surrounds our lives. We have our private rituals, our little superstitions, our symbols and fears and nightmares; and Hemingway reminds us unconsciously of the hidden worlds in which we live."

Ray West dissects him in this manner: "Frederic is the modern hero, lost between two worlds, the world of tradition and certainty which he cannot wholly relinquish, and the exciting but uncertain world of the twentieth century, where you only occasionally find something substantial to look at to make everything stop whirling, where you live for the moment, giving yourself up to sensations, for it is through the senses that you discover truth."

SWITZERLAND: Logically again, the hero of Hemingway expresses the fact that he is a man of action by his mammoth breakfast; the satisfaction of hunger and thirst is the basic clue to the contentment of the hero. It is interesting to notice how often the hero will drink and enjoy liquor as a sign of his joy of life. Carlos Baker sees in this exhilarated mood of Frederic Henry in Switzerland the resurgent imagery of the mountains as a source of strength and contentment. E. M. Halliday is less insistent on this specific interpretation and generalizes that ". . . it is undeniable that in the midst of the darkling plain of struggle and flight which was the war in Italy, Frederic Henry thinks of the Swiss Alps as a neutral refuge of peace and happiness—surely millions must have lifted their eyes to those mountains with like thoughts during both World Wars."

CATHERINE BARKLEY'S LOVE: Catherine Barkley, reappearing in Chapter XXXIV after a long absence, has suffered no change and has really not altered in her surrender of personality to her lover. This is why various critics insist upon the basic weakness of presentation of the heroines in Hemingway. Prior to the Caporetto fiasco, Catherine, always subordinated to interest in Frederic, nevertheless needed to be known and analyzed. Now there is no change; in fact, she no longer expresses her own evident worries and stresses to Frederic. It is doubtful whether the complete disavowal of individuality on Catherine's part can be fully justified. Leslie Fieldler has gone to the extreme of forecasting a dire and bleak future for the union between Frederic and Catherine: "Had Catherine lived, she could only have turned into a bitch; for this is the fate in Hemingway's imagination of all Anglo-Saxon women."

Hemingway has sketched a very romantic heroine who is an ideal mate; unfortunately, it is difficult to accept this standard as a realistic portrayal in view of the difficulties, especially the pregnancy, which Catherine is undergoing in Book Four.

COUNT GREFFI: Count Greffi is the most interesting of the minor characters and his role resembles somewhat that of Rinaldi and the priest. His air of dignity symbolizes an age which has ended with the outbreak of World War I. Of more importance, he provides justification to Frederic of the religious nature of love. It is interesting that Hemingway has selected a member of the nobility as one of the most sympathetic and important minor characters in the novel; usually, the author concentrates his sympathies with the common folk and depicts unfavorably those individuals in higher social classes.

MINOR CHARACTERS: All the Italian common people represent the deep-seated resentment and bitterness against the war among the Italians. The impression is conveyed that these poor and humble people have been deceived by the politicians and the generals —and are beginning to be aware of their plight. In Book Four, none of these individuals is "bad" in the Hemingway code; they are all "good" persons who are frantically struggling to survive the holocaust. Certainly no charge of anti-Italian bias can be leveled at Hemingway in *A Farewell to Arms*, as was attempted by some nationalistic critics. Mario Praz of the University of Rome has traced the literary fortune and influence of Hemingway in Italy. He notes in his study that Hemingway was known, respected, and imitated despite the Fascist ban on his works for almost twenty years. On the contrary, Hemingway feels sorry for the tragic situation of the people trapped in a bad strategic gamble.

The same comment may apply in part to Hemingway's depiction of the Swiss toward the end of Book Four. He is following the commonly accepted cliché that the Swiss are practical people who have preserved their way of life in the midst of war by providing comfortable service. The fact that the Swiss lieutenant becomes more amiable when he learns of their finances and that the other officials suggest good hotels and pleasant accommodations is only a humorous example of Hemingway's art. The whole peaceful and optimistic air of the last few pages of Book Four contrasts acutely with the tragic qualities of the residence in Italy.

COMMENT

ITALIAN INTERLUDE: Book Four may be conveniently divided into two sections, the residence in Italy which contrasts with the military side in Book Two, and the initiation of the Swiss stay. The trip by boat in rather uncertain weather connects the two distinctly different interludes and provides some suspense for the reader. Hemingway demonstrates again that he has carefully plotted his novel and has just as skillfully balanced the impressions he transmits to his reading audience.

Another justification may be sought in Henry's character; he is "caring" at times, still "not caring" at others. Thus, Earl Rovit writes that ". . . although Henry represses and ignores it for the most part, he does possess a strong potential 'caringness.' There are times, as we see in the excerpt, when he cares a good deal; and everything becomes 'sharp and hard and clear.'" The last few pages of the section are certainly the happiest pages for the lovers, and if Hemingway has wanted to give a thoroughly romantic conclusion to the story, he could have ended *A Farewell to Arms* with the last line of Part Four to the effect that Catherine and Henry "followed the boy with the bags into the hotel." Of course, this would have destroyed much of the effect built up throughout the four books about the power of life and death and the whole brooding backdrop of the war.

FLIGHT FROM ITALY: Hemingway employs again the now familiar symbol of the rain: he writes in the very beginning of Chapter XXXVII, the escape to Switzerland, that the rain came only in brief intervals. In other words, the trip will evidently be successful with moments of peril. At Stresa, the rain comes on occasion; when it does, Henry becomes pensive. In Chapter XXXIV, he has one of the most reflective moods in the book during an especially rainy night when they are alone in the hotel. When the sunshine appears the next day, both Catherine and he are in a gay state of mind. The only time when the two believe that they have overcome the challenge of the world, the stepping ashore in Switzerland, the rain is considered to be "cheerful" and "fine." If the rain represents the "world" in Hemingway's and Frederic's vision, or the dark forces of fate as Carlos Baker declares, then the main characters have apparently triumphed, or believe they have. Of course, if victory were assured, the novel would have been terminated at this point of near-perfect happiness.

BOOK FIVE

ANALYSIS

FREDERIC HENRY: He runs head-on to his destiny in Book Five of *A Farewell to Arms*. He must now live in the full glare of his shattering experience, and Earl Rovit writes: "Frederic Henry establishes a connection with the world in his love affair with Catherine and, in so doing, becomes humanly alive. That she dies does not negate his experience; it pushes him into the position of the Major who also had trouble in resigning himself." In Book Five, Henry basically suffers no character transformation; he has been formed in the first three books. In fact, Book Four only intensified these traits, which were formulated especially by the great retreat of Caporetto. Agony and trial come when ideals are brought to bear on specific problems. In this case, death is the ordeal to be mastered, and the theme of death is intrinsic in this novel. Death is likewise one of the dominant preoccupations in the whole opus of Ernest Hemingway.

APPARENT PEACE: There is a brilliant reversal of emphasis in Book Five because the reader has been led to fear the death of Frederic Henry in the war as the danger. The hero is plunged into the abyss of something perhaps worse: the death of Catherine, without whom he cannot have peace of mind.

He seeks no other company, no friends or social acquaintances; indeed, he cannot bear to be alone for too long. The reader is led to believe that Frederic Henry will survive and will endure; he has become a man of sensation, a man of action. He will wear the scars of his sufferings; he will be hardened and cynical; and he will expect death in any form and on any occasion to destroy his illusory security.

FREDERIC AS THE TOTAL "HEMINGWAY HERO": Frederic Henry comes to the full height of a "Hemingway Hero" in the final scenes at the hospital. He stoically challenges fate and loses, but he really does not break down. His visits to the hospital are interspersed with jaunts to the nearby cafe to eat. Some may interpret this as undue hardness and say that a man in such circumstances, especially as Catherine's condition deteriorates, would never be able to eat and drink at such a time. However, this is exactly the stance of the "Hemingway Hero." Frederic must be outwardly calm; he must accept the struggle with fate's offerings.

In Chapter XLI, the moment of truth arrives for Frederic; in a rather long paragraph of stream-of-consciousness, the possibilities of life or death are brought to the surface in a series of short sentences, often in the form of questions. Then, the import of his struggle with life is fully apparent: life is a "trap" which is baited with good fortune and some happiness until the fatal step into death.

He cannot be victorious in his journey through life but Frederic is not ready to die. He walks with burdens of grief and pessimism in the knowledge that these things signify the responsibility of being a man. Frederic Henry, however, is not only a man in his complete maturity; he is likewise the development of the "Hemingway Hero."

CATHERINE BARKLEY: Catherine Barkley comes full circle in Book Five as does her lover. She always wanted to submerge her personality into his, and she proves her mettle in the death scene. Although criticism has been leveled at her weakness as a character, her death shows her as exemplifying the stoical doctrine of Hemingway. Unfortunately, these characteristics were not revealed in any depth previously.

CATHERINE'S DEVOTION AND SACRIFICE: One may consider that the personality of Catherine remains static prior to her entry into the hospital; in the last, long chapter, she exposes her fears and her reactions, which parallel those of her lover. In other words, she has sacrificed her own feelings for his tranquility; at her moment of crisis, she shows that her personality has not only been surrendered for his sake but that her ideals are the same as his. Both have the same attitude toward life. Like Frederic, Catherine is physically brave, and this aspect is a fundamental one for the characters of Hemingway. Physical valor is the intrinsic and most evident quality of the "good" person in Hemingway's credo.

It is important to observe how closely Catherine's philosophy approximates that of Henry in the last chapter. Of course, she is likewise the romantic heroine in the tragic Chapter XLI; the lenghty description of her agony and death is typical of the romantic tradition of the past. Her philosophy demonstrates Hemingway's departure from the melodramatic; the author has inserted a profound attitude toward life and death in his heroine which rescues Catherine from some of the adverse criticism in the other books of the novel.

MINOR CHARACTERS: The minor characters are completely subordinated to the tragedy which occurs to Frederic and Catherine. In fact, most of the characters are not even named; only the Guttingens receive that recognition. There is a cloud of anonymity cast over all the persons in Book Five; in these moments, no one can provide help or a solution for the lovers. The reactions of the minor, nameless characters in Book Five reflect Hemingway's doctrine that outside society is uninterested in the struggles of others. For the author, this attitude is not of necessity bad; on the contrary, it emphasizes the aloneness of the hero and the solitary effort to achieve identity. In the confrontation with life and death, or the world, solitariness is the desired and inevitable attribute. For that reason, the Swiss, who appear in the last book, are "good"; they reflect what the "Hemingway Hero" must endure.

COMMENT

THE HEMINGWAY CREDO: Book Five comes as an anticlimax to the novel, and it is evident that if Hemingway had wished a happy ending to his story, he would have concluded after Book Four. The last part had to be brief and dramatic. At the same time, Hemingway comes to full strength in the creation of his two characters and his philosophy. Ray West views the total effect as ironical and masterful: "His life with Catherine in Switzerland and the life which they anticipated after the war were relatively devoid of conflict. Catherine and Frederic had said farewell to the life of action and struggle, but ironically their greatest test—the attempt to save the life of Catherine—came at the very moment when they seemed to have achieved a successful escape." At the beginning, the happiness of the couple continues to be on the ascendancy; and the mountains and snow of Montreux reflect this optimistic feeling. Although E. M. Halliday cannot accept Carlos Baker's insistence upon the mountains as representing goodness and joy, and his critique is especially insistent on questioning if the mountains around Caporetto could ever be so interpreted, he admits that Hemingway seems to hint at this meaning here. For example, Montreux, in the whiteness of the snow and the high mountains, is the apex of the lovers' idyll. Even the pregnancy is going well, and Catherine is exuberantly gay and optimistic. Lausanne represents a descent in all ways: the move is made because the snow is turning to rain, the mountains are yielding to the plain, symbol of trouble and unhappiness, and the hospital is located in Lausanne. The symbolism is clearest at this point: the next step down in the lovers' fortunes comes when the rains increase, spring arrives, and the hospital residence begins.

Thus, there are three distinct parts in Book Five: each denotes a diminution of happiness for Frederic and Catherine. The scenes in Montreux and Lausanne, not including the hospital episode, are high tides in the love affair, although there are signs of trouble already in the residence in Lausanne. The third part is contained within the entire last chapter; this last chapter also is exactly half the length of Book Five. It has already been mentioned that Hemingway labored long and hard in the composition of *A Farewell to Arms*; recent criticism has focused its attention on the skill which he devoted to its composition. Stewart

Sanderson praises "the closely-knit texture of the novel, and the complex structural organization which underlies and sustains its surface." Carlos Baker always calls attention to the technical arrangement of the novel and stresses that Hemingway planned his procedures with the utmost care. It is therefore interesting to bear in mind how he ordered the scenery and divisions of each book to effect the total impression.

UNITY OF STRUCTURE: Sanderson makes the point, which has been noted by other critics, that the tragedy has the artistic construction of a drama in five acts. The third act is the longest and most vital element in the determination of the play's outcome; the Caporetto episode is the key to Frederic's philosophical orientation. The war descriptions are certainly unforgettable. The first two books depict the conflict in the character of Frederic Henry; and the last two books show the apparent victory and then swift, inevitable defeat of the protagonist. The Hemingway preoccupation with death and tragedy is brought out in Book Five; the emotion is intense; and the dramatic quality is high.

SYMBOLISM OF TITLE: The meaning of the title is completely illustrated in Book Five. On the first level of meaning, *A Farewell to Arms* refers to the abandonment of war on Frederic Henry's part; this interpretation is very clear in the revulsion toward the conflict which the hero expressed in the first book. His reactions were intensified in the second book and reach the point of outburst in his desertion at the end of the third part. The war really plays no role in Book Five. The escape from Italy to Switzerland provides the excitement of Book Four but even this episode is in the background. The love affair returns to the front of the stage in the last two books. Therefore a second critical judgment has been made about the significance of the novel's title which only can be fully understood in Book Five, and particularly, in Catherine's death. Frederic in the last lines of the novel states that his farewell to the dead Catherine was like a farewell to a statue. "Arms" may logically be assumed to refer to feminine arms, that is to say, the love of Catherine. She makes the plea to Frederic on the previous page not to share their love with other women he will have in his life. Both themes, war and love, have been the two forces around which Hemingway has constructed his novel. The war would seem to be the main thread, although critics differ on the degree of stress, and certainly the first thought that comes to mind in the word "arms" is the martial reference. In addition, the second interpretation needs the reading of Book Five.

There is an equally interesting third interpretation of the title. One cannot make an armistice or a separate truce with life as Frederic Henry attempted to do with the war. His commitment must be total, and he must pay the price for winning manhood. According to critics such as Ray West, Earl Rovit, and others, the meaning of *A Farewell to Arms* is more profound and more symbolical than suspected when the novel was published in 1929. Not the war and not love but the development and passage of the "Hemingway Hero" through life and its perils are the prime elements of this book. Therefore, critical attention must follow the path of Frederic Henry as the axis around which flow the other currents of war and love. If one accepts this emphasis upon the central character rather than the themes of war and love, then the title refers ironically to the hero's tragic condition. As in the army, he has made a pact with his destiny and he cannot elude it. Only death will be the farewell that the hero can render to the human condition.

"ARMS" AS A THREE-FOLD IMAGE: Regardless of these three interpretations, and the three may be equally valid in lieu of any definitive statement from Hemingway, Book Five is highly important for the meaning of the novel. One cannot justify any statement that Hemingway composed the fifth book only for emotional catharsis or melodramatic effect. The novel is initiated on a tragic note, in the deaths of the soldiers, and in the threat of annihilation which hangs over humanity. In the last book, Hemingway has brought about a shift in the immediacy of death from the impersonal and gigantic to the personal and minute. The author wrote of war in general in the first chapter of the novel; he makes the wry and ironic observation that only seven thousand soldiers died of the cholera during the winter. By the end of Book Five, the reader is engrossed in the intimacy of Catherine's death and Frederic's loss, which has nothing to do with the outcome of the war and the terrible losses being suffered at that very time in the 1918 spring offensive of the Germans. The hero makes a passing reference to this fact shortly before Catherine enters the hospital. Thus, Hemingway has brought life and death into clear and certain terms; he may even mean in Book Five that there is a farewell to war as the critical motif in man's anxieties and agonies. Harry Levin in his study of Hemingway's stylistic achievements praises this power to extract meaning from words: "This may help to explain why it suggests a more optimistic approach to language than the presumption that since phrases can be snares and delusions, their scope should be limited to straight denotation. The powers of connotation, the possibilities of oblique suggestion and semantic association, are actually grasped by Hemingway as well as any writer of our time. Thus he can retrospectively endow a cheap and faded term like "mashing" with all the promise and poetry of awakening manhood."

Character and Concept Analyses

FREDERIC HENRY: To the positive force of love is added the growing preoccupation about the meaning of life. Thus, in the first book, Frederic passes from an introduction to love to the blossoming of the emotion in Book Two. In Book One, he was still blissfully unaware of the meaning of being a man; in Book Two, he begins to glimpse maturity because of the engagement with love. Therefore, one can trace surely and logically the trajectory of Frederic Henry's course in the first two books: the orbits of love and manhood are closely bound together.

HEMINGWAY HERO: He is also beginning to develop more completely and more deeply the characteristics of the "Hemingway Hero." At the introduction of Frederic Henry into the story in Book One and at the insights already given in these early chapters, the model is established in some degree. Frederic Henry is laconic, speaks briefly, uses simple vocabulary and syntax, and is unswayed by grandiose claims to his better nature. In this connection, the interviews with Rinaldi and the priest are the most revelatory of Frederic Henry's inner moods and intrinsic personality. If his thoughts ever come to the surface up to this point, the evidences can probably be found in these incidents. With Catherine, the hero begins to reveal his true dimensions. There exists in his soul a dichotomy between the desire for identity and the rootless nothingness he has met; and Ray West writes: "at the beginning Frederic wavers between reason and sensibility, between formal religion and 'true' Christianity, between the empty forms of love and true love. He has been thrust into a world of violent action in which choice is eventually to become necessary. . . . The Hemingway hero is, theoretically, passive, because he is allied to nature through his unreason, but his particular dilemma usually has all the appearances of active seeking." By the time Frederic returns to the war front at the end of Book Two, he has been faced with this new addition to his existence. He has still not formulated the doctrine of the "Hemingway Hero." Book Three is the baptism of fire of this "Hemingway Hero," and

Frederic's preoccupations and changed moods are sharply pinpointed in his contacts with his comrades, Rinaldi and the priest. It is important to trace exactly and surely why the hero is altered and what is the concrete outline of his personality. Frederic Henry is placed in the midst of not only a great battle but a terrible defeat. Such an awesome event has a positive and a negative result: the sufferings and physical strain wear down the stamina of any person so engaged, as proved by the desertions, cowardice, and looting described by Hemingway, and create a breaking point at which no further service is rendered. At the same time, the foundations are laid for the "Hemingway Hero." In short, he will be a man not of contemplation but of action; he will devote himself to love, happiness, and the elementary pleasures of life, such as food and drink. Each day will be enjoyed to its fullest but no hedonistic philosophy is meant here. In the back of the hero's mind is the bitterly learned knowledge that life is a farce and is absurd. The hero must find Catherine to support him in his new dimensions; without her, he cannot accede to the tremendous demands put upon him by life, or, in Hemingway's terms, the "world." Malcolm Cowley thus defines the problem of the "Hemingway Hero" and his environment: "His heroes live in a world that is like a hostile forest, full of unseen dangers, not to mention the nightmares that haunt their sleep. Death spies on them from behind every tree. Their only chance of safety lies in the faithful observance of customs they invent for themselves." However, one should always look at the two sides of a coin; the present state of Frederic Henry and his fellows does not always gain unqualified admiration for Hemingway. For instance, Sean O'Faolain lampoons the type by saying of Hemingway: "his Hero is always as near as makes no matter to being brainless, has no past, no traditions, and no memories. . . We may regret this exclusive glorification of brute courage, strength, skill and grace, but I doubt if it is literary criticism to do so." Despite adverse criticism, the popularity of the "Hemingway Hero" has never been disputed; for example, Mario Praz and Deming Brown, after analyzing the impact of Hemingway in Italy and Russia respectively, conclude that he struck a chord not only in the general reading public but also within literary circles. Be that as it may, Frederic Henry and the other Hemingway types are realistically drawn and evoke sympathy and understanding.

IRONY: There is a widespread use of irony in Hemingway, as E. M. Halliday and other critics note, and this device is brilliantly exploited in the last two books of the novel. Here are the happiest interludes for Frederic Henry. He believes momentarily that he has avoided the consequences of his duties. The progress of love for Catherine has been successful and despite minor complications and forewarnings, all seems very bright. However, he is like a mouse approaching a trap, and it is interesting to note Hemingway's frequent use of animals as symbols for his heroes. When all the complications mount and intensify, Frederic Henry reaches his stature as a "Hemingway Hero." Shortly prior to Catherine's death and at the imminence of that sad event. Frederic realizes that once man is granted the boon of life (and it is a great gift, in Hemingway's belief), he must pay the toll. Death is the end of man and it must be faced; one must learn not only to live well but to die well. Man is alone, a tragic figure, haunted by his doom and condemned by a capricious destiny. Love is the bond which can unite men but it can be broken easily by fate. These are the lessons which Frederick Henry has learned as he leaves the dead Catherine at the end; he faces the world stoically; sad and sobered by experience.

CATHERINE BARKLEY: Although Frederic Henry dominates the entire novel and Catherine never attains full development as a personality, she is the expression of love and the needed catharsis for her lover's spirit. Catherine plays no role and does not even appear in the crucial Book Three, the longest book of *A Farewell to Arms*. The analysis of this character must be sought on two levels: the changes in her prior to Caporetto and after Frederic's traumatic adventures in the disastrous retreat. She is in many ways the personification of the romantic heroine, prepared to devote herself, whatever the cost, to the ideal of love.

LOVE AS A DOMINANT IDEAL: Because of the lack of full psychological probing and depth of analysis, Hemingway has been often criticized by critics for his shallow treatment of the heroines in his novels.

Catherine is best depicted in the death scene. Then she makes a noteworthy contribution to the Hemingway doctrine about life and death and the world; she also provides a perfect complement to the attitude of Frederic Henry. Both have the same impressions: life is impossible to conquer and death is the ultimate end of the struggle. Catherine likewise expresses another key idea in Hemingway: physical courage and a stoical stance when faced by death. Hemingway, in the last chapter of Book Five, brings Catherine completely within the scope of a realistic creation. This does not mean she abandons her romanticism; on the contrary, she is prepared to sacrifice herself for love and make Frederic happy. However, in the last chapter, Catherine exposes her innermost thoughts and reactions, which were hidden except for some revelatory explanations in the first two books. Perhaps this is the high point of the dedication to Frederic on Catherine's side: union of thought, mood and spirit.

MINOR CHARACTERS: There are four minor characters who are influential in the development of the main characters: Helen Ferguson, Rinaldi, the priest, and Count Greffi. Helen Ferguson really serves as a foil to Catherine Barkley; she represents the view of morality and society about the love affair. There is also a contradictory element in the nurse's situation: she condemns the lovers but is unconsciously envious of their love. Thus, she represents two reactions of society and the outside world: criticism at the defiance of convention and jealousy at the happiness of two lovers.

RINALDI: Rinaldi symbolizes the reactions of the Italian officer class and the intellectuals to the war. Despite his overt crudity, Rinaldi is very intelligent, but his better instincts have been drowned in the blood bath of the war. He has given up all belief in the meaning of life and finds a solution for his personal agonies and those of humanity in physical pleasures, cynicism, and sarcasm. In many ways, he will explain the European attitude after World War I and the defeatism rampant throughout Italy.

THE PRIEST: Both Rinaldi and the chaplain are clearly and logically compared: the two represent contrasting reactions to the war, one abandoning any idealism or faith, and the other fighting a losing struggle to follow a set doctrine.

COUNT GREFFI: Count Greffi is the third influential character if Helen Ferguson is excluded from the list; he certainly suggests a third possible solution, in addition to Rinaldi's and the priest's, for the dilemma of Frederic Henry. Count Greffi, the symbol of a past social and political order, is a humanist; he believes in the genteel tradition and stability through appreciation of life. Of the three Italians, Count Greffi would agree very closely with Frederic's general mood, although the medical officer, the priest, and the old nobleman have all made contributions to the hero's psychological frame of mind.

There are many minor characters who are often nameless; and Hemingway generally favors their pitiful situation. He has a basic humanity which describes and observes rather than judges. He neither condemns nor approves. Hemingway shows particular sympathy for the common soldier, and, although some of the fighting men may be cowardly, he tries to understand them. His depiction of the Italians, soldiers and civilians, is very favorable, and it is evident that Hemingway sees the war as an exploitation of these people. His people, including the Swiss, are generally the "little" people, endeavoring to live out their lives in the shadow of great events; seldom are their motivations very good or very bad. They are, on the contrary, generated by basic human drives, and are on the whole kind and helpful to the lovers, Frederic and Catherine.

Sample Essay Questions and Answers

1. Discuss the use of irony in *A Farewell to Arms*.

ANSWER: The ironic contrast is found in the initial situation of Frederic Henry in the war. He represents a realistic reaction to the lofty idealism of his generation at the conflict's start. He has seen through the slogans and catchwords which have lured the young men of his age to the battlefields. At the same time his personal life is quite comfortable, far better than the lot of the ordinary soldiers whom he pities. In the third book, his close escape from execution by the military police is certainly ironical; he has dodged death from the attacking Germans and has shot one of the sergeants for desertion. Now he is seized as a deserter at the moment when he believes himself to be safely within his own lines.

The happiness of Catherine and Frederic is ironical because it is so illusory. When she is taken to the hospital to bring life into the world, she meets death. The baby, cause of all their anxieties, is born dead; Frederic remarks on this irony in the novel's last chapter. Hemingway also uses very ironical language in his descriptions, as in his first chapter, when he writes that only seven thousand soldiers died of cholera. Finally, the war setting of *A Farewell to Arms* is ironic in the historical context: after fighting doggedly for two years in a slow conquest of the mountains, the Italians are routed swiftly and lose all their costly military gains within a short time in the German and Austrian offensive.

2. How does Hemingway treat the theme of death in the novel?

ANSWER: Death is one of the important elements in the construction of *A Farewell to Arms*. There is the impersonal and the personal portrayal of death: the war obviously brings death as an everyday occurrence and Frederic's assignment as an ambulance driver has made him observe killing in the course of duty. While he is disillusioned about life in general, he still feels himself in no danger. He reflects upon the relative safety of the Italian front and his own unexposed position as a non-combatant. His first change of feeling occurs when he is wounded; then he realizes the meaning of death more closely, especially when he is removed in one of his own ambulances. The dripping of blood from a wounded soldier above him has its effect on him. Finally, in the retreat from Caporetto, Frederic Henry sees death at close hand. He learns that he can die by accident if he strays too close to the Italian rear guard or is mistaken for a spy. Brushes with death in the course of war come for soldiers and civilians alike.

3. What is meant by the statement that Hemingway employs "the art of evasion"?

ANSWER: Hemingway does not indulge in lengthy geographical and psychological description. His style has been said to lack substance because of the avoidance of direct statements and description of emotions. Hemingway relies upon the reader to interpret his meaning and only provides clues by his use of nouns without any revealing adjectives and by simple verbs. Hemingway favors action, and facts are set down in rapid succession. Seldom does the hero expound on his feelings; he is unmoved to lyrical outbursts. Instead of seeking commitment to an ideal or a cause, the characters are content to do their jobs without pondering the reasons or the consequences. If the emphasis is upon facts and acts of the will, then there is no necessity for lengthy, philosophical digressions. A character may therefore be said to evade any requirement to let the reader in on the processes of his mind. The hero, as happens to Frederic Henry, may have suffered a surfeit of flowery rhetoric and empty phrases; he is therefore wary of instituting a technique with which he is disillusioned. Evasion may refer to the lack of introspective analysis and the failure to evolve a responsibility in the characters. It takes shape in the reliance upon dialogue and the passing from one action to another in rapid succession like a motion picture setting. The characters evade engagements in order to satisfy their basic passions, such as eating, drinking, and sex—all of which are stressed in Hemingway's novels.

4. What is Hemingway's attitude toward religion in *A Farewell to Arms*?

ANSWER: Hemingway seems to say that while organized religion is not the solution of his hero's problem, nevertheless some of the tenets of Christianity may be followed with profit. Despite these rejections of religion, the lovers are religious in the sense of following the dictates of their consciences and looking upon love as the guiding motif of their lives. Some critics have written that Hemingway, in spite of his apparent naturalism, has thereby instilled a metaphysical yearning in the inquietudes of Frederic and Catherine.

5. How is Hemingway's concept of time and space depicted in *A Farewell to Arms*?

ANSWER: Hemingway ranges far afield in the novel to give the impression that locale has no bearing upon feeling and that man is the same in all places. There is no unity of place in this book: the setting changes from the Italian war front to Milan and finally to Switzerland. Within these broad areas, there are other changes of scenery which do not affect the hero and heroine. Weather may play a role, but basically geography does not, except for the mention of mountains and plains. Hemingway does not go into the minute details of the physical settings; the places are "good" or "bad" depending upon the attitude of the principal characters. The war front is bad because of the lovers' separation and the war peril; Milan is good because the two are together; and Switzerland is good because Frederic and Catherine are enjoying their happiest moments together there.

Time is concentrated in the present in Hemingway's novel; in fact, he uses the present tense a great deal within the pages of *A Farewell to Arms*. Little is known of the histories of Frederic and Catherine, and they do not reminisce about the time previous to loving each other. Likewise, little thought is given to the future. Both endeavor to live to the fullest in the present; perhaps this is an indication of the doom which is awaiting the lovers.

6. What is Hemingway's attitude toward war in *A Farewell to Arms*?

ANSWER: Hemingway has written one of the most vivid and realistic accounts of war in contemporary literature. There is no romantic or idealistic aspect to his portrayal of World War I; the conflict is an impersonal force which destroys and leads to the breakdown of rationality. Hemingway's sympathies are with the common soldier and not the generals and military commanders. He does not discuss strategy other than in terms of how the individual is caught in the trap of suffering and death at the hands of others. War brings out certain primitive instincts in man and often shows the worth of an individual. Hemingway is interested in the reactions of men facing death: their bravery or their cowardice, their regard for their comrades, and their spontaneous actions in battle. Hemingway seems to find the link of friendship and understanding as a possible result of soldiers being in the same dangerous plight. He also appears aware of the effects on civilians and tries to show humanistic actions in moments of stress. Hemingway sketches a very sharp distinction between men at war and men at peace; war exposes men to various pressures which change them drastically, as happens with the hero, Rinaldi, and the priest. Men at peace do not comprehend the problems of those in battle, as Frederic learns from the civilians after his return.

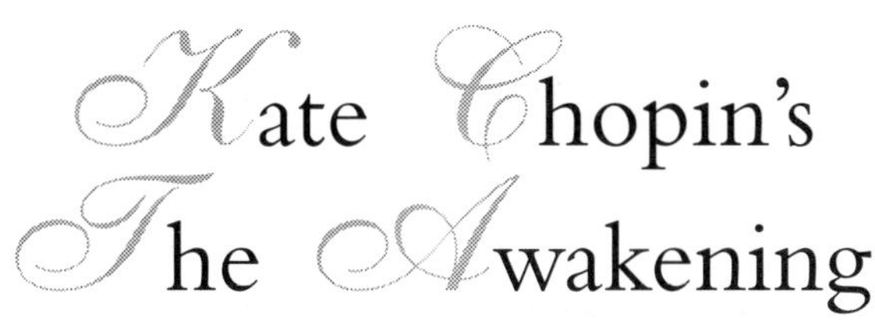

Chapter-by-Chapter Textual Analysis

CHAPTER I

BIRD SYMBOLISM AND THEME: A green and yellow parrot, hung in a cage outside the door of the main house on Grand Isle, an island fifty miles south of New Orleans, keeps repeating over and over, "Allez vous-en! Allez vous-en! Sapristi!" (Get out! Get out! Damn it!)

The parrot's command immediately establishes the theme of *The Awakening*. Edna Pontellier, the main character, who does not appear immediately in this opening chapter, will struggle to get out of her cage of marriage and motherhood. She will be damned for her struggles. The mockingbird's whistle echoes the sounds of the parrot, mocking, jeering.

LÉONCE PONTELLIER: A successful New Orleans broker, Léonce Pontellier's first action is one of impatience and even disgust. The parrot's sounds annoy him. He is restless, forty years old, of medium height, his beard is neatly trimmed. He gets up and moves away from the bird sounds. He does not want to hear them, just as he does not want to hear his wife's sounds.

POINT OF VIEW: The author lets us see Edna Pontellier through her husband's eyes. He watches her, approaching under a white sunshade and chatting with Robert Lebrun, the son of the owner of the pension on Grand Isle. Léonce's first words. "'You are burnt beyond recognition'. . . . looking at his wife as one looks at a valuable piece of personal property which has suffered some damage," show him to be a man to whom appearance is very important. His wife must take care of her looks. To get sunburned is unbecoming for a woman like Edna. She might be mistaken for a servant. This would be intolerable to Léonce. Edna is his property. One takes good care of valuable possessions. Throughout the book, Edna will struggle not to be anyone's property.

MARRIAGE: The Pontellier marriage is strained. Edna prefers the company of Robert Lebrun to that of her husband. Léonce prefers the company of the New Orleans club men at Klein's Hotel, where he can play billiards. When Edna asks whether Léonce will return to dinner, he merely shrugs. She doesn't seem to care if he eats elsewhere. Both husband and wife are indifferent to each other.

SOUNDS TO ESTABLISH SETTING: The bird sounds, the sounds of the Farival twins playing a duet on the piano, Madame Lebrun's loud orders to her servants, the sound of her starched skirts crinkling, the sounds of the children at play, all establish a summer day of warmth and ease. The sound of Edna and Robert giggling together over some private nonsense bonds them together.

CHAPTER 2

EDNA'S PHYSICAL APPEARANCE: Edna's eyes, quick and bright, yellowish brown, have about them something of the parrot. "She was rather handsome than beautiful. Her face was captivating by reason of a certain frankness of expression and a contradictory subtle play of features. Her manner was engaging." Edna's appearance, the contradictory nature of her appeal, sets her apart from the other simpler women on the island.

ROBERT'S PHYSICAL APPEARANCE: He looks something like Edna. He is clean-shaven. "There rested no shadow of care upon his open countenance." The cigar he had in his pocket was given to him by Mr. Pontellier. He does not have a lot of money and speaks frequently of going to Mexico on business. (But he will not go until he becomes frightened by Edna's feelings for him.)

SHIFT IN POINT OF VIEW: Although we first see Edna from her husband's point of view, in the second chapter the narrator's voice emerges when she comments on Edna and Robert's conversation. "Robert talked a great deal about himself. He was very young and did not know any better. Mrs. Pontellier talked a little about herself for the same reason." Authors can choose to use different points of view to tell their stories. They can use first person, which is a very limited point of view. Although we can empathize with a first-person narrator, the perspective is necessarily limited to what the "I" knows. Realizing these limitations, many authors choose to have a more flexible narrator. They decide on a third-person ("he," "she") point of view, which can be *author omniscient* (all-knowing), and can see and know what everyone is doing and thinking. An author also has the choice of using a *limited third-person point of view.* He can tell the story using "he," or "she," and we see what this one character sees and we feel what the one character feels. Chopin uses a third-person point of view. Most of the time we see Edna's point of view, but occasionally we are shifted to Léonce's point of view, and Chopin also avails herself the prerogative of authorial omniscient intrusions. *She has given herself a great deal of flexibility in using these different perspectives.*

AUTHORIAL INTRUSION: Chopin was writing in 1899. Readers were used to hearing comments from the narrator. In fact, many discerning readers enjoyed these authorial intrusions as much as they enjoyed hearing the characters. The comments on both Edna and Robert's youth are gently ironic, but kind. "He [Robert] was always intending to go to Mexico, but some way never got there." In chapter 2 we hear the author's voice for the first time. It is a voice we will come to like for its humor, its affection for the characters, with their failings, and for its steadfast intelligence.

CONVERSATION TO ESTABLISH CHARACTER: Left alone when Mr. Pontellier goes to Klein's Hotel, Edna and Robert reveal a lot about themselves through their conversation. Robert wants to go to Mexico, but somehow never gets there. He is concerned about the future. Edna talks about her father's Mississippi plantation and her home in the Old Kentucky Bluegrass Country. She talks about her sisters, her dead mother. *She seems more interested in the past.* There is a leisurely quality about the day and the conversation. It is holiday and summer and the talk is unhurried.

CHAPTER 3

CHARACTERIZATION: Léonce returns from Klein's Hotel at 11:00 that night in a very good mood. He disturbs his wife, who is already sleeping, talks to her even though she only murmurs in response. His actions show a man who is callous to his wife's needs, and utterly wrapped up in his own. He doesn't care about disturbing Edna. He is annoyed by her lack of response. This chapter starts once again with Léonce's point of view and then shifts to Edna.

IRONY: The narrator puts an unconsciously ironic thought into Léonce's head. "He thought it very discouraging that his wife, who was the sole object of his existence, evinced so little interest in things which concerned him, and valued so little his conversation." Our glimpses of Léonce, so far, hardly prepare us to think that Edna is "the sole object of his existence." The punning use of the word "object" once again emphasizes Edna's value to her husband as a possession, albeit a valuable one.

MARITAL CONFLICT AS THEME: Léonce reproaches his wife for neglecting their children, yet he has forgotten to bring back the bonbons and peanuts that he had promised to the children. Edna refuses to answer her husband. After he goes to sleep, she goes out on the porch and weeps. She feels oppressed, but does not yet blame her husband. She laments her fate, but is still unawakened. "She was just having a good cry all to herself."

SOUNDS: The hooting of an owl, the sound of the sea, the buzzing of the mosquitoes, set the scene for this marital spat. Edna is finally driven indoors by the relentless insects. The sea sounds begin to make themselves heard in this chapter, a little louder than before. The sea is *symbolic* of Edna's gradual awakening.

DEPARTURE: Mr. Pontellier eagerly leaves Grand Isle the following morning for the city where he will stay until the following Saturday. Everyone, children, servants, ladies, gentlemen, come to say goodbye. He gives his wife half of the money that he had brought away from Klein's Hotel the previous evening.

AUTHOR'S SATIRIC COMMENT: When Edna takes the money from her husband, the narrative voice comments gently, but satirically. "She liked money as well as most women." There is a wry quality to the commentary that we begin to expect and to look forward to.

GIFTS THAT SYMBOLIZE A MARRIAGE: A few days later, a box arrives for Mrs. Pontellier from her husband. It is filled with delicacies. Edna shares these gifts with the rest of the guests on the island. When everyone declares that Mr. Pontellier is the best husband in the world, "Mrs. Pontellier is forced to admit that she knew of none better." This statement, seemingly wrested from Edna's lips, says a great deal about her own husband, and about most husbands of Edna's acquaintance. The gifts look good, taste good, but are very trivial. They are also quickly gone, leaving the receiver with little. *The marriages are the same: they look good to the outsider; they are beautifully packaged.* Yet they are not substantial. Just like the gift boxes.

CHAPTER 4

CHILDREN: Edna's children, two little boys, do not rush to their mother's arms for comfort if they fall. They pick themselves up, they fight for themselves. Their nurse takes care of their physical needs. They seem surprisingly self-assured and independent, perhaps because of Edna's inability to be a "mother-woman." We see them always asking for something: food, attention. They are like children everywhere, but they are not developed as individuals. They are little animals who make enormous demands on a mother who doesn't derive great pleasure in filling their needs.

MOTHER-WOMEN: "They were women who idolized their children, worshipped their husbands, and esteemed it a holy privilege to efface themselves as individuals and grow wings as ministering angels." This commentary by the narrative voice, using words such as "idolized," "holy," "wings," "angels," is satiric in its use of religious imagery. In spite of the seeming praise, these "mother-women" do not seem admirable. They are excessive; their self-negation is a quality that neither Edna nor the narrator admires.

ADÈLE RATIGNOLLE—EMBODIMENT OF THE MOTHER-WOMAN: Adèle looks like a romantic heroine with her spun-gold hair streaming unconfined, blue eyes like sapphires, exquisite hands that are always busy sewing a child's garment. She is always concerned with her children, but uses her constant pregnancies to get attention. Edna realizes this when Adèle claims she is faint, but the color never fades from her face. Her conversation is all about her children. She is capable of showing great excitement about a pair of infant drawers. Edna cannot. Adèle seems very comfortable with her role in life. She can speak about sex and pregnancies easily. Edna cannot.

ALIENATION: Edna is not a Creole, like the other guests on Grand Isle. Even though she lives among them, she feels uncomfortable around their "absence of prudery," combined at the same time with a "lofty chastity." When she is given a rather shocking book to read, she reads it in secret while the others read it openly.

DANGER IN BOOKS: Like Flaubert's Emma Bovary, who is stimulated and enchanted by romantic novels, Edna Pontellier is easily inflamed by literature. Both *The Awakening* and *Madame Bovary* share the theme that there is considerable danger in novels that can confuse susceptible weak women.

CHAPTER 5

COURTLY LOVE: In the Middle Ages many fine ladies had a courtly suitor. This knight would prostrate himself before his lady, kiss the hem of her gown, carry her favor into battle, idealize her. The relationship was not supposed to be sexual, a matter that is still open to conjecture. Robert Lebrun devotes himself to Edna in the manner of a courtly suitor. He fetches her shawl, drinks, and books. He is constantly in attendance. This is not the first time Robert has played the devoted swain. One summer he was very attentive to Adèle Ratignolle, but she understood the game.

HYPERBOLE: Robert talks of his hopeless passion for Madame Ratignolle. He talks "of sleepless nights, of consuming flames till the very sea sizzled when he took his daily plunge." He assumes this serio-comic tone and Madame Ratignolle laughs at him. They both understand the rules of the game. Robert does not speak in this manner to Edna. Their game is a different one, even though it might look the same to the casual outsider. Edna, the alien, is not a Creole who is accustomed to passion; she is unfamiliar with the banter between a married woman and a single man that is part of the Creole tradition. *It seems to be a mock courtly love and the rules are understood by the players.* Edna, though, is not a player.

EDNA'S ART: Edna dabbles in sketching. Yet "she felt in it satisfaction of a kind which no other employment afforded her." The other "mother-women" do not seek this kind of creativity. If they play the piano, as Adèle does, they do it for the children, not for themselves. She sketches Madame Ratignolle, but is not satisfied with the portrait of her friend. It does not look like her. Does Edna see Adèle as she really is, rather than the prettified version? She destroys the sketch. The narrator tells us that her sketching showed "natural aptitude, rather than many years of work." Edna has been a dilettante. She has never disciplined herself to hard, demanding work.

CHAPTER 6

INTERNAL CONFLICT: When Madame Ratignolle leaves Edna and Robert to go to her children, Robert asks Edna if she would like to bathe. Her first response is to say no. She doesn't quite understand this answer herself, and when she finally agrees, she realizes it was what she really wanted.

SEA SYMBOLISM: The waters of the Gulf are always seductive, "never ceasing, whispering, clamoring, murmuring, inviting the soul to wander for a spell in abysses of solitude; to lose itself in mazes of inward contemplation. The voice of the sea speaks to the soul. The touch of the sea is sensuous, enfolding the body in its soft, close embrace." Edna is beginning to awaken to the spell of the sea, and to feel her own sexual birth. "A certain light was beginning to dawn dimly within her." Robert's importuning, the sea sounds, her own sensuality begin to stir in her and she agrees to swim with Robert, at a time when the other women have gone into the cottages with their children. This extremely short chapter, just one page, is important. In it Edna takes the first step to her awakening. The prose poetry of the passages of the sea are very reminiscent of Walt Whitman's "Out of the Cradle Endlessly Rocking," published some forty years before Chopin wrote. The sea, for both authors, is both seductive and symbolic of rebirth.

CHAPTER 7

A STUDY IN CONTRASTS: Edna Pontellier is described as reserved, with a noble beauty that is not readily apparent to the casual observer. Her body has long, clean lines, while Adèle, although as tall, is more feminine. Adèle has a fuller figure, is very careful of her complexion, and has to be persuaded by Edna not to bring her children along to the beach. She insists, though, in bringing her ever-present needlework.

SYMBOLISM OF SETTING: The road to the beach consists of "a long, sandy path, upon which a sporadic and tangled growth that bordered it on either side made frequent and unexpected inroads." Edna's path to full awakening is also one of sporadic and tangled growth.

LADY IN BLACK: When Edna and Adèle go to the beach together they are not alone. In the distance are the lovers, a couple seen only from afar, and the lady in black, who seems to follow the lovers wherever they go. These three characters, never developed, allowed to remain as the symbols they are, appear in many of the scenes. They do not have names; they are not three-dimensional. They are symbolic of the self-absorption of lovers, and of course, of the death that follows us all. The lady in black may be the chaperone image, or even the Freudian symbol of the superego, our conscience.

FLASHBACK TO EDNA'S CHILDHOOD: In speaking to Adèle, Edna thinks of a summer day in Kentucky, of a meadow that seemed as big as the ocean. She walked through this meadow as if she was swimming. This connection of the meadow with the sea is significant. Even as a child, Edna wanted to be free of the constrictions of her life. As she talks to Adèle, she loosens her collar. She is beginning to fling off the shackles of her upbringing, her sex, her private nature, her inability to confide in anyone. She can speak to Adèle as she has never spoken before. These confidences are as important to Edna's awakening as the swim in the Gulf with Robert. All these events are gradually loosening Edna's habitual reserve. She tells Adèle about the chilling effect of a Presbyterian service read in a spirit of gloom by her father. Obviously, her childhood lacked spontaneity. She remembers a religious period in her life and the lack of outward or spoken affectionate gestures by her family. Adèle caresses her. Edna is not comfortable with the touch of her friend's hand. She is unaccustomed to loving touches. She had few friends as a child, no confidantes. She remembers an old love, a cavalry officer, another one, someone else's fiance, and a great tragedian whose picture she still has on her desk. This flashback, told us through Edna's conversation with Adèle, helps us to understand why Edna has been so repressed all her life.

MARRIAGE TO LÉONCE PONTELLIER: He fell in love; she liked his loving her. She thought they had much in common; she was mistaken. Her father and sister objected to her marrying a Catholic. That was enough for Edna. She felt that *this kind of marriage would take her away forever from romance and foolish dreams.* We see here that Edna had a rebellious aspect even before her marriage, and that she is aware of her tendency to romance and dreams.

NARRATIVE INTRUSION: "She grew fond of her husband, realizing with some unaccountable satisfaction that no trace of passion or excessive and fictitious warmth colored her affection, thereby threatening its dissolution." This observation by the narrator makes clear that Edna was always aware that passion can destroy affection, a much more lasting emotion. She married so that passion could not confuse her. This summer on Grand Isle, the dangerous emotion once again threatens to overwhelm her, and it seems as if marriage is no safeguard.

EDNA'S FEELINGS TOWARD HER CHILDREN: She is erratic, sometimes passionately involved with them, sometimes forgetting them completely. She doesn't usually miss them when they visit their paternal grandmother, although she experiences an occasional intense longing for them. Their absence creates in Edna a feeling of relief. She realizes her fate is to have children, although she is not suited to it at all.

AWAKENING THEME: As Edna begins to reveal herself to Adèle, the taste of candor "muddled her like wine, or like a first breath of freedom." The conversation, the intimacies, confuse and frighten her, but they are at the same time exhilarating.

SYMBOLISM OF LOVERS: The lovers, often in the background, completely involved with each other, are seen again. This is what it is like to be passionately in love.

CHAPTER 8

WARNING THEME: Adèle Ratignolle tells Robert to leave Edna alone, "She is not one of us; she is not like us. She might make the unfortunate blunder of taking you seriously."

FORESHADOWING: Robert is annoyed with Adèle for speaking to him this way. He says he is not like Alcée Arobin. He then tells the story of Alcée and the consul's wife. Alcée is obviously a roué. Robert does not want to be put into the same category. This mention of scandalous affairs foreshadows what will happen in the novel.

SOUNDS: When Robert goes to his mother's room, he sees her at the sewing machine. A little black girl is sitting on the floor, working the treadle of the machine. The narrator tells us very drily that "The Creole woman does not take any chances which may be avoided of imperiling her health." This is a satiric comment on the nature of most of the women on Grand Isle. We hear the clatter of the sewing machine. *This mechanical sound is the first indication of the sterility of industrialization.* The other sounds we have heard have been of nature: birds, children, the sea, insects. With this new sound, which punctuates the conversation of Mme. Lebrun and her son, a certain tension is set up that reflects Robert's agitation. "Bang! clatter, clatter bang!" A new and disquieting element is introduced. Victor Lebrun, Robert's younger brother, described as a "tête montée," an excitable and willful fellow, who has a temper that invites violence, is discussed. Robert offers to thrash him. We are suddenly in an atmosphere of violence with the sound of the machine in the background. A Monsieur Montel is also mentioned. He has been Madame Lebrun's suitor for twenty years and sends a message to Robert that he will be in Vera Cruz next month and that maybe Robert will join him there. The tempo of the story has changed in this chapter. *There is a new quality of movement, one that has an element of danger.*

CHAPTER 9

DANGER OF MUSIC THEME: The Farival twins play the piano at a Saturday night party at which husbands, fathers, and friends are entertained. We hear the parrot's refrain again, "Get out! Get out!" Adèle Ratignolle offers to play the piano so the guests can dance. She claims that she only keeps up her music so that the children will benefit. For the "mother-women," the only reason for art, or for the mastery of an instrument, is to benefit the children. With the introduction of Mademoiselle Reisz, a gifted musician, we again are offered a contrast to Edna Pontellier.

Mademoiselle Reisz is a disagreeable woman, who doesn't like children and family, is quarrelsome, has poor taste in clothes, but is a very talented pianist. "Ask Mrs. Pontellier what she would like to hear me play." She seems to instinctively recognize in Edna a soul that will respond to her music. Edna, listening, is moved to tears.

In the past when Edna has heard a certain musical passage, she thought of the figure of a naked man standing beside a desolate rock. Music can stir the passions. The symbolism of the naked man, the freedom of nudity, is evoked by the sound of the music. The nudity of the man, the wildness of abandon is contrasted with the sterility of Edna's life.

When Mademoiselle Reisz plays, Edna sees no pictures of naked men. Instead "the very passions themselves were aroused within her soul, swaying it, lashing it, as the waves daily beat upon her splendid body. She trembled, she was choking, the tears blinded her." This is no polite, ladylike response. From the depths of Edna's soul comes a response that is overwhelming. When the musician asks her how she liked the music, Edna is overcome. She is unable to answer Mademoiselle Reisz. "You are the only one worth playing for. Those others. Bah!" says the irascible old woman. Edna has been loosened by the music, as she was before by the sea. Someone, perhaps Robert, then suggests that they take a bath in the ocean "at that mystic hour and under that mystic moon."

CHAPTER 10

GRADUAL AWAKENING: As Edna walks on her husband's arm to the water, she is acutely aware of Robert behind her. She realizes that she misses him when he is away from her just as "one misses the sun on a cloudy day without having thought much about the sun when it was shining." *The comparison of Robert to the sun makes clear how pivotal he is becoming in Edna's life.* She is gradually awakening to the fact that she is falling in love.

MUSIC: As the summer visitors to Grand Isle enter the tepid waters of the Gulf, they can hear the faint sound of music coming from Klein's Hotel.

ODORS: Strange, exotic odors assail the swimmers' senses. The sea smells, the weeds, the damp, new-plowed earth, the heavy perfume of the flowers nearby, all these combine into an aura of fecundity that is ripe with promise.

SWIMMING FOR THE FIRST TIME: Edna has attempted all summer to learn to swim. She was afraid of the water. But tonight she shouts for joy as she successfully swims for the first time. In fact, overwhelmed by her new power, she becomes reckless. "She wanted to swim far out, where no woman had swum before." There is no doubt about the author's intent here. Swimming, for Edna, is mastery. She can now exult in freedom, one that she has never known.

FORESHADOWING: She swims out. The stretch of water frightens her, and she has a quick vision of death. She manages to return to shore.

ISOLATION: Changing into dry clothes, Edna leaves the rest of the guests and begins to walk away alone. She does not pay attention to the others who call to her. Robert follows her.

THE SPIRITS OF THE TWENTY-EIGHTH OF AUGUST: "Did you think I was afraid?" askes Edna when Robert overtakes her. He answers that he knew she wasn't. She tells Robert how stirred she was by Mlle Reisz's playing. "I wonder if any night on earth will ever again be like this one." Robert tells her about the spirit that has haunted the Gulf, seeking a mortal for company. His search has been fruitless but Robert says that tonight this spirit found Edna. Edna is twenty-eight years old. The spirits only come out on the twenty-eighth of August. There is a kinship between these numbers. *Tonight Edna has been born again.* She has felt something she never experienced before. Robert and Edna sit together quietly in front of the Pontelliers' cottage. He smokes. She rocks in the hammock. It is a moment of suspended time.

CHAPTER 11

THEME OF REBELLION AGAINST MARRIAGE AND ITS CONSTRAINTS: Léonce is surprised to find his wife still up when he returns. It is after one o'clock. She refuses to go inside with him. He comes out, orders her into the house. She refuses, stubborn and resistant. She thinks back to other times when her husband ordered her to do things, and she obeyed. This time is different. A spirit of rebellion and recklessness consumes her. She tells him never to speak to her in such a patronizing manner again. Léonce decides to join her outside, takes a glass of wine, offers some to his wife. Perhaps he is trying to make believe that all is normal. She refuses his offer. He smokes cigar after cigar. Edna begins to get tired. As her sudden blaze of stubbornness leaves her, a natural fatigue sets in. She goes in. Her husband remains. *Somehow, he has won.* He has outlasted her. *In this marital skirmish, his ability to wait patiently reduces Edna's gesture to a childish tantrum.*

CHAPTER 12

SYMBOLISM OF LOVERS: Although Edna has not slept well, she is up early. Her resolve, perhaps confusing to herself, but nevertheless firm, has not vanished during the night. "She was blindly following whatever impulse moved her, as if she had placed herself in alien hands for direction, and freed her soul of responsibility." She decides to go to the Chênière for mass. The lovers are going too. The lady in black, with her prayer book, is following them. Edna does something she has never done before. She sends for Robert. This change from her usual behavior is emphasized by the *repetition in these phrases:* "She had never sent for him before. She had never asked for him. She had never seemed to want him before." He joins her with "his face suffused with a quiet glow."

THEME OF ASSERTION: With this rather royal summoning of her courtier, Edna, for the first time, takes command.

THEME OF JOURNEY: As they sail to the the Chênière Caminada, Edna feels as if she is being taken away from bondage. ". . . away from some anchorage which had held her fast, whose chains had been loosening, had snapped the night before when the mystic spirit was abroad, leaving her free to drift whithersoever she chose to set her sails."

EARTHINESS SYMBOLISM: Along with Edna, Robert, the lovers, the lady in black, who are all on the boat, is a young barefoot Spanish girl named Mariequita. She has a red kerchief on her head and a basket on her arm. Robert, who knows her, talks to her in Spanish. She is described very carefully, with special attention to her bare feet, which are broad and coarse—peasant's feet. "Edna looked at her feet, and noticed the sand and slime between her brown toes." This is an earthy detail. There is something primitive about Mariequita. *Edna is also experiencing some rather primitive feelings.*

FORESHADOWING: Mariequita asks Robert about Edna and suggests that maybe Robert and Edna are lovers. Robert hastens to assure her that Edna is married with two children. Mariequita is unimpressed with Edna's marital status. She talks about a fellow named Francisco who ran away with someone's wife, and that woman had four children. It is quite clear that to a creature such as this peasant girl, the artificial rules that men make have nothing to do with nature's rules. Edna's marriage has nothing to do with the stirrings of two animals who attract one another.

SYMBOLISM—-SAILS: Even the sails of the boat seem to swell. "The sails bellied taut, with the wind filling and overflowing them." Monsieur

Farival, the musical twins' father, a wise old man, looks at the sails, laughs knowingly. The suggestion of full bellied sails, pregnant, is symbolic of what is beginning to happen to Edna. She is also becoming pregnant with longing.

SYMBOLISM—ANIMALS: Robert invites Edna to go to Grand Terre the next day and look at the little wriggling gold snakes and watch the lizards sun themselves. *Snakes and lizards are rather obvious sexual images.* To use them in this way in 1899 was very daring. Today, of course, it seems rather tame.

ROBERT'S FUTURE PLANS: "I'll take you some night in the pirogue [a canoe hollowed out from the trunk of a tree] when the moon shines. Maybe your Gulf spirit will whisper to you in which of these islands the treasures are hidden—direct you to the very spot, perhaps." Robert, a Creole, is full of legends, myths, fantasies such as these. He and Edna banter about what they will do with the pirate gold if they find it. Edna says she will squander it and throw it to the four winds. A recklessness is growing within her that is heady. Robert responds to her expansiveness. "We'd share it, and scatter it together," he said. His face is flushed. Mariequita, who has perhaps been intimate with both Lebrun brothers, casts a look of reproach at Robert as he laughs with Edna. Her presence makes us think of women who have been used by men, then carelessly discarded.

CHAPTER 13

THEME OF OPPRESSIVE RELIGION: At the actual church service, the excuse for this outing, Edna begins to feel ill. She feels oppressed and drowsy. Her head begins to ache, and she just wants to escape the "stifling atmosphere" of the church. Robert, worried about her, suggests that she go to a Madame Antoine's where she can rest. At this stage of Edna's emergence, a church, religion, rules, orders, are not tolerable.

THEME OF LOOSENING: Madame Antoine has an immaculate tiny house. There is a huge, four-poster bed. Edna is taken to this little room, loosens her clothes, and takes off most of them. She bathes her face, neck, and arms in the basin, and takes off her shoes and stockings, climbing into the very center of the high white bed. She looks at her own round arms, and sees the texture of the skin, almost *as if she is seeing them for the first time*. And, of course, she is. This is the first time she has looked at her own body with a keen sense of sensuality. She falls asleep, aware always of Robert's presence nearby. Her body, sinking into deep sleep, is utterly relaxed, almost as if drugged. She sleeps for a long time, refreshes herself with powder, looks in the mirror, and sees a glowing face. She is very hungry, and eats a crusty brown loaf and drinks a bottle of wine. The description of her eating is detailed and sensual. There is a suggestion here of the symbolism of the Christian mass. Edna's appetite for food, for life, is growing. She senses a change in herself. "How many years have I slept?" she asks Robert.

ROBERT AS PROTECTOR: Robert tells Edna that he has been guarding her slumbers. The rest of the party they came with has all left to return to Grand Isle. Edna idly wonders whether her husband will worry about her whereabouts. Robert assures her he will not. They do not rush to return. Madame Antoine tells them wonderful Creole stories. When Edna and Robert leave, it is dark. " . . . misty spirit forms were prowling in the shadows and among the reeds, and upon the water were phantom ships, speeding to cover." The entire day has had a magical quality. Not once has Edna thought about her children.

CHAPTER 14

LÉONCE'S INDIFFERENCE: At first when Edna does not return from Chênière Caminada with the others, Léonce is "uneasy," but he is easily dissuaded from going to the island himself to look for his wife and occupies himself at Klein's, discussing "securities, exchanges, stocks, bonds, or something of the sort." Adèle Ratignolle dismisses his masculine concerns, which also reduces his activities to negligible occupations. Certainly he doesn't seem unduly worried or disturbed by his wife's absence.

THEME OF AWAKENING: Edna says good night to Robert and asks him an important question: "Do you know we have been together the whole livelong day, Robert—since early this morning?" She seems to be clarifying for herself and for Robert how special their relationship has become. She realizes that in some way she is different, is seeing things in a new way. The song she hums to herself is "Ah! Si tu savais!" and that is precisely what is happening. She is beginning to know herself.

CHAPTER 15

REVELATION: Robert decides, rather precipitously, to leave Grand Isle for Mexico. Although he has spent the day with Edna, he has not mentioned anything about his plans to her. She is dismayed and puzzled by his abrupt departure. When he comes to her cottage to say goodbye, he seems ill at ease, and eager to be off, afraid of an involvement with Edna. She recognizes her own infatuation, understands that she had feelings like this in the past, but is unable to control her growing passion for this young man.

CHAPTER 16

REBELLION THEME: After Robert leaves, Edna comforts herself by swimming. This activity provides her with the only pleasurable diversion she has now that Robert is gone. The meaning, the color have gone out of her life. She talks about Robert rather shamelessly, to everyone, going to Madame Lebrun's room and looking at his baby pictures. A letter sent to his mother fascinates her although he has not sent any special greeting to Edna. She confides to Adèle that, "I would give up the unessential; I would give my money, I would give my life for my children; but I wouldn't give myself. I can't make it more clear; it's only something which I am beginning to comprehend, which is revealing itself to me." This statement shows that Edna will fight for her independence and for freedom from the constraints of motherhood. She will not submerge her new-found self in anyone.

FOIL CHARACTER—MADEMOISELLE REISZ: Chopin uses character foils skillfully. Both Mademoiselle Reisz, the independent woman, a talented musician, unmarried and unbeholden to any man, and Adèle Ratignolle, the "mother-woman," are used for deliberate contrasts to Edna. She is like neither one of these foils and cannot become like them, even if she wished. Mademoiselle Reisz is a somewhat unpleasant woman, who won't swim, complains about the food, but becomes interested in Edna and invites her to visit when they return to New Orleans.

CHAPTER 17

CONTRAST IN SETTING: The scene shifts here to the Pontelliers' home in New Orleans, which is luxurious, meticulously tended, and utterly conventional. Here there will be restraints on Edna.

LÉONCE'S ACQUISITIVENESS: Edna's husband enjoys his home and its appointments. He is careful to maintain it, and is described as valuing his possessions, not so much for their intrinsic beauty, but because they are his. In much the same way, he values his wife.

REBELLION: On Tuesday afternoons, Edna is supposed to be "at home," which means that callers come, women who bring their calling cards, drink a liqueur or coffee, and chat. For six years Edna has been a gracious hostess. A few weeks after returning to New Orleans, Edna abruptly stops receiving guests on Tuesdays. She offers no excuse, either to her guests, or to Léonce, who is astonished at her behavior. Léonce tells Edna that he cannot afford to offend the people who come to call; he does business with them. She is unimpressed. She has defied her husband and convention. When Léonce complains about the food the cook has prepared, Edna does not try to placate her husband as she once would have done. Instead she eats alone, goes to her room, takes off her wedding ring, flings it upon the carpet, stamps her heel on it, but she is unable to make a mark on the "little glittering circlet." She breaks a glass vase. She wants to destroy something. When the maid finds the ring and gives it to Edna, she puts it back on. She is not yet ready to escape from her marriage.

CHAPTER 18

HOUSEHOLDS CONTRASTED: Edna goes to visit Adèle Ratignolle at her home in New Orleans. She intends to maintain the friendship with Adèle that blossomed on Grand Isle. The Ratignolles are very compatible, even finishing sentences for each other. "The Ratignolles understood each other perfectly. If ever the fusion of two human beings into one has been accomplished on this sphere it was surely in their union." This glimpse into another marriage depresses Edna. The domestic harmony she sees does not fill her with longing. She finds it horribly boring, and actually is filled with sympathy for her friend who lives a "colorless existence which never uplifted its possessor beyond the region of blind contentment, in which no moment of anguish ever visited her soul, in which she would never have the taste of life's delirium." Edna does not want this kind of life. She wants more.

CHAPTER 19

LÉONCE'S REACTION TO EDNA'S ART: Edna spends her time in her atelier [studio] working on her sketches. She makes no attempt to run her household in the manner she had before. Her refusal to entertain and her disinterest in returning the visits of those who call upon her anger her husband, but she refuses to accommodate his wishes. He cannot understand why she should want to spend all her time painting, when she should be taking care of her family. "I feel like painting," answered Edna. "Perhaps I shan't always feel like it." He continues to remonstrate with her. He cannot understand why she can't paint the way Adèle Ratignolle "keeps up her music." Her friend doesn't let the household deteriorate, and Léonce hastens to assure Edna that Adèle is far more of a musician than she will ever be a painter.

EDNA'S UNDERSTANDING OF HER ART: Edna does not try to defend her painting. She understands it for what it is. Léonce begins to wonder if his wife isn't becoming mentally unbalanced, but he does leave her alone. Edna spends days working in her atelier, and disrupts the entire household, demanding they all pose for her, but she is completely dissatisfied with her work. She is haunted by memories of Grand Isle, and by physical desire. In spite of this, there are days when she is very happy just to be alive. She responds to the sun, the warmth, the beauty of the city, and wanders alone exploring places that are strange and unfamiliar. She frequently sings the refrain, "Ah! si tu savais!" She is beginning to know.

CHAPTER 20

ROBERT'S YOUNGER BROTHER: Edna decides to visit Mademoiselle Reisz. She wants to hear her play again. Unfortunately, she has lost her address. It occurs to her that Mademoiselle Lebrun might have it, and since this gives her a perfect opportunity to visit the Lebruns in New Orleans, she goes to their home. The house is described as looking like a prison, with iron bars before the door and lower windows. If it is not a prison, it is a place that is tightly guarding something that

Edna wants. Victor, Robert's nineteen-year-old brother, greets Edna warmly and entertains her with slightly risqué stories of his romantic escapades. He attempts to draw Edna into his confidence by winking at her while she is speaking to his mother. The Lebruns tell Edna about two letters they have received from Robert in Mexico, but there is no mention of Edna in either one of them, and she begins to feel despondent. Victor seems to be an exaggeration of Robert—flirtatious, reckless, impetuous. Both sons have an aura about them of provocative sensuality. Victor also seems able to sense in Edna that she will listen to his tales of conquests. He titillates her the way Robert did on Grand Isle. He is a reminder of his older brother.

LOVE LETTER: Robert Lebrun has written to Mademoiselle Reisz. His letter is full of questions about Edna. He also asks Mademoiselle Reisz to play Chopin's "Impromptu" for her as this is music that has stirred him. Although he never says he is in love with Edna, this letter, full of Edna's name, is obviously a letter from a man who simply must write his beloved's name again and again. After much coaxing, Mademoiselle Reisz lets Edna see the letter. She plays the "Impromptu" while Edna reads the letter, and the combination of the music and of Robert's words reduces Edna to tears. Mademoiselle Reisz seems aware of Edna's infatuation and does not discourage her at all. She invites her to come back whenever she feels like it.

CHAPTER 21

SYMBOLISM OF MADEMOISELLE REISZ'S APARTMENT: Mademoiselle Reisz, an independent woman of great musical talent, lives in an apartment on the top floor. The rooms have plenty of windows, even though they are dingy. A great deal of light and air comes through them, and from the windows can be seen "the crescent of the river, the masts of ships and the big chimneys of the Mississippi steamers." There is a view here, unknown in other more conventional rooms. Here, there is freedom and the opportunity to see things that others do not. The apartment is symbolic of another way of life, less stifling. A magnificent grand piano crowds the apartment, asserting the importance of music to Mademoiselle Reisz.

THE COURAGEOUS SOUL: Mademoiselle Reisz banters amiably with Edna. When Edna reveals that she has been painting, Mademoiselle Reisz is scornful of her pretensions. An artist, she says, must have a courageous soul, must be willing to defy convention. She does not feel that Edna has this quality.

CHAPTER 22

THEME—MEN CANNOT UNDERSTAND WOMEN: Léonce seeks help from Doctor Mandelet, an old friend and the family physician. He complains about Edna and her attitude. "She's got some sort of notion in her head concerning the eternal rights of women; and—you understand—we meet in the morning at the breakfast table." With this admission, Léonce reveals his inability to understand his wife, and he discloses that Edna is no longer sleeping with him. Léonce also complains that Edna refuses to attend her sister's wedding, saying that a wedding "is one of the most lamentable spectacles on earth." Dr. Mandelet suggests that maybe Edna is associating with pseudo-intellectual women who are filling her head with foolish ideas. When Léonce assures him that this is not the case, that actually, Edna has stopped socializing, and does not want to associate with anyone, the doctor becomes worried. He suggests maybe there is something genetically wrong. Léonce says he chose her carefully; she comes of good sound stock. This remark clearly shows Léonce's acquisitiveness. Before he married, he checked his wife's lineage, almost as if he were checking that a horse he was purchasing would be a good breeder. The doctor sympathizes with Léonce and they agree that women are very strange. They are "moody and whimsical," and cannot be understood. He advises Léonce to take Edna with him on a business trip, if she wishes to go, or to let her stay home, if she doesn't want to accompany him.

The doctor suspects there may be another man involved, but would never suggest this possibility to a Creole husband. This chapter shows how impossible it is for either of these men to understand what Edna is and what she is going through.

CHAPTER 23

EDNA'S RELATIONSHIP WITH HER FATHER: When Edna's father comes to visit, Edna spends a great deal of time with him, not because she is so fond of him, but because they have certain tastes in common, one of them being horse racing. The father, once a colonel in the Confederate Army, still retains a military bearing, but his clothing is padded, which "gave a fictitious breadth to his shoulders and chest." His clothes make him appear to be more than he really is. He is not a substantial man, not a caring or sensitive father, and he had not been a loving husband. He agrees to pose for Edna in her atelier, but expects his daughter to be talented, simply because she is his daughter. His possessiveness seems similar to Léonce's feelings about Edna. Neither man recognizes her for what she is, but merely as an ornamental addition to himself. He does not seem particularly interested in his grandchildren either.

FLIRTATION: When Edna takes her father to the Ratignolle's for a musical evening, Adèle flirts with the Colonel until "the Colonel's old head felt thirty years younger on his padded shoulders." Edna does not understand this at all. She is not a flirt and does not have any of these feminine wiles.

ANIMAL SYMBOLISM: Doctor Mandelet is invited to the Pontellier's home to meet the Colonel. He notices a change in Edna. She is no longer the listless person he knew. She has been transformed into a radiant woman, pulsing with the forces of life. "She reminded him of some beautiful, sleek animal waking up in the sun." Edna is awakening, and it is becoming obvious to the doctor, trained as he is to be sensitive to such things. The animalism in the description of Edna, the hint of muscles rippling, of power and force, hidden, but emerging, is highly suggestive and provocative.

STORIES: The guests amuse themselves at the dinner table by telling stories. The Colonel relates stories of his escapades in the war. He, of course, always plays a very prominent part. The doctor tells of a woman, looking for new outlets, who returns to her old love. The narrator observes in this that this particular story didn't impress Edna. Edna tells a story of a woman who paddles away with her lover one night in a pirogue and never comes back. As she relates it, the people listening can actually feel the sensuous details of the southern night, the movement of the pirogue through the water, the bird's wings, the faces of the lovers. Edna's story is striking in its imagery and, of course, in *its theme of lovers escaping*. The doctor is sorry that he accepted the invitation. "He did not want the secrets of other lives thrust upon him." He feels sure that Edna has a lover. "I hope it isn't Arobin," he mutters to himself.

CHAPTER 24

REFUSAL TO ATTEND WEDDING: Edna's father and husband are horrified at her refusal to attend her sister's wedding. She offers no excuse, and when the Colonel leaves for the wedding, Edna is glad. Léonce leaves shortly to be at the wedding and to atone for Edna's action. The two men have talked about Edna's behavior and the father-in-law tells Léonce that he is far too lenient. "Authority, coercion are what is needed. Put your foot down good and hard; the only way to manage a wife. Take my word for it." Léonce feels that the

Colonel may have coerced his wife into her grave. He is certainly not as insensitive a man as his father-in-law.

EDNA'S AMBIVALENCE: Before Léonce's departure, Edna grows very affectionate and concerned about his welfare. In fact, she busies herself with his packing and clothes and underwear, quite as "Madame Ratignolle would have done under similar circumstances." She cries when he leaves, and suspects that she may join him in New York where he is going after her sister's wedding. She manifests a lot of ambivalence in her feelings toward her husband, remembering his many acts of kindness and affection.

RELIEF: The children have been taken away by the paternal grandmother and so Edna is alone. "A feeling that was unfamiliar but very delicious came over her." She explores her own home, works in the garden, plays with the dog, spends time in the kitchen with the cook and dines alone. She enjoys her dinner enormously. Although she thinks about Léonce and the children, she is content to be alone, and seems to relish her solitude. She makes up her mind to read more. She has a feeling of peace she has never had before.

CHAPTER 25

ALCÉE AROBIN: Edna goes to the races with Alcée Arobin, a young man of fashion. He spends his time at the race track, the opera, the fashionable clubs. He has a somewhat insolent manner, a good figure, is not "overburdened with depth of thought or feeling." (The narrator's offhanded comment is, as always, a welcome intrusion.) He had seen Edna before and found her unapproachable, but after meeting her at the races, recently, with her father, he decided to call on her and ask her to go to the races with him. Although they have a Mrs. Highcamp with them (the author is obviously having some fun with the name), this lady is being used by Alcée Arobin to cover him with some respectability.

EDNA'S EXCITEMENT: The races excite Edna. She is quite knowledgeable about horses, having being brought up in Kentucky horse country, and she plays for very high stakes and wins that day. She becomes feverish from excitement, and people turn to look at her, hoping for a "tip." Alcée catches Edna's excitement. They have dinner together and Alcée takes her home. He makes plans to go to the races again with Edna.

APPETITE: Edna is hungry after this evening with Alcée. Although she has eaten dinner at the Highcamps, it wasn't enough. She eats cheese and crackers, drinks beer. She is extremely restless and excited. All her senses seem to be clamoring for satisfaction. She is unable to sleep well. Her appetites are sharpening.

FIRST CONTACT WITH ALCÉE: When Alcée calls again, they go to the races alone, without Mrs. Highcamp. Alcée returns home with Edna, and he begins to woo her. He shows her an old saber scar he received in a duel outside of Paris. Obviously he is trying to impress her with his romantic, reckless past. She touches the scar, touching his palm. She is very agitated after this, and yet Alcée recognizes in her face something that does not discourage his advances. She tells him that she doesn't like him and wants him to go. Then she apologizes, saying that something in her manner must have misled him in some way. He replies that she hasn't misled him. His own emotions have done that. The narrator comments wryly that "Alcée Arobin's manner was so genuine that it often deceived even himself."

MEMORIES OF ROBERT: Edna feels she has somehow betrayed Robert. She does not think about her husband. It is not the same thing because she never loved her husband.

SENSUAL RESPONSE: Although she is upset about Alcée's presumption, she cannot forget his presence, his manners, the warmth of his glances, and above all the touch of his lips upon her hand, which has acted as a narcotic upon her. She sleeps a languorous sleep.

LANGUAGE: The language in this chapter is filled with words that evoke sensuality. Words such as "fever," "flamed," "intoxicant," "restless," "excited," "sensuousness," "narcotic," "languorous" all contribute to the heightened feelings Edna is experiencing.

CHAPTER 26

PASSION: Alcée's attentions continue. Edna allows him to speak to her in a way that shocks her at first, but "in a way that pleased her at last, appealing to the animalism that stirred impatiently within her."

EDNA'S "ROOM OF HER OWN": Edna visits Mademoiselle Reisz in an effort to quiet her inner turmoil. The musician seems fond of her and is completely aware of Edna's infatuation. One cold miserable afternoon, she announces her intention to move away from her house. Mademoiselle Reisz questions her as to where she is going, and Edna tells her that there is a little four-room house right around the corner from her husband's house. Mademoiselle Reisz wants to know why she is doing this, and Edna says that her husband's house is not hers. Because she has a little money of her own, has won money at the races, and has started to sell some of her sketches, she can afford her own place. She plans to move there with one old servant. Above all, she wants the feeling of freedom and independence. She has not told her husband.

LAST GRAND DINNER: Edna plans to give a dinner at which all of her friends shall eat, drink, sing, and laugh. This dinner will be significant for them all. It will be held at her husband's house.

ROBERT'S LETTERS: Edna reads the letters that Robert continues to send to Mademoiselle Reisz. He does not write directly to Edna. She learns that he is returning to New Orleans. She is delighted and confesses her infatuation to Mademoiselle Reisz, who points out what an ordinary young man Robert is. Edna defends him and her love. She says that women do not choose whom they fall in love with.

EDNA'S FAMILY: Edna sends candy to her children. She writes a tender message on a card. It appears to be the first time she has remembered them. She also writes to her husband, revealing her plans to leave, "for a while," and regretting that he will not be available to help her with the farewell dinner. She seems remarkably self-involved, and unaware of the effect her decision will have on her family. The narrator's comment on how cheerful and brilliant the letter is clearly reveals Edna's total immersion in herself.

CHAPTER 27

CONSUMMATION: Edna permits Alcée to take more liberties with her person. He touches her hair, her cheeks, her chin. She permits it while wondering about herself. She questions whether she is wicked. She says she cannot convince herself that she is. Mademoiselle Reisz has told her, she confides in Alcée, that in order to soar above the level plain of tradition and prejudice one must have strong wings. *Mademoiselle Reisz does not think that Edna has these wings.* Alcée continues to fondle Edna. They kiss. "It was the first kiss of her life to which her nature had really responded. It was a flaming torch that kindled desire."

CHAPTER 28

THE SHORTEST CHAPTER: Less than one page, this chapter describes Edna's feelings after that passionate kiss. Chopin is discreet about what might have happened. After all, the author was writing in 1899. As daring as Chopin is, she would not describe graphically the details of a physical relationship. It is left to the reader's imagination.

We are told that Edna cries after Alcée leaves her; she has an immense sense of irresponsibility; she feels that the unexpected and shocking have occurred. Although she thinks of her husband, she is consumed by an even fiercer love for Robert. But above all, she understands herself. She sees that life is made up of beauty and brutality. She feels neither shame nor remorse. There is regret because "it was not the kiss of love which had inflamed her, because it was not love which had held this cup of life to her lips." Certainly, this kind of reaction indicates that more than a kiss took place, even though the author continues to be guarded about the details of what happened. Edna knows herself for the first time. She knows she is capable of animal passion, completely devoid of love.

CHAPTER 29

INDEPENDENCE: Without waiting to hear from her husband and learn how he will react to her decision to quit his house, Edna hurriedly packs her things in preparation for her move to her new home. She feels uncomfortable in this house. She no longer belongs here. She must leave. She takes only her own things, not anything of her husband's.

ALCÉE'S ATTEMPT TO HELP: When Alcée visits her that afternoon (he does not seem to have to earn a living), he finds Edna absorbed in her packing. He offers to help her, and a scene follows in which he puts on a dust cap, mounts a ladder, takes down pictures and curtains, while Edna laughs at him. She seems very much in control of the situation, does not allow him to assume command. He refers to the upcoming farewell dinner as a "coup d'etat." Edna plans to let Léonce pay the bills. She allows Alcée to continue to hope for a continuation of their affair. Alcée seems puzzled at her manner. He expected her to be reproachful, or tearful. Instead she is utterly in command, ordering him around. There seems to be a complete reversal of roles. Far from being wracked with guilt at what has occurred, Edna seems independent and sure of herself.

CHAPTER 30

THE GUESTS: Edna's dinner is a small affair: ten guests. Adèle is advanced in her pregnancy and cannot attend and Mademoiselle Lebrun sends her regrets at the last minute. Alcée, Mrs. Highcamp, Mademoiselle Reisz, Monsieur Ratignolle, Victor Lebrun, a Mr. and Mrs. Merriman, characters we have not met before, along with a Miss Mayblunt, an intellectual, and a gentleman who is a journalist, are the guests. It is a rather odd assortment.

BACCHANALIAN SETTING: The table is gorgeous with a splendid pale yellow satin lace cloth, and massive candles, under yellow silk shades. Full roses glow yellow and gold, and silver and gold silverware and crystal glasses sparkle. The ordinary stiff dining-chairs have been replaced by soft luxurious ones. There is the feeling of a bacchanalian feast, of sensuous beauty, of lavishness, about the setting.

EDNA'S APPEARANCE: Edna is wearing a magnificent cluster of diamonds in her hair. She admits that it is a gift from her husband that has just arrived this morning. She is twenty-nine today. Edna is wearing a golden satin gown. Her skin has a glow of vibrancy. She looks regal.

MUSIC: Edna has hired musicians to play during the dinner. They are not in the room, but they provide an agreeable accompaniment to the conversation and to the meal. The soft splash of a fountain is heard also. A heavy odor of Jessamine (jasmine) comes through the open windows. The author's use of sensory details creates a scene that is voluptuous and stimulating.

DEPRESSION: Amidst this opulence, Edna feels a hopelessness overtaking her. It is a familiar feeling. She is filled with an acute longing to see Robert.

CHILDBIRTH: Monsieur Ratignolle has to leave early, saying his wife is momentarily expecting their child. He mentions that she has a "vague dread" which only his presence can dispel. This interjection of the physical consequences of sex for women seems to break the spell of the evening. It is a return to the mundane, away from the exotic.

VICTOR'S APPEARANCE: Mrs. Highcamp places a garland of roses, yellow and red, on Victor's black curls. It transforms him into a vision of exotic beauty. His cheeks, his eyes glow with a fire. When a white silken scarf is placed on him, he appears to be a "graven image of desire." He drinks wine, agrees to sing a song to the assembled company, and begins to sing, "Ah! Si tu savais!" Edna is very disturbed by the refrain, puts her glass down so abruptly that it shatters, but Victor continues to sing. She goes over to him, puts her hand over his mouth. He kisses her palm. The guests leave. This party has had overtones of Oriental sumptuousness, a lavish display of sensuality, and a pagan delight in the senses.

CHAPTER 31

SEXUAL SYMBOLISM: When the guests leave, Edna and Alcée straighten up the room after the party. It is a domestic scene, but Edna is disheartened and doesn't speak. She feels depressed but is much aware of Alcée's physical presence. As they walk over together to the pigeon house, she notices the "black line of his leg moving in and out so close to her against the yellow shimmer of her gown." This sexual symbolism reveals the true nature of their relationship. But there is another symbol here too. Alcée has invaded her territory. He is encroaching on her person.

THE PIGEON HOUSE: The little house that Edna has moved to is a simple place, far removed from the splendor of her husband's home. Edna has made it comfortable and habitable, but it is not luxurious. When Edna and Alcée enter this evening, Edna is surprised to find that it is filled with flowers that Alcée has sent her. She does not seem particularly pleased at this furthur invasion of Alcée into her space. She seems tired and says she is miserable. Alcée sympathizes with her and says that he will leave her, but he begins to caress her, and she allows him to remain. "He did not say good night until she had become supple to his gentle, seductive entreaties." Chopin's use of sibilants in this sentence (the repeated use of *s*) creates a mood of snake-like seduction.

CHAPTER 32

LÉONCE'S RESPONSE TO EDNA'S DEPARTURE: Léonce writes his wife a letter of disapproval. He is much concerned with what people will say. He warns her that a scandal might do damage to his business prospects. Feeling that Edna has been acting strangely, and that he must protect his reputation, he decides to hire an architect to remodel his home, and puts a notice in the papers that due to the inconvenience of having workmen in their home, the Pontelliers will be leaving New Orleans for the summer. He has managed to save face, and at the same time have some work done on his home, which he had wanted to do for a long time. Obviously, Léonce is a resourceful man, and his concern for appearances has been satisfied.

EDNA'S FEELINGS ABOUT HER NEW HOME: Edna feels happy in her modest home. "There was with her a feeling of having descended in the social scale, with a corresponding sense of having risen in the spiritual." The casting off of obligations and the indifference to other people's opinions have freed her.

VISIT TO CHILDREN: This is the only place in the book where Edna seems to have strong maternal feelings. She enjoys the feel of her children, and cannot look at her two little sons enough. Her eyes are hungry. She listens to their tales, and goes with them to see the pigs and cows; she spends a week with the children, and it seems to be the best week she has ever had with them. She tells about the house and how it is filled with workmen, and assures them about their precious possessions. They want to know about the house she is living in. Edna's mother-in-law is delighted that her grandchildren will remain with her until the renovations on the house are completed. It is difficult for Edna to part with the boys, and on the trip home, she hears their voices, and feels their cheeks. But when she returns to the pigeon house, she is alone and the children's voices have faded. At the end of this chapter, she seems, once again, to have removed herself from the children.

CHAPTER 33

ADÈLE'S WARNING: Although she is rapidly approaching the end of her pregnancy, Adèle comes to see Edna in the pigeon house. She is very curious and confused about Edna's motives for the move. She says that Edna, in many ways, is like a child, and doesn't reflect enough upon her actions. She also warns her about living alone, and allowing Alcée to spend so much time with her. She again mentions his reputation as a womanizer, but Edna does not seem concerned. Adèle begs Edna to come to her when she goes into labor, and Edna agrees to, no matter what time of day or night it is.

ROBERT'S RETURN: At Mademoiselle Reisz' apartment, one afternoon, while Edna is waiting for the musician to return, the door opens and Robert enters. He has returned from Mexico, and Edna is shocked to learn that he has been back for two days. He has not contacted her, and Edna doesn't understand why. She thought he would want to see her immediately. Robert appears to be uncomfortable, and does not act in the same manner that he had during the summer on Grand Isle. When she asks him why he didn't write to her, he says that he cannot imagine that his letters would be of any interest to her. They leave together and Edna invites Robert to have dinner with her in the pigeon house. He seems reluctant to do so, but finally agrees. When he notices a photograph of Alcée in the house, he seems shocked. Edna says that she is sketching him, and is using the photograph. She discovers that Robert was disappointed in his business ventures in Mexico, and that is why he has returned. She had hoped he returned because of her. She begins to bait him, repeating some of his own words to him, and they fall into an uncomfortable silence as they wait for dinner.

CHAPTER 34

JEALOUSY: In the pigeon house, a "certain degree of ceremony settled upon them with the announcement of dinner." There is constraint and tension between Edna and Robert due to his deliberate holding back. Edna is far more forthright about her feelings. She is confused and angered by Robert's aloofness. The only thing he admits is that he has forgotten nothing of Grand Isle. Edna notices that he is using an intricately designed tobacco pouch, and intuits that it has been given to him by a woman. She questions him about the extent of his involvement. Robert doesn't deny the pouch was a gift from a woman, but he says it was not important. Edna is filled with jealousy.

ALCÉE MEETS ROBERT: Alcée Arobin drops in with a message from Mrs. Merriman who has had to postpone a card party. He exhibits a degree of familiarity with Edna that Robert finds disturbing. A tension-filled discussion about women ensues between the two men, and Edna taunts them both about their romantic escapades. Robert gets up rather quickly to leave but he mentions Mr. Pontellier before he goes, in what sounds like a deliberate reminder to both Edna and Alcée of Edna's married state. Edna and Alcée enact a little domestic scene in which he reads items to her from the newspaper, while she straightens up the table. He again tells her how he adores her. She ignores him. His protestations of love are always amusingly cynical. When she says that he must have told the same things to many women, he says "I have said it before, but I don't think I ever came so near meaning it." When he leaves, Edna is consumed with jealousy about Robert's liaisons in Mexico. She is bitterly disappointed in their reunion.

CHAPTER 35

SYMBOLISM OF CLOTHING: When Edna awakes the next morning, she has shaken off her mood of jealousy and despondency. She convinces herself that Robert still loves her, and is confident that she will be able to break through his reserve. She knows that her passion for him will make him admit his own. Half-dressed, she eats breakfast. *It is instructive to note Chopin's use of clothing.* When Edna is feeling a sense of freedom, she casts off her clothing. We have seen this in other scenes: her first confidences to Adèle, her visit to Chênière Caminada.

BIRTH SYMBOLISM: Edna receives three letters that morning, one from her son Raoul, who tells her about the birth of ten tiny white pigs, and who asks his mother to send him candy. Birth symbolism is used frequently by Chopin. Edna is being reborn throughout the book. Adèle is about to give birth; the sow gives birth. A feeling of fecundity adds to the sensuosity of the novel.

LETTERS: Edna enjoys her son's letters. She also receives one from her husband, in which he makes plans for a trip to Europe. He assures her that this trip will be a luxurious one. He will not have to economize since he has done well in the stock market. Obviously he is trying to distract his wife with the promise of a longed-for trip. Léonce uses whatever means he can to try and lure Edna back to his home. Money is what Léonce has, and he doesn't hesitate to use it to protect his marriage. Edna answers him evasively. Arobin also writes to her. She makes no reply, but burns it. She doesn't care about him.

ROBERT'S INDIFFERENCE: Robert does not come to see her. She waits patiently for him, determined not to seek him out herself. She does continue to see Alcée Arobin.

ALCÉE'S HORSES: Although she is indifferent to Alcée, she sees him when he calls. She goes out driving with him. His horses are a little unmanageable. She finds the drive exciting. They return home early and Chopin comments that "it was late when he left her." What happened in the interim is left to the reader's imagination, but the narrator mentions that Arobin is intrigued with Edna: "... he detected the latent sensuality, which unfolded under his delicate sense of her nature's requirements like a torpid, torrid, sensitive blossom." This kind of narrative comment was heady stuff in 1899.

CHAPTER 36

GARDEN SYMBOLISM: There is a little garden in the suburbs where Edna goes to dream, to read, to think of Robert. Few people know about it. Edna has discovered it on one of her solitary walks. Few women at that time walked by themselves. Edna is unique in this small act of independence. The garden is sheltered, quiet, idyllic. It is symbolic of an innocent place where Edna can go to dream of her love.

FATE: Robert enters the garden one day, completely unexpectedly. He says he too often comes to this garden. It is fate that has brought them together again. Neither of them had planned to meet here. Edna, taken by surprise, confronts Robert and asks him why he doesn't come to see her, why he has neglected her so badly since his return from Mexico. He seems angry and asks her why she is so intent on forcing a confession from him that can result in nothing. He says she is asking him to bare a wound. Edna now realizes that he does indeed love her, and she stops questioning him.

CONFESSION: They return to Edna's home. Edna kisses Robert tenderly. He cannot help responding to her embrace. He says that he has kept away because she is married, and what good can it do to admit his love. He mentions marriage to her, if Léonce would only set her free. Edna is astonished. She tells Robert that Léonce cannot set her free. She is not one of his possessions. She is already free. "I give myself where I choose." It seems that it was never Edna's intention to marry Robert; she wants to love him. Robert is more conventional.

BREAKDOWN: A message arrives at that moment from Adèle. She has gone into labor, and wants Edna to come to her. Edna, having promised her friend, leaves Robert, who begs her to stay. He has completely broken down at this point, and wants nothing more than to caress and hold Edna. She seems much stronger than he and will not break her promise to Adèle. It is interesting to note that her marriage vows to Léonce do not concern her at all.

CHAPTER 37

SYMBOLIS OF CHILDBIRTH: Edna finds Adèle in great distress, complaining bitterly about being neglected. She has a nurse, her husband, and the doctor, but she still feels abandoned. She is restless, and berates everyone who is trying to help her. Edna begins to feel uncomfortable, thinking of her own labors, the pain, the odor of chloroform, the birth of a new life, "added to the great unnumbered multitude of souls that come and go." This childbirth scene makes her remember her own role as a mother, and it is one she prefers not to think about at this time. She feels an immense revolt against the ways of Nature, realizing how a woman who is a mother can never free herself from her responsibilities. *Edna has recently given birth to herself, as she came to understand her own nature, and this birth, for her, is the most important one, not the birth of a baby.*

ADÈLE'S REMINDER: When Adèle gives birth, she whispers to Edna, "Think of the children, Edna. Oh think of the children! Remember them." Adèle obviously senses that Edna is about to do something reckless, and in spite of her own exhaustion following the birth, warns Edna.

CHAPTER 38

EDNA'S CONFUSION: Edna walks home after the birth with Doctor Mandelet. He says that Adèle should never have demanded that Edna witness the birth. It was cruel to ask that of her friend. Edna replies that one must think of the children. The scene she has just witnessed has made her think of her own children, and of the obligation she has to them. It is not a thought she wishes to entertain. The doctor reminds Edna how Nature's only concern is to procure mothers for the race. *This conversation clarifies for Edna how transitory passion can be, and how permanent the products of passion are.* When Doctor Mandelet offers her help, she says that she doesn't want to speak of things that are troubling her. She expresses her thanks for his help, but says that she wants things her own way. That is asking for a great deal, she knows, but "I shouldn't want to trample upon the little lives. Oh! I don't know what I'm saying, Doctor. Good night. Don't blame me for anything."

ROBERT'S LETTER: Edna returns to her house and thinks again of Robert and their last passionate embraces. She once again thinks that nothing on earth could be better than "possession of the loved one." She hopes that he is waiting for her. She plans to awaken him with kisses. He is not there. Instead he has left her a brief letter. "I love you. Good-bye—because I love you." Edna does not sleep at all that night. The reader is not told what she is thinking about. We do not know at this point what she will do. The only commentary from the narrator is a description of her sleepless night, and the fact that she is still awake in the morning when her maid comes to light the fire.

CHAPTER 39

RETURN TO GRAND ISLE: The last chapter of *The Awakening* returns the reader to the setting of the first chapter. Once again we are on Grand Isle. Victor Lebrun, Robert's brother, is repairing some of the cottages on the resort island in preparation for the summer season. He and Mariequita are talking about the dinner at Mrs. Pontellier's. Victor is exaggerating every detail, and Mariequita becomes quite jealous. She feels envious of Mrs. Pontellier's beauty and easy conquest of men. The two young people are astonished when Edna Pontellier suddenly appears. They have just been talking about her. And here she is. But this is no entrancing spectacle. Edna looks tired and worn out. She tells them that she has come for a few days to rest. Before dinner, she says, she wants to take a swim. They tell her that the water is too cold, but she says she will just put her toes in.

NARRATIVE COMMENT: The reader is now told what Edna thought about during that last sleepless night. She realized that her nature meant she would want many lovers. Although she was not concerned about Léonce and the harm this would do to him, she was concerned about her sons. Since she cannot reconcile her passionate nature with that of a mother, she becomes despondent. She even realizes that her passion for Robert will one day pass. Her children seem like antagonists who will overcome, who will enslave her. She decides to elude them.

SYMBOLISM OF NUDITY: Edna walks down to the beach and removes her bathing suit. It is the first time she has ever been naked in the open air. She feels like a newborn person. Edna is about to become completely free for the first time in her life. It is fitting that she strips herself of the encumbrance of clothing.

WHITMANESQUE PASSAGE: As she steps into the ocean, she feels the sensuousness of the water, which enfolds her in a "soft, close embrace." The sea is described as "seductive, never ceasing, whispering, clamoring, murmuring, inviting the soul to wander in abysses of solitude." This passage is very similar to parts of Whitman's "Song of Myself." It is known that Chopin was an admirer of Whitman, and was familiar with his work.

FREEDOM: Edna swims out too far. She swims with long sweeping strokes. She is not afraid, except for one moment of terror, which passes. She does not look back but she thinks of Léonce and the children. They will not possess her. Her last thoughts are of her childhood, her father, her sister, the barking of a dog. She hears the hum of bees and smells the "musky odor of pinks." Her death is a deliberate, conscious decision. *There is no quality of hysteria here, but a sense of dignity and peace that bring a measure of grandeur to Edna.* Unable to go back to a life as a conventional wife and mother, Edna chooses freedom in death. It is her choice.

Character Analyses

EDNA PONTELLIER: A handsome, rather than conventionally pretty, twenty-eight-year-old woman, Edna Pontellier is vacationing on the island of Grand Isle, a resort for wealthy Creole families off the coast of Louisiana with her husband and two young sons. She is not Creole; she was born in Kentucky into a Presbyterian family. Edna's mother died when she was quite young; her father was a stern man, who ruled the household in an oppressive manner. Deprived of her mother's love at an early age, she was brought up in an atmosphere of gloom that had a chilling effect on her development as a woman. Although she had three infatuations before her marriage, none of them was ever acknowledged. She grew up without love of passion and her marriage to Léonce Pontellier is as repressive as her childhood had been. She was not in love with her husband when she married him. Nor is she in love with him now. She amuses herself flirting with Robert Lebrun, the son of the resort owner. Married women in this Creole society often play this game—it is not taken seriously by anyone. Edna is mildly titillated by Robert's attention, and she gradually begins to awaken to her own sexuality. She learns to swim during this summer, is stirred deeply by music, begins to paint more seriously than she has ever done before, and finally convinces herself that she is madly in love with Robert. She allows herself to be seduced by Alcée Arobin, a well-known roué, when Robert becomes frightened by her passion. Understanding her sensual nature, and finally facing her own sexual hunger, Edna, unable to reconcile her appetites with her role as wife and mother, swims out to sea and drowns. It is deliberately done; her death is not an accident.

LÉONCE PONTELLIER: Forty years old, a successful broker in New Orleans, Léonce is proud of his wife's beauty and considers her a possession. He expects her to be a conventional wife and to take care of their two young sons. Often, he scolds her for neglecting them. Yet, he seems more interested in playing billiards with the men at Klein's Hotel, than in spending time with his family. He is regarded very highly by all the people vacationing on the island. They think he is a perfect husband. Increasingly puzzled by his wife's refusal to play the role he has assigned to her, he goes for help to the family doctor. Léonce is critical of Edna, angry at her decision to stop the entertaining that is required of her, and shocked and embarrassed when she moves out of his house into a small house of her own. He makes up a story in order to preserve appearances that Edna has had to leave because the house they shared is being remodeled. Léonce is incapable of understanding Edna or any woman who does not fit the mold. He is far from a villain, or a brutish lout. He is just not able to accept the changes in his wife.

RAOUL AND ETIENNE PONTELLIER: Edna and Léonce's sons are not three-dimensional characters. We do not see the little boys often, but when they do appear, they always want something. Their nurse takes care of their physical needs, and Edna is not burdened unduly with them. They seem quite independent of their mother, and actually do not rush to her even when they hurt themselves. It is difficult to distinguish Raoul from Etienne. They are always together and they seem to demand something from their mother whenever they do appear. Sometimes they go to visit their paternal grandmother, where they are filled with Creole lore.

EDNA'S FATHER, THE COLONEL: The Colonel is another example of the conventional male, unable to accept a woman who is seeking independence. Although he opposed Edna's marriage to a Catholic, he seems to have accepted this by the time of his visit to New Orleans. He advises his son-in-law to be firm with Edna. His other daughters are excellent wives. He has no understanding of Edna and is quite unsympathetic to her. He was a stern, unloving father when she was growing up, and he presided over a dour household.

ROBERT LEBRUN: A rather callow Creole youth, Robert spends his summers flirting with married women, is not very successful in business, and is always planning to go to Mexico. He acts as a catalyst in stirring Edna's emotions, but he, himself, is really quite ordinary, and in time, Edna begins to understand this. He does, however, have the exoticism of the Creole male, has been raised on mystical tales, and is able to impart some of this to Edna, who responds to Robert's tales of spirits and ghosts.

VICTOR LEBRUN: Robert's younger brother is described as hotheaded and violent, but greatly beloved by his mother. He is spoiled and pampered, but at one point in the story, Edna feels herself suddenly aware of his physical beauty. He seems to be the very incarnation of desire.

MADAME LEBRUN: The owner of a summer resort on Grand Isle, Madame Lebrun is a very busy, efficient woman. Her petticoats are starched; she dresses in white. Although her husband either died or deserted her and their two small children (his whereabouts are somewhat vague), Mme Lebrun seems to have managed quite well. She has a persistent suitor, M. Montel, who has been pursuing her for twenty years.

ADÈLE RATIGNOLLE: The embodiment of the "mother-woman," Adèle Ratignolle is beautiful, plump, golden-haired, completely feminine, and utterly possessed by her motherhood. All her thoughts, plans, desires center around her children. She is pregnant this summer; she seems to be always pregnant, is constantly sewing little garments for her children, both born and unborn, and is a direct contrast to Edna Pontellier. *Chopin uses her as a foil to show how different most women are from Edna.* She becomes Edna's confidante, but is incapable of understanding a woman like Edna. When she flirts with a young, unattached man, she understands the rules that govern this game, and would never make the mistake of taking him too seriously.

ALCÉE AROBIN: Handsome, arrogant, well-known in New Orleans for his scandalous affairs with women, Alcée Arobin is the consummate roué. He knows himself, and he thinks he knows women. He consciously and deliberately sets out to seduce Edna. Obviously, he thinks she is seducible. He is a contrast to Robert, who is far more innocent and is capable of feeling love for a woman. Alcée seems to only feel desire. When he kisses Edna for the first time, Edna responds to him sexually in a way she has never done before.

MADEMOISELLE REISZ: An ugly woman, an immensely talented musician, Mademoiselle Reisz is an example of the independent woman. Her art comes first; she is blunt, outspoken, and recognizes in Edna a spirit that responds passionately to music. She does not feel that Edna has it within her to be an artist because she is not willing to make the necessary sacrifices that art demands. She gets letters from Robert Lebrun when he goes to Mexico and shows them to Edna; she encourages the younger woman in her struggle to become independent. Her apartment becomes a refuge for Edna.

DOCTOR MANDELET: Doctor Mandelet is a kindly, wise man to whom Léonce goes for advice on how to handle Edna, who is becoming increasingly difficult to understand. The doctor assures Léonce that her restlessness will pass and that women are strange creatures, not at all like men. They are willful, capricious, and need a strong hand. When Léonce complains that Edna has gotten some notions in her head concerning the eternal rights of women, and has actually moved out of his bed, *the doctor suspects that Edna has been associating with "pseudointellectual women"* who have been influencing her. He tells Léonce to let Edna alone and the mood will pass. But the thought does occur to him that there might be another man. He does not voice this though, because "he knew his Creole too well to make such a blunder as that."

MARIEQUITA: This earthy, peasant Spanish girl flirts with the Lebrun brothers and perhaps has been intimate with one or both. She is immediately antagonistic to Edna when Robert takes Edna to mass on Chênière, the island where the religious service takes place. She understands that

Edna's marriage is no deterrent to a passionate affair, nor are the two children. The detail the author gives of the "sand and slime" between Mariequita's toes symbolizes the animalism of the girl. She speaks in Spanish to Robert, who understands her. No one else on the boat going to Chênière knows what she is saying. A connection is made between Robert and Mariequita. They speak the same language, metaphorically as well as literally.

Sample Essay Questions and Answers

1. Compare Adèle Ratignolle to Edna Pontellier.

ANSWER: Adèle Ratignolle is the perfect example of the "mother-woman." A beautiful, feminine woman whose primary concern is her three children, she is pregnant again during this summer that she spends on Grand Isle. Unhappy at being parted from her children, even for a little while, she is always sewing something for them. Children's undergarments and drawers can fascinate her and provide a topic for conversation. She understands the flirtatious games played in this Creole society and knows how to fend off amorous advances made by young unmarried males, but she can still enjoy the sparring. She is utterly comfortable and fulfilled in her role as wife and mother.

Edna Pontellier is the exact opposite. She is less conventionally beautiful, is described as "handsome" and "noble" and is thinner, and is not consumed by motherhood. She pays perfunctory attention to her two young sons, who do not seem very attached to her. She is relieved when they go away for a visit. She is interested in art. She sketches, and has a natural ability. She is not Creole, was born into a repressive Presbyterian family, and does not know how to play the flirtatious games that married women and single men play on this island. She becomes infatuated with Robert, begins to awaken sexually, wants to free herself from the confines of marriage and motherhood, and is unhappy enough to commit suicide when she realizes she cannot reconcile her own needs with those of her family.

2. Compare Robert Lebrun to Alcée Arobin.

ANSWER: Robert Lebrun, an impecunious, charming bachelor, spends his summers on Grand Isle, where his mother owns a pension. He amuses himself by flirting with the married women. He is capable of an innocent flirtation with Edna, but when he feels that matters are getting too serious, he flees to Mexico. He is sensitive, exotic, touched by the magic of the Creole he has grown up with, but is not extraordinary in any way. His teasing attentions stimulate Edna and cause her to awaken from her sleep of repression. He is the catalyst in the story. Weak, impetuous, somewhat foolish, completely incapable of understanding a woman like Edna, Robert should be harmless. It is Edna's response that causes the danger.

Alcée Arobin is dangerous. A well-known roué, irresponsible, reckless, lustful, he quickly senses Edna's state of arousal and takes advantage of it. His kisses stir Edna passionately for the first time in her life. When she allows herself to be seduced by a man she knows she doesn't love, she understands what animal passion is. If Robert had seduced her, she would probably have been able to rationalize it as a culmination of a great love. She cannot delude herself about Alcée Arobin. Robert is responsible for Edna's awakening, but Alcée is partially responsible for Edna's end.

3. How is the setting of Grand Isle important in the development of the plot?

ANSWER: Grand Isle, an island fifty miles off the coast of Louisiana, is a summer resort for the wealthy members of Creole society who winter in New Orleans. Surrounded by the warm water of the Gulf of Mexico, lulled by gentle breezes, filled with the odors of jasmine, the island is Eden-like. And it is here that Edna, like the original inhabitants of the Garden of Eden, eats of the tree of knowledge. Edna, a repressed, discontented society matron, unfulfilled by her marriage and motherhood, is loosened by the sounds, smells, and primitive quality of Grand Isle and indulges in a flirtation. She is deeply stirred by music, learns to swim for the first time in the tepid waters of the Gulf, and under the spell of the setting begins to shed inhibitions. She finds out that she is a passionate animal and this self-knowledge, which she is unable to reconcile with being a wife and mother, results in her death.

4. Discuss the role of a married woman in Creole society of this time.

ANSWER: A married woman, in this Creole society at this time, was very limited. She was Catholic, so that birth control, primitive at best at that time, was forbidden. Therefore, she was pregnant frequently. She was supposed to take care of her children and household, supervise the servants, plan the menus, create a beautiful home, be able to play a musical instrument, perhaps sketch, maybe sing. She must not take any of these artistic accomplishments seriously. They were supposed to enhance the charm of her home and reflect on her husband. A wife was a possession, one to be cared for and displayed. Her needs were to be sublimated and she was supposed to be completely fulfilled by being a wife and mother. She, of course, was not responsible for contributing to the family income through working at a job. She came to the marriage with a dowry, and, perhaps, some inherited wealth.

5. Discuss the theme of man's inability to understand woman.

ANSWER: That man is incapable of understanding woman is a theme in *The Awakening*. Edna's father, a rigid, rather dour man, gave her little affection as a child and did not approve of her marriage because Léonce Pontellier was Catholic. He should have disapproved of Edna's marriage for other reasons: Léonce was twelve years older; Edna was not in love. Once Edna is married, he tells his son-in-law to be firm with her. He is utterly unsympathetic to a daughter or a wife who will not conform. It is mentioned that he hastened his wife's death through coercion.

Léonce regards his wife as a possession. He wants to display her; he wants her to adorn his home; he wants her to take care of the children and keep them from disturbing him. When Edna refuses to entertain the way she had in the past, and shows signs of rebelling, he goes for help to Doctor Mandelet.

Doctor Mandelet tells Léonce that women are moody, high-strung, irritable. They are difficult creatures to manage, but they must be handled. The doctor obviously feels that a woman must be broken, like a high-spirited horse.

Robert Lebrun flirts with Edna, teases her, fills her head with Creole lore, but is incapable of understanding her. He doesn't know what Edna really is; he doesn't really want to know. To Robert, women are enigmatic and exciting, but that's about all he understands. He could not accept Edna's independence, and if she ever married him, they both would be unhappy.

Alcée Arobin doesn't understand Edna either. He doesn't try to. He just wants to seduce her. He sees women as sexual playthings. The chase is what excites him. Not one of the men in this novel understands women: neither father, husband, lover, doctor, nor seducer.

6. Why was the public so shocked by *The Awakening*?

ANSWER: *The Awakening* was published in 1899. Readers were shocked to read about a woman who has affairs, moves out of her husband's house, is not terribly interested in her children, wants a career, wants a self. These things were scandalous at the time, years before women got the vote, were able to handle their own finances, and were encouraged to pursue careers. The sensual descriptions of water, the element that serves to awaken Edna, the sensuosity of the island itself, a paradise in which a woman is loosened of habitual restraints, the evocation of lush, unrestrained growth, both of the island and of

Edna's passionate nature, caused the book to be taken off the library shelves in St. Louis, where the author was living. She had jeopardized her reputation and her livelihood by writing such a disturbing book.

7. Discuss the use of bird symbolism in *The Awakening*.

ANSWER: From the first screeching of the caged parrot, hung outside the pension on Grand Isle, "Get out! Get out!" the symbolism of a bird in a cage is established. Edna is a bird even though her cage is gilded. She is confined by marriage and motherhood. She is described as having "quick, bright eyes." There is something bird-like about her appearance. The cry of "Get out! Get out!" is heard again in the novel and symbolizes what Edna is trying to do.

When Edna moves out of her husband's home into a tiny place of her own, her new shelter is called "the pigeon house." Pigeons are not caged; they are free to come and go, unlike the parrot who has been tamed and domesticized. Edna views the pigeon house as a place where she can be free of her habitual constraints. It is where she will taste freedom.

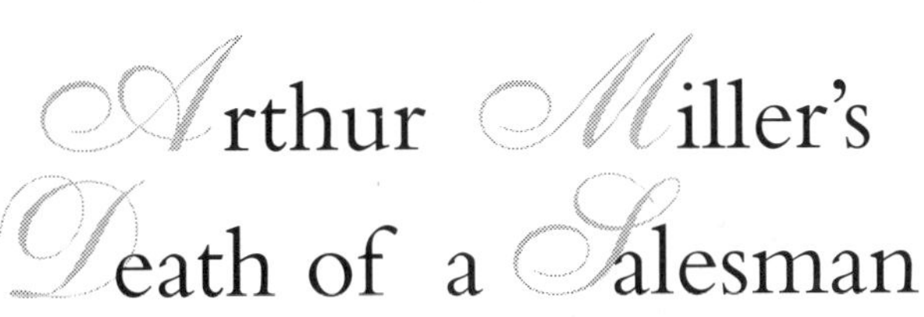

Arthur Miller's Death of a Salesman

Scene-by-Scene Summary and Analysis

ACT I, SCENE 1

Willy Loman, an aging Brooklyn salesman, returns home exhausted and irritable late one Monday night. His loyal wife, Linda, is alarmed, for by now he should be in New England on a sales trip. He tells her, however, that he could not concentrate and kept driving his car off the road. She suggests that rest might help and urges him to seek office work near home. Their grown sons, Biff and Happy, amiably reunited, are asleep upstairs. Biff, thirty-four, has just come back from one more temporary farm job. Angered and concerned, Willy cannot see how so promising a youth can be so lost. He also regrets peevishly that their house, now almost paid for, has lost its country surroundings of grass and flowers and is now hemmed in by tall apartments. He muses about the happier past, back in 1928, when the smiling, popular young Biff used to polish so expertly their old red Chevrolet.

ANALYSIS

In this opening scene significant aspects of Willy's personality are introduced, and several are effectively developed. A few of Linda's traits also are revealed, and there are brief descriptive references to the still unseen Biff, Happy, and the young boss, Howard.

WILLY: Willy appears first as a tired, worn man of sixty. His weariness is apparent in the hunched-over, stooped way in which he carries in his heavy sample cases. Besides, he himself says that he is weary, and Linda insists more than once that he needs rest and a less demanding job assignment.

He is also obviously shaken. His work as a salesman requires him to do a great deal of driving, and now he seems unable to keep his car under control. He rejects Linda's comforting assurance that it may be some easily solved problem, such as that of getting new glasses. And he is especially frightened when he realizes that although he was behind the wheel of his current Studebaker, he actually thought for a time that he was still steering the old red Chevrolet of 1928.

Thirdly, he is short-tempered. He answers Linda sharply, retorts angrily when accused of criticizing Biff, and is unreasonably irked to be offered whipped cheese instead of his customary Swiss. He testily complains about the unopened windows and condemns the builders of apartment houses for the ruining of the neighborhood.

In addition, he is worried, especially about Biff. Why has he not found himself some steady work and settled down? Is it mere laziness? Willy wants him to make a good living and is at a loss to understand why he cannot. This combination of anxiety and bewilderment has led Willy to greet his returning son with reproachful questions, and relations are strained between them. Willy also hopes that he is not causing Linda to fret, for she is his source of strength.

Finally, Willy reveals the wistfulness of a dreamer. This is emphasized subtly by the plaintive, light theme played on the flute as background music. Moreover, there is his delighted response to the pleasant scenery along the road, as well as his recollections of the lilac, wisteria, and peonies that used to give out a springtime fragrance before the apartment builders "massacred" the neighborhood. There is nostalgia, too, as he thinks of the smiling, popular younger Biff, who shined up the Chevrolet so beautifully that no one would believe it had gone eighty thousand miles.

LINDA: Willy's wife is shown here to be patient, tactful, and considerate. Even when the tired, peevish Willy is hard to please and replies rudely, she keeps her temper and tries to soothe him. Lovingly she takes off his shoes and makes every effort to restore his confidence in himself.

Yet she is clearly no mere passive helpmeet. She takes issue with Willy for talking so harshly to Biff and tells him to control himself. She would have him do nothing to dishearten further this troubled young man who is still trying to find himself. She also ventures to cut in on his tirade against the apartment builders with the remark that others have to live somewhere. Moreover, she is quite insistent that he see Howard about a less taxing position.

Although Linda, in general, murmurs reassuring words to Willy, she is shown from the first to possess a realistic awareness of the true situation. Her remark that Willy's "mind is overactive" is shrewdly perceptive, and she shows a sensitive appreciation of Biff's discouragement and confusion.

BIFF: Although only discussed here, Biff is represented as a cheerful, eager, well-liked boy who for some reason grew up to be a moody, restless young man. For over ten years now, he has gone from job to job and never made much money. That he still has some pride is hinted when Linda dodges the question of his apologizing to Willy. But that he is also sensitive is suggested by her statement that he was "crestfallen" after Willy criticized him. Her comment here also indicates that Biff admires his father and cares a great deal about the older man's opinion of him.

As for Biff's laziness, that question is left open. Willy seems undecided, and he recalls the boy Biff as energetically simonizing the car. Linda, on her part, denies that he is lazy. She describes him as "lost," but offers no helpful explanation as to how their son lost his earlier breezy confidence.

HAPPY: Virtually nothing is said of the younger son, Happy. He is clearly not on Willy's mind now and does not figure prominently in Willy's recollections, as shown up to now. He is merely said to get along well with his brother and to have taken him out with him on a date. Later it will be evident that Happy is a sensual young man, much given to casual love affairs. Here he is placed in the general family picture, but not accorded much importance.

HOWARD: Willy's young boss is the son of "old man Wagner," who held great hopes out to Willy and treated him well. With the encouragement of that masterly prince, Willy opened up the New England territory for the firm. The son, however, shows little appreciation, and this implied coldness will crucially affect Willy's life later in the play.

PLOT DEVELOPMENT: WILLY AND HIS JOB. Willy's difficulties with the car suggest that his job may be in jeopardy. Linda, for all her reassuring manner, suggests that being over sixty he cannot be expected to do so much traveling. At her urging, he agrees to go ask Howard for a New York assignment. But the references to Howard's unappreciative nature indicate that Willy may meet opposition.

WILLY AND BIFF. It is evident that relations are tense and uneasy between father and son. Remembering the smiling lively youngster Biff used to be, Willy is disgusted with the thirty-four-year-old moody drifter. Yet he does want to help Biff. So he promises Linda to hold his temper, and try to find the youth a selling job. If, however, Biff prefers to return West, he will let him go without rancor. These are good resolutions. But Willy is seen to be so irritable and impulsive that doubt is created as to whether or not further hostilities will be avoided.

TECHNIQUE: In later scenes Willy's mind will slip back to past scenes, and he will be seen talking to such memory characters as the young boy Biff or the now dead Uncle Ben. But such flashbacks might be confusing in the opening scene, when the characters are met for the first time. Even here, of course, Willy does drift back to earlier days. He thinks of his first years with the company. Biff's popularity as a boy, the former flower gardens around the house, and the 1928 car polishing. These recollections, however, are conveyed only through Willy's dialogue, with the music of the flute sometimes adding a touch of strangeness. In general, then, this first episode takes place clearly in the present and makes virtually no use of the interesting stage devices later employed to show memories being reenacted in Willy's disturbed consciousness.

IMPORTANT THEMES: "LOSTNESS." Willy says that for an instant while driving he could not remember the last few minutes. Again, he thought he was in the old Chevrolet instead of the current Studebaker. Literally, then, Willy has not known where he was—he has been lost. At sixty, moreover, he is clearly unsure of himself, worried about his job and about his son. If Biff, who cannot seem to find a satisfying way of life at thirty-four, is "lost," so, in another way, is his sixty-year-old father.

FATHER-SON CONFLICT. Willy cannot accept Linda's idea that life is a "casting off." Biff is no longer a small boy; he is a grown man thirty-four years old. Yet Willy, even meeting him at the train, angrily upbraids him for failing to succeed. He cannot stop thinking about Biff and Biff's problems and says that he will try to get him a job. Biff, according to Linda, is badly upset when his father criticizes him, but still keeps coming home, unwilling to make a break. These two men are thus extremely concerned about each other, but from the first there are also deep hostilities that will lead to more and more violent arguments.

CHANGED LIVING CONDITIONS. When the younger Willy and Linda first started making payments on their Brooklyn house, it was in a pleasant semirural area with grass and flower gardens. Vegetables, too, were grown in the backyard. Since then, however, tall apartment houses have been built that shut out the light so that plants will not grow and substitute unpleasant odors for the fragrance of lilac and wisteria. Willy's little house and the hammock he and Biff swung between the elms thus becomes the symbol of an earlier, more individualistic, more easygoing America. The big apartments in turn suggest to Willy a population "out of control" and the new "maddening" competition. Only a few buildings in a small area are involved here, but the playwright seems to suggest that the changes may be more or less typical in America.

CHANGED BUSINESS CONDITIONS. When Willy began selling for the Wagner company, he virtually "discovered" New England for them. As a young man he opened up whole new territories and was properly commended by his employer, a "prince," who was "masterful." Now, however, the business is under the direction of Howard, the old employer's son. Howard is not one to "appreciate" long, loyal service. This theme will be developed further as the play proceeds. The cold, impersonal tone of business today will be contrasted with the friendlier, more humane spirit of past transactions.

LAMENT FOR THE PAST. The tone of the play is often nostalgic. Here Willy looks back to better times when old Wagner was his boss and his house had a flourishing garden. He recalls how much admired the lighthearted Biff was as a boy and how beautiful the red Chevrolet looked when polished. The present, by contrast, is a time of darkness and suffocation, of weariness and bewilderment, of blighted hopes and bitter quarrels.

ACT I, SCENE 2

Upstairs in their old bedroom, the two sons are roused by Willy's noisy mumbling. Both are worried about him but are soon cheerfully reminiscing about their early affairs with prostitutes. Biff is ill at ease, however, aware of his father's scorn. He also feels that he should have settled down, but he has hated the routine and competition of steady jobs, and the more pleasant ranch work he has found financially unprofitable. Happy, in turn, has his own apartment, his car, and his feminine conquests. But he, too, longs for outdoor muscular work. Biff envisions a ranch they could handle together, but Happy still wants first the prestige of a large income. Biff thinks he might obtain a loan from Bill Oliver, an early employer, whom he left after stealing some basketballs. They hear Willy again, and Biff denounces him angrily.

ANALYSIS

This scene concerns the two Loman brothers almost exclusively. Only brief references are made to Willy and Linda.

WILLY: Heard by the boys to mumble about the mileage on the old Chevrolet and Biff's expert car polishing, Willy unnerves Happy and infuriates Biff. The sons' comments point up the fact that Willy's odd behavior has been going on for some time and is getting worse. Recently, Happy sent his father to Florida for a rest cure, but to no avail. Happy confirms the impression created in Scene 1 that Willy is mainly upset about Biff's drifting from job to job.

LINDA: To Happy, Linda represents the type of admirable woman he would willingly marry, as contrasted with the girls of easy virtue with whom he regularly has affairs. His mother has high standards and is incorruptible. To Biff, however, Linda appears the victim of Willy's boorish, inconsiderate actions. He is incensed that she should have to listen to his father's wild outbursts. Linda, therefore, as viewed in this scene, is the ideal wife and mother to be shielded, if possible, from the graceless behavior of Willy.

BIFF: In Scene 2 Biff shows himself antagonistic toward his father, protectively concerned about Linda, comradely toward Happy, and confused and anxious as to his own future.

At first Biff is reticent about his attitude toward Willy, although referring to him with no enthusiasm. Then, looking glum, he asks Happy why his father always seems to view him mockingly. He angrily rejects, however, his brother's suggestion that he is the cause of Willy's erratic mumbling. Later when the latter's wild talk becomes more audible, Biff reacts with fury and contempt. His father seems then only a self-centered, doltish individual who causes Linda annoyance. Still, Biff appears momentarily grief-stricken when he hears Willy refer to the old car-polishing days. There is pain as well as anger in Biff's "sour" rejection of Willy.

His references to Linda are few, but she is clearly someone he loves and admires. Although it is Happy who says he would like to find a girl like his mother, Biff also wants one who is "steady" and has "substance." And it is quite possible that he, too, sees her as an ideal type. Certainly, he is furious that she should be subjected to Willy's noisy, rambling talk. Later it will become evident why Biff's grudge against Willy has made him especially sorry for his mother.

As regards Happy, Biff seems to be genuinely fond of his younger brother. He amusedly recalls the time years ago when he first took Happy out with him on dates with whores. And his dream is to take Happy back with him out West so that they run a ranch together. He could trust Happy and they could both enjoy the outdoor work.

In general, Biff seems to Happy to have lost his old good spirits and self-confidence. For one thing, Biff is dissatisfied with his life to date. For years now he has gone from one temporary job to the next, and this he feels is the irresponsible course of a boy, not a grown man. He believes that he should marry some good, steady girl and settle down in some line of work. In this view he is thus in substantial agreement with Willy.

Yet he is uncertain which way to turn. He has held various business jobs and found them suffocating. He hated the routine and the indoor confinement, and the strong competitive spirit also disgusted him. Yet he realizes that such work pays well and makes it possible for a young man to become established. On the other hand, he has found considerable satisfaction in the open-air ranch work he has done in the West. He likes, for instance, to see the young colts in the spring. But the pay is low, and there are small future prospects.

His one solution at the moment is to try to obtain a loan and buy a ranch. In this way he could do the type of work he likes and still have some stability. He plans to approach a former employer, Bill Oliver, for the loan. Here his thinking seems somewhat fuzzy. For he quit Oliver's company shortly after stealing a carton of basketballs, and he thinks that Oliver suspected the truth. It is thus not at all clear why Oliver should lend such a dubious risk several thousand dollars. In terms, however, of Biff's mentality, the move is curiously plausible. Oliver, who once used to trust Biff, did tell him to ask him if he ever needed anything. This may well have been merely a conventional form of polite farewell, but the Lomans, both Willy and Biff, place much emphasis upon the personal bond in business. Despite all evidence to the contrary, their concept of economic relationships seems constantly to stress a man-to-man, informal, friendly meeting of individuals. Willy will talk to Howard, and all will be well. Biff will go back to the businessman who a decade or so ago put a reassuring hand on his shoulder, and will walk out with a ten-thousand-dollar loan.

Two other factors enter into Biff's vision of Oliver. Both identify Biff again as truly Willy's son. One is a streak of buoyant optimism that is hard to erase. Charley, a neighbor, will later eulogize Willy as a salesman "riding on a smile and a shoeshine." At this time in their lives both Willy and Biff are unhappy and discouraged. Yet every so often each suddenly feels an upsurge of confidence. Here, even to think of floating such a large loan from his ex-employer, Biff must have some of this hopeful enthusiasm.

There is also, however, ironically an underlying sense of desperation. Like his father, Biff at this point is beaten. He does not know what to do or where to turn. So almost any possibility that occurs to him will be seized upon with almost feverish concern. Only a man brought up to "think big" and concoct grandiose schemes could dream up the Oliver loan project. But Biff, who actually does voice misgivings, has no other prospects at all. So he will have to convince himself that Oliver did at least formerly think the world of him and may still be willing to hand him a sizable sum.

HAPPY: Like his father and Biff, Happy is described as a strong, muscular, athletic type. He holds a reasonably well-paid job in a store, but by no means finds the work itself satisfying. He, like his brother, would rather use his muscles and take on more strenuous activities in the open air. Yet he is not likely to accept Biff's invitation to join him out West.

Never Willy's favorite, Happy, the younger son, wants the respect and prestige that a lucrative job will guarantee. When the high-salaried merchandise manager enters the store, "waves part in front of him." Those who give Happy orders at work are not only "common" and "petty," but "pompous" and "self-important." Happy is determined to show them that he, too, can achieve success on their terms.

Happy, in brief, wants what his bosses possess, all the while regarding them personally with contempt. His own assumption that he is superior seems to have three bases. First of all, although this will be more apparent later, Willy always suggested that his sons were destined for greatness. As Biff says in this scene, they were not brought up to "grub for money." Secondly, Happy is very conscious of his physical strength and prowess. He thus resents being ordered around by those who cannot box so well, run so fast, or lift such heavy weights. Thirdly, he is proud of the fact that women find him attractive. He has even been able to seduce the fianceés of three store executives. He must therefore, in his view, be more virile and impressive than they are.

At the same time, he recognizes certain other deplorable aspects of his present way of life. For one thing, he is aware that material wealth does not in itself assure contentment. The merchandise manager, whom he envies, built an impressive house on Long Island, only to move out and start another within a few months. And even Happy, who can at least boast of his own apartment, his own car, and a steady supply of admiring women, admits he is often lonely and dissatisfied.

In addition, he does not like the intensely competitive spirit. If he were with someone like Biff, whom he could trust, he might be able to live up to his ideals. He would presumably be honest and would not tempt the fiancées of other men. Instead he would settle down with a good, dependable girl like his mother. As it is, all around him are corrupt, or so he claims. Hence, he takes bribes from buyers, ruins the future wives of his bosses, and eyes his fellow-workers with smoldering hostility.

A fairly sensual man, he apparently has many casual love affairs. He gets some pleasure from these dubious romances, and in addition, they help provide temporary escape from loneliness and frustration. They make him feel popular and important and—especially when the girls are the other men's fianceés—more attractive than business rivals. Yet he must admit that often there is little thrill obtained from such brief relationships. And he feels vaguely guilty about his continual self-indulgence. So he tells Biff that what he really wants is marriage with a nice, respectable girl. Yet in order to change, he would, of course, have to give up the affairs. And while these have not given him the deeper rewards of a permanent relationship, they have helped to serve as some compensation for his decidedly subordinate position at work. They act as props to Happy's ego; and despite his repeated assurances of imminent reform, he will not readily do without these minor triumphs.

Happy is not altogether ungenerous. He seems to have financed Willy's brief and unavailing Florida rest cure. And here he is not without some concern for his father's worsening condition. Yet he was never the favored son, and he is not so emotionally shattered by the situation as is Biff. He asks Biff's help because Willy's behavior is "getting embarrassing." Biff is more likely to think of his mother's sufferings, but Happy, in general, is used to looking out mainly for himself.

PLOT DEVELOPMENT: Most of this scene is taken up with exposition regarding the personalities and histories of the two sons. The only important plot element introduced here is Biff's plan to ask Oliver for a loan. This scheme will eventually have a crucial bearing upon relations between Biff and his father and will help bring about Willy's last momentous decision.

TECHNIQUE: This scene, too, is essentially one of straight dialogue. During the boys' conversation, Willy can be heard apparently addressing the boy Biff who long ago so expertly simonized the car. But there is no dramatized flashback episode here. This scene's function is essentially to introduce two more main characters, and there is little evidence of any unusual or startling stage devices. Actually, of course, having a set that shows more than one room makes it possible to show Willy muttering in the kitchen while the boys talk upstairs. But the time sequence is normal, and events are occurring objectively, not solely in Willy's mind.

IMPORTANT THEMES: "LOSTNESS." Neither Biff nor Happy is really contented. At thirty-four, Biff has no job and only the most doubtful of prospects (the Oliver plan). The outdoor work he likes offers no security and no future. The steady job that pays well has never held his interest long. He does not know what to do next. Happy is better established. He has a fair position, a car, and an apartment. But he feels that all is false around him and that he is constantly going back on his principles. Beneath his air of jaunty assurance, he, too, is anxious and confused.

FATHER-SON CONFLICT. As regards Willy, Biff appears here both "sour" and concerned as well. Toward the end, however, hearing Willy's noisy mumbling, he becomes furious at his father for disturbing his mother. Happy, too, is worried about Willy but is also annoyed because the older man's erratic behavior is "embarrassing."

CORRUPTION IN MODERN BUSINESS. Husky men both, Biff and Happy prefer working with their muscles in the outdoors. Both object to the confinement and routine of store or office work. Such attitudes may be merely matters of individual temperament, rather than indications of some flaw in the overall system. Yet throughout there is some suggestion that the wilder, freer life of those who earlier pushed Westward offered greater satisfactions to the strong individual who was good with his hands. In the indoor world, according to the resentful Happy, meaner, commoner types give orders to those whose physical prowess they could not hope to match.

Both Biff and Happy also criticize the intensely competitive spirit of business. Biff can never see why he must always try to get ahead of the next man. Happy feels that this sense of competition drives him to seduce the fiancées of store executives. Yet while he deplores this emphasis, noting that getting ahead does not guarantee bliss, he still wants to prove his worth by making more money than the merchandise manager. The brothers wish they could be business partners. Each then would have someone to trust, and they would presumably be working *with*, not *against* each other.

Taken as a whole, the views expressed by Biff and Happy are not, of course, necessarily those of the playwright. These two young men have rather obvious personality flaws. Neither is exactly a mature, sensible, truly adult individual. When, for instance, Happy sneers at his fellow employees, he is probably revealing more about his own faults than about theirs. Yet there is sufficient stress upon the coldly competitive spirit in the business world, here and elsewhere in the play, to suggest that this may be Miller's observation.

COUNTRY VERSUS CITY. Nineteenth-century Romantic poets, such as William Wordsworth, wrote that those who lived in the country, close to Nature and its wonders, were likely to be happier, nobler people than those forced to endure the ugliness of crowded cities. Here Biff's lyrical talks of the Western farm in the spring, with fifteen fine new colts, contrasts with Happy's disgruntled account of the competition, bribery, and questionable love affairs that characterize his urban world. It will be remembered that Willy remembers pleasantly the more rural Brooklyn of sweet-smelling flower gardens and feels stifled in the new city atmosphere of tall apartments with more and more people.

ACT I, SCENE 3

Willy, downstairs, urges an unseen young Biff to finish his education before taking any girl seriously. But Biff's popularity pleases him. Praising both lads for their work on the car, he is joined on stage by his sons in high-school garb. Just back from a trip, Willy surprises them with a new punching bag. Biff, in turn, displays a new football, stolen from the locker room. Willy, laughing, commends his daring. Willy himself will some day own his own business, bigger than that of their neighbor, Charley, who is less "well-liked." He tells of greeting the Mayor of Providence and promises the boys a summer ride through New England with him. The big football game is set for Saturday, and Biff pledges a special touchdown for Willy.

ANALYSIS

This scene reveals more of the personalities of Willy and Biff, with some brief glimpses of the younger Happy.

WILLY: The episode which Willy now relives occurred some fifteen years before. The fact that it is now uppermost in the salesman's troubled mind indicates the kind of life experiences that have most affected him.

First of all, it shows vividly how much he enjoyed the chance to be with his sons and to do things with them. From his admiring words to both, he thought highly of them. He taught them how to polish the car. He planned to have Biff help him chop down an overhanging branch threatening the house. He hoped to have them swing a hammock with him between some trees. He brought them a new punching bag and regaled them with his travel experiences. He was glad when they missed him and wanted their company on a summer trip along his route.

Willy is thus pictured as the devoted "family man," perhaps excessively devoted. As a traveling salesman, he was, of course, away from home a great deal. So he would undoubtedly welcome the opportunity to get together with his sons, of whom he was so proud. Yet there is here, on the part of both father and sons, an extraordinary degree of mutual affection and concern. For strapping high school boys to claim that they missed their father every minute he was away involves either exaggeration or a somewhat unusual relationship. And Willy, in turn, clearly made them, and especially Biff, his primary interest. This revelation is important because the lives of both Willy and Biff will be tragically disturbed when a break occurs between them.

Secondly, Willy is represented as a man who is capable with his hands. He gives them good, practical instructions about the care of the car. He suggests how they will remove the branch and how they will put up the hammock. He is also enthusiastic about this type of work and conveys pride in doing it well.

Thirdly, Willy places great stock in physical fitness. He does not bring his sons home a book or a science kit. He buys them a punching bag, excellent "for timing." He also talks of the advantages of jumping rope, and is keenly interested in the coming football game.

Furthermore, Willy is convinced that popularity is a strong index to success. He is delighted that the girls will even pay for the chance to be with Biff. And he is overjoyed that the coach likes Biff and that the team has chosen him captain. He suggests that the business he will someday own will be more impressive than that of their neighbor, Charley, because he, Willy, is better liked. And he emphasizes this quality in telling the boys about his New England route. He has been greeted by the Mayor of Providence. He has friends in every town. All like him and will welcome his sons when he brings them along. Even the police do not ticket his car because they recognize and respect him. Actually, Willy is bragging. He will tell Linda on another occasion that he often fears that others are laughing at him. But even if here he is engaged in wishful thinking, it is clear that he wants very much to be highly regarded. And his query as to whether or not the sons were lonesome for him indicates his desire to be well liked at home as well.

If, however, he instills in his sons the importance of personal popularity, he is not at all emphatic about the need for personal integrity. When he learns that Biff has taken the football, he tells him to return it. But he is laughing at the time and is clearly not much upset about the theft. Biff needs the ball for his practicing, and the coach will hardly disapprove. Others might be censured, but the well-liked Biff can get away with anything. Subsequently, Biff declares he will make a special touchdown for Willy. According to Happy, Biff is not supposed to do this. He has been instructed to pass. But again Willy is delighted with the intended gesture. If the boys are being given values by Willy, they are not being taught to respect the property rights or authority of others. Later we will find that Biff goes on stealing and that Happy accepts sizable bribes.

Finally, Willy reveals once more his optimistic nature. The car looks fine after the polishing, and the hammock will be hung just right. The coach will understand Biff's "borrowing" of the football and will even commend his "initiative." Someday Willy will have his own business. Meanwhile, he can take the boys on a wonderful trip. All the cities that he visits are beautiful, historic spots, with friendly, admirable people. Given even faint hopes, Willy tends to respond with enthusiasm.

BIFF: This scene emphasizes Biff's strong affection for his father, his popularity in school, and his rather questionable moral values.

Biff works hard on the car, obviously eager for Willy's praise. He is delighted with the present of the punching bag and speaks of missing his father "every minute" while the latter was in New England. He listens appreciatively to Willy's stories and is eager to go with him on the projected summer trip. He will not be worried about the big game if his father is present. And he will even go against orders to make a special touchdown just for Willy.

His popularity is suggested by the rumor heard by Willy that the girls are paying to go out with him. He is also captain of the football team, and the coach, at least according to Biff, is always encouraging him. He is sure of himself and not worried at all about the stolen ball. The fact that he is so casual about admitting the theft suggests that he is not given to guilt feelings about such moral lapses. He intends to return it anyway, he says angrily, when accused. Biff's habit of taking things, shown here, will later lead him into serious trouble. For instance, he will have to leave Oliver's employ after taking a carton of balls.

HAPPY: As compared with Biff, the young Happy receives little attention from Willy. He does tell Happy to follow Biff's lead in polishing the car, and he does throw him a word or two of praise. In general, however, Happy seems here as elsewhere to be trying to attract some attention. He lies down and pedals with his feet to show how he is losing pounds. And his "you notice, Pop?" seems to be a cry for more of Willy's regard. Willy does respond but without any continued interest. Hence, there will never be the closeness between them that develops between Willy and Biff.

CHARLEY: This next-door neighbor is mentioned here as already possessing his own business. Willy, however, does not seem impressed. Charley is not sufficiently well liked to achieve the kind of success of which Willy dreams. The contrast between the two men will be developed further in later scenes.

PLOT DEVELOPMENT: Since this is a flashback scene, it will not be as obviously one that advances the story as, for instance, those having to do with the efforts of Biff to see Oliver. Yet certainly Willy's vivid, overwhelming recollection now of earlier, less troubled times represents a further move toward his impending death. The painful contrast with the troubled present will increase the emotional strain. And gradually such memories will force him to live again with anguish a subsequent related episode that wrecked his close relationship with Biff. There is also, of course, exposition here. Biff's later stealing becomes more comprehensible in the light of his earlier, laughingly condoned purloining of the football.

TECHNIQUE: This scene is the first of the play's now famous flashback episodes. Special lighting and a thin, transparent curtain, or scrim, are often used to distinguish these past events from those going on outside of Willy's mind at the present time. There has been a lapse of some fifteen years since the car polishing and the big game actually took place. Thus all the characters in such scenes were, naturally, that much younger. Yet the same actors play the roles at both ages. The younger Linda, when she appears, will wear a ribbon in her hair. The sons, when of high-school age, will wear appropriate sweaters. Much, however, will be suggested by the skilled use of voice and gesture. Willy, for example, hunched over with weariness when he first enters with his suitcases, will walk with a springier step and use more confident tones as the earlier, less harassed salesman.

One vital distinction must be made. To some extent the scenes from the past provide exposition—necessary information to make the pre-sent action intelligible. Yet, in a very real sense, they, too, are part of the present action. They represent the memories that currently are plaguing the distressed Willy and hastening his final crack-up. Willy is collapsing mentally and emotionally, and these particular recollections, in which he loses himself completely to the horror of his family, are very real factors in his progress toward self-destruction.

One other question may be raised. These being the memories of a confused, unhappy man, how accurately do they record what actually occurred long ago? There is evidence that Biff was once very fond of his father, that Biff was a school athlete, and that Biff did steal. Yet it is virtually impossible to determine whether or not Willy has distorted the overall picture, and, if so, to what extent. All that can be stated positively is that this is what Willy's mind remembers and that this is the way the past seems to him. All in all, such scenes probably reveal more about Willy's psychological processes than they do about the factual history of the Loman family.

IMPORTANT THEMES: IMPORTANCE OF BEING WELL-LIKED. Willy is most enthusiastic about Biff's popularity and makes a slurring reference to Charley as not being liked well enough. Biff, being highly regarded, will get away with the football theft. Willy, being well thought of, will have a greater business than that of Charley. Willy's account of his recent New England trip lays stress upon the friendly reception he is always given in the cities along his route. He intimates that popularity is the key to success.

IMPORTANCE OF PHYSICAL PROWESS. Willy buys the punching bag and tells Happy that jumping rope will help his timing. He is clearly interested in the upcoming football game. In addition, the car-polishing, branch-cutting, and hammock-slinging activities mentioned are all essentially physical.

IMPORTANCE OF FAMILY TIES. Both father and sons reveal intense affection. The boys miss Willy greatly when he is away, and are eager for his praise. He wants only to take them along on his route and show them off to his New England friends. He will brag about Biff's football prowess in Boston.

QUESTIONABLE MORALITY. Willy tells Biff to return the stolen ball but tends to condone his action. For one thing, Biff needed the ball in order to practice. Secondly, the theft showed independence or daring. Finally, Biff can get away with it because the coach has a high opinion of him. In later scenes, there will be other examples in which Willy shows this same lax attitude toward obviously censurable conduct.

SYMBOLS: In various of Miller's works certain objects shown or mentioned are used to point up significant themes. In this scene the following should be noted:

THE CAR. The old Chevrolet which Biff has polished is, of course, Willy's means of carrying on his job. But here it points up the close cooperation and friendly relationship between father and sons.

THE HAMMOCK. Together with the tree trunk that must be lopped off, the hammock first recalls the countrylike atmosphere later to disappear. It is also to be one more present brought home by Willy to his beloved sons. Finally, they will put it up together—hence, it is another family project.

THE PUNCHING BAG. This is a gift indicating Willy's continual interest in his sons. He always brings them home something. It also suggests Willy's concentration upon their physical development.

THE FOOTBALL. The stolen ball, of course, ties in with Biff's preoccupation with sports. It also is used to show how dubious are some of his moral values.

ACT I, SCENE 4

As Willy's memories continue, young Bernard, Charley's son from next door, enters to warn Biff that if he does not pass mathematics he will not graduate. Willy sneers at the studious, bespectacled Bernard as anemic. Willy tells Biff to study, but is not seriously concerned. Bernard, he says, may get better marks, but Biff will be offered scholarships and succeed even as well as Willy in New England because the Lomans make a good appearance and are well liked. Happy again claims that he is losing weight by pedaling.

ANALYSIS

WILLY: Here Willy again insists that being popular and making a good impression guarantees success. He does not tell Biff not to study. He does send him over to work with Bernard. But he is clearly convinced that the handsome, athletic Biff will get what he wants without much intellectual effort. Bernard works much more earnestly and gets much better marks. But, in Willy's view, this pale, slight lad who wears glasses and is not extremely "well liked" will never have Biff's chance to forge ahead in business. As the play proceeds, it will be made clear that Biff actually fails and Bernard succeeds. This fact will distress and bewilder Willy, but as a younger man, he is quite certain as he counsels his sons.

To make his point here Willy boasts of his own sales record in New England. Once his name is mentioned, all the buyers gladly see him. And he has made great sales in Providence and Boston. Later he will admit to Linda that the trip was arduous and the returns relatively small. Why, then, does he paint here such a false picture? It is possible, of course, that in a momentary burst of enthusiasm he actually believes what he says. He is carried away with his own theory of the importance of popularity and thinks of himself as a shining example. In addition, he always seems to be courting the love and admiration of his sons. So he probably always wants to play the hero before them. With Linda, by contrast, he sometimes lowers his guard. Finally, it is at least possible that for all his bluster, Bernard's dire predictions have shaken him slightly. His scornful references to the anemic young neighbor and his glorifying of the Loman breed of muscular, personable men may be thus essentially defensive.

BIFF: Bernard says that Biff will fail mathematics and lose his chance to graduate if he does not study. Biff neither denies nor accepts this well-meant warning. Instead he seems determined to evade the issue. He shows his father how he has printed University of Virginia on one of his sneakers. He brings up the matter of Bernard's limited popularity. And he changes the subject, asking about his father's trip. He seems to have accepted Willy's values as regards the importance of being popular. He also exhibits some of Willy's dubiously grounded optimism. The name of the university is printed on his sneaker. So, of course, he is on his way. The other unpleasantness will somehow be avoided.

HAPPY: There are two brief revealing glimpses of Happy here. The first occurs when he roughly, teasingly spins the less brawny Bernard around. This is the same Happy who will later be outraged that he must take orders from weaker men whom he can outbox and outlift. And again Happy is seen pedaling and trying to get Willy to note his loss of weight. Once more Biff has been the center of attention, and Happy seems to be begging for his share.

BERNARD: In his first appearance, Bernard is seen as a thin, far from husky young man, who wears glasses. He has no cause to fear about his own marks. He may well have, as Willy says, the best grades in the school. But he is fond of Biff and worries about his friend's future. Sneered at by Willy and taunted by Happy, he still comes to offer Biff his services as math coach. Considering the cool reception he gets, he shows remarkable patience and loyalty.

PLOT DEVELOPMENT: This memory of how he reassured Biff and spoke disdainfully of

Bernard will undoubtedly help unsettle Willy still further when later he encounters Bernard as an assured, prosperous young lawyer at a time when Biff has no career at all. The matter of Biff's weakness in mathematics will also lead to the crucial subsequent Boston episode, which in turn will torment Willy and help drive him to his death.

TECHNIQUE: This is another of the flashbacks and is handled in the same way as the previous scene.

IMPORTANT THEMES: IMPORTANCE OF BEING WELL-LIKED. Biff is better looking and better liked than Bernard, says Willy. So Biff will forge far ahead of the more studious Bernard once both are out in the business world. Willy himself succeeds in New England, he claims, because people are always glad to see him. "Be liked and you will never want."

IMPORTANCE OF PHYSICAL PROWESS. The scornful references to Bernard as "anemic" and to the Loman boys as "Adonises" point up Willy's concept of the advantages pos-sessed by the man of strong physique. Happy, too, tries to claim some notice by the physical activity of pedaling and the claim of losing weight for greater fitness. Both sons, when grown, it will be remembered, make much of their muscular virility.

IMPORTANCE OF SUSTAINED EFFORT. Willy seems to have a certain contempt for Bernard's excellent marks. He dismisses him as a "pest." But the play will trace Bernard's success as contrasted with the confused floundering of all three Loman men. There is thus the implication that in the modern world, Bernard's course was the more likely to provide security, advancement, and certain other rewards.

QUESTIONABLE MORALITY. Willy seems undisturbed by the news that Biff has not been studying. The school would not dare fail anyone whose athletic achievements had led to offers of scholarships to several universities. Biff could get away with the football. So he will get away with poor grades.

FAMILY SOLIDARITY. Bernard, of course, represents a course of action opposing that of Willy. But it does seem that the three Lomans rather clannishly close ranks against him. The husky, well-liked Adonises, admiring each other, band together against the outsider.

SYMBOL: BIFF'S SNEAKERS. Biff's sports shoes, with the University of Virginia carefully printed on the sole, represent his confident dream of a bright future through athletic scholarship. When this is shattered, the sneakers will be destroyed in a fit of angry bitterness.

ACT I, SCENE 5

As Willy goes on remembering, he is joined by the younger Linda, with ribbon in hair, carrying some wash. Willy sends the boys to hang it on the line, and Biff is helped by the school crowd whom he leads. Willy boasts to Linda of enormous sales but finally admits his commissions will not run above seventy dollars. Yet they must have over a hundred for household repairs. Willy is discouraged and unsure of himself. Linda flatters him reassuringly, and he is reminded of a Boston woman with whom he had an affair. He gave her stockings and the woman promised to get him in to see the buyers.

ANALYSIS

WILLY: Willy here is extremely proud of Biff, when he hears him ordering around the other lads. He takes credit for training him to be a leader and promptly goes on to preen himself on his own extraordinary sales work. As Linda probes, however, he lowers his estimates drastically and reaches for the excuse that the stores were taking inventory. Next time, however, he will do better.

Faced with the mounting bills for car and refrigerator, washing machine and roof repair,

Willy suddenly seems to lose all the air of bravado he puts on before the boys. He is not at all sure that everyone likes him. Some do not pay heed to him at all, and others find him ridiculous. He is afraid that he talks too much, unlike Charley for whom they do have regard. Instead of being strong and godlike, he feels pudgy and fears that he looks foolish. He must work long hours for a discouragingly small return, and he gets very lonely on the road. Recalling this loneliness, he has the guilty recollection of being unfaithful to the loyal Linda with a Boston woman.

When Willy talks like this, audiences may well wonder which is the *real* personality. Is he deliberately lying to the boys? Is all the boasting a desperate attempt to mask his sense of frustration and failure? Or are these the quickly changing moods of a mercurial individual?

Certainly Willy is given to rapid shifts in judgment. In the opening scene one minute he suggests that Biff is lazy, the next that he is never lazy. Here he at first has nothing but praise for his Chevrolet, then shortly afterwards wonders why they let such cars be assembled at all. Again within a single speech he says that he is well liked and that others do not approve of him. Since he does seem to change so quickly, it may well be that his rapid transitions from hopefulness to despair are characteristic of his temperament.

As for the affair with the woman, he is not dissatisfied with Linda and does not seem proud of himself for having been unfaithful. He can usually find excuses for his actions, and here he mentally attributes his lapse to loneliness. Later he will give Biff the same reason. Yet when he is shown with the woman, he seems obviously to be enjoying himself. He relishes her flattering compliments and likes having his rather unsubtle jokes appreciated. Like Happy's conquests, the affair gives him the feeling of being a suave, irresistible man of the world. He cannot meet all the bills at home, but in Boston he can proffer a princely gift of stockings. In addition, the affair is good business, for the woman may give him entree to see more buyers.

LINDA: The younger, more sparkling Linda is as kind to Willy as her older self. She tells him encouragingly that his future sales will be better and makes the current ones sound as good as possible. She assures him that he is good-looking and commends his lively talk. Yet, however soothing her words, she is never unaware of the harsh economic facts. She knows exactly, dollar for dollar, what things cost and what Willy brings in. And when Willy talks grandly of selling thousands, her quick, instinctive query is, "Did you sell anything?" Intent upon figuring the commission so that she can pay off bills, she forces him into embarrassing admissions of failure. But she recovers quickly and works to restore his confidence. Some critics, incidentally, have suggested that had the faithful Linda been more direct and less soothing, she might have helped Willy act more maturely.

BIFF: Right before the big game, Biff is seen as the idol of the neighborhood boys. They wait around in the Loman cellar and gladly execute his orders to sweep the furnace room or hang up the wash. Both Biff and his brother are good-natured about helping out at home. They gaily agree to take over the chores from Linda.

PLOT DEVELOPMENT: This is one more pleasant memory of family happiness and cooperation, which makes more disturbing the current tensions with Biff. In addition, it recalls Biff's moment of glory as the leader among the boys, as against the present status of Biff as an insignificant drifter. At the same time, the scene has its darker side. Willy is remembering that even in his prime, he was never much of a success. And he is haunted by the Boston affair that made him feel guilty about his disloyalty to Linda and that led to his troubles with Biff. There are thus in this scene various elements that help to increase the failing Willy's current anxieties.

TECHNIQUE: The handling of this scene is somewhat unusual. The episode is a remembered one and is handled as a flashback. Within this memory, however, there is an additional one. Willy at present is recalling his past conversation with Linda. At the time, however, that he had that talk, he was reminded of a previous encounter with the woman in Boston. Special musical effects and a further use of lighting and scrim make the necessary distinctions onstage.

IMPORTANT THEMES: IMPORTANCE OF BEING WELL-LIKED. Willy is delighted here because Biff clearly is popular with the boys, who regard him as their leader. Willy sees here the proof of his theory as to what is the best qualification for success. As for himself, when he is worried about his own lack of progress, he is afraid that he is not well-enough liked.

FAMILY SOLIDARITY. The boys gladly help out with the wash or get the furnace room swept. Linda and Willy talk of paying off household bills. Willy, seeing Linda and appreciating her love, is distressed to remember his disloyalty.

THE HARD STRUGGLE OF THE AVERAGE FAMILY. There is much detailed reference here to nagging bills for car, roof, and household appliances. And Willy talks of the long hours of work necessary to make even fair commissions. *Death of a Salesman* is sometimes described as a tragedy of the "little man" or the "common man." Here the modest sums needed, that are so difficult for this family to raise, point up the low-income status of this man with the grand visions.

QUESTIONABLE MORALITY. Both Happy and Biff have been seen earlier as unmarried men who have had affairs with women. Their ideal, however, has been a stable marriage with a good, steady girl like Linda. Willy hitherto has been the hero of his sons as good husband and good father. Here, however, he is shown to be guilty of marital infidelity. His excuse is—loneliness. But again, as before, the audience is made aware that Willy's moral standards can be curiously flexible.

SYMBOLS: THE WASH. Linda, with her apron, her hair ribbon, and her basket of wash, is the housewife. Later, in Miller's play *After the Fall*, the first wife, Louise, also a woman whose main interest is the home, will usually be shown wearing an apron. Linda, with the wash, here is contrasted with the "other woman" in the hotel room.

STOCKINGS. Here the Boston woman thanks Willy for a gift of stockings. They represent Willy's attempt at cutting an impressive figure outside the home. Linda, it will be shown shortly, darns her own stockings. Given the economic straits of the Loman home, new stockings are a luxury.

ACT I, SCENE 6

Watching Linda darn her stockings, in the continued memory episode Willy angrily tells her to dispose of them. Bernard comes in with a new warning about Biff's failing. Willy also hears that Biff is being too forward with girls and is driving without a license. Willy does not want a spineless nonentity like Bernard, who will not cheat for Biff on final exams. But neither can he understand where Biff has obtained some of his dubious values.

ANALYSIS

WILLY: Willy here is seen greatly disturbed by references to Biff's youthful wildness. Essentially Willy does not want Biff to steal or cheat or act in an ungentlemanly manner. He threatens even to beat him to make him stop. Yet Willy, Biff's idol, did describe his taking of the football as "initiative." And even now Willy is pleading with Bernard to give Biff answers on the final statewide Regents examinations. So there is irony in Willy's wondering where Biff could have learned such wrong ideas. His father always gave him "decent" standards.

BIFF: Despite the warnings Biff has not been studying. Instead he is driving without a license and being rough with the girls. Also he has not returned the football. The only explanation for such behavior is Bernard's report that a teacher considers Biff "stuck up." Willy has long been praising Biff and encouraging him to think well of himself. Biff has apparently become a very confident youth, certain that he can breeze through life doing what he pleases.

BERNARD: Bernard is anxious about Biff and willing to help him before the test. He refuses, however, to run the risk of being caught on an important final examination. Bernard, apparently, is not altogether above some dishonesty on behalf of a friend. He has, in the past, given Biff some answers. But Bernard is not one to jeopardize his whole future, either. So he refuses Willy's plea and is angrily silenced by the irate salesman. For all his helpfulness, incidentally, Bernard is always quoting school gossip and generally sounds a trifle smug.

PLOT DEVELOPMENT: Here Willy's shining confidence in Biff is put to the test, and Willy characteristically tries to make excuses and even deny the manifest truth. These memories, however, are distressing ones. Biff is riding for a fall, and his school difficulties will eventually lead to the break between him and Willy. The memory of this break and the events leading up to it weigh heavily upon the older Willy's confused mind.

TECHNIQUE: This is largely straight flashback, without the overlapping effect of the previous scene. The only variation occurs when the Boston woman's laugh is heard half-mockingly amidst Willy's angry attempts to silence Biff's accusers. Willy seems particularly upset about Biff's rough behavior toward girls. Does the woman's laugh constitute a reminder of his own unauthorized romance? Or does it look ahead to the crucial break with Biff that will occur when Willy is discovered with her in compromising circumstances?

IMPORTANT THEMES: IMPORTANCE OF BEING WELL-LIKED. Even when Willy is alarmed about Biff's behavior, he still retorts that Biff has "spirit" and personality, in contrast to insignificant types like Bernard.

QUESTIONABLE MORALITY. Willy threatens to punish Biff for stealing and misbehaving with the girls. But Willy also urges Bernard to give Biff answers dishonestly on the final examination.

FATHER-SON SOLIDARITY. Even though he does not appear to be at all certain that Biff has acted admirably, Willy rudely silences Linda and angrily sends Bernard home.

SYMBOLS: THE FOOTBALL. This is mentioned again, pointing up Biff's tendency to steal. Linda says that it should be returned. Willy furiously denies that this was stealing at all. After all, Biff is bringing it back.

THE STOCKINGS. Willy irately demands that Linda throw away the stockings she is darning. Seeing her mending them makes him feel like a poor provider. He also has a sense of guilt, since he gave a box of stockings to the Boston woman. Characteristically, Willy mainly does not want to *see* Linda darning. Both he and Biff prefer to evade unpleasant reminders. Yet the memory scenes indicate that even when he can have disturbing matters removed from view, Willy can not get them out of his mind.

ACT I, SCENE 7

Back in the present, Happy comes down to coax Willy to bed. Willy laments that he never went to Alaska with his determined brother Ben and sneers at Happy's offer to finance his retirement. He is then visited by Charley, his quiet, compassionate neighbor. They play cards, and Willy scorns his friend as ignorant about vitamins and carpentry. He also proudly turns down his offer of a job. Willy then seems to see the long-dead adventurous Ben. He talks confusedly with both his vision and the bewildered Charley. Soon he insults the latter once more, and Charley resignedly goes home.

ANALYSIS

WILLY: Apparently much disturbed by the previous recollections, Willy acts irritably toward both Happy and Charley. He ridicules Happy's fine-sounding offer to "retire him for life." He knows how much his son makes and how much he spends on car, apartment, and women. Willy is not usually one to face facts squarely. But he recognizes here that his "woods are burning," and that there is small comfort in Happy's soothing assurances.

As for the affronts to Charley, there are three possible explanations. First of all, Willy is edgy with everybody. In the first scene he was irked because Linda bought a new type of cheese. Secondly, despite his kindliness, Charley always aggravates Willy's sense of failure. Charley has a good, flourishing business and a successful son. Finally, Willy keeps trying to see himself and his sons as superior beings. Charley could never put up a ceiling, but Willy is good with his hands. He finally angers even the unexcitable Charley by his rash statement that being unable to handle tools, Charley is not much of a man. But this hostile remark is in line with Willy's over-all stress upon those skills that he and his sons can claim to possess.

This scene also brings out Willy's admiration for his older brother Ben, who made a fortune in the jungle when he was young. To Willy, Ben stands for success through vision and determination. Ben knew what he wanted, went after it, and got it. He knew how to take advantage of opportunities in Alaska and Africa. Willy should have gone with him, for then he, too, would be rich. Both men represent the American dream of rising by one's own efforts from poverty and obscurity to great wealth. Ben, however, makes the daring move and realizes the ambition. Willy stays with the same small job, bragging about the past and making great predictions about the future. Ben is dream plus action; Willy is merely dream.

CHARLEY: Charley is seen here as the amiable, understanding neighbor who sees that Willy is distraught and wants to calm him down. He comes to play cards with him in the dead of night in the hope of making him tired enough to sleep. He offers him a job on the chance that having an assured income would make him less irascible. He also takes considerable abuse from the short-tempered, uneasy Willy. Yet Charley does not lack spirit. He answers Willy quite sharply when the latter suggests that his inability to handle tools makes him less of a man. Indeed, Charley's suddenly authoritative tone reminds Willy of the brisk, assertive manner of his determined brother, Ben.

Just as Charley's son, Bernard, contrasts with Biff, Charley is often seen in opposition to Willy. Charley is unassuming and unpretentious, but generally well adjusted and relatively successful. Over the years Charley's family has lived next door. The two homes, and hence the general economic background, are presumably similar. Charley, however, has not demanded as much from life as Willy, and, paradoxically, has apparently received more.

Charley and Willy are also contrasted as fathers. Here Willy confides in his friend that he is distressed about Biff's plan to return West. Willy is particularly saddened to think that he, being short of money, cannot give Biff anything. Charley, in general, feels that a thirty-four-year old son should be left to shift for himself. He urges Willy to let Biff go and "forget him." But Willy cannot do this, for his whole life is centered in his son. Later Charley and Bernard will visit on easy, friendly terms, man to man. By letting his son go, Charley keeps his pleasant relationship. Willy holds on, at least in his mind, and makes Biff and himself miserable.

HAPPY: Happy is another who tries to calm Willy. Always one to gloss over unpleasantness, he attempts to halt Willy's regrets about the past and to assure Charley that nothing is wrong. He is interested, however, almost in spite of himself, in the legend of get-rich-quick Uncle Ben. Happy, like his father, dreams of making some impressive coup. But when, momentarily carried away with the vision, he assures Willy that he will finance his retirement, Willy snorts. He may not be able to recognize his own meaningless boasts, but he can puncture Happy's. So again Happy is shown to be the less favored son.

BEN: Since Ben is seen only as one of Willy's disturbing memories, it is hard to know how far the vision represents a real person. Willy does tell Charley that his brother died recently in Africa and left seven sons. But Ben, as he appears from Willy's recollections, is a curious figure. Always hurrying off, after perfunctory questions about the family, he stands for two concepts. He is, first of all, rejected opportunity. Had Willy gone with him to Alaska, Willy would today have possessed a great fortune. Second, he is the cold, ruthless, triumphant victor over life's jungle. Ben knows what he wants, and lets nothing interfere. He is daring and unscrupulous in a way Willy could never be. There may well, of course, have been such a person. But some critics at least have wondered whether or not "Ben" was essentially a personification summing up certain of Willy's aspirations. He may well be the wild, adventurous pioneer that the more domesticated salesman at times wishes he could have been.

PLOT DEVELPOMENT: Here it becomes evident that Willy's crack-up cannot be kept within the family. Charley can hear his noisy, rambling talk from next door. And Charley also hears him talk confusedly to an unseen Ben. Another interesting development is Charley's offer of a job. Whatever is disturbing Willy, the solution cannot be found in mere economic security. Pride, of course, enters into his angry rejection of Charley's offer. But this only indicates further that Willy's sad decline is essentially a matter of inner tensions and anxieties.

TECHNIQUE: In this scene there is an even more startling use of combined objective events and Willy's mental figments. Willy at one time is conversing both with the actually present Charley and his vision of the now dead Ben. As a stage effect this is striking. There is some humor here as Charley tries to make sense out of this strange triangular parley. But it also serves to point up Willy's deteriorating condition.

IMPORTANT THEMES: SUCCESS THROUGH DARING VENTURES. Ben went into the jungle as a young man and came out with a fortune in diamonds. He never had to "grub for money." Willy regrets he never went off with Ben to Alaska for a similar rapidly acquired windfall.

FATHER-SON SOLIDARITY. Charley urges Willy to let Biff go and not worry about him further. Willy cannot do this. He wishes only that he had more to give Biff.

IMPORTANCE OF PHYSICAL PROWESS. Willy sneers bitterly at Charley for the latter cannot handle tools. Their manual skills always make the Loman men feel superior.

SYMBOLS: CEILING. Like the hammock, the overhanging bough, and the roof, the newly installed ceiling is used to emphasize Willy's skill with his hands, a type of work of which the more financially successful Charley is totally incapable. Throughout there is the suggestion that the Lomans have certain aptitudes that cannot be used remuneratively in the urban job area where they seek success.

DIAMONDS. Ben's African cache of diamonds always represents to Willy the wealth to be obtained by vision and determination.

ACT I, SCENE 8

Alone again, Willy relives Ben's one visit to Brooklyn. Ben and their father had gone off separately when Willy was a baby in South

Dakota. Their father, says Ben, was a bold, adventurous man, who toured the land selling handmade flutes. Ben alarms Linda by urging Biff never to fight fairly with strangers. But Willy calls him a great man. To fix the stoop, Willy sends Biff to steal sand from the apartment builders. They have already taken lumber. Charley and Bernard, entering, decry this thievery but are ridiculed. As Ben leaves, he again tells Willy's sons how he made a fast fortune. He also reassures Willy that he is bringing his boys up well.

ANALYSIS

WILLY: This scene emphasizes anew Willy's strong family feelings. He welcomes Ben and wants to hear more of their father. He is also eager to show how well he works with his boys by repairing the stoop while Ben waits. Again Willy shows his contempt for Charley and Bernard because they cannot work so well with their hands. And again he reveals dubious moral values by encouraging Biff's stealing. At the same time, his anxious questions to Ben as to how well he is educating his sons show the anxiety and uncertainty that plagued even the younger, more assured Willy.

BEN: Ben has a courtly graciousness as he greets Linda, but he can also be frightening. As he shows Biff how to fight, he trips him and poises his umbrella point over the boy's eye. He also is not disturbed about the stolen lumber. His sense of family responsibility also seems never to have been very strong. It appears that when he left the wagon in South Dakota as a lad of seventeen, he walked off from his mother and the very young Willy, the father having already deserted them to head for Alaska. This is his one visit to Willy, and he has to ask if their mother is still alive. Ben, however, is completely sure of himself and proud of his quickly acquired fortune in diamonds. He has never kept books, and some of his enterprises may have been questionable. But to the uncertain, struggling Willy he exudes success, and is therefore a "great man."

LINDA: Linda is not favorably impressed. She does not like Ben's insisting that Biff practice fighting. And she is horrified when he trips the boy, menaces him with the tip of his umbrella, and warns him against fighting too fairly with strangers. Linda is also worried when Biff is chased by the watchman after stealing some sand. In general, Linda's standards seem somewhat higher than Willy's. But her protests tend to be mild. Her "Biff, dear!" as she runs off, alarmed, does not sound as if she were about to be sternly unforgiving.

CHARLEY: Looking somewhat absurd in knickers, Charley comes over to warn Willy about Biff's risk of being arrested. Charley is always the good neighbor, as is his son who comes to announce that Biff is being chased by the watchman. As usual, however, the well-meant, if officious, efforts of both are scornfully repulsed. Again, too, the point is made that neither can hammer nails.

BIFF: Again the young Biff is shown eager to obey his father and to work with him on the stoop. He also is not at all annoyed that Willy should ask him to steal. He and Happy are said by Willy to be "fearless characters," with Biff possessing "nerves of iron." Such praise seems to be encouraging them to have little respect for the property rights of others.

PLOT DEVELOPMENT: Willy's memories of Ben and Ben's impressively rapid acquisition of enormous wealth will later be influential in Willy's debate with himself about committing suicide for the insurance money. Also Biff's stealing, with parental encouragement, will help to make the later Oliver episode more catastrophic.

TECHNIQUE: This is a straight flashback scene with no interweaving of action in the present.

IMPORTANT THEMES: FAMILY SOLIDARITY. Willy admires his brother and wants to hear more of their father, whom Ben describes with enthusiasm. Willy is proud of his sons as "rugged, well liked, and fearless." Ben praises Willy as a good father to his "manly" sons.

QUESTIONABLE MORALITY. Willy encourages the boys to steal sand and lumber from the construction company. He does not protest when Ben encourages Biff to fight unfairly.

IMPORTANCE OF PHYSICAL PROWESS. Willy is eager to show how he and the boys can fix the stoop. He also claims that Biff can cut down a tree. He sneers at the neighbors who cannot hammer nails.

IMPORTANCE OF BEING WELL-LIKED. Willy tells Ben that he is bringing his boys up to be popular. Ben approves of his training.

SUCCESS THROUGH DARING VENTURES. Willy holds Ben up to the boys as a great man because he made a fast fortune in the jungle. Ben praises his father because through gadgets he made more money in one week than Willy could all his life. This is undoubtedly nonsense, but Biff has said that he was never brought up to "grub for money." And Ben seems again to be stressing the quick return.

SYMBOLS: THE WASH. The younger Linda, entering with the wash, seems to personify the settled domestic life as against Ben's invitation to adventurous doings in far-off lands. Linda is hostile to Ben.

THE STOOP. This repair job of Willy's will be mentioned fondly by Biff after his father's death. It represents his expert manual skills and his interest in the home. It is also his limited answer to Ben. If he has not found a fortune in diamonds, he can at least fix a stoop. Yet even this irreproachable activity is tied in with Biff's stealing and with mean sneers at the less handy neighbors.

DIAMONDS. Again these represent the quick, fabulous fortune.

KNICKERS. Charley wears knickers that his wife picked out for him. Here the outfit contrasts Charley as a hen-pecked little man who cannot work with his hands with the more assertive Loman men who have such skills. Charley and Bernard are worried about the thefts and are clearly not "fearless characters." The contrast between the families is always somewhat ironic, but here the knickers give Willy one more chance to voice ridicule and contempt.

THE WATCH. Ben, in Willy's visions, is always looking at his watch and hurrying off. Never, apparently, having seen much of father or brother, Willy is always pleading for more help, and never getting more than a few terse statements. Ben is an elusive memory. In a sense, too, the watch seems to point up the need for quick decisions when an opportunity presents itself. Willy thinks of himself as having had only one brief chance to reach for untold wealth. He missed it. He will later see a second such chance in the suicide plan.

ACT I, SCENE 9

The vision of Ben fades, and Willy is rejoined by Linda, who reminds him that they long ago pawned Ben's diamond watch-fob gift for Biff's correspondence courses. Willy then, in slippers, goes out for a walk. The boys come down, and Linda says that Willy is worse when Biff returns. Biff promises to reform. Linda speaks lovingly of Willy. He is old and worn but deserves respect. Despite his long service, the company has put him back on straight commission, and so he secretly borrows from Charley. His sons are neglectful. She adds that Willy plans suicide. Once he smashed the car, and he still hides a rubber tube for inhaling gas. The boys are horrified. Biff will again tackle the business world, but thinks all three would be better off as carpenters working in the open air.

ANALYSIS

WILLY: This scene emphasizes Willy's disturbed personality. He insists upon going out late at night in his slippers. And, more alarmingly, he has actually tried suicide. Linda also points out that he has been a good, hard-working man deserving of some consideration. She also stresses his continued concern for his undeserving sons.

LINDA: Linda speaks affectionately and admiringly of Willy but she is not completely blind as to his limitations. She has to admit that he is not easy to live with. She knows that he deceives her about the gas device. She admits that he is not a "great man" or even the "finest character." If she is to this extent clearsighted about Willy, she is even more harsh as regards the boys. She chides them for their neglect, tells Biff to treat his father more respectfully, and speaks scornfully of Happy as a "philandering bum." She condemns both as ungrateful, and will not permit them to sympathize with her if it means attacking Willy. She may patiently soothe and encourage Willy, but to the boys she can be spirited, sharp, and uncompromising. Either Biff behaves himself or he leaves the house.

BIFF: In this scene Biff is seen to be confused and upset. He is fond of his mother and eager to please her. At the same time he obviously has some grudge against Willy, whom she so staunchly defends. He feels guilty when Linda tells him that his coming causes Willy to become more agitated. Yet if Willy needs help, Biff must stay around and get a job. He obviously hates the business world and feels ill at ease about trying to reenter it. Yet as Linda talks of Willy's misfortunes and his need for help, Biff feels miserable and promises to help. Throughout he appears to be goodhearted but very uncertain as to his course.

HAPPY: As usual, Happy tries ineffectually to make everything seem all right. He tries to reassure Linda that Biff really is devoted to Willy. He also claims, in opposition to Biff, that Willy has treated Linda with consideration. And he is sure that the insurance company was wrong in suggesting that Willy's car crashes were intentional. When, however, Biff turns on him, he answers angrily, defending Willy against his brother. Yet even he is disgusted when he learns of Willy's concealment of the gas-inhaling tube.

PLOT DEVELOPMENT: The story told by Linda of Willy's desperate plight motivates Biff more strongly to try to get a loan from Oliver. The references to the suicide attempts help to prepare for the final self-destructive course determined upon by Willy.

TECHNIQUE: Except for the scene in the boys' bedroom, this is the first in which Willy is not present. The central role is a demanding one, for Willy is on the stage most of the time. Many of the scenes in which he figures involve memories that may or may not be distorted. A scene like this, however, with only Linda and the boys is usually considered to be more objective. This, of course, takes place in the present, and no flashbacks are involved.

IMPORTANT THEMES: CORRUPTION IN MODERN BUSINESS. Willy has worked for almost thirty-six years for the company. During that time he has opened up new markets and served them faithfully. The company, however, shows no gratitude. As his production slows up with increasing age, he is deprived of a steady salary and put back on straight commission like a beginner. The treatment, as Linda sees it, is inhuman and plays havoc with a man's self-respect. Linda also notes the lack of the personal element in business now. In the past old friends used to help Willy with an occasional extra order. Now he is neither known nor welcomed.

Finally, Biff admits that he has never liked the business world. Happy says that is because he never tried to please people and because he has acted irresponsibly. Biff, it seems, used to whistle in elevators. He also took days off to go swimming, but without playing Happy's game of having others lie for him. So here there are objections to the regimentation and routine of the business world, although it must be conceded that Biff and Happy are not altogether reliable critics. Both are somewhat immature in their attitudes.

FAMILY SOLIDARITY. Linda strongly affirms her love for Willy and all but demands that the two sons help him. Otherwise they are as "ungrateful" as the company. Happy's fifty-dollar Christmas gift is scornfully judged to be insufficient. The boys accept Linda's view, and Biff promises to get a job and give his father half his paycheck.

QUESTIONABLE MORALITY. Happy claims that Biff used to take time off for swimming and thus failed to make a good impression on employers. Happy's system is to go off when he pleases but to have others lie about his whereabouts.

COUNTRY VERSUS CITY. When working in the city, Biff could not whistle in an elevator without being thought mad. Biff wishes that he, his father, and his brother could work as carpenters out on the open prairie. Then they would be free from the "nuthouse" city and free to whistle. As devotees of the outdoor life, both brothers, apparently, have skipped work on summer days to go swimming.

FATHER-SON CONFLICT. Biff is saddened to learn of Willy's plight but still harbors some deep personal resentment. His pledge to help Willy comes half from a sense of duty and half from a desire to please the adamant Linda.

SYMBOLS: DIAMOND WATCH FOB. Ben's prized gift of a diamond watch fob went to pay for Biff's courses. Willy will later think a great deal of Ben and diamonds when he plans another grand gesture to save Biff.

THE CAR. Willy's car, hitherto a means of earning his livelihood, is now seen as a possible suicide device, and it will later be used as such.

THE RUBBER TUBE. This also signifies Willy's urge toward self-destruction. But Linda's respect for Willy will not let her destroy it.

ACT I, SCENE 10

Willy returns, angered to hear Biff reduce them to carpenters. He sneers at Biff until he hears of the scheme to borrow money from Oliver. Then with enthusiasm he gives much contradictory advice. Happy says that the Loman Brothers, as a team, could sell sporting goods. Excited over the idea, Willy is rude to Linda, thus infuriating Biff. Yet Biff agrees to soothe him, before going up to bed. Biff is suddenly confident about the future.

ANALYSIS

WILLY: In this scene, Willy is rude and unreasonable. He is angry and possibly frightened because Biff has said that people laugh at Willy. So he must reassert himself as the "big shot" and set Biff down. He is also either muddled in his thinking or, as before, very changeable. He tells Biff one moment to act dignified and reserved with Oliver, the next to start the interview with some lively stories.

When he hears about the Oliver plan and also Happy's idea of the Loman Brothers business, he is immediately hopeful and enthusiastic. Yet his very optimism and feverish excitement make him even more rude and arrogant, and so the battle flares up anew.

BIFF: Although driven to defend himself, Biff tries to be patient, largely, in all probability, for Linda's sake. Only when Willy harshly silences his wife does Biff completely lose his temper. In this scene, however, there is also the old assured Biff. However slim are his actual chances with Oliver, Biff, like his father and brother, has sudden high hopes.

LINDA: At this point Linda is essentially a buffer, or peacemaker between father and son.

HAPPY: The younger son, too, tries to quell the hot tempers of Willy and Biff. He also reveals a creative idea of his own. The brothers will team up to demonstrate and sell sports equipment. Like other Loman schemes this is not altogether practicable in view of their lack of standing and lack of material resources. But as an idea it does show a certain flair. As eager as the other two, Happy says that such a partnership would permit a friendly arrangement based upon mutual trust, not cut-throat competition. And they could also take time off to go swimming. There is something brash and boyish about Happy's vision, but then all the Loman men are to some extent immature.

PLOT DEVELOPMENT: This scene raises the hopes of all, despite the personal clashes, and sends Biff off with assurance to call on Oliver. The failure of the project will plunge Willy more deeply into despair.

TECHNIQUE: There are no flashbacks here. This seems to be straight present-day action. It is a strong scene dramatically because of the intense conflicts.

IMPORTANT THEMES : FAMILY SOLIDARITY. Happy wants to work with Biff and will help him prepare for the interview. Happy and Linda try to keep peace in the family. Willy, in more tractable moments, tries to give Biff helpful advice and encouragement.

FATHER-SON CONFLICT. Willy resents what he considers Biff's contempt for him as being laughable. Willy also objects to Biff's rough talk, and Biff in turn all but accuses his father of hypocrisy. Biff also takes Linda's part when Willy shouts at her.

CORRUPTION OF MODERN BUSINESS. Happy would like to have Biff as his business partner. For then there would be "honor" and those friendly ties missing in the business world as Happy knows it. They would also have more personal freedom, for example, to go swimming, without always being afraid that someone else would take advantage of them.

ACT I, SCENE 11

Upstairs, preparing for bed, Willy complains about the defective shower. But his hopes for Biff now are high. Both sons come to bid him good night, and he again loads Biff with dubious advice. He thinks of Biff at his moment of greatness when the fans cheered at Ebbets field. Linda soothes him with a lullaby, and he agrees to see Howard in the morning and ask for a New York assignment. Meanwhile, Biff, smoking downstairs, finds and removes the rubber tubing Willy hides away as a suicide device.

ANALYSIS

WILLY: Willy continues in a highly excitable condition. He also has the optimistic notion that Biff's football success will be matched when he sees Oliver. After all, Biff has a greatness about him. Ironically, he warns Biff not to act subservient, but that is just how he himself will act with Howard, his boss.

BIFF: Troubled about Willy and yet desirous of pleasing Linda, Biff comes to say good night. Again Willy irritates him, but he controls his anger. Later he is appalled to find the rubber tubing.

LINDA: Again Linda acts with almost maternal solicitude for Willy, even singing him a lullaby. She also, however, takes advantage of his hope fulness about Biff to urge him to go to see Howard. All through this and the last scene, she patiently accepts Willy's rudeness with remarkably good grace.

HAPPY: Biff being noticeably quiet, Happy tries to make noise enough to prevent another outbreak. He also assures Linda that he is getting married. This seems a bid for attention, much like his earlier claims to Willy that he was losing weight. And it elicits the same very limited notice.

PLOT DEVELOPMENT: Linda seizes the moment of Willy's optimism regarding Biff to press him to approach Howard for an easier job. Willy listens to her and agrees to go the following morning. This crucial interview on the same day as Biff's attempt to see Oliver will accelerate Willy's downfall. In addition, Biff's finding of the tubing will intensify the young man's anxiety and strain, thus making his failure to convince Oliver seem the more devastating to him.

TECHNIQUE: Although there is no flashback here in the usual sense, an interesting effect is secured with lights. As Willy recalls Biff's day of triumph on the football field, he compares him to the Greek god Hercules, known for his strength. Linda, in turn, remembers his gold uniform. Meanwhile Biff stands on the lower stage level, outside the house, smoking. A gold light is then played upon him, and the audience sees him looking very much like Willy's bright image of his son at an earlier age. Lighting is also used to call attention to the gas heater, behind which Biff finds the length of tubing.

IMPORTANT THEMES: IMPORTANCE OF PHYSICAL PROWESS. Biff, to Willy, must have greatness in him because he was an outstanding football player.

FAMILY SOLIDARITY. The boys come in to bid Willy good night in hopes of soothing him and reestablishing general harmony.

FATHER-SON CONFLICT. Biff remains quiet, but he is obviously irked by his father's excited counsel.

QUESTIONABLE MORALITY. Willy urges Biff to lie to Oliver about his experience out West.

SYMBOL: THE RUBBER TUBE. Linda knows about the tubing, but will not remove it lest she hurt Willy's pride. Biff, however, is not so sensitive on this score. In hopes of staving off such a disaster, he takes the tubing away. Later, however, in the midst of a furious battle with his father, he will refer to it as a symbol of his father's weakness.

ACT II, SCENE 1

The next morning Willy, rested and hopeful, breakfasts with Linda. He talks of a house in the country and of building guest houses. Linda asks him to get a two-hundred-dollar advance from Howard. This will pay off their house after twenty-five years. She then tells him Biff and Happy have invited him to dinner that night. He leaves in high spirits. Biff calls, and Linda encourages him and tells him to be kind to Willy.

ANALYSIS

WILLY: Willy here hits his final peak of confidence. Buoyed up by the boys' hopes, as well as his own, he is sure that he can persuade Howard. He is somewhat discouraged to hear how much they owe. By the time they pay off refrigerator and car, both are worn out. But he shares Linda's satisfaction in at last, after a quarter of a century, making a final payment on the house. Again, too, in this scene there is the Willy who enjoys working with his hands. He talks with pride of the repairs he has made in the house, and he looks forward to building guest houses for his sons when they move to a home in the country. Finally, his deep affection for the boys is evident. He is overjoyed that they have invited him to dinner.

LINDA: In this scene Linda is her usual encouraging self, but even she seems more than usually optimistic, caught up apparently in the mood of her husband and sons. As before, she has no illusions about their needs. In nudging Willy again to see Howard, she reels off the exact amounts that they require for insurance, car repair, refrigerator, and mortgage payments. Yet in view of what she knows about the company that put the aging Willy back on straight commission, she seems remarkably naive in urging him to ask for a two-hundred-dollar advance. At this point she sounds like Biff setting out to ask for ten to fifteen thousand dollars from a man he once robbed. Her deep love for Willy, however, is also evident throughout and especially during the telephone conversation with Biff. She tells him to greet his father affectionately, for Willy is "only a little boat looking for a harbor."

PLOT DEVELOPMENT: The optimistic mood here sends the hitherto beaten and despairing Willy off to make demands upon Howard. At the same time, in view of Linda's outlining of heavy debts, it is clear that this is a last desperate chance for Willy, as is the Oliver scheme for Biff. Hence if the plea is refused, as it well may be, the consequences are likely to be grave.

TECHNIQUE: This is straight present-day conversation between Willy and Linda, but sprightly, hopeful background music is used to emphasize the mood of early-morning optimism.

IMPORTANT THEMES: COUNTRY VERSUS CITY. Willy looks forward to a house in the country where he can grow things again. He also wants to build a guest house or two there. They can raise chickens and have a vegetable garden. This would be the good life.

THE HARD STRUGGLE OF THE AVERAGE FAMILY. Much is made here of the painfully slow business of paying on the installment plan for household appliances and the car and keeping everything in repair. Insurance premiums must be met before the grace period expires, and mortgage payments must be met over a quarter of a century. Willy has never been the illustrious figure he sometimes tries to picture himself, but he has until recently met his obligations.

FAMILY SOLIDARITY. Linda encourages both Willy and Biff. Willy expresses high hopes for Biff. The boys want to entertain their father at dinner.

SYMBOLS: THE STOCKINGS. Willy sees Linda about to darn stockings and asks her not to do so while he is around. The fact that he gave stockings to the Boston woman will be brought up again significantly in a future scene.

THE RUBBER TUBING. Discovering it missing from its usual place, Linda has hopefully concluded that Willy has given up the idea of suicide. She is, therefore, somewhat deflated to hear that Biff has taken it.

SEEDS. Willy talks often of happier days when there was more light and air and they could grow flowers and vegetables. Now, feeling hopeful, he plans to buy seeds to try again. Whether it be through plants or sons, Willy wants a sense of starting something that will develop fully in the future. His one regret about the house, now practically paid for, is that strangers will take it over after he and Linda can no longer occupy it.

ACT II, SCENE 2

At the office Willy is virtually ignored by Howard, who plays fascinatedly with an expensive new tape recorder. Willy, bluffing, says he will get one too. Reminding Howard of a Christmas party pledge of an office job, he vainly requests sixty-five or even fifty dollars a week. Coldly refused, he talks glowingly of the good old days, when Dave Singleton, aged eighty-four, could still take orders by phone since business was then on a friendly, man-to-man basis. Willy adds that Howard's father promised him advancement and decries Howard's failure to honor commitments. Impatiently, Howard leaves, and Willy panics when he accidentally turns on the recorder. Howard returns, and despite Willy's pleas to be allowed to go back to Boston, discharges him altogether.

ANALYSIS

WILLY: At first Willy is the foolish braggart, talking of buying a hundred-fifty-dollar machine when he needs more than that just to cover debts. Then, begging for smaller and smaller sums just to keep going, he seems a pitiable, broken old man. Gradually, however, his anger restore his dignity. Outraged by Howard's chill indifference, he cries, "You can't eat the orange and throw the peel away." And his demand to be treated as a human being is a moving one. His subsequent shouting recalls the disturbed Willy of earlier scenes, but his nostalgic references to his family and to old Dave Singleton give him a strong human appeal in opposition to the impersonal efficiency of Howard.

HOWARD: This impatient young executive is no conventional deep-dyed villain. As compared, for instance, with the sensual Happy, he is the solid, respectable husband and father. He enjoys listening to his small son's voice on the new tape recorder, and he thinks of using the gadget to make sure that he does not miss the Jack Benny program, a comedy show. Yet to Howard, "business is business." He will talk pleasantly enough to employees. But if they do not bring in profits, they are expendable. He has no interest whatsoever in Willy's past record, his association with Wagner, Senior, or with pledges made years ago. Nor does he care how much Willy needs to feed his family. Willy's problems are his own affair. Howard's only concern is with the efficient operation of his firm. His total absorption in the tape recorder and his running off from the excited Willy suggest a shallow, rather immature man. But essentially he represents the cold, practical impersonality of modern business.

PLOT DEVELOPMENT: Although Willy's confidence was high upon leaving home and Linda, the opposition from the strictly mechanical tape recorder tends to unnerve him. He loses assurance rapidly, and even though his plea has a certain simple eloquence, he is clearly not going to be able to talk to Howard. This scene, therefore, leaves little doubt that Willy has lost his one chance. From now on, unless, of course, Biff accomplishes his improbable mission, Willy's progress will be unmistakably downhill.

TECHNIQUE: This scene in the present is interesting because of the effects secured by the tape recorder. It reveals Howard's intense personal concern with his own family and total lack of any such concern about Willy. It also works on Willy's nerves as it drones on and on. Finally, it somehow opposes the machine aspect of business dealings to the human, more personal element that Willy eulogizes.

IMPORTANT THEMES: CORRUPTION OF MODERN BUSINESS. Willy has worked for over thirty years for the Wagner Company. Even though "business is business," his plea of slightly more consideration as a human being would seem here to be justified.

LAMENT FOR THE PAST. Willy remembers with pride the self-reliance and adventurous streak of his father and his brother. He also recalls the respect and friendship with which old Dave Singleton was treated as an aging salesman, and the warm association between himself and Howard's father.

SYMBOLS: THE TAPE RECORDER. This associates Howard with a small-minded, gadget-ridden race of second-generation businessman. He obviously lacks the vision and basic generosity of his father. His pleasure is in the mechanical, and he has about him little of the humane.

DAVE SINGLETON. Old Dave, eighty-four, taking orders by telephone from his hotel room while relaxing in his green velvet slippers, represents what Willy thought and hoped would be his reward for years of hard work selling.

Actually, times have changed, and even in his sixties, Willy cannot make a living. One may ask whether this figure from the past is objectively recalled, or whether Willy has in his own mind raised Dave and perhaps brother Ben to a sort of heroic myth.

ACT II, SCENE 3

Seeing Ben again in his mind, Willy asks how he succeeded. He then recalls a past visit, in which Ben proposed that he go to Alaska. Linda, young again, carrying the wash, counters that Willy makes enough selling to be happy without leaving. She talks of Wagner's promises and of old Dave. Ben is skeptical, but Willy points to young Biff, the football hero, with scholarship offers. Willy and Biff will get their "diamonds" through being well liked by business contracts. Ben leaves.

ANALYSIS

WILLY: Here Willy appears indecisive. He wants to take Ben's offer of work supervising Alaskan timberland. But he listens when Linda talks of his great future in selling. He is convinced that selling is his best choice because he sees Biff already on the road to success, entirely on the basis of being well liked. Of course, Willy here is unduly optimistic even about Biff, since the scholarship offers from the three universities are contingent upon Biff's passing all his subjects.

BEN: As always, in a hurry, Ben talks of fighting for a fortune on the Alaskan frontier as opposed to the slow, discouraging progress made in cities. Cities have law courts, and Ben is not one to put up with hampering restrictions. He also likes the material satisfaction of owning property. He has no use for Willy's idea that building contacts will mean future security. Ben has vision, but he is also hard, practical, and ruthless.

LINDA: Seen again with the wash, Linda defends her settled domestic domain against Ben's disturbing challenge to Willy. Linda dislikes Ben and all that he stands for. She talks of Willy's popularity and of his future with the firm. She recalls old Dave Singleton, always one of Willy's ideals. And she denies that one must conquer the world in order to attain true happiness. She fights for her home and she wins.

PLOT DEVELOPMENT: Discharged by Howard, Willy is bitter and bewildered. Remembering the past when he turned down Ben's offer to settle for bright prospects in selling, he wonders whether he took the wrong course. More and more Ben's idea of the quick, decisive act, leading to a fabulous fortune, will appeal to him and help him decide to kill himself for the insurance money.

TECHNIQUE: Willy's first question to Ben as to where he went wrong is based upon his heartsick reaction to the Howard interview. This, however, leads into a flashback scene in which Ben apparently gave Willy a chance to go to Alaska, shortly before Biff's great Senior game.

IMPORTANT THEMES: COUNTRY VERSUS CITY. Willy would enjoy working with his sons out in the open in the Alaskan timberlands; there would be no installments to pay, and a man could make a fortune using his hands. Yet, prodded by Linda, Willy also finds the city challenging. Great wealth is there, too, if only those seeking it are well liked, presumably like Willy and Biff.

IMPORTANCE OF BEING WELL-LIKED. Linda says that Willy is well liked. As a result he will be happy and he will also get to be a partner in the firm. Willy picks up her argument. Great fortunes can be made if a man has good contacts who like him. The popular Biff has offers from universities and will be well received when he enters the business world.

SYMBOLS: THE WASH. This homely manifestation of Linda's concern for her household identifies her with the settled life of an ordinary urban family. What this represents is diametrically opposed to the restless, opportunistic, adventurous life offered by Ben.

VALISE AND UMBRELLA. Ben is always anxiously on the move. He is always en route to make new deals and conquer new territories. He also, one suspects, may be leaving some dubious practice as far behind him as possible. He wants nothing to do with law courts, or the regulation they impose upon rugged individuals. The umbrella might seem strange equipment for such a fearless type. But he has been seen to use it as a weapon, aiming it at Biff's eye.

DAVE SINGLETON. Again the aging salesman is used to conjure up visions of a leisurely, profitable selling career, once the contacts have been firmly established.

DIAMONDS. Willy talks of diamonds being the reward of the successful salesman as well as the successful pioneer. Because of his admiration for Ben, Willy tends always to think of fortunes in terms of diamonds. He will later think of them when he is contemplating suicide. They are his symbol for riches.

ACT II, SCENE 4

In this flashback scene, it is the day of Biff's big game. Bernard and Happy contend for the honor of carrying his helmet. If Biff wins, he will be captain of the championship city team. Charley teases Willy, who is feverishly enthusiastic, about never growing up. Willy, furious, blasts him for his ignorance.

ANALYSIS

WILLY: Enormously proud of his football-hero son, Willy is boyishly eager to get to the field and wave his pennant. If this is Biff's greatest day, it is Willy's too. He is incredulous that Charley can be so stupid as to see it as only one more game and Willy as amusingly immature. Hot-tempered throughout his life, he wants to fight Charley but contents himself with name-calling. Although he sees the game as representing personal glory for Biff, as well as for his family, he also never loses sight of possible material rewards. Previously he has often mentioned the scholarship offers. Now he suggests that some professional team may pay Biff twenty-five thousand a year, the sum paid Red Grange.

BIFF: In his few speeches, Biff is first of all eager to get started. He is also the lordly but gracious idol, as he kindly permits Bernard to carry his shoulder guards. Finally, he is Willy's devoted son, again promising to make a special touchdown just for Dad.

HAPPY AND BERNARD: Both here are Biff's satellites, vying to carry his helmet and shoulder guards and be seen with him in the clubhouse. Both are pleased just to be part of his retinue.

CHARLEY: On the whole a good, friendly neighbor, Charley here teases Willy unmercifully. Linda is probably right in her assertion that he is joking when he indicates that he did not know this was the day of the big game. But it is at least possible that his knowledge of football is limited. In any event, to him this is clearly only a boy's game, not worth all the fuss Willy makes over it. He is amusedly skeptical when Willy calls this the "greatest day" in Biff's life. Partly, then, Charley's jests stem from his own wry sense of humor, partly from the fact that his values differ markedly from Willy's.

PLOT DEVELOPMENT: Biff's sense of exaltation based on popularity and athletic prowess will be painfully lost when suddenly thereafter he is just one more student who failed a subject. And the consequences of his fall will eventually lead to Willy's self-destruction. In addition, Willy's memory of his denunciation of Charley's stupidity is one more disturbing thought as he now, penniless after losing his job, comes to seek a "loan" from the still amicable, reasonably successful Charley.

TECHNIQUE: For this flashback scene there is the bright, cheerful music of happier times. In addition, it may be noted that when Willy goes from kitchen to living room, he seemingly walks through a wall. This practice, followed in other scenes taking place now in Willy's mind, increases the effect of a sort of dream vision.

IMPORTANT THEMES: IMPORTANCE OF ATHLETIC PROWESS. Biff as champion will be cheered by thousands. His victory will mean that this is "the greatest day" of his life and may earn him a contract to be paid a great sum in professional football.

FAMILY SOLIDARITY. All the Lomans are off to the game, one to play, the other three to cheer. Biff, in turn, promises to make a special touchdown for his father.

ACT II, SCENE 5

Having walked to Charley's office, back in the present, Willy alarms Jenny, the secretary, with his wild mumbling, then tries a feeble joke or two. He then meets Bernard, now a prosperous young lawyer off to plead a case in Washington. He takes tennis rackets to play on the courts of rich friends there. He is also married, and has two sons. Willy tries to bluff about Biff's success, but finally asks Bernard why Biff lost heart. Bernard cautiously suggests that Biff's collapse really occurred not after the school failure but following a subsequent visit to Willy in Boston. After that Biff fought Bernard and burned his prized sneakers. Disturbed by Bernard's hint that he was to blame, Willy turns on him furiously.

ANALYSIS

WILLY: Several traits of Willy appear in this brief scene. First of all he is the disturbed personality, muttering something about touchdowns so that Jenny calls for help from Bernard. Then, getting hold of himself, he is again the genial salesman with a snappy quip for a pretty receptionist. Bernard's evident affluence much impresses him. To Willy material possessions are extremely significant. If Bernard's friends own tennis courts, they must be "fine people." And Bernard, having done so well, is no longer the anemic pest, but a "brilliant man." Willy as braggart is also here, for at first he tries almost pitiably to claim an equal success for Biff in the West. But soon he is again the forlorn, bewildered father, trying to understand. At the same time, he is not ready to accept any imputation of guilt, however blameworthy he actually feels. So once more his fiery temper flares.

BERNARD: Quietly assured, Bernard greets "Uncle Willy" pleasantly and asks about Biff. Generally tactful, he refrains from critical comments but tries to answer Willy's questions. In his account of Biff's erratic actions the summer after senior year, he reveals his love for Biff, despite the latter's having rarely treated him fairly. He does not know what happened in Boston but has realized that the incident there was crucial as far as Biff's later instability was concerned. Interestingly enough, however, the first explanation of Bernard, the student, was that Biff "never trained himself."

BIFF: From Bernard's account, the young Biff is shown to be highly emotional and given to dramatic gestures. The failure in school failed to daunt him particularly, but after some incident involving his father, he pummeled the inoffensive Bernard and burned his sneakers, with the University's name printed on them, as an indication that he had abandoned all his high hopes. Biff is also seen as someone who could inspire affection and loyalty even though he could be quite highhanded.

PLOT DEVELOPMENT: In this present-day scene, Bernard's obvious prosperity and settled home life with a wife and two sons make Willy even more painfully aware of Biff's unproductive existence. This adds to his desperation. In addition, Bernard's account of the past stirs up guilt feelings that he has been apparently trying to suppress. Soon, however, the Boston episode will be uppermost in his mind, and this agonizing memory also will serve to impel him toward destruction.

TECHNIQUE: This scene is played on the front of the stage to the right. The office is suggested quite simply by a receptionist's small table. Bernard's suitcase and tennis rackets are props, and the lighting directs audience attention to this stage area.

IMPORTANT THEMES: "LOSTNESS." Willy reveals to Bernard that he does not understand how so much could go wrong for Biff and begs for enlightenment.

FAMILY SOLIDARITY. Willy wants still to help Biff, his one lament being that he has "nothing to give him."

QUESTIONABLE MORALITY. Willy tries at first his usual lies, asserting that Biff is doing well out West and has actually been sent for by Oliver. Again, in talking of the teacher who failed Biff, Willy regards this action as evidence that the instructor was meanly responsible for ruining his son. For his part, while he talks of possibly having been at fault, Willy angrily denies being to blame once the idea has been broached by Bernard.

SYMBOLS: TENNIS RACKETS. To Willy these suggest the good, leisured society to which the fortunate Bernard has access. Curiously enough, Bernard, either too puny for football or too engrossed in studies, now as a man participates in athletics.

THE SNEAKERS. These shoes, as before, signify Biff's ambition to go on scholarship to the University. Burning them, he renounces his dream.

ACT II, SCENE 6

Bernard leaves, with a bottle of bourbon, a gift from Charley. Bidding Willy goodbye, he suggests that Willy "walk away" from the insoluble problem. Willy cannot. Willy is further startled to learn that Bernard will plead before the Supreme Court, although his father never lavished much attention on him. Charley again offers Willy a job and is furiously repulsed. He tells Willy to grow up and stop thinking about being well liked. Giving Willy the money he needs, he accuses him of being jealous. Thinking of his insurance, Willy says he is worth more dead. He leaves dreamily, sending apologies to Bernard and touchingly taking leave of Charley as his one and only friend.

ANALYSIS

WILLY: Here certain contradictions in Willy's nature become even more obvious. He can steadily borrow from Charley sizable sums that he may never be able to repay. Yet because he is allegedly keeping strict accounts, he feels that he is not accepting favors. If Charley objects, he will walk out haughtily. When, however, Charley offers him a job with no traveling, paying as much as he begged from Howard, he refuses with finality. At first he says that he does not need a job, then he simply says that he cannot work for his friend. Becoming an employee of the "big ignoramus" he has always scorned would be an insupportable humiliation, whereas he can still apparently convince himself that he will pay back the "loans." Willy is a proud man and as irascible as ever. Yet his last word to Charley indicates that deep within him there is some sense of gratitude.

CHARLEY: Proud of Bernard, Charley implies that he succeeded as a father because he did not smother his son with attention the way Willy did Biff. He now sends Bernard off to Washington with a friendly wave and a man-to-man gift of bourbon. Still spirited enough to fend off Willy's worst insults, Charley compassionately offers his old antagonist a job. Yet he takes issue with

Willy's insistence upon being well liked. Salesmen, he says, sell products, not themselves, and successful men are not always the most lovable types. Charley is also sharp enough to see that Willy is toying with the idea of suicide. He tries to dissuade him but Willy hardly listens. All in all, Charley stands for sensible action rather than big talk.

PLOT DEVELOPMENT: In refusing Charley's job offer, Willy proudly cuts off a final chance to maintain some self-respect as a wage-earner. In addition, in spite of himself, Charley's suggestion that his theory of being well liked is fallacious reduces his self-assurance still further. Finally, Charley's mention of the insurance premium turns his thoughts to suicide, even though he still hopes that Biff may have succeeded.

TECHNIQUE: This is played in the same stage area as the preceding scene.

IMPORTANT THEMES: IMPORTANCE OF BEING WELL-LIKED. Charley denies Willy's idea that being popular is the key to success.

CORRUPTION OF MODERN BUSINESS. Willy has harsh things to say about Howard. Charley, however, is a good, humane businessman and yet disputes Willy's claim that personal associations count for much. In apparent contradiction, however, he offers his broken friend a job.

SYMBOL: THE BOTTLE OF BOURBON. This gift from Charley to the departing Bernard suggests a pleasant, friendly relationship between the two men, both fairly prosperous. It points up their easy-going camaraderie as opposed to the tense, strained feelings between Willy and Biff, both of whom are in a difficult economic position.

ACT II, SCENE 7

Awaiting Biff and Willy for dinner at the restaurant, Happy impresses the waiter, Stanley, with his sophisticated manner. Then he suavely picks up an attractive young diner, Miss Forsythe, bragging about himself and his brother. She leaves to find a friend for Biff, who has just arrived. Biff, much upset, says that after his long wait Oliver failed to recognize him. He was, after all, never a salesman, just a clerk. Impulsively, later, Biff stole Oliver's pen and ran away. He wants to tell Willy that he now realizes his limitations. But Happy warns him not to ruin Willy's hopes.

ANALYSIS

HAPPY: This is Happy's scene. He shows a certain practiced deftness and savoir-faire in dealing with the waiter and the young prostitute, but he lies continually. There is also something cheap and second-rate in his pretensions to urbanity. He does, however, seem to be genuinely fond of his brother, and he is not without some consideration for Willy when he urges Biff not to tell him the worst. Of course, seeking the companionship of the two girls when he and Biff had asked Willy to dinner shows a certain thoughtlessness. But Happy has long concentrated upon sexual affairs, and, one feels, almost goes through the motions of setting up a date from force of habit.

BIFF: The taking of Oliver's pen recalls Biff's earlier stealing. But for all his disappointment, Biff here shows signs of growing up, of facing facts honestly. Yet in his eagerness to impart his new knowledge to Willy, thus clearing up any misapprehensions the older man may possess, he does not seem to consider at all the effect this might have upon an individual as distracted as Willy is now.

PLOT DEVELOPMENT: Biff's determination to tell Willy how insignificant the Oliver interview made him feel will prove highly disturbing to his already desperate father. In addition the date with the two girls, rather inconsiderately set up by Happy, will provide a tempting escape for the two sons when Willy's erratic actions prove embarrassing.

TECHNIQUE: The restaurant scene, also played on the front part of the stage, is suggested by light with a reddish glow, the music of a brassy orchestra, and a table and chairs brought on by the waiter and Happy.

IMPORTANT THEMES: QUESTIONABLE MORALITY. Happy boasts about his brother as a big cattleman and as a professional football star. He also tells of his mythical stay at West Point. He urges Biff to go on lying to their father. Biff, of course, has stolen again, but now he wants to admit the truth about himself.

CORRUPTION OF MODERN BUSINESS. The waiter is pleased to hear from Happy that the latter plans to go into business with his brother. In his place the bartender is always stealing from the boss.

FAMILY SOLIDARITY. Happy gets Biff a date, praising him highly. Happy tries to keep Willy happily anticipating Biff's success, while Biff thinks he will be better if he sees that Biff has failed from his own limitations and not merely to spite his father.

STEALING. Biff takes Oliver's fountain pen. This time, however, he does not pass off his action lightly. He is horrified and ashamed.

SYMBOLS: CHAMPAGNE. Happy makes much of his "overseas" champagne cocktail recipe, and sends the girl champagne to start up an acquaintance. This is obviously a proof of Happy's Continental elegance and one of his symbols of sophistication.

THE FOUNTAIN PEN. Oliver's personal pen is the sign of his executive status, something used to sign important documents. Biff, after a long wait, has been humiliatingly ignored. Taking the pen, a status symbol, is apparently almost an instinctive way of compensating for his injured pride. But the very irrationality of the act also helps to rouse Biff to realize the lie he has long been living.

ACT II, SCENE 8

Willy joins them, and they order drinks. Already mildly intoxicated, Biff tries to tell Willy the grim facts, but both boys are shocked to hear that Willy has lost his job. From then on, Willy goes on assuming that Oliver welcomed Biff, and Happy encourages this delusion. Biff wavers between keeping Willy cheerful and admitting the dismal truth. Finally, Willy gets angry, and Biff gives up.

ANALYSIS

WILLY: Bereft of all hopes and anxious to bring Linda back some good news, Willy wants only reassuring words from Biff, and therefore he angrily berates him whenever he tries to give an honest account. Willy always was enough of an optimist to make the most of the slightest encouraging sign. But here his own despair makes him try to find matter for rejoicing where none whatsoever exists. Because he is attempting the impossible, his temper is soon out of control, and he becomes increasingly harder to soothe.

BIFF: Anxious to reveal the new truths he has painfully discovered. Biff is also distressed to see his father so depressed and distraught. In addition, he is used over the years to having his mind made up for him by the strong-willed older man. Thus he finds it hard to speak his piece. Furthermore, feeling the effects of what he has been drinking, he is not altogether in a reasonable frame of mind. So as Willy continues to bait him, he finally gives up trying.

HAPPY: Happy's one concern is to calm Willy down. With this in mind, he lies continually, regardless of what Biff says, to let Willy go on thinking that Biff favorably impressed Oliver.

PLOT DEVELOPMENT: Willy's last hope has now been shattered. Excited and irritable, he will become hopelessly unmanageable and thus make impossible what was to have been a pleasant dinner party with his sons.

TECHNIQUE: This is a straight present-day scene played at the front of the stage as was the previous one.

IMPORTANT THEMES: IMPORTANCE OF BEING WELL-LIKED. Willy is certain that Oliver must have remembered Biff, because Biff formerly impressed him.

FAMILY SOLIDARITY. Willy wants good news so that Linda will suffer less. The boys are sorry for him and want to calm him. Biff favors telling him the truth; Happy leans toward the reassuring lie.

QUESTIONABLE MORALITY. Willy does not want to hear that Biff was a mere shipping clerk, not a salesman. Happy lies repeatedly about the Oliver interview.

SYMBOL: THE BURNING WOODS. Willy uses this image more than once to distinguish between the threatening total catastrophe and mere minor setbacks.

ACT II, SCENE 9

As Biff talks, Willy, distracted, hears young Bernard announcing to Linda that Biff failed mathematics and has gone to Boston to see Willy. The present-day Biff, bewildered by his father's talk of the old math failure, tries to tell him about the fountain pen. Willy slips back into his Boston memory. He is being paged in a hotel and his woman companion urges him to open the door. Biff meanwhile has been unable to make Willy see why he cannot return to talk again to Oliver. Finally, the girls return, and Willy staggers off to the men's room. Unable to cope with him further, Biff leaves, imploring Happy to stay. Happy, however, disowns his father and follows Biff with the two prostitutes after paying the bill.

ANALYSIS

WILLY: In relatively lucid moments, Willy tries to coach Biff how to lie to Oliver about having gone off with his pen. He does everything possible to avoid facing facts, and when he can no longer do so, he bitterly denounces Biff. Actually, however, in this scene he is becoming increasingly distraught, since he keeps drifting back to the Boston episode in the past.

BIFF: Confused by Willy's references to events long ago, Biff still tries to explain why he cannot again approach Oliver. Yet as Willy eyes him accusingly, Biff seems the small boy again denying that he intended to steal at all. Afterwards, alarmed at Willy's condition. Biff resorts again to less disturbing lies. But he still wants to tell Willy the truth. Eventually, unable to stand the tensions and having been struck and called names by Willy, Biff goes off. Before leaving, however, he tells the girls that Willy is really a prince.

HAPPY: Before going, Biff asks Happy to look after Willy. When the younger son demurs, Biff accuses him of not caring for their father. Happy is angered, with some justice, for he has at least made some attempts to help Willy. Yet a moment later, he goes off with the girls and even denies that Willy is his father at all. In general, he is colder than Biff. Whereas the older brother flees in agony. Happy is off to salvage a good time. Essentially, however, both reveal a certain immaturity and cowardice in so deserting the disagreeable but sadly disturbed Willy.

PLOT DEVELOPMENT: As his despair increases through Biff's revelations, Willy becomes more and more upset. His mind recalls the unhappy past when Biff failed and the Boston episode wrecked their happy relationship. Obviously, being deserted now by his sons will do nothing to restore his emotional balance. Some critics, incidentally, have questioned the plausibility both of the dating of the girls by Happy and of the abandoning of Willy by the sons. Others see it as one more evidence of the same immaturity that has kept Biff moving from job to job and Happy forever telling lies.

TECHNIQUE: This is a complicated scene technically. A soft, misty light comes up on the house as young Bernard announces Biff's failure to Linda. A trumpet note indicates that Willy has a sudden, sharp recollection. "Hearing" young Bernard's announcement, Willy in the present abuses the older Biff. Again, as they argue further, the laughter of the Boston woman is heard from the left of the stage. Willy talks sometimes to the Boston telephone operator, sometimes to the woman, sometimes to the present-day Biff.

IMPORTANT THEMES: FATHER-SON CONFLICT. When Biff tries to tell Willy the truth, Willy accuses him of spiting him and of being nothing but a "rotten little louse." Biff tries to calm him and even to see him as he used to appear to him a "pal," or a "good companion." But the relationship is now merely a torment. So Biff leaves.

QUESTIONABLE MORALITY. Willy insists that Biff lie to Oliver about taking the pen. Happy tells the girls that Willy is not his father. Biff, or course, as well as Happy, walks aways from the disturbed Willy, who was their invited guest.

SYMBOL: THE RUBBER TUBE. Before leaving, Biff takes out the tubing and shows it to Happy. He asks Happy to stop Willy from killing himself, but Happy refuses the assignment while not denying that such is Willy's intent.

ACT II, SCENE 10

In this flashback, Willy is sharing a hotel room with the Boston woman, Miss Francis. Repeated knocking at the door causes Willy to open it, after first sending her to wait in the bathroom. Biff has come to confess his failure and beg Willy to talk to his teacher, Mr. Birnbaum. He admits having missed the class and made fun of his teacher. The woman comes in, to Biff's horror, and Willy tries to invent a plausible explanation. The woman leaves but first demands her promised gift of stockings. Biff sobs, and Willy tries desperately to win him over, insisting that he was lonely. Biff, however, calls him a liar and a fake and says he does not want to go to the University. Back in the present, Stanley, the waiter, tells Willy that his sons have left. Willy tips him lavishly and sets out oddly to buy seeds.

ANALYSIS

WILLY: Even before Biff arrives, Willy is uneasy in the hotel. The knocking unnerves him, and the woman describes him as unhappy and selfish. Unexpectedly encountering Biff, he tries to bluff his way out of an embarrassing situation and all but throws the woman out. When all else fails, he resorts to the truth. But by then Biff is sadly disillusioned. As for Biff's failure, it is significant that Willy at this point does not blame Biff. In fact, he enjoys his account of how he mockingly imitated the teacher's lisp and is annoyed that Bernard did not furnish enough answers. His love for Biff is apparent throughout, but his behavior gives the boy some cause to consider him a liar.

BIFF: Young Biff first shows here a childish faith that his father can talk the teacher into giving him the points he needs to graduate. The minute he has trouble, he runs off to get help from Dad. His thinking, too, is immature: the course was failed because the teacher hated him. When afterwards Biff discovers his father's liaison, he bursts into angry tears, will listen to no explanation, and calls his fallen idol names. He is particularly distressed that Willy has given the buyer "Mama's stockings." And now that his faith has been shattered, he will do nothing about summer school and does not want to go to the University at all. There is heartbreak and disillusionment here. But Biff seems to react like a small child, rather than a young man of college age. Willy has, of course, always played the hero in front of Biff. Now Biff passionately denounces him as a fraud.

PLOT DEVELOPMENT: From Biff's first references in Act I to Willy as a "fake," an explanation has been forthcoming. Bernard's references to Boston and his question about what happened there increased the suspense. This scene explains the tensions between Willy and Biff and suggests why Biff never went on to succeed when he seemed to have such bright prospects. As a memory it involves deep feelings of guilt on Willy's part, and his reliving it at this time probably increases his sense of being lost. Some commentators have doubted that the revelation of Willy's extramarital affair could really have had such a cataclysmic effect on a normally resilient young man. Others justify this as plausible on the grounds that Willy's dubious "training" had given Biff no adequate preparation for coping with the realities of a far from perfect world. In other words, discovering Willy's perfidy was probably the bitterest possible blow that Biff could have received. But he would sooner or later have reacted similarly to other inevitable rude awakenings.

TECHNIQUE: The sensual aspect of Willy's affair is suggested by the type of musical background played. The scene is played at the front of the stage, and lighting is used to pick out the principal figures. There is otherwise no hotel-room set or furnishings.

IMPORTANT THEMES: FATHER-SON CONFLICT. Willy has done nothing directly to injure Biff. He wants only to help his son get to college. But Biff has had his illusions wrecked and is both miserable and furious. The moment before, he was blithely confident that Dad could fix anything, even a failing mark. From now on, however, the idyll is over. Biff and Willy will quarrel heatedly, be partially reconciled, then quarrel again.

THE IMPORTANCE OF BEING WELL-LIKED. Biff assures Willy that if he talks to Birmbaum in his impressive fashion, the teacher will alter the grade. Willy, for his part, enjoys hearing how Biff mimicked the teacher to the great delight of his admiring classmates.

QUESTIONABLE MORALITY. Biff has no compunction about having missed classes or cheated on exams. He is only sorry that he let his father down. Willy is annoyed that Bernard did not cheat more efficiently so that Biff could have passed. Willy lies to Biff about the woman in his room, and finally excuses his actions on the grounds that he was lonely.

SYMBOLS: THE STOCKINGS. Throughout the play Willy has been uneasy whenever he sees Linda, who has little money, darning old stockings. The boxes he gives Miss Francis are partially a business investment, for she can get him in to see buyers. They also make Willy a generous, desirable man to know and thus make him feel like the "big shot" he wants to be. To Biff, however, they represent an insult to his mother. And they thus aggravate his bitterness regarding Willy's deception.

SEEDS. Willy asks the waiter where he can buy seeds. He wants something to grow in his garden. He has just been deserted by his sons, and in a sense they were his plants, his future growth. Now he will try once more to raise vegetables from the ground, so that something that is his will grow and flourish.

ACT II, SCENE 11

Arriving home late with roses as a peace offering, the boys are met by a bitterly indignant Linda. Throwing down the flowers, she denounces the pair for deserting their father and tells both to pack and leave. Happy tries lying to gloss over the situation. Biff is remorseful and contrite. He begs to see his father before he goes. Willy, however, is out planting vegetables.

ANALYSIS

LINDA: Unyielding, almost ferocious in her denunciation of her sons, Linda will listen to no excuses. Willy is her one concern. She is more wife than mother, although she sometimes seems to mother Willy. Seemingly meek and uncomplaining whenever her husband speaks, she is here hard, relentless, even somewhat coarse. Only when she suddenly fears that she cannot by strong words stop Biff from harassing Willy further, does she adopt a milder tone and actually beg. Some critics have wondered whether or not such a positive, uncompromising woman would be likely to take so much verbal abuse from the moody Willy. Is it just that she loves him more than she does her sons? It may be noted, of course, that even though she talks soothingly to Willy, she keeps close accounts of the finances and does tend to run his life. It was she who did battle with Ben, and it was she who promoted the meeting with Howard.

HAPPY: A little afraid of the irate Linda, Happy tries as usual to lie his way out of difficulties. His assurance that Willy actually had a good time with them is obviously implausible, for Willy has come home before them. But Happy is forever trying to keep others satisfied by making free with the facts. When his lies fail to convince, he goes upstairs without apology.

BIFF: As opposed to his essentially more thick-skinned brother, Biff is conscience-stricken. He does try to tell Linda that Willy is not yet dying, but he makes no serious effort to defend his own actions. He also rudely cuts off Happy's attempts to suggest that Willy did have a pleasant evening. Humbled and remorseful, Biff still insists upon seeing Willy. And Linda is forced to recognize that Biff, too, can on occasion be a determined individual.

PLOT DEVELOPMENT: Linda's ultimatum that the boys must leave will hasten the crucial scene between Biff and Willy that will lead to the latter's suicide. The scene also reveals vital differences in the personalities of the two sons. Morally, there is some hope for Biff, little for Happy.

TECHNIQUE: This scene is played in the kitchen and living room of the house. Lighting is used effectively, especially when the boys, fearful, discover that Linda knows what has happened and she moves toward them furiously.

IMPORTANT THEMES: FAMILY SOLIDARITY. Linda has no qualms about insisting that the boys take responsibility for Willy. In view of the fact that Willy is not well and was their guest, she is obviously justified here. But, throughout, this emphasis upon obligations of parent to grown son and grown son to parent is quite pronounced. Charley and Bernard talk of letting things go and walking away. This the Lomans, with the exception of Happy, cannot seem to accept.

QUESTIONABLE MORALITY. Linda denounces the desertion of Willy as cruel and inhuman. Happy goes on lying to make Linda less angry and to make things easier for him and Biff. Linda also has harsh words for their dealing with the two prostitutes, although Happy assures her, probably truthfully for once, that all he and the girls did was follow the morose Biff and try to cheer him up.

SYMBOLS: THE ROSES. Ordinarily an attractive, fairly expensive present, these would probably be welcomed by Linda, who, as Willy has indicated, has had her share of trouble. But she roughly pushes them out of Happy's hands. As she declared in the beginning, she will not remain on friendly terms with anyone who is unkind to Willy. In rejecting the roses, she is rejecting her sons because of their having hurt her husband.

THE GARDEN. Like the seeds, in the previous scene, this is Willy's pathetic attempt to start something for the future. When Ben offered him the Alaska post, he told him he was building his fortune through his sales work. He also looked to Biff to carry on the Loman name with distinction. Now both of these hopes have faded. So in the dead of night he is out planting vegetables.

ACT II, SCENE 12

Busy planting carrots and lettuce by flashlight, Willy starts consulting a vision of Ben about killing himself for his twenty-thousand-dollar insurance money. Ben admits that this is a substantial sum but wonders about the certainty of payment and about Willy's being called a coward. Willy, however, sees the act as giving Biff a "diamond." Biff would also be impressed by Willy's funeral, with mourners from distant states. But Ben frightens him by suggesting that Biff might only hate him.

ANALYSIS

WILLY: Here Willy, gardening in the dark, is hardly rational. He is, however, obsessed with the idea of leaving a great sum to Biff. Presumably if Biff sees that his father is able to give him such a sum, then Biff will stop spiting Willy and make a success of his life. Then, after all, Willy will be assured of a sort of immortality. Willy thinks of Ben in connection with this insurance project because it involves a large fortune made instantaneously—a found "diamond," not small sums made through endless appointments. Ben also would not be one to show overconcern about the morality of the proposition. Yet, even considering the act in "practical" terms, Willy is not sure how Biff will judge him. And he does not merely want Biff to have the money. He also wants Biff to honor his memory. So in considering the possibility of committing suicide, Willy wants to be able to leave something to Biff, and also to Linda who "has suffered." But he is also, as the Boston woman long ago suggested, "self-centered" enough to want proper recognition for the sacrifice of his life. As for the morality of suicide, or of cheating insurance companies, Willy is not concerned.

For Willy has a child's view of what is fair and unfair. He has had to work hard over the years to pay his premiums. The least the company can do is pay him if he's willing to kill himself for money.

BEN: In earlier scenes Willy's memories may or may not represent the older brother, Ben, as he actually was in life. Here Ben is clearly a figment, an imaginary being. In the debate over suicide, he is actually that side of Willy's personality that has always admired swift, decisive action and looked for wealth to be obtained in an audacious coup. In addition, "Ben" always seems to personify a certain lawlessness, an impatience with the stricter requirements of ethics. And Willy has never been overly scrupulous about the property of others. Yet "Ben" also stands for a combination of selfishness and hard-headed practicality. This type of mind can appreciate material wealth in the form of diamonds or cash in lump sums. But it is skeptical about building a business through friendly contacts or counting upon a son's admiration for a suicide father. As both materialist and man of action, the "Ben" side finds self-destruction a rather negative course, and is cynical enough to wonder whether or not it would pay off at all. Speaking in his own person, Willy has some generous concern for Linda and Biff, as well as an egotistic urge to prove that he is known to many. Yet the adventurous, opportunistic "Ben" in him that prompts him to a final desperate undertaking also with its cold skepticism stays his hand.

PLOT DEVELOPMENT: Suicide has been hinted previously. Linda has spoken of other attempts to the boys; Biff has found the rubber tubing; and Charley has keenly noted Willy's reference to his being worth more dead than alive. Here, however, the plan is seen actually taking form. Willy's death thus seems imminent. Yet for the moment worries about Biff's possible reaction postpone the move. The very fact, of course, that Willy is conversing with a long-dead brother and not merely remembering indicates considerable mental disturbance.

TECHNIQUE: This scene takes place in the garden, that is, on the apron or front part of the stage. A soft blue light suggests the darkness of night and little of the surroundings can be seen. Willy uses a flashlight to read the directions on his seed packets and occasionally uses a hoe. Ben appears out of the darkness to the right. The scene is also interesting in that this is the first time that Willy holds a discussion with a figure from his past. Hitherto he has apparently just relived crucial experiences, although sometimes commenting upon them in a manner that confuses present-day characters, as when he talks to the grown Biff about failing in school.

IMPORTANT THEMES: FAMILY SOLIDARITY. Willy can talk only to his brother Ben. He wants to kill himself so that Linda and Biff will have what he can give them.

THE IMPORTANCE OF BEING WELL-LIKED. Biff will be impressed to see how well known Willy was, when all the old friends who liked him came from new England and elsewhere to attend his funeral. Willy is again engaging in grandiose visions. In fact, no one will come except family and the two neighbors.

QUESTIONABLE MORALITY. Willy seems unconcerned about any moral aspects to the question of taking one's own life. To him it is not cowardly. Yet he would not want to have Biff think him a coward or a fool. He also has no worries about whether or not he may be guilty of fraud as far as the insurance claim is concerned.

LAMENT FOR THE PAST. Willy recalls poignantly the days when the healthy young Biff used to enjoy winter sports and carry his sample cases and polish the car. How, he asks, can one recover such peaks of happiness?

SYMBOLS: SEEDS. As before, Willy's absurd planting operation represents his desperate urge to accomplish something, to build a future for his heirs.

DIAMONDS. These have throughout been Willy's symbol for great, satisfying wealth—beautiful and impressive. Here he equates his diamond with money to be paid his family by the insurance company if he kills himself. It would prove him a man worth respecting, and it would be a dazzlingly large lump sum, not little amounts pieced together by endless selling appointments.

ACT II, SCENE 13

Biff joins Willy in the garden and tells him he is leaving for good. Uneasy about facing Linda and furious that Biff will not try again to see Oliver, Willy refuses a goodbye handshake. He curses Biff for spiting him. Stung, Biff takes out the rubber tube and calls Willy a fake. As Linda and Happy watch helpless, Biff says he was in jail for stealing in Kansas City. He has always stolen because Willy made him think he must be important in a hurry. He is through running. He will go back to the West, to the work he likes. Both he and his father must face it that they are not leaders. Willy denies this irately, but Biff, no longer angry, sobs brokenly. All he asks is that Willy burn his false dreams.

ANALYSIS

WILLY: Willy here is seen roused to fury and bitterness by his sense of guilt. If Biff is failing, Biff must be still taking revenge for the Boston disillusionment because if Biff is *not* failing deliberately, then Willy is to blame, and that sort of burden Willy cannot shoulder. If, however, Biff has become a drifter out of spite, then Willy, however outraged by such ingratitude and meanness, can see himself as blameless by comparison. One lapse on his part obviously did not deserve such a long campaign of calculated insult and retribution. The third explanation, offered by Biff, namely, that he never possessed the extraordinary potential attributed to him by Willy and hence would under no circumstances have been a great leader, is almost equally obnoxious to Willy. For if Biff does not succeed magnificently, then Biff is nothing. But if Biff is nothing, so is Willy. And Willy has spent a lifetime covering up the discouraging smallness of his income by picturing himself as a dynamic, aggressive salesman universally admired and Biff as the heir apparent who would easily surpass even his father's enviable record. If he accepts Biff's less flattering appraisal of both, then he must not only give up the emotional props on which he has relied over the years. He must also admit that even if his Boston affair did not wreck Biff, his "training" of his son, of which he was so proud, left his son inadequately prepared for life. This idea, again demanding an admission of guilt, is equally insupportable. So Willy, with no job and no future, and fearful of losing all remaining shreds of self-esteem, shouts imprecations at the relentless Biff. Biff may hope to stave off Willy's suicide by making his father come to terms with reality. Willy, however, recoils with horror and fury when Biff attacks his foolish illusions.

BIFF: Highly emotional throughout this whole climactic scene, Biff's first objective is to take leave of Willy amicably, thus putting an end to the quarrels that are causing both such agony. As Willy, however, not only refuses a parting blessing but angrily denounces Biff as spiteful, the younger man becomes irate in turn and insists upon destroying once and for all Willy's false picture of both of them. The more Willy tries to shy away from unpleasant truths, the more the now remorseless Biff tries to force them upon him. Biff starts by denying that he has any wish to blame Willy. But once roused by Willy's accusations of spite, he indicates that he sees that his repeated thefts, culminating in a jail term, are traceable to Willy's having created in him a false impression that he was never meant to be a subordinate, but always an executive. While he is at it, Biff also points out that Happy is not an assistant buyer as he claims but only one of those helping the assistant buyer. In this scene Biff does show some progress toward maturity. He no longer has quite so unrealistic a picture of his own capabilities as he had. He says that he is through with stealing, and he also has recognized the kind of outdoor life he wants and will pursue it presumably without making impossible demands of it. At the same time, he still reveals some traits that do not suggest an adult personality. For one thing, he is not in command of his emotions. At one moment he is ready to strike Willy, and shortly thereafter he breaks down and sobs. Secondly, he is all too ready, when under fire, to shunt the blame onto Willy for his own criminal acts. It was Willy's fault that he stole. Finally, he tends to go to extremes. He and Willy may not be the extraordinary people Willy always envisioned, but whether they are a "dime a dozen," or even "nothing," is debatable.

PLOT DEVELOPMENT: Willy has regarded his projected suicide as a grand gesture that will marvelously impress Biff. Here Biff, in taking out the rubber tube and flinging it at Willy, denies that he will regard Willy as any hero at all. Taken with the doubts expressed by "Ben," this would seem to be a deterrent. In this scene also, however, Biff tries to make Willy give up his self-important delusions. There is no indication that he succeeds. Willy may still go ahead with his plan. Linda and Happy seem increasingly unable to influence either Biff or Willy.

TECHNIQUE: Played partially out on the stage apron (the garden), the scene moves into the kitchen. There are no flashbacks. In terms of dramatic structure, this is a great "confrontation scene," in which two antagonists face each other and take up some vital issue to settle once and for all. It might also be termed a "necessary scene." There has been much in the play about the relationship of Willy and Biff, and Biff has been relatively reticent although he has indicated the hostility he feels. Here we learn some of his true feelings, that the play, in a sense, has been promising all along.

IMPORTANT THEMES: FATHER-SON CONFLICT. Willy tries to blame Biff for spitefully refusing to succeed. Biff claims that Willy's false teaching encouraged him to steal and also to be confused about his true nature. He also calls his father a fake for toying with the idea of suicide.

QUESTIONABLE MORALITY. Biff reveals that he served a three-month jail term for stealing a suit. He blames Willy for having given him false teaching. He accuses Happy of lying and says that in the Loman house, no one ever told the truth.

SYMBOLS: THE RUBBER TUBE. To Biff this proves Willy a fraud and no hero. If Willy kills himself, Biff will have no pity for him.

THE FOUNTAIN PEN. Representing to Biff the life of a business executive, Oliver's pen now seems to him the symbol of all that he wants to reject—the stealing and the running away, the whole business world. He is going back instead to the Western open-air work that he finds satisfying.

ACT II, SCENE 14

Convinced by Biff's agonized sobs that his son loves him, Willy again sees Ben and thinks of the twenty thousand dollars. Happy, promising his mother that he'll get married, goes upstairs. Linda, after pleading with Willy to join her, follows. After she goes, Willy talks to Ben about Biff's magnificence with all that money. Ben agrees that Willy would be fetching a diamond out of the jungle. Willy thinks once more of Biff's football glory and then after a momentary panic rushes off. After the musical suggestion of a crash, the family are preparing for Willy's funeral.

ANALYSIS

WILLY: Despite the harsh words uttered in fear and anger, Willy shows here his deep love for Biff. He also still has his vision of Biff as magnificent and will realize it by getting his son the insurance money. Willy also takes tender leave of Linda, sorry that she is so tired. He is hopeful now that everything will work out for the best. In carrying off the "proposition," he will have succeeded himself and made success possible for Biff, thus pulling victory out of defeat. He is fearful but triumphant. He is also not quite sane.

LINDA: Having made her peace with her sons, Linda fearfully suspects what Willy intends to do. Yet she goes off and leaves the distracted man alone. The only preparation for this action has been her custom of leaving the rubber tubing where it was when Willy was home to help preserve his dignity. Linda does not want Willy to kill himself, but apparently cannot bring herself to interfere in order to stop him. There may be some question of plausibility here, but if Willy were determined enough, presumably he could kill himself sometime. And the requirements of drama are probably better satisfied by having the action occur at this time.

PLOT DEVELOPMENT: By an ironic twist Biff's impassioned plea, intended to convince Willy that he is a "nothing," hence not worth the sacrifice of someone's life, has just the opposite effect. Suddenly certain of Biff's love, Willy sees his son as "magnificent," needing only wealth to far outdistance Bernard. Thus he is now convinced that suicide is the answer and receives confirmation from the vision of "Ben" that this is the way to get diamonds out of the jungle.

TECHNIQUE: Light and sound effects are used here to suggest first of all Willy's distraction and momentary panic. Then music conveys the idea of a car crash and subsequently makes the transition necessary to start the family toward Willy's funeral. The grave is supposedly located at the center front of the stage apron. Thus when the characters talk around the grave, they seem almost to be talking directly to the audience.

IMPORTANT THEMES: FAMILY SOLIDARITY. Willy, by his suicide, will give Biff the chance for magnificence. Linda speaks encouragingly about both sons and indicates her love for Willy. As the funeral music starts, the family moves together, joined by Bernard and Charley.

IMPORTANCE OF PHYSICAL PROWESS. Willy's last vision of Biff is as the football hero. Biff's football is important and important people are watching him. Biff's skill at the game is still a vital element in his father's concept of his magnificence.

SYMBOLS: THE JUNGLE. Ben keeps talking of taking diamonds out of the jungle. The jungle to Willy seems to be the world in general that has made it hard for him to get ahead. The money he gets through his suicide will make jungle fighting easier for Biff. At the same time Willy has seen himself, as he remarked to Howard, as coming of a race of adventurous men with a streak of self-reliance. Such men—Ben included—tame jungles and are not tamed by them. And here Willy conquers his.

DIAMONDS. Again the insurance money is equated with diamonds. There is, first of all, a splendor about such stones, and Willy means his death to be a noble gesture. Secondly, they suggest great wealth, not small sums—and twenty thousand is more than Willy has ever had. Finally, they are made to represent a prize won by daring and initiative, by the bold stroke of an adventurous spirit. And this, too, is the way Willy regards the money he wants to leave Biff. Incidentally, the play never reveals whether or not Biff ever gets the money. It is never again mentioned.

REQUIEM

Only Linda, her sons and Charley and Bernard join at Willy's grave. Linda laments that no one else came to the funeral. She cannot understand Willy's suicide when they were almost free of debt and their needs were small. Biff remembers sadly the good old days when they all repaired the house, but insists that Willy's dreams were wrong. Charley defends Willy as a true salesman "riding on a smile and a shoeshine." Biff, unconvinced, invites Happy to head West with him. But Happy is determined to realize Willy's dream in the city. Linda, kneeling, sorrowfully bids Willy farewell. Weeping, she goes off with Biff.

ANALYSIS

LINDA. Linda expresses here the tender grief of one who had a deep love for Willy. Even if not a well-known or well-liked man—since not a single business acquaintance comes to his funeral—Willy was still someone who was loved and missed. Yet unless a certain difficulty in comprehending may be allowed in the person suddenly bereaved. Linda's comments are curious. Her remarks, for instance, to the effect that Willy's act is inexplicable because they were "free and clear" do not sound like those of the woman who was always ready to cite facts and figures and presumably knew that Willy had lost his job. From the first she knew about Willy's suicidal notions and earlier had offered some possible explanations to the boys. In terms of the drama, however, her expression of sorrow and loss is usually quite affecting.

BIFF: This scene shows that Biff has not changed his position. He can remember warmly and pleasurably the early days when Willy and his boys fixed the stoop and added a new porch. But sorrow over Willy's death has not altered his conviction that Willy's basic point of view was wrong. He is still, as he declared before, going back out West where he has been happiest. And he even tries to coax Happy into going with him. As Charley's defense of Willy suggests. Biff is still perhaps too intolerant. Must Willy's dreams have been "all, all wrong"? But Biff at least has solved his own dilemma and can now go back to his ranch life, without feeling guilty because he is not making a name for himself in the urban business world that he so hates.

HAPPY: Not unaffected by his father's death, Happy still voices the old Loman dream "to come out number one." Yet his references to not being "licked," and to showing everybody in the "racket" suggest that eventually he, too, may be headed for disaster. For Happy throughout the play has shown no inclination to work harder than ever or do his job more efficiently. All his talk has been of getting away with bribes and seducing other men's fianceés, of being slickly "covered" for unauthorized time off and of feeling nothing but contempt for those giving him orders. Even in the crucial scene of the showdown, he objected when Biff pointed out that he was only one of two assistants to the assistant buyer. Despite occasional pledges to get married, Happy does not seem to have changed at all. So his blithe assurances that he will "beat this racket" seem discouragingly hollow.

CHARLEY: In defending the man who always tended to insult him, Charley shows considerable understanding of the demands of a salesman's line of work. His line about "a smile and a shoeshine" is one of the most famous in the entire play. And Charley throughout has been a sympathetic, helpful neighbor. Yet, in a way, Charley's eulogy is confusing. For before this he tried to change Willy. He insisted, for instance, that being "well-liked" was not that important, and more than once he told Willy to "grow up." The play itself seems to point up the foolish side of Willy's visions rather than the creative side that might make a man succeed in Willy's line of work. Like Linda's tearful laments, Charley's words do add a nice touch of sentiment. And they are appropriate, probably, to the kindly old friend. But essentially they only make one lament Willy's passing and brush aside whatever critical approach has hitherto been taken.

PLOT DEVELOPMENT: The plot virtually ends with Willy's suicide. Apart from the sad or elegiac tapering off here, however, this scene rounds out the story of Willy's sons. Happy will go on following Willy's none too practical course. Biff, rejecting Willy's dream, will pursue his own less demanding objectives.

TECHNIQUE: As previously indicated, holding the requiem scene at the very front of the stage seems to bring the audience into closer contact with those making final comments. The flute music at the end and the lighting that throws into relief the tall, almost menacing apartment buildings also add their own subtle interpretive effects.

IMPORTANT THEMES: IMPORTANCE OF PHYSICAL PROWESS. Biff remembers happily the work with their hands that gave the Loman men such satisfaction. Charley and Linda agree nostalgically that Willy was excellent when manual skills were demanded.

FATHER-SON CONFLICT. Even though Willy is dead, Biff is still arguing with him. He condemns Willy's dreams at Willy's grave and tries to get his brother to give up the impossible struggle for impressive wealth and fame.

CORRUPTION OF MODERN BUSINESS. The terms in which Happy alludes to the city world—the "racket," in which he is going to show everybody that he can come out on top—recall all that has previously been said about the intense competition and low moral standards. By contrast, Biff's call to join him in the more easy-going West sounds like a last chance for health and sanity.

LAMENT FOR THE PAST. Biff remembers affectionately the old days when Willy and the boys worked happily together to fix up the house.

SYMBOL: THE HOUSE. Linda, always the woman of the house, is particularly saddened to think that now that the mortgage has been finally paid off, Willy will not be there to share the building with her. In a sense, the house represents the whole of their thirty-five hard-working years together. Their marriage has been the struggle to possess a house. Biff, too, refers to parts of the house, such as stoop, cellar, and porch. To him they represent Willy's expert carpentering skills, and hence the answer to his unrealistic or wrong dreams. And they also signify the good years of cooperative effort when family harmony prevailed.

Analyses Of Major Characters

WILLY LOMAN: In a sense there are two Willy Lomans in this play. There is the present broken, exhausted man in his sixties, soon to end his life. And there is the more confident, vigorous Willy of some fifteen years before, who appears in the flashbacks. One actor portrays both, readily shifting from one representation to the other. To some extent, of course, the personality remains constant. The younger Willy, although given to boastful blustering, does admit misgivings to Linda and loneliness to Biff. And the shattered older man, in turn, occasionally reverts to his former manner of jaunty optimism. Yet the changes are great and significant. The earlier Willy could never have been the idol of his teen-aged sons had he behaved in the perverse, distracted fashion of his older self.

Willy's agitation during his last days stems from a twofold sense of failure. He has not been able to launch successfully in the world his beloved son Biff, and he no longer can meet the demands of his own selling job. Although not altogether ignoring Linda and Happy, he is primarily concerned about the once magnificent young football star who at thirty-four drifts from one temporary ranch job to the next. Willy cannot "walk away" from Biff's problem, as Bernard suggests, nor can he accept Linda's view that "life is a casting off." Being over sixty, Willy is doubtless tiring physically. The sample cases are heavy. The seven-hundred-mile drives are arduous. And many business contacts, developed over the years, are vanishing as the men of his era die or retire. Yet the worry over Biff has obviously accelerated his collapse.

Actually, Willy's attitude toward Biff is complex. On the one hand, there is a strong personal attachment. He wants Biff to love him. He remembers yearningly the fondness shown for him by Biff as a boy, and he still craves this. At this point, however, relations are strained. Although Willy shies away from remembering so painful an episode, he knows in his heart that the Boston affair left the boy bitterly disillusioned. Feeling some sense of guilt, Willy fears that all of Biff's later difficulties may have been really attempts to get revenge. Biff has failed, in other words, mainly to "spite" Willy. Although outwardly resenting such alleged vindictiveness. Willy still wants to get back the old comradeship, even if he has to buy it dearly. "Why can't I give him something," he asks the spectral Ben, "and not have him hate me?" And his great final moment of joy and triumph occurs when he can exclaim, "Isn't that remarkable? Biff—he likes me!"

On the other hand, Willy also is emotionally involved with Biff because his son's success or failure is also his. By becoming rich and influential, the handsome, personable Biff was slated to provide Willy's victorious reply to all not sufficiently impressed with his own modest advancement. By making his fortune in the business world, Biff would prove that Willy had been right in turning down Ben's adventurous challenge to head for Alaska. He would also outshine the sensible, plodding Charley and Bernard, thus establishing once and for all Willy's theory that having personality and being "well liked" were the great requisites for preeminence. Losing his own job, Willy is naturally unhappy. But if he can still purchase success for Biff with the insurance money, he personally will yet have won. "I always knew one way or another we were gonna make it, Biff and I!"

If, however, Willy at any stage is apt to overindulge in grandiose daydreams, he is hardly the "phoney little fake" he once seems to the shocked Biff. He works steadily at one job for thirty-six years and does pay off a long-term mortgage, even if at the end he accepts some help from Charley. He takes good care of the house, too, capably making even major repairs. Although not altogether faithful, he is a reasonably satisfactory husband to Linda, who obviously respects him. He does not like to see her darn stockings or work too hard. And when he loses his job, he is sorry to think how much she has suffered. In his own way, too, he has the makings of an admirable father. He gives much attention to his boys, showing them how to do things, working with them, and praising their accomplishments. He roots for them at their games, and defends them loyally. When Biff fails, he pays for several correspondence courses, even though he has to pawn his prized diamond watch fob given him by Ben. And finally, there is genuine dignity in the man when he spiritedly speaks up for his rights with Howard.

Willy is partially a victim of circumstance. He could not have avoided getting old and tired, any more than he could have prevented the building of the apartments that hem in his house. There was even an element of mischance in Biff's inopportune visit to Boston. What's more, Willy did not originate some of the erroneous concepts and values that helped defeat him. The idea of the fast-made fortune, the "quick killing," is, to some extent, characteristically American. And our history certainly indicates that some did reach the top by combining personal attractiveness with a casual disregard for ethical practice. Moreover, Willy was hardly the first in our society to overemphasize athletic prowess at the expense of steady brain work.

Yet in placing excessive reliance upon these dubious success formulas, Willy fails to take a realistic view of his limitations and those of his son. By all but encouraging Biff's petty thievery and giving it the flattering name of "initiative," he steers Biff toward an eventual jail term and Happy toward the discreditable habit of taking bribes. By running down the importance of good grades, he prepares the way for Biff's disastrous failure. By harping upon Uncle Ben's rapid rise to fortune, he builds in both boys a distaste for the type of regular, fairly routine work that will not make anyone, as Biff says, a "big shot boss in two weeks." Finally, by encouraging them to idolize him through his blown-up accounts of their situation, he does little to help them really mature. Toward the end, Biff seems to be groping sadly toward some measure of self-knowledge. But Happy is still determined to "beat this racket" and come out "number one man." On the day of the big game, Charley ruefully asks Willy when he is going to grow up. In some ways Willy never does. His boyish enthusiasm is, of course, part of his appeal. But his persistent refusal to face facts squarely drives him at last to a violent death. Ironically, his suicide, to him the ultimate in magnificent gestures, merely leaves Linda woefully bereft and Biff more than ever sure that "he had the wrong dreams. All, all wrong."

BIFF LOMAN: At thirty-four, this husky, good-looking former star athlete is a moody, troubled man. Like Willy, he is worried both about family tensions and about his work. He is fond of his mother and saddened to see her looking older. And even though he has never regained his idolizing reverence for Willy, he would really like to meet him again on pleasant, amicable terms. In all probability he also misses the high praise with which Willy bolstered his self-confidence. Now, however, whenever he returns, obviously no success, he dreads his father's disapproval and is clearly on the defensive. Thus, when Willy "mocks" him and accuses him of failing out of spite, he is ready with an angry rejoinder. This, in turn, makes Linda antagonistic, and Biff, feeling guilty and inept, is more depressed than ever.

Having relied apparently too much in boyhood years upon the heady encouragement of an adored and adoring father, Biff seems never to have recovered fully from the Boston disillusionment. Bernard's account of Biff's burning of his "University of Virginia" sneakers suggests the dramatic finality of Biff's renunciation of all bright college plans. After that he takes various short courses but always loses heart. The ranch work, on the other hand, does give him some satisfaction. Away from his father's disappointed frowning, he likes the chance to use his physical strength in the open air.

Yet he makes very little money at such seasonal jobs, and keeps moving from one to another hoping for more. All the while, too, he cannot shake off his father's prediction of an extraordinarily great future for him. Trying better paying city work, he feels stifled by the routine and becomes impatient at the slowness of the rise to some position of security and respect. So he steals and runs off, engages in devising fantasy schemes for making a quick fortune, then drifts back to another dollar-an-hour cattle-herding stopgap. Even though this erratic program has left him increasingly anxious and disheartened, there is at least a faint hope for Biff. For Biff, at least, knows that he is "mixed up" and wants to stop acting "like a boy." After the disastrous attempt to see Oliver, he does face bravely a few more harsh facts about his limitations and resolves to give up following the old "phony dream."

Actually, Biff, like Willy, always tends to go somewhat to extremes. So his passionate insistence, toward the end, that he is "nothing," or that he and his father are both "a dime a dozen," still sounds a little like the uncompromising disclaimer of the youngster who had sobbingly burned his sneakers. Now he sees his father's dreams as "All, all wrong." Yet if he still talks a little like the grandstand hero, he is still groping toward a more realistic, more mature self-appraisal. Neither Willy nor Happy ever gets even that far.

LINDA LOMAN: Like Kate Keller in *All My Sons*, Linda is primarily wife rather than mother. Or if she is motherly, her ministrations are for Willy rather than her sons. Except when it becomes necessary for her to remind him of unpaid bills, she is forever soothing him, flattering him, tactfully suggesting courses of action, and trying to get him to eat enough and get some rest. She is almost always patient and kind to him, ignoring his minor outbursts and considerately accepting without demur such obvious deceptions as the borrowing from Charley. Linda loves her husband, respects him as a steady, hard-working man, and regards his sufferings with compassion. But she humors him as a child rather than meeting him squarely as an adult.

Yet the same mild-mannered, gentle Linda can be surprisingly blunt and harsh when she talks to her sons. She may not ever challenge Willy's grandiose talk to his face, but she reveals a clear, tough-minded recognition of the true financial picture. She rebukes Biff for failing to keep in touch and orders him either to behave pleasantly to his father or to leave. And she can coolly describe Happy as a "philandering bum." After the restaurant disaster, she denounces both fiercely, flings away their flowers and imperiously orders them out of the house. Except when they disturb or irritate Willy, she talks to them amiably enough. But she is simply not concerned about them. Her one thought is Willy. If their presence cheers him or helps him in some way, she is glad to have them around. But if what they do further upsets her already disturbed grown-up "child," then the sons must go and not return.

HAPPY LOMAN: This dashing "assistant to the assistant" buyer shares with Biff a fondness for rugged outdoor living but wants material success even more. He appears at first to have come to terms with life better than either his father or his brother. He has his own car and his own apartment. He has had considerable proof of his virile appeal to women, and has developed a glib line with which to impress them. In a small way, he is quite an accomplished liar and has all but convinced himself that he is slated to become the store's next merchandise manager.

Actually, he is by no means as well adjusted as he seems. For one thing, he cannot quiet down his own scruples. He knows that he is wrong when he takes bribes, and he has some sense of guilt as regards the seduction of other men's fianceés. In addition, he does appreciate the fact that the merchandise manager, whose success he so patently envies, is still discontented and restless. So he suspects that even reaching that pinnacle may not guarantee happiness. Moreover, he too, like Biff, feels indoor work confining. Also physically strong, he misses the exaltation of the athletic contest, and has a certain contempt for the weaklings with whom he must work.

Happy still has vestiges of old ideals. He objects to all that is false around him, even while being false himself. Even while picking up a prostitute, he remarks what a shame it is that there are so few good women. And he dreams of settling down with a decent girl like his mother. Although embarrassed by his father's odd behavior, he is not ungenerous. He did send Willy previously to Florida for a rest. And, of course, he is genuinely fond of Biff.

Yet he often refuses to face unpleasant truths and resists Biff's attempts to clear up misconceptions as bitterly as Willy does. Whatever occasional admissions he makes, he will not give up either his dream world or his shabby sensual affairs. He may talk of changing his ways and getting married, but he never sounds convincing. And his final act is to reject Biff's invitation to start anew, preferring to justify Willy's dream of coming out "number-one man." Unlike Biff, Happy learns relatively little from witnessing his father's collapse.

CHARLEY AND BERNARD: These good neighbors are notable in the play for having traits that contrast strikingly with those of the Lomans. Unlike Willy, Charley lays no claim to greatness. He goes along calmly and quietly, undistinguished but relatively content. His salvation, he declares, is that he never took any interest in anything. That, of course, is not literally true for he shows unusually generous consideration of Willy. But he obviously never developed with Bernard any such intense relationship as existed between Willy and Biff. He set himself a modest goal and is satisfied with modest achievements.

Bernard is no match physically for the athletic Loman boys, and neither he nor his father can work so well with their hands. Bernard, however, studies hard, gets good grades, and despite Willy's disparaging predictions is clearly forging ahead. At the time of Willy's breakdown, he has a wife and two sons and is pleading a fairly big law case before the Supreme Court in Washington. When Willy observes wonderingly that Bernard does not brag, Charley says that his son does not have to—his deeds speak for themselves.

Curiously enough, although opposite in temperament to the Lomans, Charley and Bernard cannot help admiring them. Bernard has no illusions as to the foolishness of Biff's neglect of math. Yet he tries constantly to be of help to him and pleads to carry his helmet or shoulder guards on the day of the big game. Charley, on his part, takes issue with Willy on such vital matters as the importance of being "well liked." Yet it is he who in the end defends Willy to Biff in almost rhapsodic terms. Willy sneered at Charley, insulted him, and then borrowed sizable sums from him. But Charley can say with vehemence, "Nobody dast blame this man."

Sample Essay Questions and Answers

1. Much of *Death of a Salesman* deals with the relationship between Willy and Biff. Could Happy have been eliminated?

ANSWER: No, for Happy is useful in providing a perspective by which the other two can be more accurately evaluated. Happy is reasonably open-handed. He will treat his father to dinner, even send him to Florida, and pledge more, if necessary. But he was never the favorite and was never caught up in the terrible disillusioning experience of Biff. For that matter, except in a general, vague fashion, Willy never seems to have expected too much from this younger son. Yet Happy has learned from his father. He has been taught the necessity of pushing to the top, of sneering at superiors and coworkers, and of not being scrupulous about an unethical practice or two. He is also an expert at bluffing, and lies almost instinctively whenever unpleasant truths threaten to prove irksome. Being harder than Willy and Biff, he has been able to work out a somewhat more satisfactory compromise. He has, after all, his car, his apartment, and his women friends, whereas both his father and his brother have almost no funds. He does have twinges of conscience but lets no troublesome sense of guilt interfere with his sensual pleasures. When Biff brings up some agonizing truths, he angrily denies them, preferring the tried and serviceable lie. Yet Willy and Biff are more poetic, more romantic, more akin to the old visionary pioneers. They love more and suffer more. And Biff may even achieve some measure of maturity. Happy has taken the worst of Willy's precepts and made them his life's code. As a character, he enables us to see Willy's errors in action. He also makes us appreciate the greater moral sensitivity of the other two Loman men.

2. If Willy's character is clearly a foolish, headstrong one, are we to assume that Charley and Bernard represent the playwright's ideal?

ANSWER: This we can assume only to a limited extent. Certainly Charley and Bernard seem to have more serene, more comfortable lives than the Lomans. Bernard has a wife and two sons, and his career is obviously thriving. His father can afford to lend Willy substantial sums, to have his own secretary, and to present a bottle of bourbon to the departing Bernard. Even with Willy in a sadly distraught condition, Charley can offer him a job. Moreover, the relationship between this father and son is friendly and untroubled. Hence, almost no negative side can be seen to their lives. And, by inference, the Lomans would be happier, more truly successful were they able to conform to the steadier, more easygoing life patterns of their neighbors.

Yet there is something heroic in the very aspirations of the Lomans. Willy speaks of his father as an "adventurous man" and talks of a "little streak of self-reliance" in his family. Willy may be born in the wrong era for his type of skills. But he does have some vestiges of the old pioneering vision, the boundless optimism, the reckless element that was part of America's heritage. Why does Charley keep coming around despite the insults? Why does young Bernard slave patiently for Biff? Neither can or will adopt the Lomans' dangerous course, but both sense here a bit of excitement, a flash of glory absent in their well-regulated lives. Like most of the far-from-sensible heroes of other eras, the Lomans live more perilously and risk more. But even failing, they are the dreamers that rescue civilization from becoming too drearily cut and dried.

3. What dramatic purpose is served by using flashbacks instead of relating events in strict chronological order?

ANSWER: The flashback scenes in *Death of a Salesman* differ from those in many other works. Ordinarily the flashback device is used primarily for exposition, that is, to convey background information needed to make the story as a whole intelligible. Of course, the scenes from the past in this play do indeed fulfill such a purpose. The episode in the Boston hotel, for instance, explains certain of the quarrels between Willy and Biff and accounts for Willy's sense of guilt. Yet such episodes also serve here another, more subtle purpose.

Willy Loman, the hero, will die at the end of the play not from old age, a dread disease, or a sniper's bullet, but in a suicidal car crash. He will kill himself because painful memories, guilt feelings, and various frustrations combine to unsettle his mind and distort his thinking. The flashbacks here are scenes from the past that torment and confuse Willy in the present. Pleasant recollections make him more agonizingly conscious of current sorrows. Disturbing ones reinforce the anxieties of the moment. Used in this fashion, episodes from Willy's past are very much a part of his later experience and, in a way, are just as essential to the main action as his crucial final encounters with Howard and Biff.

Finally, since this is to some extent a psychological drama, what Willy's confused mind instinctively recalls tells us a great deal about the kind of man he is. Would Charley, for instance, remember the football game so vividly? Thus the flashbacks here not only provide exposition but advance the plot and reveal character traits.

4. Why has Willy Loman seemed to many an unusual choice for the hero of a tragedy?

ANSWER: Tragedy as a type of drama was first successfully developed by such ancient Greek playwrights as Aeschylus, Sophocles, and Euripides. Many of our traditional concepts of tragedy derive from their handling of the form and from the commentary on their works provided by the philosopher Aristotle. The Greek tragic hero was in some respects quite different from Willy Loman.

First of all, the Greek hero was usually at the start of a play a man in an extremely fortunate position. Oedipus, for instance, is the rich and respected ruler of a state, enjoying good health, peace of mind, and the contentment of a satisfactory home life. By contrast, Willy starts as a broken, exhausted, confused "little man," bitterly at odds with his eldest son. The Greek hero fell from an exalted position, and much of the tragedy consisted in the appalling extent of his decline. But Willy has never far to fall.

Secondly, the Greek hero, although not a perfect man, seemed to sum up man's nobler aspirations. Some have felt that Willy's values are so warped and his vision so limited that he cannot qualify as a noble example of mankind. The lordly warrior Agamemnon, they maintain, would not fret about being "well liked" or get so worked up over a football game. To this Arthur Miller has replied that even poor, confused man can want with passionate intensity a sort of distinction for himself and his son, and that if he wants this enough to die for it, he achieves tragic status. Not all have accepted his contention. But some agree that since our civilization is not that of ancient Greece, our tragic hero will perhaps differ too.

5. What purposes are served by the flute music used throughout *Death of a Salesman*?

ANSWER: From the first the flute is used to create a mood or an atmosphere. Even though Willy is a heavy-set, aging man, lumbering in with weighty valises, he is also an individual forever pursuing an elusive vision or dream. And the light music of the flute, never pronounced or intrusive, keeps this side of Willy before the audience.

It is also used to provide transitions from present-day scenes to flashbacks and vice versa. Unlike many more conventional works, this play does not lower any curtain as the action moves from one place to the other, or even from one moment in time to another that occurred fifteen years before. The flute is used to smooth over the frequent shifts and to help set successive scenes.

Thirdly, the flute is connected with Willy's family history. His father, that great, "wild-hearted" man, made flutes and took his family in a wagon all over the country selling them. He was thus a craftsman, and Willy is always proud of being able to do things with his hands. He was also, of course, a salesman, and his roving, "adventurous" life has obviously signified to Willy a type of free, unencumbered existence, with profits unlimited for those who can quickly invent some such clever gadget. The sound of the flute is thus also the call Willy never wholly stops hearing to a challenging nomadic career, probably in the great West.

6. Indicate several criticisms directed in *Death of a Salesman* against contemporary American society.

ANSWER: First of all, the play suggests that modern business is so coldly competitive that decent human values are ignored. Willy gives many years of steady service to the Wagner Company. As soon, however, as his production begins to decline, he is taken off salary and put back on straight commission. Then, subsequently, he is discharged, apparently without any pension or other means of income. In addition, both Biff and Happy talk of business conditions in terms that suggest that competition encourages sharp practice or outright dishonesty.

Secondly, the work takes issue with exaggerated emphasis upon personal charm rather than upon more solid character traits. Willy keeps telling Biff that it is all important to be well liked. Biff can fail subjects and even steal with impunity provided that he has a winning smile and an attractive manner. Actually, Biff's poor grades deprive him of scholarships, and because of his lack of other necessary skills he never makes high wages. And despite his likeable personality, theft still draws him a jail term.

Thirdly, the drama seems to hint that too much stress upon certain types of white-collar work has driven those into it who would be better off working with their hands. And in general, the over-all worship of material success is seen to produce in some instances little more than a sense of failure and frustration.

7. Although *Death of a Salesman* is not poetic drama in the usual sense, it does seem to many to have a lyrical, elegiac quality, as the characters look back with sadness to happier times. What evidence is there of this lament for the past?

ANSWER: Willy Loman, when the play opens, is old, exhausted, and incapable of meeting the demands of his job. So he tends to recall a period some fifteen years earlier when life was much more pleasant. He was making more money then, and the old red Chevrolet shone, thanks to Biff's expert polishing. Biff was the popular captain of his high school football squad and was playing in a championship game. Furthermore, Biff then had excellent prospects. Three universities were making overtures about athletic scholarships. Above all, Willy was then idolized by both his boys, and peace and harmony reigned in the family.

Apart from Willy's own personal life, however, other changes have been occurring. When the Lomans first moved to Brooklyn, there were small houses and pleasant flower and vegetable gardens. The light and air were good for the spirit, and the chance for a man to plant and build increased his self-respect. Now, however, tall apartment buildings surround the small home, and, by implication, the small man. He can no longer grow vegetables or smell the flowers. He feels stifled, trapped.

In addition, the business picture has changed. There is more of the coldly mechanical even in sales transactions, whereas formerly, as when old Dave Singleton flourished, there was more evidence of respect, comradeship, and gratitude.

8. Why does Charley once remark that Willy really is a salesman and does not know it?

ANSWER: So far as Willy's actual achievements as a representative for the Wagner Company are concerned, it is hard to evaluate his record. Linda tends to flatter him, Howard is too ready to deny all his claims, and Willy himself rarely offers reliable facts about his work. Chances are, however, that at least in his prime, Willy was at least as good as the next man. He has, after all, held the job over the years. And he does support his family except for the final few months and pay off the mortgage on his house. As opposed, for example, to the Carbone family in *A View from the Bridge,* who live in a crowded tenement, the Lomans do manage to acquire property.

Yet Willy, however ordinary or average is his work for the company, is an expert at "selling" himself certain rather dubious notions. He is forever bragging about his popularity in New England and seems convinced that many will come from other states to his funeral. He is certain that Biff, having played a good game of football, will outshine everyone in the business world. And later he is certain that Oliver will lend Biff a sizable sum although his son can offer no security. At the end, he talks himself into the belief that his suicide will somehow enable Biff to take the lead once more from Bernard and become at once "magnificent." Charley's wry comment in the "Requiem," seems to take into account this astonishing facility Willy has for persuading himself and even others to buy unlikely possibilities.

9. Is there some suggestion here that both Willy and Biff are too emotionally concerned about each other's way of life?

ANSWER: Charley tries more than once to get Willy to let Biff alone to work out his own problems. After all, Biff is a man thirty-four years old. But Willy cannot heed this advice, even though he is impressed with the way Charley's hands-off policy has worked with the increasingly successful young Bernard.

Willy sees Biff's failure to settle down in some career as a spite campaign directed against him personally. Ever since Biff found him in a compromising situation in Boston, he has felt guiltily uneasy, afraid that he may inadvertently have blighted Biff's life. Yet, unwilling to admit such responsibility, he tries to blame Biff, accusing him of taking a mean and excessive revenge. Yet Willy has so identified his own interests with those of Biff that he still wants to "give him something." When Biff mentions the Oliver scheme, Willy nervously loads him with instructions as to how to behave. And once convinced of Biff's affection, Willy prepares to kill himself to give Biff the insurance money.

For his part, Biff has worries about his lack of material success that probably have nothing to do with Willy. Yet his sense of having proved a terrible disappointment to his father weighs him down further, and also stirs up defensive anger against Willy as the "fake" who let him down first. Both are grown men, in theory able to handle their own affairs. Yet both, because of strong guilt feelings, can neither achieve a mature, friendly relationship, nor let go and work out their personal problems alone.

10. How does Biff in *Death of a Salesman* compare with Chris in *All My Sons* as a key character?

ANSWER: Both young men begin by idolizing their fathers and later denounce them furiously. Chris astonished Ann and others by the extent to which he admires Joe. Yet, when he discovers Keller's part in shipping the defective materials, he is calling him the most derogatory names he can imagine. If Willy Loman's memories are at all reliable, Biff, as a high school senior, regarded Willy with astonishing hero worship. He missed him all the time Willy was away and longed to travel through New England with him. Yet at the end, unable to bear his father's taunts any longer, Biff turns on him and rejects both the man and his teachings.

Of the two, Chris starts with fewer feelings of insecurity. Chris has a good war record, likes his work at the plant, and enjoys the love of a charming and intelligent childhood sweetheart. Hence, Chris at the end can be more the stern and unforgiving accuser than Biff. And indeed Chris does seem to represent more the voice of outraged, decent individuals who discover perfidy and betrayal.

Biff, on the contrary, is poor, jobless, and discouraged. Because his disillusionment regarding Willy occurred years ago, he has had time to develop some feelings of compassion. So his outburst, provoked by Willy's unreasonable attacks, is more defensive and, in a sense, curative than severely denunciatory. And at the end Biff sobs exhaustedly, and Willy recognizes his true affection. Ironically, though, however different are their sons' rejection speeches, both fathers feel impelled to commit suicide.

Willa Cather's My Antonia

Textual Analysis

INTRODUCTION

During a hot summer's train ride through Iowa, the narrator (conceivably Willa Cather herself) meets a childhood friend, Jim Burden. Now a successful New York lawyer, Burden is married to a brisk, insensitive woman of means, who fancies herself a patron of the arts. She seems incapable of enthusiasm, and the narrator dislikes her. Jim, however, is still the romantic personality he was as a boy.

On the trip, the two friends recall Antonia, a Bohemian girl they once knew who symbolizes to both all that was fine and memorable in the Nebraska youth that they shared. Jim announces that he has been setting down all that he remembers about her. Months later, he brings his manuscript to the narrator's apartment, apologizing for its unrevised state and seeming lack of form. Deciding to add a title, he calls his piece *My Antonia.*

BOOK I—THE SHIMERDAS

PLOT: CHAPTERS 1 TO 8

Orphaned at ten, Jim makes the long train journey from his Virginia birthplace to his grandparents' farm in Nebraska. With him is Jake, a young farmhand. An amiable conductor tells him of an immigrant family in the next car. One daughter is a bright, pretty, brown-eyed girl who talks some English. Jim, however, is too shy to meet her. Arriving in Black Hawk by night, he sees the foreign group huddled amid their possessions. He himself is met by Otto, a wild-looking but kindly hired man, who drives him through the blackness to the farm.

Grandmother Burden, a lean, vigorous woman in her fifties, stands for "due order and decorum." Her white-washed kitchen is warm, clean, and inviting. Grandfather, bald but with a fine white curly beard, is reserved but gracious, and reads the Psalms beautifully.

Exploring his new terrain, Jim admires the flourishing farm but is most impressed with the unending miles of tall wine-red grass waving in the wind. Surrounded by it, he feels absorbed into something great and complete. This, he later decides, is what happiness is.

The Burdens visit the Bohemian settlers and find that their grasping countryman, Peter Krajiek, has sold them poor land and a wretched cave-like shelter. The family consists of the mother, a whining, inefficient housekeeper; 19-year-old Ambrosch, husky but sharp and wary; a small blonde girl, Yulka; a big, abnormal boy, Marek; and dark-haired 14-year-old Antonia, with large eyes and glowing skin. Gentle Mr. Shimerda, tall and slim, is a skilled weaver, who used to play the violin at weddings.

Living conditions are hard for the Shimerdas, but Jim and Antonia become fast friends as he teaches her English. He also admires her father, who seems sad and lonely. Jim rides over to see her on his pony. One chilly late fall afternoon, Antonia nurses back to life a dying insect. Its cracked voice reminds her of Old Hata, a storyteller in Bohemia. On another occasion, Jim, although terrified, kills a huge rattlesnake, and Antonia extols him to everyone.

They make friends with Pavel and Peter, two lonesome Russian settlers. Peter shares with them his precious melons. Pavel later becomes mortally ill and gasps out a tragic tale that both horrifies and fascinates the children. He and Peter once drove a sled with a bridal couple across dark, snowy Russian country. Attacked by hordes of ravenous wolves, occupants of other sleds died. Pavel sacrified the bride and groom, and the two got back safely but were forced into exile. Since then ill luck has always haunted them. Pavel dies, and Peter leaves town after all that he owns is claimed by an unscrupulous moneylender.

CHARACTER ANALYSES: CHAPTERS 1 TO 8

JIM BURDEN: In this section Jim is encountered first as a man, then as a small boy. The older Jim is described as a success in his professional life and a failure in domestic matters. He has done well as counsel for a western railroad because of his intense love of the land and his vision. His married life has proved disappointing, however, because his wife has no wish to share his enthusiasms and finds his taste for simpler pleasures merely irritating. Although disillusioned, Jim is still boyishly romantic.

At ten, Jim combines shyness with a certain love of adventure. On the train he cannot bring himself to go up to meet the foreign girl, as the conductor suggests. Yet he enjoys reading about Jesse James and cannot wait to hear how the ferocious-looking Otto lost part of an ear. Going up with his grandmother to a remote potato patch, he remains alone after she leaves, despite warnings of possible rattlers. At this time he also reveals a sensitive, vaguely spiritual nature. Traveling over the dark roads to the farm, he feels as though he were canceled out of existence. Again, seeing the windblown seas of Nebraska grass, he has the sensation of being absorbed into something great and good.

In the developing friendship between him and Antonia, the girl takes the initiative. She is, of course, four years older, but he comes to resent her rather superior airs. He is therefore much relieved when his victory over the great snake gives him a certain preeminence. Recalling the snake episode as an adult, Jim amusedly plays down the heroism of his youthful feat. After all, the snake was fat and lazy, and the frightened boy struck from instinct rather than deliberate valor. He also notes sardonically the readiness with which the young champion accepted Antonia's glowing description of his bravery. He thus makes the boy seem self-centered, pompous, and somewhat lacking in humor.

Like his grandparents, also Virginia-born, Jim is reserved. He is embarrassed by the impulsive generosity of Antonia and her father. When he teaches the girl some English, she offers him a silver ring. Later her father promises to leave him a valuable Old World gun. Jim feels merely uncomfortable.

Yet he shares a sensitivity to beauty with the Shimerda pair. With Antonia he enjoys discovering the wonders of the Nebraska countryside, and he does not laugh when she and her father try to revive the frail, dying insect and talk sadly of the old storyteller whom children loved.

ANTONIA SHIMERDA: From the start, Antonia is pictured as bright, energetic, and vivacious. She is the first in her family to learn English. Obviously the favorite of her gentle, sensitive father, she is eager to learn and grateful for any help. She is strong, healthy, good-looking, and full of life.

She is also warm-hearted and generous. She offers her ring to Jim for teaching her English. Later when Jim kills the snake, she tells everyone how heroic he was. Uniformly affectionate toward her father, she even has some feeling for the weakest and frailest of creatures, as can be seen in the incident of the dying insect.

Finally, there is indication here that Antonia will be a forceful personality. She makes the initial move in the friendship with Jim, and he notes that as her English improves she expresses opinions on everything. It is at her suggestion that Jim and she stop off to see the holes of the prairie dogs, whereupon the big snake is disturbed and coils to strike. Moreover, Jim's very annoyance at her domineering manner indicates that the immigrant girl is not lacking in spirit.

GRANDMOTHER BURDEN: This Virginia-bred farm woman is strong, intelligent, hard-working, and kindly. When Jim first sees her on the morning after his arrival, she has been crying, doubtless because the boy's father, her son, is dead. Yet she is not one to let emotions get out of control. So she briskly invites Jim down to breakfast.

She runs a good, clean, orderly home. Her bright kitchen, with its geraniums and white curtains, and sweet-smelling gingerbread, speaks well for her sense of "due order and decorum." She is also good to her immigrant neighbors, bringing them provisions to help them get started. She is, however, repelled by effusive expressions of thanks and will find it hard to understand why a woman like Mrs. Shimerda cannot run a house more efficiently. Although she tries to make allowances, she cannot grasp fully the problems of those suddenly faced with the new customs and conditions of a totally strange land.

GRANDFATHER BURDEN: In this section he is seen mainly as a dignified, industrious older man, whose white beard gives him the appearance of a patriarch from the Bible. Hardly the talkative type, he yet seems very much the head of the house. He runs his farm well and is deeply religious.

MR. SHIMERDA: Always very careful of his attire, the tall, slim Mr. Shimerda is always the gentleman, just as his wife and Ambrosch are emphatically peasants. He is fond of Antonia and most insistent that she go on learning. He takes a kindly interest in Jim and sees in the Burdens a family who may help his daughter acquire the knowledge she needs.

He suffers much because of the miserable conditions in the cave and misses his homeland greatly. Except for shared moments with the more sanguine Jim and Antonia, he is a sad, lonely, isolated figure. For a time his spirits are raised when he strikes up a friendship with Peter and Pavel, whose Russian speech he can understand. When, however, Pavel dies and Peter leaves, he is more deeply disheartened than ever.

COMMENT: CHAPTERS 1 TO 8

The brief Introduction by the author seems at first unnecessary. Jim Burden's story of Antonia is complete in itself. Nevertheless, Willa Cather within its few pages establishes certain basic lines of development.

First of all, with a few vivid descriptive phrases she establishes the importance of the natural setting. A very real part in her story will be played by the prairie country itself. By referring to "never-ending miles of ripe wheat," the ever-present red dust, the "burning wind" and the "blustery winters," she suggests those "stimulating extremes" in her novel.

Secondly, through the comments of the narrator and Jim she indicates that unlike certain other writers of her time, such as Hamlin Garland and Frank Norris, she is not going to draw a bleak, pessimistic picture of life on mid-western farms. The two friends talk of a country "green and billowy beneath a brilliant sky" and allude to the "whole adventure" of their childhood.

Thirdly, the author, by her incidental remarks about Jim's wife, makes it clear that Jim did not grow up to marry Antonia. The Bohemian girl, from the first, is not the conventional heroine of a conventional love story, even though Jim has found her unforgettable. She is intended rather to symbolize "the country, the conditions," the great adventure of growing up in rural Nebraska during the 1880s.

We are in fact to consider Antonia virtually a new type of epic figure. The earlier epic heroes, like Achilles and Aeneas, were outstanding individuals who summed up the best traits of their respective cultures. Antonia, as we shall see, is no great warrior or world leader. Yet she does, in Miss Cather's view, embody the most admirable qualities of our western immigrant pioneers.

Finally, the Introduction tells us something about the form and style of the novel. In 1918, when *My Antonia* appeared, readers were accustomed to stories with tightly constructed, often predictable plots. Miss Cather, however, was attempting something new and different. She thus has Jim say that he has written down all that he remembers about his Bohemian friend without reorganizing or revising his material. Actually, the work has been carefully planned and written by Miss Cather to develop for us gradually a well-integrated portrayal of a character and a way of life. Yet she will do this by letting Jim recall key episodes seemingly at random rather than by using the standard devices of more conventional fiction.

Incidentally, the heroine's name, Antonia, is spelled in many editions and critical works with an accent over the first letter. Because of certain printing requirements the accent will be omitted in this book. The name should be pronounced with the stress upon the first syllable (AN-ton-ee-ah). Jim also refers to her sometimes as Tony. When there is actual dialog, Antonia's English is poor at first. Later it improves, but she never speaks with the fluency of her friend Lena Lingard, another immigrant girl.

In general, *My Antonia* is a work that draws heavily upon Willa Cather's own childhood experiences. She, too, left a Virginia birthplace to join grandparents on a Nebraska farm when she was about nine years old. Thus, many of the recollections of "Jim Burden" are based upon her own memories. Recent critical studies, notably *The World of Willa Cather*, by Mildred Bennett, have identified those Nebraska friends and relatives who were the originals for certain characters. The elder Burdens, for instance, resemble her grandfather and grandmother, William and Caroline Cather (Bennett, 10-11). Antonia's family, the Shimerdas, were drawn from the immigrant Sadileks she knew in her girlhood (Bennett, 46-51). The town of Black Hawk was Red Cloud, Nebraska, as she saw it in the 1880s.

The early chapters contrast sharply the living conditions of two groups of Nebraska settlers. The Burdens represent the well-established nativeborn farmers. Capable and industrious, they have built up a flourishing homestead. Their white wooden house is warm, clean, and comfortable. They also have a windmill and barns, granaries, pig-yards, and corncribs. Grandfather works well with the hired men, and Grandmother tends her vegetable garden and presides over a neat, well-run house. The newly arrived Shimerdas, on the other hand, have poor land and the worst of accommodations. They have few provisions, poor equipment, and not much capital. In addition, they do not know the language and must rely upon Krajiek, the unscrupulous fellow-countryman who has already cheated them shamefully. Jim and Antonia arrive in Nebraska together, but it is clear at once that the immigrant girl will have a much harder struggle. Yet if she does persevere and does overcome the formidable obstacles facing her, she may well prove the more remarkable character.

As in *O Pioneers!*, her earlier novel, Willa Cather will show her American readers a strong immigrant woman enduring much and eventually contributing a great deal to her adopted country. Yet the author is not a sentimentalist suggesting that all foreign settlers are good and all native-born settlers mean or weak. Here, whereas the Burdens are friendly and try to help the newcomers, the Shimerdas are cruelly exploited by another immigrant. Moreover, even within the family group, Mrs. Shimerda is greedy and ill-natured, young Ambrosch is sly, and Marek is hardly normal. Mr. Shimerda admittedly is charming, but mournful and ineffectual. Antonia stands out as much among her own people as she will later in other circles.

If Willa Cather is not crudely lauding all immigrants at the expense of all those born in

America, neither is she indiscriminately favoring one culture rather than another. In these early chapters, a favorable portrayal is developed of Grandmother Burden, the Virginia-born standard bearer for "due order and decorum." She is a strong, able, good-hearted woman, and her orderly pleasant home is a civilizing force on the frontier. Antonia's mother is a European peasant. Physically she is sturdy. There is a toughness in her constitution that will enable her to survive rigors that will daunt her more refined, more sensitive husband. Mrs. Shimerda, Ambrosch, and Antonia all have enormous vitality. Yet Antonia's mother and brother also have the mean, grasping, small-minded natures of the peasant group at its worst. Their manners are rough, and they tend to be sly and sullen. More like her gracious father, Antonia, from the beginning, is shown to possess a warm, loving nature. As the story proceeds, however, she is subjected to two types of influence. Association with her mother and her brother has a coarsening effect. From her father, and later Mrs. Burden, she learns "nice ways." Miss Cather in this manner seems to hold up as ideal the combination of peasant vigor and determination and European or Southern American refinement, with its courtly generosity of spirit.

In this section much is made also of the emotional and imaginative response of Jim and Antonia to the natural beauty of the unspoiled land which both have suddenly come upon for the first time in their young lives. They come from vastly different backgrounds and are by no means possessed of identical personalities. Yet they do share a sensitivity to beauty, and they are both capable of enthusiasm. Miss Cather seems to approve highly of those who respond with feeling to whatever wonders they encounter. In the Introduction there is fondness suggested for the romantic Jim and none at all for his "unimpressionable" wife.

In her books Willa Cather, like such romantic poets as William Wordsworth, is much concerned with experiences that become important because some individual has felt strongly about them. The boundless prairie, with its gently blown red grass, is a fact that no Nebraskan can ignore. Yet there is is no evidence that it proves inspiring to Mrs. Shimerda or Ambrosch. Young Jim, however, is sensitive and imaginative. Alone out on the prairie, he responds to its vastness with his whole being. His enjoyment is unusually intense. He is caught up in a kind of rapture. Antonia, too, is "impressionable" and responsive. As a result, their exploratory rambles through their new region, as well as their battle with the snake and their overhearing of Pavel's deathbed confession, all become part of the great adventure of growing up. Furthermore, such exciting episodes will provide them with precious memories which will enrich their subsequent lives.

The three most notable incidents in the second half of this section are the Old Hata episode, the killing of the snake, and Pavel's story of the wolves. Each is not only interesting in itself but revealing as to the richness and complexity of Willa Cather's art.

The dying insect is revived briefly by Antonia on a chill autumn afternoon. Here the author's use of striking contrasts is most effective, as she suggests a delicate balance between warmth and coldness, joy and sadness, life and death. On the one hand, there is the flowing sunshine with the lively rabbits darting about. The young people are enjoying their pleasant friendship, and Antonia herself seems to represent vitality and warmth. She coaxes the frail insect to sing again and even momentarily rouses some spark of animation in her disheartened father. She is making progress in learning to read English, and overjoyed that the rabbits her father has shot will mean "meat for eat, skin for hat."

At the same time, death is in the air. Winter is coming, and the day gradually darkens. Antonia tells Jim of badgers torn by dogs in the old country, and she recalls the aging storyteller, Old Hata. The insect, last of the small summer creatures, has been only "lured back to life by false pretenses"; and old Mr. Shimerda, although brightening up at the sight of Antonia, is actually failing fast. The interplay here of bright and dark themes is such as to raise a most insignificant occurrence to the level of a moving and memorable experience.

As for the snake battle, the incident reveals first of all how well Miss Cather can handle a good, exciting adventure tale. The description of the rattler's loathsome writhing and the boy's sick horror is vivid, and the ensuing action is blood-curdling enough. Then the pace changes, and the author shifts to comedy, almost in the manner of Mark Twain, as Jim Burden preens himself over his heroic feat. Finally, through the rueful comments of the adult Jim, she makes us see the very slight basis for so much self-congratulations.

Actually, although she has Jim, as a man, snort skeptically at dragon slayers in general, Miss Cather is not really cynical about all heroines. Her Antonia, for instance, seems at times an epic figure. Yet her conception of the heroic emphasizes not the big, showy act in which chance may play a major part, but rather a life of courageous endurance, accepting and overcoming hardships over the years.

The third account, that of the wedding party pursued by wolves, proves that the author can do ample justice to a stark horror piece. In a sense the short narrative is independent of the main plot. It is just a story that Antonia and Jim hear. Yet the author uses it skillfully. There is contrast, for instance, between the terrible agony of the dying Pavel and the fascinated interest of the two healthy, high-spirited young people. They are not inhuman. They can be sorry for a sick, suffering man, but they still find it wonderful to be in on something so fantastic and so shocking. Knowing this weird secret is one more bond between them, one more exciting moment in their great adventure.

In addition, there is the suggestion, not infrequent in Miss Cather's works, of the operation of fate or some sort of mysterious doom. She has had Jim previously feel an awareness of the power of Destiny as he was carried through the black night to his grandparents' farm. Now, in this story, there is no indication that Peter had much to do with the death of the unfortunate bride and groom Yet, having been with Pavel at the time, he has been continually the victim of misfortune. He is pictured as a hard-working, inoffensive man, anxious to please, but he seems forever doomed to meet with ill luck.

PLOT: CHAPTERS 9 TO 15

After the first December snowfall, Jim takes Antonia and Yulka for a ride in his new sleigh, made for him by Otto, once a cabinetmaker's apprentice. The young people find the drive through the dazzling white scenery exhilarating although the girls shiver in thin dress and shawls.

The Burden home is warm and comfortable, and Grandmother sees to it that they have plenty of chicken and ham, pies, cakes, and puddings. The hired men labor hard and cheerfully, although neither will ever be rich. One night Otto tells an amusing story about his coming to America. He was asked then to look after the expectant wife of a friend. En route the lady had twins, and poor Otto had his hands full.

Some weeks later, hearing that the Shimerdas are in distress, the Burdens bring them provisions. Mrs. Shimerda embarrasses Grandmother with her tirades and tears. Antonia is more gracious, and Mr. Shimerda explains sadly that they left Bohemia with adequate funds but lost out through ruinous exchange rates and Krajiek's greed. As they leave, Mrs. Shimerda gives them a cupful of dried food, which she obviously treasures. Suspicious of anything so foreign, Mrs. Burden throws the flakes into the fire. Jim tastes one, however, and later learns that they were dried mushrooms brought from Europe.

At Christmastime, Jim makes a picture book for the Shimerda girls. Jake cuts down a small cedar, which the family trims with gingerbread, popcorn, and candles. Otto adds beautiful paper figures from Austria. On the day itself, Grandfather reads the Bible story and they breakfast on waffles and sausage. Later in the day Mr. Shimerda comes to call. He relaxes amid the civilized comforts of the Burden home and obviously returns with regret to his own cheerless hovel and self-pitying wife.

During the subsequent thaw, Mrs. Shimerda comes over with Antonia. The Bohemian woman whines enviously and seizes an iron pot. Jim is angry and reacts coldly when Antonia tells him that her father is ill and unhappy. She adds that it was her mother who insisted that they come to America to provide better opportunities for the children. Jim remains hostile, and the girl asks why his wealthy grandfather hasn't helped them with needed loans. Ambrosch, she declares, would surely pay him back.

On January 22, the Burdens learn that Mr. Shimerda has shot himself. Although the ground is frozen and travel is hard, Jim's family sends Otto for the coroner and the priest. Mrs. Burden goes over to comfort the women. Jim, alone at home, feels that Mr. Shimerda's unhappy spirit may linger in the Burden home before starting back to Bohemia. Otto cannot reach the missionary priest, but Anton Jelinek, a strong and likable young Bohemian, arrives to help. He explains to Grandfather how much having a priest means to Catholics and impresses Mr. Burden with his "manly" faith.

Otto makes a coffin. Mr. Shimerda's frozen body is then buried, after some brief prayers by Grandfather, near the crossroads, in line with an old-country superstition about suicides. During the following months, Antonia gives up her studies and works hard with Ambrosch, becoming brown and husky, but losing her "nice ways." Jim and Jake have a brief feud with her brother, but Grandfather settles things amicably and hires her for kitchen work at harvesttime.

CHARACTER ANALYSES: CHAPTERS 9 TO 15

JIM BURDEN: In this section Jim's hot temper flares more than once. At age eleven he is not overly disposed to make allowances for those whom desperate circumstances drive to behave disagreeably. Acutely aware of all that the Burdens have done to aid the Shimerdas, he is furious when Antonia's mother snatches his grandmother's iron pot. If the Bohemians are in need, it is somehow their fault. If they could not manage more successfully, they should not have come to America at all. Jim thus as a boy has little sympathy for those who won't act politely toward their benefactors.

He is angered again after Mr. Shimerda's death when the surly Ambrosch seems uninterested in returning a borrowed harness and then throws one back in poor condition. After a scuffle in which Jake knocks the Bohemian youth down, as Antonia and her mother voice fiery protests, Jim decides that he never wants to see any of these foreigners again, including Antonia. He will change his mind, of course, but on several future occasions he will again prove a young man readily roused to indignation.

He is also, however, inclined to be generous when not offended by slights. He is delighted to offer Antonia and Yulka a ride in his new horse-drawn sleigh. He even gives his long comforter or scarf to the half-frozen younger sister, thereby leaving himself open to a quinsy attack. In addition, he expends much effort in putting together an attractive picture book as a Christmas present for the two immigrant girls.

Other traits, suggested in the first section, are again evident here. First of all, Jim relishes adventure or excitement. Having liked Mr. Shimerda, he is saddened by the old man's suicide. Yet the general hubbub, the coming and going of neighbors during the period following the tragedy, he finds almost pleasurable.

Secondly, he seems sensitive here as before to beauty of various types. He enjoys the bracing drive through the snowy countryside. He finds enchanting the Christmas tree with Otto's Austrian paper decorations. He is also moved by the stark simplicity of the burial service on the bleak hillside.

Thirdly, he again gives evidence of a vaguely mystical strain. He resolutely dismisses the Catholic view that the soul of Mr. Shimerda may suffer in Purgatory because of the old man's rash action. Instead he fancifully imagines the spirit of the sad, homesick Bohemian pausing in the comfortable warmth of the Burden kitchen, then winging its way back to Europe.

ANTONIA SHIMERDA: If Jim reveals a mettlesome personality in this section, so does Antonia. When Jim criticizes her family, she replies heatedly and suggests that the Burdens could have done more to help their neighbors financially. Again, when Jake strikes the surly Ambrosch, she irately declares that she will no longer be friends with Jim and the young farmhand.

After her father's death, which leaves her heartbroken, she becomes for a time much more like her peasant mother and Ambrosch. All three work strenuously to make the farm prosper. Antonia, sunburned and strong, does the rough chores of a man and takes pride in closely rivaling her brother. Seeing her during these months, Jim finds her less feminine, more coarse in manner. Yet, in general, Antonia throughout the book is going to be held up to admiration as a woman of strength and determination. Her resolute acceptance of farm responsibilities here prepares us for her later triumphs over disasters that would destroy a weaker individual.

In addition, Antonia is refreshingly levelheaded. Despite her annoyance over the blow to Ambrosch, she comes promptly to Grandfather Burden when one of her horses seems close to death. Moreover, no false pride prevents her coming to work in Grandmother's kitchen. She is obviously delighted to be there, keeps up a cheerful clatter with the pans, and pleases everyone with her hearty good humor. In quieter moments she wistfully admits that she likes life at the Burdens. She would have the nicer, more feminine ways that Jim so admires, had she the advantages that have always been his.

GRANDMOTHER BURDEN: In this section, as before, Mrs. Burden is the ideal homemaker and good neighbor. She is especially thoughtful at the time of the Shimerda tragedy. She readily offers to go over to console the bereft women, and she urges Jake to take a good horse to ride for priest and coroner, even though the trip through the snow may overstrain the animal.

She also, on occasion, shows admirable firmness. At the funeral services when Mrs. Shimerda foolishly tries to make the terrified little Yulka bid her father good-bye, the older woman briskly and decisively intervenes.

Yet she also is shown to have a certain narrowness of outlook. She cannot see why Mrs. Shimerda, a stranger speaking little English, has not known enough to set up a hen house and keep her family supplied with eggs and poultry. She has small patience with the other woman's housekeeping methods and throws out the mushrooms. Moreover, when Mr. Shimerda kills himself, she is surprised that he could have been so inconsiderate. All in all, she never does seem to grasp very well the dire needs and problems of the uprooted Europeans.

MR. SHIMERDA: When the Burdens bring over supplies, Mr. Shimerda is grateful but deeply distressed that his family must take charity. He is a man of dignity and pride, explaining almost pathetically to his benefactors that he had some position in the old country. During the Christmastime visit, he momentarily relaxes, and we catch a glimpse of the genial Continental man of books and music he was in less rigorous climes. His suicide soon afterwards evidences his deep despair, but even before dying he goes quietly off and folds his clothes neatly, fastidious to the end.

MRS. SHIMERDA: Usually whining and disagreeable, Mrs. Shimerda shows here that she is also grasping and mean. She seizes Mrs. Burden's iron pot on the ground that her hostess has more than she has. Later she makes an absurd attempt to avoid making final payments on a cow sold to her by Grandfather.

She also seems at times not overly intelligent. She does not learn the new language or new customs easily. Her handling of the frightened Yulka at the funeral is not sensible, and her efforts to elude Mr. Burden and to repudiate her promise to pay for the cow are ludicrous.

On the other hand, she is sometimes oddly shrewd. When Jake strikes Ambrosch, she rides in to prefer charges. Moreover, after her husband's death, she encourages Antonia to compete with

Ambrosch, thus spurring the girl on to greater efforts.

Although generally an unsympathetic character, she has some good points. Her insistence upon coming to America derived from her vision of a better life for her children. In addition, she is not wholly lacking in gratitude. In fact, her emotional displays of thankfulness sometimes prove more embarrassing than her rudeness. Thirdly, she does eventually prove a fair housekeeper. When Jim visits the Shimerdas in the spring, she serves him fresh bread on an oilcloth-covered table. Finally, although superstitious about the burial of suicides at crossroads, she is also genuinely pious, praying devoutly for the soul of her husband.

GRANDFATHER BURDEN: The old patriarch has several roles to play in this section. For one thing, he is the community leader. At the time of the Shimerda tragedy, all those concerned come to his house and look to him for direction. When, for instance, Jake and the coroner suggest that Mr. Shimerda was actually murdered by Krajiek, Grandfather proves the theory untenable and establishes the fact of suicide.

Secondly, Grandfather is the peacemaker. When Jake and Jim come back furious after the fight with Ambrosch, he refuses to take the fracas seriously. He goes on helping Ambrosch to purchase the best farm animals for his needs, and he readily assists Antonia with the sick horse. Afterwards, he generously waives the final payments on the cow, and helps the brother and sister earn necessary cash by hiring both for the summer harvesting.

Thirdly, he is the man of faith, positive as regards his own religious convictions, yet capable of respecting the beliefs of others. When the Catholic Mr. Shimerda makes the Sign of the Cross while kneeling before the Christmas tree, Grandmother fears that her husband will protest. Grandfather remains silent, however, remarking quietly later, "The prayers of all good people are good." Subsequently, he argues with Anton Jelinek regarding the necessity of prayers for the dead. Yet he speaks admiringly of the young Bohemian's serious concern about such matters and treats him with grave courtesy. Then, on the day of the funeral, at the widow's request, he prays aloud for those left behind and entrusts the soul of the deceased to God's mercy.

AMBROSCH SHIMERDA: Ambrosch appears surly and disagreeable, if not irresponsible, when he misuses the borrowed harness and is rude about it to Jake. He is not, however, lazy. He is willing to take over farm burdens and to work hard. He is also strongly religious. Jim is surprised how fervently he prays for his father. Later, although he has not much money, he uses Marek's wages for Masses for Mr. Shimerda's soul.

COMMENT: CHAPTERS 9 TO 15

There is some discussion among critics as to whether this novel is essentially the story of Antonia or of both the Bohemian girl and Jim Burden. Even the title is open to more than one interpretation. What does the *my* mean in *My Antonia*? Does it mean merely that the narrator can tell us only what he knows about her? Even as a boy he is out of touch with her for considerable periods, and in later life he will make his home far from her Nebraska farm country. Or does the *my* mean that the heroine described for us is the Antonia who serves as one of the major factors in Jim's progress toward maturity? In other words is she important primarily as an interesting individual or as one of Jim's treasured memories?

Either way, the events described in this section of the work crucially affect the relationship. Hitherto, despite the economic handicaps of the Shimerdas, Jim and Antonia have been carefree young people happily exploring the countryside. The suicide of the girl's father abruptly alters everything. She was learning English quickly and might have gone on to school with Jim. And present to guide her would have been her cultivated father, who was fond of books, music, and good talk. Instead, she will have no time for further studies. She must take on the most arduous of farm chores and do the work of a man. "Things will be easy for you," she tells Jim. "But they will be hard for us." She will go on to work as a hired girl and eventually wed a poor immigrant. He will go through the university and travel much abroad. At the very end of the story Jim will talk of those "early accidents of fortune which predetermined" their lives. The great fact that sets Antonia's life course is the violent death of her beloved father.

This section also develops further the idyllic, or extremely favorable, picture of life on the Burden farm. Peace and plenty, good order, and an overall spirit of kindliness are everywhere apparent. Outside the cold winter winds may howl. Inside there can be found warmth, enough food for a feast, and happy, evenings with pop corn and taffy, song fests and story telling. As a novel, *My Antonia* is much concerned with life within the home. Within its pages three highly satisfactory households will be described. This is the first, the Burden home. The second will be that of the Harlings in Black Hawk; the third, in the final chapters, that of Antonia herself. In each instance an ideal is held up for our admiration, and the scene is described with an almost lyric enthusiasm that enhances its appeal.

By way of contrast we are also given glimpses of households far from pleasant. First, we have the Shimerda cave, dark and dismal, with a complaining, ineffectual woman doing little to make conditions better. Later we will see something of the nightmare home life of the moneylender Wick Cutter, and we have already heard of Jim's unsatisfactory domestic life with his handsome, cold-hearted wife.

One other aspect is worth noting. In these chapters much is made of the hard work and generosity of the hired men, Jake and Otto. Together they provided Jim with his delightful Christmas tree. Yet they are, and will always be, rootless men. They are regarded with pity because they will never know the solid joys of those who have homes and families of their own and can build toward a brighter future.

If, however, this is a section singing the praises of domesticity, it also provides varied examples of prejudices that can make relations between groups more difficult. One of the most revealing occurs at the time of Mr. Shimerda's death. Inasmuch as the ground is frozen and travel is extremely difficult, funeral arrangements cannot easily be made. A request is thus made to the Norwegians, who have a cemetery nearby, to let the grave be dug on their land. They refuse, whereupon Grandmother is incensed against such "clannish" foreigners. Prejudice is also shown when Jake, infuriated by Ambrosch, decides that all foreigners are the same and cannot be trusted. At that time, Jim, too, declares hotly that all are like "Krajiek and Ambrosch." On the other hand, a decent, good-hearted young man like Anton Jelinek helps to improve the community status of his people; and Grandfather, through his wise and tolerant pronouncements, also helps to end feuds and encourage friendlier attitudes. He even saves the worthless Krajiek from being charged with the one crime of which he is not guilty.

As regards the artistry of Willa Cather in handling this material, we see again how subtly she has linked the changing seasons with the events described. It is obvious, of course, that the rigors of the Nebraska winter serve to deepen Mr. Shimerda's despair and thus precipitate his suicide. Yet the vivid descriptions here of the cold bleakness of the landscape intensify the starkness of the tragedy. This is the first crucial year of the great adventure. Jim and Antonia first joyously explored Nebraska when the tall red grass was blowing in the warm September wind. Then the chill set in, and the incidents described were more somber. These included the stories of the evil snake, the dying insect, and the ravenous wolves. Now, in this section, there is the grim, bitter cold. The Shimerdas suffer in their cheerless cave, and the father kills himself. Spring, however, brings hope, and the Bohemians begin to make progress. Then by the time of the summer harvest, misunderstandings end, and Antonia and Jim are happily reunited at the Burdens. Antonia, high-spirited and healthy, enjoys getting vegetables from the garden in the morning sunshine. She and Jim admire together the wonders of a magnificent electric storm that sends thunder crashing around them one close, hot night.

If the nature descriptions are thus used skillfully to highlight successive incidents, we also find the same effective use of contrast that was evident in the earlier chapters. The most striking example of this is the Christmas scene at the Burdens. Here there is everything to make a young boy pleased with his new home. The tree, with Otto's paper ornaments, is splendid, and everyone seems eager to do his part to make the holiday festive. The visit of Mr. Shimerda, however, makes all aware of the misery of the immigrant group. For a few brief hours, this cultivated European gentleman seems to relax and almost cheer up. Yet the Burdens know, as he does, that as night falls he must return to the dark, wretched cave. Joy and sadness, warmth and cold are thus interwoven.

Other uses of contrast may also be recalled. Grandfather Burden is sensible and tolerant, as opposed to the hotheaded Jake and Jim. Anton Jelinek is the admirable young Bohemian, as against the mean disagreeable Ambrosch. The neighborly helpfulness of the Burdens and their friends is quite different from the lack of cooperation shown by the Norwegians who will not allow the burial in their cemetery.

It must again be pointed out that the Introduction spoke of the adventure that was shared by all who grew up together during the 1880s in Nebraska. The whole series of events connected with the Shimerda suicide would be likely to leave a deep impression on those closely affected by the tragedy. This Willa Cather would know well, for Francis Sadilek, the model for the fictional Mr. Shimerda, actually did commit suicide, too, and was buried near the crossroads as the novel indicates. Throughout the story the death of Antonia's father will be referred to quite frequently as Jim and the girl meet again at different stages of their lives. The burial scene on the hillside, a heartbreaking experience, is something shared, something deeply felt that will be impossible for either ever to obliterate from his memory.

It was Willa Cather's belief that the most crucial years in an individual's development, those in which he was likely to store up his most vital impressions, were those between the ages of nine or ten and about fifteen.

My Antonia is particularly interesting because it is in effect a double illustration of what she meant. In terms of the fiction, Jim as a man and later Antonia as a woman will refer to the shared experiences of their early years as the most memorable of all. In fact, the Introduction indicates that Jim is not by any means merely jotting down a few casual recollections. He may apologize for the unrevised state of his manuscript, but he makes it quite clear that he is relating events that meant much to him not only at the time that they occurred but also during the years that have passed since then.

In addition, we must keep in mind the strong autobiographical element in the work. Critics generally are convinced that a great many of the reactions and opinions attributed to Jim, are actually those of the author herself. She, too, discovered Nebraska as he did, rode around the countryside on her pony, enjoyed the company of her Virginia-born grandparents, and made many friends among the Bohemians and other groups of immigrant settlers. If her descriptions here are vivid and her scenes amazingly convincing, it seems probable that the experiences of her Nebraska girlhood, on which she drew so plentifully, did in fact leave on her a powerful permanent impression.

BOOK II—THE HIRED GIRLS

PLOT: CHAPTERS 1 TO 7

Three years after Jim's arrival in Nebraska, the Burdens rent their farm to the Widow Steavens and move into Black Hawk. There Jim can obtain further schooling. After settling the family in their new home near the edge of town, Otto heads back toward the wilder West, and Jake goes with him. Jim never sees either of these good men again.

Black Hawk is a pleasant clean little town with board sidewalks and white fences around grass plots. Jim misses the farm but likes his river view there. Because the Burden house is the first met upon entering town, country friends often stop there to leave their horses. Jim likes the company, but misses seeing Antonia. The widow Steavens says that Ambrosch is working her too hard. Grandmother hopes to get her work with their new neighbors, the Harlings.

The wife of a successful cattle merchant, Mrs. Harling was born in Norway, coming to America at age ten. A stocky, vigorous little woman, she has a fiery temper, but is also quick to laugh. She has strong feelings about everything. Her children include Charles, sixteen; the musically inclined Julia; the tomboyish Sally; and sensitive little Nina. The oldest girl, Frances, is chief clerk for her father. She knows all about credits, and her business acumen is widely respected. She works often with Grandfather Burden to save the farmers from the moneylender, Wick Cutter.

In August the Harlings lose their cook, and Grandfather recommends Antonia. Dealing with Ambrosch for the girl's services, the hearty Mrs. Harling is amused by his inept attempts to drive a hard bargain. She agrees to pay the girl three dollars a week.

Jim is jealous when Antonia obviously admires Charley Harling, baking nut cakes for him and doing his mending. In general, however, Jim has good times next door, especially when the lordly Mr. Harling is not home to demand quiet.

One evening a young blonde girl in blue, with a low, pleasant voice, arrives to visit Antonia. This is Lena Lingard, daughter of a poor Norwegian farmer, who has come to work for Mrs. Thomas, the local dressmaker. She tells them that another friend, Tiny Soderball, is set to work at the hotel, the Boys' Home. Mrs. Harling and Frances eye Lena with some suspicion, having heard stories already about her romances. Some were scandalized, for instance, when Ole Benson, married unhappily to "Crazy Mary," enjoyed talking to the gentle Lena in the fields. His wife, enraged, threatened the girl with a corn-knife. Lena denies that she did anything amiss. After this Jim sees Lena often in town, and at Christmas both help her little brother pick out presents for Mrs. Lingard.

After dreary nights on the farm, Antonia is happy at the Harlings. Evenings she contentedly sews nice clothes for herself. She also tells stories. One grim one is of a tramp denied beer at a farm where he worked at harvest-time. Wild-eyed he dove into the threshing machine and died. Another time, Jim, Antonia, and Lena visit Tiny at the hotel, when her strict employer, Mrs. Gardner, has gone to Omaha to see Booth and Barrett in a play. The young people hear a visiting Negro pianist, Blind d'Arnault, give a rhythmically exciting impromptu concert. Jim and Antonia find it thrilling.

CHARACTER ANALYSES: BOOK II, CHAPTERS 1 TO 7

JIM BURDEN: At the time of the funeral of Mr. Shimerda, Jim was not insensitive to the sadder aspects of the situation, but he did like the company that kept coming to the Burden farm. This suggestion of the lonely boy who enjoys social gatherings is developed further in these chapters. First of all, Jim is pleased that the farmers coming into town stop for a time at his house. Nor does he mind running extra errands to get extra bread or steak for them. He also finds delightful the pleasant evenings at the Harlings. As winter comes on, the town often seems cold, bleak, and dreary. Yet he finds color and warmth at their home, and happily dives through the hedge to enjoy charades, a costume party, or even a dancing lesson. He likes to hear Mrs. Harling play selections from the operas, and he listens attentively to Antonia's stories.

He mentions in passing that he has quickly become used to school life, adding that he would be as wild as any of the other boys were it not for Mrs. Harling's restraining influence. There has been previous indication that Jim can be hot-tempered, but although he mentions more than once a tendency toward wildness, it is never particularly obvious in his actions. He will, it is true, court social disapproval by associating with the hired girls, who are considered by the town to be members of a lower class. Except for this, however, he is hardly the recklessly defiant type. There is also some suggestion that he is jealous of Charley, whom Antonia admires. This, too, seems far from serious.

ANTONIA SHIMERDA: Antonia loves life. From the first she is happy at the Harlings. Young and strong, she is eager to learn, willing to work, and delighted to be part of a big, busy, cheerful household. Cooking for such a sizable group would in those days require long hours of strenuous effort. Yet Antonia is so full of youthful energy and high spirits that she is always ready to run races or take part in hay fights with the children and make them extra cookies and taffy in the evening.

This vital young Bohemian girl is also by nature creative, with an artistic strain not surprising in a violinist's daughter. Here she is seen making slippers for herself and sewing pretty clothes. When Frances teaches them all to dance, Antonia proves the most likely pupil of all. Moreover, she is a good storyteller, as is evident from her chilling yarn about the tramp and the threshing machine. Finally, both she and Jim are much moved by the rhythmical playing of Blind d'Arnault, whom they hear that Saturday night at the Boys' Home.

She is not, however, as aggressive as some of her friends. She receives Lena Lingard with only limited cordiality because she fears that Mrs. Harling may be displeased if she welcomes someone who has been the subject of gossip. Again, when asked to dance by the salesmen listening to Blind d'Arnault, Antonia seems alarmed at first and looks to the others for reassurance. Finally, she is kind and generous. Admiring Charley, she packs special lunches for his hunting trips, mends his ball-gloves, feeds his dog, and bakes his favorite nut cakes. For the others she makes candy and cookies, and she is always gentle with little Nina who so readily bursts into tears.

GRANDMOTHER BURDEN: With the move into town Mrs. Burden ceases to figure prominently in the story. She is described as busy with such community activities as church suppers and missionary society work, but Jim seems to spend most of his free time visiting the Harlings. She is, however, responsible for getting Antonia the post as cook. This good office, reveals first of all, her continuing neighborly concern. Ever since the girl lost her father, Mrs. Burden has wanted in some way to make Antonia's life a little easier.

Secondly, it indicates further how much she desires Antonia to have "nice ways." She remembers Mr. Shimerda as a "genteel old man" and shudders to think of his pretty daughter working out in the fields with rough threshers. Not one ordinarily given to asking favors, Grandmother anxiously entreats Mrs. Harling to try Antonia, for she knows that in such a pleasant environment the girl will learn much of value. For her part Antonia promises to be the kind of young woman that Grandmother will "like better," and within the month she is speaking English as well as any of the children. In later life, Antonia will tell Jim that were it not for her service at the Harlings, she might have brought up her own sons and daughters as "wild rabbits." So Mrs. Burden achieves her object.

Amusingly enough, Grandmother fears lest the disagreeable Ambrosch and his mother discourage Mrs. Harling from engaging Antonia by unreasonable demands. With this in mind, she shrewdly corners the sullen young man and suggests that it would improve his credit were his sister to work for the successful cattle dealer. Yet the younger, more vigorous, and less easily daunted Mrs. Harling sails in and good-naturedly bargains with the greedy Old World pair. She later laughingly confesses to Mrs. Burden that she is probably "more at home with that sort of bird." This is undoubtedly true. Remember how ill at ease, for all her neighborly intentions, Grandmother always was in the presence of the Shimerdas with their tears, tantrums, and extravagant expressions of gratitude? She is always a lady with a strong sense of decorum.

MRS. HARLING: Born in Norway, Mrs. Harling is stocky and vigorous, with bright, sparkling eyes and a rosy complexion. Notable for energy and enthusiasm, she is generally good natured, although she can, on occasion, reveal a fiery temper. Here she is seen as a capable homemaker, a good wife and mother. She is kind to Jim, the young boy from the next house, but will tolerate no wildness. If he causes little Nina to cry, he is sent home. She is also a good friend to Antonia, her young cook. The fact is that they are said to have much in common. Both are independent and emphatic about their preferences. Both are fond of children, animals, and music. Both are proud and generous, and both thoroughly enjoy life. Mrs. Harling's cheerful confidence in her ability to handle a situation is evident in her bargaining session with Ambrosch. It is also apparent that she is an enlightened employer for her time, since she pays fairly high wages and insists that the girl not be expected to turn back all that she earns to her brother. Finally, she is a reasonably shrewd judge of character. She likes Antonia from the first, is unimpressed by the ranting Ambrosch, and is decidedly skeptical about Lena Lingard's demure denials of frivolous leanings.

FRANCES HARLING: The oldest and least carefree of the Harling children, Frances is intelligent and hardworking. Since her brother Charley is destined for Annapolis, she has become her demanding father's business assistant. She has a good head for finance. She knows credits, as those thinking to outsmart her have learned to their sorrow. She is also, however, warm and generous. She not only saves hardpressed farmers from being cheated by the money-lender, Wick Cutter, she also takes a personal interest in their families, visiting them, attending their social functions, and sending gifts. Although her hours as clerk are long, she still finds time to teach Jim and the others dancing. She is gracious to Lena, with whose background she is thoroughly familiar, and quietly reassures the troubled Antonia that Lena will be welcome as a visitor if she behaves herself.

LENA LINGARD: A beautiful blonde girl, with a low, sweet voice, Lena is the daughter of a very poor farmer with many other children. She is sorry for her mother and happy to use her wages to assist her family. She is seen here helping her small brother choose Christmas presents. Nevertheless, she is determined never again to endure the hardships that she knew when herding her father's cattle. She has already stirred up gossip, and it is clear that she will be much admired by men. Yet, while she hopes to have a good time, she is delighted to be able to work with the local dressmaker. She likes fine fabrics and knows that she can handle them well. This means that she who formerly had only ragged clothes will be able to dress attractively. She is also ambitious and knows that by building a successful career for herself she can forever escape the farm drudgery she has come to loathe.

COMMENT: BOOK II, CHAPTERS 1 TO 7

In this section the autobiographical element is again worth noting. Willa Cather moved to Red Cloud, here known as Black Hawk, when she was eleven, in 1884, and lived there until 1890. The town when she came was about thirteen years old and numbered some 3,000 people. The houses, as mentioned, all had fences. These were to prevent stray flocks from destroying lawns.

The Harlings were the Miner family, who lived near the Cathers. Miss Cather actually dedicated *My Antonia* to two of the daughters, Carrie and Irene (Bennett, 93). Mrs. Miner, who served as model for Mrs. Harling, had died just at the time the novelist was planning the book. Her death revived many precious memories, and Miss Cather drew upon her recollections to draw an affectionate, true-to-life portrait of her old friend. Usually, like most writers of fiction, she created character by freely combining impressions of various people. Here, however, she wanted to represent Mrs. Miner as faithfully as possible (Bennett, 50-60).

Like the fictional Mrs. Harling, Mrs. Miner was Norwegian by birth. Her husband ran a general store in Red Cloud, and their daughter, Carrie, the model for Frances, served there as bookkeeper. Mary Miner suggested Julia, Margie was the tomboyish Sally, and their brother Hughie was Charley in the novel (Bennett, 44-46, 59-64). Incidentally, there was music in the Miner home, too, for the lady of the house was the daughter of an oboe soloist and had grown up to become a fairly accomplished pianist (Bennett, 59-60).

As for Antonia, the original Annie Pavelka did come to work at Mrs. Miner's. Willa Cather may have known her while the girl was still on the farm, but she became closely acquainted with her at this time. As in the book, the Bohemian family did try to claim her total wages, but Carrie Miner refused to yield. The popularity of the young servant with the children is also based on fact. Annie, too, made herself house slippers as described in the novel, and she was always willing to make Hughie's favorite nut cakes (Bennett, 48).

This section also reflects two of Willa Cather's major interests, drama and music. When the hired girls and Jim go up to the Boys' Home for the impromptu recital, they learn that Mrs. Gardner, the strong-minded woman who runs the hotel, has gone to Omaha to hear Booth and Barrett. When Willa Cather was a girl, she begged to be taken to hear Edwin Booth and Lawrence Barrett when they played in Omaha. The two famous actors, with their noteworthy Shakespearean troupe, went on tour in 1887. They played in 68 cities and towns throughout the United States. Later in Lincoln, Miss Cather worked as a drama critic. It may also be mentioned here that the Gardners, of the Boys' Home, resemble Mr. and Mrs. Holland, who ran the Holland House in Red Cloud (Bennett, 89-90).

Miss Cather also liked music, preferring, however, to hear and discuss it rather than to play it (Bennett, 153-4). Her enjoyment of the contributions of Negro entertainers is obvious here from her enthusiastic description of Blind d'Arnault. Although the portrait is a composite one, she said that she based it largely upon the life of a pianist of her day, Blind Boone (Bennett, 248). *My Antonia* was published in 1918. Today a writer might be less likely to talk in such general terms about Negroes. Miss Cather writes with admiration, but is her manner also somewhat condescending?

This section of the novel essentially is concerned with the move to town of the Burdens, Antonia, and the other hired girls. It is the ending of a way of life for them and the beginning of another. For one thing, it brings to a close the story of pioneer farming represented by the Burden household as described in the first section. When the boy Jim first came to Nebraska, his grandparents had already been there for some ten years. During that time they had subdued their portion of the wild prairie and built up a flourishing farm. Instead of the crude sod shelters of the newly arrived, they now had a warm and comfortable white frame house, as well as barns, granaries, and a windmill. They had hired help during the year and brought in extra workers at harvesttime. Their food supply was more than ample; they had plenty to share with the less fortunate.

When they move, all is changed. First of all, Jake and Otto leave, for they are no longer needed. Ordinarily this might not seem very significant. Farmhands often move from one place to another. Yet Miss Cather, through Jim, stresses repeatedly the idea that these two good, simple men, hard-working and kindly, are rootless types who will never have homes and families of their own. Attached to a solid, well-run menage like the Burdens', they acquire status in the community, and their lives somehow take on more meaning. When the poor, ignorant, hot-tempered Jake cuts down the tree for Jim or watches his language in the presence of Grandmother, he is not merely paid help. In a very real sense, he is one of the family. The same can be said of Austrian Otto when he tells his adventure yarns, provides the beautiful Christmas decorations, or puts together a coffin for Mr. Shimerda and leads the hymn singing at the funeral. With the breaking up of the farm, however, the pair head for the West, vaguely seeking adventure. After one post card from a mining camp, they are never heard from again. They have been set adrift, the book implies, to become two more restless wanderers.

Even the Burdens, however, seem to lose stature with the move. Grandfather is said to have become a church deacon. Whenever Frances Harling comes over to visit him, he is flattered, and the two work out ways of saving the farmers from the money-lender's clutches. Later Grandfather will let it be known to Anton Jelinek that he does not want Jim seen in the Bohemian's decent, respectable saloon. Both he and Grandmother are aging and might well be expected to become less active. Yet with the move into town, there is certainly a startling loss here of effectiveness as creative individuals. It is true that Mrs. Burden does make one more vital contribution by helping to free Antonia from the domination of Ambrosch. Nevertheless, it is also worth noting that she must now send her to the Harlings rather than bring her into her own home. To be sure, she will provide needed assistance during one more crisis in the girl's life, but she will also stop Jim from attending town dances patronized largely by hired help. In general, Grandmother ceases to be the forthright, energetic woman of the house and no longer dominates the domestic scene. Jim, for his part, dives through the hedge to the Harling's house.

There he finds the warmth, the companionship, and the social life that he craves. The move into town makes possible the further schooling that will enable him to go on to college and the university and build a successful career as a lawyer. Yet with the breaking up of the Burden farm household, he becomes, almost like Jake and Otto, a young man without a clearly established position in the family. At the Harlings, he is a welcome outsider, but still an outsider, and there is little to hold him in the town house of two retired old people. On the farm, he might gradually be taking over his inheritance, a junior partner in a going concern. As it is, he will flee to the East, as the hired men fled westward. And as we learned from the Introduction, he, too, will never really be able to establish a happy, productive home like that of the Burden farm.

As was mentioned before, three ideal homes are described in *My Antonia*: those of the Burdens as farmers, the Harlings, and Antonia in later life. In this section the Harling household is described. It is a well-run home, with many children, headed by an autocratic father and a strong-minded, lively, capable mother. The fact that both parents are such forceful, determined personalities might suggest the possibilities of conflict. Mrs. Harling, for instance, likes music and all the gaiety and excitement of home costume parties and dances. Mr. Harling, by contrast, likes a quiet house and demands the undivided attention of his wife. Yet a nice balance is maintained, because the lord and master is fortunately away frequently on business. In this way Miss Cather's independent and self-reliant Mrs. Harling can run things most of the time her way, and yet graciously indulge her husband's whims when he happens to be at home. Actually, when he does make an important, and rather harsh decision later concerning Antonia, Mrs. Harling, as the consistently dutiful wife, does not oppose him in any way. Yet having paid her respects in this way to traditional standards, Miss Cather still shows us her admirable homes as run by sturdy vital women. On the farm Grandfather was a man of few words and was usually out working with the hired hands. Only when the outside crisis of the Shimerda tragedy developed, did he begin to play an important role. We shall therefore not be surprised eventually to find that Antonia's husband is off attending a fair, when Jim after many years comes to call, or that he later proves to be far less decisive than the story's heroine. Incidentally, it may be noted that it is Mrs. Gardner, not her amiable Johnny, who runs the Boy's Home, that it was Mrs. Shimerda who insisted that the family come to America, and that even the assertive Ambrosch will at length be bossed by a fat wife. Miss Cather, in general, tends to draw iron-willed women. This is equally evident in others of her novels, such as *O Pioneers!* and *The Song of the Lark*.

In any event, two other admired features of the Harling home may be mentioned. First of all, although it is located in town technically, it is described as "like a little farm." It has a garden, a barn, a windmill, an orchard, and grazing land. Hence, if it is evident that if the other two idealized households are those of people close to the land, this is not far removed. Significantly enough, when Jim tries to define the "basic harmony" between Antonia and Mrs. Harling, he notes that both enjoy "digging in the earth." Secondly, the Harlings have some appreciation of the arts. Almost all play the piano, and Mrs. Harling tells them the stories of the operas from which she plays arias. They also have dancing and story-telling. Likewise in the Burden home, Grandfather read from the Bible, and Jim read for his grandmother a chapter from *The Prince of the House of David*, as well as works such as *Robinson Crusoe*, by himself. On Saturday nights, Otto would sing cowboy songs or tell tales of adventure. Finally, when years later Jim visits Antonia's house, two of her children will offer musical selections. To sum up, the good household as represented three times in *My Antonia* is one that is well stocked with provisions and efficiently run by a strong, competent, motherly woman who has kept close to nature by farming or gardening and who fosters some interest in cultural pursuits.

As for the hired girls, with whom this section is concerned, the move to town is at first glance a matter of joyous liberation. Lena, who in torn and ragged dress used to herd her father's cattle, now has nice clothes and a room of her own with a carpet. Antonia, too, who was hired out by Ambrosch to work as a field hand, is now learning to sew, to dance, and to speak English well. Up at the hotel Tiny Soderball is being given little gifts of perfume, handkerchiefs, and gloves by the kindly, generous salesmen, and is sharing these small luxuries with her friends. These immigrant girls are decent, hard-working young women, and it seems only fair that they should enjoy the very real advantages offered them by the town. Yet given Miss Cather's concept of the good life close to the soil, there is the possibility that the town may also offer certain dangers. Mrs. Harling fears lest Lena "go gadding about to dances" when she should be working and is not sure that the hotel "is a good place for a girl." Actually, as it turns out, neither of these girls will go beyond material success to become an ideal wife and mother like Mrs. Harling herself. Instead, like the hired men and Jim, they will end up individuals without strong human ties. Antonia, however, encounters the temptations of the town, at least for a time, under the sponsorship of the wise, capable, and sympathetic mistress of a happy, well-run household. This interlude will later be seen to have proved a fortunate transition.

PLOT: CHAPTERS 8 TO 15

In late spring, the Vannis, an exotic-looking Italian trio, arrive in town and set up a dancing pavilion. From then on through the summer Black Hawk evenings are more exciting. Some nights the dance floor is reserved by the exclusive Progressive Euchre Club. Jim, however, prefers the Saturday night gatherings, when he can enjoy a whirl with Antonia, Lena, Tiny, and their friends. Indeed, even the boys from the Progressive Euchre Club sometimes slip in late and risk social criticism for a waltz with the country girls.

Black Hawk has an odd social system. The townsfolk look down snobbishly upon the hired girls who have taken jobs to help their families. Yet in contrast to these strong, glowing young immigrants, with their free, assured strides, the town girls are pale and listless. Never taking any exercise, they seem to move no muscles even when dancing and grow up round-shouldered and flat-chested. Even their economic advantage is not permanent. The country girls send wages home, pay off family mortgages, and eventually marry prosperous farmers. The proud American-born maidens sit home and contribute nothing. Some town boys find the vital hired girls attractive but lack the independence to marry them. Sylvester Lovett, for instance, the banker's son, is most attentive to Lena, but terrified of possible entanglements, he runs off with a rich widow. Jim regards such youths with scorn.

Less shy than before, Antonia loves to dance and cannot wait to get to the pavilion. One night Harry Paine, a town boy soon to be married, sees her home and boldly tries to kiss her. When she furiously objects, the lordly Mr. Harling comes down and tells her to give up the dances or leave his house. Antonia defends her behavior and declares that she has a right to some fun. Despite Mrs. Harling's angry objections, she goes to work for the notorious Wick Cutter.

Wick Cutter, libertine and swindler, hypocritically quotes moral maxims and is proud of his fussy, over-decorated house. He fights continually with his wife, a wild-eyed, red-faced woman with a passion for painting flowers on china. His one fear is that she will outlive him and inherit his property.

With Lena's help, Antonia dresses better, and wears plumed hats and high heeled shoes. After the Vannis leave, Jim refuses to join the upperclass Owl Club and is bored and discontented. Discouraged by Grandfather from visiting Jelinek's saloon, he slips out to the Firemen's Hall to meet his country friends. Lena makes every dance a dreamy waltz, but a whirl with Antonia is more exciting. Sometimes she is escorted by a glib train conductor, Larry Donovan. Another time Jim tries to kiss her, but she insists that he stay away from her and Lena and go on to college.

Jim graduates, a rather lonely valedictorian, and is warmly congratulated by Antonia. That summer he studies hard alone, but on a July Sunday he goes on a picnic with the country girls. They talk of their families and of their own plans. Antonia tells him that her father had not been forced to marry her peasant mother but had done so from a high sense of honor. Jim talks of a theory that Coronado explored as far north as Nebraska. At dusk the young people are startled at the effect of a huge plow silhouetted against the sun.

In August, the Cutters go out of town, but Antonia suspects a plot. Jim reluctantly stays the night at the house, and has a bloody battle with Wick in the dark. He is angry with Antonia for having involved him in the business. Jim wants no hero's bruises.

CHARACTER ANALYSES: BOOK II, CHAPTERS 8 TO 15

JIM BURDEN: In this section Jim is seen as the lonely outsider generally at odds with the town. When he rejects the Progressive Euchre Club and its successor, the Owls, and deliberately courts criticism by associating with the country girls, he is taking a strong stand against certain Black Hawk values.

Jim, it must be remembered, was not born in Black Hawk, or even in Nebraska. He arrived as a boy of ten from a distant and very different part of the United States. So from the first, he had seen more than a single way of living, unlike those who had grown up knowing only one small area, one small group, and one narrow set of conventions. In addition, having lived on the farm and known country people, he has a high regard for healthy outdoor activities and finds stifling the closed-in town houses with their shuttered parlors. It also seems to him that the town's disdain for open air and physical fitness is but one more manifestation of its mean, small-minded, negative thinking.

If Jim has known an older Virginia culture and also the freer life of the open prairie, he has also been more closely acquainted with immigrant groups than have been many of the townsfolk. Having witnessed the early struggles of the Shimerdas, he realizes how brave and patient these people have had to be. Having liked Antonia's gentle father and been deeply affected by his tragic death, he can never again look scornfully upon all foreigners as stupid and ignorant. Moreover, having long been friendly with Antonia herself, he is well aware of her lively intelligence, her willingness to work hard, and her warm-hearted generosity, as well as her glowing beauty and her keen enjoyment of life. He therefore cannot possibly accept without question the town's apparent assumption that native-born Americans are superior in every way to immigrants and should therefore not regard them as social equals.

Jim not only holds views at variance with those of most people of Black Hawk, he, in effect, openly avows them. He coolly turns down usually coveted invitations to join clubs run by the town's social set. As a high school senior, he coaxes Antonia, Lena, and the rest into the ice cream parlor. Even they know what this implies. Norwegian Anna, one of the more dignified girls in the group, makes them all be quiet when the principal drops in to buy bread. She knows that the whisper is going through town that Jim is sly or odd, ignoring the girls of his own set in favor of the vivacious immigrants. His determined stand has its consequences. He is often lonely and becomes bored and restless. At graduation, he is class valedictorian, but only his country friends and the Harlings gather around him to offer congratulations.

Jim thus is an independent youth, with the courage necessary to withstand popular disapproval. He is good in physical combat, too. When, at his grandmother's urging, he takes over guard duty at the Cutter house because Antonia suspects a ruse, he gives a good account of himself in the battle with the midnight intruder. Yet as he rushes home battered, bruised, and partially clad, he is petrified lest someone see him, spread the story and subject him to ridicule. The next morning, feeling weary and hurt, he is in no mood for Antonia's tearful gratitude. He is merely angry that she got him into this predicament. Jim may have his heroic side, but he is not one to glory in the role of knight errant.

ANTONIA SHIMERDA: Four aspects of Antonia's character are developed in this section. First of all, there is her exuberant delight in dancing. Her zest and sparkle make her a wonderful partner, and she is immediately popular. Dancing with her, says Jim, is an adventure. She does the schottische with sprightly grace and is always inventing new steps. Her eagerness to have fun at the pavilion while she can will cost her her good position at the Harling's but it is one more proof that this girl loves life and will pursue its rewarding pleasures with unfeigned enthusiasm.

Secondly, she, too, like Jim, is an independent spirit. She likes the Harlings and is not by nature inclined to be bold or impertinent. Yet when the imperious Mr. Harling sets up what she considers unfair alternatives, she promptly gives her notice. Her going to work for Wick Cutter, a notorious seducer of young servants, is hardly a prudent move. But her assured announcement that she can take care of herself is further evidence of her habit of thinking and acting on her own initiative.

On the other hand, she is not lacking altogether in common sense as regards her amorous employer. When he makes some odd provisos about her remaining in the house alone while he and his wife are away, she shrewdly suspects that he may intend to return secretly and make unwelcome advances. Hitherto she has apparently justified her rash announcement that she could handle the situation. Now, however, she recognizes the more serious danger and does not let pride prevent her from seeking aid. Sensibly, she comes to Grandmother Burden, and with Jim's help she is saved from the fate that befell several of her predecessors in the Cutter household.

Finally, there is her loyalty and devotion to Jim. She wants him to have his chance to get further education and to have a great career in the world. She therefore encourages him constantly to go on with his studies. Although she enjoys dancing with him, she will not let him get himself romantically involved with her or with any of her friends. She is particularly concerned about the lovely, yielding Lena, whom she knows Jim finds attractive. Sternly she warns him to behave himself. Otherwise she will go to Mrs. Burden. For the most part, however, she praises warmly his accomplishments, such as his graduation speech, shares with him her precious memories of her father, and keeps assuring him that he is destined for success.

MRS. HARLING: The quick temper of Mrs. Harling flares up in this section. Having accepted her husband's ultimatum that Antonia must give up the dances or leave their employ, Mrs. Harling is hurt and angry when the girl decides to leave. Ironically enough she had become fond of Antonia because they were somewhat similar personalities. Both, for instance, were independent. Now when the younger woman's strong will clashes with her own, she is, humanly enough, furious. Subsequently, when Jim tries to defend Antonia, Mrs. Harling becomes annoyed with him too. Yet she is not one to hold grudges indefinitely. She comes to Jim's graduation and brings him a silk umbrella. Eventually, too, she becomes reconciled with Antonia.

GRANDFATHER BURDEN: Here Grandfather shows his conservatism as a Baptist deacon by letting Jelinek know that he does not want Jim seen around the Bohemian's saloon. When Jim delivers his Commencement oration, he is proud of the boy, according to Antonia, but does not tell him so. Although he has some misgivings, he does listen to Mrs. Harling's plea that young Jim be permitted to go away alone to college.

GRANDMOTHER BURDEN: Worried lest Jim acquire a poor reputation and grieved that he is sneaking out to the Firemen's Hall dances, Grandmother sheds tears. Unwilling to cause her further distress, Jim gives up the dances. When Antonia comes to her with her fears about Cutter's designs, she is sympathetic and helpful. First she suggests that Jim help keep watch. Later, after the battle, she goes with Antonia to help her pack. At that time she also soothes the irate Mrs. Cutter, who has learned of the trick attempted by her wily husband.

WICK CUTTER: First encountered when he took over all the possessions of Russian Peter, Wick here turns up as the would-be seducer of Antonia. Both actions suggest a vicious individual, but just as *My Antonia* plays down conventional heroics, so it subtly avoids the usual representation of villainy. Because of his long-term war with his wife, complete with cruel but outlandish practical jokes, Cutter is essentially a comic character. Miss Cather furnishes details that make him appear ridiculous. For example, he talks so much about his neat lawn that mischievous lads enjoy throwing dead cats over his fence. Again, he is afraid that his wife will outlive him and thus get his property for her relatives. Gleefully she insists that this is probable thanks to his dissolute habits. This alarms him, and he starts working out feverishly with dumbbells. Finally, his scheme to ruin Antonia fails, and he must sneak for a time out of town with his face striped with court-plaster, his arm in a sling.

MRS. CUTTER: A big, wild-looking woman, with long curved teeth, Mrs. Cutter is almost as bizarre a character as her husband. Nodding ceaselessly, she sometimes appears almost mad. Yet she affects a reserved manner when she pays calls in her gray brocade and plumed bonnet. Like Wick, she too has a strange sense of humor. She seems to take a peculiar pleasure out of sending him anonymous clippings about erring husbands, but she leaves the newspapers from which she cut them in plain sight for him to find. To shame Wick into giving her more money she once threatens to go around town soliciting orders for painted china, but gives this up in chagrin when he acts merely pleased. When Antonia makes herself dress like those of town social leaders, Mrs. Cutter is secretly delighted. Later outraged when Wick puts her on the wrong train so that he can return to surprise Antonia, she returns home half-hysterical, but vows to make him pay for having so wronged her. Actually, both Cutters seem almost to relish their weird hostilities.

COMMENT: BOOK II, CHAPTERS 8 TO 15

Again in this section material can be traced to the youthful experiences of the author. For one thing, Willa Cather, like Jim, delivered a commencement address, and she, too, seems to have been an independent young person unwilling to follow blindly any narrowly conventional course. In describing the social attitudes of Black Hawk, she also undoubtedly was drawing upon her memories of life in Red Cloud.

Although her portraits of the odd, squabbling Cutters are developed with considerable artistry, she based them upon actual individuals, E. C. Bentley and his wife. Bentley was Red Cloud's first money-lender and charged fantastic rates of interest. He spent a great deal on himself, but was miserly toward his wife (Bennett, 82-3).

Also based upon fact is the incident in which Antonia is peremptorily ordered by Mr. Harling to remain away from future dances. Mr. Miner found the son of a woman he disliked paying court to one of his hired girls. He forbade her to see the boy again, and the maid quit in anger (Bennett, 69). Here it is interesting to observe how Miss Cather altered the whole episode to bring out certain ideas.

First of all, the original young man proved not at all objectionable to the girl he was seeing home. In the novel, however, the youth tries to force his attentions upon Antonia. This points up the double standards of town boys, because this same Harry Paine is slated to marry quite profitably one of his own set two days later. Of course, it also indicates Antonia's sense of propriety, her independent spirit, and her feeling that she is entitled to at least some fun out of life.

These chapters in general take a long critical look at the American small town as Willa Cather knew it before the century's turn. With its shaded sidewalks and fenced-in lawns, Black Hawk (or Red Cloud) presents a neat, pleasant appearance. Yet Jim, and probably the novelist, found life there rather dull and dreary. His one haven was the Harling home, which, we recall, was like a "little farm," run by those who had been "farming people." Otherwise, whatever is interesting or entertaining seems to come from outside, from the traveling men, from Blind d'Arnault, from the Vannis. Much is made of how uneventful summer nights were in town before the pavilion was opened.

The town, however, is not only unexciting. It is narrow-minded and snobbish. Before the Vannis came, the young people could not even laugh aloud without criticism, and the lads from the Progressive Euchre Club will be censured by their set if seen dancing with the hired girls on Saturday night.

The novelist's feelings about such a rigid caste system seem to be quite vehement. At times, in fact, there is more argument than narrative in this section. Walking along the quiet streets at night, Jim thinks of all the envy and sadness in the small flimsy houses. He sees the fearful inhabitants as forever dodging, denying, and cutting corners on work merely to have more time for gossip. To him they are like frightened mice scurrying through the dark.

By contrast, the country girls are seen to typify all that is lacking in the supercilious town. They are strong and healthy, whereas the town girls are stoop-shouldered and listless. They are working hard and using their earnings constructively to help their families pay off farms. Meanwhile their town counterparts sit around gossiping meanly in stuffy parlors. These independent young women have every quality to attract young men, but the town boys are too spineless to meet the challenge. They are short-sighted, too, for the country girls will later make good homemakers and prove to be excellent wives and mothers. At one point Frances Harling accuses Jim of being a romantic and glamorizing the country girls. Frances, of course, is based upon Willa Cather's close friend, Carrie Miner. Was this, by any chance, a point on which they actually differed? Certainly, Miss Cather has sometimes been criticized for idealizing her immigrant heroines and making them seem nobler than the originals probably were. It would appear that the author was well aware of the charge. Yet she still seems to agree with Jim that the Antonias, with their natural kindliness and true hearts, were far more "real women" than the pale town girls who dreamed of "brand new little houses with best chairs that must not be sat upon."

Throughout the work, in fact, as we have seen, Willa Cather is contrasting ways of life. This is probably the reason why she goes to such lengths to prevent our being overly impressed with the wickedness of Wick Cutter, although he is undoubtedly villainous. In the usual romances of the period when *My Antonia* first appeared, much more would have been made of the rather brutal fight between Jim and Wick, especially since it was a matter of saving the heroine from an unpleasant fate. Yet, as she did in the episode of the snake fight, the novelist refuses to maintain the lofty heroic tone. Jim fleeing across town in his night clothing, fearful of being seen, is hardly the champion accepting acclaim with dignity. Cutter, too, appears almost pathetic scurrying to the depot with his face all bandaged. In *My Antonia*, there is a very real, very serious conflict between good and evil, and there is genuine heroism held up to admiration. When Jim battles town prejudice and refuses to treat his country friends as social inferiors, he subjects himself to general disapproval and must endure months of loneliness. When Antonia speaks up for what she regards as her rights, she loses her job. This type of moral victory is much more significant in the Cather works than that of striking down a snake or beating up a fatuous libertine.

Yet despite its emphasis here on social criticism, this section does introduce two new dramatic elements. The more frequent references to Lena's soft, clinging manner and willing kisses suggest a possible future relationship between her and Jim. To some extent, of course, Antonia and Lena seem to represent opposing forces as regards the boy's future. Ironically enough Jim angrily denounces town boys who lack the discrimination or the courage to choose country girls as wives. Yet Antonia insists that he go away and leave them all in order to make something of his life. The second item worth noting is a brief and casual mention of the fact that Antonia sometimes goes to dances with a smooth-talking train conductor, Larry Donovan. He will later play a crucial part in her story.

In earlier sections certain scenes were noted, such as the Old Hata and Christmas Day incidents, that exemplify Willa Cather's skilled interweaving of joy and sorrow to produce rich emotional effects. Here there is the same artistry as the country girls meet to congratulate Jim after his graduation. Having just delivered an oration that he with all due modesty considers "very good," Jim doubtless feels a certain elation. Moreover, Mrs. Harling, who has been irked with him because of his defense of Antonia, has come to the exercises, followed his speech closely, and praised him heartily. She has also given him a silk umbrella, with his name on the handle.

Afterwards he walks home alone, but in the moonlight waiting for him are Antonia, Lena, and Norwegian Anna. Antonia is most enthusiastic, and the others are friendly. Yet there is a note of sadness, too. Jim's eloquent talk reminds Antonia of her beloved father, and the boy admits that he too thought of Mr. Shimerda and dedicated his oration to him. There is also Anna's rather wistful remark that she "always wanted to go to school." These three likeable girls in their white dresses will never have the chance to go through high school, much less go on to college as Jim will presently. Yet they generously rejoice in his triumph and loyally wish him well. Recalling the event later Jim states that no later success ever pulled so at his heartstrings. As in the Old Hata scene nothing much actually happens here on the surface. Three girls stop to pay respects to an old friend who has just graduated. Yet with its setting of moonlight on maple trees, its whiteclad trio, and its brief but revealing bits of dialogue, this becomes a curiously moving encounter.

Even more memorable, however, is the chapter on the picnic, for it seems to sum up and integrate several themes developed in the story up to this point. Jim's delight in his early morning swim recalls his first joyful discovery of the Nebraska countryside. Later Antonia talks of her father's happier life of companionship and good talk in Bohemia, and her words bring back to mind the whole tragedy of the gentle Mr. Shimerda. As the day goes on, the plaintive remarks of the girls again point up the disadvantage of their limited schooling, the hard struggles of their immigrant mothers, and the problem of providing for big families. And Jim's provocative theory about the Coronado expedition that may have reached Nebraska casts a romantic aura over the outing.

Finally, there is the startling effect of the plow in the distance looming up black and huge in the sunset. It seems to be a symbol of all those solid farm families, whose daughters are Jim's friends. This magnificent descriptive passage is often cited as illustrating Miss Cather's style at its best. The scene also marks the end of Jim's Nebraska boyhood. As the sun goes down, the mood is one of exaltation.

BOOK III—LENA LINGARD

PLOT: BOOK III

At the university in Lincoln, Jim is privileged to have as Latin teacher and personal friend Gaston Cleric, a brilliant young New England scholar and poet sent West for his health. Cleric opens new realms of ideas, but Jim still finds himself vividly recalling the country people he used to know.

Only recently established, the college itself has a young optimistic spirit. Many of the students are poor farm boys, and the faculty includes ministers in hard straits and eager youths from graduate schools. Since there are no dormitories, Jim rents rooms from an elderly pioneer couple. He enjoys setting up his study and having Cleric drop in for visits. He later recalls especially the instructor's wonderful recital from memory of long passages from Dante's *Divine Comedy*.

One March evening Jim reads in Virgil's *Georgics* the sad observation that "the best days are the first to flee." He is also impressed with Virgil's idea of being the first to bring the Muse into his own "patria" or region. Then, answering a knock, he is startled to see Lena Lingard, poised and lovely in a conservative outfit of dark blue. She now has her own dress business in Lincoln. (Mrs. Burden knew this fact but did not write of it to Jim.) Lena tells him that Antonia is practically engaged to Larry Donovan, whom the Harlings and others mistrust. Lena reminds Jim that once Antonia likes someone, she tends to be fiercely loyal.

When Lena leaves, Jim decides that it is girls like her who make all poetry possible. After her call, they go often together to one-night performances of touring shows. They see *Rip Van Winkle*, *Shenandoah*, *Robin Hood*, and eventually a lavishly staged production of *Camille*, with an aging star who moves both to tears. Recalling his ecstatic walk home along lilac-scented paths, Jim the man decides that whenever *Camille* is produced, the month is always April.

Jim often meets Lena downtown, but she insists that he keep her out of sweet shops. She speaks English well, having even mastered the stilted phrases of her trade that please small-town ladies. At her lodgings Jim meets her devoted landlord, old Colonel Raleigh, and another admirer, Ordinsky, a violin teacher who worries lest Jim's intentions not be honorable. Jim reassures him, and they become friends.

Compared with Lena, Jim's studies begin to seem uninteresting. Cleric thereupon urges Jim to go on to Harvard, where the instructor will be teaching next. Trying vainly to convince himself that the move is best for everyone, Jim bids farewell to Lena. She is saddened but is at least grateful to have been his first sweetheart. At this time she also tells him that she will never marry. She has seen too much of the hardships of family life as a young girl, and wants to retain the freedom she has worked so hard to attain. Shortly thereafter Jim leaves to join Cleric in Boston.

CHARACTER ANALYSES: BOOK III

JIM BURDEN: The implication has been evident in the book up to this point that Jim is a good student. Several times he is mentioned as reading various books as a small boy, and he was able to give English lessons to the Shimerda girls when he was ten or eleven. He was valedictorian of his class and apparently delivered an original oration that much impressed those who heard it. It is therefore not surprising that he would attract the attention of the inspiring young teacher from the East. The same enthusiasm that characterized his response to the beauty of the prairie and the goodness and charm of the immigrant girls shows itself here in his initial delight in the new areas of learning to which Cleric introduces him.

Yet Jim also makes at this time some interesting and important discoveries about himself. For one thing he is astonished at the deep impression which his early experiences with Antonia, Russian Peter, and the two hired men have made upon him. This discovery startles him, for he has been stimulated by Cleric's passion for learning. He thus expects his own small past to lose significance as he comes up against the far more momentous happenings described in the classics. Actually, however, the more he reaches out for the wonders of antiquity, attempting apparently to be totally absorbed in them as he once was in the boundless plains of waving red grass, the more he is again vividly conscious of the extent to which he has been affected by his boyhood adventures.

He, therefore, half-reluctantly concedes that he will never make a scholar. Scholarship, he feels, demands that an individual be able to lose himself among things that are essentially impersonal. Jim, for his part, will be thoroughly satisfied only when he concerns himself with what he knows directly. Curiously enough, Antonia, who speculates several times about Jim's future throughout the early part of the book, never sees him as a teacher. She sees him as a doctor or a lawyer, who will some day be as rich as Mr. Harling. It may also be recalled that in the Introduction the narrator mentions that Jim has succeeded as counsel for the railroad because he loves "with a personal passion" the country through which the trains pass.

It is therefore possible that he is more affected by Cleric himself with his bursts of poetic imaginative talk than by the knowledge that Cleric imparts. Certainly, when Lena reenters his life, he loses interest in his books. Why linger over poetry when the very inspiration for poetry is so close at hand?

Is Jim in love with Lena? Speaking of Colonel Raleigh, Ordinsky, and himself, he says that all three are in love with her. Certainly he likes her. He enjoys going to the theatre with her. He likes to share Sunday breakfasts with her, play with her dog Prince, and talk over old times and mutual friends. With her around he finds it hard to concentrate on more prosaic matters, and herself she states that she is his "first sweetheart." Yet he cannot have been passionately involved to any great extent. Unlike the romantic Armand in *Camille*, he seems to suffer no heartbreak at the thought of deserting Lena for Harvard. He finds it hard to break the news to her, because he senses rightly that she will be sad. Yet he did not rush to her defense when Cleric called her "perfectly irresponsible."

Jim is called a romantic by both the narrator and the astute Frances Harling. This description does not necessarily mean, however, that he is going to be an ardent lover in the usual sense. When he is in Lincoln, he likes Cleric and Lena; but whenever he is excited intellectually, he reverts to Jake, Otto, and Russian Peter, who now stand out "strengthened and simplified" in his mind. In later life he will remain away from Antonia for some twenty years lest finding her worn and beaten might destroy some few last illusions. Some memories, he claims, are realities, and as such are superior to anything that one may ever again experience. It would thus seem that Jim derives more from his ideas of people than from the people themselves. Hence he can probably walk away from the lovely Lena with only limited regret, yet cherish for years the precious memory of her slow, "renunciatory" good-bye kiss.

LENA LINGARD: This charming young career woman is pictured, generally, as a real credit to her immigrant people. She is, first of all, extremely capable. Brought up in poverty with little or no formal education, she has become a successful dressmaker. She speaks English well and is adept at using all the standard polite phrases that induce wealthy women to become her clients. She has a genuine flair for design and now runs her own shop and hires young girls to help with the sewing. She is also extremely independent; and independence, as we have seen, is a much admired trait in this novel. She has gone off by herself and set up her shop in a town where she must make new business contacts and new friends. She refuses to let Jim pay for her ticket when they go to the theatre. In addition, she makes it clear that although she has had proposals of marriage, she has no intention of ever accepting any. This would appear to characterize her as an individualistic young woman in any age. In 1918, when *My Antonia* first appeared, it would seem even more startling.

Lena is also kind and gracious, and numbers among her admirers many different types. The lonely old Southern colonel is pleased with her gentle manners and asks her more than once to be his wife. The rather violent musician, Ordinsky, praises her for that warmth of feeling that he finds seldom among the more phlegmatic Nebraskans. Jim, too, reacts favorably to her because of her sympathetic understanding, never more in evidence than when she gracefully accepts his decision to leave.

Like Jim, she is capable of enthusiasm. He finds it always a pleasure to go with her to the theatre, for to her everything onstage is both wonderful and true. When the heroine of *Camille* nobly agrees to give up her lover at his father's request, Lena sobs. And when the young French hero, not understanding the sacrifice, denounces Marguerite bitterly, Lena cringes and covers her face. She is thus quite different from the "unimpressionable" woman who Jim later marries.

Yet despite her thoughtfulness and her sympathetic nature, Lena is only generous up to a point. She will pay her own way at the theatre and tactfully spare Jim embarrassment. She will gladly sew the torn coat of poor Ordinsky and listen patiently to the old stories of the Colonel. She will send later a substantial wedding present to Antonia and she will gladly use some of her money to build a new house for her mother and even furnish it. She will not, however, sacrifice herself for others in the way a Mrs. Harling or an Antonia will. She likes good times and enjoys a casual romantic fling. She does not want a husband who might be ill-tempered or children who would need constant care. Gaston Cleric describes her as pretty but "irresponsible." This charge is not entirely fair, in view of her concern for her mother. Yet it is true that she firmly refuses to accept the responsibilities of a home and children.

GASTON CLERIC: This brilliant but sickly Latin professor from New England is an intense, dominating personality. A man of moods, he is sometimes silent and withdrawn, sometimes brusquely sarcastic. When lecturing at his best, however, he is wonderfully imaginative. He is passionately interested in his subject and conveys the excitement of reliving ancient times to his students. Visiting the antique temples at Paestum in Italy, he is so enraptured that he remains there all night and ruins his health. He is not, however, unaware of events in Lincoln. He takes into account Jim's inability to study, with Lena present to distract him, and takes the trouble to write to the young man's grandfather to ask that he be permitted to transfer to Harvard. Jim is surprised that his grandfather agrees so readily. The question is: does the astute teacher, much concerned about the future of his promising student, tell Mr. Burden enough about the lad's friendship with Lena to insure an affirmative reply? The novel does not settle this point, but the possibility is intriguing.

ANTONIA SHIMERDA: In this section Antonia plays no direct part, but she is more than once mentioned by Lena and Jim. On her first visit, Lena says that Antonia continues her enthusiastic expectations regarding Jim's future. She is telling everyone that he will be richer than Mr. Harling. Mrs. Harling has forgiven her because little Nina is so fond of her. Yet in view of Antonia's former difficulties with her autocratic employer, is there more than mere loyalty in her hope that her champion will one day outshine in wealth that imposing gentleman? Antonia can be stubborn.

This refusal to yield to others on what seems a matter of fairness is also evident in her idolizing of Larry Donovan. Mrs. Harling and her other friends make every attempt to warn her that he is unreliable. She believes in him, however, and will listen to nothing that might discredit him.

MRS. HARLING: Despite her grievance against Antonia, Mrs. Harling magnanimously renews the friendship. She also tries to help the girl by warning her about the worthless train conductor. Incidentally, the same shrewdness that enabled her to take the measure of the blustering Ambrosch is evident in her reactions to Donovan.

COMMENT: BOOK III

Willa Cather graduated from Red Cloud High School in 1890 and went on to the University of Nebraska, founded in 1869. Her description of Jim's life there draws heavily on her own experiences. The study that the young man fixes up for himself, for instance, recalls her own accommodations as a student; and the whole picture of the fledgling university is that of her Alma Mater as she remembered it. The original for Gaston Cleric seems mainly to have been Herbert Bates, a New England teacher and poet who gave her great encouragement there. Yet the portrait may well combine traits of several stimulating professors who helped her launch her career.

Having both Jim and Lena enjoy the theatre gives Miss Cather a chance to work in more about one of her major interests. While at the University in Lincoln, she earned money by writing drama criticism for the local paper. She saw every play that came to town and was known for her severe comments (Bennett, 184).

In the chapter wherein Jim alludes to plays he has enjoyed, she lists a number of notable productions that came to Nebraska for one-night stands during her student days. Jim mentions, for instance, *Rip Van Winkle*. Starring Joseph Jefferson, a member of an old theatrical family, this was a very famous play of the era. Also noted is *The Count of Monte Cristo*. This romantic play about an escaped French prisoner who poses as a nobleman provided the greatest starring role for James O'Neill, the father of Eugene O'Neill, the well-known playwright.

Jim describes in considerable detail, however, one play in particular, *Camille*, indicating that at the time the leading actress was well past her prime. When Miss Cather attended the performance in question, she actually saw Clara Morris, an actress much acclaimed for this part, who was originally discovered by Augustin Daly, one of the most influential of American theatre managers. In her original account of the show, written during college days, Miss Cather praised the star's "terrible and relentless" realism but found the play itself "awful" (Bennett, 185). The long account in *My Antonia* certainly suggests that the acting was forceful, but Jim and Lena are far less critical of the play itself than was the young Miss Cather. Her report of their enthusiastic response is done with gentle, tolerant humor and with a perspective gained over the years. Compare the handling of this incident with Jim's story of the snake in Book I. In each we are constantly given both the boy's reaction at the time and the man's comments on the incident. Is this an effective way of handling such material? Frank O'Connor, the famed present-day Irish writer, makes good use of it also in his short stories.

Incidentally, we often find in the works of Willa Cather hints or suggestions that are most interesting yet are never fully worked out. As a novelist, Miss Cather never felt obliged to tell her readers everything she knew about her characters. She seems to have expected them to use a little imagination.

Two examples of this have already been indicated in the previous character analysis pages. Why does Antonia pointedly compare Jim with Mr. Harling? And what does Gaston Cleric include in his letter to Grandfather? Two further questions of this type, however, may be raised. For one thing, there is the matter of the romance between Jim and Lena. Certain passages suggest that it was more than merely an innocent flirtation, but the reader is left free to draw his own conclusions.

It is also worth speculating as to why, among all the plays she witnessed, Miss Cather chose to include so complete an account of *Camille*. Why not, for instance, *Rip Van Winkle* or *The Count of Monte Cristo*? *Camille* is, of course, a famous work, which would be familiar to readers. Those who had not seen the play might well have had some acquaintance with the opera *La Traviata*, which tells the same story. This would be helpful since the chapter is intended to point up the enthusiastic response of two impressionable, rather unsophisticated young people, and readers would probably know enough about the scenes in question to understand why Lena might weep uncontrollably or cower as if struck. In the Introduction the narrator suggested a vital distinction between romantic people who are capable of enthusiasm and those who are coldly insensitive. A scene like this once more places Jim and Lena squarely in the first, much favored group.

Yet it is tempting to explore a little further the idea that there may have been additional reasons for giving so much attention to *Camille*. Interestingly enough, although often Jim seems to serve as spokesman for the novelist, she has given him reactions to the play that were not quite those she expressed as a young drama critic. He is naively charmed by it all; she called it an "awful" show. We have seen that she elsewhere alters remembered material for a specific literary purpose. For instance, she adapted the incident of Mr. Miner and the maid in such a way as to bring out Antonia's independent spirit and the town boy's dubious standards. So it would seem reasonable to assume that Miss Cather may have had something more in mind when she handled the *Camille* episode in a special way.

Camille, a highly emotional drama, has a very young man of fairly high birth, Armand, fall passionately in love with Marguerite, a charming, worldly woman, notorious for illicit affairs. She is known as Camille, or the Lady of the Camelias, because she favors that flower. Because she is ill with tuberculosis, Armand persuades Marguerite to go away with him to the country, where she may recover her health. They are happy there together, until the boy's father, tearful lest his son's future be wrecked by such an association, secretly talks the good-hearted Camille into giving him up. Unaware of her noble sacrifice, Armand berates her bitterly, causing her intense suffering. After this she becomes increasingly weaker from consumption. As she lies dying, the penitent Armand, told all by his father, comes to see her. After a tearful reunion, she dies content.

Note here the curious parallels, and the equally significant variations. Jim, like Armand, is a rather unsophisticated young man of quite an upper-class family by Nebraska standards. He was, after all, invited to join the exclusive clubs in Black Hawk. Lena is somewhat older than he and already much more experienced in affairs of the heart. While Miss Cather always handles the matter reticently, there is every indication that Lena has rather flexible moral standards. Seeing her more often, Jim becomes very fond of the girl. He can, in fact, think of nothing else. Since he is an orphan, no father can intervene; but Gaston Cleric, concerned about the youth's future, certainly takes steps to remove him from the distractions offered by the "irresponsible" Lena. Lena is saddened by the parting.

Here, however, the similarities end. Miss Cather may be sympathetic to "romantics" who respond with feeling to whatever wonders they experience, such as the autumn prairie, a pathetic suicide, a strange sunset image of a plow, or a moving drama. Yet she generally takes a stand against the sentimental clichés of earlier fiction. She is a twentieth-century American writer who has little patience with the melodramatic nonsense that dazzles the emotions while making no sense whatsoever as a valid representation of life.

Here, in effect, she gives us two versions of the *Camille* story, the sentimental and a more realistic modern treatment. The one on stage tears at the hearts of sensitive young spectators but bears little relation to their own subsequent behavior.

Jim may well be in love with the amiable Lena, but he is also ambitious enough to appreciate Cleric's argument. The teacher, for his part, does not set up some kind of absurd misunderstanding by going to Lena and insisting that she make a showy gesture certain to confuse and embitter her young admirer. Lena herself is made unhappy by Jim's decision—her good-bye kiss is a slow "renunciatory" one. Yet Miss Cather does not have her suffering from some conveniently fatal malady that will guarantee a deathbed scene eulogizing her as grievously wronged. Lena has had other loves and will presumably have more in the future. She will also go on doing quite well in the dressmaking business.

It must always be remembered that when it first appeared *My Antonia* was hardly the conventional novel. It lacked the standard love story and it had nothing resembling the usual plot formulas. Its whole line was to reject false, ostentatious heroics in favor of the more solid, long-term heroism of those who lived relatively quietly and endured hardships bravely, thus strengthening their own characters and contributing something to their country by running good farms or decent businesses and raising fine big families. Viewed in this light, the *Camille* incident seems most aptly chosen to contrast the old style of writing with the new.

Finally, the two quotations from Virgil given at the start of this section are unusually apt. The one about the best days which are quickly over recalls the elegiac, or sad, note struck in the Introduction, where Jim and the narrator look back on the "adventure" of their childhood. Willa Cather seems to have felt very strongly that youth was the most glorious period, the "best days" of a person's life. Then, if ever, one had the stimulating and rewarding experiences that would be remembered gratefully all the rest of his life. This idea clearly underlies *My Antonia.* Certainly Jim constantly suggests that nothing that happened to him as a man compared with his "best days" in Nebraska, and Miss Cather drew the material for most of her own successful books from her early life in and around Red Cloud.

The second quotation about being the first to bring the Muse, or the light of literature, to one's "patria" is also interesting. Willa Cather, although she lived elsewhere in later life, seems to have felt aways that she belonged in a special way to the prairie country. This was her neighborhood, her "patria," and in her stories she gives literary status to the region and its people. She immortalizes Nebraska just as Virgil praised his native countryside, near Mincio, in the *Georgics.*

BOOK IV—THE PIONEER WOMAN'S STORY

PLOT: BOOK IV

Graduated from Harvard after two years, Jim comes home before starting law school. Frances Harling is now married, but his grandparents seem unchanged. People talk pityingly of Antonia. Having gone off to marry Donovan, she was deserted by him and now has an illegitimate child. Jim wonders why she could not have done so well as Tiny or Lena.

The town also sneers at Tiny, who went to Seattle to open a hotel for sailors. Looking back, the elder Jim admits that then no one could have predicted her later history of dangerous but profitable ventures.

After the gold strike in Alaska, she makes the difficult journey to Dawson City, opening there a restaurant and later another hotel. Having taken care of a fatally injured Swedish prospector, she falls heir to his claim. After ten hard years of mining and real estate deals, she returns rich to San Francisco. Meeting her in 1908, Jim finds her a slight, severe looking woman who cares only about money. Lena has joined her, still gossiped about but cautious enough. She sees to it that Tiny is always well dressed but sends her sizable bills. Tiny, who used to dance gaily, now limps, having lost three toes because of frostbite in Alaska. She is not very excited over her success. In fact, she no longer seems much interested in anything.

Back in town, Jim sees a large framed picture of Antonia's baby in the photographer's window. How like her not to be ashamed of the child. Jim still wonders angrily how she could have gone off with the lordly, self-pitying conductor. To find out more, he drives out to see the Widow Steavens, noting with pleasure how the open prairie he knew now boasts many prosperous farms.

The Widow Steavens relates how happy Antonia was before the ill-fated trip and how eagerly she sewed her trousseau. Even Ambrosch was moved to give her plated silver and three hundred dollars. Tricked and then abandoned, she returned home pregnant after a month. Never going into town, even to see a dentist, she herded Ambrosch's cattle until December and then, without help, bore her child. Ambrosch nastily suggested drowning it, thus evoking an angry warning from the Widow. Antonia, however, loved her baby just as much as if she had been married.

Jim meets Antonia in the fields. She is worn and thin but still vital. They talk of Mr. Shimerda and of Cleric's recent death. Jim is leaving for good, but to her he will seem near as does her father. She would never like living in a city. Jim says that he would like to have had her as sweetheart, wife, mother, or sister. As the moon rises, he holds her strong brown hands, thinking that hers is a genuine woman's face. Most are only shadows. Promising to return, he walks back alone, hearing from the past a laughing boy and girl.

CHARACTER ANALYSIS: BOOK IV

JIM BURDEN: In the previous section, Jim spoke of his discovery that as he read more of the classics the country people he had known as a boy stood out "strengthened and simplified" just as the plow had seemed to stand out against the sun. He then added that they were so alive in him that he seldom wondered whether they were alive elsewhere. In other words, Jim has such vivid memories of these friends of his youth that they go on being part of his life long after he has ceased to see them in the flesh. Among those he mentioned earlier were Jake, Otto, and Russian Peter. He hadn't seen or heard from any of them since he started to go to high school. Yet these old friends, or rather their images, accompany him in his new experiences and seem very much alive in him.

Jim throughout the work is a rather lonely individual, often the outsider. Hence these memory friends mean a great deal to him. In the Introduction, when the narrator first talks of Jim and Antonia, she says, "His mind was full of her that day." As a lad he walks the Black Hawk streets at night, solitary and aloof: as a man he travels on trains through the West, putting distance between himself and a loveless marriage. Thanks, however, to his romantic disposition, he can draw spiritual strength or renewal of hope by mentally rejoining once more the reliable, unchanging old acquaintances "strengthened and simplified" in his consciousness to represent solid, homely virtues.

Once we understand generally how Jim regards these remembered figures, we can better appreciate his reaction here to Antonia's misfortune. She has been good to him over the years and has praised him extravagantly to others. They have, in fact, been fairly close friends. Yet when he hears that she has been deserted and disgraced and is back on the farm drudging for Ambrosch, his feeling is not profound sympathy but bitter disappointment. He cannot forgive her for having exposed herself to the pity of others. He has his mental picture of her as the joyous girl who used to race through the countryside with him and as the real woman, with "warm, sweet face . . . kind arms, and . . . true heart." This is *his* Antonia, and he does not want his vision destroyed. If Antonia is in actuality going to be a foolish girl who throws her love away on a worthless braggart, thus courting public scorn, he wants only to shut her out of his mind.

He relents somewhat when he sees her baby's picture in the photographer's window. As a young lad in Black Hawk, Jim had little respect for the townspeople. He regarded them as narrow-minded snobs, too terrified of gossip ever to think for themselves. The picture, however, a crayon enlargement in an expensive gilt frame, means that Antonia is not keeping her child hidden away, but is showing pride in her offspring. This gesture of independence helps to reestablish Jim's favorable image of Antonia. He is still disgusted with her for her folly, but at least he will go to see her.

When he subsequently meets her after hearing the full story from the Widow Steavens, he quickly responds to her friendly interest and tells her all about himself. Then he assures her that when he was away he thought of her often. He would, in fact, have liked to have her as sweetheart, wife, mother, or sister, "anything that a woman can be to a man." He then makes two highly significant statements. "The idea of you is a part of my mind," he says, and adds, "You really are a part of me." Before he leaves, he holds her hands, thinking of the past, and scans her face, which he intends always to "carry with" him. Then he leaves, almost believing that he is accompanied by the young, laughing Jim and Antonia.

There is no indication that he asks about her baby or her family, the state of her health, or her plans for the future. If he leaves in an exalted frame of mind, it is because he once more has "his" Antonia, a vital person with warm, brown hands and a grave, strong expression, whose kindly concern about his friends, his way of living, and his hopes, is pleasantly reassuring. If Jim's peace of mind depends much upon happy memories, this meeting renews treasured recollections of a happy childhood and provides material for future reveries. Even at the time he looks closely at her face to fix it firmly in his consciousness.

What then are we to make of his ardent declaration that he wishes he could have had her as sweetheart, wife, mother, or sister? It probably should be taken largely as a sincere but rather vague outburst of sentiment. There is no evidence that he ever seriously tried to court her. For that matter, were he now in earnest, they are both still young and unmarried. But for all his genuinely democratic urges, she is an unschooled Bohemian immigrant farm woman with an out-of-wedlock child, and he is a Virginia-born university student. They move in different circles, and both tacitly recognize the fact. Moreover, if he cannot really decide whether even in theory he would have liked her as wife, mother, or sister, he has no definite relationship in mind. All in all, the idea of Antonia is what Jim needs and wants.

ANTONIA SHIMERDA: The account given Jim by the Widow Steavens reveals much about Antonia. As a young girl in love, preparing for her wedding, she was joy personified. Gaily she would use the Widow's sewing machine, "pedaling the life out of it, all the while singing merry Bohemian songs. As always she worked very hard determined to run a good home for her future husband. She regarded herself as a country girl and disliked having to live in a city but she went off with happy tears when Donovan wrote her to come. Everything in this part of her story points up Antonia's high spirits, unlimited energy, and eagerness to do things well.

After her unfortunate experience, she is "crushed and quiet" but not one to weep self-pityingly and demand that others sympathize. Neither does she go around angrily denouncing her betrayer or even sink into lethargy or despair. Unwilling to subject herself to the town's patronizing airs, she stays at home even when plagued by ulcerated teeth. So it is clear that she is sensitive about her loss of reputation. Yet she bears herself with dignity, exercises good control over her feelings, and patiently endures her mother's muttering and Ambrosch's surliness, as well as her other afflictions. She is more than ever a strong character.

She is also strong physically. During the months of her pregnancy, when many women would limit activities, she goes on doing heavy farm work. Right up to the end, she herds cattle, even during a December snowfall. Then at night she goes in alone to her room and "without a groan" bears her child. When the Widow Steavens is summoned by the flustered Mrs. Shimerda, Antonia calmly directs her where to find the proper soap.

Strong morally and physically, Antonia seems somehow to draw her extraordinary vigor from the land. More than once in this section does she speak of how much being close to the soil means to her. She is troubled when she learns that she may have to live in Denver, afraid that she will not be able to manage so well without chickens or a cow.

Upon her return, the Widow notes that when watching her cattle Antonia likes to be alone and sun herself on the grassy banks. Uncertain as to how long she may live, she recalls her happier childhood and enjoys the autumn. When Jim makes his visit, she declares that she would always feel lonely and miserable in a city. She wants to live and die where she knows every stack and tree and "where all the ground is friendly."

Despite all that she has suffered, Antonia retains her warm, loving interest in others. She is glad to talk things over with the Widow and has no harsh words to say about the man who tricked and deserted her. She loves her baby dearly, and has its picture taken and beautifully framed. No child, says the Widow, ever received better care. Finally, when Jim arrives, she receives him graciously and insists upon hearing all about his friends, his way of living and his plans. At that time she also indicates her determination to see that her little daughter gets a good start.

In general, Antonia seems to look ahead more than does Jim. When he was in high school, she was always speculating about his future and urging him to go away and achieve success. After he left, she went on telling people that one day he would be richer than Mr. Harling. After her sad experience, she thinks of happier days with Jim and her father, and she tells her friend later that she is grateful that they had each other when they were small. Yet she is most interested in his hopes and dreams. She also has one of her own. She wants to give her child a better chance than she had. The Widow calls Antonia a "natural-born mother." As such, she has reason to anticipate a busy, useful life in the years to come.

THE WIDOW STEAVENS: Although mentioned as being present at the Shimerda funeral and later as renting the Burden farm, the Widow is much more fully delineated in this section. She is another of Miss Cather's sturdy, independent, kindly farm women. Jim describes her as brown as an Indian, tall and strong. Mrs. Harling called her a good talker with an excellent memory. And she does, in fact, tell Antonia's story in lively fashion with dialogue and revealing details.

First of all, she is a warmly sympathetic person. She rejoices in Antonia's marriage prospects, lets her run her sewing machine, and teaches her hemstitching and other skills. When Antonia returns, abandoned and shamed, the Widow, far from snubbing her, drives over promptly. As she listens to the girl's tale of woe, she is so "heart-broke" that she cries "like a young thing."

The Widow is also a woman of spirit. Hearing of Antonia's misfortune, she wonders tartly why such a "bad one" as Lena Lingard can walk proudly in her silks and satins. She does admit, however, that Lena is good to her mother. She also praises Ambrosch for acting like a man when he gives Antonia the silver and the three hundred dollars. Yet she warns him in no uncertain terms when he later says something about putting the infant in the rainbarrel. "I pride myself," she tells Jim, "I cowed him." The good Widow probably did, for the baby waxes strong and healthy, and Ambrosch is expected to pick up its framed picture at the photographer's!

LARRY DONOVAN: The character of the train conductor who seduces Antonia is only lightly sketched. Except for Antonia, who is fairly reticent, all who mention him are hostile. Lena says that she and others could relate "things" about him and implies that the Harlings do not like him. Jim calls him a "professional ladies' man." Elsewhere, Jim speaks of him scornfully as a "train-crew aristocrat" who will not even condescend to open a window for a passenger. Cultivating an air of "official aloofness," he changes his uniform as soon as his run comes to an end. He never talks much to men but gravely confides in women how sadly his merits are unappreciated by the railroad, which has yet to make him a passenger agent. Antonia quietly adds the information that he is dishonest. Discharged for allowing passengers to ride at lower than authorized rates, he sent for Antonia without letting her know the facts. He was ill, and she took care of him. Then when her money had all been spent, he left without a word. She believes that he has gone down into Old Mexico where many conductors cheat the inhabitants and thus get rich. This is the man Antonia used to talk of proudly as if he were president of the whole railroad.

TINY SODERBALL: Of the three hired girls, whose story is told at some length, Tiny is the most aggressive and most daring. Except for her disastrous romance with Larry, Antonia remains in and around Black Hawk. Lena moves only to Lincoln, until summoned by Tiny to the West Coast. Tiny, however, the hotel waitress who danced trippingly and yet could always keep customers in their place, goes far afield. Venturing first to Seattle, she goes on to the wilds of Alaska. She has some goodness of heart, since she took care of the dying Swedish prospector. Yet she is also a shrewd, hard-headed business woman, as is evident from her successful operations in real estate and mining. In devoting her life, however, to the accumulation of wealth, she seems to have missed out on many deeper satisfactions. Were it not for Lena, she would not even dress like a woman of means. When Jim sees her, she is pleased with her achievements, but not much excited about them or anything else.

COMMENT: BOOK IV

This section consists of two separate stories. The one tells of Tiny Soderball's rise from hired girl in a Black Hawk hotel to a wealthy resident of San Francisco. The other describes the lamentable failure of Antonia's marriage plans and Jim's last meeting with her before going on to law school and settling in New York. Hitherto we have noted repeatedly that this novel avoids the usual or conventional form. It may be worthwhile at this point to consider how the different sections are related and how taken together they form an integrated study of life.

Book I, *The Shimerdas*, shows the ideal farm household as developed over a fairly long period by the well-established American settlers. By contrast it also describes the prodigious handicaps with which the European immigrants start to achieve this good life. So awesome are the obstacles that a fine, intelligent man is driven to suicide. Yet young people like Antonia and Ambrosch go bravely to work, and gradually their lot improves.

Book II, *The Hired Girls*, moves the action to Black Hawk. Having given up their farm, the Burdens no longer represent Nebraska settlers at their most productive. The Harlings alone manage to bring into the town the happy, wholesome atmosphere of the farm. The country girls come into Black Hawk to work, and it is soon seen that the social lines are sharply drawn. Jim, however, having known an admirable farm set-up and having followed with admiration the hard-won progress of the immigrant group, refuses to accept the town's narrow standards. In defiantly adopting a democratic attitude and treating the hired girls as his equals, he in effect wagers that these vital, bright-eyed young women are capable of accomplishing at least as much as, and probably more than, those native-born Americans who scorn them as stupid, ignorant foreigners.

The next two books, *Lena Lingard* and *The Pioneer Woman's Story*, provide impressive support for his contention. Here the town's delusions of superiority are dealt with on its own terms. Inasmuch as no evidence is forthcoming that the smug citizenry of Black Hawk demonstrated unusual talent or capability, the inescapable conclusion is that their claims to belong to an upper class rest mainly on the fact that they are better off financially than the immigrants. They have fussier houses and more expensive clothes. Their men have made good livings in various lines of business, and they therefore enjoy a certain prestige. Coming from foreign families, Tiny and Lena start with nothing but their own intelligence, energy, and determination. Lena becomes a fashionable dressmaker who can attract as admirers American men of substance. Tiny, by her own efforts, accumulates a considerable fortune. If Black Hawk rates people on the basis of their material progress, Lena and Tiny score highly for the country girls.

How then does Antonia fit into the debate? In some ways she never even approaches the records set by her two friends. Even her English retains a slight accent. Moreover, although she does avoid the unwanted attentions of Cutter and the impudent town lad, she encounters nothing but misery when she accepts a marriage proposal from a native-born trainman. Even when regarding her with some pity, the town would seem to have some cause to dismiss this immigrant girl as naively imprudent. Yet the next and climactic book, *Cusak's Boys*, gives her the last word. Eventually, after long years of painful struggle, she will achieve the economic level required for some respect from the town. It will be mentioned in passing that the school has its picnic each year on her farm. Yet she will have done even more in the end than Lena or Tiny, or for that matter than the type of townsfolk that so wearied Jim. For she with her happy home and many children will have gone on to a fuller, richer life, with far deeper satisfactions. Succeeding the Burdens and the Harlings, she will add those special admirable traits that were part of her European heritage. All three hired girls thus refute the town's claim to automatic superiority in the three final sections of *My Antonia.* Lena and Tiny make impressive material gains. Antonia does well materially but also proves at length morally and spiritually greater than those who looked down upon her and friends.

A second question that arises in connection with the fourth section is that of Antonia's involvement with Donovan. Hitherto Antonia has been a fair judge of character. She was not fooled by Wick Cutter or Lena, and she was outraged when the engaged young man tried to kiss her. She also seems to have had fairly strict standards. She may have liked to dance, but she was never one for casual love affairs. The Widow Steavens makes a sharp distinction between the "good" Antonia and the "bad" Lena.

Actually, we are safe in assuming that if Willa Cather leaves so much about this affair unexplained, she probably does not want it overemphasized. Taken generally, it serves several purposes. First of all, it plays up the contaminating element of the town. Everything about the train conductor is shallow, petty, and false. His very insignificance is used to bring out more sharply Antonia's heroic nature. Even her misdirected loyalty reveals her strong, loving nature. Moreover, the hardships endured in consequence of Donovan's perfidy merely make manifest even further the noble qualities of her indomitable spirit. The fact is that the train man is treated throughout as a minor nuisance that can momentarily daunt but not destroy this vital personality who typifies all that is creative or life-giving, who is, in truth, a natural-born mother.

Yet a few suggestions may be advanced as to why Antonia did choose this particular worthless figure as love object. Allowing for the possibility that an infatuation can be irrational, we may note certain facts. First of all, the two men whom she always idolized were her father and Jim. Fastidious types both, they were certainly refined. Moreover, Grandmother Burden and Mrs. Harling combined to wrench Antonia away from rough farmers and the uncouth Ambrosch so that she might learn "nice ways." With such formulative influences she would be likely to look for a man with a cultivated manner. In addition, both her father and Jim were not hard-driving, aggressive individuals. Her sad father committed suicide. Jim walks his solitary way and is, to her way of thinking, largely unappreciated. After graduation she makes a point of stopping to tell the boy's grandfather how splendid his speech was; and, according to Lena, she is always bragging about him and his prospects while he is away at school. Yet Jim, it is clear, is not hers to marry. Where will she find another "refined" young admirer? The Black Hawk boys with any education and community standing simply do not wed immigrant farm girls. Then along comes Donovan.

Willa Cather is famous for her economical style that wastes no words on unimportant facts or unnecessary details. Hence the details actually given are likely to be significant ones. We have seen that relatively little information is supplied about Donovan. Yet we are told that he makes a point of changing his clothes as soon as he leaves the train. Considering the dusty atmosphere of old-fashioned rail coaches — Jim himself talks of being "sticky and grimy" on one — Donovan would seem to be careful about his appearance. Secondly, he adopts a "dignified" and "aloof" air. Mr. Shimerda certainly had dignity, and Jim, one of the Burdens from Virginia, always is somewhat reserved. Finally, Donovan claims that he has failed to receive important railroad posts, for which he is qualified because "rough shod" men have been preferred. Here, too, Antonia would be reminded of her gentle, ineffectual father and Jim who had yet to make his mark.

One final aspect may be noted. Although Antonia has as an ideal a refined, gentlemanly type like her father or Jim, she seems at times curiously humble. Her mother, after all, was a peasant who married above her station in the Old Country, and Antonia tends to be grateful for kind words from the elite. After her return home, when Jim tells her that he has thought of her often, she asks tearfully, "How can it be like that, when you know so many people, and when I've disappointed you so?" They are longtime friends. She has him in mind frequently, but is amazed that he should think of her. Her attitude toward Donovan seems similar. Before she leaves, she worries lest in the city she will not be able to "manage so well for him." Upon her return, she admits that she never pressed him to marry her, hoping that if he saw how well she could "do for him," he would want to stay with her. If she was in love with him, it would seem that this was an almost servile devotion roused through superficial resemblances between him and the two men of whom she had long been genuinely fond. Interestingly enough, when she does marry, she chooses no "rough shod" man, but a former Viennese furrier who likes "theatres and lighted streets and music."

Also in this section, Jim notes with delight the progress made by the farm families since he first arrived in Nebraska as a small boy. The land, enriched and mellowed by the changing seasons, has become increasingly productive as a result of sustained human effort. Man, working in harmony with Nature, achieves deep satisfactions. Both adults and children, thinks Jim, are fortunate when this cooperative enterprise, giving rise to "sweeping lines of fertility," restores beauty and harmony to the world.

Antonia, the "natural-born mother," is clearly in this picture. Donovan is just the opposite. He takes and does not give. He is all that is shabby, mean, and essentially destructive. Yet while he can cause Antonia grief, she is too much in harmony with all that is life-giving or creative in the land to be permanently wrecked. Her spirit is strong and unquenchable. Incidentally, here again the town is contrasted with the country. Larry takes Antonia away from the farmland she loves to the city. There life is hard for her, and she finds that even her clothes cannot be cleaned properly. Is the literal dirt used to signify other less clean aspects of urban life? She returns, and her clothes are washed and dried in the sun. From the earth Antonia draws the strength to accept her disappointments and go on, like the other productive farm people, to contribute to the country's progress.

The last point to be considered is Miss Cather's use of the Widow Steavens as narrator for the story of Antonia's sad affair. The rich vernacular speech of this spry, spirited older woman is pleasant in itself, and the character is beautifully drawn. This also permits the novelist to handle the recital with both sympathy and reticence. The Widow, after all, will not be expected to know everything about the relationship, and Jim will not be one to pry. This way we are given the bare facts of the situation, permitted briefly to cry "like a young one" over Antonia's misfortune, and then briskly encouraged to observe that since then, and despite difficulties, the girl has "got on fine."

BOOK V—CUZAK'S BOYS

PLOT: BOOK V

Not for twenty years does Jim keeps his promise to come back to Antonia. He knows that she married a young Bohemian cousin of Anton Jelinek. He has heard, too, that they had many children and for years were not prosperous because her husband lacked force. Jim once sent her pictures of her native village from abroad, but has hitherto avoided visits for fear of finding her old and worn. He prizes his early memories and wants no more illusions shattered.

Eventually, however, he receives happier reports from Lena and Tiny and decides to stop over in Nebraska. According to Lena, Anton Cuzak, whom Antonia married, is not a hard-driving type, but she is fond of him and proud of their ten or eleven children.

Approaching the Cuzak farm, Jim meets three small boys, one of whom looks full of mischief. Two older girls in the kitchen greet him politely and seek their mother. Strong, sunburned, somewhat grayed, Antonia has the same unforgettable eyes. Still, vigorous, she seems "battered but not diminished." After failing at first to recognize him, she receives him with all the old warmth and introduces her children. Their father is with the oldest boy at a street fair in Wilbur. She is distressed to learn that Jim has no children.

Jim is later taken to view the new fruit cave, near the house. As the youngsters afterwards race out into the sun, Jim sees then as an "explosion of life out of the dark cave." He then is shown the flourishing groves and orchards, as well as a charming grape arbor, all of which Antonia has lovingly tended. The early years were difficult, she admits, because her husband became easily discouraged. She worked hard, however, and later the children helped. Her first baby, Martha, is now married and has a son. She loves the farm, but does not regret having learned "nice ways" at the Harlings. She will never, however, send her daughters out to be hired girls, nor will she have to.

That evening, Jim is shown family pictures, and Leo the impish boy who is Antonia's favorite, plays old Mr. Shimerda's violin. The next day, Cuzak returns, a short, rumpled man with a black curly mustache. He and young Rudolph tell of the fair. Later the lad recounts how Wick Cutter finally shot his wife and then committed suicide, making sure that having survived her even briefly he could still dispose of his wealth. Cuzak also tells Jim about his early life in Europe. He misses the bright lights but loves and admires Antonia. Jim leaves, and spends a disappointing day in Black Hawk. Walking out into the country, he remembers the early days and thinks how Destiny shaped the lives of Antonia and the boy Jim. He will now see more of her and her family, for she shares with him the precious past.

CHARACTER ANALYSES: BOOK V

JIM BURDEN: In this section, Jim's reluctance to risk any clouding of his bright image of Antonia as strong and indomitable is brought out. As a successful lawyer and an old friend, he might have come to offer some assistance when he heard that she was poor and had a large family. Willa Cather herself made every effort to send thoughtful gifts of money or sometimes even seed to old Nebraska farm friends when times were hard. Jim, however, mails some pictures from Bohemia, but stays away lest he see Antonia "aged and broken." Only when Lena gives him a "cheerful" account of Antonia's situation does he finally get up the courage to pay a call.

Meeting her again, he is deeply moved. As he feared, she does look older after twenty years of intense effort, but as a personality she still has undiminished vigor. This he finds reassuring. She has, of course, lost teeth, but he is consoled to discover that she has retained the "fire of life." Meeting all her well-mannered, handsome children and admiring her neat house and flourishing farm, Jim is much affected. Watching the young people streak out of the dark cave, he feels for the moment dizzy.

He is particularly taken with the older sons. They make him feel like a boy again, and he finds long-forgotten interests revived in him. He tells them that he was once very much in love with their mother. As he lies down to sleep with the boys, he is again aware of the vivid images Antonia has always left in his mind. She represents timeless and universal human attitudes and stimulates the imagination. She makes one feel the meaning of ordinary happenings, the wonders of making things grow. Generous in every way, she is to Jim a "rich mine of life." From this it can be seen that Jim still values her more as a symbol than as a person. Her image, "strengthened and simplified," as were those of Otto and Russian Peter when he read the classics in Lincoln, has been one of the sustaining forces of his life. Fortunately, when he at last dares to return, he finds that she is still the great spirit he had envisioned over the years.

Cuzak he regards as interesting and companionable. His description of "Papa" as a "crumpled little man" with a quaint habit of looking at one sidewise, after the manner of a work-horse, seems tinged with condescension. Yet he likes talking to him about Vienna and the gay city life that the Bohemian so misses. He looks forward to taking the boys on camping trips and enjoying long walks in the future with Cuzak. If his reactions to Antonia are those of a man who depends much upon idealized memories and inspiring symbols, his response to the hospitable men of the family suggests that here is a lonely, childless individual ready to adopt a whole ready-made family.

Finally, there is still in Jim the vaguely mystical strain evident in the earlier chapters. Returning to the countryside near Black Hawk, he again feels the sensation of being obliterated. Once again, too, he is conscious of the force of destiny and more aware than ever how much his first childhood years exploring the prairie with Antonia have meant to him as a man.

ANTONIA SHIMERDA CUZAK: When Jim meets her again, Antonia is pleased and excited. As she asks him to stay to meet her husband and her oldest son, she is "panting with excitement." Obviously, Antonia has remained capable of enthusiasm. She is, in fact, so "stirred up," she can hardly talk. She goes on to say that she feels as young as ever and can do as much work. She is happy and very pleased with her family and her home. She jokes about her fondness for the prankish Leo and soothes the tearful little boy whose dog has just died. She talks with awed satisfaction of all the bread she has to bake and confesses that she loves her trees as if they were people. She thanks God for her good health and calmly declares that had it not been for her strength they would never have been able to keep the farm going during the hard years when Cuzak was ready to give up. She herself has never been discouraged and never lonely. Life may have been easier in town, but while there she used to be confused and ill at ease. Here she works unceasingly, but is never sad. She evidently runs a good home. The children are happy and healthy, and the older ones help the younger. She encourages Leo to play his grandfather's violin, and she tells them all stories of the old days. She is fond of her husband and delighted to have him enjoy such little excursions as the one to the street fair. As for herself, she is a wonderfully contented wife and mother who has had all her own dreams come true and now labors cheerfully to give her many children the best possible chances.

ANTON CUZAK: A good-humored, philosophical man, Cuzak is kindly and intelligent. He too enjoys life. His glowing description of the acrobats and dancing bear at the Fair reveals his capacity for experiencing joy. He is also considerate. Polite enough to substitute English for Bohemian since Jim is their guest, he cannot wait to tell Antonia about those who sent greetings to her from town. He also presents his gift of a paper snake gently to little Jan so as not to frighten the shy child. He is proud of his large family. He likes his children and seems to find them amusing. He misses the joys of city life, but has stayed on the farm and worked hard because of Antonia. She is so warm-hearted that he has been able to survive the isolation. Now he has his sons as companions. By no means so forceful as Antonia, Cuzak is not an unworthy husband for her. He seems to be bright, fairly cultivated, gentle, and hard-working. He may not be Mr. Shimerda or Jim, but neither is he a plodding farm hand.

LEO CUZAK: Antonia's favorite child, twelve-year-old Leo, is an independent, saucy young rascal. Curly-headed and handsome, he insists that his mother tell Jim that he was born on Easter Day. When she forgets, he butts her with his head. He is given to occasional scornful remarks and reminds Jim sometimes of the skeptical Mrs. Shimerda. He plays the violin fairly well for a self-taught boy, and seems both deeply sensitive and unusually daring. He appears to enjoy things more than other people and hates to make deliberate judgments. When Jim leaves, Leo runs off without saying good-bye. He may have been sorry to see Jim go, or he may have been jealous because Antonia showed the visitor so much attention. No one knows, says his older brother, Ambrosch.

WICK CUTTER: As an old man, Wick looks like a dried-up little monkey but still quarrels unceasingly with his palsied wife. More and more he becomes obsessed with the dread that she will inherit from him, since under the law a surviving wife can at least claim one-third. So he buys a pistol ostensibly to shoot a cat, and one night when there are many within earshot kills his wife. He then shoots himself, but times his shot so that he is alive after she is and can tell this to the horrified men who rush into the house. Antonia is amazed that anyone could have such a cold heart. Wick to the end, however, shows a perverse kind of mental alertness and courage, as well as a macabre sense of humor. Although his actions are dreadful, he still seems an oddly comic creation.

COMMENT: BOOK V

Anton Cuzak is based on a young Bohemian named Pavelka, who married the original Annie Sadilek. He also suggested the hero for Miss Cather's famous short story "Neighbor Rosicky" and was quite proud of the honor (Bennett, 50). The Pavelkas, like the Cuzaks in the story, had a great many children. Whenever she returned on visits to Nebraska, the novelist enjoyed going out to see them on their farm. She was particularly impressed with the good manners of the young people. Incidentally, she, too, sent her Bohemian friend pictures from Czechoslovakia, which the family continued to cherish (Bennett, 49-53).

The bizarre deaths of Wick Cutter and his wife also are based upon actual happenings. M. R. Bentley, the original Red Cloud money-lender, did kill his wife and himself in this manner. The only striking difference in the fictional accounts is that Wick leaves only a relatively small estate, whereas Bentley's was considerably greater (Bennett, 84-5). Again, however, the author intends to make a point. Cutter, the mean, avaricious individual, shrivels physically and dies wretchedly to deprive his wife of a rather insignificant sum. Antonia, warm and generous, who was once his intended victim, lives on to be happy and prosperous.

In many of her stories Willa Cather depicts heroines who are stronger and abler than their men. It is clear that Cuzak is by no means a contemptible figure. He is intelligent, good-natured, affectionate, and hardworking. Yet there can be little doubt as to who runs things on the Cuzak farm. Antonia is clearly the more dynamic, the more vigorous of the two. She says flatly that had it not been for her physical hardihood they could never have kept the farm going during the difficult early years. It was she also who, after her husband was asleep, went down to water the young trees that eventually formed the beautiful orchards that Jim admires. Far from denying her claim, Cuzak readily admits that he would have given up long ago had it not been for his warm-hearted, determined wife. Jim describes Cuzak graphically as the "instrument" of Antonia's life mission.

Interestingly enough, there is no indication that Jim envies Cuzak. He seems, in fact, to be almost sorry for the little man. Although Jim's admiration for Antonia as the symbol of motherhood at its best may be almost boundless, he sees at once that the lot of her devoted husband may be far from ideal. His first impression of Cuzak is of a "humorous philosopher who had hitched up one shoulder under the burdens of life." He notes that the Cuzaks are on the friendliest of terms but sees Anton as the "corrective" and his wife as the main "impulse." Cuzak's own words have a wistful quality. He guesses that Antonia was right to keep them on the farm. He is grateful that she is not too strict with him, allowing him occasionally an extra beer in town. All in all, she is "a good wife for a poor man." Yet he does miss the sociable evenings in the city. This is particularly interesting when we recall how desperately homesick Mr. Shimerda was for his old cronies who used to talk with him "about music, and the woods, and about God." The dilemma is clear. Antonia wanted a husband as much as possible like her father and Jim. Yet neither of these men ever wanted to live permanently far from urban life. When she found a man who met her standards, he did not really want an isolated farm existence either. Love for her and for their children has kept him out in the country for over twenty years, but his mildly regretful tone causes Jim to wonder if the life that is desirable for one is ever perfect for another. Jim himself has had his difficulties with an energetic, executive wife. Here he seems almost to join forces with Cuzak. Both, being cosmopolitan in spirit, can talk of Vienna together.

The point has been made previously that *My Antonia* is to a great extent autobiographical. The underlying question posed at the end seems to be one that Miss Cather herself had to answer. The more she saw of urban life in the America of her time, the more she came to dislike it. This attitude is particularly apparent in such novels as *One of Ours* and *The Professor's House*. Life there was meanly materialistic and small-minded, in contrast with the happy creative home life of a Burden or Cuzak farm. Yet from the first, she herself was attracted by the richer cultural opportunities offered in the great cities. She liked the theatre and the concert hall. She enjoyed talking with cultivated people. She also took pleasure in visiting other lands. Although discouraging distracting intrusions upon her privacy, she delighted in entertaining close friends and serving them delicacies and fine wines. All that Mr. Shimerda and poor Cuzak longed for, she too would have sadly missed. Yet she still maintained that a life close to nature, such as that developed by Antonia, was ideally the most rewarding. In the marriage of Antonia and Cuzak, the two modes of existence are merged. Yet Miss Cather cannot honestly report that the situation equally satisfies both parties. She herself settled for the city, but went off to a remote resort or the sparsely populated Southwest or back to visit Nebraska whenever she felt the need for a spiritual tonic.

The use of symbols is particularly noteworthy in this final section. Antonia's secluded grape arbor with its benches for repose seems to sum up fittingly the serene, orderly, fruitful life that Jim's friend has worked out for herself. The old Shimerda violin, played by Leo, along with the carefully described photographs of former friends, suggests Antonia's resolve to pass on cherished traditions to her descendants. Above all, the striking picture of the children racing up from the dark cave into the sunlight is significant. On the one hand, it represents the good things growing out of the farm's dark soil. On the other, it calls to mind the wretched conditions in the gloomy Shimerda cave during the first bitter winter. These healthy, laughing young people are Shimerda grandchildren.

As the story ends, Jim, who is childless, seems to plan to treat the Cuzak boys almost as foster sons. Antonia in the past has often been kind to him. Is she now about to provide him with some of the needed satisfactions of a solid, family life? For that matter is this what in a limited way old friends like the Pavelkas did for Willa Cather?

As Jim sees life after all his extensive travels, the small town is depressing and the city cold. Here, however, among these country people, with their strength and warmth, good humor and unflagging enthusiasm, he feels at last at home. With his cosmopolitan experience, he brings the great world to their small farm, and this they welcome. They, in turn, give him a reassuring sense that life can have rich positive values which produce peace and contentment.

In the last chapter there is an artistic rounding out of the work, with three themes re-introduced that were sounded at the beginning of the story. First of all, there is the golden beauty of the prairie in autumn that rouses a feeling of exaltation. Secondly, there is the awesome idea of being so absorbed into the vastness of nature as to feel obliterated or blotted out. Finally, there is the concept of destiny as a great mysterious force that determines the course of lives. Whatever difficulties and disappointments this fate originally ordained for Jim and Antonia, it at least made it possible for them as children to share a succession of wonderful adventures. Such stimulating experiences later sustained them individually and established between them an imperishable bond.

Although many lively incidents are vividly described in *My Antonia*, the episodes are related not so much for their intrinsic interest as for the effect they have upon those participating. This is essentially a psychological novel about two highly impressionable people temperamentally capable of enthusiasm. Its main appeal will probably always be to readers who feel strongly about things and go on regarding life as a great adventure to be enjoyed to the hilt.

Character Analyses

NOTE: In Willa Cather's novels the good, or admirable characters often reveal the same basic traits, and the less agreeable figures, too, also have certain qualities in common. The outline form has been used here to make this more apparent. It is also worth remarking, however, that even favorably drawn individuals are shown to have some faults, and that less noble ones are not always seen at their worst.

ANTONIA SHIMERDA

1. *is generous.* She offers Jim her ring for teaching her some English, lavishly praises his killing of the snake, never spares herself when working for those she likes.

2. *is intelligent.* She learns quickly, asks questions, and even as a girl has opinions on everything.

3. *is independent.* She is not cowed by the strongminded Mr. Harling, and she does not hide away her first child.

4. *is courageous.* She weathers well such disasters as her father's suicide and Donovan's treachery, and keeps up her husband's spirits during years of poor crops.

5. *is hard-working.* She does a man's work in the fields and later energetically labors to build up the Cuzak place.

6. *is good to children.* She is the loyal big sister to Jim, makes candy for the young Harlings, and is obviously a wonderful mother to her own big family.

7. *likes animals and plants.* She tends the dying insect, gives up hunting, and cultivates a splendid garden.

8. *has respect for order.* Her house is well run, with the older children trained to help the younger.

9. *has respect for tradition.* She remembers fondly stories of her father and of Jim and passes them on.

10. *has a feeling for beauty.* She likes music and dancing, draws inspiration and solace from the land, and creates a lovely, peaceful garden.

Negatively she also

11. *can be foolhardy.* She is unwise to go to work for Wick Cutter.

12. *can be unreasonably loyal.* She will not listen to friends who distrust Donovan.

JIM BURDEN

1. *is generous.* He offers his scarf to Yulka, gives up the dances to please his grandmother, rejoices in Antonia's prosperity.

2. *is intelligent.* He recognizes early the fine qualities of Mr. Shimerda and rejects the narrow views of many in Black Hawk.

3. *is independent.* He ignores the snobbish younger set and chooses the country girls as friends.

4. *is courageous.* He does kill the snake and fight Cutter, and he refuses to conform with Black Hawk prejudices.

5. *is hard-working.* He studies much alone when preparing for the University, taking off only the day of the picnic.

6. *has respect for tradition.* Like Antonia, he treasures the memory of Mr. Shimerda.

7. *has a feeling for beauty.* He describes often his joy in the changing splendors of the Nebraska landscape.

Negatively, he also

8. *can judge harshly.* He dislikes foreigners after Jake's fight with Ambrosch, and is angry when Antonia lets herself be deceived by Larry.

9. *can act selfishly.* He leaves Lena rather abruptly and stays away for twenty years lest he be dismayed at finding Antonia no longer triumphant.

GRANDFATHER BURDEN

1. *is generous.* He is good to Jim and helps the Shimerdas even when they seem mean and ungrateful.

2. *is intelligent.* Although convinced that his type of religion and his way of living are good, he can appreciate the views of the manly Jelinek and the Catholic piety of a Mr. Shimerda.

3. *is hard-working.* Although aging, he labors with the hired men.

Negatively, he also

4. *can be narrow-minded.* Even Grandmother worries about his strong views on religion, and he keeps Jelinek away from Jim, although the Bohemian's saloon is respectable.

GRANDMOTHER BURDEN

1. *is generous.* She is kind to Jim and to Antonia, and even to the disagreeable Mrs. Shimerda. She also lets the horse be sacrificed when help must be obtained.

2. *is intelligent.* Even when her patience is strained, she sees something in the Shimerda viewpoint.

3. *is courageous.* She fights snakes with her cane and braves Mrs. Shimerda's ire to keep Yulka from being frightened at the burial service.

4. *likes animals.* She will not let the badger be killed.

5. *has a feeling for order and beauty.* Her house is clean and attractive, and she works hard to keep it so.

Negatively, she also

6. *can be narrow-minded.* She is impatient with the sorely beset Shimerdas and won't try their unfamiliar mushrooms. She also stops Jim from going to the dances attended by the country girls and their friends.

MR. SHIMERDA

1. *is generous.* He marries his wife to protect her good name, gives up his friends for her and the children, and hopes to give Jim his prized gun.

2. *is intelligent.* He has read much and is always delighted in amicable discussions.

3. *has a feeling for order and beauty.* He hates the dark, depressing Shimerda cave and appreciates the Burdens' hospitality. He is also a musician.

Negatively, he also

4. *lacks force.* Although he knows more, he cannot handle his wife and Ambrosch.

5. *lacks stamina.* He gives in to despair and kills himself.

MRS. HARLING

1. *is generous.* She is good to Antonia and Jim, even forgiving them for having strongly opposed her.

2. *is intelligent.* Note how quickly she takes the measure of Ambrosch and Mrs. Shimerda, and also of Donovan.

3. *is hard-working.* She attacks domestic chores vigorously.

4. *has respect for order.* Her household is well conducted.

5. *has a feeling for beauty.* She likes music and can appreciate Antonia's enjoyment of good threshing weather.

Negatively, she also

6. *has a fiery temper.* She is furious when defied.

LENA LINGARD

1. *is generous.* She is kind to her little brother and builds her mother a house. She lets Jim go gracefully and sends wedding gifts to Antonia, who tried to keep Jim away from her.

2. *is intelligent.* She runs her business and her life efficiently. She learns all that she needs to know for success.

3. *is independent.* She leaves town to start her own business, rejects offers of marriage to stay free, and pays her own way.

4. *has a feeling for beauty.* She creates good-looking clothes and enjoys the theatre. She likes to dance.

5. *shows warm sympathy for people.* She acts understandingly toward Ole Benson, the Colonel, and Ordinsky, as well as Jim. She even suffers with characters in plays.

Negatively, she also

6. *falls short of Antonia's selflessness.* She enjoys the attentions of male admirers but wants none of the responsibilities of marriage.

ANTON CUZAK

1. *is generous.* He gives his wife full credit for their prosperity, is hospitable to Jim, and brings home gifts to his children.

2. *is intelligent.* He takes an interest in Jim's travels and asks interesting questions.

3. *is hard-working.* He may sometimes have become discouraged but he struggled along with Antonia to make the farm pay.

4. *has artistic interests.* He speaks of opera singers and Vienna and misses the cultural advantages of the city.

Negatively, he also

5. *seems less forceful than his wife.* During the hard years he lost heart, but she never faltered.

MRS. SHIMERDA

1. *is mean-spirited.* She whines and complains, envies the Burdens, and resents their generosity.

2. *is greedy.* She snatches Mrs. Burden's iron pot and is unwilling to pay fully for the cow.

3. *is stupid.* Despite a certain shrewdness, or cunning, she does not plan efficiently or run her home well.

Positively, she also

4. *has some initiative.* She insisted that the family emigrate.

5. *has force and stamina.* She does not collapse after her husband's death, but goads her children on to work, and labors along with them.

AMBROSCH SHIMERDA

1. *is mean-spirited.* He has a surly manner, ruins the harness and will not admit it, works his sister hard, sneers at Antonia's baby, and drives off the Widow Steavens.

2. *is greedy.* He tries to get his hands on most of Antonia's wages but is prevented by Mrs. Harling.

3. *is disagreeable.* He has none of the social graces.

Positively, he also

4. *is hard-working.* He is never shown to be lazy.

5. *is pious.* He prays for his father and has Masses said.

6. *gives Antonia a fair dowry.* He also at least takes her in again when she returns home in disgrace.

WICK CUTTER

1. *is mean-spirited.* He takes unfair advantage of immigrant farmers with limited resources and little knowledge of mortgage regulations.

2. *is greedy.* He cheats many farmers and does not even want to leave his wife or her family any of his money when he dies. So he kills her and then himself.

3. *is sensually corrupt.* He seduces two hired girls and plans to add Antonia to his victims but is prevented by Jim.

4. *is hypocritical.* He mouths moral maxims and ostentatiously contributes to the church.

5. *is clever.* He taxes the best efforts of Frances Harling and Grandfather Burden to extricate the farmers from his clutches. His scheme to surprise Antonia is ingenious, and his final gruesome jest at least shows planning.

6. *is almost perversely good-humored.* He enjoys his wife's taking orders for painted china, cheerfully puts her on the wrong train, and even dies with a comic flourish.

Sample Essay Questions and Answers

1. The heroism of Miss Cather's pioneers consists in surviving hardships and overcoming obstacles. Indicate the different types of difficulties encountered by the immigrants in *My Antonia*.

ANSWER: First of all, there is the language barrier. Unable to communicate, the newly arrived Shimerdas cannot ask for needed help, make friends easily, or avoid relying upon a scoundrel like Krajiek. Second, there is the rigorous Nebraska climate. Were the winter less severe, Mr. Shimerda and his sons might have been able to escape the prolonged unpleasantness of life in the cave and to arrange for a more adequate food supply. Third, there is the lack of cooperation among the immigrants themselves. Krajiek, already well established, wants only to cheat his countrymen. Otto, the Austrian, distrusts the Czechs, and the Norwegians refuse to permit the burial of Mr. Shimerda in their cemetery. Fourth, there is prejudice on the part of the native-born Americans. Even the kindly and tolerant Burdens find some of the older European customs hard to tolerate, and the Black Hawk snobs regard all foreigners as inferiors. Finally, some problems stem from individual personality traits. Mr. Shimerda's painful loneliness, his wife's whining manner and general inefficiency, Ambrosch's sullen rudeness, and even poor Russian Peter's shyness, all help to worsen the plight of those already at a severe disadvantage. Many, however, do go on to achieve an eventual solid prosperity. And their struggle, to Miss Cather, is the measure of their greatness.

2. What part does Antonia's European background play in the formation of her strong, creative personality?

ANSWER: Arriving in America as a girl of fourteen, Antonia has already acquired excellent values from the gentle, cultivated father she so passionately admires. At home he was a violinist who delighted in the company of fellow musicians. He also read many books and liked to talk over stimulating ideas with old friends in a pleasant garden setting. From him she undoubtedly obtained her feeling for music and her eagerness to learn. His whole nature is noble and generous. He married her mother only because he thought it the honorable thing to do, and he suffers greatly when he must accept charity from the Burdens. He understands, too, Antonia's warm-hearted urge to keep life in the frail insect. Affectionate to her, courteous to all, he suggests always that same greatness of spirit that later distinguishes her from the petty snobs of Black Hawk. From her mother, on the other hand, Antonia doubtless derives her rugeed constitution. Mrs. Shimerda may be somewhat incompetent and often disagreeable, but she is determined and does survive the worst of winters. To make her way in the world and wrest victory from the soil, Antonia would have to be far stronger than the listless town girls. Actually she has both her mother's peasant toughness and her father's vision, but none of the older residents cramping prejudices. Thus she can put in years of incredibly hard physical effort and eventually achieve the good life originally outlined for her by her Old World father. The secluded Cuzak garden would have charmed him, and his grandson now plays his beloved violin.

3. In *My Antonia* does the author idealize all European immigrants at the expense of native-born Nebraska settlers?

ANSWER: As in her other stories about immigrant pioneers, Willa Cather here does stress the admirable qualities of people from non-English-speaking lands. Her portrayal of Antonia, for instance, emphasizes the Bohemian girl's kindness, generosity, courage, perseverance, and amiable good nature. Lena and Tiny also possess commendable traits, as do the other hired girls, Russian Peter, the Austrian Otto, and, among the Bohemians, Mr. Shimerda, Anton Jelinek, and Anton Cuzak. By contrast the Black Hawk townspeople seem pale and dull, if not narrow-minded or snobbish. Young men like Harry Paine and Sylvester Lovett are regarded with contempt, and Wick Cutter is, of course, a scoundrel.

On the other hand, not all Europeans are noble, and not all native Americans base. Within the Shimerda group, the father is a suicide, the mother is meanly spiteful, Ambrosch is sullen, and Marek weakminded. Krajiek is greedy and unscrupulous, and the Norwegians are uncooperative at the time of the Shimerda funeral. Among the early settlers, the Burdens are kindly, tolerant, and generally helpful. The Harlings, too, are above reproach, and the Widow Steavens is a true friend in need. Others in the community also volunteer aid at the time of burial. Hence, while the heroine and certain other favorably drawn characters are Europeans, not all immigrants are represented as intellectually or morally superior to their neighbors born in this country.

4. For much of his life Jim Burden lives far from Antonia and moves in circles far different from hers. Why has she meant so much to him?

ANSWER: Youth to Willa Cather is the period when deepest, most lasting impressions are formed. Jim meets Antonia when he is ten and she is four years older. They have both been uprooted from their birthplaces and set down in a wild new country. Everything to them is novel and exciting, and, except for little Yulka, there are no other children near. They therefore share uniquely the joys of exploration and discovery. In addition, they are together during such startling episodes as the killing of the snake and the deathbed horror tale of Pavel. Later in Black Hawk, Jim must share her with the Harlings, the hired girls, and various male escorts. Nevertheless, she still takes a strong interest in his welfare, and he, in turn, considers her the best dancer in town, typifying all that is vivacious and gay in the country girls.

From the first, Antonia, ever generous, gives the lonely boy the praise and encouragement he needs. She extols him to everyone for killing the snake. She urges him to study hard and insists that he will succeed. She also keeps him from becoming too friendly with Lena so that he will have the chance to forge ahead. Finally she is the daughter of Mr. Shimerda, of whom he thought a great deal. She is thus, in a sense, his link with the rich culture of the Old World, which her father represented. Jim is therefore especially pleased at the end to find out that Antonia has kept faith magnificently with the noblest ideals for which the old violinist stood.

5. Heroism is often represented in fiction in terms of individual spectacular feats. In *My Antonia* does this type of showy accomplishment receive major emphasis?

ANSWER: On at least two occasions Jim Burden is heroic in this conventional sense. He kills a rattlesnake, and he bests a midnight assailant in brutal hand-to-hand combat. In booth instances, however, the nobler aspects of the boy's achievements are played down. The account of the snake episode brings out the element of blind chance, the boy's instinctive rather than deliberate action, the weakness and torpor of the old snake, the foolish vanity of the young victor, and the exaggerated praise of him by the loyal and generous Antonia. In the fight with Wick Cutter there is stress upon Jim's distaste for the role of gallant protector, his wild flight across town afterwards in his night clothes, his terror lest the town hear of the matter and laugh at him, and his fury at Antonia for getting him into it. In some ways Jim is a genuine romantic, but he is hardly the usual shining knight. In minor episodes, such as Jake's quarrel with Ambrosch, the treatment is no more serious. Far more impressive throughout is the heroism of determination and endurance represented by Antonia. Her father's death deprives her of schooling and plunges her into exhausting farm work, but she proudly takes on man-sized tasks without complaint. Later, when she returns home, unwed and abandoned, to bear her child, she feels keenly the shattering of her dreams and the scorn of the townsfolk. Once again, however, she accepts her hard lot, and prepares to make the best life possible for her baby. Finally, after she marries Cuzak, there are years of poor crops and small returns. Never daunted, she keeps up her husband's spirits and helps him build up a flourishing farm. This, to Willa Cather, is indeed heroism.

6. Antonia marries a Bohemian immigrant, and her growing family speaks little English at home. Was she then virtually unaffected by her contacts as a girl with those born in this country?

ANSWER: Antonia as wife and mother may speak English rarely and prepare such Bohemian pastry treats as kolaches, but she has actually gained much from her friendships with Americans born here. Her mother was hardly the best of homemakers. Grandmother Burden, by contrast, was capable and efficient. Antonia evidently learned much about the domestic arts from this wise old Virginia lady. She also acquired those refinements and graces of manner summed up in the expression "nice ways." Note how much cruder and rougher she seems when restricted for a time to the company of her mother and Ambrosch. Later, when she works for the Harlings, she becomes part of a well-run household in which there are several children. After her father's death, her life at home was grim and cheerless. Now she is a member of a happy family group. She has long known how to work; she learns at this time how to play. At pleasant evening gatherings she is encouraged to tell stories, and she gladly makes candy and cookies. Moreover, the Harlings like music, and they introduce her to opera arias and plots. In town, too, she learns how to dance and how to dress, and subsequently the Widow Steavens helps her before and after she leaves with Donovan. Above all, she learns from Jim. He was her first teacher of English, and his respect for her father establishes a strong bond. Afterwards, as he goes on to college and law school and then travels extensively, he is her link with the great world beyond her farm. She is proud of all he has accomplished and talks of him admiringly to her children. Mrs. Cuzak is no copy of Mrs. Shimerda. Her sons, one feels, will go ahead, like Jim, to get the education she had to miss.

7. After Antonia, Lena Lingard is the immigrant character whose history is related at the greatest length. What significant contributions does this character make to the novel as a whole?

ANSWER: The beautiful blonde Norwegian is, first of all, one of Jim's answers to those taking a contemptuous view of immigrant girls who work for a time as servants. Lena becomes a successful businesswoman among Americans and on strictly American terms. She is a talented dressmaker with creative ability. She works hard, learns to speak English well, and deals capably with employees and customers. There is also nothing crude or coarse about her. With her soft voice and gentle manner she attracts not only poor Ole Benson, or even the wild violinist, Ordinsky, but also the banker's son, Sylvester Lovett, the courtly Colonel Raleigh, and Jim himself. Remaining single, she does so strictly by choice.

Secondly, she has a special role to play in Jim's life. During his student days in Lincoln, she gives him the feminine companionship he needs. She is an attractive girl who can sob with him over *Camille*, prepare him a pleasant dinner, and give him news of home. She asks little in return, even paying her own way at the theatre, and lets him go gracefully when he must leave for Harvard. Her charm and sympathetic understanding have helped him mature. In love with her lightly and briefly, he learns for the first time what poetry is all about.

Finally, she serves as contrast to Antonia, who is even more selfless and generous. Lena builds a house for her mother, but has no wish to sacrifice herself for husband and children. Given the facts of her childhood poverty and misery, it is understandable that she values her personal freedom. Yet she obviously falls short, as does the wealthy Tiny, of Antonia's greatness of heart.

8. *My Antonia* lacks a conventional plot. How does Willa Cather unify her varied material?

ANSWER: In the Introduction, Jim Burden declares that he has set down almost at random what he remembers of Antonia and the whole adventure of their childhood in Nebraska. We are thus warned not to expect a tightly knit plot. Yet his statement suggests three unifying factors. First of all, these are the memories of one man, Jim, already identified as a romantic personality. Most events will thus be seen from a single point of view and interpreted according to one person's standards or values. Secondly, there is Antonia herself. Although not present in all chapters, she is rarely altogether forgotten. Tiny Soderball's story, for instance, presents a kind of material success to be later contrasted with Antonia's deeper satisfactions; and Lena refers to her several times in the Lincoln scenes with Jim. Finally, the idea that the book will point up the "adventure" of early youth indicates a common element in such dissimilar experiences as the killing of the snake and the summertime picnic.

Two other devices, however, may also be considered. One is the use of minor characters as links. The Widow Steavens is mentioned several times in early sections although she will be important only when Antonia has her baby. Similar references are made to Larry Donovan and Anton Jelinek. On the other hand, Jake and Otto are recalled long after they have left the scene. Lastly, the progress of the seasons, so eloquently described, seems to carry the work along. The Nebraska landscape is essentially the same, but there is a kind of natural development as seed is planted and then crops are harvested, and as winter miseries yield to the hopefulness of spring.

9. In *My Antonia* Willa Cather creates memorable scenes rich in such contrasting moods as sorrow and joy, hope and despair. Indicate how more than one emotion is suggested in several major episodes.

ANSWER: One of the most striking examples is the incident in which Antonia revives the failing insect. There is a chill in the air, and the girl herself is thinly clad. Yet her kind, affectionate nature seems briefly to restore life and hope. The insect's weak chirping in turn recalls memories of happy evenings in Europe when eager children gathered around the fire to hear Old Hata. Those days, however have vanished, and with them Mr. Shimerda's hour of glory when he played at the weddings of noble benefactors.

Another such scene is that of the Christmas celebration. Thanks to the generous hired men, young Jim has a beautiful tree, with Otto's Austrian paper decorations adding a touch of enchantment.

Arriving for a visit, the sad Mr. Shimerda is warmly greeted and graciously entertained. A sociable man, he relaxes and for once seems almost cheerful. Nevertheless, all are aware that he must soon go out again into the bitter cold and that he will find the wretched Shimerda cave now more discouraging than ever.

The snake episode combines genuine terror with almost satiric humor as the shaken victor begins at once to strut with pride. Later at the Harling house, a sudden chill strikes during a pleasant social evening as Antonia tells of the tramp who killed himself at harvest time. On Commencement Day, Jim gives a good speech and is glad to be reconciled with Mrs. Harling. Yet afterwards he seems very much alone, and there is something wistful in the friendly tributes of the hired girls, who never had the chance to complete their schooling. Finally, the work as a whole consists of the happy memories of a man who went on to suffer many disappointments.

Harper Lee's To Kill a Mockingbird

Textual Summary and Comment

CHAPTER 1

Scout (Jean Louise) Finch narrates the story, beginning with a brief family history. Simon Finch, a fur-trapping apothecary, journeyed from England to Alabama, establishing the family, which made its living from cotton on Simon's homestead, Finch's Landing. The Civil War left the family only its land, which was the source of family incomes until the twentieth century when Atticus Finch (Scout's father) and his brother Jack left the land for careers in law and medicine. Atticus settled in Maycomb, the county seat of Maycomb County, with a reasonably successful law practice about twenty miles from Finch's Landing, where his sister Alexandra still lived.

Scout describes Maycomb as a lethargic, hot, colorless, narrow-minded town where she lives with her father, brother Jem (four years older), and the family cook, Calpurnia. Scout's mother had died when she was two.

When Scout was five, she and Jem found a new friend, Dill Harris ("Goin' on seven"), next door in Miss Rachel Haverford's collard patch. Dill was Miss Rachel's nephew from Meridian, Mississippi, who spent summers in Maycomb.

In the summertime, Jem, Scout and Dill usually played within the boundaries of Mrs. Henry Dubose's house (two doors north) and the Radley place (three doors south). The Radley place fascinated the children, because it was a popular subject of gossip and superstition in Maycomb. Arthur Radley had gotten into trouble with the law when he was a boy. Instead of being sent to the state industrial school, his father took custody of him within their house. He was not seen again for fifteen years. Many legends grew up about the Radley house and about what went on inside. Miss Stephanie Crawford, a neighborhood gossip, added fuel to the fire—a fire which included stories of crime, mutilation, curses, and insanity.

Dill was fascinated by these stories, and gave Scout and Jem the idea of making Boo Radley come out of seclusion. When Dill, always eager for some new adventure, dared Jem to run up to the house and touch it, Jem thought things over for a few days. Finally, filled with fear, he accepted the dare. He ran up, touched the house, and ran back. As the three children stared at the old house, they thought they saw an inside shutter move.

COMMENT: Many themes and plot-themes emerge in Chapter 1. Great emphasis is placed on the world of Scout, Jem, and Dill—a small world bounded by a few houses and composed of only a few people. From the limited knowledge of this small childish world at the novel's opening, Jem and Scout broaden with the passing of years and events. By the time the novel reaches its conclusion, they will have learned much more about human nature. Also, Miss Lee emphasizes the Radley family. They are the focal point for the development of numerous themes to come. For example, when old Mr. Radley died, Calpurnia did something she had never been known to do before. She spoke evil about a white man when she said, "There goes the meanest man ever God blew breath into." Finally, there are the themes relating to family and the Maycomb setting. They increase in importance from chapter to chapter.

CHAPTERS 2–3

Dill returned to Mississippi at the end of the summer. Although she was looking forward to school more than anything in her life, Scout's first day at school was a disappointment. When Miss Caroline tried to teach reading, Scout was bored. Much to Miss Caroline's dismay, Scout was already accomplished at reading and writing. She told Scout to tell her father not to teach her anything more because it would interfere with her reading. Later, at lunch time, Walter Cunningham had no food with him. When the teacher tried to give him a quarter, the boy would not take it. Scout made the mistake of trying to explain the reason to Miss Caroline. The Cunninghams were poor country folks who had been hit hard by the Depression and were too proud to accept charity. For her trouble, Scout got her fingers cracked. Thinking that Walter Cunningham was the cause of her difficulty, Scout tried to beat him up. Jem would not let her. Instead, he invited the boy to lunch at their house.

That afternoon, Miss Caroline saw a cootie crawl out of Burris Ewell's hair. She was shocked by this and told the boy to go home and wash his hair. The boy really did not care, however, and became abusive, since he was in school only because the truant officer had made him come. He did not plan to return. That night Scout had a talk with her father. She said she hoped that Atticus would allow her to stay home from school like Burris Ewell. However, he explained to her that the Ewells were a different kind of people. They did not care about learning and had been a disgrace to Maycomb for generations. Then Atticus made a bargain with his daughter. He told Scout that he would continue to read to her every night provided she would go back to school and promise not to tell her teacher about it.

COMMENT: These two chapters can be considered together for they contain the story of Scout's first experience away from her narrow world at home. The reader must remember that although she was bright for her age, Scout was only six. Whatever she had learned thus far, she had learned at home from her father, her brother, Calpurnia, and a few neighbors. Therefore, she had much to learn from and about the rest of the world. For example, Scout was a town girl and not a farm girl like many of the other children in the class. Miss Caroline, the teacher, was not from Maycomb, and could not be expected to know or to understand the peculiarities of the people of Maycomb. The little girl could not comprehend why Miss Caroline did not have a better understanding. With her limited experience, Scout thought that people were alike everywhere. Therefore, she thought that her teacher should automatically know that the Cunninghams were poor. Also she thought that her teacher should understand that the Cunninghams, and other people of Maycomb, were too proud to accept anything that they could not pay back. But Maycomb was farm country, and farmers were a "set breed of men," prizing independence more than a full stomach. Miss Caroline was from the city; Scout learned that city people were different.

Note, however, that Miss Caroline seemed to have learned something that first day at school too. In the morning, she became disturbed when Scout tried to tell her about Walter Cunningham. In the afternoon she was quite willing to listen to one of the older children when he explained to her about Burris Ewell. Thus the reader will find this entire novel is a series of experiences in which one character will gain new insights from his association with the others.

There are two important new names introduced in these chapter—Walter Cunningham and Burris Ewell. Both are from the poor, rural section of the county. However, the reader should notice the difference in their characters. Walter is proud and independent; he won't accept charity. He apologizes for still being in the first grade. At lunch Atticus speaks to him about farming as though he were a grown man. On the other hand, Burris Ewell is surly. He dares Miss Caroline to make him do anything. Here, therefore, the author presents the reader with the first series of character contrasts. These will be important to the reader throughout the entire novel, especially if he expects to be able to understand fully the theme of the story.

CHAPTERS 4–6

Because Scout was in the first grade, she got out of school thirty minutes earlier than her brother. This meant a walk home alone past the dreaded Radley house. Usually she would run by it. There were two giant oaks on the Radley property. One day as Scout was running past, she noticed something shiny in a knothole of one of the trees. Examining it, she found two pieces of chewing gum. When she decided they were all right to eat, she put them into her mouth. When Jem came home, he made her spit out the gum. Anything found on the Radley place might be poison. On the last day of school the children found a box with two pennies in it. They did not know what to make of the situation, but they decided to keep the pennies.

Two days later Dill arrived. As usual he was full of wild stories and anxious to play games of make-believe. The group decided to play a game modeled on the life of Boo Radley. One of the stories about him was that he had stabbed his father with a pair of scissors, so the children began to act this out every day. They continued until Atticus caught them and took away the scissors.

While the two boys played a scissorless version of their Boo Radley game, Scout became friendly with Miss Maudie Atkinson, a benevolent neighbor who had grown up with Atticus's brother Jack. The two of them would sit on Miss Maudie's porch and talk. One day they had a talk about Boo Radley, and Miss Maudie tried to explain the mystery of the Radley family. Recalling that Arthur had been nice to her as a boy, she called the Radley house a sad place. She denied the rumors about Boo as "three-fourth colored folks and one-fourth Stephanie Crawford." The next morning Jem and Dill decided they would try to drop a note into the Radley house by using a fishing pole. While they were doing this, Atticus came by and once more warned them about bothering the Radleys.

On the last night before Dill had to return home to Mississippi, the boys hatched a plot. They decided to sneak through the back of the Radley property and take a peak through one of the windows. While doing this, they saw the shadow of a man pass by. As they ran toward the back fence, a shotgun blast went off. The three of them hurried even more and managed to escape. However, when they got home, Jem realized that he had lost his pants. He had had to squirm out of them while crawling under the Radley fence. Thus he found himself faced with another problem. That night, after everyone had gone to bed, he went back after his pants. Luckily, they were still there.

COMMENT: These chapters reveal the children's reaction to the Radley place and to the Radleys themselves. It is a typically childish viewpoint. For example, Scout could not eat the gum because anything found on the Radley place might be poison. Also in these chapters there is childish imitation. The life which the Radleys led was very unusual. The family remained almost constantly in the house. The children, with a natural inclination to imitate the unusual in the adult world, wanted to play the Radley game. The Radley game was their Maycomb substitute for playing cowboys and Indians. With a typical childlike love of adventure and a curiosity to discover the unknown, Scout, Jem, and Dill longed to discover the answer to the Radley mystery. They could not understand it as Atticus or Miss Maudie did. They had to try to find out for themselves what went on inside the secretive home. Thus the incident of the note on the end of the fishing pole and the night visit. Notice, however, that although the children are curious, they are not foolishly brave. For example, they have the length of the fishing pole between them and the house. Also they chose the darkness of night to sneak up to the window.

CHAPTER 7

School started again. "The second grade was as bad as the first, only worse." One afternoon, Jem told Scout that when he returned to get his pants, they were hanging over the fence. Some one had mended the tear—"Not like a lady sewed 'em, . . . All crooked." After this, the children began to find more things in the tree. First a ball of twine, then two soap dolls, and finally an old watch. They decided they should write a thank-you note to whoever was giving them these things. However, when they went to put the note into the knothole, Jem and Scout found that it had been filled in with cement. Nathan Radley, Boo's brother, said he had done this because the tree was dying and this was the way to save it. Atticus came home from work and told Jem, "That tree's as healthy as you are." Scout noticed that Jem had been crying when he came in that night.

COMMENT: In this chapter the children begin to stop taking things for granted. They try to figure out how the articles in the tree got there. When they conclude that it is probably Boo Radley who is putting them there, they do the logical thing. They write a note which they intend to put into the tree. There is a difference, however, in the way in which each one reacts to the cement. Scout is still very young. She knows that Nathan Radley is being mean, but it does not affect her personally. On the other hand, the older Jem is more sensitive and feels things more deeply. He cries not for himself but for Boo Radley. He cannot comprehend how one man can be deliberately cruel to another. In his childlike way, Jem realizes that Boo Radley must have enjoyed putting those articles into the tree for them. Jem also realizes that the Boo Bradley was very considerate to sew his pants. Because of his youth, he does not know how to fight adult cruelty. Thus he cries.

CHAPTER 8

Usually Maycomb had hot summers and mild winters. When snow fell one night, Scout thought it was the end of the world. She had never seen it before. Because of this unexpected cold weather, everyone had fires going at home. During the night, Miss Maudie's house caught fire. Since all the houses were old wooden ones, everyone had to go out into the cold night. While Scout was watching the firemen at work, someone slipped a blanket around her shoulders. Later, first Jem and then Atticus realize that Boo Radley must have done this. Jem is afraid to return the blanket; he is afraid of what Nathan may do to Boo. Atticus agrees that they should keep the blanket and the incident to themselves.

COMMENT: Kindness is a prominent theme in this chapter. There is the unexpected kindness of Boo Radley. An air of mystery pervades the blanket incident because no one realizes at the time that the action is being taken. The effect on Scout is typical. She is all right until it dawns on her what has happened. Then she is sick with fright at the thought that Boo Radley stood right behind her and touched her. On the other hand, Jem reacts differently again. His first concern is Boo. In a babbling attempt to defend him, Jem blurts out the story of his pants to Atticus. His compassion is genuine. He is afraid of what Nathan may do to Boo. As soon as his fear for Boo is relieved, however, he relaxes and makes a joke at Scout's expense—he re-enacts the scene for her benefit, frightening her terribly.

Courage is also an important theme, embodied in Miss Maudie's character. The day after her house burned down, she did not wallow in self-pity. She laughed and said that she was glad that the whole thing had happened. Now she would be able to build a smaller house, take in roomers, and have more room for the plants which she loved so dearly. The children were perplexed by her unexpected good humor, but they admired her good-natured bravery in the face of personal tragedy.

CHAPTER 9

Chapter 9 introduces the reader to the main action of the story—Atticus Finch's defense of the Negro Tom Robinson. "Maycomb's usual disease," as Atticus calls it, begins to show itself. The narrow-minded bigotry of the townspeople and of the Finch family is hard for Scout to cope with. First there was Cecil Jacobs who announced in the schoolyard that Scout's daddy defended "niggers." Scout denied it, but ran home to get an explanation. Atticus told her that he was going to defend Tom Robinson, a member of Calpurnia's church. He explains that the case is very important to him personally, and requests that Jem and Scout try to ignore the talk they will hear around town. Next day, Scout is ready to fight Cecil Jacobs again, but remembers Atticus' request and walks away from a fight for the first time in her life.

Some time later they left for Finch's Landing for the customary family Christmas celebration with Uncle Jack, Aunt Alexandra, and cousin Francis. Francis taunts Scout by calling Atticus a "nigger-lover," saying that "he's ruinin' the family." Scout flies to her father's defense with fists and "bathroom invective," but gets a spanking from Uncle Jack. Later he apologizes when he hears her side of the story, and promises not to tell Atticus what Scout and Francis really fought about.

COMMENT: This chapter is very important if the reader is going to understand the full meaning of this novel. Atticus has been appointed to defend a Negro. Scout is ridiculed by one of her schoolmates because of this. Here is shown the attitude of the townspeople toward the Negroes. Then on Christmas Scout hears the same talk from her cousin Francis. This shows the attitude of the Finch family itself about the problem. Both Cecil Jacobs and Francis are, of course, echoing what they have heard the adults say on the subject. Obviously, to both family and townspeople it seems that Atticus Finch is making a mistake. How does Scout act about this matter: She wants to fight with her fists. But she soon learns that this is not the way to combat a dispute over ideas. Uncle Jack spanks her, but in her mind he has been unfair. Uncle Jack had not listened to her side of the story. When she can tell him about it in the quiet of her room, he says that he is sorry.

What then is the picture of the world in the mind of this child, and how does it foreshadow the future events of the story? At first Scout fights with her fists because she does not know how to fight any other way. Then she sees adult injustice applied to her by Uncle Jack, someone whom she loves. She begins to realize that lack of knowledge and lack of forethought often lead people to do things that they might not otherwise do. Later, when Scout sees the injustice performed by the people against the Negro Tom Robinson, she is going to be able to have just a little bit better understanding of the reasons for it.

CHAPTER 10

The first nine chapters give us a picture of Atticus Finch as a kind and understanding man. He is also an upright man who is trying to raise his children properly. In this chapter we get a clearer picture of him. First we see him through the eyes of his children. To them he is old and feeble because he can't play football. Then an event occurs to change this picture. A mad dog comes down the street. It is Atticus who is called upon to do the shooting. His children see him now as a brave man. Scout wants to brag about this to all her friends, but Jem tells her not to.

COMMENT: To the reader this chapter might seem out of place. It appears to be an unrelated incident. However, it serves to help prepare the reader for what is to follow. In a sense, it sums up the character of Atticus Finch. Thus far we have seen him as a very quiet and serious person. Now the author shows another side of his character. He is brave but in a different way. He does the day-to-day actions so well that when he is called upon to do an extraordinary action, its performance comes naturally to him.

Again we see a contrast in the attitude of the two children. The younger Scout still cannot understand why things should or should not be done. For example, she cannot understand why Atticus never told his children about his ability to shoot. On the other hand, Jem, the older child, is beginning to have a sense of values. He realizes that being a man, and more importantly, a gentleman, is not just in acting and talking. It is knowing when to act and when to talk. In childlike simplicity he says, "Atticus is a gentleman, just like me." More than ever he wants to be like his father.

CHAPTER 11

Mrs. Henry Lafayette Dubose, an old lady who lived near the Finch house, made a point of being cantankerous and scolded Jem and Scout every time she saw them. Sometimes she would scold them for something they did; sometimes for the way they were dressed. The children, of course, hated her, but there was nothing they could do about it. One day she made some remarks about Atticus, calling him a "nigger-lover." On the way home that day, Jem took the baton which he had bought for his sister and used it to wreck all of Mrs. Dubose's camellias. When Atticus learned of this, he made Jem apologize. Jem had to read to Mrs. Dubose every day for a month. During this time she had repeated fits which frightened Scout. Soon after, Mrs. Dubose died. Atticus then explained to the children that she had been a morphine addict. When she found out that she did not have long to live, she determined to break the habit. The purpose of Jem's reading was to distract her attention while she was having her fits. By the time of her death, she had won her battle.

COMMENT: At the close of this chapter, Atticus refers to Mrs. Dubose as the bravest person he ever knew. This statement is difficult to understand, especially since it comes from a man whom she had openly abused. But Jem learns that sometimes people say and do things because they cannot help themselves. For example, Mrs. Dubose was a sick old lady. She took out her suffering on Scout and Jem. Yet fundamentally she was a courageous person. Atticus admired her strength of will and determination to die "beholden to nothing and nobody." This was adult bravery. Atticus wanted the children to understand that courage is more than "a man with a gun in his hand." The camellia which she sent to Jem was a symbol of strength. Jem had tried to destroy the shrubs, but they grew back because they were strong. Mrs. Dubose had almost been destroyed by morphine, but she conquered it finally. She was as strong as her camellias.

Chapter 11 brings Part I of this novel to a close. The children have seen three examples of adult bravery. First there was Miss Maudie who faced the difficulty of rebuilding her house after the fire. Then there was Atticus who never bragged about his ability to shoot. But when he was needed, he was unafraid to face the mad dog. Finally there was Mrs. Dubois who faced bravely the prospect of a painful death. Now Jem and Scout must come face to face with the greatest test of their young lives—the trial of Tom Robinson.

CHAPTER 12

This chapter introduces the reader to the second part of the novel. Atticus was away at the state capital, so Calpurnia asked the children if they wanted to go to church with her. Scout and Jem thus enter into the world of the Negro. There are many things that are strange to them. The Negroes, for example, do not sing from hymn books. Also Reverend Sykes is quite open about the way he addresses his parishioners, even calling out the names of certain people who had done wrong. The collection that Sunday was for Helen Robinson, Tom's wife. Because Scout did not understand why she did not go to work, Reverend Sykes explained that no white person wanted to hire Tom Robinson's wife. Later, when Calpurnia and the children arrived home, they found Aunt Alexandra on the front porch waiting for them.

COMMENT: There are many interesting little points in this chapter that the reader should not pass over if he is going to appreciate its value to the story. First, there is the greater distance which is developing between the older Jem and the little sister. He understands more easily and tries to be more serious than she. Furthermore, he is beginning adopt a superior attitude where she is concerned. Secondly, there is the comment that Calpurnia makes to Lulu. This woman resented Jem and Scout coming to the Negro church. Calpurnia told her that it was the same God. Thirdly, when Reverend Sykes asked for more money for Helen, Jem insisted to Calpurnia that he and Scout use their own rather than what she wanted to give them. This shows his desire to be like the adults. Fourthly, there is the attitude of Calpurnia about the way she acts. She wants to be educated and to speak like the white folks; and yet with her own people, she acts and speaks as they do. All of these facts put Jem and Scout right into the middle of the Tom Robinson plot. Jem is trying to be mature, but Scout still does not understand many things. Both children are amazed by what they see in the Negro Church. They are also surprised by Calpurnia's actions. Scout cannot understand why the Negro woman would hide her knowledge when she was among her own people. But Calpurnia had her reasons, and they were good ones.

In this chapter the reader might make a contrast between Calpurnia and Lulu. Calpurnia seemed to realize that if she were to be accepted by the white people, she would have to improve herself. Thus she had learned to read, and she had also taught her son Zeebo. On the other hand, not only did Lulu not want to be accepted by the white people, but she did not want to accept them when they came to her. The result was that Calpurnia did find a place where she was welcome. This is not to say that she was accepted into white society in general. However, she had become an important part of a white family which was willing to accept her for what she was personally. In fact, Atticus Finch looked upon Calpurnia not as a servant, but as a very necessary and much-loved member of his family.

CHAPTER 13

Aunt Alexandra came to spend the summer with her brother's family. Jem and Scout weren't very happy about this arrangement, Atticus knew that he would need all the help he could get during the trial of Tom Robinson. Aunt Alexandra made herself right at home, determined to have a "feminine influence" on Scout. Scout resigned herself to a long summer. Aunt Alexandra tries to tell the children about their family background and how proud they should be of it. Atticus at first told Jem and Scout that they should listen to her. However, he realized afterwards that her "preoccupation with heredity" and "gentle breeding " stemmed from a false sense of values. He told the children to forget it.

COMMENT: This chapter introduces the theme of the importance of family background and the caste system in Maycomb. Aunt Alexandra is impressed by a good name. To her this means a family who can trace its ancestry, and who has lived on the same land for a long period of time. Of course, she regards the Finch family and their estate, Finch's Landing, as inviolate proof of their moral and social worth. She would carefully conceal any black marks on the family name. For example, she is shocked to discover that the children know the story of their Cousin Joshua, who had been in jail for having tried to shoot another man. In contrast to his sister, Atticus gave little thought to family breeding. He was more interested in the personal value of an individual. He never told Jem and Scout much about the family background because he did not think it important enough to discuss. He did the best he could to give them a genuine sense of values and behavior.

CHAPTER 14

A few days later Aunt Alexandra overheard Scout ask Atticus about going to visit at Calpurnia's house. Upset by this request, Alexandra urges her brother to fire the Negro cook, but he won't do it. Calpurnia has been a faithful member of the family too long. After the quarrel, Jem tells Scout that she should avoid upsetting Atticus because he's got a great deal to worry about with the trial. Scout thinks that Atticus wouldn't worry about anything. That night the children discovered Dill under Scout's bed. He had run away from home, and he related a fictional tale of his neglect by his new father. He wasn't happy and wanted to be with his friends. Jem's act of treason in telling Atticus about Dill is forgiven when Atticus gets permission for Dill to stay.

COMMENT: This chapter reemphasizes Aunt Alexandra's feelings about Negroes. She does not want her family associated with them in any way. Alexandra's main concern was the preservation of a good family name in order to keep one's place in society. When her two brothers left Finch's Landing, she stayed on to take care of the place. But her life was far from happy, for she had made an unfortunate marriage. Her husband was more interested in fishing than in anything else. Now she sees the family name in danger of being completely ruined by the Tom Robinson affair and by Calpurnia's influence.

Dill provides a contrast to Aunt Alexandra. Where she puts faith in a family name, at the expense of truth and personal happiness, Dill ran away from home to find happiness. The remarriage of his mother should have given him security. Instead it gave him a greater feeling of not being wanted. In other words, mere home and family name were not enough. Dill had the courage to seek happiness, instead of resigning to a false value system.

CHAPTER 15

One night some men from town came and stood outside the Finch house. Jem could hear them talking with his father, but he did not know what about. He was frightened because he thought a mob had come after Atticus. But these were friends who had come to warn Atticus that there might be trouble when they moved Tom into the county jail next evening. The next night Atticus took the car and drove away. Later Jem, Scout, and Dill got dressed and went into town. There they found Atticus sitting in front of the jail. They did not go near him, however. When they saw some men get out of cars, Jem was again frightened and he and Scout ran to their father's side. Atticus was frightened for the children and tried to get them to go home, but they would not. A man grabbed Jem by the collar to send him home, but Scout kicked him. She spotted Walter Cunningham's father in the crowd and began chatting loudly about Walter and the Cunningham money troubles. Scout made Mr. Cunningham ashamed. He turned to the other men, and they all left together. Atticus was relieved, but he was also proud of his children because they had wanted to be with him when he was in trouble. The children were not at first aware that Mr. Underwood, editor of the Maycomb *Tribune*, had been watching the proceedings with a loaded double-barreled shotgun.

COMMENT: In this chapter the author describes contrasting scenes—the crowd outside the Finch house and the mob outside the jail. Jem is witness to both of these, and he is frightened in both cases. In the first scene, it is ignorance that makes him afraid. He cannot see who the men in the crowd are, nor can he hear what they are saying. His imagination runs wild with thoughts about the Ku Klux Klan and other lynch mobs that he has read about, but never seen. In the second case, it is the sight of real danger that makes him afraid. He sees the mob approach his father, and he knows what they want. Jem's reaction to fear in the first scene is to panic. He screams at his father that the phone is ringing. His reaction in the jail scene is to run to his father's side and staunchly refuse to leave. Knowledge has given Jem a sense of control over the situation. He does not lose control of himself or become blinded by emotion. The crowd is blinded by emotion and ignorance. But in their case, the ignorance is self-imposed, not simply lack of knowledge of the facts. Scout shames them by her innocent guilelessness.

CHAPTER 16

Monday, the day for Tom Robinson's trial finally arrived. Atticus told the children not to go downtown; so they had to wait until lunchtime for news. To Scout the day seemed just like a Saturday. The whole county appeared to be coming into Maycomb for the trial. Miss Maudie thought it was morbid, the way everyone acted as though it was a Roman carnival, but Jem told her that the trial had to be public. When Atticus came home for lunch, he told the children that the jury had been selected. After he returned to town, Jem, Scout, and Dill followed. They had to be careful that Atticus did not see them; so they waited until all the white folks had gone into the courthouse. But there wasn't even standing room left. Luckily they met Reverend Sykes who took them with him to the Negro balcony where they were able to find seats.

COMMENT: This chapter yields yet another series of contrasts. On the one hand, there is the ever present snob—Aunt Alexandra—who thinks of the Negro only as a servant. She cautions Atticus against discussing things in front of Calpurnia. She tolerates the presence of a Negro because it's convenient. On the other hand, there is Braxton Bragg Underwood, an intense, profane man, who "despises Negroes, won't have one near him." Yet he is the one who, with his shotgun, made the evening watch with Atticus. It might be argued that he was protecting Atticus, not Tom Robinson. But Atticus was guarding the Negro, and many townspeople were highly critical of them for defending Tom. Miss Lee reinforces this contrast with numerous other examples, illustrating two typical sides of the Southern dilemma. For example, there is the incident of Miss Maudie and the narrow-minded foot-washing Baptists who hate her garden as a sinful display of vanity. Yet she refuses to go to the trial because she thinks it is a spectacle. They are marching on to see "justice done." There is also Mr. Dolphus Raymond who lives with a Negro woman. In spite of local criticism, he does what he wants to do and what he feels is right. Finally, there is Atticus himself. He did not ask for this case, he was appointed to it. However, he does not use that as an excuse for not doing the best job he can. He intends to defend Tom Robinson no matter what anyone might say. The case has become a matter of conscience with him. The author's sympathies, revealed through Scout's naive eyes, obviously lie with Atticus and men like him, who have the courage to do what they consider morally right, even though distasteful.

CHAPTERS 17–18

The trial began, Judge Taylor presiding. Mr. Gilmer, the solicitor, called two witnesses. The first, Sheriff Heck Tate, reported the routine facts of the case. Mr. Ewell had come to get him. The sheriff found the girl badly bruised. She identified Robinson as her attacker. He testifies that the bruises on Mayella Ewell are on the right side of her face. The second witness, Bob Ewell, tells his version of the rape. He relates how he came home and found Tom Robinson with his daughter. His attitude is surly, but Judge Taylor makes him answer all the questions. The most important part of his testimony occurs when Atticus tricks him into showing that he is lefthanded. Jem is jubilant about this because he feels that his father now has a very good chance of winning the case, if he can prove that Mayella was beaten by her father.

When Mayella comes to the witness stand, she is very nervous. She is afraid of Atticus and of what he is going to ask her. Her story is that she had asked Tom Robinson to break up a chiffarobe for her. When she went into the house to get something, Tom followed her. She turned around, and he attacked her. After Atticus had her repeat her story very carefully, he asked Tom Robinson to stand up. As it turned out, Tom had only one good arm, his right. The left had been mangled in a cotton gin when he was a boy. It was obvious to everyone that for him to rape a strong country girl like Mayella would have been very difficult.

COMMENT: In these two chapters, the author gives a vivid picture of the other side of the case. The Ewells, we discovered earlier in the story, were ignorant country folk. They did not go to school, and they were not clean. Bob Ewell was a surly man who spent his relief checks on liquor rather than on food. Mayella, as we see in Chapter 18, is a lonely, frightened girl. She has no friends of her own age, and little social life.

The contrast between these poor whites and the Negroes is immediately apparent. Even though the colored people were outcasts, they had self-respect. Calpurnia had learned to read, and she had taught Zeebo to read. The Negro church-goers were poor, but they contributed their dimes to help Helen Robinson. The question that arises in the mind of the reader is why Bob Ewell should be so anxious to accuse a Negro of raping his daughter. The implication is that he did it as a cover-up for the fact that he had himself beaten Mayella. Bob Ewell is a white man, but he is not accepted by his own group. He is surly in court because he feels inferior to Atticus and to Judge Taylor. He is dirty and poor because he is too lazy to be anything else. He is, in fact, lower than the Negroes, and hates them more for it. The only way he can maintain his white superiority is by persecuting a Negro. Tom Robinson becomes the scapegoat in Ewell's battle for pseudo-self-respect, the only means Ewell has of achieving social equality with the other whites. For him, it will justify his squalid, unproductive life. Unfortunately for him, however, he has met his match in Atticus Finch. Instead of emerging as a hero, Bob Ewell emerges as a fool. Atticus has proven publicly that the Ewells were lying about Tom Robinson.

CHAPTER 19

When Tom Robinson gets on the witness stand, he tells a very different story. He describes how Mayella had been asking him for help for several months. On the day of the alleged rape, Mayella had put her arms around him and kissed him. She tried to get him to kiss her, but he was too frightened to do anything but run when he got the chance. Mr. Gilmer, of course, tried to make Tom look like a liar. The vicious manner in which he did this caused Dill to burst into tears. Scout had to take him outside so he would not disturb the whole courtroom.

COMMENT: This chapter paints a vivid picture of loneliness and of the desperation to which it can drive a person. Mayella Ewell waited for months for a chance to get some true affection. But Tom Robinson's life hangs in the balance because of her. Being a Negro, he could not yield to Mayella without getting the blame for her actions. By the same token, he did not dare strike her or push her in order to get away. If he had done so, he still could have been accused of attacking a white woman. Finally, the fact that he did run away when Bob Ewell appeared made it possible for the Ewells to say anything they wanted about him. Because he was a Negro in a white community he could count on no safety whatsoever. The townspeople always rallied to the defense of a white person, no matter how despicable. The fact that Tom Robinson, a Negro, should help Mayella Ewell, a white girl, because he felt sorry for her, was ironic. Mr. Gilmer sneered at him for suggesting that this was what he had done.

The contrasting reactions of Dill and Scout are revealed in this chapter. Dill is himself an outcast of a sort. The author does not tell us much about his life in Meridian, but we do know that Dill's real father is not dead. We also know that Dill had been shuffled from relative to relative. When his mother remarried, he still did not feel wanted; so he ran away. Thus, Dill could not bear the sight of another outcast, Tom, being mistreated. It made him sick and caused him to weep. On the other hand, Scout had always been loved, had always had the security of a home. Her reaction is that, after all, this is Mr. Gilmer's job. Tom Robinson is just a Negro. True, she does realize that Mayella Ewell is probably the loneliest person in the world, and that Atticus is much kinder than Mr. Gilmer, but she is not particularly moved to pity by what she sees.

CHAPTER 20

Outside the courthouse, Scout and Dill met Mr. Dolphus Raymond. He gave Dill a sip from the bottle he carried in a paper sack. The townspeople had always thought that Mr. Dolphus had whiskey in that bottle, but it was really only Coca-Cola. Feeling better, Dill returned to the courtroom with Scout. Atticus was addressing the jury and pointing out that the prosecutor had proven nothing against Tom. In fact, the truth was obviously the opposite of what the Ewells claimed. Atticus ended his speech with a plea to the jury to believe him in the name of God.

COMMENT: We can compare the story of Mr. Dolphus with the speech made by Atticus Finch. Mr. Dolphus was, in a certain sense, lying to the townspeople. He created for their benefit the impression that he was a drunk. In this way, although they disapproved of his life, they left him alone. They said he could not help himself. The same may be said of the case against Tom Robinson. The townspeople do not approve of the Ewells, but the Ewells are white. Because of this, they can be forgiven their way of life. The evidence is against the Negro because, just as nobody could see inside the paper sack where Mr. Dolphus hid his Coca-Cola, so nobody saw inside the Ewell cabin. Mr. Dolphus could pretend whiskey, and Bob Ewell could pretend rape. However, God created everybody with an equal right to justice. Therefore, Atticus pleads with the jury, in the name of God, to make a just decision to free the Negro.

CHAPTERS 21–22

When Calpurnia came to the courtroom, it was the first time that Atticus was aware that the children were present. He sent them home for supper. After eating, they returned to town to await the jury's decision. The obvious happens and Tom Robinson is convicted. As Atticus walked out, all the Negroes stood up, as a gesture of respect for him. The next morning the back porch is covered with gifts of food that the colored folks had sent. Atticus is so overcome with emotion that he cannot eat. Later, downtown, Bob Ewell spit in his face and swore to get him. Although he had lost the case, Atticus had proven that Bob Ewell was a liar.

COMMENT: In these two chapters we see the reaction of the characters to the trial. That Tom Robinson would be found guilty was a foregone conclusion. That Jem would weep because of it was not. He had been so certain that Atticus would win the case that the verdict of guilty caused tears of indignation. His own moral rectitude and innocence had made him believe that everyone must see the truth and have the courage to do right. He learned that night that adults sometimes have integrity only when it is expedient. When Miss Maudie cut him a piece from the large cake, it was a sign that he had taken a giant step toward manhood.

On the other hand, Dill's reaction is perhaps more to be expected. He had already seen much of the adult world and had suffered personally from it. That he should become cynical is not surprising. He had given up the hope of expecting adults to be rational. His desire to become a clown and to laugh at the ways of adults is an example of this cynicism.

Miss Maudie and Miss Stephanie give us the contrasting views of the townspeople. Miss Maudie is their conscience for she sees the right and realizes that Atticus stands for it. Miss Stephanie represents their self-righteousness. She is blinded to justice and spends her mental energy being shocked by such things as the children sitting in the Negro balcony. Bob Ewell represents the bitterness of the townspeople. Like them he pretends to be good, but malevolence lurks under the surface. When the cloak of false virtue was removed from him by Atticus Finch, he struck back in the only way he knew. He promised more malevolent violence.

CHAPTER 23

There is very little action in this chapter. Because of Bob Ewell's threat to kill Atticus, the children are frightened. He calms them by telling them that Bob Ewell is all talk. There is a general discussion of the trial and of how Jem and Scout react to it.

COMMENT: Miss Lee reemphasizes Atticus's rational judgment in the discussion he has with the children. He explains that Tom would have gone free had twelve boys like Jem been on the jury. Jem is reasonable, but at Tom's trial they saw what happens when something comes between a man and his reason. Atticus also tells them how despicable he thinks it is to take advantage of a Negro's ignorance. For the first time, the children find out that one member of the jury, a Cunningham, had originally fought for acquittal. Scout is thrilled and announces plans to get to know Walter better and invite him to dinner. Aunt Alexandra gets upset, calling him "trash." As the children review the events of the past few weeks and months, they try to understand adults and their behavior. Scout decides that all this talk about classes of people is nonsense. "There's just one kind of folks, folks." Jem reflects that if people are all alike, why do they go out of their way to despise one another? He says, "I think I'm beginning to understand why Boo Radley's stayed shut up. . . . Its because he *wants* to stay inside."

CHAPTER 24

Late in August of that summer, Aunt Alexandra was having a missionary tea. Jem and Dill were off swimming. Scout was helping to entertain the ladies. The talk was about the pagan Mrunas. The ladies were sorry for these poor, far-off people who lived such a savage life. They had no sympathy, however, for Tom Robinson, his wife, and the other Negroes. Suddenly, Atticus came home and called Alexandra into the kitchen. Tom Robinson was dead. He had tried to escape from the prison farm, and the guards had shot him.

COMMENT: The irony of this chapter is quite obvious. The Mrunas were far away and posed no threat. It was quite all right for the missionary ladies to feel sorry for their uncivilized and un-Christian life. On the other hand, the Negroes were close by and most of them tried to lead Christian lives. Tom Robinson was in jail on an unjust charge. Even in the face of this contradiction, the ladies felt justified in viewing the Negroes as inferiors. They agreed that Atticus had been wrong in trying to defend one of them. Even Alexandra, who had previously opposed her brother, could see the evasion in this type of thinking.

The character most affected by the missionary tea was Scout. She was in the world of adults—a world which often mystified her. But she did learn a lesson from her aunt. After Atticus left with Calpurnia to go to the Robinson cabin, Aunt Alexandra had to do the serving. Nevertheless, she did not allow her emotions to show. She would not appear before these other women as anything but a lady. Scout learned a lesson in bravery. She also learned that Aunt Alexandra knew how to handle herself in a difficult situation. In other words, Scout concluded that background did mean something. Aunt Alexandra was able to continue with the missionary tea because she had been trained in a certain tradition. One part of that tradition was that one never allows a personal problem or feeling to interfere with the courteous treatment of other people.

CHAPTER 25

Atticus had picked up Jem and Dill on the way to Tom's, so they were present when Helen Robinson learned of the death of her husband. She fainted and had to be carried into her house. The town reacted to the death in its usual manner—with indifference. This was just one more "nigger" who had "cut and run." Mr. Underwood wrote an editorial in his paper likening Tom's death to the "senseless slaughter of songbirds by hunters and children." Bob Ewell "said it made one down and about two more to go."

COMMENT: This chapter is a bitter comment on the people of Maycomb. There was little sorrow that a man had died needlessly. Even Mr. Underwood's editorial made little impression on these people. They would forgive him his attempt at being dramatic. No one would cancel either subscriptions or advertising because of it. Scout finally realized the significance of the whole situation. Once Mayella Ewell started screaming, Tom Robinson was a dead man, Scout realized that "in the secret courts of men's hearts Atticus had no case." In these circumstances, no Negro had the slightest chance of winning. It was color that determined right and wrong, truth and falsehood, and Tom Robinson was unfortunately black.

CHAPTER 26

At school that fall, during a discussion of current events, Miss Gates mentioned how terrible it was that Hitler was persecuting the Jews. Yet, on the night of the trial, Scout had heard her say that it was about time that somebody had taught the Negroes a lesson. The little girl could not understand how her teacher could hate Hitler so much, and then turn around and persecute the Negroes at home.

COMMENT: Miss Lee relentlessly pursues the contradictions and evasions of the bigoted mind. Miss Gates is well educated, but this does not seem to have helped her to be reasonable. Jem is upset by what Scout tells him, but not because of Miss Gates. He is trying to put the whole trial incident out of his mind. His youthful idealism was outraged by the jury's decision. Now he wants to try to forget the entire affair.

CHAPTER 27

Although things were pretty quiet after the trial, three things happened in Maycomb that indirectly affected the Finches. First, Bob Ewell got and quickly lost a job with the WPA. He blamed Atticus for his being fired. Then, one Sunday night, Ewell tried to burglarize Judge Taylor's house. Ewell also started annoying Helen Robinson. Link Deas, who had given her a job, had to threaten Ewell with jail in order to make him stop.

COMMENT: The events of this chapter foreshadow the final action of the novel. Bob Ewell had threatened to get Atticus Finch. After the death of Tom Robinson, he had said that there was one down and two to go. He tried to get Judge Taylor by burglarizing his house. But the judge was at home, and the attempt was not successful. Then Ewell tried to get at Atticus by annoying Helen Robinson. Thus, the scene is now set for the final blow. It is Halloween, and Scout and Jem must go out alone past the Radley place to the school.

CHAPTER 28

Walking by the two big oaks on the Radley place, Scout and Jem are frightened by Cecil Jacobs who jumps out at them. Later, at the school, Scout falls asleep and misses her cue to come out on stage. She is too embarrassed to let anyone see her. Jem agrees to wait until everyone has left before taking Scout home. Because Scout has her costume on, Jem must lead her toward home. On the way, they sense that someone is following them. Suddenly they are attacked. When Scout finally gets herself untangled, she sees a strange man carrying Jem across the street. Running home, she finds that her brother is hurt. When Sheriff Tate arrives, he finds Bob Ewell lying dead under the oak tree.

COMMENT: The author carefully builds the suspense on the night of Ewell's death. First the two children are frightened by Cecil Jacobs. They come home alone in the dark. The Radley house lurks in the background. A stranger comes to their rescue when they are attacked. Thus the climax of the story is reached. Bob Ewell had sworn to get Atticus Finch. He had tried and failed. Now he lies dead under the oak tree on the Radley place.

There is a certain significance in the pageant too. It had been written to commemorate the glories of Maycomb. The people were self-satisfied and complacent about the way they lived. The auditorium was bright and gaily decorated for the presentation. But outside there was darkness, and evil lurked nearby. This is what the people of Maycomb had ignored. They had done Bob Ewell's dirty work by disposing of Tom Robinson, but they had not paid the slightest attention to the evil Ewell himself. In a similar way they had a detached interest in the Mrunas and in Hitler's persecution of the Jews. These were safely far away, and they could simply ignore injustices at home. They were too self-satisfied to think that real evil could threaten them.

CHAPTERS 29–31

Heck Tate and Atticus discuss what had happened. At first, Atticus thinks that it was Jem who killed Bob Ewell. Of course, it was not. Boo Radley was the mysterious stranger, and it was he who had saved the children. After Doctor Reynolds told them that Jem was going to be all right, Scout walked Boo Radley home. Standing on his porch, she saw the town from a different angle. Finally, she realized that Atticus was right. You can't understand other people until you get into their skin for a minute.

COMMENT: The story ends as it should. Justice has finally been done. Scout's understanding of the adult world has grown. For example, Boo Radley had always been a mystery to her before. She never knew the reason why he did not come out of his house. Now she sees him in a different light. All the while the children thought that they were spying on him, he was watching them. In spite of what they tried to do to annoy him, he came to their aid when they needed him. Somehow they had become his children, and he had protected them. Boo Radley, the alleged haunt, has been the instrument of justice for a town too cowardly to face the truth.

CONCLUDING THOUGHT: In the first chapter, it was mentioned that the world of the children was limited by a few houses. Their view of life was also limited. As the story progressed, the children learned much from their experiences. In the last chapter, Scout stands on the Radley porch. From it the neighborhood looks different to her. This is Boo Radley's view of the world. Scout has learned the lesson of tolerance. Atticus had told her that there were many different viewpoints in the world, and that she should never judge anyone else's ideas until she had looked at them from his point of view.

Character Analyses

JEAN LOUISE FINCH: This character is probably the most important one in the story for the reader, because we view the action through her eyes and get her opinions about what is happening. Very aptly she is nicknamed Scout. At the beginning of the story she is six years old, and at the end she is eight. Scout is a very unusual little girl for many reasons. First of all, she is a tomboy but is not difficult for the reader to understand. After all, her mother is dead, she idolizes her father, and she has her older brother as her only playmate throughout most of the story. Secondly, Scout is above average in intelligence. The reader knows this because when Scout starts to school, she already knows how to read and to write. However, there is no indication in the story about how well she can do either of these; only that she can. Thus we don't have to conclude that she is in the genius class. We know that she picked up the reading from constantly being with her father, and the writing from Calpurnia. Thirdly, Scout is perceptive. By this is meant that she notices what is going on around her, and she has a certain ability to observe it. For example, at the trial she realized that Mayella Ewell must be the loneliest person in the world, and she was moved to sympathy by that thought. Lastly, Scout has a temper which gets her into occasional trouble. She would rather fight first and ask questions later. This gives her a sense of equality with her brother as she says about their fight in Chapter 14.

THE WOMAN AND THE GIRL: In studying the character of Scout, the reader must be careful. Actually there are two characters who are in reality one person. There is the grown Jean Louise who is telling the story, and there is the little girl Scout who is a part of the story. The reader should try to keep these two separate. The one is recalling what happened to her as a child. The other is the child herself going through the actions.

ATTICUS FINCH: Atticus, Scout's father, is the central figure in the plot of the novel. The meaning of his name gives a clue to his character. Atticus is a term which refers to the ancient Greek city of Athens. It implies learning, culture, and heroism. Atticus Finch represents all of these things and more. To his children, he is a father whom they can love and respect, and to whom they can look for comfort and reasonable advice. To Tom Robinson and the other Negroes, he is a source of strength and of help. They respect him because they know he recognizes their personal dignity and that he will fight to protect it. To the townspeople, he is a symbol of integrity. Even though they criticize him for defending the Negro, they still reelect him to the state legislature. Unconsciously, they know that they can count on him to do those things for them that they lack the courage to do for themselves.

JEREMY FINCH: Jeremy is Scout's older brother. A boy of ten when the story opens, he is about thirteen when it ends. The events of the story parallel his transition from child to young man. His nickname, Jem, is appropriate. At the beginning of the story, he is a gem, a diamond in the rough that will be polished by the events in Maycomb. He emerges at the end of his experience completely changed by his contact with the adult world.

Of all the characters in the novel, Jem is the one who changes most during the course of the story. In the first chapters he is a rough and tumble boy, who accepts Dill's dare to run up to the Radley house. He tries to put the note through the shutter with the fishing pole. He sneaks into the Radley place at night in order to look into the window. As the story progresses, he becomes more sensitive to the meaning of the happenings around him. He develops a compassionate attitude toward Atticus, Tom, Boo Radley, and Mrs. Dubose because of a growing adult awareness of their problems. He has a more adult understanding of the Tom Robinson case than Scout and Dill. He wants his father to win it. In the courtroom, he listens attentively. However, when the jury convicts the Negro, he is shocked. His boyhood ideals of justice and honor have been shattered. He broods over man's ability to be so obviously unjust to his fellow man.

CHARLES BAKER HARRIS: Charles Baker Harris is the character whom the reader might regard as the outside influence on the story. He is the only important character who is not from Maycomb. Like the other characters discussed so far, his name indicates his part in the story. Throughout the story he is referred to as Dill. The reader who is familiar with these matters knows that dill is a plant whose seeds are used to flavor other food, for example, the dill pickle. Thus Dill Harris is put into the story to flavor it. The reader does not know much about his background. The author tells us that he has been shuffled from relative to relative. Also, after his mother remarries, he does not feel that she really wants him. From the narrative the reader realizes that Dill is both imaginative and sensitive.

DILL'S PLACE IN THE NOVEL: Dill has three important parts in this novel. First is that which concerns Boo Radley. Before Dill arrived on the scene, Jem and Scout merely wondered about the Radley place. They did not go near it. However, one of the first interests of Dill was to find out what was going on inside the house. It is he who dares Jem to act. If we say that the Radley house in this instance represents Maycomb, and the Radleys the townspeople who don't want their lives disturbed by anything unusual, then we can say that Dill represents the disturbing element. When we consider that he is an outcast of sorts, we might say that he represents the Tom Robinson case. This is the incident that disturbs the otherwise quiet town.

Secondly, Dill is a spectator at the trial. He is the outsider watching how Maycomb's system of justice works. What is the effect on him. It makes him sick, and then it makes him cynical. In this sense he represents another point of view. The people of Maycomb don't want their white-black society disturbed. But they cannot see it for the rotten thing that it is. They are too close to it. The outsider Dill, however, can see the gross injustice of it all, and he is disturbed by what he sees.

Thirdly, Dill is another child in the story. He provides a companion for both Jem and Scout. As a boy, he can play boy's games with Jem. However, since he is closer in age to Scout than to the older Jem, he can share her problems better. He and Scout have a few talks together, such as the one on the night when he ran away from home.

ARTHUR RADLEY: Known to the children as Boo, Arthur appears only once in the story, at the end when he rescues Jem and Scout from Bob Ewell. Therefore, the reader does not know much about his personality except that he is a shy man, living in total seclusion. His real place in the story is as a symbol. He is a phantom that goes out only at night. In the beginning of the story, he is the symbol of the unknown. The children wonder about him and want to find out all they can about his life. At first they ask questions; later they invade the Radley property to satisfy their curiosity. Boo Radley becomes a symbol of kindness as he leaves various things in the tree for the children to find and then covers Scout with a blanket on the night of Miss Maudie's fire. He becomes, in addition, a symbol of bravery. In the scene describing the Ewell attack on the children, Scout sees a strange man under the street light. He is walking as though carrying a burden too heavy for him. Even though a physically weaker man, Boo had no fear of the stronger Ewell. The irony of it all is that Boo Radley, the town freak, has a more genuine sense of values and greater compassion than most of the citizens of Maycomb. The children learn lessons of greater importance from Boo than they do from almost anyone else. They learn to judge him by his actions and not by town gossip.

AUNT ALEXANDRA: Aunt Alexandra, Atticus's sister, represents the traditional values of the South—home, family, heredity, gentility, and white supremacy. She maintains all of these values even at the end of the novel. It is not she who changes, but Scout. Scout meets her aunt halfway. Aunt Alexandra represents the crucial problem of the South, then as now—an unwillingness to forsake a false value structure even in the face of evidence that it is meaningless and unjust.

CALPURNIA: Calpurnia, the Finch family cook, is the link between the black and white worlds of Maycomb. She has a dual personality, acting in one way with her friends and in another with the Finches. She is practically accepted as a member of the Finch family. She treats the children as though they were her own. She does not spoil them; she helps Scout learn to write; she listens to their problems. Atticus is not afraid to talk openly in front of her because he knows that she understands. The author suggests that the Negro can be a valuable part of white society, if white men will only judge him on the basis of individual merit. Calpurnia's character also suggests a lesson for Negroes. They must learn to admire individual achievements, not as the aping of the white man's world, but as a necessity of dignified human life. Because both whites and blacks are guilty of racism, by not judging men individually, Cal must hide her achievements from both.

MISS MAUDIE ATKINSON: Although this character does not play a great part in the story, she is perhaps one of the most colorful people in it. She is a benevolent, brave woman who loves floral beauty and the Finch children. Her bravery at the time of the fire foreshadows her valiant support of Atticus's defense of Tom. She is the most rational feminine character in the novel, one who repudiates Aunt Alexandra's value system.

BOB EWELL: Ewell represents the poor white trash of Maycomb. He is ignorant, irrational, slovenly, and totally unwilling to take any steps to improve himself. His hatred of the Negro is greater than anyone else's in Maycomb because he knows he is inferior by any rational standard of comparison. He trades on the fact that Maycomb's standards are not rational, and that it will support his hunt for a scapegoat. He hopes to gain a self-respect he never earned by degrading Tom Robinson.

MAYELLA EWELL: Scout described Bob Ewell's daughter as the loneliest person in the world. In a sense she was the victim of circumstances. Her father's attitude prevented her from behaving like a normal person. Her desire for affection was genuine. Her lies were the result of fear of her father. In spite of what she does, the reader is sympathetic toward this poor girl who in some ways suffers more deeply than the Negroes of Maycomb.

MRS. HENRY LAFAYETTE DUBOSE: This character is important only in relation to Scout and Jem. They learned a valuable lesson from her bravery in the face of impossible odds. They also learned that judgment of another human being requires that the context be known and evaluated.

MISS STEPHANIE CRAWFORD: She represents the self-righteousness of the townspeople. Her stock in trade is vicious gossip aimed at almost anyone who offends her concepts of the status quo.

JUDGE TAYLOR: Judge Taylor is an elderly man well versed in the law. He seems to want to see justice done, but he is limited because the ultimate decision rests with the jury.

TOM ROBINSON: Tom's character is not well-drawn. He is a two-dimensional figure who seems to be a kind person. However, his ignorance and his position as a Negro cause his ultimate downfall.

MR. DOLPHUS RAYMOND: He appears only briefly in the story, during the trial. Because he lives with a Negro woman, he is an outcast. But his children are the ones who suffer most because of this. Half black and half white, they belong to neither race and neither wants them. Both whites and blacks are guilty of intolerance.

LINK DEAS, HECK TATE, MR. UNDERWOOD: These are minor characters who figure in the trial sequences. They are one segment of the white society in Maycomb, however, who seem to have a proper sense of justice.

UNCLE JACK: He is Atticus's brother. Scout is very fond of him because he is kind and genial. He supports his brother's decision to defend Tom.

UNCLE JIMMIE: He is Aunt Alexandra's husband. He is an ineffectual husband and father, but Alexandra preserves the marriage at all costs to protect the family name.

FRANCIS: Francis is Aunt Alexandra's grandson, who first gives the reader the family's reaction to the Tom Robinson case. He taunts Scout by calling Atticus a "nigger-lover."

THE CUNNINGHAMS: They are a poor white family. They provide a contrast to the Ewells. They are industrious, proud, independent people who never accept anything they cannot repay. One of the Cunninghams is almost responsible for a hung jury at the trial.

Sample Essay Questions and Answers

1. Explain the historical background of the story.

ANSWER: *To Kill A Mockingbird* takes place in the early 1930s. This is the time of the Great Depression in the United States. It is also a period of great social change, a time that has a great influence on the plot itself. For example, farmers, like the Cunninghams, were hurt by the depression. They depended solely upon their crops to make a living. When they could not sell their crops, the farmers became very poor. The crops rotted and there was little money to buy new seed. The only choice the farmers had was to leave their land and go to the city to find work. This was something that the Cunninghams, for example, did not want to do. Also, since Maycomb was a farm area and the town itself depended upon the farmers, the entire area was very poor.

The author makes reference to what is going on in Washington at the time. By this she means the social changes that the Roosevelt administration was making in the lives of the people of the United States. Things such as the NRA and the WPA were government designed to help restore economic growth. The implication is that the people of Maycomb needed to reexamine their way of life. Perhaps it was time that they broke with some of their rural traditions.

2. Why can Atticus Finch be described as the central figure in the story?

ANSWER: Atticus Finch can be described as the central figure in the story because he embodies the theme. He fights for justice and tolerance. Throughout the story he is the one who advises the children to try to see the other person's point of view. He is the image of good with which the children contrast the evil they see around them. Atticus is also the chief protagonist of the plot. In some ways he represents the conscience of Maycomb, or whatever is left of it.

3. Describe the background of the Finch family.

ANSWER: Simon Finch migrated from England to Philadelphia. He had been irritated at home by the persecution of the Methodists by the other Protestant sects. Eventually, Simon bought some slaves and settled on the banks of the Alabama River. There he established his homestead, Finch's Landing. For years it had been the custom of the men of the family to stay at the homestead and make their living from cotton. However, Atticus and his brother Jack broke with this tradition. The one left to practice law, the other to practice medicine. Alexandra, their sister, remained at Finch's Landing.

4. Why was Aunt Alexandra so concerned about family and background?

ANSWER: Atticus had said that Alexandra was concerned about family and background because this was all she had left. There was not a dime of the family fortune remaining to his generation. This is a typical Southern reaction. Many people in the South, victims of "genteel poverty," cling to the past to give the illusion of security and position in the world. Aunt Alexandra had found neither of these with her husband, who was not interested in anything but his fishing. Atticus and Jack found new careers, new ways of life, and a new means to give them a sense of identity. Atticus found this in his law career, and in being both father and mother to his children. Jack Finch found it in medicine. But Alexandra had nothing but tradition.

5. Explain some of the strengths and weaknesses of the novel.

ANSWER: Generally speaking, the novel is well written. The action moves along at a good pace and does not get bogged down at any point. The theme of the novel is clear and well illustrated throughout the book. All of the major ideas are convincingly dramatized. The author never gets "preachy" but lets the reader judge for himself the morality of the issues. Perhaps the main weakness of the book lies in the character of Scout. Her reactions are not always as childlike as they should be. The author, who is telling the story in the first person, does not always capture a childish point of view. Occasionally, therefore, Scout appears too adult.

6. Why is Dill a major character?

ANSWER: Dill is a major character because he represents an outside influence on the action of the story. When he arrives on the scene, his imagination and desire for adventure move the other children to try new things. For example, Dill's curiosity about the Radley place leads them to attempt to find out what Boo Radley looks like. Since Dill is not a resident of Maycomb, he is not really a part of what is happening. He is only an observer. In other words, through him the author is giving a picture of what outsiders think of Southern "justice." When Dill cries and gets upset at the trial, he is a symbol of the outsider who gets disturbed when he sees what the Southerner is doing to the Negro.

7. Explain the role of Jem in the story.

ANSWER: Jem reflects the mood of the story and of its theme. At the beginning of the story, when all is well, he is a happy child. As the story progresses, Jem grows into young manhood, going through a series of physical and mental changes. This represents the change of attitude that some modern Southerners are taking towards the Negro question. When the second part of the book takes up the story of Tom Robinson, Jem becomes moody and serious. At the trial he listens attentively. When the situation looks good for Tom, Jem is the one who shows confidence. Later, after Tom is convicted, Jem is the one who cries. Finally, when Bob Ewell attacks the children, Jem is the one who gets hurt. In fact, he will never fully recover from the effects of his broken arm. In other words, Jem represents the Southerner who does not approve of what his fellows are doing. However, just as he will always have the scars of his fight with Bob Ewell, so it seems he will never be able to escape the injustices of the Southern community.

8. What type of novel is *To Kill A Mockingbird* and why?

ANSWER: *To Kill A Mockingbird* can be classified as a realistic novel because the author tries to faithfully record the situation just as it existed in the South at the time. She does not try to excuse the evil that she pictures in the book. There is no idealization—people are prejudiced and indifferent. However, she also shows that there are some reasonable people who do not sanction what is happening, and who try to do something about it. Maycomb is a place that could very well exist since there are towns in the South exactly like it. The author has captured the speech of the Southerner, the climate, and the prevalent attitudes. She records, she does not pass first-hand judgment.

Mark Twain's The Adventures of Huckleberry Finn

Summary and Comment

CHAPTER 1. I MEET MOSES AND THE BULRUSHERS

Mark Twain's *Huckleberry Finn* opens with the hero of the story (Huck Finn) introducing himself as one of the characters who figured in another book by Mark Twain, *Tom Sawyer.* Huck tells us that "Mr. Mark Twain" was more or less truthful in telling the story of *Tom Sawyer.* On occasion Twain "dressed up" the story, but by and large he told it accurately. After all, Huck says, everybody lies once in a while—except maybe Tom Sawyer's Aunt Polly, or the Widow Douglas (the woman who took Huck into her home in an attempt to raise him), or Tom's cousin Mary.

At any rate, Huck continues, at the end of the other book he and Tom are rich because they found a robber's cave in which there was loot amounting to $12,000. With this money set out at interest, each of the boys gets a dollar a day spending money, "more than a body could tell what to do with." Huck tells us he soon tired of living a respectable life with the widow, so "when I couldn't stand it no longer I lit out." He found his old hogshead (the large barrel he slept in during his free and easy days) and was content again. Content, that is, until Tom Sawyer talked him into going back to the widow's house in order to put up a respectable "front." Tom, you see, was starting a band of robbers (another of Tom Sawyer's games), and Huck could join if he had a good reputation.

Huck then tells us how he felt cramped in the clothes he had to wear at the widow's house—he preferred his old rags, at least he didn't itch and sweat in them. When the widow tried to teach him Bible stories (particularly "Moses and the Bulrushers"), Huck was interested until he found out that Moses was dead. When he learned that, he says, "I didn't care no more about him, because I don't take no stock in dead people."

Things got rougher when Huck asked the widow to let him smoke his corncob pipe, and she said no because smoking was crude and dirty. What Huck couldn't understand was that the widow thought that snuff taking was all right because she did it herself.

Huck got into trouble with the widow's old maid sister, Miss Watson, who came to live with the widow about this time. Miss Watson tried to teach Huck to spell, but Huck couldn't stand it. When Miss Watson told him about Hell, Huck said he wished he were there—he felt he needed a change. But Miss Watson didn't understand, so she lectured Huck about evil and good and Heaven. Huck comments, "Well, I couldn't see no advantage in going where she was going [that is, to Heaven], so I made up my mind I wouldn't try for it." And anyway, Huck was glad he wouldn't get to Heaven because Miss Watson didn't think Tom Sawyer would get there.

At the end of the evening, Miss Watson and the widow call the slaves in and say prayers. Then everybody goes to bed. Alone in his room, Huck begins to feel lonesome and scared. His fear grows on him as he listens to the sounds in the night and finds superstitious meaning in such noises as the hooting of an owl and the baying of a dog. When he flips a spider off his shoulder into the flame of a candle where it shrivels up, Huck becomes more down-hearted than ever.

He lights up his pipe—no one will know because everyone is asleep—and settles down with the stillness of the night. Then he hears twigs snapping and a quiet "me-yow! me-yow!" out in the yard. His mood brightens. He answers the call, puts out the light, shinnies down to the ground, and finds Tom Sawyer waiting for him.

COMMENT: This chapter gives us an idea of the kind of person Huck Finn is. For all practical purposes he is an orphan: his mother is dead, and his father is the village drunkard—a mean person whom we'll meet in the next few chapters. As a result of his background, Huck has grown into a free-wheeling sort of person who is happiest when he has fewest social responsibilities. He doesn't think about religion the way other people do, because he seems more interested in the comforts of the moment. Huck is essentially superstitious, but he isn't hypocritical or sneaky. He doesn't like to get people excited, especially if it would do no good. He wants mainly to be left to his own devices, to sleep in his hogshead, to wear his old rags, and to eat his food all mixed up (because "the juice kind of swaps around, and the things go better").

CHAPTER 2. OUR GANG'S DARK OATH

Tom and Huck start making their way through the widow's backyard when Huck trips and makes a noise. Miss Watson's slave Jim, who is sitting in the kitchen doorway, hears the noise, but because the light is behind him he can't see Tom and Huck. He calls out into the darkness. Since he gets no answer, he decides to outwait whoever is in among the trees. He sits with his back against a tree, about halfway between the two boys. Huck notices that whenever he's in a situation like this, where it isn't smart to move around, he begins to itch. But just as he thinks he can't stand the itching (in eleven different places) any longer, Jim begins to snore.

The boys crawl away, but before they leave, Tom sneaks into the kitchen and takes three candles. He puts a nickel on the table to pay for them. Then he crawls back to where Jim is sleeping and puts Jim's hat on a branch above his head. Huck explains that because of this game of Tom's, Jim thinks he's been "witched." He tells the rest of the slaves that the nickel he found in the kitchen is a charm given him by the devil. As a result of this night's adventure, Jim is highly respected by his comrades who are as superstitious as he is. Jim "stretches" the truth even more by saying that witches rode him all over the world.

The boys go to a hill overlooking the village. Here they meet Joe Harper and Ben Rogers and two or three more of their friends. They take a skiff—a clumsy, flat-bottomed boat—and go two and a half miles downstream, where they land. Tom makes everybody swear secrecy; then he shows them a cave in the hillside. The boys crawl into it. After going about 200 yards, they find their way into a large room, "all damp and sweaty and cold. . . ."

Here Tom explains his plan for forming a robber gang. He says, "Now, we'll start this band of robbers and call it Tom Sawyer's Gang. Everybody that wants to join has got to take an oath, and write his name in blood." Tom reads the oath—a gruesome one—and everybody signs. One of the articles of the oath is that the family of any gangmember who tells the gang's secrets must be killed. This leaves Huck out; he hasn't any family—since his father hasn't been seen in the village in over a year, everybody thinks he's dead. Huck remembers Miss Watson. He offers to let the gang kill her if he tells any secrets. The gang accepts Huck's offer, and he is allowed to mark his sign (Huck can't write, remember) in blood on the oath.

The boys discuss gang policy for a while. They decide—rather, Tom Sawyer decides—that they are highwaymen, not burglars. The reason is that highwaymen have more "class." This is also the reason why they will always kill their victims—there's more "style" in a gang that kills the people it robs than in one that doesn't. After some talk about ransoming victims—talk that shows Tom's knowledge is from books he doesn't understand too well—the gang goes home because little Tommy Barnes got scared and wanted his mother and threatened to tell all the gang's secrets. Tom bribes Tommy Barnes with a nickel. The meeting then breaks up with the gang resolving to "meet next week, and rob somebody and kill some people."

COMMENT: In this chapter we are introduced to Tom Sawyer and Jim, Miss Watson's Negro slave. We note that Jim seems to be a stereotype of others of his race and station in the Southern states during the early nineteenth century. (Much more will be said about Jim later in the book.) Tom is interesting, though. He is a leader among the boys of the village, and he has high romantic ideas. He especially likes to play games on people, as Huck says. We see this in the trick Tom pulls on Jim by placing Jim's hat in the tree, and in the oath taken by the boys when they form the robber gang. There is no chance at all of the boy's killing anyone, or stealing anything of great value—not while one of them is still crying for his mommy, and getting bribed to keep the gang's secrets. By and large we see that Tom Sawyer is different from Huck Finn in that Tom plays at rebelling against society, whereas Huck, as we saw in the last chapter, really wants to "get out from under" civilization.

CHAPTER 3. WE AMBUSCADE THE A-RABS

The next morning Huck gets a "going over" from the widow's sister, Miss Watson, because his clothes are all dirty from climbing around the cave the night before. The widow herself doesn't scold; she cleans off the clothes. Huck resolves to behave on the widow's account. He tells us that he can't see any reason for "hooking up" to Miss Watson's kind of religion. Whenever he prays he doesn't get what he wants. And as for the widow's kind of religion, Huck doesn't think he'll be a credit to it, "seeing I was so ignorant, and so kind of low-down and ornery."

Although Huck's drunkard father hasn't been seen in some time, and although the rumors are that he died—drowned in the river 12 miles north of the village—Huck is not so sure his father won't be coming back soon. He is unhappy when he thinks that his father may come back, because his father beats him and mistreats him.

At any rate, Huck and Tom and the rest of the boys play robber for about a month, until finally Huck and most of the other boys quit. They "hadn't robbed nobody, hadn't killed any people, but only just pretended." Tom explains to Huck that the gang never gets loot because the travelers—particularly the last ones, the A-rab caravan—have magic rings and magic lamps which they use to call genies to their aid. Huck doesn't believe all this. All he knows is that the A-rab caravan turned out to be a group of Sunday school children on an outing. However, he took a ring and an old whale oil lamp into the woods with him "and rubbed and rubbed till I sweat like an Injun...but it warn't no use, none of the genies come." Huck concludes that Tom Sawyer was lying. He says, "I reckoned he believed in the A-rabs and the elephants, but as for me I think different. It had all the marks of a Sunday school."

COMMENT: This chapter continues giving the background information we are getting of Huck Finn and the people he is involved with. Huck is no enemy of organized religion; he just can't understand how it will do him any good. Notice how neither Tom Sawyer's magic lamps nor Miss Watson's prayers give him any satisfaction. Huck prays for fishing gear, but only gets the line—which is useless without hooks. He rubs the lamp, calculating to have a genie build him a palace he can sell, but no genie comes. Notice also Huck's attitude of letting every man believe what he wants to. Huck doesn't tell Tom the truth about the Sunday school outing; he says instead, "I think different." A similar thing happened in Chapter One, when Huck felt there was no percentage in Miss Watson's religion, but didn't tell her so because it would only get her excited and wouldn't do any good. This feeling that certain things are useless because they don't do anybody any good is an indication of Huck's pragmatic leanings.

Our first hint of trouble comes when Huck talks about his father, "pap" as Huck calls him. From the fact that Huck doesn't believe his father drowned, we come to expect "pap" to show up any day.

CHAPTER 4. THE HAIR-BALL ORACLE

Three or four months later, sometime in the winter, Huck is going to school, learning to read and write. The widow feels he is coming along slowly but surely, getting "sivilised." Huck is getting tolerant of his "new ways," his bed and clothes and food.

One morning, however, he sees a set of footprints in the snow outside the widow's house. He recognizes the cross made with big nails in the left boot heel. His father is back in the village!

Huck runs to Judge Thatcher, the lawyer who has his money in trust for him, and sells the Judge his rights to both his share of the $12,000 and the interest (about $300 a year). The Judge gives Huck $1.00 for the money.

Then Huck goes to Miss Watson's slave Jim, who has a magic hair-ball which he uses for telling fortunes. For a quarter (a counterfeit quarter, but Jim knows how to fix it by putting it between pieces of a raw potato) the hair-ball prophesies to Jim and Jim repeats to Huck. The "fortune" is this (Jim is telling Huck):

> *"Yo' ole father doan' know yit what he's a-gwyne to do. Sometimes he spec he'll go 'way, en den agin he spec he'll stay. De bes' way is to res' easy en let de ole man take his own way. Dey's two angels hoverin' roun' 'bout him. One uv 'em is white en shiny, en t'other one is black. De white one gits him to go right a little while, den de black one sails in en bust it all up. A body can't tell yit which one gwyne to fetch him at de las'. But you is all right. You gwyne to have considerable trouble in yo' life, en considerable joy. Sometimes you gwyne to git hurt, en sometimes you gwyne to git sick; but every time you's gwyne to git well ag'in. Dey's two gals flyin' 'bout you in yo' life. One uv 'em's light en t'other one is dark. One is rich and t'other is po'. You's gwyne to marry de po' one fust en de rich one by en by. You wants to keep 'way fum de water as much as you kin, en don't run no resk, 'kase it's down in de bills dat you's gwyne to git hung."*

Huck returns to the widow's house. When he goes up to his room at night, he finds his father sitting there.

COMMENT: The story is beginning to get off the ground. Huck seems to be changing, to be settling down to his new life. He has a safe investment and is living in the home of a woman who loves him with something very much like a mother's love. "She said she warn't ashamed of me," is the way Huck recognizes this love. But then, in the middle of what look like good days, Huck's father appears. Huck is so frightened of his father that he sells out his share of the wealth he and Tom found. He goes to Jim looking for help from spirits, that is, Huck goes to Jim because Jim has a reputation for his knowledge of spirits, witches, and devils. This totally uneducated superstition seems to be the kind of religion Huck trusts.

Be especially careful to note the "fortune." It doesn't tell Huck what to do about his "pap," but it does tell him to stay clear of the water. In the next couple of chapters we will see that the village believes Huck was drowned. Then we will see Huck and Jim escape on the river by means of a raft.

CHAPTER 5. PAP STARTS IN ON A NEW LIFE

When Huck walks into his room, he doesn't see that his father is there until after he shuts the door and turns around. With a shock he realizes his father is sitting there, a very pale white ("a tree-toad white, a fish-belly white," Huck says) with long, greasy black hair and long "mixed-up" whiskers. He is wearing filthy rags and shoes through which his toes show. Huck's father accuses him of putting on airs and "frills" in order to be better than his family. He raves that since none of the family knew how to read, Huck is being disrespectful in learning how to read. Pap tears up a picture Huck received as a prize for his schoolwork, takes Huck's last dollar (the dollar Huck got from Judge Thatcher that morning), forbids Huck to go to school, and threatens to cause trouble for Judge Thatcher unless the Judge gives him Huck's share of the $12,000.

Because they want to protect Huck from his father, Judge Thatcher and the widow try to get him appointed their ward. That is, they want to be his legal guardians. But the court in the village has a new judge, one who is unfamiliar with Huck's pap. This new judge decides not to separate Huck from his parent, because it's not a good thing to break up families. This decision boosts pap's pride and makes him so happy that he gets drunk on three dollars he forced Huck to borrow from Judge Thatcher. As a result of his spree the old man is jailed for a week. The new judge tries to reform pap by taking him into his house, cleaning him up, and making him respectable. Pap swears off liquor. He is welcomed into the new judge's family like a repentant sinner, and is given a spare room. But that night he gets thirsty, crawls out the window, trades his jacket for a jug of "forty-rod" (a cheap whiskey, something like "white lightning"), crawls back into his room, gets drunk, crawls out again, and breaks his left arm in two places. In getting drunk he practically destroys the spare room. The judge is disgusted with him.

COMMENT: In this chapter we get our first full-length view of Huck's father in action. Besides learning of his dirtiness and drunkenness, we are struck by the old man's meanness. We also note the peculiar pride he has in his ignorance and slovenliness. Just how Huck understands his relationship with his father is made clear when Huck says he continued to go to school after his father's appearance mainly in order to spite his father. The last picture we get of Huck's father in this chapter is that of a bedraggled, smelly drunk with a broken arm, lying helpless in the gutter. It looks as though the black angel of Jim's prophecy in the last chapter is going to win out. The satire on "enlightened" systems of justice is obvious.

CHAPTER 6. PAP STRUGGLES WITH THE DEATH ANGEL

When pap gets well again, he begins chasing Huck and beating him for going to school. Huck borrows money from Judge Thatcher, gives it to pap who gets drunk, "tears up the town," and lands in jail.

Pap begins to hang around the widow's house, "laying for" Huck. When the widow tells him she'll make trouble for him, he threatens to show who's Huck Finn's boss. One spring day he catches Huck and takes him three miles up river to a log cabin in a thickly wooded spot on the Illinois shore, where nobody can find him.

Huck enjoys his captivity. For one thing, no one ever bothers him about studying or cleaning up. Life is carefree and lazy, except for the beatings Huck gets when his father is drunk. Huck accepts the beatings as part of life—for a while, at least.

But when pap takes to going off to town and locking Huck in the cabin for three or four days at a time, and when the beatings get more and more frequent, Huck decides he has to get away somehow.

One time while he is locked in the cabin, he finds an old, rusty saw blade which he uses in an attempt to cut his way through one of the logs at the back of the cabin. Pap comes back before he's free, so Huck hides his saw and disguises the log he's sawed through. Pap tells Huck that the widow and Judge Thatcher have another lawsuit against him and it looks as though they'll win this time. Huck decides to escape before then, because he no longer wants to be civilized. He's too comfortable now to go back to the widow's. Then pap settles down to get drunk while Huck brings in the supplies and cooks supper.

The drunker pap gets, the more he "cusses" the government for treating him so badly while it lets freed Negroes vote. He gets so excited about what he's saying that he doesn't watch where he's walking. He trips over the salt pork tub, and curses louder and more violently while hopping up and down trying to soothe his barked shins. Finally he drinks himself into a stupor.

Huck manages to fall asleep for a while, but is awakened by a shriek. Pap is thrashing around yelling about snakes crawling over him. Then he shouts that he hears the footsteps of the dead. Then he thinks that Huck is the Angel of Death coming for him. He attacks Huck with an axe, but Huck runs around the cabin until pap gets tired and falls asleep. Huck takes down the gun, makes sure it's loaded, steadies it on the turnip barrel, aims it at pap, and waits for the dawn.

COMMENT: It is in this chapter that we see Huck's resolve to escape. This escape is going to give rise to all his adventures: those on the river and off it. Huck's motives for wanting to escape are pretty clear: (1) he won't be safe with his father; (2) he can't tolerate "civilization"—not after the vacation from it he's taking now.

CHAPTER 7. I FOOL PAP AND GET AWAY

The next morning pap doesn't remember his struggle with the "Death Angel," so Huck explains that he took the gun down because someone tried to break into the cabin. Pap sends Huck out to check the fish lines to see if they caught anything for breakfast. As he walks along the river bank, Huck notices the floating tree limbs and driftwood—a sure sign that the river is on the rise. Then he sees an empty canoe—13 or 14 feet long. He jumps into the river, clothes and all, and salvages it and hides it in a little creek, thinking that when the time comes for his escape he'll use the boat to go about 50 miles downstream instead of hiking through the woods. He doesn't tell pap about the canoe, but explains his wet clothes by saying he fell in the river.

After breakfast, Huck and pap rest awhile. About noon they go out to see if anything of value is floating down the river. They get part of a raft—nine logs fastened together—which pap will take down to the village sawmill and sell. Huck is locked in again while pap goes to the village. He takes out his saw, and starts cutting away at the back of the cabin again. When he is free, he takes the sack of cornmeal, side of bacon, whiskey-jug, coffee and sugar, ammunition, wadding, bucket, gourd, dipper, tincup, the saw, two blankets, skillet, coffee-pot, fishlines, matches, and "everything that was worth a cent." All these things he puts in the canoe. Then he fixes up the ground he marked up crawling out of the hole when he dragged all these things out. He puts the log back in place so no one will be able to tell it has been cut through. Then he goes into the woods and shoots a wild hog; next, he takes the axe from the woodpile and smashes in the front door. He drags the pig into the cabin and hacks its throat with the axe so it will bleed all over the cabin floor. He drags a sackful of rocks over the ground to the river, so it will appear that something was dragged from the cabin and dumped in the river. Then he sticks some of his hair to the bloody axe and flings the axe into a corner of the cabin. He gets rid of the pig, then using the sack of cornmeal, he leaves a false trail going away from river, so it will look as though someone carried a leaking sack of cornmeal into the woods. Finally, Huck waits till dark, certain that when he leaves people will think he's been killed by robbers who escaped in the direction away from the river. He dozes for a while, and when he wakes it is late, and he sees pap rowing back from the village.

Huck sets his canoe adrift. Pretty soon he is passing the ferry landing where he can hear the distant voices of people talking but they seem a long way off. Soon he can only hear a mumble and an occasional laugh as he lies in the bottom of the canoe, looking up at the deep sky.

He lands the canoe at Jackson's Island, where he hides it and lies down for a nap before breakfast.

COMMENT: This chapter is interesting in two ways. First, notice all the details involved in Huck's escape from pap. The kind of planning involved to make things appear as though Huck were killed by robbers is not the kind of planning we expect from Huck Finn. Instead, we think of Tom Sawyer as the kind of fellow who lays out this sort of plan. Huck realizes this, too. For just after he drags the pig and the rocks around, Huck says: "I did wish Tom Sawyer was there; I knowed he would take an interest in this kind of business, and throw in the fancy touches. Nobody could spread himself like Tom Sawyer in such a thing like that." The important thing to remember is that Tom would have done these things as a game; but Huck, on the other hand, does them in dead earnest.

Secondly, it is in this chapter that we get our first deep glimpse into Huck's feeling for the river. (In the second chapter, when the boys are on the hill overlooking the river, Huck mentions how beautiful the river is, but he doesn't explain himself, as he does here.) The river is awfully quiet, awfully strong, and awfully big—about a mile wide at this point. But you can hear a long way on it. You can, in a way, be part of what's happening on the shore (by listening), while you are separated from those happenings by a half-mile of water. When Huck, on Jackson's Island, hears the man on the lumber-raft give orders, he says with some surprise, "I heard that just as plain as if the man was by my side."

CHAPTER 8. I SPARE MISS WATSON'S JIM

Huck wakes up about eight o'clock feeling "powerful lazy and comfortable." Just as he's getting ready to turn over for 40 more winks, he hears a "boom!" up the river. It's the ferry boat, firing a cannon over the water to make Huck's body rise to the top. The people on the ferry boat set loaves of bread with quicksilver in them afloat on the river. The idea is that the loaves will come to a stop over the body. Huck is hungry, so he snags one of the loaves and eats it while he watches the boat full of villagers looking for his body. After rounding the island looking for the body, the boat with its occupants heads back to the village. Huck feels more secure now knowing that people believe he is dead and will no longer come looking for him.

For three days and nights Huck hangs around the island getting more and more bored and lonesome since he has nothing to do and no one to talk to. The next day he goes exploring on the island and stumbles across a smoldering campfire. In a panic he rushes back to his camp, packs his gear into the canoe, ready to be off and running on short notice, and climbs into a tree to hide. When he gets hungry, he goes across to the Illinois bank and cooks supper. His fear of the unknown person on the island keeps him from sleeping; so that night he decides to go looking for the other man. Once he makes this decision he feels better. He wanders a while until he comes to where he stumbled across the campfire. He sees a man sleeping beside the fire. When the man awakes, he stretches himself. Huck recognizes Miss Watson's Jim! Huck is so glad to see that the unknown person he feared is someone he trusts that he steps out of the woods and greets him. Jim is not so glad to see Huck. He had heard Huck was dead, so he thinks that what he sees is a ghost. Huck convinces Jim that he's not a ghost, and after providing breakfast for the two of them—Jim hasn't eaten anything but berries for at least four days—Huck tells Jim how he escaped from pap. Then Huck asks Jim what he is doing on the island. After making Huck promise not to tell on him, Jim says that he has run away from Miss Watson. Huck is shocked. Jim reminds him of his promise:

> *"But mind, you said you wouldn't tell—you know you said you wouldn't tell, Huck."*
>
> *"Well, I did. I said I wouldn't, and I'll stick to it. Honest injun, I will. People would call me a lowdown Abolitionist and despise me for keeping mum—but that don't make no difference. I ain't a-going to tell, and I ain't a-going back there, anyways."*

Jim explains that he ran away because he overheard Miss Watson tell the widow that a New Orleans slave trader offered her $800 for him. Although she didn't like the idea of selling a slave down the river (where slaves were less humanely treated than they were higher north), the amount of money was too much for her to turn down.

After telling Huck how he managed to escape and of the hardships he encountered on the island, Jim notes some omens, or superstitious signs, and tells Huck about some of the many signs and omens he knows. He tells Huck that his hairy arms and breast means he will be rich someday. As it is, he is worth $800, and he wishes he could spend some of it.

COMMENT: Huck feels secure when he sees the ferry boat give up the search for his remains. He points out that the bread had been prayed over by the widow or the parson so that it would find him. It found him—Huck ate it. The prayers were answered, Huck figures, because the right kind of people did the praying. Notice the irony here. Huck doesn't say that the purpose of the bread being set afloat was to find his body so it could be buried. What Huck seems to be telling us is that whether your prayers are answered or not depends on how you look at things.

The most important event in this chapter, though, is Huck's promise to Jim. Huck, willfully and with full knowledge of the consequences of his promise, places himself outside the social order. He can't go back to the village (society) now, because he will protect a runaway slave. Huck is really "dead" now, so far as society is concerned.

CHAPTER 9. THE HOUSE OF DEATH FLOATS BY

Against Huck's wishes, he and Jim carry their gear up to a cave in a 40 foot ridge on the island. The cave is high enough for Jim to stand up in, and as big as two or three rooms of a house. It has an outcropping beyond the opening so that Huck and Jim can build a fire. In a little while the sky starts to darken, and it begins to thunder and lightning. Huck is impressed by the beauty of the stormy weather, especially when the wind whips the treetops and the lightning illuminates them for a flash. Jim reminds him that if he had been left to his own devices, he would still be down on the island, soaking wet in this storm.

The river continues to rise and to bring with it debris from flooded areas farther north. One night Huck and Jim catch a raft of pine planks, 12 by 16 feet, solid and well built.

Another night, just before daylight, they see a two-story frame house floating down the river. They paddle out to it, and find a dead man in it, shot in the back. The floor of the house is littered with whiskey bottles, greasy playing cards, and masks made out of black cloth. Jim and Huck ransack the house for candles, knives, tin-cups, and other materials they can use. Then they set off for their island again. By this time it is daylight. Jim has to hide in the bottom of the canoe covered with an old bed quilt taken from the house, while Huck paddles back to the island. They get home safe.

COMMENT: In this chapter Huck and Jim share their first common experience on the river. This new partnership between these social outcasts is rewarding to both parties. Huck, by allowing himself to be advised by Jim, is saved the loss of all his gear in the storm and the flooding which follows it. Jim finds equipment in the house floating down the river.

The dead man in the house turns out to be Huck's pap, as we learn in the very last chapter of the novel. That is the reason why Jim didn't want Huck to enter the house until the dead man's face was covered. One other item was picked up out of the river by Huck and Jim: the raft. It is on this raft—a gift of the river—that the two will make their journey.

CHAPTER 10. WHAT COMES OF HANDLIN' SNAKESKIN

Huck and Jim have breakfast and then settle down to inspect their haul. Huck wants to know something about the dead man, but Jim says it's bad luck to talk about the dead, especially since they might come to haunt. They find $8 sewed in the lining of a coat they took from the house, and Huck begins to boast of their good luck. Two days earlier Huck had handled a snakeskin. Jim told him it was bad luck. Huck now says he wishes he could have more bad luck like that. Jim replies that the bad luck is yet to come.

Four days later Huck kills a rattlesnake and as a joke coils the snake up on the foot of Jim's blanket. Unknown to Huck, the rattlesnake's mate coils up on the blanket, next to the dead snake. When Jim lies down that night he is bitten by the snake. For four days and nights his foot and leg are swollen, and he is out of his head from the pain and from the whiskey he drinks to ward off the poison.

Finally the river begins to go down between its banks again. The first thing Huck and Jim do is bait a line with a skinned rabbit. They catch a catfish six feet two inches long, weighing over 200 pounds. It's as big a fish as was ever caught in the Mississippi.

The next morning Huck decides to go into the village to see what's happening there. Jim has him go at night, disguised as a girl, in some of the clothes they took from the floating house. Huck notices a light in the window of an old shack that had been abandoned last time he was in the village. He peeps in at the window and sees a 40-year old woman there, knitting. She is a stranger who never met him. He reminds himself to behave like a girl, then knocks at the door.

COMMENT: The dominant theme of this chapter is superstition. The luck of finding the rich haul in the house and the luck of catching the huge catfish are balanced against Jim's snakebite. Just as Jim foretold the heavy rains by watching the flight of birds, so he foretells the snakebite by noting that it's bad luck to touch snakeskin with bare hands. Huck is repentant and vows never to touch snakeskin again.

Notice how neither Huck nor Jim distinguish between what is probable and what isn't. One might be able to tell something about the weather by watching the flight of birds. But handling snakeskin does not necessarily mean one is going to have bad luck.

Mark Twain uses superstition in three ways. First of all he uses it to indicate that the characters are plain, simple folks in the sense of being primitive and therefore uncluttered, who do a great deal of thinking through to the reality of things. The people are crude, but they are also sincere, honest and innocent.

Secondly, Twain makes comic use of superstition. This book was written by a writer who gloried in being called "America's funny man." The comic element of *Huckleberry Finn* is a very important one, although it is often overlooked because of its obviousness. Twain uses humor, low comedy, satire, all to good effect.

Thirdly, the element of superstition is used to carry the theme of Fate through the novel. Instances of this use of superstition are the snakeskin, and Jim's belief that a hairy chest indicates future wealth.

CHAPTER 11. THEY'RE AFTER US!

The woman invites Huck into the house. He tells her his name is Sarah Williams and he's from Hookerville, a little village seven miles below St. Petersburg. He and the woman get to talking. She tells him all about the murder of Huck Finn, and how the village folk at first thought pap had killed his son to get the $6,000 from Judge Thatcher without having to go through the courts for it. But when the villagers discovered Jim had run away, they then suspected him. Then Huck's father borrowed money from Judge Thatcher to outfit a search party to look for Huck's killer. Then pap disappeared. A reward of $300 was posted for Jim, and one of $200 for pap. The woman tells Huck she thinks Jim is hiding out on Jackson's Island because she saw smoke rising from there a few days ago. Her husband has gone off to get a boat and a gun. He and a friend are going to the island tonight to capture Jim.

Huck gets nervous and gives himself away—the woman discovers that he is not a girl. He tells her that he is an orphan apprenticed to a mean farmer and that he has run away. She sympathizes with him, explains some things he should do to act more like a girl, and sees him off.

Huck hears the clock strike eleven. In an hour the woman's husband will be going to the island to fetch Jim. Huck heads for the island, wakes Jim, and they load their gear on the raft and glide silently off down the river.

COMMENT: The adventure on the Mississippi river—one of the most fascinating voyages in literature—is about to begin.

CHAPTER 12. BETTER LET BLAME' WELL ALONE

Huck and Jim escape down the river on the raft, towing the canoe after them. Huck started a camp-fire on the island to decoy the men who were hunting Jim. He says, "I played it as low down on them as could." They run all night and rest up during the day, watching the rafts and steamboats going up and down river. Jim fixes up the raft, making a kind of wigwam on it to keep out the weather and a fire-box so they can keep warm in cold and sloppy weather. The fifth night out they pass St. Louis, and five nights after that they spot a steamboat "that had killed herself on a rock."

Huck is gripped by a spirit of adventure and wants to investigate the boat. Jim doesn't want to go, but Huck argues and wins. Huck wishes Tom Sawyer were there, to enjoy the adventure.

When they board the steamboat, they discover that someone else is on it. There are three bandits on the boat, two of whom are about to kill their partner for threatening to squeal on them. The two decide not to shoot their partner, but rather to maroon him on the boat and let him drown when the boat breaks up. The reason is that to shoot the man would get them hanged, and besides "it ain't good morals."

Huck decides to cut the robbers' boat loose and maroon them all until he can get a sheriff to come and get them. At this point Jim discovers that the raft has broken loose.

COMMENT: This chapter is full of references to the idyllic life Huck and Jim are living. They float down the river, stopping here and there to buy some supplies or "borrow" a chicken or watermelon or pumpkin. When they meet adventure, Jim tells Huck "Better let blame' well alone." But Huck, in the spirit of idealized adventure which is characteristic of Tom Sawyer, must seek out adventure. The gang of robbers that he runs into on the steamboat is the real thing. With them there is no such thing as bribing one of the gang who threatened to squeal—they will kill him. Compare Tom Sawyer's gang to this. Tommy Barnes (in Chapter Two) was lucky that Tom Sawyer only played make-believe.

CHAPTER 13. HONEST LOOT FROM THE "WALTER SCOTT"

Unless Huck and Jim find the robbers' skiff, they too will drown with the robbers. After a tense search they find the skiff, but before they can get in it, two of the robbers come out, throw some loot in it, and get in themselves, preparing to leave their comrade to his death. But one of the two remembers that the man in the steamboat still has his share of the money, so they go back to get it. Huck and Jim take advantage of their absence to scramble into the skiff and cut loose from the wreck. The swift current takes them quickly out of sight of the wreck. Then Jim takes to the oars, and sets off trying to catch up with their raft. As they glide rapidly along, Huck has time to stop and think. He begins to worry about the robbers, and "how dreadful it was, even for murderers, to be in such a fix." So he decides to have Jim put him ashore at the first light, and he will send help to the wreck, then meet Jim later, down river. But the plan doesn't work, because they catch up with the raft before they see a light on the shore. After they transfer the robber's loot to the raft Huck takes the skiff and goes to a ferry slip nearby. He talks the captain of the ferry into going out to the wreck by telling him there are relatives of a rich man on board it. Before the ferry can get to the wreck, Huck sees the wreck floating down the river, breaking up. Huck feels sure the robbers are dead.

By the time Huck gets back to the raft, it is beginning to get light, and so he and Jim hide the raft on an island, sink the skiff, and sleep "like dead people."

COMMENT: The elements of drama, suspense, and adventure dominate this chapter. The action is swift, the pace of the narrative is rapid—as rapid as the current that bears Huck and Jim away from the wreck.

This chapter and the one before it provide a further contrast between Huck Finn and the world around him. Once again he meets people who lack any quality of humanity. In resolving to send some kind of help to the robbers, Huck shows a moral sense far superior to that of any character he's met so far. Neither the ferry captain nor the woman in St. Petersburg think of doing good unless some immediate reward is forthcoming. Huck alone seems not to put a price on his efforts.

The *Walter Scott* is a den of thieves. This name is an indication of what Mark Twain thought of romantic novelists.

CHAPTER 14. WAS SOLOMON WISE?

When they awake, Huck and Jim sort out the goods that the gang stole from the wreck. They find boots, blankets, books, clothes, cigars—all sorts of things. They lounge around all afternoon, talking and lazing. Huck tells Jim about the conversation he overheard on the steamboat, and says that this kind of thing is real adventure. Jim says he'd rather do without adventures, because when he discovered that the raft was missing he thought he was either dead or sold down river for sure. Huck reflects: "Well, he was right; he was most always right; he had an uncommon level head for a nigger."

He reads to Jim about kings and dukes and people like that, and they get into a discussion about the only example they both are familiar with: King Solomon. Jim doesn't think much of Solomon because Solomon didn't know that cutting a child in half doesn't answer the question about who the child belongs to. When Huck comes to understand that Jim can't be reasoned with on this subject, he changes the topic to French kings. This lead to a discussion of the French language. Jim argues that Frenchmen ought to speak English like everybody else. At this point Huck gives up.

COMMENT: In this chapter we see Huck feeling superior to Jim. Huck with his white man's education and "civilized" outlook doesn't understand Jim's reasoning, even though he realizes (in the beginning of this chapter) that Jim has practical common sense. Huck is still an adherent to the standards of his surroundings. We shall see him learn this, and try to change himself in the next few chapters.

Of course, the humor in this chapter is obvious. It is based on Twain's device of contrasting appearance with reality: Jim's literalness and the spirit of things in this case.

CHAPTER 15. FOOLING POOR OLD JIM

Huck and Jim decide that they will travel on the raft to Cairo, Illinois, where the Mississippi River joins the Ohio River. There they'll sell the raft and take passage on a steamboat up the Ohio to the Free States. They figure they'll be in Cairo in three days.

On the second night they run into a heavy fog which causes them to tie up. Huck takes a line from the raft and paddles ahead in the canoe to find something to tie to. The current is so swift that the raft tears out the sapling he'd tied it to; Huck in the canoe is separated from Jim on the raft. Before Huck can take out after the raft, the fog closes in so thickly that he can't see 20 yards ahead of him. For the greater part of the night Huck and Jim shout to each other trying to locate each other. When they become further separated by a group of small islands and swirling currents, they both become exhausted and fall asleep. Huck wakes up under a clear, bright night sky in the wide river. He sets out to look for the raft, and after being misled by floating debris finally finds it. Jim is still sleeping, and the deck of the raft is covered with dirt, leaves and other "rubbage." Seeing the condition of the raft, Huck thinks of the difficult time Jim must have had.

Nonetheless, Huck tries to fool Jim into thinking that there wasn't any fog, that they weren't separated, and that all that Jim went through was only a dream. Jim is convinced that it was all a bad dream, and he proceeds to interpret it. Huck then asks Jim to interpret the meaning of the debris that covers the deck.

Jim is abashed and taken aback. He tells Huck that the joke isn't funny, since he was really afraid only for Huck's welfare in the fog. He says: "Dat truck dah is *trash*; en trash is what people is dat puts dirt on de head er dey fren's en makes em ashamed." He gets up and walks to the wigwam.

Huck continues: "But that was enough . . . It was fifteen minutes before I could work myself up to go and humble myself to a nigger; but I done it and I warn't ever sorry for it afterward, neither."

COMMENT: In this chapter Huck Finn seems to grow to the realization of what friendship is. He pulls a trick on Jim similar to the trick Tom Sawyer pulled on Jim in Chapter Two. Jim, as he did in Chapter Two, explains and "dresses up" the adventure he met with. But this time Huck is around to see the results of "playing games" with other people's feelings. He resolves not to play these tricks any more.

In addition, Huck realizes that he must right the wrong he has done. And although it is against everything he has ever learned about relations between white men and Negroes (let us always remember that Mark Twain is portraying a small boy born and raised in the South during the 1830s), Huck humbles himself to Jim. This is Huck's first real victory over himself. He is now really better than his father—remember how pap cussed because a free Negro could vote—because he puts aside all the conventional notions of relations between men, and begins to treat Jim with the dignity that belongs to a human being. Huck is the real idealist. Tom Sawyer only plays at romantic games.

But Huck's trials and his growth are not over, not by a long shot.

CHAPTER 16. THE RATTLESNAKE SKIN DOES ITS WORK

When they set out the next morning, Huck and Jim follow a big raft downstream. They're full of excitement about getting to Cairo. Huck begins to feel guilty because he's helping a slave to escape. Miss Watson never did him any harm, Huck thinks. And here he is, helping her property get away. He feels even more guilty when he hears Jim's plans for buying his wife out of slavery, and for stealing his children if their owner won't sell them. Huck feels that Jim will be doing an injustice by stealing his children. Huck is highly sensitive to the fact that he is helping Jim. And when Jim tells Huck his plan for stealing the children, Huck adds to himself, "I was sorry to hear Jim say that, it was such a lowering of him."

Huck decides to tell on Jim. His opportunity arises when he sets out in the canoe to check on their location. Before he's very far from the raft, he meets two armed men in a skiff who ask if he's seen any runaway slaves. Huck tries to squeal on Jim but can't, because he remembers that Jim called him "de bes' fren' Jim's ever had; . . . de on'y white genlman dat ever kep' his promise to ole Jim." Because the men suspect Huck of hiding slaves on the raft, they decide to search it. Before they get to it, however, Huck gives them the impression that there's a man with smallpox on board. They back off rapidly, but give Huck $40 (which they put on a piece of driftwood that floats to him).

Huck goes back to the raft, "feeling bad and low" because he didn't do right—that is, he didn't turn Jim in. But then he thinks that if he had turned Jim in, he'd feel just as bad as he does now.

He finds Jim hiding in the water with just his nose sticking out, and calls him up. They figure they have about 20 miles to go, and that won't take them too long to cover. Then they'll be in Cairo, where they'll catch a steamboat heading North.

But the bad luck of the snakeskin catches up with them once more. During the foggy night they had passed Cairo, and are now miles downstream, heading deeper into slave territory. Downhearted and dejected, they decide to abandon the raft and take the canoe—which can be paddled against the current—upstream to Cairo. They discover that the canoe has broken loose from the raft. More bad luck from the snakeskin!

The only thing to do now is to continue downstream on the raft until they come to a place where they can buy a canoe to go north in. After dark, they set off again. The night is murky and gray, and they light their lantern when they see a steamboat approaching them. The steamboat pilot apparently doesn't see the raft, and runs it down. As Huck dives overboard on one side of the raft he sees Jim go overboard on the other side. The steamboat slashes straight up the center. Huck dives deep to escape the paddlewheel. When he comes to the surface, he calls for Jim, but doesn't get an answer. Huck manages to get to shore. After "poking along" for about a quarter of a mile, he comes upon an old fashioned log hut. Before he can run by and get away from it, he is cornered by a pack of dogs. He stands still, very still.

COMMENT: In the early part of this chapter, Mark Twain makes use of irony, that is, his characters say one thing, when Twain himself obviously means to call our attention to the exact opposite. This irony is in the scene where Huck thinks of Jim, his wife, and children as the property of other people. The fact that Jim's children belong to some other person seems quite right, natural, and proper to Huck. Yet, by making so much of the point, by emphasizing it the way he does, Twain suggests to us how unjust it is that a man should be "lowered" by having to "steal" his children in order to keep his family together. People consider—as Huck Finn here considers—the injustice to the slave-owner, but not the injustice to the slave.

Huck, in feeling guilty about helping Jim escape, is still a child of his time. He is aware of right and wrong as his society explains it to him. He has a long way to go, and many adventures to experience before he finally matures as a man who can think for himself and withstand the social pressures which result in injustice. That he is moving in the right direction is made clear when he tells us that if he were to turn Jim in, he would feel just as bad as he does because he doesn't turn Jim in. Huck feels himself caught between two devils. He feels that men should stick together and help one another in times of trouble. He feels that to turn Jim in after he has given his word not to, and after Jim has suffered a great deal for him, would be the last act of cowardice. As outcasts on the river they must support each other.

The bad luck that comes of handling snakeskin finally comes upon them in all its terrible force. Not only do the refugees overshoot Cairo, but they lose their canoe and raft, and they lose contact with each other. (We spoke—in the last paragraph—of men helping each other in times of trouble. Notice that the steamboat doesn't bother to stop to help any survivors after it smashes the raft.) In terms of the narrative thread, or plot of the story, this superstition makes a series of events believable which could otherwise seem merely coincidental.

CHAPTER 17. THE GRANGERFORDS TAKE ME IN

The noise of the dogs awakens the occupants of the house, who greet Huck at the ends of their rifles. Cautiously they let him into the house and search him before they give him dry clothing and food. Huck tells them he fell off the steamboat, and invents a family background. He notices, in the meantime that the Grangerford house is well decorated (with brass knobs instead of iron or wood ones, and paintings on the wall and the like) for a country home. He concludes that they are a "nice family." Huck describes Emmeline Grangerford, a daughter who died when she was fifteen years old. He describes her as a painter and a poet, but he notices that most of what she's painted and written has been sad, on the theme of death. She seemed to be very sentimental about dead people, the kind of girl you'd go to if you wanted to cry; and she was happy mainly in times of sorrow.

COMMENT: The Grangerfords are an aristocratic Southern family representative of the fine families of the Old South in the days before the Civil War. This chapter and Chapter 18 contain a great deal of ironic comment on the social elite of plantation life. Notice how Huck admires the decorations of the Grangerford house. Notice also that the decorations are mawkish, trite, and really tasteless. But Huck is also aware of one other item—the food is good, and there are bushels of it.

CHAPTER 18. WHY HARNEY RODE AWAY FOR HIS HAT

Huck describes the head of the house, Colonel Grangerford, in just the terms we would expect to be used in describing an old-time Southern plantation owner. When he scowls, nothing goes wrong for a weak. He is head of a large family—there are Bob and Tom and Buck, Miss Charlotte and Miss Sophia. In addition, three sons were killed and Emmeline died young. The family—together with cousins from miles around—gathers frequently for social calls. The colonel owns hundreds of acres of farmland, and well over 100 slaves. He is carrying on a feud with a neighboring aristocratic family, the Shepherdsons. We learn about this feud when Huck and Buck (who is Huck's age, about 13 or 14), out in the woods hunting, see Harney Shepherdson riding along on his horse. Buck shoots at Harney, but misses him and only knocks his hat off. Despite the fact that he has a clear target, Harney doesn't shoot back. Instead, he rides off after his hat. When Huck asks Buck why the shooting occurred, Buck tells him about the feud.

Huck describes how the Grangerfords go to church the following Sunday, carrying their rifles. They hear a very good sermon on brotherly love. On the way home they talk about theological subjects.

Later that Sunday, Miss Sophia asks Huck to go to the church and get her Bible for her. Huck doesn't know it, but the Bible has a note in it from Harney Shepherdson, the man Sophia is in love with. The note tells the hour when Harney and Sophia will elope, go across the river and be married.

That afternoon, the slave who is assigned to wait on Huck takes him out to the woods and leads him to a cleared spot. Huck looks around and finds Jim. The two are reunited, and Jim tells Huck that he has repaired the raft. They can be on their way again.

The next morning, when Huck wakes up, he learns that the Grangerfords have all ridden out to intercept Sophia and Harney before they can cross the river. He follows after and sees a gunfight in which Buck and his cousin Joe (who at this point are the last living male members of the Grangerford family) are cut down. The shooting, Huck tells us, "made me so sick I most fell out of the tree [where he was hiding]. I ain't agoing to tell *all* that happened—it would make me sick again if I was to do that. I wished I hadn't ever come ashore that night to see such things. I ain't ever going to get shut of them—lots of times I dream about them." When it gets dark, Huck climbs down from his tree, finds Buck's body, covers its face, and goes to where Jim has the raft hidden. After a moment of panic when he doesn't see the raft because Jim has moved it to a place where they can move out swiftly, Huck finds Jim and the raft. They glide out into the river—at this place a mile and a half broad—and Huck feels "free and easy and comfortable" again.

COMMENT: In Chapters 17 and 18 we are given a picture of life among civilized people. The theme of man's inhumanity to man is well developed. The proud, fierce Grangerfords and Shepherdsons fight over some incident that no one can now recall. They respect each other, but they kill each other. They go to church and hear sermons on brotherly love, then set ambushes for each other. The churchgoing incident illustrates the underlying problem and underscores it ironically.

The love affair between Sophia and Harney reminds us of the love in Shakespeare's *Romeo and Juliet.* Both Romeo and Juliet were members of feuding families; the difference between Shakespeare's characters and Twain's is that Shakespeare's Romeo and Juliet died before they could enjoy their married life together, and their deaths brought the feuding families together in peace.

It is important to notice how Huck is happy when he gets to the river, the raft, and Jim again. The sordidness, the bloodthirstiness, and the cruelty and stupidity of these highly respectable families makes him feel sick inside.

CHAPTER 19. THE DUKE AND THE DAUPHIN COME ABOARD

Huck and Jim spend some quiet days and nights on the river, which are ended the morning that Huck picks up two men running from a mob of angry townspeople. They are obviously con-men who have been found out by their victims. Huck brings these men to the raft. The younger of the two men, about thirty years old, says he is the rightful claimant to the title of Duke of Bridgewater, but that he has been cheated out of his inheritance. He moans and sighs for awhile, until Huck and Jim offer to make him feel better by calling him by titles of respect ("Your Grace," and the like), and by waiting on him. By and by, it turns out that the other man, who is about seventy years old, is the rightful claimant to the throne of France, the Dauphin. The only way Huck and Jim can make *him* feel good is to call him "Your Majesty" and stand until he tells them they can sit.

Huck realizes that the two men aren't really royalty, but he says nothing because it wouldn't pay. All he wants to do is keep peace in the family. He adds, "If I never learnt nothing else out of pap, I learnt that the best way to get along with his kind of people is to let them have their own way."

COMMENT: The idyllic journey Huck describes in the opening paragraphs of this chapter is about to be interrupted for good by the appearance of the king and the duke. The description of the river at daybreak is a song of appreciation of the simple beauty and goodness of Nature, marred only where it has been touched by the hand of man. Huck enjoys the stillness, the calm and the quiet of the river.

Contrasted with this mood is the behavior of the king and duke, the two river characters who make their livings swindling the simple village folk.

Huck's love for peace and quiet is further brought out in this chapter when, after he notices that the two men are frauds, he decides to keep quiet, because to do otherwise would only cause trouble. By keeping quiet about what he knows, Huck is in a favorable position so far as his dealings with the scoundrels are concerned. He knows they are frauds; they think he doesn't know. Beginning with this chapter the theme of Jim's escape from slavery is dropped into the background. It comes up later in the story where it forms the nucleus of the farcical escapade that Huck engages in with Tom Sawyer on the farm of Silas Phelps.

CHAPTER 20. WHAT ROYALTY DID TO PARKVILLE

By asking them if they think a runaway slave would run South, Huck convinces the king and the duke that Jim is not a runaway. He then makes up a story about his family, telling them that Jim is the only piece of property he has left. The reason they run only at night, Huck says, is that too many people have tried to board the raft and take Jim, accusing him of being a runaway.

The king and the duke—being "royalty"—take over the beds in the raft's wigwam, leaving Huck and Jim to sleep outside. Huck notices how Jim stands watch for himself and Huck too. He understands that Jim is his friend.

Next day the duke proposes to put on *Romeo and Juliet* in the villages they run across. The king agrees with him, and sets about learning his parts. Later the king and the duke take Huck into a small village down around the bend. They discover from an old Negro that almost everybody is down at a prayer-meeting. Leaving the duke in the village's printing shop (which is empty, since the whole population went to the meeting), the king and Huck go to the prayer-meeting. There they hear a preacher delivering an emotional sermon. The king stands up and confesses that he is a pirate captain come from the Indian Ocean to find men for a crew. He cries and blubbers about his sins, and promises that he will raise money to go back and devote his life to missionary work among the pirates. The villagers, emotionally excited, take up a collection, netting him $87.75, and a three-gallon jug of whiskey he manages to steal from its resting place under a wagon.

The duke in the meantime had set up some jobs in the printing office and made money from people who thought he was the shop owner. In addition, he designed a poster advertising a reward for a runaway slave. Using this as evidence, he says, they can say that Jim is a runaway being returned to his rightful owner. That way the raft can be run in the daytime. All four agree that this is a good idea.

At four in the morning when Jim calls Huck to take the watch, he tells Huck he hopes they don't run into any more royalty. He doesn't like the two they have.

COMMENT: In this chapter we are introduced to the workings of frauds. They think nothing of breaking the people's confidence and making fools of the villagers. This behavior is the real life extension of Tom Sawyer's make-believe and "game" playing.

CHAPTER 21. AN ARKANSAW DIFFICULTY

The duke undertakes serious rehearsals for the production of the balcony scene from *Romeo and Juliet*. He adds—for excitement—a sword fight scene from *Richard III* and Hamlet's soliloquy. He teaches the king a botched-up version of the soliloquy. One morning he goes into a little village where he gets handbills printed up announcing the presentation of the three scenes. On the handbills he represents himself as David Garrick, the Younger, and the king as Edmund Kean, the Elder.

They come across a little village which is being visited by a circus—a stroke of luck, they feel, since all the country-folk will be coming into town for the circus, and so may stay for the Shakespearean presentation.

Huck describes the town and its inhabitants. The place is obviously a one-horse village. The streets are a foot deep in mud in places, and the villagers are lazy ne'er-do-wells. As the town fills up with people coming in from the country, the villagers get more and more rowdy. Finally a country character named Boggs who has a reputation for threatening people but doing nothing about his threats comes into town.

He is high-spirited as a result of heavy drinking. He rides up to the biggest store in town and insults its owner, a Colonel Sherburn. Sherburn comes out of the store and tells Boggs he has until one o'clock to continue the insults. After that time Sherburn will hunt him down. At one o'clock Boggs is still "cussing." The villagers send for his daughter to calm him down. Before she can come, however, Sherburn finds Boggs and shoots him down in cold blood before the horrified eyes of the villagers and country-folk. Boggs is carried to the village drugstore, where he dies surrounded by a crowd of curious onlookers. Witnesses to the action begin describing and acting it out to the latecomers. In a little while the crowd gets worked up, and somebody suggests lynching Colonel Sherburn. The mob takes up the cry, and storms toward Sherburn's house, snatching up clotheslines to do the hanging with.

COMMENT: In this chapter Mark Twain describes the typical early nineteenth-century sleepy village in the South. Its laziness, slowness, dirt, and ignorance make it fit game for con-men like the king and duke who try to pass themselves off as once-famous British actors. By the 1830s Garrick was long dead and Kean had died in 1833. The soliloquy which the duke teaches the king is obviously a half-remembered mish-mash of snatches of phrases from several of Shakespeare's plays. Notice how the duke seems to take over as the leader of the two frauds.

Boggs doesn't insult Sherburn after one o'clock. Not only that, but Sherburn shoots Boggs twice. This makes it seem that Sherburn was deliberately trying to upset the calm of the village.

Notice also that when Boggs dies, several of the villagers begin imitating Sherburn—one in particular is good at it. By describing the actions of the villagers before, during, and after the shooting, Twain gives us a picture of the mob which makes it seem to be made up of fools and cowards.

CHAPTER 22. WHY THE LYNCHING BEE FAILED

The mob storms Sherburn's house, trampling the fence that stands in its way. Then Sherburn steps out on the roof of his porch with a shotgun in his hand. Scornfully he rebukes the crowd for its cowardliness in coming for him illegally instead of having him arrested. He points out the cowardice of the average man—in the North for allowing himself to be downtrodden in the South for needing the protection of the mob in lynching parties. He singles out the leader of the mob—a person named Buck Harkness—whom he refers to as a half-a-man. Finally he orders the mob to disperse and "take your half-a-man with you."

Huck leaves too and goes to the circus. He is impressed by the glitter of the parade, and when a "drunk" gets into the act and tries to ride a circus horse, Huck feels embarrassed for him. But it turns out that the "drunk" is a member of the troupe. Huck feels sorry for the ringmaster who, he says, was put upon by one of his performers.

That night the king and the duke put on their show, and draw twelve people who obviously don't appreciate their brand of Shakespeare. The duke makes up a sign advertising another show, "The Thrilling Tragedy of the King's Cameleopard or The Royal Nonesuch . . . Ladies and Children Not Admitted."

COMMENT: The sudden fury of the mob and its equally sudden dispersal are illustrations of the totally herd-like quality of the villagers. The people behave like cattle who are easily led and easily frightened. Sherburn's speech is straightforwardly cynical; it thoroughly dispirits the mob and destroys its self-righteous anger. The fact that Huck is still a small village boy at heart is made clear in his comment about the ringmaster. Huck can't tell the difference here between showmanship and reality. He thinks the ringmaster was really fooled by the clown pretending to be a drunken country boy. It is obvious that the whole scene was part of the circus' entertainment. Huck can't be entertained by that kind of pretense.

CHAPTER 23. THE ORNERINESS OF KINGS

The next day the king and the duke put on their show. The audience, attracted by the last line of the handbill—"Ladies and Children Not Admitted"—is a large one. The show consists of the king hopping around the stage on all fours, naked. When the duke announces that the show is over, the audience feels that it has been cheated and is about to attack the duke and the king. One man in the audience gets up and tells the rest that it wouldn't be smart to admit they were made fools of because they would be the laughing-stocks of the village. He tells the rest of the audience to go out and praise the show, getting the rest of the villagers to come. Then everyone in the village will be in the same boat. So the audience leaves peacefully. The second night the same thing happens. On the third night Huck stands near the door where the duke is collecting admissions. He notices that the crowd is much larger, made up of many people who have seen the show on one of the other two nights. He notices also the smell of "sickly eggs," "rotten cabbages and such things." The duke gives a by-stander a quarter to tend the door while he goes backstage. Instead of going there, however, the duke and Huck head for the raft as fast as they can. Huck figures the king is in for trouble. But when they reach the raft and set out toward mid-stream, the king crawls out of the wigwam and asks them how things went. Huck is surprised to learn that he had never been to town. The king and the duke laugh over the stupidity of the townspeople who paid out $465.00 in the three nights, and were cheated out of their revenge.

When the king and duke fall asleep, Jim asks Huck if he isn't surprised by the way they carry on. Huck doesn't see any reason for telling Jim that the men aren't real royalty; it would do no good. Besides, he adds, you probably couldn't tell the real ones from these frauds.

Huck falls asleep, and Jim doesn't wake him when it's his turn to stand watch. When Huck awakens by himself at daybreak, he hears Jim bemoaning his children. Huck gets Jim to talking about his wife and family, and learns that Jim feels very bad because he once punished his little girl 'Lizabeth for not closing the door when he told her to. After he punished her, he discovered that she was deaf as a result of scarlet fever.

COMMENT: The "orneriness" of human nature is the theme of this chapter. The king and the duke cheat the villagers by appealing to their lower appetites. The villagers cheat their neighbors in order not to appear foolish. Then all the villagers are left high and dry when they come back for revenge, because the duke is more clever than they are. Jim, alone, is aware that the king and the duke don't represent the ordinary run of human beings. Huck feels there is nothing you can do; they (people in general) are all alike. It isn't too difficult to see that Huck is here acting as a mouthpiece for Mark Twain, himself.

Notice that Jim is remorseful when he's reminded of the incident of his daughter. In a poignant and touching confession he tells us that he can never forgive himself for being cruel to the poor deaf child, even though he wasn't really cruel, and he had no way of knowing beforehand that the child didn't hear him tell her to shut the door. Contrast the cruelty of Huck's pap with what Jim takes to be his own cruel action towards 'Lizabeth.

CHAPTER 24. THE KING TURNS PARSON

The king and the duke plot to "work" the villagers on either side of the river where the raft is tied up. They can't decide on a "project"; they're afraid to try the "Nonesuch" because word might have leaked down from the last village they tried it in. So while the duke stays aboard the raft to scheme something up, the king takes Huck out in the canoe to see if he can make anything. The king directs Huck to head for a steamboat laying up about three miles above the town. Huck is happy because he wants a steamboat ride. But before they get to the boat, the king sees a country boy walking along the shore, and invites him into the canoe where he asks him questions about the village and everybody in it. The boy, innocent and unsuspicious, tells the king everything he knows. Among the things that he tells the king is the fact that Peter Wilks, a villager, just died, and the rest of the villagers are expecting his brothers—Harvey, a clergyman, and William, a deaf-mute—to arrive from England at any moment. The brothers will take over Peter's estate when they arrive and administer it for Peter's nieces, Mary Jane, Susan, and Joanna. The king learns that the country boy is going to New Orleans to take passage to South America. When they get to the steamboat, the king puts the country boy on it, and has Huck paddle him another mile up the river before sending Huck back to the raft to fetch the duke. Huck knows what's going to happen, but he doesn't let on. When Huck brings the duke back, the king explains that he plans to impersonate the brothers of the dead Peter Wilks. The duke will be the deaf-mute, and the king will be the preacher.

They flag down a big steamer and have it land them at the village. They go into the main street, with Huck as their servant, as though they don't know that Peter's dead. Upon learning that their "brother" is dead, the king and duke sob and cry and carry-on. Huck is disgusted. He says, "It was enough to make a body ashamed of the human race."

COMMENT: By playing on the innocence and inexperience of a country boy, the king and duke are about to attempt their biggest confidence fraud yet. They are counting on the ignorance of the townspeople and the emotional upset caused by their uncle's death to separate the girls from their proper inheritance. Huck is about to rebel against the atrocious behavior of the king and duke. The fact that he is disgusted with their trifling with human beings makes him steal from them in a later chapter.

Huck's disgust is also a reflection of Mark Twain's attitude toward fraud and inhumanity.

CHAPTER 25. ALL FULL OF TEARS AND FLAP DOODLE

The news of the arrival of Peter's "brothers" travels rapidly, and when they get to the house, they are greeted by an enthusiastic throng of villagers, together with the three girls. After making a great and public display of sorrow, the king and duke get down to their serious business—finding out how much money Peter had. Mary Jane, the eldest niece, hands over the letter Peter left, telling where the money is hidden. Three thousand dollars and the house are to be given to the girls, and three thousand dollars and George's tanyard—George is another brother, the girls' father; he died shortly before Peter did—are to go to the brothers. When the king and duke go down the cellar to get the money, they discover that $415 is missing. They do not want to appear dishonest, and so they make it up out of the money they made at "The Royal Nonesuch." To make a "splash" the king gives the money to the girls, saying he and his brother feel that since the girls are poor orphans they should have it all. While he's at it, he makes a speech which is interrupted by the village doctor, Doctor Robinson, who accuses him of being a fraud. But the townspeople are too firmly convinced that the king and duke are Peter's brothers. They argue and try to quiet him. Finally the doctor tells the girls not to trust the imposters. But Mary Jane shows her "spunk" by giving the king the $6,000, telling him to invest it for her and her sisters without giving them a receipt for it. The doctor again warns the townspeople and the girls of the foolish mistake they're making, and goes away.

COMMENT: The hypocritical and inhumane dishonesty of Huck's "royalty" is made crystal clear in this chapter. Mark Twain strikes out at the blundering ignorance and the unthinking sentimentality of the villagers, and especially of the eldest of the three girls—Mary Jane—who, because of her sentimentalized hospitality, practically begs to be swindled.

Doctor Robinson represents the rational element in the human race, the element Mark Twain came more and more strongly to identify himself with. This rational segment believes things only when documented proofs have been presented to it. It is probably no accident that this doctor has the same name as the doctor who was murdered while robbing a grave in *Tom Sawyer.* The reason the Doctor Robinson in *Tom Sawyer* was robbing graves is that he wanted bodies to experiment with and to dissect. Nowadays people will their bodies to medical schools for just such purposes, but in the nineteenth century and earlier it was sometimes considered criminal to dissect human cadavers. Hence, people who wanted to advance science and dispel ignorance had to get their materials any way they could.

What is important to note is that Mark Twain sets up a conflict between the lone reasonable man and the crowd of unthinking, materialistic, sentimental common people.

CHAPTER 26. I STEAL THE KING'S PLUNDER

The king and the duke intend to stay overnight in the girl's house, and so they ask Mary Jane for rooms. She puts Uncle William (the duke) in the spare room, Huck in the cubbyhole in the attic, and Uncle Harvey (the king) in her room, although it has her dresses and things hanging on the wall.

Huck eats supper that night with Joanna, the 14-year-old who has a hare-lip. She asks him questions about England, and he blunders through her questioning with answers that are contradictory. She notices this, and accuses him of lying. Mary Jane and Susan (the 15-year-old) overhear this accusation and make Joanna apologize to Huck. Huck feels "low and mean" because he's helping the king and duke steal their money. He feels even worse because the girls are going out of their way to make him feel at home and among friends. He wants to tell on the king and duke, but he's afraid to go to the doctor because he doesn't want word to get out about his telling. He feels he can't tell Mary Jane because she's so honest—all her feelings show in her face. He decides to steal the money.

After searching the duke's room and not finding the money, he goes to the king's. Before he can search the room thoroughly, the sound of footsteps sends him running for a hiding-place behind the dresses hanging on the wall. He overhears a conversation between the king and duke, in which the duke tries to convince the king that they should steal just the $6,000, and run away in the middle of the night. But the king thinks it's silly to run off with the cash and leave the money that can be gotten from selling old Peter's property. He convinces the duke that they should sell the house, tanyard, and slaves, and take all the money. They will say they are taking the girls to England with them, and this will give them the excuse they need to sell the property quickly. After they run off, people will realize that the sales were illegal, and the girls will get their property back.

The duke agrees to this. He cautions the king about hiding the money they already have. The king takes the money from its hiding place among the dresses—about a foot away from where Huck is hiding—and stuffs it into the mattress. When they leave the room, Huck takes the money up to his cubbyhole and waits for everyone in the house to fall asleep. Then he slips quietly down the stairs.

COMMENT: The king's argument that the sales will be held to be illegal and that the girls will get their property back is not realistic; it is a sign of his and the duke's greed. The duke gives in to this false reasoning a little too easily. For although the girls may get their property back, the proceedings involved are long and costly.

Huck is touched by the girls' position as orphans and by their basic goodness and unselfishness. He decides to help them. Notice how Mark Twain has the action develop by means of a series of coincidences. Huck accidentally overhears the king and the duke hatch their plot; he hides behind the dresses which are left in the room for no specific reason; he doesn't hide under the bed because it happens to be a low bed, and so he escapes getting caught. Using coincidences like this is usually considered a flaw in a literary work. But Mark Twain paces the action so swiftly that the flaw—if in this instance it is one—is hardly noticeable. Not only that, but he makes the coincidental action work for him by providing a way to heighten the suspense. This structural looseness is a mark of the picaresque elements in Twain's novel.

CHAPTER 27. DEAD PETER HAS HIS GOLD

Huck tries to get outside to hide the money, but the front door is locked. Then he hears somebody coming. There is no place for him to go. He hides the money in the coffin, with Peter. After he tucks the money away and gets out of sight behind the door, he sees Mary Jane enter and kneel in front of the coffin and cry. He slips out of the room without being seen and goes back up to bed, where he lies awake all night worrying what to do next. He's afraid to go down and get the money out of the coffin because somebody might catch him. He's sure the money will be found when the undertaker screws the lid on the coffin. Then the king will have it, and there will be no second chance to steal it.

Finally the hour of the funeral comes, and as Huck sweats with worry over the money in the coffin, the undertaker slides the lid over Peter and screws it down. Now Huck is in a fix. He doesn't know whether the money is still in the coffin, or whether someone found it and took it away without mentioning it. Because he's unsure, he doesn't know whether there would be any use in writing Mary Jane a letter telling her that the money was put into the coffin.

That evening the king sets up the sale of the girls' property by telling people that he and William have to get back to England and want to take the girls with them. The girls are all excited, and can't wait to get going. However, their spirits are considerably dampened the next day when the king sells their Negroes to slave traders—the two sons up the river and the mother down the river. The girls think it was cruel of the king to separate the family. Huck consoles himself with the knowledge that the sale is illegal, and the family will be back together again shortly. But the townspeople are upset.

The next morning the king and duke notice that the money is missing from the king's mattress. They question Huck, who tells them that he's seen the slaves going in and out of the room, but didn't think anything of it at the time. He leads the two frauds to believe that the Negroes who were sold the day before may have taken the money with them. The duke blames the king for being so greedy that he sold the slaves off too quickly. If they were still around the house, he argues, the money would be, too. The king and duke argue for a while; then the king curses Huck and himself for not understanding what the slaves were doing.

COMMENT: The humorous situation concerning the noises in the basement during the funeral service provides Huck with an opportunity to admire the calmness and composure of the undertaker. Note how easily the crowd is distracted from the immediate proceedings, and note also how the undertaker is careful to satisfy the crowd's curiosity.

CHAPTER 28. OVERREACHING DON'T PAY

Next morning as Huck is going downstairs, he hears Mary Jane crying in her room while she's packing for the trip to England. He asks what's bothering her, and she tells him that she's upset over the inhuman treatment shown the slaves. He blurts out that the family will be reunited within two weeks. She wants him to repeat what he's just said, and he does. But first he makes her promise to leave the house that very morning, before breakfast, and visit friends for three or four days. He's afraid the truth will show on her face, and people will force her to tell them; then he and Jim will be in trouble.

He outlines a plan to her. She will stay at her friends' house outside town until 9:00 or 9:30 that night. Then she'll come back and put a candle in the window. If Huck doesn't show up by eleven, she's to have the king and the duke jailed. If Huck is to get caught, she's to have him released. In order to make sure the king and the duke get jailed as frauds Huck gives her a slip of paper with "Royal Nonesuch, Bricksville" written on it. He tells her to send to Bricksville to find out all she needs to know about the frauds. As he's seeing her off, he gives her another note telling her where he put the money.

Huck explains Mary Jane's absence to Susan and Joanna by saying she went across the river to visit some sick friends. He warns them not to tell the king and duke why she went because that would only postpone the trip to England—they would be quarantined because the illness is catching. Instead he suggests that they tell the "uncles" their sister went across the river to convince some friends to come to the auction and buy the house.

At the auction that afternoon the king and duke sell off everything. While they're selling the last item—a graveyard plot—a steamboat lands two men who claim to be Peter Wilks' brothers.

COMMENT: Compare Huck's plan for saving the girls' fortune with Tom Sawyer's plan for liberating Jim in Chapter 34 and following. Huck's plans are simpler, more realistic than Tom's. This is an important way in which the boys differ. Huck is concerned with results, Tom with methods.

It is important to note that the greed of the king and duke gets them into trouble—and this trouble could land them in the penitentiary.

CHAPTER 29. I LIGHT OUT IN THE STORM

The two men who claim to be Peter's brothers are "nice looking." The one who claims to be Harvey is older than the other, who has his arm in a sling. They say they will wait till their baggage comes in to prove they are who they say they are. The doctor and the lawyer (Levi Bell, who has just returned from a business trip) and a man named Hines (he saw the king and Huck pick up the country boy) side with the newcomers and claim that the king and duke are frauds. The king denies this. He argues that the newcomers are frauds. After some inconclusive argument, the old gentleman asks the king to describe the tattoo on Peter's breast. The king thinks quickly and says it's a thin blue line you can't see if you don't look closely. The newcomer says it's a small, dim P-B-W. Since the men who laid Peter out for burial didn't see either the line or the P-B-W, Levi Bell suggests they all go down to the graveyard and dig Peter up. The crowd collars all four men and Huck, and heads for the cemetery. It is now dark, and beginning to thunder and lighten, and rain begins to fall. In a flash of lightning somebody sees the bag of gold and sings out. The man who is holding Huck jumps forward for a look and, in the excitement, releases him. Huck escapes. As he is running through town he sees a light flash in Mary Jane's window, and his heart swells up. He gets to the river and takes a canoe. He heads for the towhead in midriver where the raft is tied up. As he jumps aboard the raft, he tells Jim to cut loose—they're free of the king and the duke.

His joy is short-lived, however, for while he's dancing around he hears the sound of oars. The lightning shows him the king and the duke heading for the raft. "So I wilted right down onto the planks, then, and give up; and it was all I could do to keep from crying."

COMMENT: The element of coincidence saves not only Huck and the king and the duke, but it also saves the girls' money. Were it not for the coincidental arrival of the real brothers, the king and duke might have got clean away. But the newcomers arrived at the last possible moment; even the reader has stopped expecting them to show up. And were it not for the tattoo which nobody noticed, the men wouldn't have been taken to the graveyard. And of course the sudden thunderstorm is the perfect weather for digging up corpses.

When the king is confronted with the question of the tattoo on Peter's breast, he brashly attempts to bluff it out. In the next chapter the duke is going to praise the king for this sudden inspiration. In what kind of person is such quick thinking praiseworthy? This kind of bluff is an important part of the king's character.

Throughout the chapters dealing with the Wilks affair, Huck has a feeling for the girls—particularly Mary Jane—quite unlike his feelings for any one else in the book. His feeling for Jim is different, as is his feeling for Aunt Sally (see Chapters 40, 41). He admires Mary Jane's "spunk" or "sand." We suspect he might fall in love with her if he were a different sort of fellow. Notice how the vagueness and inexactness of the word "sand" in this context is precisely the kind of vagueness one expects from a boy like Huck in this situation.

CHAPTER 30. THE GOLD SAVES THE THIEVES

When the king and the duke get aboard the raft, the king shakes Huck, accusing him of trying to run out on them. But the duke tells the king to let Huck alone—neither the king nor the duke stopped to save Huck when they got their opportunities to escape from the crowd. So they have no reason to expect that Huck would look around and try to save them when his chance came.

The two frauds begin to argue about the money. They have not only lost the Wilks fortune, but they lost the money they made from the "Royal Nonesuch" to boot. They accuse each other of stealing the money and hiding it in the coffin. Huck is uneasy, until the duke forces the king to confess that he stole it. The king confesses—an outright lie, because we know Huck stole it—only after the duke takes him by the throat and throttles him. After this incident, the men curl up with their whiskey, and within a half hour they are friendly again.

COMMENT: This chapter does two things: it develops the characters of the king and the duke, and it serves as a transition between the Wilks episode and the next affair. Note how the king tries to take out his anger on Huck; note how the duke confesses that he planned to steal the money, and forces a similar confession from the king. The duke bullies the king just as the king bullied Huck. Compare the results of this adventure with the king's boast earlier that he likes to trust to "Providence." He ends up losing money instead of making it.

CHAPTER 31. YOU CAN'T PRAY A LIE

After lying low for a while, the king and duke begin stopping at villages again, but with little success. Their attempts at running dancing schools, prayer meetings, temperance clinics, and the like meet with failure. Huck notices that they are broke and desperate. They plot and scheme together for two and three hours at a time. He and Jim decide to rid themselves of their royalty the first chance they get. One morning they stop near a little village called Pikesville, where the king goes ashore to see if the people have heard of "The Royal Nonesuch." He says that if he isn't back by noon, the duke and Huck are to come into town.

The king doesn't come back by noon, and so the duke and Huck go into town where they find the king drunk. While the king and duke are arguing, Huck runs back to the raft figuring that while the frauds are fighting he and Jim will make their getaway.

When he goes to the raft, he finds that Jim is gone. He shouts for him and searches the woods, but can't find him. Heartbroken by what he fears has happened to Jim, he sits down and cries.

After a while he goes out onto the road where he sees a boy walking. He asks the boy whether he's seen a man fitting Jim's description. The boys says he has seen a runaway slave who was taken to Silas Phelps' farm. It seems the king told Phelps that Jim is a runaway from below New Orleans, and that there is a $200 reward for him. The king sells his interest in the reward to Phelps for $40, because he is in a hurry to go up river and can't wait around for the owner to come and claim Jim.

Huck is grieved by the doublecross the king and the duke pulled on Jim. He decides that Jim would be better off at Miss Watson's than down river, and so he resolves to write a letter to Tom Sawyer telling him to inform Miss Watson of Jim's whereabouts. But he reconsiders. He knows that Jim would be despised because he ran away, and would probably be sold down river anyway. Also, he thinks that everybody will find out that he helped Jim escape. He wouldn't be able to face his friends.

He decides to reform himself. He kneels down and tries to pray, but can't find words—because he wasn't really going to give Jim up. So he writes the letter, and immediately feels better. Before he prays, however, he begins thinking of all the good and bad times he and Jim shared on the river. He remembers that Jim called him "the only friend ol' Jim ever had." He thinks: If ever Jim needed a friend, he needs one now. His eye lights on the letter he has just written. He thinks to himself:

> *"It was a close place. I took it up, and held it in my hand. I was a-trembling, because I'd got to decide, forever, betwixt two things, and I knowed it. I studied a minute, sort of holding my breath, and then says to myself: 'All right, then, I'll go to hell'—and tore it up. It was awful words, but they was said. And I let them stay said; and never thought no more about reforming."*

Huck decides to go to work to steal Jim out of slavery again. He hides the raft on an island. The next morning he dresses in his good clothes, eats, bundles some belongings and goes ashore in the canoe. He hides his bundle and canoe and begins walking toward Silas Phelps' place. Before he gets there, he meets the duke who is putting up "Royal Nonesuch" posters. He tells the duke a story about the raft being lost—pretending he thought the king and the duke took Jim and ran off without him the day before. The duke explains that the king sold Jim and spent the $40 drinking and gambling. The duke is obviously afraid that Huck might expose the "Royal Nonesuch" fraud, and so he gives him directions to a non-existent farm forty miles away. Huck pretends to believe him and sets out in the direction the duke points. But he doubles back through the woods toward the Phelps place. He wants to get to Jim and tell him to keep mum about the "Royal Nonesuch." He is afraid of what the frauds might do to anyone who squeals on them.

COMMENT: In this chapter Mark Twain again takes up the story of Jim's escape from slavery. He has left it alone for a while in order to recount the adventures of the king and the duke. The entire emphasis of this section of Jim's story will be different from what it was before, as we shall see in the following chapters.

Huck's moment of crisis comes when he finally resolves to follow his heart instead of his head. He will save Jim—which is, as far as he is concerned, wrong. He has been taught that the right thing to do is to turn Jim in. This chapter restates with emphasis the theme of Chapters 15 and 16, in which Huck arrives at the same conclusion. Huck's determination not to unsay what he has said is a clear indication of his basic honesty and integrity. Whatever he is—Abolitionist, or worse—he is not a hypocrite. "You can't pray a lie," he says. He might like to do wrong and get away with it; but since that obviously won't work, he isn't going to do right for the wrong reason. He decides, and accepts the consequences of his decision: "'All right, then, I'll go to hell'—. . . . It was awful thoughts and awful words. . . ."

For all his courage in making this resolution, note that he is nevertheless reluctant to cause trouble for the king and the duke. This is not because he likes the two frauds, but, rather, because he wants to keep out of trouble so he can work out Jim's escape.

CHAPTER 32. I HAVE A NEW NAME

When Huck gets to the Phelps farm, he finds that it is "one of these little one-horse plantations, and they all look alike." He describes the place in some detail. Before he gets to the house, however, he is surrounded by yammering dogs. One of the slaves rescues him by calling off the dogs. Then he is called to the house by a woman who mistakes him for her nephew, coming for a visit. He lets her think he is her nephew—she is supposed to be his Aunt Sally—and makes up a story about his steamboat trip down river to her place. When the woman's husband comes home, she hides Huck under the bed until the proper moment. The man is worried because something may have happened to the boy. After teasing her husband for a while, she hauls Huck out from under the bed. Her husband asks, "Who's that?" She replies, "It's Tom Sawyer!" Huck almost faints with relief. He knows enough about the Sawyer family to be able to lie without getting caught. When he hears a steamboat whistle, though, he gets nervous. The real Tom Sawyer may turn up and give him away. He has to get to the landing before Tom gets to the plantation. He tells the Phelps family that he wants to go get his luggage from the place he's hidden it.

COMMENT: Elsewhere Mark Twain tells us that Phelps' farm is a fairly good picture of a farm owned by his uncle. Note how Mark Twain's first-hand experience helps him write a vivid and concrete description of the kind of farm he is describing.

The whole chapter here is an introduction to Jim's escape from slavery. Since Huck's luck in landing at Tom's uncle's farm is highly unlikely—improbable—Mark Twain slides over it by emphasizing not Huck's good fortune, but Huck's discomfort while he's trying to find out who he's supposed to be. To do this Twain builds up a great deal of suspense by having Huck forced to lie about his journey without knowing where he was to have come from, or who he was supposed to be.

CHAPTER 33. THE PITIFUL ENDING OF ROYALTY

Huck is given one of Phelps' wagons, and he heads for town. Halfway there, he meets Tom Sawyer, who thinks Huck is a ghost. After proving he isn't dead and never was, Huck explains his situation to Tom. Tom tells Huck to take the trunk he has in his wagon, and go back to the farm. Tom will arrive a little later, and Huck is to pretend not to know him. Huck tells Tom that he is going to steal Miss Watson's Jim out of slavery, and asks Tom not to tell on him. He is shocked and surprised when Tom offers to help steal Jim. Huck is so excited by this offer from a boy he considers good, that he gets back to the farm too soon. But Phelps is not a suspicious man, and so everything's all right. A little while later Tom arrives, and after making up a long story about being a stranger and telling where he is from, finally kisses Aunt Sally. Since she doesn't know who he really is, she scolds him. Tom then identifies himself as Sid, his half-brother, who is back in St. Petersburg.

After dinner Huck finds out that Jim has already told Silas Phelps about the fraudulence of "The Royal Nonesuch." He and Tom climb out of their bedroom that night and head for town. They want to warn the king and duke. But it's too late. On their way into town they are passed by a procession of people who have tarred and feathered the king and duke, and are riding them out of town on a fence rail. Huck says: "It was a dreadful thing to see. Human beings can be awful cruel to one another."

Huck feels guilty, even though he hasn't done anything wrong. He decides that a person's conscience doesn't have any sense. It takes up a lot of room, but doesn't do any good.

COMMENT: In this chapter we see Huck still following his emotions instead of his reason. He does so because he is by now firmly convinced that theory or reason is a poor adviser and that experiences and feelings are more likely to lead a person right. Although the king and duke used him and Jim shamefully, he is sorry to see them mistreated and cruelly punished.

With Tom Sawyer's return to the story we can expect some more "romantic" games, similar to Tom's teasing of his Aunt Sally. Notice how Tom keeps even Huck in the dark about his plans for pretending to be Sid.

It is important to understand the kind of people Sally and Silas Phelps are. Remember that in the last chapter (32) Sally remarked it was lucky no people were killed in the steamboat explosion? Even though she is portrayed as a kind-hearted, loving and warm, humane woman, she evidently didn't consider the Negro a person. Remember, too, that Silas is a good man, innocent and religious—even though he plans to sell Jim for the reward money.

CHAPTER 34. WE CHEER UP JIM

On their way home, Huck and Tom decide that Jim is probably kept in a hut in the back of the farm, because they saw food being taken there, and the slave that took the food down used a key to unlock and lock the hut. Tom tells Huck to think of a plan to steal Jim, but Huck realizes that Tom is going to come up with a plan that has lots of "style." This is just what happens. Tom discards Huck's plan because it is too simple and easy. Tom's plan, Huck says, "was worth fifteen of mine for style, and would make Jim just as free a man as mine would, and maybe get us all killed besides." When they get home, they examine the hut where they think Jim is kept, and then they go to bed. Huck enters the house by the unlocked door; Tom, however, climbs up the lightning rod—after several unsuccessful attempts.

The next morning they get to see Jim by tagging along with the slave who takes the food down. When Jim sees them he sings out, but they act as though they don't know him. By this they let him understand they are going to do something for him.

COMMENT: In this chapter Tom Sawyer takes over. Notice that the slaves—particularly Jim—seem to fade into the background. They become mainly props, minstrel show Negroes. Tom is not concerned with Jim as a person, or as a friend—the way Huck is. He is interested in a make-believe adventure. Huck knows this, although he doesn't quite understand it. He says that Tom's plan would free Jim just as effectively as his would. What he means is that his simple, direct plan would free Jim just as effectively as Tom's complicated, confusing one. Not only that, but his plan would be a lot less dangerous, and require a lot less work.

The reason for this difference between the two plans is that Tom is interested in method, while Huck is interested in results.

CHAPTER 35. DARK, DEEP-LAID PLANS

Huck and Tom discuss the plans to dig Jim out of the hut he's locked in. They could easily tear the lock off the door, but Tom wants something more exciting. Huck keeps suggesting quick and easy ways of getting Jim loose, but Tom won't hear of it. He says these methods are too "unregular." Huck must steal a sheet to make a rope ladder (even though there's nothing Jim can possibly climb); he must steal a shirt so Jim can keep a diary in his own blood (even though Jim can't write); he must steal table-knives to dig Jim out with (even though there are picks and shovels nearby).

COMMENT: Note how Tom uses his wide reading to dredge up the rules for a proper escape. His reading seems to have consisted entirely of the kind of romantic classics—"Baron Trenck," "Cassanova," "Bevenuto Chelleeny," "Henri IV"—which Mark Twain satirizes elsewhere. Notice how Tom is willing to pretend that the job takes thirty-seven years, yet is not willing to pretend a saw is a knife. In the next two chapters we will see what happens to this "integrity."

The contrast between Huck's world and Tom's world is made sharper in the passage dealing with stealing. Note how Huck can't understand why it's so wrong for him to steal a watermelon, while it's all right for him to steal sheets, shirts, knives, and the like.

CHAPTER 36. TRYING TO HELP JIM

When they think the household is asleep, Huck and Tom climb down the lightning rod, shut themselves in the lean-to next to Jim's hut, and begin digging up the dirt floor next to the wall of Jim's prison. After a long session of digging with the knives, Tom admits that they have to use the picks and shovels, and pretend they're digging with knives. Tom doesn't feel right about it, however. He'd like to use the knives, but his hands are too blistered.

Next day Tom steals a pewter spoon and brass candlestick to make pens out of so that Jim can write a journal in blood. That night they finish the tunnel under the wall, and get into Jim's prison hut. Jim is glad to see them and wants to leave his prison immediately. Tom convinces him that to escape like that would be highly irregular. Jim agrees to go along with Tom's plan, although he doesn't understand such things and how they belong in the white man's world. At any rate, he's comfortable and well looked after, so he'll put up with his imprisonment. Tom tells him that they'll smuggle in equipment (a rope ladder, etc.) by Nat, the slave who feeds Jim, and by Silas and Sally, who visit him to cheer him up and pray with him.

Next morning the boys smuggle a piece of candlestick to Jim by stuffing it into his bread. They go along to see how it works, Huck says: "when Jim but into it most mashed all his teeth out; and there warn't ever anything could 'a' worked better. Tom said so himself." While they're standing there, about eleven dogs crawl into the room through the tunnel, which comes out under Jim's bed. Nat thinks he's being witched, so he faints. Tom gets rid of the dogs and locks the lean-to door. He then sets things up for getting the rope ladder to Jim by telling Nat that he and Huck will get rid of the witches by putting something into a "witch pie."

COMMENT: The emphasis in this chapter is on the contrast between Huck's level-headed realism and Tom's romantic nonsense. Notice that Tom complains about the morality of using picks and shovels. Tom does not mean the same thing by "moral" that Huck does when he says that people are cruel to each other.

Note that Huck, who has had real adventures on the river—boarding the Walter Scott, the house of death, being involved with the Grangerfords who all get wiped out by the Shepherdsons, and being involved with the king and the duke—doesn't seem to realize that those were real adventures. Instead he enters into the spirit of Tom's make-believe excitement, just as he was completely fooled by the make-believe excitement of the circus (Chapter 22).

Notice also that Jim is no longer treated as a warm, feeling human being. He is relegated to an inferior position, mainly because the story is no longer about his escape to freedom. Mark Twain has shifted the emphasis away from Jim's escape to freedom, and placed it on the attitudes and points of view of Huck and Tom. These attitudes and these viewpoints are responsible for the cultural sterility and the ignorant inhumanity of the little backwater villages. As Mark Twain says in another place, if it weren't for "romantic" literature of the type Tom Sawyer loves, the Civil War might never have happened. This is probably why the wrecked steamboat, the den of thieves, is called the *Walter Scott*.

CHAPTER 37. JIM GETS HIS WITCH PIE

Tom is bent and determined on making Jim's escape follow all the rules he's distilled from his adventure books. He has to send Jim odds and ends of things like a ropeladder baked in a pie, pens made out of candlesticks and spoons, and many other items, all useless to Jim in his present circumstances. The Phelps household is too well run to permit Tom and Huck to steal the spoons and sheets and shirts they need. Finally, in order to overcome the great risk of detection, they steal things and put them back when they are discovered missing. The boys do this over and over again, until Aunt Sally doesn't know what she has or how much of it. On top of this, they so confuse the poor old woman that she doesn't care whether the whole house or any part of it is carried off.

Tom and Huck bake the pie in a brass warming pan of Silas'. They found the pan in the attic amongst the rest of the family "relics." By telling Nat the pie will keep the witches away, they are able to get him to carry it to Jim on the tray with Jim's food. The boys also put tin plates stolen from the slave quarters on the tray. Jim hides the rope ladder in his bed, and scratches marks on the plates and throws them out the window hole of his hut.

COMMENT: Notice in this chapter how Tom's plans usually get changed a little due to the need for practicality. The plans are always bigger than the reality, in which Tom ends up "pretending" something is done his way, while it is actually done more realistically.

CHAPTER 38. HERE A CAPTIVE HEART BUSTED

Tom draws up a coat of arms for Jim, part of which makes sense and part of which doesn't. He refuses to explain the arms to Huck. Huck says, "If it didn't suit him to explain a thing to you, he wouldn't do it."

Then Tom says Jim has to carve sorrowful inscriptions on a rock. Since there are no rocks in Jim's hut, Tom and Huck go to get a grindstone. They are almost squashed by it when it topples over as they are rolling it to the hut. So, they get Jim out of the hut and have him help them. When they get the stone in the hut, they chain Jim up again, and have him start carving the inscriptions. Since Jim can't read or write, Tom has to outline the inscriptions on the rock and let Jim follow the lines. Finally Tom decides to bring Jim spiders, rats, and snakes to keep him company. According to the rules, all prisoners must tame and make pets of whatever animal life infests the prison. If none infests it, some must be imported. Also, according to Tom's rules, every prisoner raises flowers in his cell by watering them with his tears. The boys will have to bring Jim a little weed which grows without sunlight. Jim will have to use onions to draw his tears, and he will have to pretend the tears are produced by his "deep sorrow."

COMMENT: The silly escapades in this chapter—including the release of Jim and his re-imprisonment—point up the character of Tom Sawyer and establish the realistic character of Huck by the strong ironic comment. It is obvious that Jim can be freed at any time, and Tom frees him. But Tom pretends that Jim cannot be freed. He makes a game of the "evasion," as he calls it. Jim is a stage prop, like the case-knives, and the weed, and the rats, snakes and spiders. There is confusion over the importance of the *thing* to be done and the *way* it is to be done.

Huck isn't aware that Tom doesn't know what the coat of arms signifies. Compare Tom's coat of arms with the soliloquy the duke teaches the king in Chapter 21. Notice the resemblance in the fact that both the speech and coat of arms are half-remembered, imperfectly understood collections of jargon and cliché. Notice also that Huck is taken in by both just as neatly as he was taken in by the clown in the circus. The fact that Tom can make himself believed in spite of his obvious ignorance and the fact that Huck got involved with the king and the duke in spite of their obvious fraudulence come close to stating explicitly the central themes of most of Mark Twain's works. This is that the human race will get itself into hot water no matter what rewards are offered for staying out of hot water.

CHAPTER 39. TOM WRITES 'NONNAMOUS LETTERS

The boys catch rats and snakes and spiders to take to Jim. The vermin get loose in the house, upsetting Aunt Sally no end. Finally—three weeks later—everything is ready for the "evasion." It must come soon because Silas Phleps has written to the plantation the king told him Jim escaped from. Since the plantation does not exist, he naturally gets no answer. So he decides to advertise Jim in the St. Louis and New Orleans newspapers. Huck wants to free Jim immediately.

In order to make the escape a proper one, Tom insists on writing anonymous letters to the Phelpses, telling them that Jim is going to be stolen by a group of "cutthroats from over in the Indian Territory." Then he dresses Huck in a frock belonging to one of the slave girls and has him sneak around slipping the letters under the door.

The result is that the family is nervous and jumpy, especially Aunt Sally.

COMMENT: Tom is not happy with having Jim escape easily. He writes the letters in order to give the plot away. He does not have Huck deliver the final letter (which tells the day and time of the "robbery"), but delivers it himself for the excitement and adventure involved. The Phelpses have stationed a Negro outside to guard the family. Tom doesn't even notice that the excitement is somewhat toned down since the guard is sleeping soundly enough to allow Tom to slip the note down the back of his neck.

CHAPTER 40. A MIXED-UP AND SPLENDID RESCUE

On the day preceding the night they set for Jim's escape, Tom and Huck go fishing and check out the raft. They get home late for supper and notice that the whole family is edgy on account of the last letter. Up in their bedroom after supper Tom discovers that Huck forgot to take butter for the lunch they put together to eat after the getaway. He sends Huck down to the cellar to get it. While Huck is getting the butter, Aunt Sally comes down into the cellar. He quickly hides the butter (and the bread he was carrying it on) under his hat. But Aunt Sally sees him and makes him go to the "setting-room" to wait till she comes and has a chance to question him about why he's been down there at this hour. When Huck gets to the "setting-room" he finds it full of farmers—fifteen of them—with guns! He concludes that Tom's letters have ruined the escape.

By the time Aunt Sally comes to question him, the butter under his hat has melted and started oozing down the side of his head. Aunt Sally sees the oozing butter and, after panicking because she thinks his brains are leaking out, pulls his hat off. When she realizes it's only butter, she lets him go, saying that if she'd known all along he wanted something to eat she wouldn't have objected to his being in the cellar.

Once he's free of the "setting-room," Huck goes up to bed as he's told. But instead of settling down for the night, he climbs down the lightning rod, runs to Jim's and tells Tom about the band of armed farmers. Tom, instead of being frightened, is happy. His plan will be "gaudily" successful. Before they can get moving, however, the hut they are in is surrounded by the farmers. They manage to escape, anyway, with Tom pushing Jim first and Huck second. Tom is last to leave. They manage to evade the farmers who by now are chasing them and shooting, and they make their way to the raft.

Huck and Jim discover that Tom has been shot through the leg, but Tom doesn't mind—he's happy; his plan was successful. Huck and Jim, however, are not so happy. Jim decides to risk his freedom in order to get a doctor for Tom. Huck and Jim override Tom's objections. Tom then gives Huck directions about the proper way to bring a doctor. The directions are as unrealistic as the whole plan to rescue Jim. Huck agrees with Tom and leaves after telling Jim to hide in the woods when he sees the doctor coming.

COMMENT: After the escape, the character of Jim comes once more into the foreground. He is no longer the backdrop for Tom Sawyer's silly adventure-game. He is a person in his own right, acting in a way consistent with the pattern of action he established during the voyage with Huck in the earlier chapters of the novel. Not only is he considerate to the point of sacrificing his freedom for the wounded Tom Sawyer, but he is a personality strong enough to overcome Tom's objections. No one—at least not Huck or Jim—has been able to rule Tom Sawyer up to this point.

When Jim makes the offer to sacrifice his freedom, and when Huck realizes he means it, he says the best thing of Jim he can think of: "I knowed he was white inside, and I reckoned he'd say what he did say...." Jim's loyalty is the kind of loyalty Huck admires and tries to live up to throughout the story. Jim is Huck's teacher in this respect. For as with the superstition, so with ideas of social justice: Huck does not believe in superstitions he hasn't seen come true. Those he's seen coming true—the rattlesnake skin, for instance—he believes in. The others—Miss Watson's praying, for instance—he is skeptical of because they didn't do anything.

CHAPTER 41. "MUST 'A' BEEN SPERITS"

Huck finds a doctor and sends him out to the raft. The doctor won't go with Huck because he doesn't think the canoe will hold them both. While he's waiting on shore for the doctor to return, Huck falls asleep. It is broad daylight when he awakes. Fearing that the doctor may have gone home, he checks the house but finds that the doctor hasn't been back since he left last night. Before he can get out to the raft to see what the trouble is, he runs into Silas who takes him home after he explains that he and Tom joined in the hunt but got separated during the night. At home he sees all the family's friends and neighbors sitting around, eating the Phelpses out of hearth and home, talking about the excitement of the night before. (This is where the title of this chapter is taken from. The neighbors actually enter into the spirit of Tom Sawyer's plan, and enjoy it for the kind of plan it was, though they do claim Jim must have been out of his mind to do all the crazy stuff.) No one suspects the boys of helping Jim escape.

When he sees how worried Silas and Sally are, Huck feels ashamed. He is so ashamed that when he promises Sally he won't climb down the lightning rod to go hunt for Tom—who everybody thinks is lost—he doesn't. But he does slide down the rod three times that night to peep in the window of the front room where he sees Sally waiting up for Tom with tears in her eyes.

COMMENT: Huck is a changed person. The lies he tells the doctor are not so convincing as all the rest he's told so far in the novel. Once he promises Aunt Sally he won't run out on her, he doesn't run out—even though he wants to join his comrades more than anything he's wanted to do so far.

The neighbors' discussion of the events of the night before parallels in a way the description and acting out by the village loafers of the shooting of Boggs in Chapter 21. The reaction to the real adventure in Chapter 21 is the same as the reaction to the bogus adventure in the chapter before this one. Note Huck's attitude toward the assembled neighbors. Does he understand what's going on? Do you think he understands the similarity to the crowd that went to lynch Sherburn?

CHAPTER 42. WHY THEY DIDN'T HANG JIM

After breakfast the next morning, Silas goes into town to look for Tom, but comes back without him. He remembers, though, to give his wife the letter he got from the post office the day before, when he found Huck. Before Aunt Sally can open the letter, however, she sees the doctor coming, followed by Tom, carried on a mattress, and Jim, chained. Tom is out of his head from the bullet wound. Silas and the doctor take Tom into the house. Huck follows the men to see what they're going to do with Jim. They are going to hang him, until someone remembers that his owner might show up. When he does come, they will have to pay for Jim. They settle for hitting him—"they give him a cuff or two the side of the head"—and cussing him. He is chained tightly this time.

The doctor comes out and tells the men to go easy on Jim because he helped to save Tom's life at the expense of his freedom. Not only that, he says, but Jim was a good and a faithful nurse. The men leave off the cussing.

Next day Tom wakes up in his right mind, and tells Aunt Sally the whole story of how he and Huck "liberated" Jim. When he finds out that Jim is in chains and under guard, insists that Jim be let loose immediately. It seems Miss Watson died two months ago and set him free in her will. She was sorry she ever considered selling him down river. While he's explaining that he wanted to set Jim free for the adventure of it, his Aunt Polly comes in. She came down from St. Petersburg because Aunt Sally wrote that Tom and Sid had arrived safely. Polly knew that Sid was nowhere near the Phelpses, and so she went down to investigate. She identifies Tom and Huck.

COMMENT: It is interesting to compare this chapter with Chapter 22, where the mob is turned away by Colonel Sherburn. This mob doesn't hang Jim because it might cost them money. There is no question of justice for Jim. The laws of economics prevail: if you destroy a man's property, you pay for it. There is no one here to ask what Jim is charged with, let alone anyone qualified to ask whether he's guilty and to what degree. Only the doctor is respected enough to be listened to. He alone tries to make things easier for Jim. But he's not very effective, is he? The men stop cussing. They keep the chains on, however, as though they have extended a great mercy to Jim. Jim is saved only because of practical considerations.

And what is Huck's reaction? Huck reports the goings-on, and is sympathetic to Jim. But he doesn't make the connection between the injustice being done Jim and the responsibility these men have to see that Jim is treated humanely.

The coincidental death of Mrs. Watson and her equally coincidental will have been regarded by some people as a flaw in the novel. This ending is thought to be weak and fortuitous. In modification of this opinion it ought to be noted that this ending does help explain Tom Sawyer's motives. Huck sees now why Tom Sawyer would be acting like a "low-down Abolitionist." Remember: Tom seems to be Huck's hero all through the book. Every time he has an adventure, or does something "gaudy," he wishes Tom were there to see him and approve. Tom is the young boy who will grow up to be the respectable and successful man in his day. We shall see in the next chapter what is going to become of Huck.

The arrival of Aunt Polly is as fortuitous as the announcement of Jim's emancipation. However, she rounds out the story by confirming Tom's report, thereby guaranteeing Jim's freedom, and by identifying Huck, thereby motivating Aunt Sally to try to adopt him in the next chapter.

CHAPTER THE LAST. NOTHING MORE TO WRITE

Huck asks Tom what he thought they were going to do after they set a free slave free. Tom says he thought they'd continue down the river, then come up again and have a parade in St. Petersburg to honor Jim for escaping from slavery. Considering that St. Petersburg is in slave territory, Huck figures things ended well as they did.

Jim is released from his chains; Tom gives him $40 for being a good prisoner. Jim reminds Huck of the time he said he'd be rich again, and here he is, rich. Then Tom suggests they all buy outfits and set out for the Indian territory in search of adventures. Huck is agreeable, but says he doesn't have any money; pap's likely got it all from Judge Thatcher by now. Jim tells Huck that pap was the dead man they saw in the floating house.

Now that Tom is almost well, he carries his bullet "around his neck on a watch-guard for a watch, and is always seeing what time it is, and so there ain't nothing more to write about, and I am rotten glad of it, because if I'd 'a' knowed what trouble it was to make a book I wouldn't 'a' tackled it and ain't a-going to no more. . . ."

COMMENT: Everything is neatly wound up in this "Chapter the Last." Jim is free; Tom has his bullet to impress people with; and Huck is setting off for the Indian Territory ahead of the others, because Aunt Sally wants to adopt and civilize him, and he's "been there before."

Notice that so far as his social "adjustment" is concerned, Huck is just about where he was in the beginning of the novel: looking for some way to "get out from under" civilization, and to escape its stifling restrictions.

With pap dead, it turns out that Jim has been Huck's closest companion and a kind of alternate father to him. All during the trip, Jim has looked out for Huck and taught him all the things he should learn in growing up. He stood Huck's watches, and he taught Huck the ways of the birds, and he provided the closest thing Huck has to a religion: the superstition that really works. It works well enough to seem to Huck, the narrator, a proper causal force to keep things going along.

Character Analyses

HUCKLEBERRY FINN: Huck is the central figure of the novel, the son of the town drunkard. He is essentially good-hearted, but he is looked down upon by the rest of the village. He dislikes civilized ways because they are personally restrictive and hard. He is generally ignorant of book-learning, but he has a sharply developed sensibility. He is imaginative and clever, and has a sharp eye for detail, though he doesn't always understand everything he sees, or its significance. This enables Mark Twain to make great use of the device of irony. Huck is essentially a realist. He knows only what he sees and experiences. He doesn't have a great deal of faith in things he reads or hears. He must experiment to find out what is true and what isn't. With his sharply observant personality he is able to believe Jim's superstition at some times, to scoff at it at others.

THE WIDOW DOUGLAS: The wife of the late Justice of the Peace of St. Petersburg—the village which provides the story's setting. Huck likes her because she's kind to him and feeds him when he's hungry. Her attempts to "civilize" him fail when Huck prefers to live in the woods with his father. He doesn't like to wear the shoes she buys him, and he doesn't like his food cooked the way hers is.

MISS WATSON: The Widow's maiden sister. She leads Huck to wish he were dead on several occasions by trying to teach him things. Her favorite subject is the Bible. She owns Jim and considers selling him down river. This causes Jim to run away. Filled with sorrow for driving Jim to this extreme, Miss Watson sets him free in her will.

TOM SAWYER: Huck's friend. A boy with a wild imagination who likes to play "games." He reads a lot, mainly romantic and sentimental novels about pirates and robbers and royalty. He seldom understands all he reads; this is obvious when he tries to translate his reading into action. He doesn't know what "ransoming" is: he supposes it to be a way of killing prisoners. He has a great deal of drive, and can get people to do things his way.

JIM: Miss Watson's slave, and the one really significant human character Huck meets in the novel. Though he is referred to as Miss Watson's "nigger," it is clear that the expression is used as a literary device—it is part of the Missouri dialect of the nineteenth century. Aside from Huck, Jim stands head and shoulders above all the characters in the book, in every respect. He is moral, realistic, and knowing in the ways of human nature. He appears at times as a substitute father for Huck, looking after him, helping him, and teaching him about the world around him. The injustices perpetrated by the institution of slavery are given deep expression in his pathos.

PAP: Huck's father, the town drunkard. He is in every respect the opposite of Jim. He is sadistic in his behavior toward his child. He is dirty, greedy, and dies violently because of his involvement with criminals. He is typical of the "white trash" of the day. Pap is an example of what Mark Twain thought the human race was: unreformable. A person is what he is, for good or bad, and nothing can change him.

JUDGE THATCHER: The guardian of Tom's and Huck's money. He is very wealthy, and the most respected man in the village. He becomes involved in a lawsuit to protect Huck from the cruelty of his father.

THE GRANGERFORD FAMILY: Southern aristocrats of the pre-Civil War south. They are portrayed as men who are jealous of their honor and cold-blooded in revenge. They are excellent horsemen and good fighters, and they respect their enemies as being the same. Their women are sentimental, but accustomed to hard living. Their taste runs to plaster of paris imitations of things and melancholy poetry. The general influence of Sir Walter Scott's romantic novels is clearly seen in the details of these people's daily lives.

THE KING AND THE DUKE: Two river tramps and con-men who pass themselves off to Huck and Jim as the lost Dauphin of France and the unfortunate Duke of Bridgewater (Bilgewater). They make their living off suckers they find in the small, dirty, ignorant Southern villages. Of the two men, the duke is less cruel and more imaginative than the king, though neither has any moral sensitivity worth mentioning. These men represent the starkly materialistic ideals of "the man who can sell himself" in their most logical extreme. Mark Twain holds them up as examples of the anti-social tendencies of the human race. Readers are usually satisfied when they come to the part of the story where these two get tarred and feathered and driven out of town on a fence rail. Huck is more humane about their suffering.

THE WILKS GIRLS: Nieces of Peter Wilks, a dead man. The king and the duke try unsuccessfully to rob the girls' inheritance. Mary Jane, the eldest, causes Huck to almost fall in love with her. He admires her spunk, or "sand." Susan is the middle sister, and Joanna, the "Harelip," is the youngest. Joanna questions Huck about his fictive life in England. His discomfort at being caught in a situation where he can't lie very easily is removed by Mary Jane and Susan who berate Joanna for upsetting the peace and quiet of their guest. The girls are innocent sheep, ready for snatching by the king and duke. Only Huck of the three "visitors from England" feels sorry for their plight.

THE PHELPSES: Tom Sawyer's uncle and aunt. They buy Jim from the king and the duke. Kind, gentle people who do right as their consciences dictate. Sally is going to adopt Huck, but he would rather go live among the Indians.

AUNT POLLY: The aunt with whom Tom lives. She is fairly well off, a member of the middle class. With a nephew like Tom, she is long-suffering.

SID: Tom Sawyer's half-brother. He doesn't figure in this story, except that Tom uses his name because the Phelps family thinks Huck is Tom.

Sample Essay Questions and Answers

1. What is Huck's attitude toward people he disagrees with? What does this tell us about Huck?

ANSWER: Huck says he learned one thing from pap: never disagree with his kind of people. Let him have his own way. You won't learn anything by disagreeing with him; you'll suffer less in the long run by simply letting him go along his own business, no matter how disagreeable it is to you. Huck says the same thing about Miss Watson. While she describes Heaven to him, he keeps thinking he'd "rather go to the other place." But he doesn't tell her, because it would only get her excited and would do no good. He thinks the same thing when he decides not to tell Jim that the king and the duke are frauds.

In general then, Huck's attitude seems to be that if you let other people alone, they won't come around disturbing your peace and quiet. There doesn't seem to be any percentage in stirring up trouble by getting people all excited. Things won't be changed. An illustration of this is supplied by Dr. Robinson's warning to the Wilks girls that the king and duke are frauds. In spite of this reasonable man's warning, the girls trust the king and duke until the truth becomes painfully obvious to them. They could have spared themselves a great deal of sorrow if they had listened to the voice of reason.

This tells us that Huck enjoys peace and contentment, that he probably has too little of it in his life, and goes to the mighty, sliding river to escape from the harassment of the widow and her sister and the cruelty of his pap.

2. Does Huck change at all during the course of the novel? In what way?

ANSWER: Yes, Huck becomes more mature, more humane, more self-reliant as a result of his experience and his association with Jim. Huck learns what real friendship means, and he grows to value and cherish his friendship with Jim. In the beginning of the novel he joins Tom in playing a joke on Jim. But towards the end, he cries when Jim is sold to the Phelps family by the king and the duke. The turning point in Huck's relationship with Jim came when Huck humbled himself after he played the game on Jim the night they were separated on the foggy river.

As a result of this friendship, Huck comes to place more trust in his experiences, rather than in what he's been taught. What he learns out of books is too far removed from daily life to be of any use to him.

He points out to Tom Sawyer that he's interested in *results,* not formalities, when it comes to helping Jim escape. This is a change from what he believed when he joined Tom Sawyer's robber gang in the beginning of the book.

3. What use does Mark Twain make of concrete details of description and character portrayal?

ANSWER: Mark Twain depicts life and people realistically by choosing important concrete details that characterize the people or things he is describing. His description of Silas Phelps' farm, for instance, is drawn in great detail, ranging from the dogs that form the spokes of a wheel around Huck to such a small detail as the logs that form steps over the fence. A character is sketched in by Mark Twain by a few deft touches of dialectal comment, and a short speech. The realism of Mark Twain's writing is a result of his eye for detail and his use of detail in description and analysis.

Little things like the decorations of the Grangerford house add up to give the reader an overall impression of the family. By using the family to represent the finest traditions of the pre-Civil War South, Mark Twain adds concreteness to his comment on conditions there.

4. To what extent is *The Adventures of Huckleberry Finn* a book of social criticism?

ANSWER: By reflecting Mark Twain's attitudes towards the individuals responsible for the injustices and inhumanities done to the poor and helpless, the book contains much that can be called social comment. In its literary form this comment is called satire. That is, its purpose is to make people recognize their own flaws and laugh at them; by laughing at their own follies and faults, people can be made to change their ways.

In a more direct way, *Huck Finn* is a book of social criticism insofar as Mark Twain describes intolerable ignorance and crudity from Huck's point of view, and has Huck comment on the stupidity and cruelty which underlie them. Huck is quick to see the cruelty of tarring and feathering the king and duke, and of chaining Jim in double irons and putting him on a ration of bread and water.

Huck is the vehicle of Twain's comment even in those passages where he does not understand what's going on. He admires the art of Emmeline Grangerford. But from the way Huck describes the drawings, the reader can only smile at Huck's lack of education and deplore the bad taste of the South's finest families.

5. In what way can Jim be said to be a father to Huck?

ANSWER: We first see Jim in a father-role when he teaches Huck about the ways of the birds. Huck doesn't believe Jim at first, but is forced to admit the wisdom of Jim's lore when the rain comes down and forces the heroes to flee to higher ground. Jim exercises power as Huck's protector and defender in this instance. He helps Huck learn something about the nature of the river and the weather, and he aids him in saving his equipment.

In another way Jim is Huck's father. He provides the standards by which Huck can judge the rightness of people's behavior. Huck didn't learn these things from his father; he couldn't subscribe to the widow's or Miss Watson's religion; he could only learn from Jim. And the way he does this tells us about Huck. Huck believes only what he sees. If he's told a thing, he suspends judgment on it until he sees it come true. This is the case with the rattlesnake skin, and it is the case with the bird-lore Jim teaches him.

Finally, Jim looks after Huck by taking his watches for him, allowing Huck to sleep longer. His care for Huck's safety and comfort is almost the same as he would expend on his own children.

6. To what purpose does Mark Twain devote so much space to Tom Sawyer's fraudulent scheme to free Jim?

ANSWER: Mark Twain develops the contrast between Tom and Huck in the final chapters which deal with Tom's scheme to free Jim. The impersonal approach that Tom takes is perhaps the most striking quality of his plan. He does not care, really, whether Jim is uncomfortable or suffering. He wants the escape to be according to the rules. To this end he is willing to steal things from the Phelpses, although he won't let Huck steal a watermelon for his own comfort and pleasure. This single-minded pursuit of glory and "gaudy" effects is the most important characteristic of the king and the duke, who are Tom Sawyer's grown-up counterparts.

The contrast is perhaps better stated by saying that Huck is more interested in freeing Jim than Tom is. Indeed, after he learns that Tom knew Jim was free all the time, Huck comments that he always knew Tom was too good to be a low-down Abolitionist. Tom is interested in the adventure of the thing, Huck in the result of the adventure.

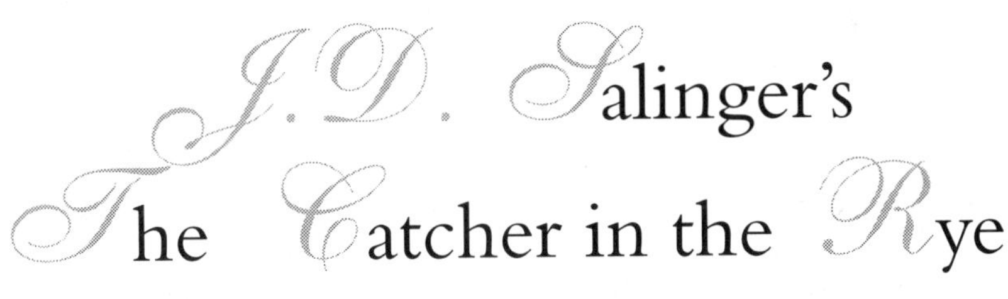

J. D. Salinger's The Catcher in the Rye

Analysis and Comment

CHAPTERS 1 AND 2

FIRST PERSON: An element of prime importance to the effect that this novel has on the reader is the fact that it is told in the first person. The use of this method of telling a story lends verisimilitude to the details while, at the same time, the reader is made to feel that he knows more about what is happening than does the narrator. A major reason for the fact that *Huckleberry Finn* is the only literary sequel in history that surpasses its antecedent is that Huck was allowed to tell his own story, while Tom Sawyer's adventures were related by an adult. The result was that in *Tom Sawyer*, the author constantly interposes himself between Tom and the reader. We are told, instead of being allowed to discover for ourselves, what emotions it was intended that we feel in a given situation. We never really get to know Tom because we see him through the eyes of another person; when we read *Huckleberry Finn*, it is almost as though we are living through his experiences ourselves.

The same is true in the case of Holden Caulfield. Because he is allowed to relate his own story in and on his own terms, we feel an empathy for him that could not have been otherwise achieved. The reader is granted an introspective view of the story; at the same time, because his background is not the same as Holden's, the reader retains his objectivity. Thus, he learns more about Holden than Holden himself knows.

AUTOBIOGRAPHY: A pitfall to be avoided is the conclusion that since many of the details about a fictional character agree with actual aspects of the author, the story is an autobiography. It is true that Pencey Prep reminds us of Valley Forge Military Academy—in Pennsylvania—which Salinger attended; it is true that Holden mentions an older brother who is a writer (who seems similar to Salinger himself) and to whom Holden always refers by his initials—D.B., not J.D.; there are, no doubt, many other characters and events that Salinger drew from his own life. It does not, however, necessarily follow that the story is autobiographical in every particular. Salinger follows the precepts of one accepted literary practice and writes about what he knows best. It is well known that A. Conan Doyle drew Sherlock Holmes from his own imagination, but it is to be doubted that Sir Arthur had a tithe of the adventures he so vividly described.

HOLDEN'S HONESTY: Holden exhibits a cynical self-awareness as he retraces the events that led up to his present position. He has a good many strong opinions, yet he tries to look at both sides—or, in fact, the many sides—of a question, and, what is perhaps most important, he *feels* and tries to express his feelings. Holden's view of what is facile, unreflecting and cliché-ridden in the adult world is to figure largely in the rest of the novel. Holden's reaction—amusement rather than resentment—to the circumstances that cause his expulsion, is another indication of his innate honesty.

HOLDEN'S LANGUAGE: Holden's colloquial—not to mention slangy—manner of speaking, as well as his boyish repetitions, stresses on certain words and his self-admitted vocabulary deficiencies all attract attention at first. In time, however, the reader is acclimated to Holden's narrative style. More important are Holden's reasons—that is to say, the author's reasons—for relating his story in such a manner. It is evident that the language of this account must remain consistent with the teenager who tells it. Holden's verbal limitations are related to the verities about him and about his world that emerge from this approach. Holden's account of what his teachers say and what his schoolmates say is also important. It is necessary that the reader accommodate himself to Holden's manner of speaking, if he is to understand the entire commentary of the novel.

THE IMPORTANCE OF FEELINGS: Holden's involvement with feelings is established early in the novel. His discussion of farewells is touching; moreover, it is important, since, from that discussion is adduced more information about various elements of Holden's personality. He is casual in his disclosure of matters that are surely important to him—his leaving school, for instance, or the theft of his personal belongings. We wonder whether or not Holden is keeping himself from feeling too strongly about things; or is he, perhaps, afraid to feel strong emotions? We may also speculate whether his indifference to people's opinions is not actually a means of hiding his fear that they won't like him.

Holden often searches for feelings; he tries to affect a sadness at leaving places, usually without success. This attempt to counterfeit emotions, and some of his apparently unmotivated antics give us further insight into his character. He would be the first to scoff at such a suggestion, but it is quite possible that Holden is trying to *find* himself.

CYNICISM: Holden is cynical beyond his years, to an extent that may be quite disconcerting at first. Although we may feel that this cynicism is born of hidden insecurity and frustration, there is no gainsaying the fact that Holden's pithy comments are often apt and biting. In his account of his conversations with his teacher and the head of the school, the adults' remarks do not seem terribly profound. We can see that although they are well-meaning people, they tend to speak, as well as think, in clichés. There is an element of truth in what they say—clichés get to be clichés because the truths that they express are manifest—but that truth is rendered unpalatable for Holden by his inability to take these adults seriously. They represent the fatuousness and shallowness so often found in the middle-class world.

We say that Holden is "cynical beyond his years" advisedly. Because of Salinger's artistry, it is easy to forget that it is not a boy of seventeen who is telling this story, but an adult, and a perspicacious adult, at that. The language used is that of an intelligent, though troubled, boy; the wisdom and sentiments expressed are those of a worldly wise man.

"BLACK-AND-WHITE," EITHER/OR THINKING: One of the reasons adults and adolescents fail to communicate, as represented in Holden's exchange with Mr. Spencer, is the inflexibility of the rules and conventions of the adult world. Mind-sets, we might call them, a failure to perceive any middle possibilities between "either/or," a failure, in fact, to recognize the complexities of life.

Holden is on rather sound philosophical ground here. He is following the tenets of the famous American psychologist-philosopher, William James, who regarded the universe as "pluralistic," that is, many-faceted, in spite of man's stubborn desire to classify and categorize it. Furthermore, according to James' philosophy, a person who admits this complexity, or the lack of neat "either/or's," is a pragmatist—that is, he is able to look at the world as it really is, even though this is less orderly, perhaps even frustrating in its lack of clear "yes or no" answers, and he is able to accommodate to changes in his world, whether external or in his own consciousness. We might be justified, therefore, in calling Holden Caulfield a pragmatist—a rather sophisticated and realistic thinker.

EMPHASIS ON FACTS: Despite his favorable qualities, Mr. Spencer demonstrates another aspect of adult inflexibility—that which overemphasizes factual knowledge. (Salinger's distaste for this method of educating young people seems to have expanded into a theory of education, stressing the desirability of *showing* rather than telling and labeling, so as not to stifle a person's naturalness or individuality; the story "Teddy" explores this theory.) With needless irritating repetition, Mr. Spencer dwells upon Holden's inadequate grasp of historical facts, but we are left with the feeling that Holden knows as much about ancient Egypt as he cares, or needs, to know.

One gets the impression that Mr. Spencer's approach to history is static rather than dynamic, that he stresses separate fragmented facts in a pedantic and uninteresting manner, and that he himself lacks historical perspective and has not even perceived how Egyptian history might be made interesting for his students so that they would be anxious to learn about it. Thus, Holden, in his awareness of the pluralistic universe that is being absorbed constantly into a new present, may be better equipped than Mr. Spencer to perceive reality. Yet, Holden is made to feel that he is wrong; he feels apologetic about his supposed inadequacies. This is bound to have unsalutary effects on his psychological well-being.

HEALTH: The reader is given no specific diagnosis of Holden's ailments. Since he is telling the story while he is a resident of a rest home, we conclude that there is something wrong with him but we are never told what it is. This ambiguity is well executed by Salinger. He is aware that, in young people especially, there is a connection between physical and psychological health. Certainly Holden differs considerably from the traditional hero, who is physically and psychologically unblemished.

MENDACITY: We find that one of the most oft-used words in Holden's lexicon is "phony." He is constantly detecting sham motives in the people around him. The advertisement for Pencey Prep disturbs him; the picture of a horse jumping over a fence gives in his opinion, a false image of the school. In Holden's judgment, Pencey is a home for dishonest, spoiled children, and not for idealized horsemen-to-be. Also held up to ridicule is the spurious picture of life that is found in Hollywood movies. Salinger's relationship with the movie industry was not extensive but it apparently left its mark. The reader may be reminded of the comments of other authors whose opinions of Hollywood were less than laudatory. S. J. Perelman called it "Bridgeport with palms" and P. G. Wodehouse referred to it as "Dottyville-on-the-Pacific."

Holden is deeply concerned with the fact that his older brother, D. B., has prostituted his writing talent by going out to California; he feels that D. B. is being untrue to himself and his convictions in his pursuit of material success. Holden thus exhibits his involvement with broad questions. This problem of the fate of talent, ideals and sensitivity in a materialistic society becomes one of Holden's preoccupations in the novel.

COMMUNICATION: Salinger is concerned with the lack of communication in the adult world. An illustration of this is the magazine that Mr. Spencer tries to toss on the bed; he misses, and the magazine is picked up by Holden. The magazine, which falls to the floor, is meant, perhaps, to represent adult knowledge and experience; the "toss-and-miss" game demonstrates the lack of connection between the worlds of the adult and the adolescent.

IRONY: Although Mr. Spencer regrets the necessity of giving Holden a failing mark, he cannot restrain himself from reading aloud Holden's inadequate examination composition. Thus, instead of assuaging the boy's discomfort, he adds to it. Holden, on the other hand, tries to alleviate the teacher's embarrassment by engaging him in aimless conversation. We see that their relationship is ironically inverted. Holden has more sympathy for and interest in people than does Mr. Spencer.

Holden's attempt to put his teacher at ease fails, in part, because although he has a great awareness, his immaturity precludes his channeling it into actual communication. Instead, Holden thinks, while chatting, about the ducks in Central Park. This delicate concern for the creatures of nature and sensitivity to the mysteries of nature are beyond Mr. Spencer's perspective ability. The teacher lives in another world.

Another ironic circumstance is exposed when Holden reminisces about Elkton Hills. The headmaster of Elkton Hills spoke only to those parents who had the proper social graces; the materialistic or naively factualistic aspects of the teaching profession are thus adduced. Holden is more attuned to reality than are his mentors, but he is incapable of handling his own world; nor are they capable of guiding him.

Holden leaves Mr. Spencer after consoling him and advising him not to worry, and the traditional image of the mild, harmless teacher has been established. We must realize, however, that Holden is also taking a one-sided view of things here. Mr. Spencer's failure to communicate and the Elkton Hills headmaster's hypocrisy are not necessarily the condition of the adult world, but Holden is too young and hypersensitive to see that, yet. In this sense there is a double irony in Holden's point of view.

CHAPTERS 3–5

ESCAPISM: Holden is aware that he has a habit of lying and he ostensibly deprecates this fault. He is not entirely sincere in his self-castigation, however; he enjoys his fantasies, his imaginative escapes, and he is aware that his lies are of little significance. Salinger uses Holden's escapist tendencies to satirize the typical content of Hollywood movies; Holden projects himself into the unreal celluloid world by visualizing himself as the hero in a melange of typical Hollywood plots. We also see, here, a touch of exhibitionism in Holden; he cannot seem to help trying to draw attention to himself, even of people whom he does not particularly admire.

THE RED HUNTING HAT: The theme of escape through fantasy is continued when Holden toys with his red hunting cap. When Holden is interrupted in his reading, by Ackley, who interrogates him about the lost fencing equipment, he is annoyed and covers his face with the cap. He makes believe that he is blind and calls out to his mother to give him her hand. We can see that Holden is caught up and trapped in his own imaginary games. He wears the cap backwards while he reads, thus asserting his own individuality; the cap thereby becomes a part of the fantasy world that he enters while reading, at the same time suggesting his own personal "hunting" or searching for companionship—with books or with real people. Furthermore, the cap, because of its similarity to a baseball cap, probably reminds him of Allie's baseball mitt, and thus of Allie, and suggests ultimately the theme of the "catcher in the rye," or protector of childlike innocence and purity.

STATUS SEEKING: The Cadillac-driving Mr. Ossenburger, after whom Holden's dormitory is named, is a typical representative of the status-seeking, mealy-mouthed middle class. Holden cannot take seriously the wealthy undertaker's sermon about God being our buddy, for he feels that the man's status and dignity are false. The expensive automobile, the financial donation to the school—for which the dormitory in his name is a *quid pro quo*—and his career of profiting on death all underscore Holden's mocking picture of adult society. Holden accuses the adult sermonizer of being too preoccupied with financial gain and his own status to be worthy of instructing others on religious or moral matters; this indictment could, of course, be applied to the large number of people who have merited it. This is a theme of Salinger's that recurs—in various guises—throughout his works. Salinger's characters that he seems most to admire are those who do not wish to appear to others any different than they are.

Holden's description of and reactions to the undertaker's inflated rhetoric are amusing, but they serve a more profound purpose; they deepen our appreciation of Holden's serious concerns and sharpen our vision of his abundant empathy. We can see just what it is that is contributing to turning Holden into the champion and protector of young innocence. Although we must always be aware of Holden's tendency to oversimplify, due to his own innocence, we cannot but respond to his horror of the crassness of the world and its social snobbery.

ACKLEY: It is not only the adult world that Holden finds displeasing; it is not a simple case of youth and age being mutually antagonistic. Ackley, an introvert, is depicted as being weird and nasty; his physical attributes are repugnant to boot. He is a social outcast at school, not only because of his poor grooming, but because he appears to be uncooperative and unfriendly. Being an introvert, he is driven more and more into himself because he is rejected. It is interesting to speculate on the fact that, despite their seemingly antithetical personalities, Holden and Ackley are alike in many respects. Neither boy is respected or accepted by his fellows. They both tend to withdraw into themselves and they both evince their lack of concern for the opinions of others—Holden by his iconoclastic capers and Ackley by his personal habits. We may come to the conclusion that the element in Holden's make-up that saves him from being as repellent to us as Ackley is Holden's native intelligence.

STRADLATER: Perhaps nowhere in the world can unpleasant personal habits be more egregious than in school dormitory; Holden has already clearly delineated the disgust that Ackley fills him with. The case of Stradlater is a bit more complicated. Stradlater is representative of the athletically and socially successful boy whose accomplishments have gone to his head. Holden is upset by the disparity between appearance and reality; he feels that Stradlater is clean only on the surface and that underneath that surface he is a "secret slob." Ackley, on the other hand, makes no pretence of being anything but slovenly; at least he is not hypocritical about his personal habits.

LONELINESS: Holden is hypersensitive to anything tawdry, and we see that he is repelled by the contrasting shapes that tawdriness can take in the persons of Ackley and Stradlater. Yet, in spite of his being critical of people, his loneliness draws him to them, and he really seeks companionship with both boys. Unfortunately, however, he can find no common ground on which to meet either boy.

LITERATURE: Holden's conception of what constitutes great literature is an interesting one: that a great book, when read, will cause the reader to wish that he could telephone the author and talk to him. This is further evidence of Holden's desire for warmth and human relationship. This theme of a lonely youth searching for friendship, for deep personal relationships with his fellow man is central to this and, of course, to many other novels, It manifests itself in such diverse examples of the genre as Charles Dickens' *David Copperfield* and Nelson Algren's *The Man With The Golden Arm.*

JANE GALLAGHER: Salinger has a knack for allowing the reader a glimpse of an interesting character, but only, as it were, at second hand. Sometimes this can prove to be almost frustrating, as is true in the case of Jane Gallagher. From Holden's description of the way Jane plays checkers, with more regard for the symmetry of the pieces on the board than for the outcome of the game, we wish that she might have been introduced into the action of the novel. In Holden's great fear of Jane's fate at the hands of Stradlater we find the seed of the "catcher in the rye" image. He wants to protect her innocence from the potentially corrupting influence of Stradlater. Thus, the lonely youth seeking to establish human companionship is simultaneously concerned with protecting innocence. The two activities work hand in hand.

ALLIE: The book's most delightful character never actually appears in the novel at all. Salinger uses a device similar to that of Truman Capote in his *Children On Their Birthdays*—the fact that a precocious child is no longer alive is the first thing the reader learns about that character; as the author fills in details about him, the reader's regret that he could not have met that character personally increases. The episode of Allie and the baseball glove is one of the most moving in the novel, for it beautifully conveys to us the extent of Holden's loss without violating the superficially offhand, sentimental tone that has been established as Holden's attitude toward the outside world.

ADULT DISTRUST: An adult world that does not trust Holden because it cannot understand him is seen in the incident of the snowball. After making a snowball, Holden looks around for something to act as a target for it, but the snow-covered objects outside his window all look so pristinely lovely that he can't bring himself to destroy the symmetry of the beautiful scene. He carries the snowball to the bus, but when the bus driver refuses to believe that he does not intend to throw it, Holden feels defeated; in so many ways he is the soul of integrity and once again his integrity is questioned.

Another incident that is revelatory of the unsympathetic adult world revolves around Allie's death. Because Holden broke all the windows in the garage, and then tried to break the car windows, his parents spoke of sending him to a psychiatrist. The adult world cannot seem to understand the deep sense of loss that can be felt by an adolescent. Holden contrasts his lovely and likeable little redheaded brother with the less attractive people surrounding him; this sharpens his already keen sense of bereavement. It is possible that Holden's recollections of Allie are colored by the fact that he is gone; nevertheless, we are quite willing to take Holden's word for it when he assures us that we would have liked Allie.

CHAPTERS 6–8

AMBIVALENCE: Holden's feelings about Jane are ambivalent in two ways. He does not seem to be at all sure of what he wants their relationship to be, and he is equally unsure how Jane will conduct herself on a date with a self-acknowledged rake like Stradlater. It is typical of Holden that when he is unhappy, he seeks out the companionship of anyone who is close at hand—even the despised Ackley. (Careful reading, by the way, will disclose the fact that Salinger has inadvertently assigned two different names to Ackley's roommate. Possibly this was due to sections of two different versions of the story being subjoined. The best of authors occasionally err in this fashion—in *Huckleberry Finn* Tom Sawyer's girlfriend is called Bessie Thatcher, instead of Becky.)

It is difficult for us to take seriously Holden's confession of cowardice; he himself doesn't seem to be sure about it. We also do not know whether to list the results of Holden's encounter with Stradlater as a victory for the former or for the latter. Holden lost the physical battle, but he won a moral victory because he championed chivalry and virtue; he has been defeated but not dishonored.

QUIXOTISM: As noted above, Holden attacks the cult of athletic prowess, whose motto is "might makes right." His knightly behavior is redolent of the madness of Don Quixote, at least insofar as ideals are concerned; the battlefield is far more prosaic. This fight, which is like a duel, establishes Holden's quest to attain a moral order. (To be as fanciful as Holden himself, one might say that the red hunting cap, which he puts on backwards, symbolizes a *tarnhelm*, the magical powers of which enable its wearer to become invisible.) Holden asserts himself as an adolescent caught between the anxiety of childhood and the hoped for assimilation into the adult world.

GENEROSITY: Apparently, Holden cannot help being generous, no matter how unworthy are the recipients of his gifts. His willingness that almost amounts to an eagerness to oblige in granting favors—although he sometimes keeps caste by affecting reluctance—is indicative of his desperate need for fellowship. His generosity is not limited to material possessions—he gives of his time and company, often against his own inclinations.

Another aspect of Holden's generosity is his tendency to try to find some good in most people, even if only a miniscule amount. Thus, Stradlater's self-centeredness is transformed into the ability to keep a secret.

ALIENATION: Holden's departure from Pencey Prep is a recapitulation of a scene that he has played many times before, when he was forced to leave his temporary and shifting home, school. Still depressed about Jane's putative fate at the hands of Stradlater, he is rebuffed in his attempt to seek solace in conversation with Ackley. Salinger uses this inability to relate to a fellow student, a religious vocation or prep school to exemplify Holden's deep alienation from society. He cannot even go home to his family—at least, not yet; he puts it off as long as he can—because they will not understand him emotionally. Holden is thus driven more and more into himself, cut off from the social world; he reacts by putting on his childish symbol of escape and passivity, the red hunting cap.

AVOIDANCE: Holden's chance meeting with the mother of a schoolmate leads him into the perpetration of another tangled skein of lies. Part of the psychological justification for this act—for which he feels remorse, even when committing it—arises from his inability to inflict pain; he does not want to make life difficult for people. This oversimplified easy way out appeals to his fertile imagination, but he seems to enjoy his imposture more than he should. (Note the resemblance to Huckleberry Finn; Huck could never come across a stranger without creating an entirely new autobiography for himself. He was often impelled to do this by reasons of self-preservation, but he seemed to enjoy himself mightily, too.)

Holden has the typical youthful predilection for feeling that he has the problems of the world on his shoulders, a natural concomitant of his view of himself as the focal point of all society. Thus, he feels responsible for far more situations than he could possibly control, let alone affect. Part of Holden's problem is that he has an overabundant supply of empathy, quite often for people who neither desire it nor appreciate it.

ACCEPTANCE: Holden's attempts to be accepted into the adult world are a bit ludicrous. Mrs. Morrow is apparently unimpressed by his talking about going for a drink or by his display of his prematurely gray hair. Like any other child, and like many an adult too, Holden has an overwhelming desire and need to be noticed.

MOTHERS: Salinger makes some trenchant observations about maternal affection and the blind spots it can cause. For all of Salinger's love—amounting at times almost to deification—of youthful innocence, he can see clearly how easily a mother's view of her children can be warped by love and pride. Of course, Salinger's comments are mild compared to what Philip Wylie has written on an allied subject; the latter's excoriating denunciation of what he termed "momism" is well known.

CHAPTERS 9–11

COMPANIONSHIP: More clearly than ever, we sense Holden's desperate need for companionship of almost any kind. His slip of the tongue in giving the cab driver his home address is revelatory of his subconscious desire to go home—although that particular repressed desire is vying within him with other, antithetical desires. That Holden is starved for companionship is revealed by the fact that many of the people with whom he attempts—or only considers the attempt—to strike up a conversation obviously have so little in common with him. This is even more clearly seen when he does elicit a response; the resulting conversation is usually perfectly inane.

ATTRACTION OF VULGARITY: Holden's ambivalent nature is further adduced by his actions after he reaches New York. Although he is familiar with what we might call "the better things in life," he constantly manages to be drawn into vulgarity. (It is noteworthy that his familiarity with motion picture clichés is not consistent with his contempt for that medium.) With scores of hotels to choose from, he selects one that seems to be rife with perverts. He finds excuses not to call people he admires, but he telephones a girl he doesn't even know because he was told she was of easy virtue—and then he makes a botch of the conversation.

His continued quest for female companionship has similar results in the tawdry night club. His ideal of innocence and fun, Phoebe, with whom he hopes to find solace, is compared with these dull-witted girls who worship movie idols. Holden disdains and pities these vacuous creatures and yet he tries to prolong their stay in his company as long as possible. (Note that Salinger is guilty of an error in the nightclub scene: the legal minimum age at which one could consume liquor in New York at that time was eighteen, not twenty-one.)

PHOEBE AND JANE: It is becoming apparent that there are only two females whose companionship Holden really enjoys. One is his ten-year-old sister and the other a girl with whom his relationship has been, in the main, platonic.

Phoebe is a delightful child; there are not many like her in literature, let alone in life. She has more than red hair in common with her brother Allie; she is charming, intelligent, vivacious and, most of all, fun. In fact, one might say that Salinger is eating his cake and having it too; he gave us the tragedy of Allie's death, but he brought him back to life in Phoebe.

We get the impression that insofar as he has ever been in love with any girl, Holden loves Jane. She can be trusted to share the innermost secrets of Holden's life, for example a look at Allie's glove. Jane is the book's only character who is Holden's age or older to whom Salinger does not impute a loss of innocence. However much he may care for Jane, though, Holden never lacks for an excuse to defer talking to or seeing her. There seems to be an integral part of Holden's psyche that refuses to allow him to find happiness.

CHAPTERS 12–14

HORWITZ: Salinger's treatment of the interplay between the young boy and the hard-bitten cab driver is quite effective. Curiosity about the vagaries of nature is a leveling factor in man; to paraphrase Shakespeare, the love of nature makes the whole world kin. We see two kinds of innocence in contrast: Holden's youthful ingenuousness and the uneducated cabbie's simplicity. Horwitz is upset by Holden's questions at first, but soon his imagination is stimulated. Salinger deftly pokes fun at the myth of the omniscient New York cab driver by having Horwitz aver that he knows that fish are protected by Mother Nature; they eat through their pores while frozen in the lake. Perhaps Horwitz arrives at this conclusion so that he may feel secure in the knowledge that Mother Nature is looking after him.

ERNIE: Because Ernie now seems so self-conscious in the tinselly atmosphere that he has surrounded himself with and because he now seems concerned only with projecting a flattering image of himself, Holden feels that Ernie—like D.B.—has knuckled under to the forces of crass materialism. This theme—the commercialization of art—exemplifies what Holden feels about the adult involvement with materialism that surrounds human acts and has the power to destroy anything worthwhile that man may create. The saddest thing about artists who succumb to the temptation of self-gratification is that they lose the ability to distinguish between art and entertainment.

LILLIAN: Lillian Simmons is another example of the shallowness of society. She cares more about being seen and heard that about communicating with people. Her motives and deceptions are so pitifully transparent that we must emulate Holden in his pity for her.

SUNNY: Emotion is so important to Holden that he is appalled by the prospect of commercialized sex. While the physical aspects of love are very meaningful to him, they mean nothing if they are rendered impersonal and cold. Holden wants to talk with Sunny for a while; he wants to share her experiences and find out what made her what she is, but she is unable to respond. Once again he finds that people do not care about him as he would like to care about them. The encounter with the prostitute, showing first Holden's brash temerity, followed in turn by misgivings, qualms and then horror of the vulgarity of the situation, is well delineated. It serves to reinforce the image we have of Holden as an innocent youth being initiated into the cold and calculating world of the adult society.

RELIGION: In the increasing seriousness of his reflections, Holden ponders on religion. He evinces a pragmatic bent in such matters; his value judgments of the Disciples are from a strictly twentieth-century point of view. Christ is accepted by Holden as a pure ideal, but the lesser representatives of Christianity are, as Holden sees them, the frail human element that corrupts. Thus, they are harsher judges of their fellow man than God would be.

MAURICE: Although Holden has certainly told more than his share of lies, he has a very definite code of honor; he lives up to it and he expects other people to live up to theirs. When Holden faces up to Maurice, it is not for the sake of the money—as we have seen, Holden does not know the value of money—but because Holden cannot abide that kind of dishonesty. Salinger has taken great pains to prepare the reader for Holden's courageous stand. Holden has previously admitted that he is not physically aggressive, and because he shies away from fights he considers himself to be a coward. This battle, however, involves truth; consequently, Holden abandons all precautions. It is a moral conflict fought out in a most unconventional setting. Although Holden loses the physical encounter with Maurice he has successfully defended his honor.

FANTASY: After the fight, Holden takes refuge in the world of fantasy. It is interesting to note that this lad, who despises the fraudulent celluloid world, often thinks in terms of Hollywood images. Salinger seems to be satirizing a world that is becoming unable to distinguish reality from fantasy—a world in which an actor who plays a doctor on television receives countless letters begging him for medical advice.

CHAPTERS 15 AND 16

MATERIALISM: We find that Holden is not afflicted with pride in material possessions; the philosophy of "conspicuous consumption" means nothing to him. He tells us of the time when he was embarrassed because his suitcases were so much nicer than his roommate's. Displaying his characteristic empathy, Holden tried to hide his suitcases, in consideration of his roomate's feelings. This thoughtful act did not achieve its desired effect, however, because his roommate wanted the suitcases to be seen so that it would appear as though he owned them. This simple tale illustrates the entire process of jockeying for a superior materialistic image in our society. It is not necessary actually to own things; the *appearance* of ownership suffices. At about the time that Salinger was writing this book, people who could not afford Cadillacs (the status symbol *par excellence*) were buying tail fins to make their Chevrolets look like Cadillacs; people who did not own television sets were putting dummy television antennas on their roofs.

CHARITY: The nuns have not fallen victim to this false philosophy; they stand for a measure of self-sacrifice that extends far beyond the "society charities," which Holden feels are all based on self-indulgence. This conflict between true charity—or a total commitment—bothers the youthful protagonist. He rejects internal self-gratification as a fraud and demands that false ego be purged. Of course Holden himself is not being entirely consistent here, since the money that he gave the nuns meant nothing to him, but it must be admitted that he did for them what he could. Holden feels that money is a demeaning influence on society—or, as the New Testament has it, "The love of money is the root of all evil."

Salinger is telling us that a charitable act is deserving of the name only if the performer of the act is giving up something that he values and getting nothing in return. When Mr. Ossenburger donated money to Pencey, for instance, it was not charity; his name was immortalized—or so it would have seemed to him—on the dormitory building. Thus, he was making a simple purchase. The egotism behind a charitable act destroys the value of the act, reducing it to self-gratification.

SALLY HAYES: Holden's masochism manifests itself again when he seeks out Sally Hayes. She is attractive and superficially intelligent, but she does not have the qualities that Holden most admires—emotional profundity and an involvement with people. He further flagellates himself by taking her to places he does not like, among people he detests.

THE POOR FAMILY: When Holden follows the poor family along the street, it shows his subconscious quest for home life, and a spiritual father. Holden's mention of his father is conspicuous by its almost total absence from the novel. He has said that his father is quite wealthy but also quite busy; they do not seem to share many experiences. This lack of affection from his father has a profound effect on Holden's life. Psychologists might say that he is failing in his school work in order to gain the attention of his father and to command his father's love. This partial explanation has a bearing on the plot as well as on other events and circumstances that contribute to Holden's failure. Nevertheless, he is responsible for his own deeds, no matter how mitigating the circumstances may be. Holden must contrive to channel this responsibility in a meaningful direction. To bridge the gap between adolescence and manhood demands an assimilation of values and experiences that are at present but a jumble to Holden. The process has been and is going to be slow and painful.

This poor family represents innocence to Holden—the child is singing just "for the hell of it." There is no sense of shame attached to his actions; a spiritual purity surrounds his singing. The song itself becomes identified with Holden's desire in life, as we shall see later.

MUTABILITY: When Holden searches for Phoebe, one of the first places he goes is to the museum. He recalls the days when he attended her school and he recollects the occasions when he visited the museum. The nostalgia of childhood remembrances gives him a warm feeling, but he recognizes, perhaps for the first time, that many years have passed and things are no longer the same. He is older now; he is a different person. Although Phoebe is going to the same school and the same museum, her experiences, in varying degrees, will differ from his. This realization has a profound effect on Holden. Change—mutability—is a reality. Life goes on and the past seems quite distant to him now. The transitory quality of life makes him realize that he is not a child any more. His decision not to enter the museum is different from previous occasions in the novel when he backed away from an experience; he really no longer has the urge to enter. It does not appeal to him now. He cannot go home again to the world of childhood; he must cross the threshold into the world of adulthood.

Salinger expands on the desirability of immutability when he describes the various exhibits in the museum and notes the comforting fact that they never change. A boy could grow into manhood, marry and have children of his own, or even grandchildren, but the same Eskimo would still be fishing through the same hole in the ice. The exhibits are thus an expression of immortality in a mortal world. Poets have, of course, long dilated on this and similar themes. In "The Rubáiyát of

Omar Khayyam" we find:

Come, fill the Cup, and in the fire of Spring
Your Winter-garment of Repentance fling:
The Bird of Time has but a little way
To flutter—and the Bird is on the Wing.

The seventeenth-century English poet Andrew Marvell, in his "To His Coy Mistress," said:

But always at my back I hear
Times winged chariot drawing near,
And yonder all before us lie
Deserts of vast eternity.

The latter poet's solution, incidentally, was not to keep fleeing ineffectually, but to turn the tables and make "time run," or in short, to seize each new day and live it vigorously and affirmatively.

CHAPTERS 17–19

SINCERITY: Superficial social engagements are repellent to Holden, but he continually makes and keeps them. He cannot understand why he blurts out that he loves Sally; he almost convinces himself that it is true at the time, but in his heart he knows that it is not. His desire to be sincere is forever trapping him and leading him to be quite insincere.

The conversation at the theatre annoys him greatly because it seems to contain cultural involvement and great significance; in reality, as Holden knows, it is hollow and trivial. The audience at the theatre is like a large portion of the audience at an opera or concert; they go not to hear the music but to engage in a contest to see who can be the first to destroy an emotion-filled moment with premature applause.

The lack of true warmth in social relationships disturbs Holden because he desires to love, to be an adult, to be a person who is committed emotionally and psychologically to another person.

SEARCH FOR STABILITY: Sally's desire for admiration of her physical attributes leads Holden and Sally to a popular skating rink where their efforts to ice-skate are ludicrous. Since they are both very poor skaters they are forced to give up the social pretense and leave the ice. In the ensuing conversation—as well as throughout the novel—Holden seeks to be understood by and establish a relationship with a female. He is searching for stability. But the more he tries to explain to Sally whence comes his dissatisfaction with his life, the more he becomes unrealistic and confusing. His request that Sally run off with him would have offended a far more understanding person than she. This romantic request illustrates his urge to break through conventions and be an adult, but it is indicative of how childish he still is.

Holden's almost incoherent conversation with Sally articulates his disenchantment with the adult world and its demands and conformities. As such, it is a fairly compact account of the complaints of many of Salinger's protagonists, adolescent and adult, as seen in *Nine Stories*. They are all unhappy in a world they never made.

ESCAPE: Although Holden desires stability and is willing to commit himself to a meaningful life he cannot bring himself to compromise his ideals. He still wants to escape what he would call a "phony" future; he wants no part of the settled life of the ordinary college graduate—the routine quest for material acquisitions. Sally, of course, cannot comprehend all this—it is, after all, Holden's personal crisis—so their parting is unhappy and angry. Their argument ends Holden's attempts for the moment to establish this kind of relationship.

VALUES IN ENTERTAINMENT: The great majority of movies—foreign, as well as American—create an unreal world that Holden finds unacceptable. The story of the particular movies recounted by Holden, is a glorification of material success in typical soap opera fashion; false sorrows and happy endings are strewn about with a lavish hand. Holden refuses to be overwhelmed by the sheer weight of the stage show; he would rather pay attention to personal, individual performances. For example, he believes that Jesus would also hate the meretricious Christmas show but He would appreciate the orchestra's tympani player. Holden's brother Allie liked that musician so much he sent him a postcard from Washington, D.C. To appreciate an unsensational but profoundly true performance is a beautiful thing, in Holden's eyes. This, of course, is diametrically opposed to the philosophy of the mass media, which glorifies the sensational and false.

CARL LUCE: Carl knows a great deal about relationships with women, but only the physical aspects. He is an expert on sex, not love. He rebuffs Holden's attempts to engage him in a personal and serious conversation and continues to play the role of the superior being who is the final arbiter on any matter he wishes to discuss. His spurious intellectualism can be discerned through Holden's remarks. When they were at school, Carl saw that his informal seminars on sex were dispersed when he was tired; he wanted to make sure that no conversations took place while he was absent, so that he would continue to be the one that everyone sought when they desired information on any aspect of sex, homosexual or heterosexual. Carl loved to play the oracle, but he was never a sincere intellectual who gloried in the give and take of discussion and who admired genuine inquiry and developing self-awareness. He wanted control of any situation by being in possession of all the "facts." Salinger caricatures this type of knowledge by having Holden inform us that Carl had a large vocabulary, the best at school; or, at least, so indicated the tests. The lack of relationship between good marks and genuine character and personal development is the horror implicit in many modern educational practices.

SPIRITUAL EXPERIENCE: The only common ground found between Carl and Holden is their agreement that sex is both a physical and a spiritual experience. (It must be admitted, of course, that Holden has no first hand knowledge about the matter, as yet.) This idea excites Holden, who asks if this is why Carl now has an Eastern girlfriend. The lack of unity of the physical and spiritual elements in Holden's life is at the core of his own basic problem. Nevertheless, the middle ground between these two extremes of human attraction is man's abode, just as Holden is caught between childhood and adulthood, between anxiety and assimilation.

Carl advises Holden to undergo psychoanalysis; this is a foreshadowing of Holden's real needs. He informs Holden that he himself does not need analysis because he has adjusted to life through his father's advice. Holden proceeds to punish himself—in response to amorphous guilt feelings—by getting drunk. In his musings concerning guilt and sadness he arrives again at thoughts concerning Allie's death. Perhaps Salinger is saying here that Holden, being an impressionable adolescent, holds himself responsible for not being able to prevent death; this is why he fails in school and cannot abide institutions. In order to eschew culpability he tries to pass himself off as an adult, but he is not accepted as one because of his youthful mannerisms.

QUEST FOR ANSWERS: In this internal quest of Holden Caulfield, we see his burgeoning preoccupation with the mysteries of life. He is searching for the answers to profound questions—his curiosity concerning where the ducks in the park go in winter time symbolizes his desire to learn the way nature functions and, by extension, the secrets of nature. When he escapes into fantasy through his imaginary bullet wound we see the natural processes of solace, relief and escape from pain that come through the exercise of imagination. Holden is lonely and depressed; he feels sorry for his mother and father, especially his mother who, he feels, has yet to get over Allie's death.

CHAPTERS 20–23

HUNTER AND HUNTED: Holden's red hunting cap seems to symbolize both the hunter and the hunted—that is, Holden's seeking life and being pursued by it. His fantasy of being wounded has some reality about it since it is becoming manifest that he is headed for the nervous breakdown that was hinted at earlier, because of the conflicts between idealism and reality, and because of his inability to assume control over his hitherto purposeless life. The hunting cap represents his passive resistance to many unpleasant aspects of life; he bought it when his schoolmates ostracized him and he dons it whenever he wants to retreat from unpleasant happenings.

HOME: His decision to sneak home to Phoebe shows us his tremendous desire to be at home again and thus establish a relationship with someone he can love and will love him. He realizes that his pathological introversion is becoming dangerous to his mental and spiritual health. His recollection of the rain falling at Allie's funeral gives a glimpse into his ironic thoughts; in his deep sorrow he speculated on the people, who should feel privileged at being among the living, running for cover from the rain.

CATCHER IN THE RYE: One of the most important and revealing sections of the novel involves Holden's arrival at his home. At last Holden is beginning to formulate his thoughts—a bit incoherently, it is true—about what he wants to do with his life. The "catcher in the rye" is the guardian of innocence and the protector of innocents. Thus, we discern Salinger's oft-implied creed—the human animal is pure in his childhood; he is not corrupted until he enters adult society. Whatever unpleasant characteristics a child may display are the results of premature exposure to adult influence—which may remind us of Holden's prematurely gray hair. This idea is a slight variation of Rousseau's concept of the "Noble Savage."

We can see Holden's great attachment to Phoebe's childish innocence and preternatural wisdom. She wants to protect Holden and also make him grapple with his responsibilities. Salinger artistically juxtaposes Phoebe's smallness against the enormous furniture of the room—D.B.'s—she chooses to sleep in. The large, venal world and the small, innocent child are symbolic of the problems that Holden must learn to face.

INSIGHT: The arguments against the usefulness of school that Holden presents to Phoebe represent the visceral insight that he has been developing during the course of the novel. He sees himself as a romantic hero challenging the institutionalized academic ogre. He is depressed at the thought that he may prove unequal to the struggle; he does not want to become what we call today an "organization man."

CONCEPTION OF GOOD: When Phoebe challenges Holden to name something that he thinks is good, he thinks of the nuns. Their spiritual dedication to the cause of charity is summed up physically for Holden in their black habits and the steel-rimmed glasses of one of them. In his eyes, the physical and spiritual are united in their total commitment. Holden is not aware that although the nuns were not motivated by materialistic status-seeking, they were not altogether free of spiritual status-seeking in their motivations. Holden is impressionable; he follows his moral instincts in his evaluation of people.

When asked what he wants to be, he is unable to think of a practical occupation. He answers by telling what he wants to *do* with his life, in broad general terms; he cannot envision *becoming* something other than what he is now. His philosophy does permit him to choose here and now to do something in the future. His choice involves the key image of the novel; he wants to be the catcher in the rye, to save innocent children from falling into the abyss of adult corruption. He yearns for philosophical significance in his life—to have a great moral purpose above and beyond practical truths. The mission takes on the godlike proportions of a savior. Without sacrilegious intent, he wishes to save humanity from the evil of its ways.

IDENTIFICATION: Salinger uses a clever device by having Phoebe demonstrate her belching ability immediately after Holden states his philosophy. This absurd juxtaposition of the lofty and the mundane serves to heighten the mood of the profound situation that Salinger is depicting. The technique lends verisimilitude to the novel and enables the reader to identify Holden's world with his own. Salinger's artistry causes the novel to be a mature work of art, and not merely a book for youngsters. At the same time, of course, young people find the novel eminently enjoyable and understandable. Being closer to Holden's age, they may find it easier to identify with him and his problems.

CENTRAL IMAGE: As we have said, they key to the meaning of the novel is in the image of the "catcher in the rye." The actual line of Burns' poem is "if a body *meet* a body," but Holden does not have the exact words, although he has the words that interest him. His mishearing of the words may be symbolic of his incapacity to perceive reality accurately—that is, respond to the world as it really is, rather than as he wishes it were. However, careful reading will disclose that, as Holden relates the story, he is aware that he had the wrong words and that Phoebe is correct in telling him that it was "meet." Thus, Salinger is indicating that Holden has a new-found ability to come to terms with reality. Holden has changed, as we shall see in our perusal of the remainder of the book.

FAMILY RELATIONSHIPS: Holden, who likes to dance, says the Phoebe is a wonderful dancer. Her ability to perform this social ritual has a great significance for Holden; it is one of the innocent pleasures of life that he likes to recall. In its way, perhaps, it is a way to participate in the pleasures of the adult world. In any event, he and Phoebe can perform together very well. They have an ability to exercise their talents in an harmonious and disciplined manner. This fact is important for proper comprehension of the novel—Holden needs Phoebe; his relationship with her will serve as a basis for a solution to his problems.

While Holden is with Phoebe, Mrs. Caulfield appears for the first and only time in the novel. Holden has spoken about her; we learn that she is kind, but somewhat insecure. A poor sleeper whose worry and concern is constant, she has never really recovered from her grief at Allie's death. Her reaction to Phoebe's (supposed) smoking is the only evidence we see that she can display parental authority. Her reproof is surprisingly mild; Salinger cloaks her response in ambiguity. It could mean that she is being psychologically clever by not attaching too much importance to Phoebe's act, but this seems doubtful. It could be evidence of laxness on her part, or perhaps gratification that Phoebe did not take refuge in a lie (which, if true, is ironic because Phoebe did lie). Mrs. Caulfield's sense of parental responsibility cannot really be judged from this specific instance because it is inconclusive; but an overall observation is permissible. Phoebe said she smoked because she was unable to sleep, which might indicate that she was psychologically or physically uncomfortable. Once she finds that Phoebe is warm enough and therefore physically comfortable, Mrs. Caulfield makes no further effort to learn whether Phoebe is lonely for disturbed in any way. On the surface, it would seem that Mrs. Caulfield does not try to give her children psychological or spiritual warmth. She seems to be somewhat troubled herself—she has constant headaches—and not very capable of spiritual understanding. Holden may have been driven to the refuge of hypersensitivity by his parent's incapable handling of his problems.

THE LIE: Phoebe's lie to her mother about smoking poses an interesting moral question: should one condone or condemn her behavior? The answer would depend on one's attitude toward Holden. If he is conceived of as a wrongdoer who deserves to be caught, Phoebe should have told the truth; if one has sympathy for Holden's plight, the conclusion is that Phoebe told a sweet, unselfish lie.

The moral dilemma presented here parallels that of Huck Finn, when he protects the runaway slave by telling a lie. Huck castigates himself afterward and believes that he is doomed because of his lie; the reader, however, knows better. Mark Twain, who was always closely associated with the philosophy of the lie, also wrote a short story called "Was It Heaven—Or Hell," in which the question of the moral acceptance of the precept of an "unselfish lie" is thoroughly threshed out.

In *The Catcher in the Rye* the problem is not germane to an appreciation of the entire novel, but it does have relevance. In order properly to evaluate Holden Caulfield, one must ask oneself where moral responsibility resides—in the individual or in society. Certainly, the complex interrelationship of the two makes a simple solution impossible; Salinger wisely leaves the decision to the reader.

PHOEBE AND HOLDEN: In addition to the moral problem raised here, which permeates the entire novel, one can see a direct contrast between Phoebe and Holden. Holden tells lies in order to escape painfully embarrassing situations, at times, but more often his lies are completely purposeless. Phoebe's lie has a tangible motivation; she is more down to earth than is Holden. Phoebe is responsible person who uses the device with continence and deliberateness.

When Phoebe asks Holden to promise to see her play and he acquiesces, one sees his final resolution adumbrated. Holden loves his little sister, and does not want to hurt her.

CATHARSIS: It is this love for Phoebe—and, really, for his entire family—that causes Holden to break into cathartic tears. Phoebe has given him her Christmas gift money, and he is leaving home. This ambivalent exit—he is unable to make up his mind whether or not he really wants to be caught—is preceded by a symbolic gesture; Holden gives his red cap to Phoebe. The reason he now eschews the hat, which has been symbolic of his passive—though rebellious—idealism lies in Holden's realization that his quest for moral responsibility is over, in a sense; the quarry has been sighted and he no longer needs his hunting cap.

CHAPTER 24

MR. ANTOLINI: The story comes full circle when Holden again seeks contact with a figure of authority as embodied by a teacher. His visit to Mr. Antolini parallels the events in the opening section of the novel, when Holden visits Mr. Spencer, Mr. Antolini is much younger than Spencer; he is a very articulate man and very much in contact with reality.

Just as Salinger used separate bedrooms as a device to symbolize the lack of communication between Mr. and Mrs. Spencer, he implies a lack of communication between Mr. and Mrs. Antolini by having them always shouting at each other from different rooms in their apartment; they are rarely found in the same room. This distance between man and wife is an aspect of the loneliness and isolation that Holden often perceives in life. Mr. Antolini's psychic struggles are denoted by his chain smoking and heavy drinking; he is not as impervious to the vicissitudes of life as we had first thought.

THEORIES OF EDUCATION: Holden tries to explain to Mr. Antolini why he failed school. Emerging from his almost incoherent discourse is his distaste for arbitrary rules. Mr. Antolini argues that there must be some order, that there is a time and a place for everything, but Holden points out that sometimes the realization of just what interests a person is born when that person is talking about something else entirely. This approach to the positive through the negative shows Holden's acute perception. He concludes that the speech teacher, Mr. Vinson, was very intelligent but was not possessed of "much brains." This is further evidence of Holden's (or Salinger's) acute perception. The thesis is, of course, that wisdom is superior to mere intelligence; wisdom is the use and application of intelligence in a compassionate manner.

Thus summed up is a major portion of Holden's problems at school. He believes that wisdom is—or should be—the school's primary concern. Knowledge should make one happier and wiser; the *information* he received at school did not make Holden happier and was, therefore, not knowledge in its truest sense.

ADVICE: Mr. Antolini warns Holden that the youth is heading for a fall; this foreshadows Holden's breakdown and echoes the symbol of catching children as they fall over the cliff. The physical manifestation of Holden's collapse is his increasing inability to concentrate and his nagging headache.

Mr. Antolini's advice to Holden is epitomized in his quotation of Wilhelm Stekel, the psychiatrist:

> *The mark of the immature man is that he wants to die nobly for a cause, while the mark of the mature man is that he wants to live humbly for one.*

This affirmative advice is quite applicable to Holden's case; to accept this philosophy would mean to accept, in a constructive way, his role in the world. Thus far, of course, Holden has not accepted life; he has, instead, rebelled against school and family in the "immature" spirit of "dying nobly for a cause."

SEARCH FOR TRUTH: Since the plot of the novel revolves around school—and thereby knowledge—it is fitting that a teacher should discuss Holden's attitude toward learning. As Mr. Antolini says, Holden is in love with knowledge; this is true but, as was said above, Holden rejects the educational system because it does not help him in his passionate search for truth. This search is one of the major themes of the novel—that is, Holden's quest for wisdom, in order to establish a moral order by asserting himself. Holden's involvement with moral and intellectual truth renders him vulnerable to the false and unjust elements of life.

MR. ANTOLINI'S GESTURE: Mr. Antolini has asked Holden about the state of his acquaintanceship with girls. Holden's response, which deprecates Sally's worth and shows a renewed interest in Jane, evinces his willingness to attempt to establish a mature relationship with a girl. It is a natural question for Mr. Antolini to ask, but the aftermath makes it seem more dramatic, in retrospect.

We are never quite sure just why Mr. Antolini came and put his hand on Holden's head while the boy was asleep. Salinger is deliberately ambiguous about the matter and it must be admitted that the point is not a vital one. If Mr. Antolini is a homosexual, that fact only serves as ironic comment on his sound moral advice. If he is not, and Holden mistook the import of the gesture, it is further evidence of how Holden's hypersensitivity adds to his difficulty in entering into honest human relationships.

CHAPTERS 25 AND 26

NOTE: The last section of the book is probably the fullest in content and the tightest in structure. Because the themes are resolved as the novel comes to its conclusion, any interpretation of the events and symbols of the entire novel will depend on a close reading of this section.

AWARENESS: Holden's second thoughts about Mr. Antolini indicate an emerging awareness. After he casts doubt on his early conclusions as to what had occurred at the apartment, Holden is forced to concede that Mr. Antolini showed true charity to him, giving of his time and attention, regardless of the interpretation that might be placed on his later actions. As usual, Holden is capable of seeing more than one side of a matter.

NEVER TO RETURN HOME: Holden next decides that he will never return home. Spiritually, at least, it is true that he will never return home because he is undergoing the profound metamorphosis from adolescence to maturity; he will never return to childhood nor will he escape any more into the world of fantasy. He must go forward and grow up and thus break away from his emotional attachment to the past.

FANTASY: With characteristic ambivalence, Holden, while preparing to enter the adult world, indulges in fantastic daydreams. His dream of escaping from reality as an anonymous deaf-mute to an idyllic cabin in the woods mirrors the romantic dreams of the poets. His vision of the beautiful and unreal girl he will marry is typical of his sentimental solutions to the problems of life.

VICE: Holden's wish to say goodbye to Phoebe brings him to the school that he attended years ago. Ironically, this attempted farewell will lead him home as well as to the destruction of his false conception of the ideal of childhood innocence. The obscene graffiti he discovers on the walls of the school, he mistakenly assumes are the work of perverted adults. His inability to perceive that children are responsible contains a certain amount of pathos; he is so anxious to defend the pristine purity of childhood—to be the catcher in the rye. There is further irony in Holden's mistaken equation of vulgarity with vice. He is too ready to assume that innocence is capable to being corrupted with a word.

THE TOMB: Holden's touching concern for children is seen in his conversation with the boys he meets at the museum. When he tells them all about Egyptian mummies, he is making use of, in a very practical way, the knowledge he gained in Mr. Spencer's history class. This is an amusing link to the opening section of the book—at last Holden finds that those hard-won facts are of some use.

The two boys are frightened and run away from the Egyptian tomb; it is quite appropriate that they should fear the mysterious and the unknown. Holden's fear is of the unknown—to him—adult world, and of the brutality and violence he is sure is there. Left alone, Holden sees the same obscene phrase in the tomb itself, causing him to speculate on the ubiquity of vulgarity; he feels that it will accompany him to his grave.

CLIMAX: Phoebe's arrival marks the dramatic conclusion of the novel. She is wearing the red cap, thus symbolically changing places with Holden. Now it is Phoebe who acts irresponsibly and irrationally, by wanting to run away; Holden perforce becomes the apostle of common sense. Thus, Phoebe—presumably unwittingly—becomes the catalytic agent that causes Holden, willy-nilly, to accept responsibility.

CONCLUSION: Holden had told us at the beginning of the book that he would tell us no more than he had told D.B.; he has done this, and we know now the events that precipitated his breakdown. True to his word, Holden will say no more. We may recall that at the conclusion of *Huckleberry Finn* Huck says:

> *. . . there ain't nothing more to write about, and I am rotten glad of it, because if I'd 'a' knowed what a trouble it was to make a book I wouldn't 'a' tackled it, and ain't a-going to no more.*

These seem to be Holden's sentiments, exactly.

Character Analyses

HOLDEN CAULFIELD: The central character and the sole source of information for the events in the book. We learn everything only as it comes through Holden, the narrator and protagonist. In general, Holden's environment can be considered unstable and superficial. He rejects the traditions of school because they are artificial, lacking depth and warmth. His loneliness and rebellion come from his passive rejection of the false conventions and materialistic values that surround him. Because Holden fails in school, uses vulgar expressions, gets drunk, and is very interested in sex we might consider him to have low moral standards. Although these common adolescent characteristics may not fit in with our idealistic conception of a teen-ager, Holden represents the lonely American youth seeking to establish a moral code based on transcendent values. Holden's wealthy background, however, allows him to skip over all the middle-class materialistic concerns of our society. Holden's ambition to be the "catcher in the rye" symbolizes his desire to establish a moral order. (His name is a pun upon this theme: "hold" in "field.") Humorous as well as honest but by no means perfect, Holden searches for some purposeful relationship, but he is not yet prepared for an adult role in society.

His interest in everything stems from his youthful search for experience and freedom. This general but undefined interest in things demonstrates his undeveloped sensibilities. It is important to realize that other characters can be seen and understood only through this sensibility, i.e., Holden's consciousness is the consciousness of the entire novel—characters emerge only as they mirrored in this consciousness. On the surface we know only what Holden tells us about these people.

Is he defeated by society or will he change society? His general breakdown may have been brought about by society, but it does lead him back to reality with a new awareness. Holden's new awareness, however, will not change society. Like Huck Finn, Holden is a youth whose social significance must be evaluated in practical terms. Huck Finn did not establish racial equality everywhere, and Holden Caulfield does not give society a moral vision that transcends the false power and false security that materialism offers as the *raison d'etre* of our society. What he does gain for himself is the recognition that no man is an island.

PHOEBE CAULFIELD: She epitomizes the child prodigy type that Salinger so frequently creates. Her childish whimsy is mixed with serious perceptions that force Holden to reevaluate his actions and probe his conscience. In the novel, Phoebe receives Holden's full esteem, as she represents the continued flow of children who must be cared for, the life process that is man's responsibility. Her unselfishness stems from a basic innocence which Holden understands but which overwhelms him.

ACKLEY: He is neither ambitious nor generous. Rather, Ackley is an unfriendly, unsophisticated youth who reacts with scorn because he does not fit into society. His character is drawn to perfection by Salinger. His reaction to alienation contrasts with Holden's. The apathy and cynicism he express cover up his deep resentment at his rejection by society.

ALLIE CAULFIELD: Salinger creates another off-stage prodigy. Allie is another of the near perfect, precocious, young people who populate his fiction. He functions almost as an alter ego to Holden who compares everything to him.

MR. SPENCER: He yearns to be sympathetic but fails. He represents an older generation of sweet but befuddled teachers who have lost contact with the realities of life. In Holden's eyes he would be classed as a nice but depressing guy.

Mr. Spencer's genuineness as a person can be seen beneath his fumbling ways. The Indian blanket that he and his wife bought on a vacation symbolizes his sincere but simple delights. The Indian blanket also shows his honest but uncommunicable love of history and culture.

MR. ANTOLINI: A younger man who left the Elkton Hills school to teach at N.Y.U., he is more articulate than Spencer, and thus is able to communicate a good deal with Holden and show him how even idealism can be put to constructive rather than self-destructive use, and how necessary it eventually becomes to reach some compromise with the rest of the world, however vulgar it seems, and to establish some order within oneself.

It is one of Holden's more significant lessons that, though Mr. Antolini may not be perfect, he can be helpful. Thus, this teacher weakens Holden's tenacious grip on the either/or reasoning that often results in a paralysis of action, or in escapism.

STRADLATER: There has to be such a character in order to suggest all the qualities in American society that Holden despises, from the exaggerated evaluation of athletic ability and masculine parade of virility to personal egotism, superficial even callous thinking, worship of materialism and amoral ethical position. Stradlater, though, is popular, successful with girls, a leader of boys; he is not, however, a person to be looked up to according to the more subtle but more desirable standards Salinger details in his writings.

SALLY HAYES: For the most part she is representative of the wealthy, superficial world of Holden's own background. Through knowing her, he learned how to distinguish a surface knowledge and culture from true depth and understanding. Certainly he is not able to communicate to Sally any of his deepest problems.

[There are of course other lesser but interesting characters, particularly those mentioned who appear little, if at all: Jane Gallagher; Mr. and Mrs. Caulfield; Allie, the near-perfect dead brother.]

Sample Essay Questions and Answers

I. THE IDEAS IN *THE CATCHER IN THE RYE*

1. What is the theme of *The Catcher in the Rye*?

ANSWER: The theme of any work of art is arrived at by first deciding what the subject is. In *The Catcher in the Rye*, the subject is growing up. Now, the attitude that the author puts forth about his subject is what we call the theme. Therefore, the theme, in its broadest sense, would be the difficulty of growing up, the lonely and arduous voyage from innocence to experience.

2. Is this theme in the mainstream of American literature?

ANSWER: Yes. Perhaps because our nation and traditions are so young, many prominent American novelists have used the theme of a young person's initiation to experience. The loneliness that Holden feels in his quest is also the reason that Ishmael in Melville's *Moby-Dick* goes on the whaling voyage. The adventures and moral quest in Twain's *Huckleberry Finn* also parallel the continual search for order that Holden undertakes. Crane's *The Red Badge of Courage*, as well as other novels, shows the same preoccupation with psychological growth and moral awareness as does *The Catcher in the Rye*. The rebellion against genteel language and the subjective, individualistic way of telling the story also are very American. It is probable that in his use of colloquial language, Salinger was radically influenced by Ring Lardner.

3. Should Holden be considered a typical or an unusual American youth?

ANSWER: Although Holden's sensitivity and intelligence are heightened for the purpose of dramatizing his character, he shares, to a considerable extent, the problems of all American youth.

4. What are some of the chief difficulties that Holden faces as an adolescent?

ANSWER: Holden's main problems are honesty and egotism. Holden cannot really accept the death of his brother Allie. He idealizes him to the point where it interferes with his ability to make new friendships. He desires to be honest, which demands facing the problems of life, but he wants to protect all other children from having to face them. His sincerity leads him to lie, which beclouds his honesty, and forces him to wonder about his ability to be honest. This general pattern, i.e., a self-conscious examination of himself, leads him to doubt all his motivations, as when he dismisses the notion of being a lawyer. Holden feels that self-gratifying motives cannot be separated from any good intention. Holden, preoccupied with self, has a confused vision of the real objects in life. One of the evidences of Holden's growth is stated in the last chapter when Holden finally learns how to miss people.

5. What does Holden's concern for the ducks symbolize?

ANSWER: Holden identifies with the innocent creatures and wants to know what fate has in store for them. It is symbolic of his desire to know about nature.

6. What is the significance of Holden's relationship with his parents?

ANSWER: His relationship with his parents intensifies his general alienation because they do not seem to give him personal direction and warmth. He fails to see that their way of life can offer any solution for his problems.

7. Does Holden change?

ANSWER: Yes. At the end of the book he does not desire to run away from home, and his concern for people has become more positive.

8. Is the novel pessimistic or optimistic?

ANSWER: If one accepts Holden's growth of vision, then the novel must be considered optimistic. If, however, a reader feels that the growth does not counterbalance the painful struggle, the Holden's adolescence is both pessimistic and pathetic. The novel, of course, would be very pessimistic if Holden did not develop a new vision and purpose in life through his difficulties.

The answer also may vary according to whether the reader is afraid that Holden will be—or will not be—cured in the rest home.

9. May a novel about an adolescent be significant to adults?

ANSWER: Yes. The universality of the theme cannot be overstated. If adult society cannot identify with the struggles of the young attempting to reach maturity, then adult society has no hope of maintaining a position of leadership. Without leadership, institutions would no longer give direction but merely propagandize. Social progress and communication is a two-way street which demands that the young understand the old and vice versa. Holden's growth in awareness and responsible acceptance is the most dramatic event in the book, but it must be matched by a mutual movement of comprehension on the part of adult society if it is to mean anything.

10. What is Holden's attitude toward religion?

ANSWER: Holden satirizes the sermon by the wealthy undertaker. He sees the false image that is created in the connection between spirituality and material success. For the same reason he admires the charity of the nuns. He fells that they are directly committed to the principle of charity. Yet he pities them, even though they stand in direct contrast with the false, "ego" satisfying charity of some of his socialite neighbors, because they appear out of touch with reality.

11. What is Holden's attitude toward sex?

ANSWER: Holden's sensitivity and normal teenage preoccupation with it can be seen throughout the novel. He is always talking of "flits" and he runs from Antolini's house in fear of being attacked.

12. Is Holden a snob?

ANSWER: No. Holden is too genuinely concerned about people. In fact he is quite the opposite of a snob because he feels sorry for those who are not as privileged as he is. Although Holden's taste occasionally shows that he comes from a wealthy family, he does not express a feeling of superiority on the basis of wealth or social advantage.

II. THE FORM OF *THE CATCHER IN THE RYE*

1. What is the overall structural pattern of the novel?

ANSWER: The novel's shape is that of a circle. It begins in a California rest home, where Holden starts telling about the experiences which lead to his breakdown. The end of the novel returns to the rest home, completing the circle. Salinger intensifies and rounds out the circular structure of the novel by repeating the same symbols and themes at the conclusion of the novel that he used at the beginning.

2. In what literary tradition can *The Catcher in the Rye* be placed?

ANSWER: *The Catcher in the Rye* is a novel about the development or maturation of the hero. There are many examples of this type in American and world literature, such as Twain's *The Adventures of Huckleberry Finn*, Crane's *The Red Badge of Courage*, Joyce's *A Portrait of the Artist as a Young Man*, Lawrence's *Sons and Lovers*, Faulkner's *The Bear*, and Mann's *The Magic Mountain*. In a rapidly changing world this type of novel has a strong universal appeal.

3. What effects come from Salinger's use of point of view?

ANSWER: *The Catcher in the Rye* is an example of subjective, first-person narrative. Everything we learn comes from and through Holden, who is the major character. The effect is not only to engage the reader directly in the novel but also to create depth. The reader must realize that Holden can only present things as a seventeen-year-old; it is up to the reader to evaluate Holden's personality and character through what he does choose to present. This places a burden on the reader to dig deeply into the meaning of things.

4. What role does language play in the development of character and action in *The Catcher in the Rye*?

ANSWER: The colloquial and slang language serves to heighten the characterization of Holden Caulfield as well as control the pace of the novel. Holden's off-hand speech serves to demonstrate his inarticulate yet rebellious personality. He uses the same word in many different contexts, which forces the reader to pay close attention in order to appreciate the exact shades of meaning Holden intends.

5. What are some of the more important symbols in the novel?

ANSWER: The three most important symbols are the song by Robert Burns, the red hunting hat, and the sports imagery which appears throughout. The title, which comes from a mishearing of the song, indicates Holden's great desire to have a transcendent moral purpose, to save children from any loss of innocence. Linked with the song title is the cap worn in reverse, which is the distinctive apparel of a baseball catcher. This inversion of the hunting cap, a symbol of man as the hunter, indicates that Salinger sees the hunting instinct in a different manner now. Man's struggle is elevated to the level of a moral quest. The red hat links Holden with the tradition of hunter, but Holden's passivity obviously makes him a new kind of hunter. Indeed, he is more the hunted than the hunter. The hunting hat is also linked to the general game and sport imagery in the novel. How you play the game, or whether you play the game, indicates your attitude to life. Holden, the reformer as well as the rebel, wants to make the rules more human, more acceptable to man.

6. Is the structure of *The Catcher in the Rye* well balanced?

ANSWER: Some critics have argued that the structure of the book falls apart when Holden does not follow through with his plan to run away. Phoebe, they argue, does not provide sufficient motivation for Holden's dramatic reversal. This criticism came quite early in the reception of the novel, and has since been well refuted. There are several reasons for Holden's reversal. Holden is very attached to his family; his tenderness for Phoebe and his memories of Allie are the most forceful relationships he has. Furthermore, Holden is running away from responsibility, not an unbearable family life. His struggle does not take the form of a direct clash between personalities. Holden's desire to escape his fraudulent environment is not without a sense of the loss of family that will accompany this separation. Therefore, when Holden decides not to leave because of his responsibility to Phoebe, this comes quite naturally to him. The motivation is subtle and complex just as the characterization of Holden is. The book is carefully and successfully well balanced.

7. Is Holden an heroic figure?

ANSWER: Certainly Holden is not heroic in the traditional sense. Rather, he fits into the modern anti-heroic hero. He is not conventionally successful in his undertakings. Obviously Holden's strength does not rest in the traditional successes. Instead he is functioning on a different level, he is fighting a Don Quixote type of battle in order to restore moral order. Holden is heroic in the deepest sense because he truly battles against sham and corruption. His nobility does not reside in his external success but rather in his spiritual struggle.

Arthur Miller's The Crucible

Plot Summary

ACT I (AN OVERTURE)

In the spring of 1692, Reverend Samuel Parris, the petty, irritable minister of Salem, Massachusetts, is worried about his small daughter, Betty. She has slept, seemingly in a trance, since he caught her with his teen-aged niece, Abigail, and other girls dancing in the forest the night before. With them was his Barbados slave, Tituba, but Abigail denies that there was any Devil-worship or conjuring. Someone already has summoned the Reverend John Hale, a witchcraft specialist from nearby Beverly. But Abigail insists that she is virtuous, even though she was lately discharged as servant by John Proctor's wife. The latter, she claims, is a spiteful liar.

Thomas Putnam, a shrewd, ruthless landowner, arrives with Ann, his gloomy, neurotic wife. Their daughter, too, is sick, and Mrs. Putnam is certain that witchcraft is abroad. Why else would she have lost so many babies, all dying soon after birth? Parris disputes her theory since his own niece and daughter took part in the now-admitted conjuring. But Mary Warren, the Proctor's present servant, enters to announce excitedly that talk of witches is all over Salem. Left alone briefly with Abigail, the girls, including Mary, the awakened Betty, and Mercy Lewis, the Putnam's crafty maid, worry about how much more they should admit. Abby, however, warns them to say no more or she will make them pay dearly.

John Proctor, a vigorous, independent farmer, enters and irately orders home his servant, Mary, who leaves followed by Mercy. John jests briefly about the scare with Abigail, with whom he has had an affair. He firmly denies, however, that he still loves her, and is angered by her vindictive references to his wife. At this point a psalm is heard sung by villagers, Betty starts screaming, and Parris and the Putnams return.

Also arriving now are two elderly personages—cantankerous Giles Corey and gentle, dignified Rebecca Nurse. Rebecca easily soothes the agitated child. She antagonizes the Putnams, however, who have often been at odds with her family, by her common-sense refusal to get overly exercised over a youngster's hysteria. Rebecca has twenty-six grandchildren! A quarrel then breaks out between Proctor, lining up with Rebecca, and the Putnams, intent upon proving diabolical influence. It is also evident that Proctor dislikes the fiery sermons and mean avarice of the Reverend Mr. Parris. In addition, Proctor and Corey rouse Putnam's ire further by claiming lumber that he says belongs to him.

Arriving with several weighty books, the Reverend John Hale energetically proposes to sift the whole witchcraft question. Sure of himself and of his learning, he listens attentively to the Putnams and even to crotchety old Corey's suspicions that his wife, Martha, reads too much. Hale is appalled to learn of the forest rites and sends for Tituba. Terrified for her life, the slave heeds the minister's leading questions and confesses with imaginative gusto. Pressed to name witches, she cooperatively accuses two questionable old women, Sarah Good and Sarah Osburn. The bystanders are impressed. And Abigail, exalted and aglow, also piously confesses, adding more names, as does the feverish

Betty. Putnam, triumphant, goes to call the marshal to arrest those listed and to put them in chains. Parris prays thankfully.

ACT II

One night a week later, at Proctor's farm, John talks with his wife, Elizabeth. She tries to be dutiful and even agreeable, but clearly cannot forget his infidelity. Proctor is alarmed to learn that many have been arrested in Salem, that notable judges have come, and that there is talk of hangings. Elizabeth urges him to denounce the formidable Abigail. When he hesitates, she eyes him accusingly, and he, in turn, rebukes her for being cold and unforgiving.

Timorous Mary Warren, now a lofty court official, enters, giving Elizabeth a hand-made poppet, or rag doll. Obviously horrified and sick, Mary tells them that Goody Osburn is set to hang, Sarah Good having saved herself by confessing. She adds that Elizabeth herself was mentioned, but that she loyally came to her defense. Proctor's wife now knows that Abigail seeks her life. John is incredulous, but agrees now to go and testify that Abigail admitted the fraud to him.

Suddenly Hale appears to do some investigating on his own initiative. He notes Proctor's limited church attendance, refusing to grant that disliking Parris is any valid excuse. Challenged to repeat the Ten Commandments, John ironically forgets the one against adultery. At Elizabeth's prodding, he tells Hale of Abigail's falsehoods. As for himself, he cautiously avoids rejecting the possibility of witches. But Elizabeth firmly declares that if she can be accused, then there are no real witches.

Corey and Nurse arrive, angry and disturbed, to report the arrest of their wives. Even Hale is shocked to hear Rebecca charged with supernaturally slaying the Putnam infants. Two court officials, Cheever and Herrick, then come to take Elizabeth, whom Abigail has finally charged. Mary's doll is urged as evidence, for a needle stuck in the doll could be a witch's way of inflicting stabbing pains in her victim. The story is largely disproved, but despite John's outraged objections, his wife is taken and chained. Hale promises to plead for her, however, and John warns the petrified Mary to tell the truth and save her mistress.

ACT III

In the meeting-house vestry room, now a court antechamber, Corey, noisy and contentious, is barred from offering evidence to save his wife. Stern Judges Hawthorne and Danforth accuse him of trying to undermine the court. Corey, Nurse, and Proctor then bring in the frightened Mary Warren to declare all the girls liars.

Questioning Proctor closely, the suave Danforth assures him that he need not try this to save Elizabeth. She claims to be an expectant mother and will not be executed for some time. Proctor, however, will not desert his friends. The men present an affidavit, with over ninety signatures, asserting the high opinion held by neighbors of all the accused wives. They are shocked, however, to hear that all those loyal friends will be hauled into court. Corey, in turn, charges Putnam with backing the accusations to gain lands. Unable, in conscience, to name his source for this charge, Corey is arrested for contempt.

Mary then fearfully testifies, and the girls are brought in to confront her. Abigail coolly accuses her of lying. As a test, the judges order Mary to faint as she did in court, but Mary cannot oblige. Unable to rouse interest enough in the forest revels, Proctor desperately admits his adultery to discredit Abigail. He adds that his wife, who never lies, will support his contention. Hastily summoned, Elizabeth charitably shields his good name, thus unintentionally blasting his case. Emboldened, Abigail leads her set in a wild, frenzied outburst to frighten the wits out of Mary. Weakening, the quavering girl rejoins the rest and accuses Proctor. Hale tries to intercede for him, but the judges send Proctor and Corey to prison.

ACT IV

In the Salem jail three months later, Marshal Herrick thrusts Sarah Good and Tituba out of a cell so that Danforth and Hawthorne may confer there. The two women, leaving, chatter crazily of good times with the Devil in sunny Barbados. The jail stench is foul. Herrick is drunk, and confusion and misery are rife in Salem. Hale has been ministering to those about to hang, and Parris looks gaunt and a little mad. Abigail and her friend Mercy fled Salem recently, taking money from his strongbox with them. Broken, Parris pleads for a postponement of the executions, especially of the much respected Proctor and Rebecca, but the judges remain obdurate. Hale says that none will confess, despite his efforts.

In hopes that she will induce Proctor to admit his guilt, Elizabeth is brought in. She is thin, pale, and dirty, but retains a quiet dignity. Hale, horrified at the havoc everywhere, urges her to get John to lie. John then arrives, bearded, grimy, and worn, having been kept chained in the dungeon. They talk privately, and he is saddened to learn that Giles Corey is dead. The old man was pressed with great stones, since he would not plead in a way that would surely disinherit his sons.

Proctor declares that he is not a saint like Rebecca, and asks Elizabeth how she would feel if he lied to save his life. Humbly, she refuses to judge him, admitting that she, too, has sinned. Unsure of herself, she was cold to him, thus driving him into Abigail's arms.

Proctor decides to confess, and Hawthorne and the other judges are delighted. He does not like, however, their publishing his shame in the village and he adamantly refuses to name anyone else accusingly. He balks further at signing his name to the dishonorable confession. Then, with newfound courage, he joins the brave Rebecca and goes to his doom. Hale begs Elizabeth to call him back, but she will not take from him his painfully acquired "goodness." There is an ominous roll of drums, and Hale weeps.

Character Analyses

JOHN PROCTOR: This plain-spoken, vigorous farmer would seem to represent the good, average citizen who may upon occasion be moved to take heroic action. He would not normally be considered a saintly individual, and he has no great eagerness to be a martyr. Yet when put to the final test, the meaning here of "crucible," he will go to his death rather than irrevocably compromise his integrity.

His human frailty is established early in the play. Although normally a good husband and father, he is said to have seduced the beautiful and very young Abigail, when she was a servant girl at his farm. In a community that places much emphasis upon church attendance, he has not been the most faithful of worshippers. In addition, as the Reverend Mr. Hale easily ascertains, he cannot readily recite his Ten Commandments.

Furthermore, he is by no means desirous of courting trouble. He may speak up boldly to Parris, for whom he has contempt, but he is decidedly cautious when questioned by Hale. Whatever private opinions he entertains on the subject of witchcraft, he makes his replies as ambiguous as possible to avoid drawing the minister's censure. He also tries to stop Elizabeth from speaking too freely.

On three other occasions there is abundant evidence that he is not naturally given to rash or bold gestures. For one thing, he is quite reluctant to heed his wife's urging to denounce Abigail to the court. Apart from the fact that he has loved her, he considers the move dangerous. He might not be believed. Again, when the judges tell him that he need not keep forcing upon them the unwelcome deposition, since his wife claims to be pregnant, he is, for the moment, unsure. Clearly he is tempted to withdraw, but loyalty to his friends finally wins out. Lastly, after suffering torture and close confinement for several months, he is disposed to sign a confession. This is not entirely selfish, for he wants to care for his wife and children. Yet it is consistent with his overall inclination to avoid heroics. He himself says that since he is not of heroic mold, it would almost be hypocritical of him to stand up and play the hero.

In spite, however, of his humble awareness of guilt and unwillingness to run foolishly into jeopardy, he is a forceful individual given to decisive action. He bluntly opposes Parris and Putnam. He tears up Herrick's warrant and tries to prevent the officers from arresting and chaining his wife. He works extremely hard to get Mary Warren to change her story, and joins with Nurse and Corey in obtaining the deposition favoring the accused women. When all else fails, he speaks up and reveals his shameful act of adultery to the judges. Even in prison he does not accept defeat easily. He struggles bravely until restrained by fetters, and will talk to no one, only deigning to occasionally take some food.

When, therefore, he suggests toward the end that only in destroying his lying confession does he reveal some goodness, he is not being fair to himself. He has hitherto fought hard and ably for justice; and in admitting publicly his sin with Abigail to save Elizabeth, he has already shown himself capable of generous self-sacrifice. Because he has a lively conscience, he may, in fact, have followed Elizabeth's lead and undervalued his own merits because of his one sensual lapse.

At the same time, when he must choose either the lie and life, or the truth and death, he is understandably uncertain. Certain factors, however, combine to help him arrive at his final noble decision. First of all, Elizabeth, while giving him no directive, lets him know that she thinks him a good man. And she herself, of course, has not surrendered. Secondly, he is more than ever impressed with the fanatical harshness of the judges. They will leave him no shred of self-respect if he yields. Thirdly, he thinks of his children and dreads willing them a dishonored name. Fourthly, he is shamed by the courage of Rebecca and the others who have not freed themselves by lying. Fifthly, he feels, as before, a strong sense of loyalty. He certainly will not implicate his friends in any confession. But will not any confession be a form of disloyalty? Finally, he comes to see that his own consciousness of integrity is supremely important. And it is this sudden awareness—that he cannot even to save his life deny all that he stands for—that enables him to leave his now-more-than-ever beloved wife and accept his fate with courage.

Proctor, of course, is not altogether "average." He is, from the first, a forceful individual. But only after much suffering and painful doubt does he recognize fully his dignity as a man and defend his truth to the death.

ELIZABETH PROCTOR: Elizabeth is sometimes in the play called Goody Proctor, the word "Goody" being a conventional title for a married woman. She is first mentioned by the hostile Abigail as being a cold, bitter liar. Afterwards the beautiful and passionate Abby attacks her again to John Proctor himself. And while he loyally defends his wife, he does not seem entirely to disagree.

In Act II, Elizabeth herself appears and does little at first to make a much more favorable impression. She goes about her household duties with an injured air and finally provokes even the penitent Proctor's anger with her stony, unforgiving manner. She is perhaps trying to be more agreeable, and she has undoubtedly been hurt by his infidelity. But when she urges him to go and denounce Abigail, she is almost too ready to see in his understandable hesitation more evidence of his weakness.

In the scene with Hale, however, Elizabeth begins to win more sympathy. She shows more spirit than Proctor in rejecting any suggestion that she has failed in her religious obligations. She has lived up to her creed and knows it. If she can be thought a witch, then there is no such thing as witchcraft. Afterwards when the men come to arrest her, she speaks up firmly about Mary's poppet or doll. Faced with the inevitable, however, she leaves with quiet dignity, having first left instructions about the care of the house and the children. Actually, she is afraid, but resolutely declares that she will not fear.

She measures up well, also, when she is summoned to court. It is known already that she has made no confession but has informed the court promptly of her pregnancy, probably aware that they might not readily execute a woman expecting a child. Respected by her husband because she has always told the truth, she is suddenly called upon, without warning, to testify as to his relationship with Abigail. Whatever she may have said to him in private, Elizabeth cannot bring herself to injure John's reputation. She stretches the truth as far as possible and thus, ironically, destroys his chance to defeat Abigail. Here, however, it is clear that Elizabeth loves her husband enough to go against her own strict code.

In her final appearance it becomes evident that as a result of her cruel imprisonment she has become wiser, more understanding. She has come to appreciate John's goodness, whereas formerly she saw only his betrayal. In addition, she has recognized her own part in his fall from grace. Because she was unsure of herself, believing she was plain and unattractive, she was tense and anxious, as well as easily jealous. Had she been warmer, more loving, he might not have strayed.

Elizabeth has also realized, however, that she cannot tell her husband what to do. For one thing, she no longer feels so ominiscient and above reproach. For another, she knows that he must settle matters with his own conscience. Loving him now more than ever, she desperately wants him to live and knows that she can probably persuade him to do so. Yet having assured him that she will respect him whatever he decides, she heartbrokenly refuses to urge him to follow Hale's counsel of compromise. This means exercising iron control, but Elizabeth knows that John must achieve some peace of soul even if it means his death. Always a good woman, she too achieves here an act of heroic renunciation.

JOHN HALE: The Reverend Mr. Hale, minister of Beverly, is another character who moves from a comforting sense of goodness and capability to a humbling awareness of limitations. When he arrives at the Parris home with his armload of learned volumes, he is in the best of spirits. He knows that whatever problems may have arisen to disturb these worthy but uninformed villagers, he has all the answers. He may have to investigate carefully and sift evidence. He realizes that some may not have his training and not be so apt at separating truth from falsehood. But he will be patient, tolerant, and firm until all mists are cleared away. Hale, in short, is seen at first as a well-meaning but conceited young man of learning.

His vulnerability soon becomes apparent. He talks much of sifting facts and consulting reliable sources. But he also has high hopes of getting prompt, impressive results. Hence when the startling, highly emotional revelations of Tituba shock the assemblage, he jumps at the chance for a showy conversion and orders those accused into irons. Proctor and Rebecca have already urged caution; there are obvious tensions between them and the Putnams; Abigail has already been proved to have engaged in questionable activities; and Tituba is a terrified slave. Yet Hale excited announces that the powers of evil have been defeated.

By Act II, however, he is less certain. Events he helped to set in motion are now causing him anxiety. So he comes by night to question the Proctors. He is somewhat severe with John because of his poor record of church attendance, but he is impressed with his sensible manner and shaken when he accuses Abigail of fakery. He is also favorably disposed toward Elizabeth after hearing her spirited defense of her life as a conscientious Christian woman. So he is surprised and disturbed when the marshal comes to arrest her. Proctor, of course, suspects that he came to trap them. But Hale avows his ignorance and promises to speak on her behalf. He still, however, declares that the courts are just and will free the innocent. Actually, he feels guilty and uncertain. He cannot see how one girl like Abigail could cause so much havoc, and he does not want to accept Proctor's angry charge that he, Hale, is a coward. Much troubled, he takes refuge in the theory that the whole village must in some way have offended God and thus drawn down divine wrath.

From then on he tries to be of some help to Proctor and his friends. He makes excuses for Proctor's Sunday plowing, and mentions the overall panic to explain why some fear to give evidence. He suggests that the men's petition be placed in a more acceptable legal form, and urges that Mary Warren's accusations against Abigail be very carefully weighed. When Elizabeth's reticence weakens John's case against Abigail, Hale again comes to John's defense, claiming that he has always suspected Abigail of lying. Unimpressed with the final screaming that causes Proctor's arrest, he walks out of the court, denouncing the proceedings.

It might then be assumed that Hale turns into an admirable figure. After one act of folly, he perceives his error and tries to save those accused. Yet in the long run Hale, for all his decent instincts, comes off badly because he represents the side of unworthy compromise. Having failed to obtain any postponement of the executions, he pleads with those condemned to make lying confessions. His argument is that no faith justifies the sacrificing of life, God's most precious gift. Those who will not yield, even under such impossible conditions as those prevailing in Salem, may be damned for pride. Elizabeth replies that he thus takes the Devil's side. Despite his urging and her own love for Proctor, she will not accept his teachings. And at the end, she, recognizing John's heroism, stands inspired, while Hale weeps.

As compared then with the stern, heartless Danforth and Hawthorne, Hale is more human, more open-minded, and more capable of admitting that he could be wrong. He also shows some courage in coming to the defense of the Proctors and in irately quitting the court. Yet, when measured against the uncompromising valor of Corey, Rebecca Nurse, and both Proctors, he is seen as a moral failure. A minister pledged to uphold the truth, he counsels deliberate lying, and his emotional reasoning rings false. Harshly tested, as are the rest, he denies his principles, and is last seen a pitiable lost man, rejected by all.

MARY WARREN: This weak, frightened young girl plays a more crucial role in the play itself than the domineering Abby. She is not mean or vindictive. Neither is she callous, for she comes home sick and horrified when the first executions are set. She also does make some attempt to stand up bravely and confess her "pretense."

Usually, however, she tends to yield to stronger personalities. Badly frightened when Abby threatens, she jumps when ordered home by the angry Proctor. For a brief time, of course, she does make a pathetic effort to assert her dignity as someone of importance. She is a court official who has dined with the great and cannot be sent to bed like an unruly child. But her confidence quickly evaporates, and she is bewildered and alarmed when the poppet Abby induced her to give her mistress is produced as evidence of witchcraft.

Like John Proctor himself, she mistakenly assumes that all her false testimony in court was a simple matter of lying. Yet she cannot seem to simulate one more fainting spell when so commanded by the judge. Actually, as in the subsequent episode in which she screamingly denounces Proctor, she is probably at times hysterical. When under Abby's baleful influence, being timorous anyway by nature, she undoubtedly is often a prey to uncontrollable emotions.

ABIGAIL WILLIAMS: Abigail is shown generally as a cool, resourceful schemer taking advantage of a peculiar situation to advance her own plans. At the outset it is not at all clear why she led the midnight revels in the forest. Idle and restless since her dismissal from the Proctors, she undoubtedly craves excitement. She may, however, also have had some belief in Tituba's magic. Betty Parris says that Abby drank blood as a charm to kill Elizabeth.

When questioned, she weighs answers carefully, telling as little as necessary, hotly defending her virtue in general, and blaming everyone else whenever she can. The plot involving Mary's presentation of the doll is well planned and executed, and she seems to have no compunction about causing others to die. She has been, in her opinion, badly treated, and she will brazenly cut down any who now challenge her veracity. She even warns the formidable judge, Danforth, that in questioning her he may be calling down upon himself God's wrath for allowing Hell to confuse him.

In the early scene with Proctor, it is true, she does give some hint of softer feelings. He has, she says, taught her how to love, and she lives only for the embraces he has since denied her. Shortly afterwards, however, she is cleverly fending off Hale's questions. Abigail once tells the girls by way of threat that she knows how to provide a "pointy reckoning," having seen her own parents brutally slain by Indians. And she subsequently proves herself a dangerous foe, until the day she flees Salem with her friend Mercy and her uncle's carefully hoarded savings.

One final question remains. Is Abigail herself, for all her cold plotting, sometimes partly hysterical? Her outcries following Tituba's confession have in them a note of wild glee. And when, under great tension later, she turns on Mary Warren, she seems genuinely frightened and her hands are icy. Abby is, in general, the hard opportunist who leads the young accusers. But the Putnams and other older villagers are also stirring up enmities. And it is possible that she, too, is sometimes caught up in the feverish excitement that grips all of Salem.

REBECCA NURSE: This aged and revered grandmother is used throughout to point up the criminal absurdity of Salem's witchcraft proceedings. Even before coming to Salem from Beverly, Hale has heard of her many charitable works. And when later he learns of her arrest, he is shocked. For if she should be proved corrupt, then nothing will prevent "the whole green world from burning."

Regarding the outbreak of trouble, Rebecca is the peacemaker, trying to restore sanity and friendlier feelings. She soothes the screaming Betty by her very serenity and strength, without saying a word. And she urges the distraught Mrs. Putnam to worry less. Rebecca knows about excitable children and has seen most of their crises overcome with time and patience. When the Putnams continue to talk of witchcraft, she urges them to seek solace in prayer. This advice rouses their ire, since they envy her flourishing family.

She is quietly in agreement with Proctor's charge that Parris's fiery sermons discourage those with children from coming to church. But she tries to get the resentful Proctor to make his peace with Parris, regardless. She is horrified to learn the Goody Putnam sent a small daughter to conjure with Tituba, and she hopes that Hale's strenuous efforts to drive out demons will not hurt the little Parris girl. When she leaves them to go to her prayers, they all know that she is not at all certain that good will be accomplished by Hale's ministrations.

In the last act, when Proctor must decide what course to take, he always has Rebecca as the standard of heroic silence. Others may break down, but the frail, aged Rebecca is a saint, already with "one foot in heaven." When she is told that John has confessed, Rebecca is stunned. She could not tell a lie to damn herself. How could he? And the moral force she exerts helps to make him change his mind. Rebecca is last seen, feebly but with courage, going to her death, with Proctor holding her arm. He now repays with physical support the moral support she has given him.

Sample Essay Questions and Answers

1. Compare the characters of John Proctor and John Hale as they are gradually developed in *The Crucible.*

ANSWER: At the outset, Proctor and Hale are both vigorous young men in their thirties. Hale is as trained scholar, and Proctor is a farmer who cannot easily recite the Commandments. Both, however, exude confidence. Proctor talks quite assertively to Parris and Putnam. Hale is quite sure that he and his books can solve Salem's problems.

By Act II, both have been somewhat shaken. Proctor, having heard Mary Warren's account of the madness abroad, and being very uneasy about what Abigail may try next, quite cautiously answers Hale's questions. Hale, on his part, has undertaken the investigation because he is no longer quite so certain of their guilt as he was when he ordered all those accused by Tituba and Abigail to be arrested and chained. He is impressed by the answers of the Proctors, and not at all pleased when Elizabeth is seized. But he wins Proctor's contempt as he tries to tell himself and the rest that justice will surely be done.

From then on Proctor fights valiantly to free his wife. Hale, however, tries to play both sides. He signs death warrants of those condemned, and yet he timidly does try to help Proctor and Nurse. Eventually he does angrily leave the proceedings, but his brave defiance comes too late.

At the end, Hale comes out firmly for moral compromise—lying to save one's life. And the Proctors reject his counsel as unworthy.

Thus, Proctor goes to his death with shining integrity. Hale lives, a beaten, rejected symbol of principles betrayed.

2. Why does the weak Mary Warren, rather than the ruthless Abigail, receive more attention in the play?

ANSWER: There are several reasons why this nervous, unstable girl is given so much prominence. First of all, in dramatic terms, the uncertain character makes possible more suspense. The very coldness and cleverness of Abigail that make her formidable also make any surprising change on her part unlikely. But Mary, essentially well-meaning and decent, is torn between her loyalty to the Proctors and her fearful dependence upon Abigail. The audience can, therefore, not be wholly sure which side she will finally support. This makes her an interesting figure.

In addition, she is used to illustrate how the weak can sometimes be used by more dominating unscrupulous individuals to bring about grave injustices. Mary Warren is sick with horror at the idea of the death warrants. Moreover, her gift of the doll to Elizabeth seems to have been well-meant. But she has clearly been used as a pawn to get her mistress convicted of witchcraft. Later, when Abigail starts the outcry against her, she screams out her accusations against Proctor largely from hysterical terror. She then simply cannot help herself.

Finally, the character is used to bring out how valueless may be the testimony of the badly frightened. Mary Warren may wish to be a good girl and not lie. Yet she cannot pretend to faint. On the other hand, virtually against her will she may launch terrible accusations. Evidence must be evaluated whence it comes. And even the well-intentioned, the play suggests, may be caught up in the hysteria of the moment and do inestimable damage.

3. What is the significance of the title *The Crucible*?

ANSWER: A crucible is literally a container used in the process of heating and melting metals. When subjected to great heat while in such a container, the more valuable metals are separated from the baser. When used figuratively, the word "crucible" means a hard test or severe trial.

In this play, not metals but men and women are made to undergo a sort of smelting process. When the Proctors, the Coreys, and Rebecca Nurse are arrested and forced to face dreadful accusations, they are, in effect, told to confess or die.

These people do not want to lose their lives. On the other hand, they are not accustomed to swearing to what is untrue. Their religion tells them that in doing so they court damnation. And even their ordinary self-respect normally demands of them that they speak the truth and keep their word. Yet if they will "confess" and satisfy their judges, they can live. If they tell the truth, they will be hanged. For average farm people not used to thinking of themselves as heroes, this is a formidable choice to have to make.

Despite some natural hesitation, however, the Proctors, Rebecca, and Giles all live up to their code. Choosing death rather than perjury, they prove themselves to be the most precious metals in the American ore.

4. The first act of *The Crucible* is subtitled an "overture." Why is it so designated, and how has it been received critically?

ANSWER: The term "overture" means normally an opening or introductory part of a musical composition or a literary work. In a sense, of course, any play's initial scenes must be concerned with giving necessary background material and identifying characters and situations so that the audience can follow the plot. But in this drama the procedure is somewhat different.

Although *The Crucible* has several extremely admirable figures, the main character or actual hero would seem to be John Proctor. Along with most of the other leading participants in the central conflict, Proctor does appear in the first act or overture. But he by no means stands out as he does during the rest of the play. Moreover, much of the later action will deal with the complex relationship between him and his wife, Elizabeth. But Goody Proctor, while mentioned, does not appear in this opening act at all.

In setting up *The Crucible*, Miller was very much aware of the differences between the theocratic civilization of seventeenth-century New England and the more secularist society of our own times. So he decided to give a great deal of background and establish well his period atmosphere before setting the Proctor plot fully in motion. Some critics have felt that this postpones unnecessarily the main action of the play. Others have commended the dramatist for taking a novel approach in solving the technical problems in this unique work.

5. What dramatic purposes are served by the role of Giles Corey?

ANSWER: Cranky, obstreperous old Giles adds, first of all, an elements of humor to a generally somber drama. A rather fussy, eccentric character, he is proud of his many bouts with the law, much to the amusement of his friend Proctor and the annoyance of the grimly acquisitive Putnams.

Secondly, Giles, with his innocent but foolish questions, is used to show on what absurd pretexts charges might be leveled against harmless people, once the fear of witchcraft had been roused. Much gratified to be able to get a bit of free information from the learned visitor, the Reverend Mr. Hale, Giles inquires why his wife Martha is always reading books that she will not let him see. Later, when Martha has been arrested, the heartbroken old man will rue his unfortunate remarks. Yet in more normal times, no one at all would have taken his querulous complaints seriously at all.

Finally, he emerges, for all his cantankerous quirks, as a man of integrity and courage. Having given his word to protect his source for the accusation against Putnam, he refuses to divulge the name even when accused of contempt. And he goes to his painful death in silence, refusing to plead at all, in order to protect the rights of his children. Tested in the crucible of the witchcraft trials, this crotchety old farmer acquits himself well as a decent human being.

6. When Proctor, Nurse, and Corey try to introduce evidence for the defense, why is their attempt doomed almost from the start?

ANSWER: Some of their difficulties seem to stem from the court procedures of the time, which apparently were not designed to protect adequately the rights of those accused. But there are other factors also operating against them.

First of all, there is the nature of the witchcraft charge. As is pointed out by the judges, since the alleged offense involves matters of subtle spiritual influences, ordinary rules of evidence cannot apply. A person, in theory, could apparently be peaceably at home minding his own affairs, and yet be sending his spirit out to harass someone else. Great reliance would therefore be placed upon the word of the presumed victim.

Secondly, the presence of fear in both community and court helps to hinder their efforts. The good people who could attest to the innocence of the women accused stay fearfully away from the proceedings and beg that no names of theirs be used, lest they in turn be arrested. And the judges themselves seem afraid. Perhaps the whole authority of the courts is being threatened by these angry petitioners. And again, should they be proved right, will this mean that the court has already condemned innocent people?

Thirdly, there are personal grudges involved. Parris certainly has no love for Proctor, who criticized him as unworthy to hold the town's religious services. Putnan is not only greedy for land, but is anxious to protect the reputation of his daughter, one of the girls making the charges. And Abigail wants her revenge against the Proctors and is also determined to avoid being charged herself.

Finally, there are two almost accidental elements that help wreck the Proctor case. Normally, Elizabeth would tell the whole truth, and Proctor would be safe in avowing that she would validate his confession. For once, however, her wifely compassion acts to make her at least stretch the truth a bit to save her husband's good name. And this half-lie ironically helps to doom him. Moreover, were Mary Warren a slightly stronger personality, she might not have recanted her testimony. But, being a frightened, neurotic girl, she is easily dominated by the inexorable Abigail.

7. How does the relationship of John and Elizabeth change throughout the play?

ANSWER: In the first scene with Abigail, John firmly announces that he will not in the future prove unfaithful to his wife; but he does not with any great conviction deny the girl's charge that his wife is cold and severe. In Act II, Proctor is seen humbly trying to conciliate Elizabeth, but she remains frosty and clearly resentful. As a result, Proctor finally becomes angry and protests the harsh manner in which she never lets him forget his act of infidelity.

Once Hale arrives, however, to question the couple, the atmosphere begins to change. Whatever their private differences, John and Elizabeth are united in their efforts to convince the minister of their solid Christian convictions. And when Elizabeth becomes rather dangerously candid in opposing some of the witchcraft proceedings, John tries to make her answer sound less provocative. When, subsequently, men come to arrest her, John tears up the warrant and tries in vain to stop them.

At the time of the trial, he proves that he has made every effort to get evidence to save her, and eventually even confesses his shame to secure her release. She, in turn, goes against her priciples to avoid injuring his good name. By the last act, when both have suffered rigorous confinements, the love and admiration between them is more than ever obvious. Both know their faults and want only to take up life together again, with their now deepened insights. But John finally goes to his death for the truth, and Elizabeth heartbrokenly understands and commends his heroism.

8. Can *The Crucible* be legitimately classified as a social drama, as the term is customarily used?

ANSWER: Social dramas in the Ibsen tradition usually deal with current problems and make use of contemporary settings and characters. *The Crucible*, by contrast, is clearly an historical work, and there is no reason to assume that it is some simple allegory exactly mirroring any modern situation. Yet it still fulfills certain requisites of social drama.

First of all, the questions that it raises, while not exclusively applicable to any era, are, or at least have been, of vital interest in our day. While people today have not been arrested for witchcraft, they have been accused of pursuing courses detrimental to the community. And there has been much discussion as to the validity of such charges and the methods employed in conducting related investigations. Since such matters involve both cherished individual rights and possible grave danger to the nation, a play like *The Crucible* can seem quite timely.

Furthermore, in other works, such as *All My Sons*, Miller has indicated the need for a thoroughly responsible citizenry at all times in order to safeguard the future of free men. Here the brave decisions of the Proctors and the other heroic characters are made to seem just as relevant to our own day as that of the Austrian prince in the Miller drama, *Incident at Vichy*.

9. To what extent has Arthur Miller followed the facts of history in writing *The Crucible*?

ANSWER: In preparing his drama, the playwright engaged in extensive research; there is much in the play that is taken directly from the early history of New England. First of all, most of the leading characters were based upon people living in Salem at the time of the trials. John Proctor, Giles Corey, and Rebecca Nurse, as well as Parris, the Putnams, and the judges at the proceedings, were all taken from history. And the fate of Proctor and his friends is that of the originals. In addition, there is much valid information included as to the beliefs, customs, and practices of the time.

Certain elements, however, have been introduced to make the work more effective dramatically. Abigail has been made somewhat older, and there is no historic basis for the romance between her and John. As a result, the tensions existing between him and his wife were also invented by Miller. In fact, according to the playwright, only the skimpiest indications exist as to the character of John Proctor. So the playwright has done much to develop and reveal the personality of his hero.

Finally, there are doubtless some contemporary emphases. Miller himself has questioned whether or not the Proctors may be more aware of their own psychological states than would have been possible in their early era. And the language, although it sounds authentic, is essentially an effective stage idiom with period flavor.

10. Suggest some reasons why *The Crucible* is an effective drama on the stage, even apart from possible contemporary implications.

ANSWER: First of all, there are several scenes of strong conflict; and lively differences often form the basis for good theatre. Proctor and Corey align themselves against Putnam and Parris. John and Elizabeth have matters of disagreement; and Proctor takes issue with Mary Warren. The trial scene, of course, involves a number of bitter dispute; and then there is Proctor's final debate with the judges.

Secondly, good suspense is maintained. Inasmuch as the penalty for conviction in the trials is death, the stakes throughout are high. And at several points there seems to be some chance that injustice will be prevented. Will Mary Warren's testimony be accepted? Will Proctor's confession be confirmed by Elizabeth? Will Hale be able to postpone the executions? And then finally, of course, there is the question of Proctor's own decision.

Thirdly, there are quite a few attractive and appealing characters. The Proctors, old Giles, and Rebecca Nurse all have admirable human traits; and even Hale and poor Mary Warren win occasional sympathy. Ordinarily a play becomes more interesting if the audience cares about the characters. And as *The Crucible* proceeds, spectators find themselves much concerned with the fate of the men and women of principle whose lives are so unjustly in jeopardy.

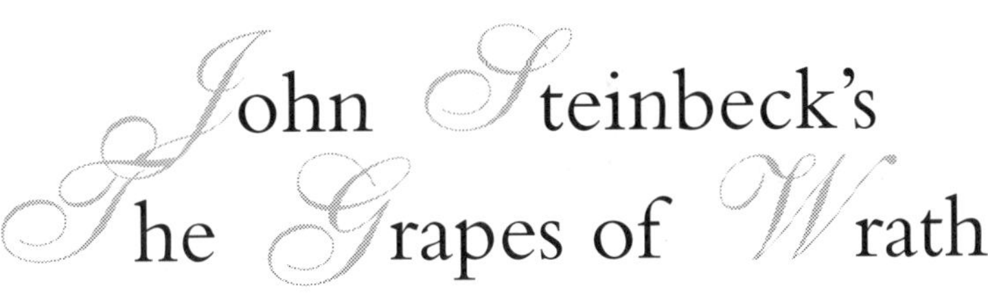

John Steinbeck's The Grapes of Wrath

Plot Summary and Comment

CHAPTERS 1–3

The first chapter of the novel establishes a situation and an atmosphere from which will emerge the people and the happenings: the devastation of the drought to the land is described in detail, along with the effect it has had upon the people and their lives. They huddle in their houses, or protect themselves from the seeping dust when they go out, for the wind viciously raises the dust from time to time. The women and children watch the men to see if they are going to stand up under the strain; for the moment they do. Into this ominous atmosphere walks Tom Joad, in the second chapter, hitch-hiking home from prison in cheap, new clothes, released on parole after serving four years of a seven-year sentence for homicide. Although the red transport truck carries a sticker stating "No Riders," Tom talks the driver into a ride when he emerges from the restaurant, because the driver wants to be considered a "good guy," one who can't be kicked around by "rich bastards." As the two men roar down the road together, the truckdriver confides his ambitions to get ahead and, none too subtly, elicits the facts of Tom's immediate past. As they part, he wishes Tom luck. Chapter Three carefully details the progress of a horny-beaked land turtle up onto the highway embankment and along the road. A woman driving a sedan swerves to avoid hitting the turtle, but the driver of the truck which has just put down Tom Joad tries, unsuccessfully, to hit it.

COMMENT

DESCRIPTION OF THE DROUGHT: The opening paragraph of the novel—indeed, the entire first chapter—is an exquisitely worked out prelude to the whole action and outcome of *The Grapes of Wrath*. (The passage of course has become rather well-known as a classic of prose style, and is often anthologized). Beginning with "to the red country and part of the gray country of Oklahoma, the last rains came gently, and they did not cut the scarred earth," the author chronicles in the initial paragraph, chiefly through use of colors, the progressive destruction of the drought: "the surface of the earth crusted, a thin hard crust, and as the sky became pale, so the earth became pale, pink in the red country and white in the gray country." The fact that the color of a whole countryside could be changed by burning sun and lack of rain has an overwhelming effect on the reader: red turns to pink, gray to white, green to brown; the ploughed earth becomes thin hard crust. It is a growth cycle grimly reversed.

The oppressive atmosphere builds with the dawn which depressingly brings no day, and with the picture of men and women huddled in their houses. "The dawn came, but no day. In the gray sky a red sun appeared, a dim red circle that gave a little light, like dusk; and as that day advanced, the dusk slipped back toward darkness, and the wind cried and whimpered over the fallen corn." In this pathetic and poetic paragraph, the sun and the wind seem as much like actors in some silent drama as the huddled people who lie and wait for the dust to settle. Nor does the concluding passage of Chapter One relieve the heavy mood established by Steinbeck: the people come out of their houses tense and watchful, and there is grim decision in the air, hanging on the question of whether or not the men will "break." "The women studied the men's faces secretly, for the corn could go, as long as something else remained." And for the moment the tension is dissipated. "After a while the faces of the watching men lost their bemused perplexity and became hard and angry and resistant. Then the women knew that they were safe and that there was no break. . . . Women and children knew deep in themselves that no misfortune was too great to bear if their men were whole. The women went into the houses to their work, and the children began to play, but cautiously at first. As the day went forward the sun became less red. It flared down on the dust-blanketed land. The men sat in the doorways of their houses; their hands were busy with sticks and little rocks. The men sat still—thinking—figuring."

WHAT IS ESTABLISHED IN CHAPTER ONE, A SITUATION OF EPIC PROPORTIONS: The effect of the graphic, even anguished, description of the physical state of things and, by implication, the mental state, is to make the reader aware of pending crises as yet unseen and whole worlds or ways of life hanging in the balance. We note that no particular people have yet been introduced—i.e., the Joads—and the rather generalized men, women and children who stand about bewildered in the dust seem almost to be pantomimists in some ageless and universal drama. Immediately, and wisely from a literary point of view, the author is going to particularize the action into a crisis for the Joad family; but the first lines of the novel suggest significantly that the problem of survival is timeless, elemental, and common to all mankind.

Another theme, related to the one of survival, is established here, in the threatened loss of human dignity. The immediate crisis is essentially economic but is seen as closely related to loss of morale: the primary concern of the women is that their men remain whole, that they give battle to adverse circumstance. The twin themes of economic and moral decline are of course integral to the novel; they will clash throughout with the lingering impetus to survive. (One of the things which Steinbeck was most vigorously outspoken about in the newspaper articles published as the pamphlet *Their Blood Is Strong* was this slow but steady demoralization and loss of personal esteem in the men, customarily regarded as heads of the family unit. More recent commentators on the conditions of poverty—for instance, Michael Harrington in *The Other America*—also cite the deep psychological damage to the man which often begins with loss of the means of livelihood, whether through losing his job and being unable to get another one or, here, having his land destroyed or much diminished in value and ultimately being dispossessed of it.)

THE DUST AS A SYMBOL: The word *dust* is repeated 27 times in Chapter One, and such repetition reinforces one of the themes—or in fact the twin themes mentioned above: economic decline which will accumulate into disaster, and deteriorating morale which will at length split up the family unit. The dust is all-pervading, and can be said to symbolize the downward-settling fortunes of the Joad family, and of all the people caught up in its destructive swirl. It is out of the land that the novel's action develops, and the land has turned to dust. Note the following examples of the author's utilization of every possible visual and aural (the same consonant or vowel sounds) effect with *dust,* along with the invariable association of dust with what is dying or dead: "the earth dusted down in dry little streams"; "every moving thing lifted the dust into the air"; "the dust from the roads fluffed up"; "the sky was darkened by the mixing dust, and the wind felt over the earth, loosened the dust, and carried it away"; "the stars could not pierce the dust to get down." Other examples of similar sounds are *crust, fluffed, brushed, muffled.* The wind becomes an agent of the demonic dust, almost personified as it "feels" over the earth, assisting the dust to dominate the other natural elements of air, sky, sun, stars. The women must battle the dust on their windows and door sills, the children are obliged to play in it—"they drew careful lines in the dust with their toes"—and the endurance of the men is tested as they face the "ruined corn, drying fast now, only a little green showing through the film of dust."

INTERCHAPTERS IN *THE GRAPES OF WRATH*: Chapter One introduces Steinbeck's use of what are usually termed "interchapters" in this novel. There are 16 interchapters altogether, spanning about 100 pages. Most of these interchapters furnish social background which illuminates the actions of the Joad family (i.e., the conflict between the banks and the farmers; buying a car; selling household goods); a few provide historical or other information (the history of migrant labor; land ownership in California; Highway #66). The description of the drought and later, of the rains, of course records dynamic natural phenomena out of which socio-economic changes are forcibly wrought. The interchapters are always interwoven with chapters before and after, in a manner which will be explained in the commentaries following.

AN ACTUAL ACCOUNT OF DROUGHT IN OKLAHOMA: For those who have never visited the dust bowl or experienced a dust storm it will be of interest to quote briefly from one of a series of "Letters from the Dust Bowl" written during the summer of 1935 by Mrs. Caroline A. Henderson and subsequently published in *The Atlantic Monthly*. Mrs. Henderson speaks first to her friend "Evelyn" of the startling "transition from rain-soaked eastern Kansas with its green pastures, luxuriant foliage, abundance of flowers, and promise of a generous harvest, to the dust-covered desolation of No Man's Land." She describes their present conditions: "Wearing our shade hats, with handkerchiefs tied over our faces and Vaseline in our nostrils, we have been trying to rescue our home from the accumulations of wind-blown dust which penetrates wherever air can go. It is an almost hopeless task, for there is rarely a day when at some time the dust clouds do not roll over. 'Visibility' approaches zero and everything is covered again with a siltlike deposit which may vary in depth from a film to actual ripples on the kitchen floor. I keep oiled cloths on the window sills and between the upper and lower sashes." Mrs. Henderson also remarks with sympathy, incidentally, on the number of families who have been forced out of the area, describing the "pitiful reminders of broken hopes and apparently wasted effort" she encountered driving through the countryside. "Little abandoned homes where people had drilled deep wells for the precious water, had set trees and vines, built reservoirs, and fenced in gardens—with everything now walled in or half buried by banks of drifted soil—told a painful story of loss and disappointment." (This series of letters, and other invaluable and interesting background to *The Grapes of Wrath*, can be found in Warren French, *A Companion to The Grapes of Wrath*, New York, 1963. French, a biographer of John Steinbeck, divides his small and useful volume into Background, Reception and Reputation of the novel, and provides answers to such intriguing questions as What Was the Dust Bowl? Who Were the "Okies"? How Was *The Grapes of Wrath* Received at Home? Was *The Grapes of Wrath* Answered? Is the Movie Like the Book? etc.)

CHAPTER THREE, THE TURTLE: When total chapters, even short ones, are devoted to turtles, we are obliged to look for significance. Just as Chapter One was a masterpiece of poetic, almost biblical, evocation, so Chapter Three—an interchapter—is a masterly specimen of scientific-like observation of the turtle's minutest movements. First of all, then, the chapter has value as technique, as excellent realistic description. It is clear, though, that the activities of the turtle are not to be discounted; and indeed, he reappears in the next chapter, picked up by Tom Joad and commented upon by that character who is of such philosophical importance in the novel, Jim Casy. (The reappearance of the turtle in Chapter Four is in fact a simple instance of the way Steinbeck interlocks chapters and interchapters, as suggested above. Such repetitions, in other words, are ways of unifying a novel, and are especially meaningful if the recurring thing or idea is of thematic or symbolic value.)

If we examine the brief adventure of the turtle, we find that he covers the grass, "leaving a beaten trail behind him." Then he confronts a hill—the highway embankment—and methodically negotiates it to the flat and easier going surface of the highway, having mastered—straining, slipping, lifting—the 4-inch concrete wall which borders the road, no mean achievement, we are made to see through the detail, for a turtle. And we note that the turtle has crushed a red ant in his climb. He is also dragging along with his front legs a head of wild oats—the "beards" mentioned in the first paragraph, which contain seeds. The rest of his adventure is comprised of crossing the highway, where a woman swerves (with some danger to herself—"the wheels screamed . . . two wheels lifted for a moment and then settled") to avoid hitting him but the truck driver who has just dropped off Tom Joad (which is a unifying link with the foregoing chapter) tries to smash him. Another matter worth noting is that the turtle is emphasized in his ancient, enduring, almost primieval qualities: "high-domed shell . . . hard legs and yellow-nailed feet . . . horny beak . . . old humorous frowning eyes."

The turtle, of course, stands for survival, for the mysterious and instinctive life force which prompts him to begin over again each time, despite setbacks, his laborious progress and which likewise will impel the Joads onward to California. The turtle crushes a red ant which gets in the way of his armored shell, and survives the truck driver's attempt to crush him. (And at this point we recall the aggressiveness of the driver: his delight in probing the secrets out of people; his desire to train his mind all the time, and to take some correspondence school courses; his yearning to "tell other guys to drive trucks." He is a man who intends, at least in a vague way—"just study a few easy lessons at home. I'm thinkin' of it"—to get ahead.) Similarly, the Joads will endure and overcome the obstacles to their journey to California. Even more significant to our understanding of the symbolic value of the turtle is the fact that when he had regained his upright position on the other side of the road, "the wild oat head fell out and three of the spearhead seeds stuck in the ground. And as the turtle crawled on down the embankment, its shell dragged dirt over the seeds." The turtle in his laborious progress yet perpetuates life, assists in the initiation of a new growth cycle. The important idea of rebirth in the analogy between the turtle and the Joads can be discussed more fully in our interpretation of the ending of the novel.

CHAPTERS 4–6

Young Tom Joad, having removed his uncomfortable shoes to pad in the dust, sights the familiar land turtle and picks it up. Under the shade of the tree he heads for to seek relief from the boiling sun, he discovers a figure from his past, the preacher Jim Casy. (It is the preacher in fact that he has referred to a few minutes ago as a man who knew big words; again, unity is strengthened by the link through "preacher" between Chapters 2 and 4, especially since Casy will figure largely in the action of the novel.) But Jim Casy, always a thinker, has now thought himself out of being a preacher. He has decided that in good conscience he can no longer preach, although he asserts "I got the call to lead the people, an' no place to lead 'em." He loves people, he says, but he has lost faith in religion. Together Casy and Tom come upon the deserted Joad homestead, the reasons for its desertion having been eloquently explained in the previous interchapter, which traces the developments by which the land was taken out of the hands of the tenants by the owners, or rather by the twin inanimate monsters of the tractor and the bank. Tom and the reverend are at a loss to discover why the Joads have left, without any word to their absent son, however, until a former neighbor, Muley Graves, happens along and relates to them what has been happening. Tom hears how his grampa and pa put up a good fight before eviction, but that the events "took somepin outa Tom." Muley's existence has been warped into strangeness by the changes too: all his folks have gone on to California, but he could not bring himself to leave the land; he wanders around sleeping and eating in a fugitive fashion—"'like a damn ol' graveyard ghos,'" he says. On this occasion he shares with the other two men his trappings of the day—two cottontails and a jackrabbit—and there is some philosophizing around the fire until the three are forced to hide by authorities who have seen their light and come to check on "trespassers." They sleep that night in the bottom of the dried-up gulch.

COMMENT

JIM CASY, PHILOSOPHER, PROPHET: From the moment Jim Casy reveals that he isn't preaching anymore—"Ain't got the call no more. Got a lot of sinful ideas—but they seem kinda sensible"—there is the implication, soon borne out, that he is to function as some sort of spokesman for reorientations, for new ideas. As he talks on, it becomes clear that he has been and is experiencing a sort of spiritual rebirth; and in fact the theme of rebirth, suggested in the seeds dropped by the turtle, is now picked up by Casy. Steinbeck dwells for a moment upon the habits of the turtle, always "goin' someplace," to implant the idea of Jim Casy's future leadership. Casy points out. "Nobody can't keep a turtle though. They work at it and work at it, and at last one day they get out and away they go—off somewheres. [This syndrome is demonstrated by the turtle, in Chapter Six.] It's like me. I wouldn' take the good ol' gospel that was just layin' there to my hand. I got to be pickin' at it an' workin' at it until I got it all tore down. Here I got the sperit sometimes an' nothin' to preach about. I got the call to lead the people, an' no place to lead 'em." Jim is so bothered by this thought that he applies it again to the passing dog that ignores Tom's friendly whistle. "'Goin' someplace," he repeated 'That's right, he's goin' someplace. Me—I don't know where I'm goin'." Jim is clearly searching for a place, a new and worthwhile function.

The subject of Jim's reorientation is brought up again; for he still claims to have "the sperit" but he has been forced to examine himself on a number of matters connected with religion as he has formerly practiced it. For one thing, his sensuality has disturbed him; he has not, for example, been able to fit sex and his relish for it—particularly after riproaring revivalist meetings with the girls from his audience—into the context of his religion. But he ponders, "Maybe it ain't a sin. Maybe it's just the way folks is. Maybe we been whippin' the hell out of ourselves for nothin'." And he wrestles with definitions of sin and virtue. It is the nature of "sperit" which most puzzles and consumes him, though; at one point he asserts (significantly, for Jim Casy is being shaped for the reader into a humanist), "It's love. I love people so much I'm fit to bust, sometimes." But it is in the question of "Jesus" that his supposed heresy rests. "An' I says, 'Don't you love Jesus?' Well, I thought an' thought, an' finally I says, 'No, I don't know nobody name' Jesus. I know a bunch of stories, but I only love people." In fact—and this is the core of the philosophical stand which Jim Casy will take throughout the novel—he has "figgered" a lot about "the Holy Sperit and the Jesus road. I figgered, 'Why do we got to hang it on God or Jesus? Maybe,' I figgered, 'maybe it's all men an' all women we love; maybe that's the Holy Sperit—the human sperit—the whole shebang. Maybe all men got one big soul ever'body's a part of.'" Jim's revelation, which he knows "deep down" is true, actually has a rather fancy name in the history of American philosophical thought: he has just announced his intuition of the "Transcendental Oversoul," but in somewhat earthier terms than his unseen mentor and chief proponent of the concept, Ralph Waldo Emerson, ever spoke.

In short, one of the strands of the social philosophy which Steinbeck develops during the novel can be traced to American Transcendentalism, with its concept of the Oversoul—"one big soul ever'body's part of"—with its faith in the common man and in self-reliance. The philosophy will be most often spoken by the "prophet," Jim Casy, and it will be acted out by the Joads and their fellows. For Jim's new calling, of course, will be to follow the trek westward, since he decides that these people "gonna need help no preachin' can give 'em. Hope of heaven when their lives ain't lived? Holy Sperit when their own sperit is downcast an' sad? They gonna need help. They got to live before they can afford to die." And in this statement Jim places a most ironic finger on the inadequate, unrealistic and even hypocritical premises of his religion as he has come to view it: he can no longer continue his pat offers of future paradise or his hair-raising portrayals of hellfire and brimstone before the present and nauseatingly real wretchedness of his people.

NOTES OF PATHOS: The ideas of humanism, love of mankind introduced in these chapters are reinforced by notes of pathos here and there. Tom Joad, for example, has picked up the turtle to take to his little brother, because he knows "kids like turtles." He retrieves the turtle once, in fact, before at last releasing it when he finds his family departed, explaining, "I ain't got no present for the kids. . . . Nothin' but this ol' turtle." Also, there is a pathetically human absurdity in Granma's Christmas card to Tom in prison, which caused his cellmates to call him "Jesus meek"; as Tom points out, again demonstrating his awareness of the human condition (evidence that he, like Jim Casy, may eventually undergo some sort of education and conversion during the novel): "I guess Granma never read it. Prob'ly got it from a drummer an' picked out the one with the mos' shiny stuff on it. . . . Granma never meant it funny; she jus' figgered it was so purty she wouldn't bother to read it. She lost her glasses the year I went up. Maybe she never did find 'em." Tom shows compassion here, just as he does a few pages later when he mentions his hope to have found his sister Rose of Sharon helping take some of the burden of work from his mother.

Also, the theme of human dignity—preservation or loss of it—again arises in these chapters. The dispossessed and bewildered Muley Graves is a pathethic figure. He insists he was unable to accompany his folks to California—"Somepin jus' wouldn' let me"—yet he is only half-alive, like an old graveyard ghost, and when asked to come along the next day to Uncle John's and perhaps westward he replies, "Huh? No. I don't go no place, an' I don't leave no place." And at night there is his womblike withdrawal into his protective cave: "Muley pulled at the covering brush and crawled into his cave. 'I like it in here,' he called. 'I feel like nobody can come at me.'" In spite of his companions' protests to the contrary, Muley is one who has indeed become a little "touched" by the upheavals which have occurred. Old Tom's self-esteem has suffered, too—"it took somepin outa Tom"—although young Tom resists hiding in the cotton from the deputy sheriff, exclaiming "Jesus, I hate to get pushed around!" Perhaps the tenant in Chapter 5 assesses pretty well the deep-rooted attachment of these men, especially the older ones, to their land, and the trauma of being uprooted: "Funny thing how it is. If a man owns a little property, that property is him, it's part of him, and it's like him. If he owns property only so he can walk on it and handle it and be sad when it isn't doing well, and feel fine when the rain falls on it, that property is him, and some way he's bigger because he owns it."

INTERCHAPTER FIVE, FORECLOSURES: Although it is a dialogue between the owners of the land, or their representatives, and the tenants, this interchapter presents groups—the classes involved in the conflict, we might say—rather than particular people such as the Joads. Such a presentation emphasizes the far-reaching effect of the changes wrought by bank foreclosures and tractors: the reader perceives a panoramic mass of dispossessed people just as he had a panoramic vision of the dust in Chapter 1. And, of course, Steinbeck has chosen here to contrast heavily the humaneness of the tenants and their attachment to the land with the inhuman remoteness of the banks and inanimate monstrosity of the tractors, including their gloved and goggled drivers, regarded by the farmers as traitors to the land and to their own folks. Of the tractor driver—"Joe Davis's boy"—it is said that the "monster" in the background—bank, agency, company—had "goggled his mind, muzzled his speech, goggled his perception, muzzled his protest." The chapter provides social background for the narrative in the sense that it is the foreclosures, of course, which force the emigration.

CHAPTERS 7–9

It is a depressing prospect, for the unwilling emigrants at least—"in the towns, on the edges of the towns, in fields, in vacant lots, the used-car yards, the wreckers' yards, the garages with blazoned signs"—the glaring image presented in Chapter 7 of the used car hustlers, most of them "outsiders" who have hurried into the country to capitalize on the dire necessities of these dispossessed. Meanwhile, in Chapter 8, Tom and Jim Casy make their way toward Uncle John's, whose sad life story is related, and the structure of the Joad family is bit by bit unfolded as young Tom is reunited first with his father—"at last he touched Tom, but touched him on the shoulder, timidly, and instantly took his hand away"—then his mother—"she moved toward him lithely, soundlessly in her bare feet, and her face was full of wonder"—then the rest of the family, all of whom have changed in his four years' absence: Rose of Sharon married and pregnant, Al a tomcatting 16-year-old, Ruthie a young lady of 12, Winfield still gauche. They all breakfast together energetically, after a curious and meditative grace by their former preacher. But the necessary prelude to the long trek westward is to strip themselves of all but the necessary implements of utensils, bedding, clothes. The interchapter 9 poignantly images the general scene: an $18 Sears Roebuck plow, a fine team of mules with braided manes and forelocks, a dirty rag doll, a book called Pilgrim's Progress—all to be sold disastrously cheap, or discarded. "How can we live without our lives? How will we know it's us without our past? No. Leave it. Burn it." And of course take the rifle: "Wouldn't go out naked of a rifle."

COMMENT

INTERCHAPTER 7, BUYING A USED CAR: The ironic picture here of the imported used car dealers' exploitation of the evicted tenants is an interesting instance of the variety of Steinbeck's prose style. The sentence structure in this chapter has been referred to by one critic as "staccato"; it is an abrupt and blunt style which the author utilizes throughout the novel, from time to time, often to achieve the effect of harsh, mechanical facts of life which frustrate bewildered people like the Joads. "Used Cars, Good Used Cars. Cheap transportation, three trailers. '27 Ford, clean. Checked cars, guaranteed cars. Free radio. Car with 100 gallons of gas free. Come in and look. Used Cars. No overhead. . . . Old monsters with deep upholstery—you can cut her into a truck easy. Two-wheel trailers, axles rusty in the hard afternoon sun. Used Cars. Good Used Cars. Clean, runs good. Don't pump oil." The short running sentences suggest the hustling and pressuring of the salesmen, while the repetitions emphasize the depressing frequency with which such scenes were enacted. The fast pace also reminds us of how the tenant-buyer was out of his element in such a setting, at a disadvantage, too "nice" as the salesman points out: "Get 'em under obligation. Make 'em take up your time. Don't let 'em forget they're takin' your time. People are nice, mostly. They hate to put you out. Make 'em put you out, an' then sock it to 'em." And the man searching among the glittering machines for one which will get him to California asks himself, "How do you buy a car, What does it cost? Watch the children, now. I wonder how much for this one? We'll ask. It don't cost money to ask. We can ask, can't we?" (This style of writing, incidentally, is reminiscent of what is called the "newsreel technique" of John dos Passos, American contemporary to Steinbeck; in the staccato quality and the pattern of repetition there is also a hint of the poetry of Carl Sandburg.)

GROUP, OR UNIT, INSTEAD OF INDIVIDUAL, A THEME: One of the positive themes of the novel is suggested in Chapter 8 (the "negative" themes are those of economic and moral decline—shattering of the family unit and deteriorating self-esteem), a theme which by the end has become social prophecy. While it is true that the Joads are at first bound together as a family—and this is the structure that Ma in particular is stubbornly determined to preserve, although she sees it disintegrating around her (with the death of Grampa, the disappearance of Noah, etc.)—there is a glimpse in Chapter 8, again through the eyes of Ma, whose matriarchal position enables her to understand the psychological and therefore real force of separate persons banded together, of the protection and power which might come out of group action. She has perceived the ineffectiveness of any one small, scared and angry man against the present adverse circumstances: "Tommy, don't you go fightin' 'em alone," she declares passionately. "I got to thinkin' an' dreamin' an' wonderin'. They say there's a hun'erd thousand of us shoved out. If we was all mad the same way, Tommy—they would't hunt nobody down . . ." Tom seems to understand this somewhat revolutionary notion of Ma's, because he immediately asks if "many folks feel that way?" It is a theme, the idea that survival might rest in group action, which will pick up more and more momentum in the ensuing chapters, first when the Wilsons and the Joads join forces for their common welfare, later in the almost idyllic (it turns out) sanity of the government camp (where "community organization," as we know it today in the fight on poverty, is in full and effective operation), and of course in the ultimate reorientation of Tom Joad from a kind of primitive individualism—"I climb fences when I got fences to climb"—to his faltering conviction of Jim Casy's "one big soul" and of a notion of "social welfare"—"all work together for our own thing"—to be realized, unfortunately, in Tom's time only through social warfare.

MA, JIM CASY, AND THE THEME OF LOVE: Jim Casy's not-so-amateur philosophy of love, linked with his theory of "one big soul," was mentioned in Chapter 4. And his philosophy is actually a combination of the Transcendental "Over-soul" explored by Emerson, based on intuition (which the ex-preacher would be likely to regard as revelation), and the ideas of mass democracy, love of all men, found in the poetry of Walt Whitman (we can look upon the Whitmanesque tone in fact as the second strand of Steinbeck's "philosophy" in the novel). It was previously suggested, too, that Jim Casy predominantly prophesies whereas the Joads essentially act out such philosophy as we find in *The Grapes of Wrath*. But there is from the first an important line of communication open between Ma and Jim Casy; for Ma too is intuitive, and Ma is probably the most important symbol of love in the book. (To a lesser extent, Sairy Wilson also represents intuition, and human love.) It can be said in fact that Tom Joad's reeducation and "conversion" to a new way of thinking is the result of his communication with both Jim Casy and Ma.

"Ma watched the preacher as he ate, and her eyes were questioning, probing and understanding. She watched him as though he were suddenly a spirit, not human any more, a voice out of the ground." Ma recognizes in Casy something different and detached, the quality which turns him more and more into a commentator and comforter, which makes possible such insights as he offers, for example, at Grampa's death (Chapter 13): Casy tells them, "Grampa didn't die tonight. He died the minute you took 'im off the place. . . . He didn' suffer none. Not after fust thing this mornin'. He's jus' stayin' with the lan'. He couldn' leave it." Jim Casy denies in good conscience that he has a God, but he practices brotherly love; this is why Sairy Wilson (Chapter18) turns to him on her deathbed for truly human fellowship, a closeness to fellow humans she had once upon a time experienced through music, through singing. Sairy answers Casy, "You got a God. Don't make no difference if you don' know what he looks like." And after Casy had bowed his head and "talked to himself" instead of actually praying, she says, "That's good. That's what I needed. Somebody close enough—to pray."

God, then, is love, to Jim Casy and in actuality, to such figures as Ma and Sairy, because their *actions* are based on this love principle—intuitively, of course, rather than consciously. Jim Casy cannot in honesty claim he is sure of God, but he is sure of men and how they respond to brotherly love. Thus Casy is a pragmatist (pragmatism, in fact—the "is" thinking mentioned in the Introduction as one of Steinbeck's credos, is the third philosophical strand to be traced through *The Grapes of Wrath*. "Is" instead of "why" or "what should be"—this is what Jim Casy has voiced in Chapter 6 with his conviction that the emigrants are going to need help on their journey, but a kind of spiritual help geared to actualities rather than to preconceived notions: "Hope of heaven when their lives ain't lived?" Casy asks in exasperation. "They got to live before they can afford to die."

Ma, too, is a pragmatist, who takes things as they happen, and then of course acts from the love principle. She assesses (at the same time typically minimizing) her role to Al, for example (Chapter 13), as they ride along together. He has asked her timidly if she is scared about their new life. "A little," she honestly replies. "Only it ain't like scared so much. I'm jus' a settin' here waitin'. When somepin happens that I got to do somepin—I'll do it." Thus she does what she has to, staggeringly, when Granma dies as they cross the desert, lying all night beside the dead woman until she is certain that the family is safely across. Ma's act moves Jim Casy to an awed comment: "All night long, an' she was along. . . . John, there's a woman so great with love—she scares me." Ma walks within the magic circle of brotherly love. But her response to the untimely death of Granma is no more than could have been expected from our introduction to her and her position in the Joad family unit in Chapter 8: "Her hazel eyes seemed to have experienced all possible tragedy and to have mounted pain and suffering like steps into a high calm and a superhuman understanding. She seemed to know, to accept, to welcome her position, the citadel of the family, the strong place that could not be taken. And since old Tom and the children could not know hurt or fear unless she acknowledged hurt and fear, she had practiced denying them in herself. And since, when a joyful thing happened, they looked to see whether joy was on her, it was her habit to build up laughter out of inadequate materials." (Note the almost biblical tone of the prose which describes Ma. There is in fact an Old Testament resonance to a sizeable portion of the prose in the novel.) From Ma's answer to a wondering remark of Tom's in this same chapter, we understand very well that she can be expected to "do what she has to," to fight, as it becomes necessary. Tom says with some amusement, "Ma, you never was like this before!" Ma replies sharply. "I never had my house pushed over. I never had my fambly stuck out on the road. I never had to sell—ever'thing."

INTERCHAPTER 9, AMASSED BITTERNESS: We have referred above to the growing social awareness of Jim Casy, Tom Joad, and Ma, the development in them of an understanding that little people can gain power and security by acting as a group toward their common welfare. It is interesting that this idea, and the impetus for it, is generalized (just as all the interchapters deal with universally applicable social background, with unidentifiable actors in masks who seem to present in tableau the fate of all Joads, all Wilsons, all Davises). Of starting over again, the faceless, unseen "Everyman" of the Okies declares, "But you can't start. Only a baby can start. You and me—why, we're all that's been. The anger of a moment, the thousand pictures, that's us. This land, this red land, is us; and the flood years and the dust years and the drought years are us. We can't start again. The bitterness we sold to the junk man—he got it all right, but we have it still. And when the owner men told us to go, that's us; and when the tractor hit the house, that's us until we're dead. To California or any place—every one a drum major leading a parade of hurts, marching with our bitterness. And some day—the armies of bitterness will all be going the same way. And they'll all walk together, and there'll be a dead terror from it." (The image here is strongly suggestive of some of the lines from "Battle Hymn of the Republic," which Steinbeck had at one time intended to have printed along with the novel. The first four lines provide an especially vivid link with the unmistakeably socialistic vision offered here of the downtrodden poor arising in anger: "Mine eyes have seen the glory of the coming of the Lord,/ He is trampling out the vintage where the grapes of wrath are stored;/ He hath loosed the fateful lightning of his terrible swift sword,/ His truth is marching on.")

CHAPTERS 10–12

Having sold their remaining possessions dirt cheap, the Joads suddenly feel a sense of urgency about departing; they butcher the shoat, pack up everything, and are off in the dawn, leaving the forlorn Muley Graves standing in their dooryard watching. The desolation of the deserted houses and land is depicted in Chapter 11, an interchapter, which also contains harsh comments on the loveless mechanism of the tractors and their drivers: "when a horse stops work and goes into the barn there is a life and a vitality left, there is a breathing and a warmth, and the feet shift on the straw, and the jaws champ on the hay, and the ears and the eyes are alive. There is a warmth of life in the barn, and the heat and smell of life. But when the motor of a tractor stops, it is as dead as the ore it came from." Chapter 12 describes that "main migrant road," Highway 66; it marks the transition between roughly the first and second portions of the novel, introducing the journey or "exodus" (as the first part has been, in the biblical analogy, the "oppression in Egypt"). Highway 66 is a world in itself, and a vast, various one, reaching across the Texas Panhandle into the mountains, bleaching desert, then more mountains into the fantastic luxuriance of California. Trekking on 66 is no joke for drivers anxiously listening to motors and wheels or watching heat and oil gauges. Strange contradictory rumors about the Promised Land float from its two-bit service stations and restaurants. Over this pavement 250,000 people are in flight.

COMMENT

THE FAMILY UNIT: In Chapter 10 we see the Joad family unit functioning intact for almost the last time. Ma jokes communicatively with Tom as she scrubs clothes and kids the spluttering and unbuttoned Grampa about "they don't let people run aroun' with their clothes unbutton' in California." In two different passages there is conveyed the sense that the men of the family still maintain their dignity, are still "whole." For example, Ma, powerful as she indubitably is, adheres to the ritual of letting the men decide if Jim Casy is to accompany them. "Ma looked to Tom to speak, because he was a man, but Tom did not speak. She let him have the chance that was his right, and then she said, 'Why, we'd be proud to have you. 'Course I can't say right now; Pa says all the men'll talk tonight and figger when we gonna start. I guess maybe we better not say till all the men come.'" And, as the truck returns from its ignominious mission of disposing of the remaining possessions, we see that "Al sat bent over the wheel, proud and serious and efficient, and Pa and Uncle John, as befitted the heads of the clan, had the honor seats beside the driver." Later in the evening, "the family met at the most important place, near the truck. The house was dead, and the fields were dead; but this truck was the active thing, the living principle." The clan is regrouping around its "new hearth, the living center of the family." Again, in the question of Casy's traveling with them, the ritual is preserved as they all wait out of politeness—"his position was honorary and a matter of custom"—for Grampa to voice his opinion. Afterwards the squatting men and the standing women may enter the discussion. There is an echo of Steinbeck's pamphlet title, *"Their Blood Is Strong,"* in Ma's prideful answer to whether or not they can feed an extra mouth. "It ain't kin we? It's will we? As far as 'kin', 'we can't do nothin', not go to California or nothin'; but as far as 'will,' why, we'll do what we will. An' as far as 'will'—it's a long time our folks been here and east before, an' I never heard tell of no Joads or no Hazletts, neither, ever refusin' food an' shelter or a lift on the road to anybody that asked." Her tone makes Pa ashamed, and the issue of Jim Casy is of course settled.

JIM CASY, A PROPHET GROWS IN STATURE: Two characters who relate and communicate with Jim Casy—Ma and Tom—make further observations in Chapter 10 about what kind of man he seems to be. Ma reiterates in another way her feeling that he is changed, more spirit than man. "Watch the look in his eye," she declares. "He looks baptized. Got that look they call lookin' through. He sure looks baptized. An' a-walkin' with his head down, a-starin' at nothin' on the groun'. There *is* a man that's baptized." It is as if she were describing one who fasts and meditates (and indeed, a bit later, Jim himself brings up in a half-deprecating manner the analogy to Christ in the Wilderness), and to say that he gives tangible evidence of his "baptism" is her highest praise. Jim of course has discovered his "someplace to go." He has to go where "the folks is goin'." Insisting that he will never "preach" again, he tries to articulate his new-found "humanism." "I ain't gonna try to teach 'em nothin'. I'm gonna try to learn. Gonna learn why the folks walks in the grass, gonna hear 'em talk, gonna hear 'em sing. . . . Gonna lay in the grass, open an' honest with anybody that'll have me. Gonna cuss an' swear an' hear the poetry of folks talkin'. All that's holy, all that's what I didn' understand'." (Once more Jim's exuberant declaration of love for the people is in the spirit of Walt Whitman.) Tom Joad's contribution to the discussion of what is, or isn't "preachin'" is ironically complimentary to Casy too: "Preachin's a kinda tone a voice. . . . Preachin's bein' good to folks when they wanna kill yar for it. Las' Christmus in McAlester, Salvation Army come an' done us good. Three solid hours a cornet music, an' we set there. They was bein' nice to us. But if one of us tried to walk out, we'd a-drawed solitary. That's preachin'. . . . No, you ain't no preacher."

STEINBECK'S AGRARIAN THEORIES: One of the harshest contrasts drawn so far by the author has been that of life close to the land as opposed to cold mechanisms like tractors, their inhuman drivers goggled and muzzled, and in the background the indifferent manipulations of depersonalized ownership. In this respect Chapter 11 can be cross-referenced to Chapter 5, both interchapters. Here again the "deadness" of steel is contrasted to the warmth of land and animals and growing things. The author is quite insistent on his point that man is not a machine. "But the machine man, driving a dead tractor on land he does not know and love, understands only chemistry; and he is contemptuous of the land and of himself. When the corrugated iron doors are shut, he goes home, and his home is not the land." This has been said in greater length in Chapter 5 in describing the gloved and goggled man in the iron seat who has come to violate the land and its people. This man cannot touch, smell, feel. "He sat in an iron seat and stepped on iron pedals. He could not cheer or beat or curse or encourage the extension of his power, and because of this he could not cheer or whip or curse or encourage himself. He did not know or own or trust or beseech the land. . . . The land bore under iron, and under iron gradually died; for it was not loved or hated, it had no prayers or curses." Now, while this may be an exaggerated version of what happened ultimately to the land of the dust bowl, for it had simply been too long overworked in crops whether by hand or by machine, it is a powerful statement of what has been referred to as Steinbeck's agrarianism (or more specifically, Jeffersonian agrarianism). It is a form of democracy, and its focus is on the man's identification with the land. But actual contact with the land is essential for such a democracy to work, for it is in this closeness to the very cycles of growth, whether frustrating or gratifying, that a man's measure of himself, his dignity, resides. Thus a form of human erosion—and a disastrous one psychically—is being uprooted from the land as the dust bowl people were. As will be seen in comments following on later chapters, this philosophy—of the psychic hold the land gets on a man, of the meaningfulness of agrarianism as a way of life—is strongly urged throughout the novel.

CHAPTERS 13–15

"I dunno what we're comin' to," the fat filling station attendant on Highway 66 keeps saying, who has had people begging gasoline from him or trading chickens and bedsteads for it. And it turns out that he too is ready to pull out and go west. The first camp site for the Joads is a significant one, for they meet the Wilsons, with whom they form an alliance. Grampa dies abruptly of a stroke in their tent, and it is a blank page from their family Bible which is offered to record the facts that accompany Grampa to his grave in a glass jar, so that nobody will think he was murdered. The Wilsons' kindness is returned by Al's offer to help them repair their ailing car. A relationship has in fact been established by their acting together in sorrow, and they decide to travel together, which will enable them to space the load more easily over the two automobiles. Two ideas are significantly stressed in the short following interchapter: "The Western States are nervous under the beginning change," and "this is the beginning—from 'I' to 'We'." In other words, social revolution is in the air, clattering down Highway 66, where Mae and Al, along with innumerable others, run a restaurant whose reputation and economic security rests—quite legitimately—on what the truck drivers think of it. There is a poignant scene in which a migrant stops to buy ten cents worth of bread. Mae, tough as she tries to appear, ends by giving his children "nickel apiece" candy for a penny. Then the truck driver customers who observe her kindness tip her liberally on their way out.

COMMENT

FROM "I" TO "WE": The steady emergence of a concept of "we"—group action in the public sense, human compassion for one's fellows in the personal sense—is really the whole thematic concentration of these three chapters. Steinbeck is developing more and more what he has taken pains to establish in the previous chapters: the anger and terror, and accumulated bitterness of these people—"the people in flight from the terror behind—strange things happen to them, some bitterly cruel and some so beautiful that the faith is refired forever;" the "beautiful happenings" that sometimes refire faith—the kindness of a toughened roadside waitress to a couple of yearning kids, repaid in turn by the tough truck drivers who observed the incident; a trailer built of junk and loaded with a family of twelve and their possessions, waiting in innocence and desperation of Highway 66 for a car to pull them to California, and a car does pick them up; a man like Jim Casy who feels the change in the air, senses that the people are "goin' someplace" and that they will need help. In short, given such a psychically charged situation, something will give, something has to give—and the direction will be one of love or hate. The first step toward "we" (not including the Joad family's joint decision to let Jim Casy accompany them) is the alliance with the Wilsons, founded on the deepest sort of kinship which is not of one's own blood: their acting together in a time of trouble (here, death; but it could have been birth too). Sairy Wilson voices her folk philosophy on the subject: "We're proud to help. I ain't felt so—safe in a long time. People needs—to help." This attitude is reinforced—formalized, we might say—by Jim Casy in his words for Grampa; in fact Jim's words seem to summarize his growing philosophy of humanism: "This here ol' man jus' lived a life an' jus' died out of it. I don't know whether he was good or bad, but that don't matter much. He was alive, an' that's what matters. An' now he's dead, an' that don't matter. Heard a fella tell a poem one time, an' he says 'All that lives is holy.' Got to thinkin', an' purty soon it means more than the words says. An' I wouldn' pray for a ol' fella that's dead. He's awright. He got a job to do, but it's all laid out for 'im an' there's on'y one way to do it. But us, we got a job to do, an' they's a thousan' ways, an' we don' know which one to take. An' if I was to pray, it'd be for the folks that don' know which way to turn." Again, Jim sounds like a pragmatist: the main thing is to be alive, and just as important, to help one's brother know "where to turn." Perhaps fittingly, it is Ma who solidifies the compact between the Joads and the Wilsons: "You won't be no burden. Each'll help each, an' we'll all git to California."

Thus interchapter 14 elaborates in a general way—partly through a kind of choric repetition (like a Greek chorus, which often fills in background, comments on the direction things are going, etc.). It is another way of saying the owners, the seemingly big and powerful, on one side and the little people on the other, when the two ideas are repeated: "the western land, nervous under the beginning change"; and "this is the beginning—from 'I' to 'we.'" The rest is elaboration: "The Western States, nervous as horses before a thunder storm. The great owners, nervous, sensing a change, knowing nothing of the nature of the change. The great owners, striking at the immediate thing, the widening government, the growing labor unity; striking at new taxes, at plans; not knowing these things are results, not causes." And the causes, the causes for the new "we" formations, put simply, are "a hunger in a stomach, multiplied a million times; a hunger in a single soul, hunger for joy and some security, multiplied a million times. . . ."

CHAPTERS 16–18

As the Joads and the Wilsons crawl on toward California in their two vehicles, there are more and more crises. The touring car of the Wilsons' breaks down, needing a new con-rod bearing, which will amount to a time-consuming repair job by Tom or Al. The Wilsons insist that the Joads go on without them. Tom offers an alternate plan, that the truck go ahead to California while they, Tom and Jim Casey, remain behind to repair the car and catch up with them. It is an appealing plan in that it would enable most of the adults to get work sooner. But, in her first and surprising show of violence, Ma puts her foot down. She amazes everybody with her "I ain't a'gonna go," and grabs a jack handle to back up her statement to Pa. Ma's strong instinct to survive requires that the family unit stay intact, a choice which takes precedence over mere expediency. Tom and Jim Casy stay behind to repair the car, which proves easier than they had anticipated, then join the family up the road at a camp, where there is more unpleasantness: a fifty cent charge, stubbornly applied to each car; a ragged man who is on his way back from California, having failed to make a living there.

The many roadside camps are described, where "in the evening a strange thing happened: the twenty families became one family, the children were the children of all. The loss of home became one loss . . . ." In the camps unwritten laws—"right"—emerge, through practical experience and common sense. Passed by the border patrol, they enter California with a prospect of the Painted Desert, to be crossed. They encamp by a river to rest for a night crossing, and there are more setbacks and crises: another man on his way back from California, saying it's nice country but it "was stole a long time ago"; a fanatical Jehovite woman, like a bad omen, who frightens Rosasharn and strains Ma's nerves, tight from tending the ailing Granma—Ma is forced to assert, "We ain't gonna have no meetin' in this here tent." Ma's second moment of violent anger comes in her confrontation of the policeman in khaki and boots and pistol who stops at the tent and informs her they must get out; this time she grabs an iron skillet to reinforce her scornful words to the challenger. The men bathe in the river, where the strange and silent Noah informs Tom he will remain by the river and catch fish, instead of going on with them. When it is time to start into the desert, it is discovered that Sairy Wilson, never well, is at last too ill to go on. Jim Casy comforts her, and most reluctantly they leave the Wilsons behind. At midnight they reach an inspection station in the desert, where there is a demand to look over their possessions, to unload the vehicles. Again Ma steps forth with a kind of hysterically dogged refusal to allow the search, insisting that Granma is too sick; yet when Tom speeds up to the next town, Barstow, where the inspectors have said a doctor can be found, Ma begs them to go on across. In the dawn they come out of the desert, creep into the mountains and at last pause to get out and look down into the green valleys of California. It is then that they discover that Granma has lain dead in Ma's arms all through the night.

COMMENT

TOM JOAD, ORIENTATION TOWARD CONVERSION: In his response to Jim Casy's social prophecy, as they work together on the old sedan, Tom Joad is common sensical—a pragmatist too, we might say— and somewhat individualist—to each his own. Just as Tom refuses to look ahead, and worry, Jim Casy is insisting that things are moving ahead anyhow. "If ya listen," he says, "you'll hear a movin', an' a sneakin', an' a rustlin', an'—an' a res'lessness. They's stuff goin' on that the folks doin' it don't know nothin' about—yet. They's gonna come somepin outa all these folks goin' wes'—outa all their farms lef' lonely. They's gonna come a thing that's gonna change the whole country." This is when Tom repeats "I'm still layin' my dogs down one at a time," and "I climb fences when I got fences to climb." Yet Tom is being pulled more and more into the changes, and into meditating about the changes, toward that end point when, Jim Casy having in effect laid down his life for Tom, Tom becomes a disciple and a fighter. Furthermore, Tom's strain of stoic realism is useful to his growing philosophical awareness; for example the manner in which he shakes up the whining, self-pitiful one-eyed service station attendant by trying to show him how he really appears and how he could appear seems to have some effect, for he asks Tom softly, "Think—somebody'd like—me?" And at the end of Chapter 18, Tom speaks to his parents stoically but compassionately about Grampa and Granma, now dead. His mother looks at the green and gold country of California lying before them and observes how "purty" it is, wishing the old folks could have seen it. Tom's answer parallels Jim Casy's earlier observation about how Grampa really died, in his heart, before ever leaving the homestead. "They was too old. They wouldn't of saw nothin' that's here. Grampa would a been a-seein' the Injuns an' the prairie country when he was a young fella. An' Granma would a remembered an' seen the first home she lived in. They was too ol'. Who's really seein' it is Ruthie an' Winfiel'."

DETERIORATING UNITY, MA FIGHTS DESTRUCTIVE ELEMENTS: We have seen that Ma's anger and violence are aroused when there is a real crisis involving preserving and protecting her family: she rises up against Pa with a jack handle to prevent him from separating the two loaded cars as they travel; she orders out of her tent the fanatical Jehovite woman because she threatens to become a disruptive influence, especially to Rosasharn, since her ideas of sin are a bit rigid and upsetting to the pregnant girl; she grabs an iron skillet and is about to take a swing of indignation at the cold and contemptuous uniformed stranger who intrudes upon the privacy of the tent and calls her a strangely derogatory name, "Okie"; and she takes her solitary initiative in the middle of the desert at night to prevent the inspectors from unloading the truck and discovering Granma's death before they are safely across the desert.

Ma's violence can be looked upon as a last-ditch stand, as she senses the growing desperateness and futility of the situation. Her awareness that the family seems to be falling apart and her hidden feelings of helplessness at the frustrations brought from outside forces are seen in these chapters too. Ma never gives way—publicly. But after the iron skillet incident, "Rose of Sharon watched her secretly. And when she saw Ma fighting with her face, Rose of Sharon closed her eyes and pretended to be asleep." Ma is dazed at Tom's news of Noah's disappearance, turning "stunned eyes toward the river. 'I jus' can't seem to think no more,'" is her answer. As they all prepared to leave that night, because the policeman has stated that they must be out of there by morning, Ma voices to Tom—or to nobody in particular—her sense of lowered morale. "'I pray God we gonna get some res'. I pray Jesus we gonna lay down in a nice place.' The sun sank toward the baked and broken hills to the west. The pot over the fire bubbled furiously. Ma went under the tarpaulin and came out with an apronful of potatoes, and she dropped them into the boiling water. 'I pray God we gonna be let to wash some clothes. We ain't never been dirty like this. Don't even wash potatoes 'fore we boil 'em. I wonder why? Seems like the heart's took out of us.'" And, since Ma is the core or center of the family, her reflections ring grimly true.

PRAGMATISM: The pragmatic attitudes seen in Tom Joad and Jim Casy are reflected in the first experiences of the families at the campsites. That is, as the families adjust to the new and very different life of the road and the camp, fashioning unwritten laws or rights to fit the present circumstances, they are behaving pragmatically. "The families learned what rights must be observed the right of privacy in the tent; the right to keep the black past hidden in the heart; the right to talk and to listen; the right to refuse help or to accept, to offer help or to decline it. . . ." These are positive rights, just as there are also prohibitions, negative rights, which come to be understood: do not intrude upon a man's privacy; keep quiet while the camp sleeps; the customary protection against theft and murder must prevail. It is important to emphasize again from time to time this philosophical strand of the novel—pragmatism—in order to realize that those people who could learn a new way, who proved most flexible, had the best chance of survival. And in such an attitude the people might even have a weapon against "the owners," those awaiting so "nervously" in the West, those who in effect are mentally "running scared." As the discouraged fellow who is on his way back east points out, "They hate you 'cause they're scairt. They know a hungry fella gonna get food even if he got to take it. They know that fallow lan's a sin an' somebody' gonna take it." These men, the owners, are not flexible, are not pragmatists, as was suggested in Chapter 14; for they strike out in panic at the "immediate thing," not able to see the causes for the sullenly rebellious army of people creeping across the West. Steinbeck seems to be saying that ownership "freezes" these people into *in*flexibility; thus they fear the two men squatting in a ditch, conferring, "figgering," because it bodes change and revolution—they must separate these two men, and fear them, without comprehension. The comment in this chapter applies throughout: "If you who own the things people must have could understand this, you might preserve yourself. . . . But that you cannot know. For the quality of owning freezes you forever into 'I,' and cuts you off forever from the 'we.'"

CHAPTERS 19–22

As a transition into the third part of the novel, the sojourn in California, there is the historical/social information provided in Chapter 19—the land of California stolen from the Mexicans who were weaker, the first squatters who thus became owners, and later, exploiters of other weak people: Chinese, Japanese, Mexicans, Filipinos—and Okies. The Joads are still hurt over Granma's "county" burial—they could spare but $5 for her painted box—as they set up camp in their first Hooverville and learn immediately that work is scarce and constant harassment from the local police is to be expected. Connie Rivers experiences at this point his definitive disillusionment, declaring sullenly, "If I'd of knowed it would be like this I wouldn' of came. I'd a studied nights 'bout tractors back home an' got me a three-dollar job." He disappears into the woods not to return. Ma is horrified by the cluster of hungry children who gather around her stew pot, in which there is barely enough to feed her own family; her dilemma between compassion and practicability is touching. A man named Floyd, whom Al helps with grinding the points on his car, fills him and Tom in on the situation. There is trouble, when a contractor, accompanied by a deputy sheriff, comes into the camp ostensibly looking for workers; the way the authorities operate by intimidation and coercion is demonstrated when Floyd questions their legal authority, asking for assurance about wages (since they invariably go down when the number of applicants increases, a situation the owners purposely set up), and is called "red" and "agitator"—by witness of the deputy—and arrested. He hits the deputy, runs, is shot at (a woman's hand catches the .45 bullet); Tom and Jim Casy enter the fray, and in the end Jim Casy takes the blame, and the arrest, for Tom, who had hit the deputy from behind. It is one of the occasions when Uncle John is so troubled, supposedly by his shame at not acting as Jim Casy did, that he has to get drunk on some of his little store of money. Aware that the camp is to be burned out before morning—a common occurrence—the Joads head for the incredibly decent government camp at Weedpatch. For the almost idyllic period of their stay in this government camp—which is run along the lines of the modern Israeli *kibbutz*—the family pride of the Joads is restored. From the moment Tom drives the truck through the entrance, barely avoiding damage to the old car because of a hump placed purposely in the roadway to cause drivers to slow down for the children often playing there, the atmosphere is different, decent and human. There are Sanitary Units with hot water and toilet facilities (the experiments of young Ruthie and Winfield with the curiosity of a flushing toilet—when it flushes, they assume it is broken—are pathetically amusing), a series of elected committees which govern the camp community, and a regular social life—square dances on Saturday, known to the people around (for the camp people may invite friends among the small farmers) as the only dance to which a man can bring his wife and children. They can work out, if they wish, the dollar a week the camp costs, and they can get credit through a co-op plan for up to $5 at the camp grocery, where the prices are also fair (instead of invariably higher than "in town," as at all other camps). Since the camp officially is "United States" rather than "California," no police are permitted to enter unless there is a riot. Ma eagerly sets about pulling her family back together, getting them clean and well-fed, and anticipating with a nervous womanly pride the visit of the Ladies Committee. Perhaps she sums up the government camp—what it means to be addressed as "Mrs. Joad" again, as well as what the author is saying in terms of social theory—by her sigh, "Why, I feel like people again."

COMMENT

AGRARIANISM OVER CAPITALISM: Chapter 19 fills in historical information of social significance about the settling of California, explaining how the land taken from the Mexicans, once planted and harvested and inhabited, became "possession, and possession was ownership." But the real purpose of this interchapter is to trace the insidious process by which love of the land was replaced by "shopkeeping" and "manufacturing" attitudes toward the land. (And it is well to recall here that the author by his long residence in California from childhood was in a position to comment on these changes.) "And all their love was thinned with money, and all their fierceness dribbled away in interest until they were no longer farmers at all, but little shopkeepers of crops, little manufacturers who must sell before they can make. Then those farmers who were not good shopkeepers lost their land to good shopkeepers. No matter how clever, how loving a man might be with earth and growing things, he could not survive if he were not also a good shopkeeper. And as time went on, the business men had the farms, and the farms grew larger, but there were fewer of them." As farming became an industry, the crops changed more and more to concentration on money-making types, and there was increasing exploitation of workers used to low wages—foreigners, outsiders, although the Okies fiercely felt they were Americans, in America seven generations back, having fought in the Revolution and the Civil War. The sympathetic reassertion here of the agrarian way of life is evidenced by the crimes enumerated: the "imported slaves"—"they live on rice and beans, the business men said. They don't need much. They wouldn't know what to do with good wages. Why, look how they live. Why, look what they eat. And if they get funny—deport them;" the crime of fallow land where people are hungry—"And a homeless hungry man, driving the roads with his wife beside him and his thin children in the back seat, could look at the fallow fields which might produce food but not profit, and that man could know how a fallow field is a sin and the unused land a crime against the thin children;" and, "oranges to be dumped if the price was low"—a situation devastatingly elaborated in Chapter 25, which begins "the spring is beautiful in California" but ends with the bitter-as-gall statement of facts; "Burn coffee for fuel in the ships. Burn corn to keep warm, it makes a hot fire. Dump potatoes in the rivers and place guards along the banks to keep the hungry people from fishing them out. Slaughter the pigs and bury them, and let the putrescence drip down into the earth."

OAKIES: Steinbeck expands a little in Chapter 19 on the "concept" of "Okies"—the reasons of their "Americanness" (as contrasted to the Chinese, Japanese, Filipinos and Mexican migrants) as well as of their desperation which might contrive to amass them into a social force. One paragraph in particular assesses their accumulating grievances, an accumulation which we observe grows more and more explosive in the third section of the book, culminating in the various disasters and decisions at the end. "They were hungry, and they were fierce. And they had hoped to find a home, and they found only hatred. Okies—the owners hated them because the owners knew they were soft and the Okies strong, that they were fed and the Okies hungry; and perhaps the owners had heard from their grandfathers how easy it is to steal land from a soft man if you are fierce and hungry and armed. . . . And in the towns, the storekeepers hated them because they had no money to spend. There is no shorter path to a storekeeper's contempt. . . . The town men, little bankers, hated Okies because there was nothing to gain from them." It is a way of saying, "their blood is strong," and they may turn out to be the very ones who will rise effectively in social protest.

THE SOCIAL LESSON—AMELIORATION OR EXPLOSION: One anecdote, well depicted, serves as well as any to measure the increasing frustrations of downtrodden people like the Okies: the patch of garden in the Jimson weeds—"Now and then a man tried; crept on the land and cleared a piece, trying like a thief to steal a little richness from the earth. Secret gardens hidden in the weeds. A package of carrot seeds and a few turnips. Planted potato skins, crept out in the evening secretly to hoe in the stolen earth." (Notice the poetic quality through sound effects, consonance and assonance.) But the deputy sheriff kicks off the carrot tops and tramples the turnip greens and remarks, "Did ya see his face when we kicked them turnips out? Why, he'd kill a fella soon's he look at him. We got to keep these here people down or they'll take the country." Fear piled on top of fear, anger on top of anger. Or the representative newsclipping: "In Lawrenceville a deputy sheriff evicted a squatter, and the squatter resisted, making it necessary for the officer to use force. The eleven-year-old son of the squatter shot and killed the deputy with a .22 rifle."

As they camp in their first California Hooverville, Tom Joad, who has heard from Floyd Knowles the harsh facts of their situation, comes to talk to Jim Casy about it. As usual Jim Casy has had it "figgered" out for a long time. "Listen all the time. That's why I been thinkin'. Listen to people a-talkin', an' purty soon I hear the way folks are feelin'. Goin' on all the time. I hear 'em an' feel 'em; an' they're beating their wings like a bird in an attic. Gonna bust their wings on a dusty winda tryin' ta get out." (Jim reiterates, incidentally, on this occasion, his latter-day conviction of the inadequacy of religion and prayer for such real-life problems: "I use ta think that'd cut 'er. . . . Use ta rip off a prayer an' all the troubles'd stick to that prayer like flies on flypaper, an' the prayer'd go a-sailin' off, a-takin' them troubles along. But it don' work no more.")

Tom, in his reflections voiced to the somewhat demoralized and skeptical Floyd Knowles, puts his finger once again on the concept of group action. "Well, s'pose them people got together an' says, 'Let 'em rot.' Wouldn' be long 'fore the price went up, by God!" As Floyd points out, such actions have been tried, and stopped by the greater power of the local officials. But lurking in this conversation and others, of course, is the idea of unions and striking, which Jim Casy comes to believe in enough to fight for and lose his life for.

The ideal for these people is presented in Weedpatch, the humane government camp, where the Joads begin to feel like people again and hope is temporarily restored. Washed, clean, fed, warm, almost comfortable for a change, Ma, the spokesman for endurance—"Why, Tom, we're the people that live. They ain't gonna wipe us out. Why, we're the people—we go on"—begins to hope and plan again, as if such feelings are natural to humans when they have a modest sense of well-being: "Wouldn' it be nice if the menfolks all got work? Them a-workin', an' a little money comin' in? Them a-workin', an' us a-workin' here, an' all them nice people. Fust thing we get a little ahead I'd get me a little stove—nice one. They don' cost much. . . . An' Sat'dy night we'll go to the dancin'. They says you can invite folks if you want. I wisht we had some frien's to invite." At Weedpatch people pay if they can, and work it out if they can't. And those who can't go out into the fields are assigned other jobs, such as caring for small children. The government is formed out of the people themselves. A brilliant example of the psychological efficacy of such a social structure, as the author sees it, is provided in the incident of Ruthie's rude intrusion on the game of croquet going on among the children. In profound childish mistrust of her own social acceptability, exhibiting the hostility which is the inevitable outcome of the rejection and diminished self-esteem increasingly thrust upon her family and therefore upon her, she insists upon playing in the game presently in progress, in spite of the assurance from the pig-tailed little girl that she can play "next game." She slaps the girl and wrests the mallet from her. At this point the elderly lady observing all intervenes and tells the children to let Ruthie play, by which she means that they *all* drop their mallets and exit from the court, leaving Ruthie to play alone, in false and lonely satisfaction. At length she flings down the mallet and flies home in tears. The old woman says wisely to the children returning to the court (one could only wish most play supervisors were as wise as she, and question, critically, whether Steinbeck is idealizing a bit): "When she comes back an' wants to be decent, you let her. You was mean yourself, Amy." But the basic point is valid: people, lives, however damaged, can be rehabilitated, through attitudes which are at once pragmatic and compassionate.

Also, in the description of the Weedpatch system of government, the distinction between "charity" and "communal living" is carefully established. The amusing core of the story is that somebody has been stealing toilet paper from Unit Four. "We got our troubles with toilet paper," says Jessie Bullitt, member of the Ladies' Committee of Sanitary Unit Number Four. "Rule says you can't take none away from here. . . . Whole camp chips in for toilet paper. . . . Number Four is usin' more than any other. Somebody's a-stealin' it. Come up in general ladies' meetin'. Ladies' side, Unit Number Four is usin' too much. Come right up in meetin'!" But this time three little girls are not cutting paper dolls from it, as on the last occasion; for a "flushed, perspiring woman" steps to a doorway to "confess" that her five children have probably been using too much because they have all had the skitters (diarrhea), from eating green grapes, because they are short of money. At which the admirable Jessie Bullitt announces, "Now you hol' up your head. That ain't no crime. You jes waltz right over t' the Weedpatch store an' git you some groceries. The camp got twenty dollars, credit there. You git yourself fi' dollars' worth. An' you kin pay it back to the Central Committee when you git work." To Mrs. Joyce's protest that "we ain't never took no charity," there is the vigorous reply that such is not charity, for the credit belongs to the camp jointly and may be dispensed to anyone. This is in contrast to Annie Littlefield's embittered comments on the Salvation Army, where her family was made to feel it *was* charity: "Las' winter; an' we was a-starvin'—me an' the little fellas. An' it was a-rainin'. Fella tol' us to go to the Salvation Army. . . . We was hungry—they made us crawl for our dinner. They took our dignity. . . . Mis' Joad, we don't allow nobody in this camp to build theirself up that-a-way. We don't allow nobody to give nothing to another person. They can give it to the camp, an' the camp can pass it out. We won't have no charity!" Her voice was fierce and hoarse. "I hate 'em," she said. "I ain't never seen my man beat before, but them—them Salvation Army done it to 'im." (It is probably the *concept* of charity with its damage to the psyche which is being lambasted here more than the Salvation Army per se.)

PROSE STYLE IN CHAPTER 19: It was suggested earlier that Steinbeck's style is here and there indebted to the Old Testament. One of Steinbeck's critics, for example—Peter Lisca—has arranged in phrases, like poetry, some of the lines in Chapter 11, which sets forth the author's agrarian philosophy; the effect is that of reading from a page of the Old Testament. It is interesting that in Chapter 19, which also deals with agrarianism, the love of the land contrasted to merely "shopkeeping" the land and working it only with an eye toward larger and larger profit, the lines read similarly and could be arranged thus:

And all the time the farms grew larger and the owners fewer.
And there were pitifully few farmers on the land anymore.
And the imported serfs were beaten and frightened
And starved until some went home again,
And some grew fierce and were killed or driven from the country.
And the farms grew larger and the owners fewer.
And the crops changed.
Fruit trees took the place of grain fields,
And vegetables to feed the world spread out on the bottoms:
Lettuce, cauliflower, artichokes, potatoes—stoop crops.
A man may stand to use a scythe, a plow, a pitchfork;
But he must crawl like a bug between the rows of lettuce,
He must bend his back and pull his long bag between the cotton rows,
He must go on his knees like a penitent across a cauliflower patch.
And it came about that. . . .

Steinbeck is clearly influenced by Biblical style, and the analogy between the Joads and Israel in Egypt: as we have seen, the three parts of the novel divide roughly into oppression, exodus and the land of Canaan.

CHAPTERS 23–25

Chapter 23, gently ironic, placed between those chapters which describe the Weedpatch idyl, depicts the pleasures of the migrant people. "The migrant people, scuttling for work, scrabbling to live, looked always for pleasure, dug for pleasure, manufactured pleasure, and they were hungry for amusement. Sometimes amusement lay in speech, and they climbed up their lives with jokes." Or there were the folk three: harmonica, fiddle and guitar. And if a man had a little money, there was liquor, "the hard edges gone, and the warmth. Then there was no loneliness, for a man could people his brain with friends, and he could find his enemies and destroy them. . . . Failures dulled and the future was no threat. And hunger did not skulk about. . . ." Chapter 24 is another cheerful interlude in the lives of the Joads, except for the incident at the dance of the three young men who have been hired to start a fight and cause trouble for the government camp. Saturday is wash day: first the children, then the men, last the women, get clean and ready for the night's dancing. There is a poignant moment when Rose of Sharon—young, married, pregnant and deserted—expresses to Ma her fearful longing to attend the dance. Ma as usual fixes things; that is, she arranges it so that the lonely girl can stay out of trouble. "Know what you an' me's gonna do? We're a-goin' to that dance, an' we're a-gonna set there and watch. If anybody says to come dance—why, I'll say you ain't strong enough. I'll say you're poorly. An' you can hear the music an' all like that." The men meanwhile plot to thwart the anticipated attempt from the outside to disrupt their camp, and they worry together about job prospects. Chapter 25 speaks for itself its contrasts: the language of growth, which is beautiful—"the spring is beautiful in California"—at war with the language of destruction, which is ugly—"burn coffee. . . . dump potatoes. . . . slaughter pigs."

COMMENT

SOCIAL PROTEST THROUGH GROUP ACTION: The successful routing of the three potential rioters at the Saturday dance in Weedpatch government camp is of course an instance of the effectiveness of group action, made possible, we ought to note in passing, by the sense of fellowship demonstrated by the small farmer Mr. Thomas who leaks the plan to Tom and his colleagues who work for him briefly (Thomas of course is one of those being squeezed out by price-setting and other power moves of the bigger operators). And, although their frustrations remain just as great as ever, once the resolve is made to handle the incident and the three intruders without violence, that resolve is upheld. Afterwards, though, the men squat together discussing the "change a-comin'" which all of them are just about agreed upon by now. Pa, so far pretty passive, says "They's change a-comin'. I don't know what. Maybe we won't live to see her. But she's a-comin'. They's res'less feelin'." And the man in the black hat relates the impressive anecdote of the revolt of the mountain people against the rubber companies in Akron, Ohio. The chronicle of persecution of the "outsiders" by the local people seems to have been the same: a union formed, the great hue and cry of Red!; storekeepers and legioners and preachers out in military drill with pick handles. Then, "Well, sir—it was las' March, an' one Sunday five thousan' of them mountain men had a turkey shoot outside of town. Five thousan' of 'em jes' marched through town with their rifles. An' they had their turkey shoot, an' then they marched back. An' that's all they done. Well, sir, they ain't been no trouble sence then. These here citizens committees give back the pick handles, an' the storekeepers keep their stores, an' nobody been clubbed nor tarred an' feathered, an' nobody been killed." In the silence that follows, Black Hat brings forth his inevitable point: "They're gettin' purty mean out here. Burned that camp an' beat up folks. I been thinkin'. All our folks got guns. I been thinkin' maybe we ought to git up a turkey shootin' club an' have meetin's ever' Sunday." A lot of such "thinkin'," and the moving restless feet of the men who listen, and we are not far from the actions which will be initiated by men like Jim Casy who at length take it upon themselves to act out what they have thought out.

It is fitting that the author includes his most vigorous and poetic social protest statement in the following chapter (25). The ironic contrast is apparent. The quite paradisical vision of spring in California, the ripening of all growing things for the good harvest—"the first tendrils of the grapes, swelling from the old gnarled vines, cascade down to cover the trunks"; "petals drop from the fruit trees and carpet the earth with pink and white"; "the centers of the blossoms swell and grow and color." The earnest men "of understanding and knowledge and skill" who experiment and watch and nurture toward the perfect crop. Then the awesome awareness that such quickening and ripening has been born and nourished to rot:

cherries, prunes, pears, grapes. The price is too low to pay wages to pick them; the wine must be cheaply and cheatingly made, with rotten or wasp-stung grapes and chemicals. The little farmers will be inevitably overcome by debt. Decay, physical and moral, is the keynote of the atmosphere. The chapter concludes on such crimes against nature and men most bitterly and eloquently. "There is a crime here that goes beyond denunciation. There is a sorrow here that weeping cannot symbolize. There is a failure here that topples all our success. The fertile earth, the straight tree rows, the sturdy trunks, and the ripe fruit. And children dying of pellagra must die because a profit cannot be taken from an orange. . . . The people come with nets to fish for potatoes in the river, and the guards hold them back; they come in rattling cars to get the dumped oranges, but the kerosene is sprayed. And they stand still and watch the potatoes float by, listen to the screaming pigs being killed in a ditch and covered with quicklime, watch the mountains of oranges slop down to a putrefying ooze; and in the eyes of the people there is the failure; and in the eyes of the hungry there is a growing wrath. In the souls of the people the grapes of wrath are filling and growing heavy, growing heavy for the vintage."

CHAPTERS 26–28

Life at the Weedpatch camp could breed apathy, however, out of its very decency: although there was no work to be found in the area, the families could not bear to leave. But one night after supper Ma pins down her men to discussing specifically just what they are going to do now. She reminds them of what they have avoided bringing out in the open: Winfield jerking and twisting in his sleep; "one day' more grease an' two days' flour, an' ten potatoes"; meals of fried dough. But it is a psychological and emotional impasse: the men claim, in truth, that "we been a-lookin', Ma. Been walkin' out sence we can't use the gas no more. Been goin' in ever' gate, walkin' up to ever' house. . . . Puts a weight on ya. Goin' out lookin' for somepin you know you ain't gonna find." Ma's position is just as clear, and true: "You ain't got the right to get discouraged. This here fambly's goin' under. You jus' ain't got the right." The upshot of the conference is that they are up and out of the camp before dawn the next morning. At the advice of a smiling well-dressed man in a roadster who directs them they head 40 miles north to the Hooper ranch to pick peaches. Although the tight security check of name and license by the armed deputies strikes them as strange when they enter the ranch premises and set up in a dirty little one-room shack, it is only later that they become aware that they are "strikebreakers," that they have been hired in the place of exasperated men who joined together in rebellion against the 2½ ¢ a box they were offered to pick peaches. But they know it is an unfriendly place, with inhabitants who seem ashamed of being there. When Ma takes the hard-earned slip for one dollar—the joint earnings of the family for the day—to the man at the little store, she discovers painfully that all items are overpriced in comparison to town shopping, and the dollar is easily eaten up in one night's dinner.

Tom walks out to explore the curious situation after supper and comes across a tent hidden in a deep ravine, from which to his surprise emerges Jim Casy. For Jim the time in jail has been like Christ's days in the wilderness, he says, for he has finally worked out things in his mind. He reasons that even decent people will steal when there is absolutely no other way to get what they need. And he relates how one day when sour beans were served the prisoners, their mass protest obtained results. Casy leaves his point up to Tom to figure out, but it turns out that the preacher has gained a small reputation for himself in the current strike and union activities. This is unfortunately proved by the violence which follows. The nervous men hear noises and when they go to look, come upon two searchers with pick handles. They are after Jim Casy, whom they recognize. One of them crushes Casy's skull with the pick handle, as he is saying, "Listen, you fellas don' know what you're doin'. You're helpin' to starve kids. . . . You don't know what you're a-doin'." As Tom looks at the preacher, who is undoubtedly dead, he knows what to do. He grabs the pick handle, pounds at the man who has assailed Jim Casy, and, struck a glancing blow, makes an escape down the stream. Tom creeps into the shack and lies in pain with his crushed nose until the dawn, when he is obliged to relate to Ma what has happened. The first day he hides there in the house (for it is certain then that he has killed the deputy); after that the family apprehensively moves on, stopping at a point where they hope to pick some cotton, and hiding Tom in a culvert with a blanket. They take up their last residence in some boxcars, sharing the long boxcar with the Wainwrights. While the cotton lasts they are able to earn well and eat well. However, because little Ruthie in an argument with another child over some Cracker Jacks has revealed that her brother is a killer hiding out, it is considered too dangerous for Tom to remain there, and Ma bids him a painful farewell. He tells her that, although he hopes to keep from getting killed, he intends to do now "what Casy done." As Ma walks back to the camp a man catches up with her and offers a small picking job to her and her family. It turns out to be the last picking they get. As they finish the job and start back to camp the next day, the rains begin. Yet life goes on: Al Joad and Aggie Wainwright are engaged, and Rose of Sharon's time is almost due.

COMMENT

TOM JOAD, THE NEW PROPHET AND LEADER: In Chapter 26 Ma explains that she has just been "a-treadin'" on Pa to make him mad, to get him to act, but that it is really Tom she leans on. "You got more sense, Tom. 'I don' need to make you mad. I got to lean on you. Them others—they're kinda strangers, all but you. You won't give up, Tom." Perhaps because he is a pragmatist—because he *has* "got more sense," Tom takes the job reluctantly, asserting "I don' like it. I wanta go out like Al. An' I wanta get mad like Pa, an' I wanta get drunk like Uncle John." But Ma insists that Tom is not like the others, never has been—he is "more than himself." "Ever'thing you do is more'n you. When they sent you up to prison I knowed it. You're spoke for." This is the same as to say, especially since Jim Casy has just died a martyr's death, that Tom is the new prophet. This is borne out in the parting scene between Ma and Tom, where he describes to her the death of Casy, and tells her what he is going to do. In his hiding place in the brush he has been thinking about all the things Casy ever said (it can be said, in fact, that when Tom goes forth from the solitary ravine he is emerging from his own Biblical "wilderness"). As Tom sets forth his thoughts to Ma it is clear that he has got hold of Jim Casy's concept of the "oversoul," and of Jim's late conviction of the promise of group action. "But now I been thinkin'what he said, an' I can remember—all of it. Says one time he went out in the wilderness to find his own soul, an' he foun' he didn' have no soul that was his'n. Says he foun' he jus' got a little piece of a great big soul. Says a wilderness ain't no good, 'cause his little piece of a soul wasn't no good 'less it was with the rest, an' was whole. Funny how I remember. Didn' think I was even listenin'. But I know now a fella ain't no good alone." That Tom remarks he wasn't listening, he thought, is another hint that his knowledge has been "intuitive," almost "divine revelation." (It should also be pointed out that Tom's "cave" is a womblike place, his state there is somewhat "prenatal," and his emergence, especially after the confrontation with Ma, is like a rebirth.) He has absorbed Jim Casy's message that "two are better than one," and now relates it to the agrarian philosophy and the concept of group action. "I been thinkin' how it was in that gov'ment camp, how our folks took care a theirselves, an' if they was a fight they fixed it theirself; an' they wasn't no cops wagglin' their guns, but they was better order than them cops ever give. I been a-wonderin' why we can't do that all over. Throw out the cops that ain't our people. All work together for our own thing—all farm our own lan'." When Ma expresses her fears that he will kill or be killed, he reverts to the concept of the Oversoul. "Well, maybe like Casy says, a fella ain't got a soul of his own, but on'y a piece of a big one—an' then. . . . Then it don' matter. Then I'll be all aroun' in the dark. I'll be ever'where—wherever you look. Wherever they's a fight so hungry people can eat, I'll be there. Wherever they's a cop beatin' up a guy, I'll be there. If Casy knowed, why, I'll be in the way guys yell when they're mad an'—I'll be in the ways kids laugh when they're hungry an' they know supper's ready. An' when our folks eat the stuff they raise an' live in the houses they build—why, I'll be there." Tom's speech is pretty much Biblical paraphrase—he has practically said "Lo, I am with you always, even unto the ends of the earth"—and he has declared his spiritual oneness with his brothers, moving beyond personal material considerations to action from ethical principle and inner conviction. (Jim Casy's martyrdom, incidentally, and his stature as Christ-like prophet, has been made pretty clear through Tom's description of his death to Ma, who demands to know, so she can "figger how it was"—in other words, assure herself about Tom's innocence or guilt. Tom repeats Casy's last words: "You got no right to starve people. . . . You don' know what you're a-doin'." As if to make no mistake Ma too repeats the words: "Tha's what he said—'You don' know what you're doin''?" So we have a paraphrase of Christ's last words on the cross, "Forgive them, Lord, for they know not what they do.")

CONTROL OF THE FAMILY: In the last chapters of the book Ma has taken over control of the family, although she remains compassionate in the role. In Chapter 26, after she has forced the menfolk to consider what moves they must make to survive, Pa sniffles: "Seems like times is changed. Time was when a man said what we'd do. Seems like women is tellin' now. Seems like it's purty near time to get out a stick." Ma answers, "You get your stick, Pa. Times when they's food an' a place to set, then maybe you can use your stick an' keep your skin whole. But you ain't a-doin your job, either a-thinkin' or a-workin'." At this point Ma contends afterward to Tom that she did it to "rile" Pa, that things are still all right. "He's all right. He ain't beat. He's like as not to take a smack at me." But later, when she begs Tom to stay with them, after he has killed the deputy, her reasons indicate her doubts: "Tom! They's a whole lot I don' un'erstan'. . . . They was a time when we was on the lan'. They was a boundary to us then. Ol' folks died off, an' little fellas come, an' we was always one thing—we was the fambly—kinda whole and clear. An' now we ain't clear no more. I can't get straight. They ain't nothin' keeps us clear. Al—he's a-hankerin' an' a-jibbitin' to go off on his own. An' Uncle John is jus' a-draggin' along. Pa's lost his place. He ain't the head no more. We're crackin' up, Tom. There ain't no fambly now." And at length, in Chapter 28, the issue is brought out into the open between Pa and Ma. When the Wainwrights express their fears to the Joads about the deepening relationship between Aggie and Al, Ma answers, "Pa'll talk to Al. Or if Pa won't, I will." Later she apologizes to Pa. "I didn' mean no harm a-sayin' I'd talk to Al." "I know," is Pa's quiet answer. "I ain't no good any more. Spen' all my time a-thinkin' how it use' ta be." He goes on to reflect how, even though as Ma points out, the new land is "purtier," he has been escaping dreamily into the past. Of this new but painful land he remarks, "I never even see it, thinkin' how the willow's los' its leaves now. Sometimes figgerin' to mend that hole in the south fence. Funny! Woman takin' over the fambly. Woman sayin' we'll do this here, an' we'll go there. An' I don' even care." These are desolate words, to which Ma answers with intuition and compassion. "Woman can change better'n a man. Woman got all her life in her arms. Man got it all in his head. Don' you mind. Maybe—well, maybe nex' year we can get a place."

CHAPTERS 29 AND 30

It settles down to steady rain, and the boxcar camp is bit by bit flooded out. First the people in tents flee the water; then those privileged folks in the boxcars watch with panic and indecision as the water rises around their vehicles and toward the floors of the boxcars: to leave, or to throw up a protective wall of earth and stick it out? The issue is somewhat accidentally decided by the beginning of Rose of Sharon's birth pains: the Joads must stay, and they convince the others to work at the wall. At first the man made levee successfully holds back the rising waters. Then disaster strikes (ironically, it is just after Rose of Sharon's baby has been born dead) in the form of sheer chance: a cottonwood is struck down by lightening, and its roots tear into the levee, and the water creeps, then flows through. Al dashes frantically to the truck, to try to start it and get it to higher ground; but he is too late, and the water has conquered them all. The rest is chaotic. Uncle John takes the shriveled little infant in the apple box and floats it down the floodtide, muttering in dull anger, "Go down an' tell 'em. Go down in the street an' rot an' tell 'em that way. That's the way you can talk. . . . Go on down now, an' lay in the street. Maybe they'll know then." Pa asks Ma, pleadingly, "Did we slip up? Is they anything we could of did?" Al's idea of tearing out the sides of the truck to build a platform on the floor of the boxcar, where they can move their stuff three or four feet higher and sit on top of it, out of the water, is put into operation. During the day and the night the families huddle on the damp platforms; in the dawn Ma asserts that they must go to higher ground. They start out through the deep water, the adults carrying the little ones on their backs and helping the weak Rose of Sharon. After walking along the highway they spot a barn and head for it. There is hay there. And in one of its corners there is a young boy crouching with his father. At Ma's request he offers a dirty comforter to dry Rose of Sharon. The little boy's answer to Ma's question about the deathly looking fellow with him is that he's starving. The boy explains bleakly that his pa hasn't eaten for six days: "Says he wasn' hungry, or he jus' et. Give me the food. Now he's too weak. Can't hardly move." The boy adds that when he realized the man was starving he stole some bread and made him eat it; but the man has not been able to keep the food down, and he needs soup or milk. Ma and her daughter exchange a deep look, and Rose of Sharon asks the rest of them to leave. They go into the tool shed. Then Rose of Sharon lies down beside the starving man and offers him the saving milk from her breast.

COMMENT

INTERPRETATION OF THE ENDING: As critics of Steinbeck have pointed out in some detail (especially Peter Lisca, *The Wide World of John Steinbeck*) the entire novel, and especially the ending, is filled with Biblical analogy and symbolism. The grapes, for example, have figured largely both as symbols of bitterness and of plenty (Lisca cites Biblical parallels: Revelation, Deuteronomy, Jeremiah, Numbers, Canticles). In particular Grampa before his death was continually evoking a vision of plenty through his allusions to the huge bunches of grapes he was going to devour when he got to California. It would seem that, as Lisca points out, Grampa "is symbolically present through the anonymous old man in the barn (stable), who is saved from starvation by Rosasharn's breasts. . . ." Two passages from Canticles bear this out: "This thy stature is like to a palm tree, and thy breasts to clusters of grapes"; (7.7) "I [Christ] am the rose of Sharon, and the lily of the valleys." (2:1) In giving new life to the starving man, Rose of Sharon is participating in a Christ-like way in the rebirth of a whole people (we recall here the ritual of communion, too—"Take, eat; this is my body. . . . drink, this is my blood"—symbolic spiritual rebirth through the symbolic absorption of Christ's body). We can say that Rose of Sharon comes to represent physical revitalization through Jesus Christ just as Jim Casy (whose initials are J. C.) stands for the philosophical prophecy of Christ. (Lisca cites analogues for Rose of Sharon's gesture in art, literature.

Character Analyses

THE JOAD FAMILY

GRAMPA: Grampa Joad is like a character out of Chaucers' "The Miller's Tale"—he is lecherous, loud, cantankerous, and the Joads seem to secretly relish his consistency in this. In the early pages of the novel he repeatedly insists on his intention to gorge himself on grapes when he reaches California. "Know what I'm a-gonna do?" he says. "I'm gonna pick me a wash tub full a grapes, an' I'm gonna set in 'em, an' scrooge aroun', an' let the juice run down my pants." Grampa is an old ripper, and his *joie de vivre* is earthily and convincingly pictured. Ironically, though, Grampa panics at the time of departure, has to be drugged with cough medicine, and dies of a sudden stroke on the first night out, to be buried on his homeground of Oklahoma.

GRANMA: She is Grampa's spirited equal, whether eating, cussing or praying. There is a characteristic anecdote told about her: once after a church meeting when she was talking in tongues she grabbed the shotgun and fired away part of Grampa's backside. This insured her rights with him for the duration of their long life together. Flighty as Granma appears, her affection for her husband is obvious in, for example, the chaotic moments in the Wilsons' tent before Grampa's death, when she hops about "like a chicken" shouting frantically at Jim Casy, "Pray, you. Pray, I tell ya. . . . Pray, goddamn you!" After Grampa's death she retires more and more into a dream world, until she dies in Ma's arms during the night as they drive across the desert.

UNCLE JOHN: Pa Joad's older brother, Uncle John can be regarded as the black sheep of the family, in that he is an eccentric loner, and a lonely guilt-ridden man. His story explains his actions: long ago his young wife, who was pregnant, had told him one night that she had a stomachache, which he ignored to the extent that he suggested she take some medicine. She died that night of a burst appendix. The pattern of Uncle John's life alternates between periods of severe abstinence and brief binges, alcoholic and sexual. Also, he has always tried to assuage his guilt by being good to people—candy and gum for the kids, a sack of flour dropped off on somebody's porch.

PA: The elder Tom Joad is a man who, when we meet him, is finding it hard to accept the brute fact of his eviction from the land, where he has labored all his life. His wife and children continue to show respect for him as the head of the family, but in point of fact the leadership slowly passes out of his hands into Ma's and Tom's. He is presented as a stunned, bewildered figure, sometimes angry, sometimes passive.

MA: Ma is a powerful though unassuming figure in the Joad clan. She is probably the ideal mother figure. She is patient in her unending labors, and in her determination to keep down fear and encourage joy in her family. She has a sense of humor and on occasion a kind of girlishness. Yet she can act, and act vigorously, in opposition to the menfolk when it is for the sake of preserving the family unit. Throughout the novel she emerges as a symbol of love, as a person who instinctively practices brotherly love. She is a person of insight and intuition, and is able to communicate with the philosopher of the novel, Jim Casy, and his unconscious "disciple," her son Tom.

NOAH: Nobody ever knows what Noah thinks or feels, or even whether he is slightly feeble-minded, as Pa fears, because of an accident at his birth. He does his work reliably and never raises his voice in anger. On the day before the family sets out across the desert, as they encamp by a river, Noah announces to Tom his decision to remain by the river and fish. And indeed, the parting vision of such a placid existence for Noah is a natural one.

TOM: Tom is a central character, and perhaps the one who develops most—and survives—in the novel. He is individualistic and quick to anger if he feels he is being pushed around; he is also kind, sometimes witty, and potentially strong in the moral and intuitive sense that his mother is. In effect Jim Casy becomes his teacher, converting him by word and by his own example to the idea that a man cannot just look after himself but in the spirit of compassion is obligated to help others. Although he is still an outlaw of society at the end of the book, his status is actually changed: he is fighting for social amelioration, a better way of life for his people and for all struggling people. Tom, in other words, experiences reeducation and rebirth in the novel.

ROSASHARN (ROSE OF SHARON): In the four years of young Tom Joad's absence his sister Rosasharn grew up and married a local fellow, Connie Rivers. During the early part of the journey these two giggle and dream their way westward, as she carefully carries their unborn child. Most of Rosasharn's existence in the story is centered upon this child, who at length, because of inadequate diet, unsanitary and harrassing living conditions, and perhaps because of Connie's eventual desertion, is born dead in the last pages of the novel.

AL: Sixteen-year-old Al is expert at two things: tomcatting and mechanics. He worries about his responsibility for the old Hudson, but his judgments prove sound and dependable for the family. Typically, Al is an admirer of his older brother Tom and wishes to imitate him. At the end of the story he has become engaged to Aggie Wainwright, whose family has shared a boxcar with the Joads.

RUTHIE: She is 12, and seen in the novel at that point of suspension between girlhood and womanhood, ranging from ladylike composure which excludes her young brother Winfield to giggling, frantic games and exploits with him.

WINFIELD: He is 10, and realistically depicted in the gaucheries, the awkwardness, the mischievousness of a 10 year old.

OTHER CHARACTERS

JIM CASY: The ex-preacher is revealed from the first as an introspective man who retains the respect of the community in spite of—later, because of—the fact that he now refuses to preach. He has examined himself, he says, and has found that although he still strongly feels a call to lead and help the people, he can no longer in good conscience preach the religious gospel they are accustomed to. It emerges that he does not believe the old-time hell-fire and promise-of-heaven religion is realistic for their present needs. Jim Casy, who is the Christ-figure prophet until his martyr's death, speaks thoughts which reflect various philosophies: Transcendentalism, humanism, pragmatism, socialism. He does in fact lead and comfort the people; and he lays down his life for Tom Joad, who has in effect become his disciple and eventually takes over his work for social betterment.

MULEY GRAVES: He is a neighbor of the Joads in Oklahoma, and he represents one of the pathetic directions in which the ruined lives of the Okies ran. Although his family has migrated to California, "somepin'" kept him from accompanying them. The way he now roams the countryside, living almost like an animal off the land—"like an' ole' graveyard ghos'," as he confesses—he seems a little touched. He is a sad figure to all, as we get our final glimpse of him standing forlornly in the dooryard of the Joad homestead.

SAIRY AND IVY WILSON: This couple from Kansas link their fortunes with the Joads' on the first night out, when Grampa dies and they offer their help and possessions. Al fixes their car, and the families split their load into the two vehicles and travel on. Sairy Wilson is frail and ill, and in California, when they are ready to tackle the desert, it becomes apparent that she is at last too sick to travel. The Joads unhappily leave the Wilsons behind, knowing that Sairy's death is imminent and Mr. Wilson's survival alone uncertain.

FLOYD KNOWLES: He is a young man who can be singled out from among the various men encountered by the Joads as a commentator on the conditions of the migrants. They meet him in the first Hooverville camp in California. He bitterly describes the exploitation of the workers by the owners, and the injustice and brutality of officials. His commentary is immediately borne out, for when a contractor comes into the camp looking for workers, accompanied by one of the innumerable deputy sheriffs, Floyd speaks up and demands his legal rights, and he is immediately arrested on the false charges of "red agitator."

THE WAINWRIGHTS: In that last of the Hoovervilles, the Wainwright family shares a long boxcar with the Joads, while they all pick cotton. Al Joad begins to court their daughter Aggie and the two become engaged. Mrs. Wainwright assists in the birth of Rosasharn's stillborn child, and when the Joads leave to take Rosasharn and the children, Ruthie and Winfield, to higher ground, Al remains behind in the water-logged boxcar with the Wainwrights.

JESSIE BULLITT, ANNIE LITTLEFIELD, AND ELLA SUMMERS: These women are members of the Ladies' Committee of Sanitary Unit Number Four who come to call on Ma in the Weedpatch government camp on their first day there. In their very human mixture of common sense, bustling self-importance, little personal jealousies, genuine good intentions and actual hard work they may be taken as prototypes of the figures who can be expected to rise to leadership and function effectively when the people are given choice and power.

MRS. ELIZABETH SANDRY: This woman should be mentioned as representative as a particular element which was a carry-over from the Bible evangelism, stomping and hollering religion from which the Joads emerged. A fanatical, sin-obsessed, spirit-stifling woman, she is not portrayed sympathetically. She viciously frightens Rosasharn with the contention that her baby will be deformed if she has "sinned" by "hug-dancing," and Ma tells her to be on her way. The manager explains to Ma that the woman will probably not bother them again; her system is always to call on and try to convert the newcomers to camp. We would find Mrs. Sandry among the "sin-mongers" who sit by in rigid disapproval of the Saturday square dance in the Weedpatch camp.

EZRA HUSTON AND WILLIE EATON: These men are chairmen, respectively, of the Central Committee and the Entertainment Committee of the Weedpatch camp. Here too their actions in warding off the riot attempt by outsiders at the Saturday night square dance may be regarded as symbolic of the progress which can be accomplished when the people run their own affairs. The survival of the good reputation of the camp—hence the survival of all the people there—was involved in the prevention of trouble that night, and the elected leaders of the people handled it.

JIM RAWLEY: Rawley is the humane manager of the government camp. In all his actions—from reassuring Ma about the intrusion by the amateur evangelist functioning as midwife in the delivery of babies—he behaves as a pragmatist (with common sense and a notion of realities) and a humanist (with compassion).

TIMOTHY WALLACE AND WILKIE WALLACE: These two men take Tom with them for a brief pipe laying job with Mr. Thomas right after his arrival in the government camp.

MR. THOMAS: Thomas is an interesting representative—a good man—of the small farmer or small businessman contingent in the hierarchy of laborers, owners, bankers, officials, etc. He is sympathetic to the situation of the migrants—for example, he himself is ashamed and angered that he must reduce their pay from thirty cents to twenty-five cents, and he does them the important favor of revealing the plan to cause a riot at the Saturday dance. He is one of the little men who will probably be squeezed out eventually by larger business interests; as it is, he is obliged to lower the wages because he is under the power of the Farmers' Association, which in turn is controlled by The Bank of the West. The power interests will not hesitate to wipe him out if he resists.

COMMENT: As is obvious from a reading of the novel, there are innumerable faceless or nameless actors in the drama of *The Grapes Of Wrath*: i.e., the tractor drivers, the truck driver who gives Tom a lift, Mae and Al and the two truckers in the roadside restaurant, the one-eyed filling station attendant who hates his boss, the auto dealers, camp officials, sheriffs, storekeepers. All of them in a small way at least are to be regarded as commentators on the social situation in the novel.

Sample Essay Questions and Answers

1. Discuss the idea of a Transcendental "Oversoul" as it appears in the novel.

ANSWER: It is Jim Casy who first brings up, in folk idiom, the concept that, translated, resembles the Oversoul propounded by the American Transcendentalists, especially Ralph Waldo Emerson. The Transcendentalists defined "Oversoul" as a sense of oneness with God, with nature and with other individuals. The discovery of the Oversoul had to be made through intuition; that is, a person felt or sensed this truth, rather than saw it as a tangible fact. Jim Casy, the ex-preacher who has been doing a lot of thinking, has found the religion of Bible-belt evangelism no longer adequate to his needs or the needs of his people. He has come up with the idea that the "sperit of God"—for in his country any version of religion has always included the idea of "sperit" and "getting the sperit"—may be instead the human spirit. And instead of separate souls, every single person's soul—and I believe the word *sperit* can be used synonymously—may go to make up part of "one big soul." At several points in the novel he renews the discussion of one big inclusive soul that holds together, unites all people. It can be seen that such an idea also fits in with the concept of the family unit and the social philosophy of group action developed in the book.

2. What would you say is the social philosophy developed in *The Grapes of Wrath*?

ANSWER: Theoretically viewed, it is probably based upon the ideas of Marx and Lenin and other socialist thinkers of the past and present. Yet the social philosophy which develops in this novel is also peculiarly American, founded on what might be termed loosely "the American Dream": the principle of democracy, of course, including the rights due to all under such a system; the pioneer spirit of endurance which first explored and settled the Middle West and the West; the will to forge ahead and succeed—drive (even though the undesirable effects of this same urge are revealed in the form of grasping materialism and ruthless power interests in the novel). Specifically, the social theory which develops and is realized in action in *The Grapes of Wrath*—through the efforts of the Jim Casys, the Tom Joads and those who choose to follow them—is that which urges that the small people, the poor people, those most in a position to be exploited and denied by the power of the profit hungry, must amass strength through banding together and taking group action. As the novel progresses, this idea first takes the form of worried, angry conversations among the frustrated men: "We have guns. What if we banded together to fight the owners, the banks, the deputy sheriffs?" There are some past examples before them—i.e., the mountain men who revolted successfully in Akron, Ohio against rubber companies. There is the present working example of the essentially socialist community of the government camp at Weedpatch: there the people manage all their own affairs—government, economy, policing, health, recreation (along the lines of the modern Israeli *kibbutz*)—and they also keep out unwarranted intrusion and intimidation from outsiders to the camp. "Advanced" social theory (for the period under consideration—the depression and post-depression years) is also realized, at length, in that the jobless and starving men come to understand the nature of "unions" and "strikes," along with the violence of "strikebreaking," unfortunately. At the end of the novel Tom Joad, who has killed a deputy sheriff in defense of Jim Casy, brutally murdered for his "agitation" for a union and for strikes to get fair wages, has set forth to work toward this same social ideal. For the one ruthless social lesson learned by the Joads and their like in the novel is that "separately we are weak, together we have strength."

3. Briefly describe the biographical and historical background which produced *The Grapes of Wrath*. Given this context, how was the novel received at its publication, and more recently?

ANSWER: First of all, John Steinbeck knew intimately the country and the people about which he wrote. Born and raised in the Salinas Valley in California, he lived most of his first forty years there (and much of his writing until recently was set in that locale). Furthermore, in the mid-thirties he became aware of and disturbed about the conditions of migrant workers in general (he had observed them in his own countryside, in California) and the plight of those who were forced to flee from the Dust Bowl of parts of Kansas and Oklahoma in particular. He wrote newspaper articles on the subject in 1935 and 1937, having gone to Oklahoma and made the westward trek to California with the migrant workers themselves. (The latter series of articles was published as a pamphlet called *Their Blood Is Strong*.) It needs hardly be added that other published commentary of the period—excepting that which defended certain ownership and public interests in the states most involved, such as California and Oklahoma—corroborates Steinbeck's journalistic findings which he metamorphosed into fiction.

At its publication in 1939 the novel was received essentially as a social document and a work of social protest, by both its admirers and its detractors. It was acclaimed, even in the form of a Pulitzer Prize to Steinbeck; it was widely discussed and debated in newspapers, magazines and on the radio; it was of course turned into a movie; and it was in some places banned and burned, for its so-called revolutionary socio-economic theories (for the charge of "Red!" was as panicked, as all-inclusive and as vaguely defined at that period of American history as it has been in more recent years), for its so-called unfair and untrue report of the conditions of migrant laborers, and for its so-called dirty language.

When some of the first furor over the novel died down, however, critics began to look at it from an artistic point of view and to ask the question which is still being asked and answered pro and con—is it art or propaganda? Or, in fact, does one have to choose between the two? Critics of each decade since its publication have tended to look upon it with the going critical attitudes and habits of their group, with a general shift from the sociological readings toward artistic critiques which include everything from Steinbeck's various philosophies (humanism, pragmatism, biological theory of man, non-teleological thought, agrarianism—how well these come across in the context of the novel), his alternations between the dreamlike and the real (fantasy, allegory, symbolism), his ideas of good and evil, the individuality or universality of his characters, his mystical symbolism.

4. How can the word *humanism* be applied to *The Grapes of Wrath*?

ANSWER: All the major characters in the novel, with Jim Casy and later, Tom Joad leading, seem to move from a religiously based to a humanly based philosophy of life in the novel. It is clear, of course, as soon as Jim Casy begins to explain to everyone why he cannot be a "preacher" any longer that he more and more finds the religious precepts of his and his people's immediate past untenable in their present realities: some of Jim's most memorable speeches early in the book are his declarations that he wants to help and comfort the people still, he feels things are changing and they are going someplace, but he can no longer look upon sin in the conventional Bible-belt evangelical way nor can he offer facile prayers or parade future heavenly glory to people whose lives are materially and psychically wretched in the present. In another important speech he claims the "sperit"—a feeling of which has always figured so largely in local religion—seems now to him to be more of a *human* spirit than the spirit of a remote God; at any rate it is this human spirit which he now feels sure of, just as he feels certain that the souls of all the people go to make up one great soul: the Oversoul spoken of before.

Tom Joad moves toward a philosophy of humanism in the novel, too. At the beginning, although he is a sensitive, kind and communicative person, he is still, rather naturally, "out for himself"—individualistic, we might say, focusing on his own personal and material well-being and of course, the welfare of the Joad family. His actions, that is, stem more from particular causes and crises rather than from any sense of general principles. As he says, "I put one foot down in front of the other," and "I climb fences when I got to climb fences." He is, however, an admirer and disciple of Jim Casy's almost from the beginning, too, since Jim is the first person from his past whom Tom encounters on his way home from prison. Tom always listens with curiosity and interest to Jim Casy, and later he realizes, as he tells his mother, that he has absorbed more of Casy's philosophizing than he knew. He takes over Jim Casy's philosophy and his tasks, too, at that point after Casy's martyrdom when he quotes the preacher and takes up his credo that "Two are better than one." He speaks in terms of "our people," of doing something so that they may live decently and happily again. Tom Joad has thus enlarged his compassion to all human beings, beyond the family unit.

The women like Ma and Sairy Wilson can of course be included among the "humanists" in the novel too, for (first of all as mothers) all their actions are outgoing and predominantly selfless. Ma Joad cares about human beings and understands them strikingly well. There are countless examples of her insight and understanding: after Grampa's death, later in the evening, she instructs Rosasharn to go and lie by Granma because "she'll be feelin' lonesome now"; she is constantly attuned to the complex emotions which come with Rosasharn's pregnancy, compounded by the desertion of her husband Connie—Ma prevents Tom from needling her, yet encourages her to see Tom's jokes about her swelling body as affectionate, which they are; she comprehends that the girl in her loneliness wants to enjoy the Saturday dance at Weedpatch but desperately fears the temptation of her flesh, so that she and Ma go and sit together, Rosasharn secure in Ma's promise to keep her out of trouble; and at the very lowest ebb of her daughter's morale, shortly before her baby is due, Ma makes exactly the right move by giving Rosasharn the gift of gold earrings, one of the few family possessions salvaged, and further distracts her from her troubles by piercing her ears on the spot. Ma silently and without judgment whatsoever acknowledges Uncle John's absolute need to get drunk on the night Jim Casy has stepped forward to go to prison in place of Tom; on another occasion, she breaks down with reasonable and sympathetic words the pathetic defenses of the mother whose hungry children have licked the Joad stew pot and gone home to brag and ask questions about it. One of the prime instances of Ma's insight into and compassion for humanity is her exchange with the scared little storekeeper at the Hooper ranch, where her hard-earned dollar is so swiftly absorbed by the exorbitant prices set by the Hooper controls. She has complained with perfect justice about the unfair price on each item of her purchases. When finished shopping and on her way out, she realizes that she still has no sugar, which she has promised the family. She asks the man to trust her for the dime's worth of sugar, which her family is earning at the moment out in the orchards. He cannot: company rule. Not even for a dime, Ma asks? "He looked pleadingly at her. And then his face lost its fear. He took ten cents from his pocket and rang it up in the cash register. 'There,' he said with relief." While he cannot go against the owners, out of fear, he can loan money from his own pocket. As Ma gratefully acknowledges his huge gesture, in relative terms, she makes her point about "humanism" among the poor people in general: I'm learnin' one thing good. Learnin' it all a time, ever' day. If you're in trouble or hurt or need—go to poor people. They're the only ones that'll help—the only ones."

It might be added that the humanistic philosophy we find in *The Grapes of Wrath* has been attributed to the influence of Transcendental philosophy, which stresses man's worth and dignity and potential depth of character, and to Walt Whitman's exuberant belief in the masses and love of one's fellow man.

5. What is meant by the application of the term "agrarian philosophy" to *The Grapes of Wrath*?

ANSWER: Such a philosophy, or thematic strain, which has been linked to what is known as Jeffersonian agrarianism—a form of democracy and a way of life—is everpresent in the novel. That is, Steinbeck elevates farming as a way of life, if it is accompanied by love of, respect for the land. For those who love the land and make it a way of life it takes on symbolic meaning: the people identify with cycles of natural growth and contrastingly, when the soil erodes and is worn out it is at the same time the spirit of the people eroding and wearing out. Ideally, then, the land can be a unifying thing, holding people together and bringing serenity and well-being—and importantly, a sense of human dignity. As it is said at one point in the novel, "I am the land, the land is me." But likewise, if the land is taken away, then a man's identity—and so his self-esteem—is taken away. And if the people are uprooted from the land, then their unity is destroyed, proven in the novel as we witness the disintegration of the Joad family unit. One of the most eloquent pleas for agrarianism comes in an interchapter late in the novel, wherein the spring and the exquisite ripening of all growing things in California is described, then harshly and bitterly contrasted with the wilful destruction of nature's perfections by those who care only to make profit from the orange or the grape—what the author calls the shopkeepers and manufacturers of the land, who have replaced, for profit's sake, the genuine farmers.

6. How can the word *pragmatism* be related to *The Grapes of Wrath*?

ANSWER: Pragmatism is generally considered to be one strand of the philosophy found in the novel. As Steinbeck has himself put it, it is also referred to as "non-teleological" or "is" thinking. It means, in brief, looking at things and trying to evaluate them and act upon them as they really *are* instead of as our various preconceived notions or theories tell us they *should* be (hence the distrust of certain conventional "shoulds" of religion in the novel, and their replacement with the realities of human existence and need, "is" thinking). Jim Casy, Tom Joad, Ma are all in varying degrees examples of pragmatists: they try to look at life as it really is, without invariably applying standards they have learned somewhere, which are often inapplicable (the many questions about what is or is not "sin" which arise and are resolved through personal reasoning and judgment rather than by preconceived rules illustrate the pragmatic direction of thought in the novel); they are also flexible, noticing the details of one situation which make it different—hence its result or resolution different—from another. At one point, for example, Ma declares that she will take things as they come (when Al has asked her if she is scared about the new life); she will do what she has to do when something happens to require her action: this is exactly the rule of action she adheres to throughout. The shouting religionists say it is a sin to get drunk; yet Uncle John, in his life and deeds one of the kindest men known, sometimes finds it absolutely necessary to his psychic survival to go on a drunk—Ma, as we have seen, does not condemn such an action. Or, for another example, Ma carefully adjusts her behavior in the progress of the Joad family disaster toward Pa, by custom and right the head of the family but by necessity a figure more and more regarded as passive: Ma notes each alteration, judges and acts accordingly. Jim Casy has looked around him, and "listened to the people," as he so often says; and from what he has seen and heard he has had to change his notions of what "sin" is: fleshly pleasure, for instance, especially among people who work hard, assume family responsibilities, help their neighbors, suffer sometimes incredible hardships, he no longer can look upon as sinful. All that is a part of life must be taken into the consciousness and dealt with; and life is various.

7. Comment briefly on symbolism in *The Grapes of Wrath.*

ANSWER: The dust, the turtle, and the grapes can be singled out, and two characters in particular—Jim Casy and Rose of Sharon. The dust symbolizes the erosion of the land and the erosion of the lives of the people. As we see at the beginning of the novel, it has pervaded, discolored, choked and ruined everything. The dust of course is synonymous with "deadness." The land is ruined, a way of life is shattered, and the lives are uprooted. More remotely, the dust also stands for the profiteering owners in the background, who are "dead"—i.e., indifferent—to the life and love of the land, and who are the ultimate cause of the change from fruitful to barren soil. The soil, and the people, have been drained and exploited. (We might hazard a guess that the rain at the end of the novel, which is of course excessive, in a way completes the cycle of the dust, which was also excessive. In this way nature has restored a balance and has initiated a new growth cycle. This ties in with other examples of the "rebirth" idea in the ending.)

The turtle, which appears and reappears several times early in the novel, stands for survival, for the driving life force in all mankind. For the turtle ploddingly but steadily advances past every obstacle he encounters: the red ant in his path, the truck which tries to crush him, being imprisoned temporarily in Tom Joad's jacket (and he advances, incidentally, toward the southwest, the direction of the mass migration). Also, the turtle is consistently pictured as ancient, lasting, almost primieval, with its horny head, yellowed toenails, indestructible high dome of a shell, humorous old eyes.

The grapes seem to symbolize both bitterness and plenty (and critics have found Biblical analogies—of both line and situation—for these ambivalent meanings). The title of the novel of course is taken from the song, "Battle Hymn of the Republic," which evokes in image and in feeling an invincible army marching on to victory. And so the Joads and their brothers, in their increasing frustrations and sufferings, are depicted, as an army growing in ever more militant wrath toward an irrevocable demand for restitution and comfort. Grampa, the oldest member of the clan, is the chief spokesman for the grapes as symbols of plenty: all his descriptions of what he is going to do with those luscious grapes out in California vividly suggest largesse, content, freedom.

It has been suggested by critics that the old man (although not so old as Grampa was when he died) who receives sustenance from Rosasharn's breast at the end is a kind of surrogate, or substitute, for

Grampa; and since he is saved from starvation, hence from death, this constitutes a rebirth for the Joad clan (Grampa being the actual "father") and for the whole people figuratively viewed. In line with this view we have Rosasharn as not only a mother giving nourishment but almost a Christ-figure (there is a passage from Canticles referring to Christ as Rose of Sharon, and suggestive of revitalization; the notion of rebirth through Christ's physical body is of course symbolized in the ritual of communion, also, with the "bread" and the "wine" which stand for Christ's body and his blood). The clearest figure of the Christ-like prophet, of course, is the philosophizing Jim Casy. His symbolic function can be verified in a number of ways: the initials of his name, of course; his continual soul-searching, culminating in what he himself refers to as his time in the "wilderness" when in prison; his life as an example of what he comes to believe; the discipleship of Tom Joad toward him, which he hardly solicits but which Tom seeks in the light of his goodness; the substitution of his own body—symbolically, his life—for Tom's to go to prison, to "save" Tom (since for him to go to prison, having broken parole, would be disastrous); and finally, his actual death, which is in essence a martyrdom for the people whom he has lead and comforted and fought for, in which he paraphrases (as he has previously done) the last words of Christ on the cross: "They don' know what they're doin'."

8. Comment briefly on John Steinbeck's style of writing.

ANSWER: In general, Steinbeck seems to alternate between passages of description (frequently included in short separate chapters called interchapters) and narrative consisting of dialogue and action. The descriptions are often filled with exquisitely observed detail, whether of nature or of the material, man-made world or of human nature. There is a great variety of style in *The Grapes of Wrath*, and it has been attributed to a number of influences, of which the following seem valid: the Bible, particularly the Old Testament (this is substantiated by the fact of the many paraphrases and analogues to the Old Testament in the novel); American poets such as Walt Whitman and Carl Sandburg; John Dos Passos and his so-called "newsreel technique" (the chapter treating the used car dealers, for example); the chanting, repetitive technique of the chorus in Greek tragedy; and of course the folk idiom itself, from which the dialogue is realistically reproduced.

F. Scott Fitzgerald's The Great Gatsby

Analysis and Comment

CHAPTER I

Very important to *The Great Gatsby* is the voice of the narrator, Nick Carroway, a young man of good Mid-western family who had "gone east" to New York for a career in stocks and bonds after serving in World War I. Nick actually narrates the entire novel, which is written in "first person": that is, the person of Nick himself. The fact that *The Great Gatsby* is "told" through the mind and personality of Nick Carroway is basic to the structure—and meaning—of the book.

THE MEANING OF NICK: Nick is far more than an "objective" or non-involved spectator; he is deeply involved in the action. For this reason, the reader must understand Nick while Nick comments upon Jay Gatsby and the other characters of the novel. In a very basic sense, *The Great Gatsby* is a novel with a "dual hero"—the story is "about" Nick no less than it is about Jay Gatsby, and both men ultimately emerge as moral symbols: Gatsby as the embodiment of spiritual desolation or waste, and Nick as a hope for moral and spiritual growth.

Ever since his return to the Midwest from the "East" and his experience with Gatsby, Nick has been attempting to define this experience for himself; the flashback method of narrative employed by Fitzgerald is really a means to clarify Nick's own "education." For Nick Carroway is searching for a world in which some sort of moral *code* is possible, a world in which "conduct" and moral values involve something more than the mere gratification of impulse. Nick, indeed, remarks that when he returned to the Midwest he wanted "the world to be in uniform and at a sort of moral attention forever."

What Nick desires is a *foundation* for moral action, for he had found in the East—and in the person and fate of Jay Gatsby—only a "foul dust" of illusion, of "gorgeous" dreams rather than substance, of "gesture" rather than emotions, and promises rather than life. As for Gatsby himself: despite the fact that Nick despises his vulgar ambitions and schemes, there remains a pathetic tragedy about the man—pathetic because all of Gatsby's energy and "extraordinary gift" had been devoted to emptiness; and tragic because the very basis of Gatsby's idealism made its own degradation inevitable.

If Tom is at home in the world of wealth—his by inheritance and right—and uses it like the splendid and mindless animal he is, Jay Gatsby attempts to make of his own wealth a kind of magic key to a dream palace of idealized bliss. This is a basic contrast: the fact that material wealth is, for Tom, what a toy is to a brutal and spoiled child; while for Gatsby material wealth is what a holy "vision" is to a religious mystic. For Gatsby, indeed, material "success" is itself an ideal, and this is the paradox at the heart of Gatsby's "romance." Tom, who uses wealth as he would a woman or a horse, survives through his materialism; Jay Gatsby, who would make of materialism a spiritual ideal, is ultimately destroyed by his own dreams. Nick's very first visit to the Buchanan mansion is highly charged with symbolic description and symbolic action.

SURFACE WITHOUT SUBSTANCE: The description of this scene is important because it introduces several themes or "motifs" of the novel. Basic to *The Great Gatsby* is Fitzgerald's rendering—through Nick—of a world in which appearance is not only mistaken for reality, but actually replaces it, so that the surface of things, or of people, rules out the substance of either. Nick, for example, tells us at the very beginning of the novel, that Gatsby's life had been "an unbroken series of successful gestures"—and a "gesture" is, by definition, the appearance of emotion without the emotion itself.

Throughout the book Fitzgerald reinforces this theme of "promise" that produces nothing, of "confidence" produced by fear (that is, the exact opposite of everything the word "confidence" implies), of "friends" without friendship, of "smiles" that are pasted on faces like labels on boxes of detergent, of "good times" that are manufactured like "caterers' productions," or "romance" without love, "pleasure" without enjoyment, "winning" without victory, "thrills" without consummation, and motion without meaning. Like the muscles of a frog that twitch to mechanical stimuli, all emotions are reduced to reactions, and all reactions are prepackaged according to sentimentalized ideals.

THE FITZGERALD WOMAN: The essential *coldness* of both Daisy and Jordan is another basic theme of *The Great Gatsby* and indeed, Fitzgerald's work as a whole: that is, the view of American women as lovely, graceful, shallow, "romantic" but childishly selfish, childishly destructive, and—perhaps most important—*emotionally frigid* despite (or because of) their "romantic" and sentimental charm—a charm that is a *gesture* of life rather than a quality of living.

Fitzgerald very cleverly sets up a contrast between Tom's immense tension, his violence, and the awkward and bumbling manner in which he states his position—a position which (like all other positions in the novel) is little more than a parody: in this case of both politics and science. Tom's attempts to "talk," indeed, are parodies of intellect just as the "love" between Gatsby and Daisy is a parody of love itself.

DAISY AS ILLUSION: Daisy's voice, like Daisy herself, is an illusion, a "trick" which—as Nick understands—is little more than a device to "exact a contributor emotion"—or rather, the *effect* of emotion.

The as yet vague feeling that the world of the Buchanans represents some sort of moral rottenness, is reinforced by Nick's realization that Jordan (to whom he is physically attracted) is *the* Jordan Baker, a well-known amateur golfer. To Jordan, "victory" is a matter of mere appearance—a role to be played—and we come to understand that for her, as for Daisy, *gesture* has replaced internal no less than external truth, and illusion has itself become reality.

The result, of course, is that for Jordan Baker neither the illusion nor the reality is capable of providing true pride, or true satisfaction; hating the very idea of not "winning," she is nevertheless willing to obtain "victory" by means which make it impossible for the victory to have any meaning. And so Jordan too suffers from a kind of personal, almost spiritual hunger; a creature of illusion, she at once fears reality and yearns for it, and attempts to manipulate illusion in a pathetic and childish effort to secure the satisfaction of reality without its bothersome details.

THE APPEARANCE OF GATSBY: Very important in defining the basic themes of *The Great Gatsby* is the fact that Nick's first view of Gatsby himself is a peculiar one: the latter seems almost to be engaged in some sort of mystic rite, and Nick actually continues on home without speaking to him. For as Nick watches, Gatsby turns toward the Buchanan mansion across the bay—where a single green light gleams on the Buchanan dock. Slowly he stretches out his hands to the green light, in a gesture like that of a worshipper before a shrine. And then he vanishes, leaving Nick alone in the "unquiet darkness." And indeed Gatsby is a worshipper before a shrine: for we discover (as the novel progresses), that his shrine-and-Goddess is Daisy Buchanan; Gatsby is a worshipper of, and a pilgrim to, a vaguely realized image of some "beauty" which in truth is a mere vacuum.

CHAPTER II

Vital to the majestic structure of *The Great Gatsby* is the introductory descriptive passage in chapter II, which contains one of the most memorable images in the fiction of F. Scott Fitzgerald: a landscape of desolation over which presides—like a squat and obscene parody of God—the billboard face of Doctor T.J. Eckleburg.

Critics have made much of this scene, and with good reason. Travelling through the "valley of ashes," Nick is, in a basic sense, travelling through an inferno of the Damned—an inferno which exists side-by-side with the white and unreal dream of Gatsby's Fairy Princess—Daisy herself. And while Jay Gatsby (as the reader later discovers) is incapable of recognizing the "ashes" of what Daisy represents—and indeed, takes the emptiness for substance, and the ashes for some jewel of ultimate value—Nick Carroway sees all too clearly the spiritual desolation of the Buchanan world, and the tragedy so inevitable when Gatsby attempts to find in this world "the stuff that dreams are made of."

Even the colors of this landscape are echoes of Daisy: the "yellow" of Doctor Eckleburg's spectacles, the "yellow" brick of the houses on the street where Tom's mistress—Mrs. Wilson—makes her home. The color yellow, of course, is one of decay—but it is also one of riches as well: the color of sunlight and gold. And just as the gray dust of Doctor Eckleburg's landscape relates to the white "purity" of Daisy, so too does the yellow of Mrs. Wilson's street relate to the sordid and empty reality of Gatsby's dream.

In the Wasteland, it is people like Tom Buchanan and Mrs. Wilson, "consumers" in the most appalling sense of the word, who survive: feeding upon the dreams, the sentiments, or the fears of other human beings, they move like profane machines of flesh, using and breaking, and discarding all that gets in their path.

That George Wilson is to be the instrument of Jay Gatsby's destruction is one of the chief elements of structural symmetry in Fitzgerald's novel. For Wilson has this in common with Gatsby: neither is defined solely in terms of appetite or impulse. And in the world of the Buchanans and Mrs. Wilson, appetite and impulse—the gratification of ego or flesh—become the sole values of existence. Any remnant of idealism, no matter how diluted by a misguided worship of material surface, and any remnant of human love, personal commitment, or moral pride, is—in the Wasteland—a source of weakness rather than strength.

WILSON AND GATSBY: If Wilson is, as Tom says, "dumb" because of his love for and faith in his wife, so too is Jay Gatsby "dumb" in his idealization of Daisy. But while both men are wrong in their ideals, and are ultimately destroyed by the Ideal itself, it is precisely their mistakes which cause them to emerge as individuals finer, and more human, than those who survive them: In a basic sense, then, Jay Gatsby and Gorge Wilson are "balanced" against Daisy, Tom Buchanan, and Myrtle Wilson: on one side the echo—distorted, perhaps, and cheapened, but still vaguely (and helplessly) fine—of the old ideals of devotion and *giving*; on the other side, a process of mere *taking*, of "genteel" or vulgar consumption.

It is indeed the cry of "I want" that defines both Myrtle and Tom—the "I want" of an insatiable infant, picking up and breaking and throwing a way according to the impulses without emotion, and desire without meaning.

That both Gatsby's ideal and Myrtle's impulse are equally futile, is a clue to the essential tragedy of Gatsby's dream—and the "American Dream" itself, which, represented by Gatsby, is a Golden Palace built either on a dung-heap or a mountain of cotton-candy.

Nick, of course, who represents the "Midwestern" aspect of Fitzgerald's vision, is all too aware of the moral vacuum in which he finds himself—a world of verbal gestures, of false "ecstasies" and shallow opinion. The fact that he is not quite sober is actually a rather clever narrative device: since the scene is viewed through his point of view (as narrator), the result is both a heightened sensitivity and blurred impressionism which contributes to the effect, and the ludicrous horror, of this small scene of The Wasteland in action.

The very conversation in Myrtle's apartment serves as ironic definition of the sentimental but essentially destructive and parasitic "romance" of Daisy Buchanan herself—and of the "Fitzgerald Woman" in general. Myrtle of course, like other citizens of the Wasteland, reacts to appearance only; for her too, surface has replaced substance, the "suit" indeed "makes the man"—and one is reminded of the lines by the poet T.S. Eliot: "We are the hollow men, we are the stuffed men, head-pieces filled with straw. . . ." That George Wilson, however, is indeed a "gentleman" or, rather, the emptied shell of one, is what sets up his own tragedy and the tragedy of Jay Gatsby.

A CRESCENDO OF BLOOD: Like all of the "good times" in the world of the moral Wasteland, Myrtle's party ends in disaffection and violence—a *Walpurgisnacht* of sordid and drunken unreality.

CHAPTER III

A deservedly famous section of *The Great Gatsby* is Chapter III, for in this brief account of the Gatsby "parties" Fitzgerald defines not only Jay Gatsby as an individual, but the perverted idealism and pathetic optimism of "the American Dream" itself. It is with this chapter too that the imagery of "enchantment" and unreality so basic to the novel is clarified: the theme of illusion and in evitable failure—inevitable because any illusion taken for reality contains the seeds of its own destruction.

THE ENCHANTED PALACE: Crates of oranges and lemons arrive before the weekend, and crates of pulpless halves—the assorted garbage of Gatsby's "productions"—leave after each weekend is over; and there is something almost obscenely ludicrous in the very juxtaposition of crates filled with fruit and cars filled with people—both consumed and discharged like the raw material and end product of some gigantic, meaningless digestive tract.

Nothing, somehow, is fixed to any sort of reality; there is laughter without amusement, "enthusiasm" between strangers, a disembodied and baroque celebration of some nameless holiday that had never occurred—and never will. And the guests themselves (most of whom Gatsby had never seen) act as though they were in "an amusement park"—a Coney Island for adults. The pathos, of course, is that for these adults—as for Gatsby—the "Coney Island" represents the only "high" life they know; it is indeed (as Nick remarks) a "simplicity of heart" and vague expectation, or hope, that is always waiting for some sort of ecstatic fulfillment—and always disappointed when the caterers depart, and all the golden coaches become once again the sordid pumpkins of reality.

TOURING THE "CATERER'S PRODUCTION": When the gentleman calls Gatsby "a regular Belasco" (referring to a famous theatrical producer) the result is a definition of the entire Gatsby world: a theatricalism calculated solely for *effect*, a gigantic and somehow absurd (and perhaps touching in its absurdity) *gesture* of "the good life." It is all an elaborate "backdrop," a piece of stage-machinery against which Jay Gatsby plays out the tragicomic masquerade of his own dreams.

THE GATSBY SMILE: Nick's description of Gatsby at this point is very important. For one thing, it reinforces our awareness of Gatsby as not only a "producer" of elaborate and meaningless theatrical effects, but as being, in his own person, no less an "effect" than his pseudo-gothic mansion or unused books. Gatsby, in short, has in a basic sense "created" his own identity from personal romanticism based on socially prepackaged labels; so completely does he carry out the ritualistic surface of the role he has created for himself, that the role ultimately replaces the self, and there is nothing left of Gatsby at all but the "act" of what he wishes to become.

The Gatsby smile, one should note, "builds" and grows more radiant, more intense, as though it were leading to a climax . . . that quite simply never occurs. And this too is a basic quality of the Gatsby dream, the Gatsby romanticism (and the romanticism of the American dream itself). Always there is *process* without consummation, the gradual inflation of a huge, glowing, balloon of hope, or expectation, or ecstasy, until the balloon itself is suddenly punctured for one reason or another, and flops down to earth. And then there is nothing to do but wait for another balloon—if one has any breath left, or if the supply of ballons has not been exhausted.

GATSBY'S ISOLATION: Amid all the "Coney Island" celebration, indeed, Gatsby is a remote and almost "pure"—or at least, self-contained figure; and once again we have the clear impression that for Jay Gatsby the baroque "good times" he makes available for others is little more than a means to an end—an end involving some sort of Ideal that transcends, in a urgent yet undefined manner, the "good times" themselves.

JORDAN AND NICK: Sensing the core of honesty and moral firmness in Nick (who himself represents the old traditions of "conduct" and ethical responsibility, just as Gatsby represents a new world of moral expediency and false dreams), Jordan realizes that it is only with a man like Nick that she would be able to "go her own way." Nick, indeed, would always be there to pick up the pieces of whatever mess Jordan has made.

For Jordan Baker, in short, her "love" for Nick is simply one more calculation among many. Like Daisy and Tom Buchanan, she neither desires nor needs to be "careful" of anything or anyone; if the Buchanans rely on their money as a means of achieving what might be called freedom of *impulse*, Jordan understands that with a man like Nick Carroway she would achieve the same privilege. And Nick, infatuated with Jordan's beauty and charm, almost succumbs. That he ultimately does not succumb, is one of the essential differences between his nature and that of Jay Gatsby; drawing on the Mid-western traditions which both bind and protect him, Nick has the basic "soundness" which enables him to "go back home." For Nick Carroway is only an observer of the world of infernal enchantment. He has not become one of its inhabitants, and for this reason (protected by the bulwark of his own moral traditions) he can finally escape from the arms of even the most charming demon of the moral Inferno itself.

CHAPTER IV

GATSBY'S "NONMATERIAL MATERIALISM": When Gatsby calls for Nick one morning in his "gorgeous" car, one notes that the automobile has a very special meaning indeed. Like all of Gatsby's possessions, it is far more than a material object; it is a "sign" of the pathetic mystique which serves Gatsby—the representative of "The American Dream"—as he worships a kind of Ultimate Value that far transcends any material object at all. Gatsby's attitude toward material objects, again, differs sharply from the fleshly materialism of a man like Tom Buchanan; for Gatsby the material world is somehow elevated to a spiritual dimension, and the acquisition of material objects becomes almost a religious ritual. This is precisely what sets up Gatsby's ultimate doom: the fact that his "materialism" is itself a romantic "faith" in a kind of vaguely glowing perfection which the material world can never offer.

For Jay Gatsby, in short, "materialism" is itself an ideal, a romantic dream of unnamed spiritual ecstasy, a perpetual expectation which somehow turns to ashes when the "object" (whether a car, a mansion, or a woman) is actually achieved. In this respect he resembles another famous character of American fiction written during the twenties: the celebrated Babbitt of Sinclair Lewis' novel. Both Babbitt and Gatsby are caught up in a self-destructive paradox: they attempt to make spiritual affirmations of material *things*, and in the process find themselves with neither the spiritual dimension nor the values of materialism itself. Just as Babbitt makes of his office a "business cathedral" (and so degrades one and is disaffected with the other), so Jay Gatsby attempts to make of his cars, and his mansion, and his "silk shirts," and his dream of Daisy Buchanan, an act of worship. It is this "non-material materialism" which sets up Gatsby's ultimate destruction.

The car itself is described with an interesting series of adjectives—adjectives which communicate a sense not only of opulence, but of combined brittleness and softness, almost of decay. And Gatsby himself is emotionally infected with a perpetual restlessness, a kind of insistent disaffection or impatience. Whatever wealth has brought to Jay Gatsby, one thing is clear: it has brought him neither peace nor any real pleasure.

ILLUSION INTO REALITY: GATSBY'S SELF-HYPNOSIS: Gatsby's "autobiography" is memorable for something far more important than its elaborate falsehood. The significance of his manufactured "identity" is not simply that it is untrue, but rather that Gatsby has been attempting—with all the means at his disposal—to convince himself that what he knows to be false is actually true. He is, in short, involved in a sort of self-hypnosis; given the "right" stage-props, the right surface and facade, it is indeed possible for Gatsby to "double-think" himself into a kind of perverted "faith" in an *ideal* Jay Gatsby. That this ideal never in fact existed makes no difference; armed with stage-props and rituals, Gatsby is indeed (as Nick later remarks) trying to "fulfill his Platonic conception of himself."

So completely has Gatsby surrounded himself with the *appearance* of his own ideal, that he almost believes in it himself. Left to his own resources, however, Gatsby cannot complete the magical metamorphosis; the "conjurer's trick" he is attempting requires something more than his own faith in the "trick" itself. What it requires is the faith of *others*; not until he arranges the illusion so that it becomes reality in the minds of other human beings, can Gatsby rest secure in his own fantastic re-creation of life. Once other people "believe" him, the magic can indeed turn lead into gold—but first he requires that the image he has created be reflected from other heads.

Gatsby, in short, lives in a world of mirrors, a world in which illusion can become reality only if the transformation is *publicly* acclaimed; reality, indeed, thus becomes *external* rather than internal, and "anything goes"—anything is "possible" if private desire can be manipulated into public assent.

THE FRAGILE "ENCHANTMENT": The problem, of course, is that false identities do depend essentially on externals, and the result is personal vacuum. Combined with Gatsby's optimistic "faith" that every desire can be turned into reality with the right stage-props, with the right *gestures* or "productions," there remains the nagging fear, the inevitable panic resulting from the fact that the "enchantment" itself can last only so long as the external appearance remains intact. Given any change in external circumstances; given any sudden eruption of crisis, or intrusion of real emotion, and the entire edifice must collapse; the "enchantment" fades away like cheap neon light, and the result is . . . nothing at all.

There is no room, in an Enchanted Palace, for the sordid demands and necessary commitments of reality, and it is for this reason that Gatsby's protection of Daisy at the end of the novel represents something far more profound than chivalry; in protecting his Ideal, he is literally fighting for his own survival. For Jay Gatsby has so "enchanted" his own vision that without the enchantment he quite simply does not exist. Defined by externals, there is nothing beneath the surface; without his "faith" in material acquisition—the stage props—as a means of securing his enchanted ideal, his glowing "promise," there is nothing but the Valley of Ashes, with the yellow eyes of Doctor Eckleburg peering over a desolated landscape from which all the fairy girls and golden hosts have long since fled.

That Gatsby does have the Ideal, however, at once defines his non-reality and somehow redeems it as well, for it is by means of the Ideal that Gatsby transcends his own materialism—unlike the merely gross flesh of a Tom Buchanan. And it is for this reason that Nick, despite the fact that he finds Gatsby absurd and even offensive, nevertheless remembers the "purity" of Gatsby himself; the peculiar innocence and childlike hope, the sense of wonder that Gatsby radiates even in his complete inability to distinguish between truth and falsehood, between the real and unreal.

GATSBY AND DAISY: A creature of "whiteness" indeed, Daisy is the "fairy girl" of Gatsby's dreams in more ways than one—and her essential *lack* of emotion provides an important link in the chain of perverted "Ideals," pathetically futile gestures, and sordid circumstances that finally destroy Gatsby and his dreams. Gatsby's relationship with Daisy in this matter, it must be emphasized, resembles Fitzgerald's own relationship with his "fairy girl" of real life: Zelda, who was to be both his wife and his despair, and whose love he had to "earn" with "success." As we have already noted in our introduction to *The Great Gatsby*, Fitzgerald knew all too well the power exerted by wealth or the appearance of "success" even on the hearts of sweet young girls and the "romance" of love; the ironic relationship between money, now matter how achieved, and the Ideal of Beauty is a basic theme of his work and a basic comment on American culture as Fitzgerald saw it.

CHAPTER V

Once Nick understands the Gatsby-Daisy relationship, he (and the reader) also understands that Gatsby's entire "production" is aimed at the winning of an ideal, and there is a marked increase in *urgency* when Nick discovers the entire area of West Egg ablaze one evening with "unreal" light. It is Gatsby's mansion, where the lights have been turned on in every room. This is a very effective image, an example of the narrative economy of Fitzgerald at his best. For the blaze of "unreal" light communicates both the intensity of Gatsby's emotion, and the illusion which is the basis for the emotion itself. Some sort of climax is obviously in the offing—and if this climax turns into an absurdity, into an anticlimax of pathetic tragedy (as indeed it will), the cause is to be found in the nature of Gatsby's dream—a dream which (as we have so often remarked) contains the inevitability of its own destruction.

GATSBY'S GRATITUDE: The *resources* of Gatsby himself are so completely without a standard of either moral code or social perception, that his attempt to express himself becomes little more than a vulgarity. For in sincerely wanting to "thank" Nick, he offers to cut him in on a lucrative stock deal.

Under the circumstances, however, Nick has no choice but to refuse Gatsby's offer—for the offer itself would turn an act of friendship into a "business deal," and so become an act of degradation. That Nick perceives this, and Gatsby does not, defines the gulf separating a world in which all of human emotion—love or friendship, or gratitude—is little more than "business" and material acquisition, from a world (Nick's world of the Midwest) where there are still areas of human life which are simply not to be bought or sold.

The point to remember is that Gatsby does not mean to be sordid or insulting; he is using the only means at his disposal—the only "magic" he has at his command: material acquisition. It is, indeed, the same "magic" with which he hopes to achieve his Ideal of Beauty: Daisy Buchanan.

"GRAND PASSION" AND LOW COMEDY: Nick tries to comfort him, and finally becomes impatient: "You're acting like a little boy," he says to Jay Gatsby, the Prince of the Golden Palace, and this single remark defines much of Gatsby's peculiar charm—and pathos. For Gatsby, despite (or because of) his wealth, and his dreams, is indeed a "little boy"—a worshipper of toys which he takes to be signs of Divinity. For boy-men like Jay Gatsby, the trivial must be always elevated to the Cosmically Significant, and it is precisely this quality of "boyish" idealization demonstrated by Gatsby, that other American writers (Ernest Hemingway, for example) came to see as the unique "charm"—and maddening weakness—of so many of their countrymen.

THE PALACE OF ENCHANTMENT: And how does Gatsby react to the fact that he has at last captured his Butterfly Queen with a "net of gold"? He simply moves like a man sleepwalking through a dream that has suddenly become flesh. His very possessions, accumulated with such effort, suddenly become almost "unreal" in Daisy's presence; and indeed they are important only as they succeed or fail to succeed in giving her delight.

It is important to note, however, that the very realization of Gatsby's dream has in some way "spoiled" the dream itself; at this moment which he had idealized for so long, when his emotion is at "an inconceivable pitch of intensity," Gatsby somehow is beginning to feel a loss—a loss of something he cannot name or identify. "He was running down like an overwound clock," Nick observes—and the image, with all its absurd deflation, is indeed a description of Gatsby's ultimate fate.

GATSBY'S MAGIC SHIRTS: Gatsby's silk shirts as many critics have noted, are actually far more important than any mere garment ever spun by machine or man. For these shirts, to Jay Gatsby (like his car or his mansion), are important not in themselves, but for what they represent—and what they represent is the shrine of "success" and Ideal value made possible by success itself. Gatsby does not merely "wear" these shirts; he *worships* them, or uses them as *sacred objects* in a ritual whose meaning is, paradoxically enough, spiritual rather than materialistic.

To Tom Buchanan, for example, a shirt, even a silk shirt, would be—quite simply—a shirt. For Jay Gatsby the material object transcends itself; it becomes a mystic sign and spiritual endowment. This is what Daisy senses in this memorable scene—for as Gatsby continues to pile the rainbow of silk cloth higher and higher, Daisy literally collapses in a kind of ecstatic moaning; bending her head into the shirts, she begins to cry "stormily," declaring their beauty with sobs of mingled delight and sadness: like a music lover rhapsodizing over a violin solo by Bach.

The *meaning* of Gatsby's shirts, in other words, despite the peculiar absurdity of the entire scene, is that of a man who brings to his Dream a preoccupation with materialism which in some way has been transformed into enchantment; hence the relevance of the dedication on the flyleaf of *The Great Gatsby*, the bit of verse from the work of Thomas Park D'Invilliers:

Then wear the gold hat, if that will move her;
If you can bounce high, bounce for her too,
Till she cry "Lover, gold-hatted, high-bouncing lover,
I must have you!"

GATSBY'S "HYMN": After what might be called the "ecstasy of the shirts," however, Gatsby's mood of exultation somehow darkens and returns to a lower pitch. For having shown Daisy his palace, having reached her at last—knowing that she will be his—there must inevitably be a loss of enchantment itself. Daisy's fascination for Gatsby, after all, had rested in large part upon her very unavailability; made available once again, turned from an Ultimate Cause to simply another possession, Daisy must suffer a considerable loss in status. Gatsby senses this, a "loss" to which Nick refers when, describing Gatsby's appearance, he remarks that "his count of enchanted objects had diminished by one."

"Enchanted objects," after all, by definition disappear when touched; and this is precisely the measure of Gatsby's success—and his loss.

CHAPTER VI

GATSBY'S IDENTITY—AND THE AMERICAN DREAM: At this point Nick's analysis of the Gatsby character provides a basic insight not only into the character of the namesake of the novel, but into "The American Dream" of enchanted "success." For the dream of the 17-year-old James Gatz—the vision of "a vast, vulgar, meretricious beauty" that in some way was Divine as well as merely materialistic, is precisely the dream of Jay Gatsby as a man.

The pathos, of course, is that the fevered dreams and hope for some iridescent and glowing "glory" that one might expect from a 17-year-old drifter possessed of a keen imagination, is precisely the dream of the adult man as well. The result is a kind of nursery turned into a cathedral; a world in which the fairy-stories of adolescence (themselves based on pulp fiction) become the sole motivation of manhood, and are given an almost spiritual sanctification because they are the only Holy Cause which James Gatz—and the world which shaped him—can offer to human aspiration.

From his adolescence, in short, Gatz-Gatsby had been pursuing the Holy Glow of some vaguely imagined "success," an "identity" gleaming like a mirage just over the horizon of tomorrow. The result is both complete romanticism and complete lack of any real identity at all; obsessed (as Nick remarks) with "a promise that the rock of the world was founded securely on a fairy's wing" and viewing his own identity through fashion-magazine spectacles, Jay Gatsby—the Prince of Enchantment—indeed "sprang from his Platonic conception of himself."

It is, however, a "Platonic Idealism" whose only means of self-realization is material acquisition at any cost; it is an identity founded on facade, and a "self" which depends for its very existence upon illusion. This is the core of the Gatsby paradox, and the paradox of The American Dream itself: a unique *kind* of materialism that in a basic sense never "grows up," that is elevated into a perpetual, adolescent, romantic, and spiritual value. And because Gatsby's materialism—like American materialism—is all of these things, the result must be destructive; when material goals are reduced (or elevated) to spiritual cotton candy, they dissolve at the touch.

The smile itself, of course, is still another symbol of the vacuum beneath the surface of Gatsby's appearance. Representing not a state of emotion but a state of ambition, the "smile" is an instrument to be deliberately manipulated; it is a social weapon rather than a personal tribute, and as such is no more meaningful than are the bright, "perky" and vacuous "smiles" which so often infest college campuses on sorority-pledge day.

GATSBY'S APPRENTICESHIP: Cody, however, was taken in by the Gatsby smile—for he was himself a creature of emptiness, an opportunist whose wealth was based on certain "lucky" transactions in the mine-fields of Montana.

But Gatsby was, in some basic way, made of finer stuff than his "mentor"; a romanticist even as a youth, he had remained apart from the worst dissipation, and indeed had at this time acquired a dislike for liquor which was to last all his life.

THE BUCHANANS AT GATSBY'S PARTY: The guests at the party contribute to the effect we have already discussed: a kind of kaleidoscope of insubstantial "fun" and meaningless charm, together with a hint—and perhaps more than a hint—of nightmare or vacuum beneath all the colored lights and "perfect" moon.

Fitzgerald, all through this scene, introduces images which serve to reinforce the lack of substance in the Gatsby-Daisy relationship, and so delicately does he combine fragile "beauty" with absurd pomp, that the result is an indirect definition—or redefinition—of character.

IMAGERY OF GESTURE: For Daisy Buchanan, indeed, emotion itself is a matter of "gesture," and anything too *real* is likely to prove "offensive" in more ways than one.

THE BASIS OF THE GATSBY-DAISY "LOVE": Daisy, in short, is "in love" less with Jay Gatsby the man, than with Jay Gatsby the "Knight Errant"; one might say that she loves *the gesture which Gatsby has made*, the "romance" of unrequited love and noble devotion. This attitude, of course, is itself a paradox, for in loving the *gesture* of Gatsby, Daisy must—inevitably—find the romance of the gesture dissolving if she ever gives herself to him in the flesh. That flesh is precisely what she does *not* want, is a basic irony of the book.

Gatsby himself, furthermore has no less difficulty in "loving" Daisy as a woman. So completely has she been for him an ideal, a Holy Cause, that to accept her for a woman with a real life and a real past—a past complete with a husband and a child—is no longer possible. In a basic sense, Gatsby has not only idealized reality, but has replaced reality with the Ideal.

Gatsby's insistence that one can indeed "repeat the past" is an important clue to his essential adolescence—an adolescence which he has never outgrown. For Gatsby no less than for Myrtle Wilson or Tom Buchanan it is "I want" that must serve as a theme for living; the difference between them is that what Gatsby "wants" is based on illusion, on ideal, while Buchanan or Myrtle recognizes no ideal at all.

Gatsby, at any rate, does not "want" Daisy *as she exists*; he wants his Golden Girl, his Golden Dream of five years before. That this Dream has actually lived with another man for five years, and—even more intolerable—had actually borne a child by him—has no part in his vision. One cannot, after all, imagine a "dream girl" in a state of pregnancy. Gatsby, again , has devoted all his "magic" to an image which no longer exists; he is indeed watching over "nothing"—and this defines both the purity of his romanticism, and the pathos of his innocence.

CHAPTER VII

DAISY'S LITTLE GIRL: The little girl's appearance is itself a finely wrought irony. For Daisy's relationship to her child is hardly that of a mother to a daughter; the role of Pammy in Daisy's life is all too obviously that of a "darling" little toy—a toy to be "played with" and removed by the hired help when its presence is no longer convenient. "You dream, you" cries Daisy to the little girl, and for Daisy Buchanan her child is indeed a "dream"—a mere shape or decorative object in her life, the echo rather than substance of emotion.

Daisy's emotions, of course, are completely superficial; indeed, her very praise of Gatsby (that he looks like a man in an advertisement!) defines the nature of her "emotion"—or rather, her infatuation with the entire *gesture* of "having" a love affair.

A VOICE FULL OF MONEY: Daisy, of course, has been rather indiscreet; in the world of impulse, however, caution is itself vulgar, and Daisy is simply too much of a child to control her delight in her enchanting new plaything: Jay Gatsby himself.

The voice of Daisy Buchanan, says Gatsby in one of the most important sentences of the novel, is a voice "full of money." And we immediately perceive the truth of this comment—the key to all the "magic" of Daisy Buchanan.

It is all a fairy story, a parody of some child's tale of enchantment grown more ruthless—and more dangerous—because of the absurd misdirection of power which resides in wealth itself. And if Daisy Buchanan is "the king's daughter" of some real-life myth, Gatsby is for Daisy the Enchanted Prince of some real-life epic; when crisis intrudes, and demonstrates all too clearly that the Princess is a creature of flesh, and that the Prince is neither royal nor enchanted, all the dreams must—inevitably—go smash.

TWO CUCKOLDS: Where Wilson is deeply hurt, however, almost physically ill because of his wife's betrayal, Tom Buchanan is merely angry, furious, like an overgrown infant deprived of "his" property. This is a vital difference between the two men, and is a basic reason why Tom will ultimately survive.

Wilson's "weakness" is precisely the fact that he loves his wife too deeply; for Tom Buchanan, on the other hand, "love" is itself a matter of ego and appetite, and if he is furious that Gatsby has engaged the affections of his wife, he is no less angry that Wilson is planning to deprive him of a mistress. It is men like Wilson and Gatsby—men defined by emotion or Ideals—who are ultimately destroyed; in the Wasteland of modern America, it is the flesh-ridden "realists" like Tom Buchanan who accommodate—and survive.

THE RIVALS: This is not to say, however, that Tom does not care for Daisy—or, for that matter, for Myrtle Wilson. It is, rather, that his love is on a different level; incapable of loving (or hating) an *Ideal*, his very emotions are in a basic sense *pragmatic*: that is, *realistic*. Unlike Gatsby, who tries to recreate the world according to a dream, and unlike George Wilson, who is ruled by his emotions, Tom is rich enough, and "simple minded" enough—to hold only those ideals which are useful to his own position in life, and to ruthlessly eliminate any emotion which becomes a threat rather than a pleasure.

THE SOURCE OF GATSBY'S "GOLD": The pathos is that while Tom has the "goods" on Gatsby, he has not really described him at all—for everything that Gatsby did, he did for the sake of his Golden Girl, his Dream of Purity and Enchantment: Daisy herself.

THE END OF A DREAM: The paradox is one which lies at the very heart of American culture: in attempting to achieve a Golden Dream of Idealistic Beauty through the only means available to him, Gatsby represents a world in which means have become totally subordinate to ends, where "success" is the only moral reality, and where the end itself—the Dream—is by this very fact reduced to a parody of any "purpose" whatsoever.

That Gatsby's Dream is itself a pathetic illusion, is dramatized by the reaction of Daisy Buchanan—who suddenly finds that her Fabled Lover, her long lost Prince Charming, far from being "above" the sordid reality of the world, has spun his "enchantment" from the most sordid and most vulgar element of the reality itself. And so Daisy Buchanan "withdraws" from Gatsby, withdraws from the sudden smash of her romantic infatuation like a sorority girl in white lace avoiding a puddle of grease. Everything is over; everything, indeed, is "dead."

THE DEATH OF MYRTLE: The scene is a vitally important one, for two reasons: first, it demonstrates that for all of Daisy's love of "romance" she is actually far closer to the brutal selfishness of Tom Buchanan—the selfishness and carelessness of the very rich than she is to the Idealism of Jay Gatsby.

The second point of major significance in the scene is the fact that while Daisy and Tom draw closer together—while they "conspire" to destroy Gatsby himself—Jay Gatsby remains under the fatal illusion that Daisy is still "his" girl, his Fairy Princess. And this illusion—as foolish as it is, and as pathetic as it is—once again defines the paradox of Jay Gatsby both as a man and as symbol. For it is Gatsby the bootlegger, the man who has literally sacrificed his entire life to the pursuit of an *ideal*, and who has made of material acquisition a shrine for the worship of that ideal, who is ultimately the one who *gives* rather than takes.

All of Gatsby's vulgarity, in other words, all of his "materialism" and single-minded pursuit of wealth, has been, in a very basic sense, founded upon his willingness to *sacrifice* himself for that in which he believes: the Ideal Beauty to be achieved through work, and effort, and purity of *devotion*. It is Tom Buchanan and Daisy who, completely without ideals or any spiritual dimension, simply "retreat into their money" at any eruption of crisis.

Such is the nature of Gatsby's purity, that the "something" in him which Nick perceives as spiritual rather than material, leads him to self-sacrifice rather than to self-protection; all that he has done—all the evil that he has perpetuated—has been done not for himself, but for others—for the sanctification of his Dream. And this, of course, is a paradox not only of Gatsby, but—

as we have indicated, what sociologists and critics have termed "The American Dream"—a kind of materialism devoted to spiritual values.

A WASTE OF POWER: That Gatsby's spiritual value—his Ideal Cause—is the amoral sentiment and the random impulse of Daisy Buchanan, is itself the deepest horror of his situation. And this situation, again, is grounded not in "evil," but rather is *wasted goodness*: the goodness of devotion, in almost religious terms, to a "Goddess" made of tinfoil and rotten gumdrops. This theme of *waste*—a waste of devotion, a waste of human resources, a waste of ambition—is basic to *The Great Gatsby* as a novel. It is also a basic theme of the work of Fitzgerald and of other American writers as well. From Henry James to John Steinbeck, from Mark Twain to Sinclair Lewis, American writers have been obsessed with the image of America as a *power for good* somehow diverted into an *instrument of the false and the trivial.*

Just so does Jay Gatsby, the pathetic, the vulgar, and yet—in some way—noble "knight errant," mobilize his own resources to "protect" his ideal: Daisy Buchanan. And it is for this reason that Nick Carroway remarks, while Gatsby "watches" over the Buchanan house (where, unknown to him, Daisy and her husband are "conspiring" for his destruction), that Gatsby is watching over "nothing"—a nothingness which is indeed the essence of the dream of Jay Gatsby, and perhaps the dream of American "Success" as well.

CHAPTER VIII

FLASHBACK TO A HOLY GRAIL: But something unexpected happened: instead of taking Daisy and forgetting her, he had found that she became, for him, a total definition of value—self-value no less than ego-value. He had begun to love Daisy like a man "committed . . . to the following of a grail": and from that moment Jay Gatsby conceived of the mysterious world of wealth as itself a magical *ideal* of perfection and purity.

NICK'S JUDGMENT OF GATSBY: As Nick says good-bye to Gatsby, he senses the core of idealism at the heart of his vulgar ostentation and indeed remarks on the "incorruptible dream" shaping the nature of Gatsby's material corruption.

In the final analysis it is Jay Gatsby who tried to keep some sort of spiritual value alive in the moral "ashheap" ruled by the Buchanans.

THE DEATH OF GATSBY: Gatsby's death, like his life, is the product of an illusion; Wilson's death, like his life, is the product of misplaced faith and a love which—in the Wasteland—can achieve no greater dignity than hysteria.

CHAPTER IX

FINAL EULOGY: The last chapter of *The Great Gatsby* actually serves as an epilogue, a final comment on the futility and emptiness of all that James Gatz—the dreaming Minnesota adolescent—had "succeeded" in accomplishing.

It is Gatsby's father, however—a bedraggled little man from a little town in Minnesota—who provides the final note of pathos. In New York for Gatsby's funeral, Henry C. Gatz sadly tells Nick that his son could have been "a great man." And indeed he could—given a different *purpose* to his life, or rather, given a world where dreams need not be confused with reality, and where material acquisition and material display need not be elevated into some sort of pseudo-spiritual "happiness."

GATSBY AS SYMBOL: For the central truth about Jay Gatsby was that he was a knight-errant devoting himself to a pilgrimage in which the only "Jerusalem" is the moral and spiritual vacuum represented by Daisy Buchanan; he was, indeed, a Sir Lancelot of epic resources, faced with a world in which the Holy Grail had been reduced to a blinking neon light.

THE "AMERICAN DREAM" WASTED: Self-protection, like self-indulgence, is the only absolute commandment which the Buchanans, kings and inhabitants of the Wasteland, can possibly recognize. "Careless" with the power that comes with wealth; completely self-centered with the total egotism of moral primitives, people like Daisy and Tom "smashed things up . . . and let other people clean up the mess they had made."

RETREAT TO THE PAST: Ultimately, it is the "capacity for wonder" and devotion to an ideal which had made America great; and it is the loss of this "wonder," and the degradation of the ideal, which had turned the "green land" to the ashheaps of Doctor Eckleburg. Nick understands all too well that the story of Jay Gatsby represents far more than the fate of a poor boy who had tried to get enough money to marry his "true love." For the story of Gatsby is also the story of wonder, and power, and devotion, turned into instruments of a machine of false values, a machine which first spawns and then eats its own children, and exists for no other purpose than its own digestion.

Such is the world which had destroyed "Jay Gatsby"—a senseless arrangement of vulgar appetites in which motion has replaced direction, impulse has replaced moral choice, and "love" has become little more than a process of mutual cannibalism. And the tragedy of the book is that Nick's return to the Midwest is, in a profound sense, less a hope for America's future, than a retreat into America's past.

Character Analyses

NICK CARROWAY: The narrator of the novel, Nick, represents the traditional *moral codes* of America. Himself from the Midwest (which contrasts to the East of Long Island and the world of the Buchanans), Nick is attracted by the beauty, the wealth, and the sophistication of "The Wasteland"—but comes to understand the essential emptiness, the gaudy display of "nothingness" which characterizes the Wasteland itself. As the critic Arthur Mizener remarks, the novel is, in a basic sense, Nick's story as well as Gatsby's, for it is Nick who at last achieves a "gradual penetration of the charm and grace of Tom and Daisy's world. What he penetrates to is corruption, grossness, and cowardice."

It is Nick too who perceives the essential pathos of Jay Gatsby, the romantic idealism which shapes his very materialism, and so sets him off sharply from the gross and fleshly Tom Buchanan. Nick, indeed, who says that he wishes the world "to stand at moral attention forever," understands that Gatsby is motivated not by selfishness, but rather by devotion—devotion to an ideal rendered false by the appetites and moral vacuum of the Wasteland. Alone among all of Gatsby's "friends" (with the exception of the character called "Owl-Eyes") to pay a final tribute to the pathetic bootlegger-Idealist, Nick sees Gatsby as being a symbol of the American Dream gone sour, an "innocent" destroyed by a corrupt world. And when Nick leaves the East, he does so with the hope of finding some remnant of a moral and personal reality "back home."

JAY GATSBY: The "subject" of the novel, Jay Gatsby is a dramatic symbol of the Idealism which makes of materialism itself a type of romantic expectation—a uniquely American "non-material materialism." Gatsby, indeed, is a kind of pathetic "Don Quixote" tilting at non-existent windmills and counting his silk shirts as though they were rosaries; attempting to achieve a glow of vague spiritual "enchantment" through material acquisition, Gatsby represents the paradox—and the pathos—of spiritual values reduced to vulgarity and futility in the moral Wasteland.

The essential tragedy of Gatsby is, in a profound sense, the tragedy of American Idealism itself: the waste of enormous energies, even self-sacrifice, to self-illusion and (as Nick remarks) the service of a "vast, vulgar meretricious beauty." Gatsby, furthermore, has no *means* to communicate his Idealism, or fulfill it, aside from the false standards of the Buchanan world itself.

Perhaps the chief element in Gatsby's inevitable destruction is the fact that his romanticism, his misplaced "faith" in material success (as a kind of spiritual rite and proof of identity), is so intense, that he ultimately believes that he can indeed recreate reality according to his heart's desire. A "magician" in a world of sordid appetite and cowardice, Gatsby's "dream" is—by the conditions of its own existence—doomed to failure. For he cannot "regain" Daisy simply because he pursues her not really as a woman, but as an Ideal. And as an Ideal, Daisy Buchanan—and all she represents—must vanish like spiritual cotton candy at the first eruption of crisis.

TOM BUCHANAN: The husband of Daisy and lover of the gross and fleshly Myrtle Wilson, Tom is both ruler and representative of the moral Wasteland which has replaced American Idealism. Tom is a creature of brute appetite and direct "action" based on self-preservation and self-interest rather than any idealism whatsoever. He is "strong" because in the moral Wasteland idealism itself is a source of weakness rather than strength; devoted to nothing but the impulses of his own flesh and the demands of his own ego, completely without any concept of either a moral code or personal loyalty.

For Tom and Daisy Buchanan there is no moral responsibility whatsoever; they "retreat into their money" at any crisis, and "leave other people to clean up the mess."

DAISY BUCHANAN: Gatsby's "Golden Girl," the dream and "Cause" of his wasted idealism, Daisy falls into a familiar pattern of Fitzgerald women. These women are lovely, delicate, and "romantic"—but essentially parasitic, and emotionally frigid despite (or because of) their sentimentality. Critics, indeed, have noted that Fitzgerald's attitude toward women is very ambivalent; perhaps because of his traumatic experience with Zelda, he combined an extremely romantic "worship" of them (much like Gatsby's) with an equally extreme distrust of them—a distrust which approaches actual fear.

Arthur Mizener, for example, notes that Fitzgerald "never loved merely the particular woman; what he loved was her embodiment for him of all the splendid possibilities of life he could, in his romantic hopefulness, imagine." On the other hand, a critic like Charles E. Shain notes the procession of "mercenary" and "fatally irresponsible" women in Fitzgerald's work—women who are "as dangerous to men as classical sorceresses." So too William Goldhurst notes that Fitzgerald imaged the American woman as "physically attractive," but having a "destructive influence on the man with whom she is associated."

Daisy Buchanan, motivated by weakness rather than passion, and by sentiment rather than emotion, is simply impelled by any force ready to determine her direction, and to protect her from either emotional discomfort or emotional commitment. The basic fact of Daisy is her *lack of substance*, and *The Great Gatsby* is filled with images which reinforce this *emptiness*, images which follow Daisy Buchanan through Fitzgerald's pages like the gossamer cloth "floating" around her face. Loyal only to sentiment and the *gesture* of love, she deserts Gatsby at the eruption of crisis like a sorority girl in white lace avoiding a puddle of grease.

JORDAN BAKER: Jordan is no less a creature of the moral Wasteland than is Daisy or Tom Buchanan. A "lovely" girl who (like Daisy) dresses in "white" and always seems to be "cool," Jordan is an opportunist in her own way. Nick is attracted to her, but ultimately breaks with her because he sees in Jordan that same ability for irresponsible exploitation that he sees in Daisy and Tom.

MYRTLE WILSON: Myrtle is one of the "users" of the Wasteland—just as her husband is one of the used. A creature of impulse (she met

Tom on a train and just "had" to have him), she is blood-rich and full, loud and sentimental—with ludicrous mannerisms of borrowed "refinement." Myrtle too is a kind of parasite on the misplaced idealism of George Wilson, who appears and reappears in the novel like a man being slowly eaten by a vampire. It is symbolically fitting that Myrtle Wilson dies as she had lived: violently, with a gush of blood, killed by a car driven by Daisy Buchanan.

GEORGE WILSON: Myrtle's husband, a hapless shadow of what once had been a handsome man, George—like Gatsby himself—is destroyed by the fact that he holds to ideals of honor, and actually loves his wife. In the moral Wasteland, those with ideals and those who truly love are alike vulnerable, and it is ironically apt that it is George Wilson who shoots Gatsby before taking his own life. Like Gatsby, Wilson is, in his own way, a romanticist.

MEYER WOLFSHEIM: Wolfsheim is a memorable figure, and his very "sentiment" creates a kind of absurd horror—like modern "syndicate" gangsters who are "nice" citizens in their own community, and who contribute to boy scout troops while controlling the sale of narcotics.

PAMMY: When Daisy calls her daughter a "dream" she is indeed defining her own incapacity for any sort of real emotion.

HENRY G. GATZ: Gatsby's father, who comes to New York for the funeral, and shows Nick the pathetic excerpt from Gatsby's diary—an excerpt replete with laudable virtues and Franklin-like resolutions. It is Mr. Gatz who remarks that his son could have been "a great man"—and indeed the waste of the resources of energy and idealism is a basic theme of the novel.

DOCTOR J. ECKLEBURG: Eckleburg's face, indeed, is taken by George Wilson as being "the eyes of God"—and this is one of the most memorable absurdities of the book. As an image, Doctor Eckleburg is extraordinarily effective; the monstrous face and yellow eyes become a parody of Divinity.

Sample Essay Questions and Answers

1. Discuss the meaning of Idealistic or "non-material" materialism in *The Great Gatsby*.

ANSWER: Idealistic or "non-material" materialism refers to the fact that for Jay Gatsby, materialism is raised to a romantic ideal, a kind of glowing expectation of some vague and magic "happiness" to be obtained through materialism itself. The paradox, of course, is that idealized materialism "promises" what it can never provide: that is, a spiritual glory. In the person of Jay Gatsby we have a dramatic representation of the uniquely romantic materialism of America, a king of innocence according to which men attempt to create a glowing Ideal from material acquisition, and attempt to convince themselves that *desire* can define reality, that *gesture* can define action, and that *sentiment* can define emotion.

2. Explain *The Great Gatsby* as a novel with a "dual hero."

ANSWER: *The Great Gatsby* is a novel with a "dual hero" because Nick Carroway, the narrator, is in many respects no less important to the book than is Jay Gatsby himself. Nick, indeed, represents at least an awareness of the traditional values and moral codes that made America great. A spectator rather than inhabitant of the moral Wasteland of the Buchanan world, Nick provides a definition-through-contrast of the wasteland itself. He also serves as a means of defining the essential idealism of Jay Gatsby, and the waste of energy and devotion which Gatsby's "worship" of Daisy represents.

3. In what way does Daisy Buchanan represent "the Fitzgerald woman"?

ANSWER: Daisy Buchanan, whose voice "is full of money," is one of a long line of Fitzgerald women who are both idealized for their beauty, and feared because of their fatal irresponsibility, their parasitism, their lack of any personal substance, and their destructively "romantic" commitment to mere gesture. Daisy, indeed, is a kind of gorgeous "balloon" of loveliness—but a balloon, after all, is a charming surface surrounding empty space. Just so does Daisy "drift" in and out of "love"; lacking any authentic impulse of her own, Daisy is essentially frigid despite (or because of) "her romanticism." She moves, or rather is impelled, in the direction of whatever force—whether of personality or money—seems "in control" at the moment. A creature without loyalty or moral responsibility, she is indeed a "Fairy Princess" who belongs to anyone with the proper magic wand.

4. What is the significance of the billboard face of Doctor T. J. Eckleburg?

ANSWER: The huge face of Doctor Eckleburg is a kind of presiding deity of the Wasteland. Doctor Eckleburg's staring yellow eyes, indeed, are mistaken for "the eyes of God" by the hapless George Wilson. The billboard is a basic—and extraordinarily provocative—image, a dramatic parody of a moral and spiritual Wasteland lost both to the affirmation of God and the affirmation of man.

5. Discuss the significance of Gatsby's "diary."

ANSWER: The excerpt from the diary of Jay Gatsby—written while he was still a boy named Jimmy Gatz—is a dramatization of the decay of the American Dream. The excerpt, shown to Nick by Gatsby's father, is filled with Franklin-like plans for earnest "self-improvement" and hard work. The diary, in short, reinforces a basic theme of the novel: the theme of wasted devotion, wasted power, and wasted potential.

6. *The Great Gatsby* has often been considered a *parody* of "The American Dream." Discuss this concept.

ANSWER: The "American Dream" is a kind of romantic expectation, a belief in the possibility of achieving some sort of glowing future with hard work and sincere devotion. Fitzgerald's novel is a "parody" of this dream because in the person of Jay Gatsby we have the corruption of the Dream itself: that is, the traditional devotions wasted on spiritual gum-drops and material trivialities.

The American Dream, in short, becomes corrupted into the moral Wasteland of the Buchanans on one hand (a wasteland where impulse and appetite replace moral code and spiritual value), and diluted into the unfocused romanticism of Jay Gatsby on the other. The parody, in other words, is created by the fact that Gatsby serves the "vast, vulgar, meretricious beauty" represented by Daisy Buchanan through the modes, and even the gestures, of the American Dream itself. It is for this reason that Nick, at the end of the novel, makes an implicit comparison between Gatsby and the early explorers of the New World. Gatsby too is a man of ideals and self-sacrifice; both the ideals and the sacrifice, however, in the Wasteland lead only to absurd illusion: the worship of Daisy Buchanan, the silver "balloon" of surface without substance.

Stephen Crane's The Red Badge of Courage

Analysis and Comment

PART I: BEFORE THE BATTLE CHAPTER 1

The opening chapter of *The Red Badge of Courage* begins with a striking variant version of a conventional literary "beginning," that of the *reverdie,* or "welcome to Spring." The opening of Chaucer's *Canterbury Tales* is a famous example of a high rhetorical treatment of the motif, as is Surrey's poem, "Description of Spring, Wherein Each Thing Renews Save Only the Lover":

The soote season that bud and bloom forth brings
With green hath clad the hill and eke the vale,
The nightingale with feathers new she sings,
The turtle to her make hath told her tale . . .

T. S. Eliot, in *The Waste Land,* alters the traditional imagery for ironic effect:

April is the cruellest month, breeding
Lilacs out of the dead land, mixing
Memory and desire, stirring
Dull roots with spring rain . . .

Crane's opening words, like Eliot's, invert the traditional attitude, for, while he is ostensibly speaking of the transition from dawn to day, his imagery suggests the green awakening of Spring and ironically equates the military reveille to the surging of some giant in the earth vivified by the returning sun: "The cold passed reluctantly from the earth, and the retiring fogs revealed an army stretched out on the hills, resting. As the landscape changed from brown to green, the army awakened, and began to tremble with eagerness at the noise of rumors. It cast its eyes upon the roads, which were growing from long troughs of liquid mud to proper thoroughfares. A river, amber-tinted in the shadow of its banks, purled at the army's feet . . . ." This personification is continued in the image of the enemy camp at night, which appears as a "red, eyelike gleam of hostile camp fires set in the low brows of distant hills." After this generalized and symbolic introduction, the scene is focused more sharply as the narrator reports the appearance of "a certain tall soldier" waving a shirt like a banner as he returns from a brook where he had gone to wash it. Actually, the narrator is far from being a disinterested recorder of fact, and we note here a certain flippant, even sarcastic tone in his remark that the tall soldier had "developed virtues and went resolutely to wash a shirt," that he "came flying back" from the brook with news of a move on the next day, was "swelled with a tale he had heard," had "adopted [an] important air," spoke pompously, and so forth.

COMMENT: To define the narrator's *tone* of address with precision, and thus to establish his *attitude* toward the facts he reports is essential to the interpretation of all works of fiction—especially so of *The Red Badge of Courage.* A central critical problem in Crane criticism, in fact, is the attempt to determine his attitude at different points in the narrative toward nature, toward his main character, Henry Fleming, and toward such abstractions as "courage" and "war." Here, the narrator's somewhat supercilious attitude toward the tall soldier and his comrades is a first inkling of his later treatment of the theme of the puniness of individual determination in the face of the uncontrollable forces of nature and of institutions.

The following paragraph sees the tall soldier smugly mapping out a campaign based upon the fragment of information he has come by, and the two score soldiers who had just been "hilariously" encouraging the dancing of a Negro teamster reduced to small arguing groups, an event which implies the sudden and random shifts of mood and intention characteristic of men herded together for the purpose of waging war. This paragraph ends on the impressionistic detail: "Smoke drifted lazily from a multitude of quaint chimneys."

COMMENT: Basically, the *impressionist* author attempts to record the scene as it has momentarily impressed him—that is, to record those details of color, shape, and arrangement which have stood out in his vision as most suggestive of the mood inspired in him. Here, the lazily drifting smoke is perhaps meant to suggest the languid emotions of the soldiers, and the "multitude of quaint chimneys" something of the unreal, fairy-tale atmosphere which war engenders.

Another private, with a smooth flushed face, loudly denounces the report as a "thunderin' lie," and nearly comes to blows over it with the tall soldier. The narrator next reports the reactions of a certain corporal, and by choosing a deliberately inflated style and vocabulary for him (far above the dialect we assume to be natural to him) achieves the ironic effect of a viewpoint which perceives the absurdity which underlies all individual human designs: "He had just put a costly board floor in his house, he said. During the early spring he refrained from adding extensively to the comfort of his environment because he had felt that the army might start on the march at any moment." This tone of ironic superiority is the narrator's most frequent device, especially in the first half of the book. He goes on to remark, for instance, that many of the men now engaged in a "spirited debate"; that one outlined the commanding general's plans in a "peculiarly lucid manner"; and that some "advocated other plans of campaign." This is followed by a report of their conversation with the tall soldier (now called "Jim"), in a dialect which is plainly meant to suggest their farmerish origins.

COMMENT: This rapid alternation of colloquial dialogue with expository passages couched in a comparatively learned and abstract vocabulary is itself an aspect of the book's style, and thus an index to its meaning. The reader quickly perceives the disparity between the two types of discourse and takes it as a symbol of the disparity between ambition and realization in those same individuals.

Listening to the remarks of the tall soldier and the comments of his comrades was "a certain youthful private" (Henry Fleming, though we do not learn his name until later—his last name not until Chapter 12. He is most often referred to as "the youth"). The youth repairs to his hut and crawls through an "intricate hole" to the interior in order to mull over some "new thoughts" (perhaps suggestive of a descent into the unconscious, though the whole question of the extent to which *The Red Badge* may be submitted to analysis as a "psychological quest" is in need of further study. Other aspects of this theme will be dealt with as they arise). The youth lies down on a wide bunk, and we are given a description of the hut. Cracker boxes, grouped about the fireplace, serve as chairs. A magazine illustration hangs on the wall, as do three rifles on pegs. A folded tent serves as a roof, while the sun makes it glow a light yellow. Smoke curls from the fire, and the "flimsy chimney of clay and sticks made endless threats to set ablaze the whole establishment." The youth, in a "trance of astonishment," considers his situation in a reverie which verges from ultra-romantic clichés about marital glory on the one hand, to sanguine predictions about modern "civilized" strife on the other. He dwells upon the idea of battles as "great affairs," as "vague and bloody conflicts that had thrilled him with their sweep and fire," in which he played the role of protector with "eagle-eyed prowess." But he had long ago dismissed these visions as "crimson blotches" on the world's history, as distant as crowns and castles. "He had long despaired of witnessing a Greeklike struggle. . . . Secular and religious education had effaced the throat-grappling instinct, or else firm finance held in check the passions."

COMMENT: Both the suppressed desire to participate in heroic combats, and the glib sociological truisms are forms of romantic or idealistic attitudes which show the youth as immature. His attitudinizing, moreover, is indicated by the obviously "poetical" and rhythmical quality of these sentences. Note particularly the almost regular rhythm of the final clause, the consonance on the *s*, *c*, and *f* sounds (especially the alliteration in "firm finance"), the *e* assonance in "sec," "ed," "eff," "else," "held," and "check" (most particularly, the careful sound balance between "sec" and "check"). This sentence is repeated verbatim several pages later.

The next paragraph is almost a tableau in words. War, as it existed in the stylized daydreams of the youth, was nothing but "tales of great movements . . . marches, sieges, conflicts . . . large pictures extravagant in color, lurid with breathless deeds." The youth's reverie becomes in effect a flashback, as the narrator now contrasts his grandiose vision with his mother's prosaic analysis of the matter. She had discouraged him, with contempt for his ardor and numerous reasons to prove his greater importance to the farm than to the army, but the newspapers, gossip, and his own imaginings had aroused him beyond recall. (Apparently with some sarcasm, the narrator notes that the youth's decision was aided by daily newspaper accounts of decisive victories.) In bed one night, he heard the church bells "as some enthusiast jerked the rope frantically" to report news of a battle, and the outcries of the people as they rejoiced made him "shiver in a prolonged ecstasy of excitement." The next morning he enlisted.

COMMENT: It is important to note that the decision to enlist is the immediate result of a compulsive nervous reaction (the "shiver of ecstasy"), itself provoked by an act which is so described as to suggest that it, too, has a compulsive quality ("some enthusiast jerked the rope frantically"). An enthusiast, strictly speaking, is one possessed by a god, and the clear implication here is that war (or the god of war) radiates impulses which actually stimulate behavior beyond the power of the individual will to control, at least the will which is sensitive enough to imaginative stimuli such as the "clangoring of the church bell." ("Clangor," in this context, recalls John Dryden's famous line on the power of music: "The trumpet's loud clangor excites us to arms.")

Henry's announcement that he had enlisted was greeted by his mother's stoic reply, "The Lord's will be done," while she continued to milk the brindle cow (though the youth did observe two tears to fall from her eyes). She had disappointed him by saying nothing about "returning with his shield or on it." This, of course, is the command that Spartan mothers are alleged to have issued to their famous warrior sons as they set out for battle, but Henry's mother, doggedly peeling potatoes, is a far cry from the romantic image he has dimly anticipated. Telling him not to try and "lick the hull rebel army," and to "keep quiet an' do what they tell yeh," she sends him off with eight pairs of socks and a cup of blackberry jam. Her parting speech, a long catalogue of the bad influences a young man will be exposed to in the army, makes Henry impatient and uneasy. His departure is attended by feelings partly of relief and partly of shame, while he watches her brown, tear-stained face as she knelt among the potato parings. He goes to bid farewell to his schoolmates and meets the same sort of ambiguous response to his heroic gesture. Henry, and some others who had enlisted, strutted about in the wave of privileges they enjoyed for the afternoon, but there is an uneasy note in the "vivacious fun" which a certain dark girl made at his martial spirit, offset only by the vision of another girl who (it seemed to him) "grew demure and sad at sight of his blue and brass," and who became flustered when he spied her watching his departure from a window. On the trip to Washington, the fanfare, attention, smiles, and compliments the regiment received had the youth believing he must really be a hero. The narrator now briefly disposes of several ensuing months by remarking that "after complicated journeying with many pauses, there had come months of monotonous life in a camp," and indicating the onset of disillusionment in the youth—he had previously thought of war as a constant series of death struggles, but found that he had actually had little to do but sit and try to keep warm. This inactivity merely brought him back to his earlier theory about the disappearance of Greeklike struggles, and "firm finance" holding in check the passions. "He had grown to regard himself merely as a part of a vast blue demonstration."

COMMENT: This idea of the army and its movements as a "blue demonstration" is a thought which recurs in the youth's mind a number of times throughout the book. It suggests the impersonal character of warfare, the machinelike process of a military campaign, and the purposeless—almost academic—relationship it appears to bear to the intentions of the individual will. Warfare comes to seem a perfunctory organization of color and form, a natural phenomenon not vastly different from the annual burgeoning of spring, which might in its turn almost be termed a "green demonstration."

The youth, amid all the drilling and reviewing, seemed to have no other purpose than to look out for his personal comfort. The only enemies he had seen were some pickets along a river bank, a "philosophical lot," who occasionally shot "reflectively" at the blue pickets. There was actually a jaunty current of good-humored badinage which passed back and forth between the two lines, such exchanges as a reproach by the blue soldiers for having been shot at, and a reply by the gray that their guns had exploded without their permission. The youth even got on rather friendly terms with one of them, a fact which made him rather regret war temporarily.

COMMENT: The fact that this is the American Civil War (though Crane, of course, never explicitly admits it) points up the antithesis between the official national "emotion" of hatred for the enemy and the potential counter emotion of friendship for the individual foe. There are reliable accounts from other sources (for example, A. G. Empey's *Over the Top*, a memoir of the First World War) of opposing forces engaging each other in light-hearted conversation and even calling temporary truces during which they exchanged visits. Thomas Hardy's poem, "The Man He Killed," is a memorable expression of the same sentiment:

Had he and I but met
By some old ancient inn,
We should have set us down to wet
Right many a nipperkin!
But ranged as infantry,
And staring face to face,
I shot at him as he at me,
And killed him in his place . . .

Encounters of this sort were balanced by the tales he heard from veterans about gray, relentless hordes sweeping along like Huns, or of eternally hungry men whose "red, live bones" stuck out through rents in their uniforms. But he realized that recruits were prey to veterans' horror stories, which were not to be trusted. At this point he began to analyze the question of his own courage—to prove to himself mathematically that he would never run from battle. A slight panic grew in his mind as he anticipated an actual battle, "contemplated the lurking menaces of the future," and he began to waver in his belief in his own stout heart. His law of life and his knowledge of himself would be of no avail in a crisis, he felt. He was an "unknown quantity"; he would have to "experiment" again, and "accumulate information" about himself lest he should act in a way to bring disgrace upon him.

COMMENT: Crane is perhaps suggesting, through the "mathematical" and "scientific" terms which the youth here employs in his introspection, that the question of courage will not submit itself to this sort of analysis; that as long as Henry approaches the performance of brave deeds through an abstract process of rationalization about "courage" he will fail to achieve them.

At this point the tall soldier and the loud soldier enter the hut (the tall soldier does this "dexterously" through the same "intricate hole" Henry has previously entered—perhaps an indication of his greater mastery of self-knowledge). They are arguing about the rumored move, and to the youth's question, "Going to be a battle, sure, is there, Jim?", the tall one replies in the affirmative with the air of a man "about to exhibit a battle for the benefit of his friends." (We see how easily a clear perception of the danger and horror is dispelled by the personal triumph of "being right" in the matter. But when asked how he thinks the regiment will perform, he replies, "Oh, they'll fight all right, I guess," upon which the narrator sarcastically intones, "He made a fine use of the third person.") Under the youth's prodding the tall soldier (Jim) gives his opinion about the probable bravery of the members of the regiment. It is a masterpiece of uncertainty and ambiguity. A few might run . . . or the whole regiment might turn tail . . . then again they might stay "and fight like fun" . . . they'll fight "better than some if worse than others" . . . most of them will "fight like sin" after they once get shooting—and so forth. When Henry, in a half-joking fashion, asks Jim if he ever thought he might run himself the loud soldier giggles nervously, while Jim answers by saying that he would probably run if others did, but that if everybody stood and fought, why then he would stand and fight, too. "By jiminey, I would. I'll bet on it."

COMMENT: Jim's reply is hardly an example of supreme self-assurance. His uncertainty gratifies and reassures the youth, who had feared that all the untried men were confident of their future bravery. Furthermore, his speech points up the problem of collective versus individual action. "Everybody" is, after all, an abstraction. A rout and a charge both must begin in the determined act of a single individual.

SUMMARY: From the outset we are confronted by the book's basic method of description and exposition—a deliberate vagueness about names, places, and times (even the opposing armies are not identified); broad strokes of description, selected for impressionistic and symbolic effect; and a consistent detachment on the part of the narrator, which takes the form of an ironic objectivity toward all characters except the youth, into whose mind we gain a limited access. The effect is to render with concrete particularity (from *within* the scene) the welter of thoughts and emotions which is characteristic of men in training for a battle. In addition, the following observations about character, theme, and style are worthy of note:

1. Three of the main characters are introduced: Henry Fleming, Jim Conklin, and Wilson, though they are referred to most often merely as the youth, the tall soldier, and the loud soldier (the youth sometimes as Henry; Wilson's name is not yet mentioned).

2. The primary issue in the book—the youth's dilemma over courage and cowardice—is presented in the form of self-analysis as well as dialogue with the tall soldier. He arrives at the point of being satisfied that his own uncertainties are typical of the rest of the untried men.

3. Sentence structure in general tends to be simple and uncomplicated, reflecting Crane's attempt to render reality with blunt objectivity. There is, however, a discernible undercurrent of more involved rhetorical structures, generally for ironic effect.

4. The author makes a marked use of color imagery (red, for instance, for allusions to war, glory, derring-do, etc.; yellow for the pall cast on romantic notions by mundane actualities such as the mother's discouraging reaction). Metaphor, and especially personification, is used frequently to suggest a kind of immanent will in nature itself (for example, "the chimney . . . made endless threats to set ablaze the whole establishment").

5. There are frequent allusions to the trappings and motifs of the heroic ages (Greeklike struggles, the Spartan mothers, the horde of the Huns), which contribute to a pattern of ironic contrast between the youth's initial idealism and his growing disillusionment.

6. Vocabulary: the narrator often resorts to an elevated vocabulary to call attention to ironic contrasts—that, for example, between the mother's deep moral rectitude and the effect the banality of her expression has on Henry's idealism: "Moreover, on her side, was his belief that her ethical motive in the argument was impregnable."

7. "Poeticism": Crane occasionally slips into a markedly rhythmical form of expression, characterized by a high degree of sound patterning (such as alliteration) and colorful language, usually as an accompaniment to some high—flown sentiment. The effect is normally felt as irony. For instance: "He could not accept with assurance an omen that he was about to mingle in one of those great affairs of the earth."

CHAPTER 2

The next morning revealed that the tall soldier had been mistaken about the move. Scoffed at and sneered at, he had to defend his reputation by beating one of his detractors in a fist fight. This in no way solved the youth's problem. His self-questioning had to be postponed, as he resumed once more his "blue demonstration" theory. Days of "ceaseless calculations" proved nothing. He decided he would have to enter the "blaze" and make an objective consideration of the way his body behaved. Mental arithmetic would have to give way to a kind of chemical analysis—blaze, blood, and danger being, in effect, the chemist's precipitating acids. Even so, he tried "to measure himself" by his comrades, particularly by the tall soldier, a man he had known since early youth. How could Jim Conklin accomplish anything that Henry Fleming was incapable of doing? Perhaps Conklin had a false opinion of himself—on the other hand, perhaps he was indeed destined to achieve glory in combat.

COMMENT: There is a glancing, partial illumination in the youth's conclusion that only blaze, blood, and danger can give him the answer he seeks. (It is also an unwitting bit of prophecy.) Even his preference for a chemical rather than an arithmetic metaphor is something of an improvement in personal insight, though he still continues to "calculate," "measure," and "fathom" the depths of his problem.

The youth hoped to discover a comrade who had the same doubts as he, and tried to lure others into a confession of similar misgivings. He failed to do so. Moreover, he feared to tell his secret to anyone lest he prove to be an unworthy confidant, thus leaving himself open to derision. As for his companions, he alternated between two opinions, sometimes believing them all to be heroes, men of superior qualities who wore their courage without ostentation, at other times comforting himself in the belief that secretly they were all as terrified as he. Outwardly, they took the prospect of battle lightly, and he suspected that they might be liars. For these thoughts, however, he reproached himself as a sinner against the "gods of traditions."

The slowness of the generals seemed to him intolerable. They had no conception of his great problem, and his anger occasionally caused him to grumble about like a veteran. One morning, however, before daybreak, whispered rumors caused some uneasiness in the ranks. Against a yellow patch in the sky (which looked like a rug laid for the coming sun) was silhouetted the figure of the colonel on his horse. Vague tramplings and mysterious shadows added to the youth's impatience. Suddenly the "mystic gloom" was pierced by battle sounds, and he saw the colonel calmly stroking his moustache. Suddenly he heard the clatter—the "clickety-click"—of a horse's hooves, and a jangling rider appeared to deliver a message to the colonel. As he rode off he shouted back (to the youth's astonishment), "Don't forget that box of cigars."

COMMENT: The youth is mystified because, in his inexperience, he cannot comprehend the casual attitude of the professional soldier toward what to him is an encounter charged with romance, mystery, and extraordinary personal involvement.

As the regiment moved off it resembled a monster "wending with many feet." (Crane's choice of the archaic verb "wend" [meaning "walk," with the additional connotation of "turning"] reinforces in a minor way the motif of fairy-tale unreality.) The men stumbled along, muttering and arguing, until one fell down and another stepped on his hand. In a brief parody of the style of epic "naming" the narrator refers to him as "he of the injured fingers," and reports that he swore bitterly, to which the rest responded with nervous laughter. As they strode along, a "dark regiment" in front of them and a "tinkle of equipment" behind came to be seen in the rising dawn as two thin, black lines disappearing over a hill before them and into a wood behind. They resembled "two serpents crawling from the cavern of the night." The river, however, was nowhere in sight, so that the tall soldier (the narrator remarks) "burst into praises of what he thought to be his powers of perception."

COMMENT: Here again we notice the deliberate rhetoric of an elevated vocabulary and alliterative phrasing being used to comment ironically on the self-deluding pomposity of certain characters.

Some agree with Jim Conklin; some offer other theories. But the youth continues in his own "eternal debate." He becomes gloomy and suspicious, looking anxiously ahead for signs of combat. He sees nothing but a dun-colored cloud of smoke floating in a sky of fairy blue, and is disappointed to see not a melancholy aspect like his own but a gleeful look on the faces of the others in his regiment. They spoke with assurance of victory, "felicitating themselves upon being a part of a blasting host."

COMMENT: The strong suggestion of the idea of "blight" (in the word "blast"—compare, for instance, John Milton's "O fairest flower, no sooner blown but blasted") is perhaps the faint beginning of a pattern of flowery imagery Crane employs to convey the sense of war as outrageous floral growth—a satanic form of nature—on the earth's face. It is ironic that the regiment here congratulates itself on "blasting" the enemy, but will soon pitch camp and "sprout" wildly. "Tents sprang up," says the narrator, "like strange plants. Camp fires, like red, peculiar blossoms, dotted the night."

It is here that the youth's sense of isolation intensifies. As the rest rejoice on being "part of host," and laugh merrily at the company wags even to the point of forgetting their mission, the youth is saddened by their blithe demeanor. "Whole brigades grinned in unison, and regiments laughed," but his separation becomes more total. In counterpoint to his growing seriousness the regiment as a whole begins to treat the entire affair as a lark—a schoolboy escapade. A fat soldier attempts to steal a horse from a dooryard but is routed by a young girl, and the regiment whoops and enter "whole-souled upon the side of the maiden." They jeer at the private and give the girl enthusiastic support. When they pitch camp that night the youth keeps to himself, and wanders into the gloom. The numerous fires, we are told, "with the black forms of men passing to and fro before the crimson rays, made weird and satanic effects." As he lay in the grass, enveloped by night and caressed by winds, he felt a "vast pity" for himself and imagined that the surrounding mood was that of an encompassing sympathy for him.

Henry reflects on his life at home, and wishes that despite the tedious round of tasks in barn and house he could be back there once again. In his present vision the brindle cow and her mates each have a "halo of happiness" about their heads, and he would have give anything to return to them and put a great distance between himself and those men who were now "dodging implike around the fires."

COMMENT: The "implike" men and the "weird and satanic effects" they produce are certainly meant to suggest the devotees of an unholy creed, just as the "halo of happiness" about the cows' heads is a whimsical suggestion of farm duties as a form of "religion." It is important for the reader to notice even the casual manifestations of the religious metaphor Crane brings into play if he wishes to respond properly to the representation of Jim Conklin's death in Chapter 9. (Just before Jim falls, for instance, he is seen in the grip of "implike enthusiasm.")

Suddenly the loud soldier (Wilson) approached, and began to speak in an optimistic way of their chances in the coming battle. Gleeful and exultant, he exclaims "this time—we'll lick'em good!" His face is described as boyish, he walks with an elastic step, and he speaks with youthful enthusiasm: "Gee rod! how we will thump 'em!" His pride and boisterous anticipation of success provoke only bitter sarcasm from Henry, who asks how he can be sure he will not run, and follows up Wilson's denial with a reminder that many good men have run from battle in the past. He finally stirs Wilson to the angry rejoinder, "Who are you, anyhow? You talk as if you thought you was Napoleon Bonaparte."

Failing to discover a sympathetic chord in Wilson, he becomes more wretched than before, and goes to his tent, where he falls asleep by the side of the tall soldier. Fear takes the form in his mind of a thousand-tongued monster he could never hope to cope with, even though others might go about the business of war with absolute coolness. He sweats in anguish at these visions, while the voices of his comrades, who are calmly gambling nearby, float to him on the night air. The youth stares at the "red, shivering reflection of a fire" on the wall of his tent until he falls asleep.

SUMMARY: There is very little action in Chapter 2. The first dozen paragraphs show the regiment encamped for an unspecified period of time, during which the youth has time to consider his problem at length. Then the regiment advances up the bank of the river; a man falls and injures his hand; a fat soldier tries unsuccessfully to steal a horse; and, finally, the regiment pitches camp for the night. Additional points:

1. The youth, in trying to forecast his reactions in battle, goes about it as a problem to be "calculated," though he has a dim intuition that an abstract solution of it is beyond him. He remains isolated in his spiritual suffering.

2. The religious metaphor is continued in such images as:

a. the "mystic gloom" of morning with the colonel silhouetted against a yellow path of sky which almost resembles an oriental prayer rug.
b. the weird, satanic effects created by implike shadows in the firelight.

3. There are a number of minor images which provide partial, ironic perspectives on a variety of human attitudes toward war:

a. the tall soldier is called the "fast flying messenger of a mistake," as if he were some ignoble Hermes.
b. some of the men talk excitedly about the battle "as of a drama they were about to witness."
c. the youth tends to interpret distant figures as "monsters," "dragons," "reptiles," or "serpents," all images which convey his complicated sense of the horror and yet the romance of war.

CHAPTER 3

On the next night the columns of marching men, looking like purple streaks, filed across a river, the waters of which appear wine-tinted by a glaring fire. (One of Homer's constant epithets for the sea in his *Iliad* is "the wine-dark sea".) The fire also caused occasional gleams of gold or silver among the troops, while out of the mysterious shadows cast by the hills of the farther shore came the "solemn" song of insects.

COMMENT: The Impressionistic choice of details here ("purple streaks," "wine-tinted water," "gleams of gold," "solemn song" of insects, and so on) suggest strongly that the approach to battle is to be taken as a kind of dark, satanic sacrament, in which the marching columns have the aspect of a sacrificial offering, and thus continues the thread of "religious" imagery.

The youth, fearing an immediate assault, watched the woods carefully, but the regiment arrived at a camping place and "its soldiers slept the brave sleep of wearied men."

COMMENT: "Brave sleep" is an excellent example of the vigor and freshness of Crane's language. It probably owes something to the famous couplet from William Collins' "Ode Written in the Year 1746,"

> *How sleep the brave, who sink to rest*
> *By all their country's wishes bless'd!*

Yet, for Crane, it is not the men but the sleep which is "brave"; he thus questions ironically the very meaning of "bravery" (which, in fact, in earlier periods of the English language, meant "bravado," or even merely "insulting cheek").

In the morning they were aroused once more, and led further into the forest, losing as they marched many of the signs of a new command. Aching feet and perspiration led to grumblings. Knapsacks and thick shirts were shed. Soon only the most necessary equipment was being carried. "You can now eat and shoot," said the tall soldier, "that's all you want to do." (This divestiture of clothing, which certainly represents the increasing hold which nature is exerting over the soldiers, is not an uncommon form of literary symbolism. There are examples as diverse as Eugene O'Neill's *The Emperor Jones,* in which Jones' loss of his clothing accompanies a reversion to savagery—to the primitive roots of his psyche—and Shakespeare's *King Lear,* in which Lear's nakedness during the storm on the heath symbolizes unaccommodated man standing powerless before nature.) Even so, the narrator's attitude remains ambiguous, and he calls himself back from any possible hint of overseriousness with the comment, "But there was much loss of valuable knapsacks, and, on the whole, very good shirts."

For all that, they did not yet look like veterans, and they had to put up with the jibes of returning warriors directed against their unspoiled ranks and the newness of their uniforms. Given a while to rest, the youth, moved by the odor of "peaceful pines," the monotony of axe blows, and the "crooning" of insects, returned to his theory of a "blue demonstration." Suddenly, early one morning, he was awakened by being kicked in the leg by the tall soldier, and found himself running down a road surrounded by other panting men. His canteen banged "rhythmically" on his thigh and his haversack "bobbed softly," while all around he could hear men whispering "jerky" sentences of complaint and reproach. (This is perhaps a suggestion of an opposition between the rhythm of instinctual motions and the relatively disordered pattern of analytical thought.) The damp fog and sudden spattering of firing bewildered him. He could not think, and merely felt himself carried along by a mob. The sun now spread "disclosing rays" and, one after another, "regiments burst into view like armed men just born of the earth."

COMMENT: This is unquestionably an allusion to the myth of Cadmus, who, as he prepared to sacrifice a cow to Athene, was set upon by the serpent which guarded the Castalian spring. The serpent having killed almost all of Cadmus' men, he crushed its head with a rock and (at Athene's command) sowed its teeth in the ground, whereupon armed men sprang up. Cadmus escaped by throwing a rock among them, causing a brawl in which nearly all were killed. To what extent the part played by cow and serpent in this myth may be related to Crane's symbolic use of the mother's brindle cows and his serpentine imagery is a question worthy of consideration.

The youth felt that his moment had come. He was about to be measured, and he found himself in a "moving box" bound by the iron rules of tradition and law. He began to complain of his fate. He had been dragooned into the army by a merciless government, and now he was going to be slaughtered. The regiment moved across a little stream and climbed a hill on the opposite side, amid the boom of artillery. Quickly his fear gave way to curiosity, and he scrambled up the bank eagerly, expecting to find a battle scene. (Crane is not explicit at this point, but it is clear that the youth's romantic dreams have gotten the upper hand momentarily, and that he is swiftly disappointed by the prosaic scene of confusion which greets his eyes.) Some fields are squeezed in by a forest; there are "knots" of skirmishers running "hither and thither," and firing aimlessly. Other regiments "flounder" up the bank, as skirmishers continually "melt into the scene" only to reappear in other places. They were always "busy as bees," absorbed in their "little combat."

COMMENT: The phrase "busy as bees" (in its proverbial application at least as old as the sixteenth-century writer John Lyly's *Euphues,* which refers to "an old man, as busy as a bee") well illustrates the ironic extremes to which Crane's tone verges. On the one hand it has the absurd connotations of diminutiveness, perhaps mainly due to Isaac Watts' sentimental poem,

How doth the little busy bee
Improve each shining hour
And gather honey all the day
From every opening flower!

But it also suggests the analogy between the human and the bee communities, a matter which has long been the subject of serious investigation, and thus tends to define warfare as another instance of blind, instinctual forces.

The youth tried to avoid obstacles, but his "forgotten feet" knocked against stones or became entangled in thorns (another indication of a merging with nature itself). In short, instead of coming upon a tapestry depicting a heroic battle fought by dashing, splendidly dressed warriors, he became "aware that these battalions with their commotions were woven red and startling into the gentle fabric of softened greens and browns."

Once the youth encountered the body of a dead soldier, dressed in an awkward, yellowish suit, and worn shoes from which a dead foot "projected piteously." The ranks had to open to avoid the corpse. The youth peered vainly at the ashen face and tawny beard for an answer to his great Question. Now his ardor had faded and his curiosity was satisfied. (Crane now provides a short expository comment, which is an important key to the youth's later failure of nerve: ". . . If an intense scene had caught him with its wild swing as he came to the top of the bank, he might have gone roaring on. This advance upon Nature was too calm. He had an opportunity to reflect. He had time in which to wonder about himself and to attempt to probe his sensations."

COMMENT: Surely the comparison with Shakespeare's Prince Hamlet is an apt one here. In his failure to take decisive action, Hamlet soliloquizes:

Thus conscience does make cowards of us all;
And thus the native hue of resolution
Is sicklied o'er with the pale cast of thought,
And enterprises of great pith and moment

With this regard their currents turn awry,
And lose the name of action.

Indeed, the question of whether the youth has acted as a "coward" has hardly more relevance to Crane's theme than the identical question as put to the actions of Hamlet, or even of Shakespeare's Falstaff (*1 Henry IV*). Crane is more concerned with such things as the relationship between native sensitivity and "crowd psychology," or between feeling and thought as opportunity makes room for one or the other to dominate.

The landscape appeared to threaten him, a coldness crept over his back, and his legs seemed not to fit in his trousers at all. A distant house took on an ominous look. He doubted the competence of the generals, and imagined that they were all about to be sacrificed. He expected the "stealthy approach of death." The youth wanted to warn his comrades of the generals' idiocy—to step forth and make a "passionate speech." But the line of soldiers went calmly on, most of them wearing expressions of intense interest, appearing absorbed in what they were doing. They "were going to look at war, the red animal—war, the blood-swollen god. And they were deeply engrossed in this march." The words stuck in his throat, as he saw that they would only laugh at his warning. So he adopted the air of a doomed and isolated witness to tragic omens. This mood was sharply interrupted by the young lieutenant, who began to beat him with the flat of his sword and accuse him of lagging behind.

The brigade halted after a time, and the "religious" metaphor once more occupies the youth's mind. The gloom of the forest is a "cathedral light"; the "floating smoke" (from the rifles) goes up in white, compact balls. A number of the men began to build little protective mounds. They even argued about the merits of small ones over large ones, and over the correct postures to be assumed during combat. (The veterans, meanwhile, were "digging at the ground like terriers.") In a short time they were ordered to move on. The youth's loud complaints at this lack of consideration were met by the tall soldier's calm explanation. Soon, in another place, they had erected another line of entrenchments, ate their noon meal behind still another, and were moved from that in turn. They seemed to be wandering about aimlessly. The youth had been taught that man became "another thing" in battle, and in this change he saw his salvation. His impatience inevitably led him back to his theory that this was all a "blue demonstration." He wished either to return to camp or to go into battle and discover that he was indeed "a man of traditional courage." The tall soldier chewed philosophically on a sandwich of cracker and pork, while the loud soldier grunted sarcastically and the youth continued to fidget. The loud soldier declared his desire to get into a fight, while the tall soldier, "red-faced, swallowed another sandwich as if taking poison in despair." But as he chewed he became quiet, lost in blissful contemplation of the food he had swallowed. "His spirit seemed to be communing with the viands." His equanimity appeared to be a result of his eating at every opportunity. He had not even raised his voice when he had been ordered to leave behind the little entrenchments he had made, "each of which had been an engineering feat worthy of being made sacred to the name of his grandmother."

COMMENT: Any interpretation of the tall soldier's meaning to the story (especially the significance of the manner of his death at the end of Chapter 9) must face up to these earlier suggestions of his status as a "communicant" in some unspecified religion. (Crane later refers to him, in fact, as a "devotee of some mad religion.") A widely held opinion (which originated with R. W. Stallman) is that Jim Conklin is a symbol of Jesus Christ, and that his death is a sacrificial death through which Henry Fleming achieves his redemption. But here we note clearly that the tall soldier is defined as a "communicant," not as a sacrificial object.

The regiment moved out in the afternoon and the youth continued to grapple with his problem. Even death appeared to him as a welcome conclusion. It was, after all, nothing but rest, and he was surprised that he had made such a stir about it. Meanwhile the skirmishing went on, and he heard cheering mingled with the sound of distant firing. Then the skirmishers appeared on the run, rifle flashes were to be seen, clouds of smoke rolled "insolently" across the field, and the battle din increased to a tremendous roar. The youth was spellbound, his eyes wide and busy, and his mouth hanging open. In his astonishment he felt a "heavy and sad hand" on his shoulder. It was the loud soldier. Pale, his lips trembling, he handed the youth a packet enclosed in a yellow envelope. The youth started in surprise, but the other "gave him a glance as from the depths of a tomb, and raised his limp hand in a prophetic manner and turned away."

COMMENT: It should be noted that the religious metaphor is not confined (among the human figures) to Jim Conklin. It is here used of Wilson, who is momentarily regarded as a "prophet," crying "from the depths" (perhaps a hint of Psalm 129—*De profundis clamavi*, "Out of the depths I have cried unto thee, O Lord!", or possibly of the story of Lazarus, speaking from the tomb).

SUMMARY:

1. Action: The regiment has marched for another day, and crosses the river at nightfall. After some days they are plunged into battle, where the youth confronts its ugliness and chaos. The youth continues to ponder; Conklin maintains a philosophical calm; and Wilson is overcome by maudlin and gloomy thoughts of death.

2. The regiment comes further under the influence of nature (the clothes-shedding episode) and thus of instinctual response, but they remain "fresh fish" in the eyes of the veterans (as the similarity of headgear suggests).

3. The tension between instinct and calculation is pointed up in the sudden starts and pauses in the chapter, wherein the youth is sometimes forced to act on impulse, and must make greater efforts to find leisure for reflection. The same antithesis is indicated in the contrast between the recruits who argue about proper postures, and the veterans who dig like terriers.

4. Continued image patterns:

a. The classical-heroic theme—here seen mainly in the allusion to the myth of Cadmus, but also in such casual epithets as that of the "wine-tinted water."
b. The religious metaphor—references to the "blood-swollen god of war," the "cathedral light of the forest," to Wilson as a "prophet," and especially to Conklin as a "communicant" in "blissful contemplation."

5. Stylistic effects:

a. Verbal irony—such phrases as "busy as bees," and "projected piteously."
b. Personification—for example, "the smoke clouds went slowly and insolently."
c. Elevated style—Conklin's trenches, for instance, being called "engineering feats worthy of being made sacred," etc.

6. Characterization: By far the most important detail in the chapter is the youth's sudden aspiration to see a glorious scene of battle and his consequent disappointment at the actual confusion which greeted him, together with the psychological depression which followed.

PART II: BATTLE AND FLIGHT
CHAPTER 4

The brigade halted at the edge of a grove, and the new recruits passed rumors about eagerly. There is some agitated gossip about various officers (Perry, Carrott, Hannis, and Hasbrouck), a rumor that the general promised to take command of the 304th himself, and a report of a boast made by one of the 148th Maine regiment about the "five thousand" of the enemy they had just killed. (The Maine soldier is referred to as Bill, and he turns out to be the man whose foot was trod on during the march.) Bill is reported as having been willing to give up his hand for his country, but reluctant to have "every dumb bushwacker in th' kentry walkin' 'round on it." He went to the hospital, regardless of the fight; the doctor wanted to amputate three fingers, but "he raised a heluva row," the reporting soldier continued, "he's a funny feller."

COMMENT: The concepts of courage, mere heroics, and cowardice are here presented in an uneasy poise. Bill is alleged not to be "easily scared," yet his willingness to give "his hand to his country" jibes oddly with such genuinely heroic offers as Nathan Hale's to "give his life for his country." And his willingness to go to the hospital as well as the row over having the fingers amputated (which appears to have been an instant cure for malingering) suggest that he is far from a model of bravery. Furthermore, the reference to amputation anticipates the youth's later thought (Chapter 5) that he might save himself from annihilation by "amputating" himself from the regiment, while the noncommittal description of Bill as "a funny feller" looks forward to such appraisals as that the tattered man makes of the tall soldier in death: "Well, he was a reg'lar jim-dandy . . . It was a funny thing." This is a minor manifestation of the theme that war does extraordinary things to the emotions—brings about a severe psychological wrenching.

As the men crouched there, the din of battle swelled, shells screamed overhead, and bullets whistled through the trees. The lieutenant of the company was shot in the hand, and he swore so magnificently that a nervous laugh broke out along the line—his profanity relieved the tensions of the moment. "He held the wounded member carefully away from his side so that the blood would not drip upon his trousers."

COMMENT: The word "member," here used of the hand—in fact, the very idea of the relationship of members to an organic whole—looks ahead to the youth's embodiment of his problem of courage in the image of the relationship of members and whole, individual part and total unit, and is related also to the amputation motif just alluded to.

While the captain and the lieutenant dispute about how to bind the wound, the battle flag is seen in the distance being "jerked about madly," seeming to try "to free itself from an agony." Men emerge from the smoke fleeing, and the flag sinks down, as if in a "gesture of despair." As the soldiers of the 304th retreat (the youth is at the rear, with the reserves) they hear jeers and catcalls from the veterans on the flanks. The youth saw officers, cursing like highwaymen, striking about in an effort to stem the rout. One raged like a spoiled child. Another looked as if he had been roused from bed to go to a fire. Oaths and grim jokes went unheeded by the "mad current" of soldiery on its way to the rear. The youth thought that he must certainly flee, if only he could get control of his legs. The stampede seemed to be a flood that could drag sticks, stones and men from the ground. The "monster" that caused the flight did not immediately appear, or (so the youth thought) he would very likely take to his heels.

SUMMARY: This short chapter occupies a very short period of time—only a few minutes before an encounter, and a few (perhaps only seconds) during it. It has the following specific functions:

1. It brings the youth a step nearer to actual combat, and allows him enough leisure to decide that flight from battle is a distinct possibility for him.

2. It provides serious and comic (the "Bill" episode) versions of courageous actions.

3. It introduces the terminology of "amputation" and "members," which will be elaborated upon in later chapters.

4. It presents a concrete picture of the literal and the emotional turbulence of battle, in the nightmarish picture of cursing officers, jeering veterans, and terrified recruits.

CHAPTER 5

The fifth chapter opens in the lull before the counterattack by the soldiers in gray. Phantasms from his early boyhood thronged in upon the youth's mind—the circus parade, with a dingy lady on a white horse, a band in a faded chariot, and an old fellow on a cracker box in front of a store, a "thousand details of color and form." The cry arose, "Here they come," and there was a feverish flurry to have cartridges at hand and guns ready. Suddenly they came running, a "brown swarm" of yelling men swinging rifles and following a flag which was tilted forward. The youth began to wonder if his gun was actually loaded, when his thoughts were interrupted by the vision of a hatless general exhorting the colonel of the 304th to hold them back, and the colonel stammering in reply that they would do their best. The general rode off, making a "passionate gesture," the colonel scolded like a "wet parrot," and the captain of the youth's company "coaxed in schoolmistress fashion." The youth was perspiring freely, his mouth hanging open. One glance at the foe and he forgot to wonder about his gun being loaded, but began to fire it as if it were an automatic affair. "He suddenly lost concern for himself, and forgot to look at a menacing fate. He became not a man but a member . . . He was welded into a common personality which was dominated by a single desire. For some moments he could not flee, no more than a little finger can commit a revolution from a hand."

COMMENT: It is significant that the youth's temporary "courage" at this point (he will of course flee before long) is a result of a feeling of membership in a common personality. But the feeling is still too much the result of reflection, and too much dependent on the closeness and solidity of the other members.

The noise gives him assurance; his sense of the regiment as a firework proceeding "superior to circumstance," the consciousness of his comrades' presence, and his sense of a "subtle battle brotherhood" seem necessary to sustain his nerve. Furthermore, it is a courage as yet untried by any real challenges. These are soon to begin, as his blistering sweat, cracking eyeballs, and roaring ears are followed by a red rage. His one-shot rifle gives him a feeling of impotency against the "swirling battle phantoms." He had to fight for air, as a babe who is being smothered fights the deadly blankets.

COMMENT: The comparison with the smothering baby is far from casual. (Shortly after, in fact, the man at his elbow is described as "babbling . . . soft and tender like the monologue of a babe.") Battle reduces the youth to a condition of psychological infancy, necessitating the "education" which his later experiences provide.

In addition to the babbling man, there are sounds of snarling, imprecation, and prayer, forming a chantlike undercurrent to the war march (that is, the sounds of rifles and cannon). The tall soldier swore "curious oaths," and another man plaintively wondered aloud why they had not been given support. The youth listened to all this through the haze of a "battle sleep." None of the heroic poses which he had earlier envisioned were at all in evidence. Men were "surging" in impossible attitudes, cartridge-box flaps "bobbed idiotically," and rifles were jerked and fired aimlessly at forms which had been increasing in size "like puppets under a magician's hand" (even the "war as drama" metaphor here degenerates into a puppet show). The officers, too, appear ridiculous, looking like awkward and boisterous children as they bob to and fro, give vent to extraordinary howls, and practically stand on their heads in excitement. The lieutenant had to pummel a deserting soldier back into line and even help him to load his gun. The captain had been killed earlier, and his face bore an "astonished and sorrowful look"; the babbling man, his head grazed by a bullet, was bleeding freely; another man, shot in the stomach, sat down with a rueful gaze.

At last the attack was turned back. The enemy departed, leaving their debris behind. Some of the youth's regiment whooped in a frenzy; others remained silent. The youth became aware of the suffocating atmosphere and took a long drink of the warm water in his canteen. Along the line went the triumphant claim, "We've helt 'em back; derned if we haven't." And the narrator remarks, "The men said it blissfully, leering at each other with dirty smiles."

COMMENT: A leer is (according to a common dictionary definition) "a sly look or sidewise glance expressing salacious desire, malicious intent, knowing complicity, etc." While "dirty smiles" may refer merely to the grime on the men's faces, there is a certain ambiguity about the entire sentence; it may well be meant by Crane to suggest (what is a psychological commonplace) that there is a subtle sexual aspect to the martial drive, just as there is to the enthusiastic frenzies of certain primitive religious rites (both of which ideas enter into the pattern of imagery in the closing chapters of the book).

At last finding leisure to look about, the youth noticed ghastly bodies lying in grotesquely twisted attitudes. From the rear of the grove came a volley of shells from a number of guns which "squatted in a row like savage chiefs" as if they were holding a "grim pow-wow." Processions of wounded men, masses of troops, sounds of cheering and combat, the noise of guns, all gradually relinquish their hold on the youth's attention, and he suddenly notices with a thrill the striped emblem of his country, looking "like a beautiful bird undaunted in a storm." His gaze turns upward, and he notices in astonishment the blue, pure sky and the gleaming sun. "It was surprising that Nature had gone tranquilly on with her golden process in the midst of so much devilment."

SUMMARY: This chapter covers the first attack to which the youth is directly exposed. He is among the reserves of the 304th, who stand firm and repulse the enemy. It is mainly concerned with the youth's physiological responses to combat, and the psychological changes they bring. Specifically:

1. As before, characters are put before us in brief, epitomizing phrases: a hatless general who makes a "passionate gesture" and gallops away; a stammering, petulant colonel: the captain who coaxes his troops like a schoolmistress, and tells them to hold their fire until they are close up (ironically, he is among the first to be killed); the valiant lieutenant.

2. The question of the youth's "courage" is related to his sense of "membership" in a common personality, and is thus tied in with earlier images of bodily "members" and "amputation."

3. Imagery:

a. The "religious" metaphor is not prominent except for an allusion to the imprecations of the men as a "chantlike" undercurrent to the war march.

b. The "infancy" figure appears in the simile which compares the youth to a choking baby, as well as in the childlike actions of the officers, and the babbling man.

c. The "war as drama" figure is seen in the "puppet" metaphor, and in the lieutenant's "acting a little isolated scene" with a deserter.

4. Perhaps the finest contribution this chapter makes is to present the ghastly, phantasmagoric pattern of sound (cannon din, curious oaths, infantile monologue), form (idiotic jerks, bobbings, and contortions), and color (black figures of gunners, dominating red of the flag, pure blue sky) which assails the youth's senses.

CHAPTER 6

This chapter opens with the youth in a mood of elation—a premature "ecstasy of self-satisfaction." He saw himself as a magnificent warrior, a fine fellow, who had achieved ideals which he had formerly considered beyond him. Amid a general atmosphere of sociability, of handshakings and earnest conversations, the youth luxuriated. In amazed consternation they were suddenly forced to hear the cry of "Here they come ag'in," and to look toward the wood to see the tilted flag speeding forward once more. Once more, too, the bursting shells and the din. They groaned, fretted, and complained. A voice expressed the wish that its hand had been trodden on by Bill Smithers, instead of the reverse, after which the narrator remarks that the "sore joints of the regiment creaked as it . . . floundered into position." The youth half expected the enemy to apologize and retire gracefully. But the firing began, and the sheets of flame and clouds of smoke arose again. Crane describes the youth at this point in one of his most objective bits of description: "Into the youth's eyes there came a look that one can see in the orbs of a jaded horse. His neck was quivering with nervous weakness and the muscles of his arms felt numb and bloodless. His hands, too, seemed large and awkward as if he was wearing invisible mittens. And there was a great uncertainty about his knee joints."

His comrades' earlier complaints came back to him, and he began to exaggerate the skill and bravery of the enemy, who, he thought, must be machines, "wound up perhaps to fight until sundown." He was reeling from exhaustion, but he fired at an approaching cluster, then stopped. He caught glimpses of men running like pursued imps, and the whole scene became for him "an onslaught of redoubtable dragons. He became like the man who lost his legs at the approach of the red and green monster" (apparently an allusion to some folklore or fairy-tale motif). A man who had been firing by his side, suddenly stopped and fled, while another lad, who a moment before had been a paragon of courage, broke and ran. The youth seemed to receive a sudden illumination—a revelation. "He, too, threw down his gun and fled. There was no shame in his face. He ran like a rabbit." Others also scampered away from the fight, and Henry, yelling in fright, swung about and ran.

COMMENT: Crane is at considerable pains to point out the reflexive, compulsive nature of the youth's act. He has been taken by surprise; he is exhausted; his imagination is at its most susceptible. Indeed, all his former speculations about losing control of his legs, as well as the multiplicity of images depicting the enemy as a serpent or dragon of some sort, blend in his vision of himself as the man who lost his legs at the monster's approach. Furthermore, the "mystic brotherhood" or organic *member*-ship of his regiment is shattered not by the youth, but by the feverish rifleman and the courageous lad nearby, both of whom turn tail and run.

In his panic the youth takes "great leaps" toward the rear, abandoning rifle and cap on the way. Running like a blind man, he first avoids the sword of the bawling lieutenant, then later falls heavily against a tree. As he ran his fears magnified, and he thought the battle noises were stones about to crush him. Striving not to be one of the dragon's initial mouthfuls, he sprinted insanely to the rear. Crossing a field he found himself amidst exploding shells, so that he was forced to go twisting off through some bushes. The sight of a battery firing methodically and coolly aroused in him only a sort of scornful pity, as did the face of a youthful rider, and even the very guns themselves—"six good comrades, in a bold row." He found it hard to understand the reason why a brigade should be going to the help of its fellows, hastening forward to be swallowed up by the war god. Either they were some wondrous breed of men, or else they were outright fools. As he went on the youth slackened his pace, since he had left "the place of noises."

After a time he came upon a general seated on horseback—a quiet man, who looked like a business man in a fluctuating market. The youth even imagined that the general might call upon him for advice. He felt like thrashing him for standing so calmly in one spot, and making no effort to save life by ordering a retreat. Skulking about, he overheard the general issuing orders, through a messenger on a fine chestnut horse, for a regiment to be detached to back up the center. Shortly thereafter the general bounced excitedly in his saddle, joyous with the realization that the line had held. After sending word to follow up this success, he "beamed upon the earth like a sun," and "held a little carnival of joy on horseback."

COMMENT: Crane's ironic reflections on the youth for his failure to comprehend the necessity of professional calm on the part of the general suddenly turn against the general himself, as we perceive that his speech patterns, his instant enthusiasm, and his almost boyish glee at his success are not vastly different from that of the men themselves at their earlier success.

SUMMARY: Chapter 6 treats of the temporary respite enjoyed by the reserves of the 304th, the second charge by the gray line, the boy's flight, and his reactions as he flees to two encounters: the "precise gunners" of a battery; and a quiet general on horseback. His first reaction is one of pity and scorn, but by the end of the chapter there is a slight shaking of his smugness.

1. This crucial chapter provides the reader with an insight into the psychology of flight. The youth is surprised and exhausted (he is compared to a jaded horse). Two staunch comrades at his side flee unabashedly—one runs "like a rabbit," others "scamper away through the smoke," and the youth himself is compared to the "proverbial chicken" (presumably, the "chicken with his head chopped off," who runs about wildly on surviving nervous impulses). Furthermore, it appears to him that the "regiment is leaving *him* behind," rather than the reverse.

2. A number of thematic images reappear in forms which anticipate the youth's desertion:

> **a.** The "god of war"—"the slaves toiling in the temple of this god began to feel rebellion at his harsh tasks."
> **b.** The regiment as "body"—"the sore joints of the regiment creaked as it painfully floundered into position to repulse."
> **c.** The enemy as "serpent"—the youth "became like the man who lost his legs at the approach of the red and green monster."
> **d.** The "automation" figure—it is now the enemy which the youth imagines to be "machines of steel . . . wound up to fight until sundown."

CHAPTER 7

With mingled feelings of shame, amazement, and anger, the youth listened to the cheers which told of a blue success. He tried to tell himself that he had done right in rescuing himself—one little piece which could later rejoin its fellows. His action, he felt, had been correct, commendable, wise. As he thought of his comrades who had remained, his feelings turned to bitterness at their stupidity—a stupidity which had betrayed him. His own enlightened farsightedness had been betrayed by fools. Angry rationalization suddenly passed into apprehension, as he wondered what howls of derision would greet him when he returned to camp, then into acute pity, and finally into a "dull, animal-like rebellion against his fellows." With head bowed, brain in an agonized confusion, and guilt-ridden eyes, he shambled along.

Leaving the open fields, he entered a thick wood, trying to escape the sounds of the rifles. Vines and bushes were spread out like bouquets. Sprays and saplings "cried out" as he trampled among them. "He could not conciliate the forest," and, afraid lest the sounds should bring men to see him "he went far, seeking dark and intricate places."

COMMENT: The "intricate" places may be compared to the "intricate" hole which served as a door to his hut in Chapter 1, both suggestive of penetration into the dimmer regions of the psyche.

The sounds of war grow faint in the distance, and the sun, "suddenly apparent, blazed among the trees," while insects made rhythmical noises in unison. Nature now appears to him in a most idealized form. The landscape is a "fair field holding life"; Nature is a "woman with a deep aversion to tragedy." Throwing a pine cone at a squirrel, he watched it run in fear, and was convinced that this was the law. Danger means flight. The youth "wended, feeling that Nature was of his mind."

COMMENT: The picture the youth entertains is of course false, and will be shattered by the shocking confrontation with the corpse which quickly ensues. The scene as he now views it is the typical "ideal landscape" of so many medieval poems, in which green banks, singing birds, and burgeoning trees are presided over by the goddess *Natura.* The "fair field holding life" is like fourteenth-century writer William Langland's "faire fielde ful of folke" at the opening of his *Piers Ploughman*; the medieval pageantry of the scene is underlined by the archaic connotations of the verb "wended."

There is a glancing reference to another, less favorable, aspect of nature in the swamp, bog tufts, and oily mire which he has to pass through, but at length he reached an enclosure, a "chapel" formed by arching boughs, carpeted with pine needles, and illuminated in a "religious half light." Horror-stricken, he observed a corpse with its back against a tree. The blue uniform had faded to a melancholy green (perhaps it is being reassumed into nature). The eyes were fishlike, the mouth an appalling yellow, and ants crawled along the face. The youth shrieked and stood immobile for several moments exchanging glances with the thing, then cautiously retreated, while his feet caught in brambles and his mind subtly offered the perverse suggestion that he go back and touch the corpse. Finally, he fled.

COMMENT: The "religious metaphor" and the nature imagery come into shocking collision in this scene. The youth, thinking he is escaping from the "swollen war god" into an idyllic earthly paradise (and unconscious of the painful reminders in the blazing sun and the oily mire) stumbles into the very heart of nature and discovers there that She is in effect the divinity to whom war makes its sacrifices. Ironically, even the sacrifice lacks the clean barbarism of knife and bleeding victim, and is instead merely the deposit of a putrescent mass.

SUMMARY: This short chapter contains one of the two or three most shocking episodes which contribute to the maturing of the youth's emotional and intellectual attitudes toward war and courage. He begins by congratulating himself on his sagacious intellect, and escapes from the nagging sense of guilt by burying himself in the bosom of Nature, where he at first finds confirmation of the rightness of his actions, but soon undergoes a horrifying shaking of his purpose, when he encounters the decaying body of the soldier.

CHAPTER 8

The sardonic voice of the narrator opens this chapter by continued references to the hymns chanted by the trees. Suddenly, a "crimson roar" was heard in the distance. His mind was again in a turmoil, and he began to run toward the battle, telling himself that one ought to be a spectator at such a tremendous clash. The ear-shaking thunder of the battle caused him to reflect that the fight he had been involved in was nothing but "perfunctory popping." He began to take his own and his mates' initial attitude of seriousness toward the battle with a sort of wry humor. They had supposed that their deeds of glory would cut their names "deep into everlasting tablets of brass," and that their reputations would be forever enshrined "in the hearts of their countrymen." But he reflected that perhaps even such illusions might be good, if they prevented wholesale flight from battle.

COMMENT: This echo of Henry Lee's eulogy on George Washington—"first in war, first in peace, and first in the hearts of his countrymen"—epitomizes the publicly accepted standard of heroism. As he thus formulates it, the youth appears to be thinking ironically, but his irony is neither total nor absolute, and he begins to see good in gestures of heroism.

As the youth hastened on, the brambles and trees formed chains which held him back and he reflected with a "fine bitterness" on the new resistance of the forest (to letting him pass into battle) considering its previous hostility (its interference as he had run away, and the horror of the "chapel" scene). Obstinately he pressed on, fascinated by the image of battle as "the grinding of an immense and terrible machine," producing corpses. He passed through a field littered with clothes and guns, a newspaper, and a group of corpses "keeping mournful company." He felt like an invader in the place, and hurried on. Finally, the youth arrived at a road, along which came a "blood stained crowd" of men, whose curses and groans mingled with the cheers of others and the "courageous words of the artillery and the spiteful sentences of the musketry." Against the stupendous din and pageantry of the battle, this "steady current of the maimed" appeared like a parade of contorted puppets. A man with a shoeful of blood hopped like a schoolboy in a game; another appeared to be imitating "some sublime drum major." Still another had the gray seal of death on his face (this is Jim Conklin, though the youth doesn't recognize him); his hands were bloody, he stalked like a specter, staring into the unknown.

A wounded officer peevishly criticized his bearers and bellowed at those blocking his way. In reply, they told him to be damned. The shoulder of one of the bearers knocked against the spectral soldier (Conklin). At this point the youth fell in with the melancholy march.

A tattered man, stained with blood and powder, trudged along "listening with eagerness and much humility to the lurid descriptions of a bearded sergeant. His lean features wore an expression of awe and admiration. He was like a listener in a country store to wondrous tales told among the sugar barrels . . . His mouth was agape in yokel fashion."

COMMENT: This description well illustrates the problem of deciding whether the narrator is reporting his own interpretation of events, or the youth's. On the one hand we are given a number of idealizing details: the formulaic description "the tattered man"; his "humility" and "lean features"; his comparison to a "listener . . . to wondrous tales." On the other hand, we note the reference to the country store and the sugar barrels, the entire description terminating in the sharply contrasted sentences, "He eyed the story-teller with unspeakable wonder," and "His mouth was agape in yokel fashion." It is probably best to consider this kind of antithesis as a reflection of the tension in the youth's own conflicting attitudes. He vacillates between a vision of heroic warriors, whose deeds and postures are charged with a kind of sanctified significance, and a vision of aimlessly cavorting puppets.

The youth noted that the tattered soldier had a gentle voice, pleading eyes, and wounds in his head and arm. In an apologetic manner, he tried to engage Fleming in conversation about the battle. He had much praise for the way the boys had fought, and after recounting a dialogue in which a Georgia soldier had told him across a picket line that the blue soldiers would run at the sound of a gun, he ended, "No, sir! They fit, an' fit, an' fit." For a while his homely face "was suffused with a light of love" for the army; then, suddenly, he turned to the youth and inquired where he was hit. In a panic Fleming turned and slid away, forehead flushed and fingers nervously picking at a button.

SUMMARY: This brief chapter advances the plot in a few specific ways:

1. The youth's certainty that he was right in fleeing is seen to be modified.

2. He meets the "spectral soldier"—Conklin, though he doesn't recognize him—and this underscores the terrible metamorphosis which war brings about in persons.

3. His encounter with the tattered soldier is the beginning of his suffering of the shame of his flight.

PART III: THE RETURN TO CAMP
CHAPTER 9

The youth fell back in the procession of the wounded, out of sight of the tattered soldier. Amidst the bleeding throng he felt that his shame was on display, and he glanced about furtively. He was envious of them; he wished that he, too, had "a wound, a red badge of courage."

COMMENT: This is the first time that the phrase "red badge of courage" has appeared in the book.

The spectral soldier stalked at his side, his gray face causing others to gather about and slow their pace to his. With lips tightly closed, he signed them to go on; he seemed to be "taking infinite care not to arouse the passion of his wounds." Suddenly the youth recognized his waxlike features and screamed in horror, "Gawd! Jim Conklin!" Jim made a commonplace gesture and held out his gory hand. As the youth lamented over him in an inarticulate way, Conklin made gestures of concern about the youth's own adventures in the day's fighting. He seemed bewildered about his own wound, and as Henry put forth arms to assist him, he appeared to be overcome by terror and his face turned to "a semblance of gray paste." In a shaky whisper he confided to Henry his fear of being run over by the artillery wagons, and the youth promised to take care of him, though the gulpings in his throat made him speak somewhat inaccurately. The tall soldier clung "babelike" to the youth's arm, and began to whine for assistance. Sobbing in anguish, Henry could only make fantastic gestures to express his loyalty. All of a sudden, the tall soldier recovered himself and went forward with "mysterious purpose." At the suggestion of the tattered soldier Henry tried to grasp Jim's arm and lead him off the road, out of the way of an approaching artillery battery. Wrenching free, Conklin dashed off through the field toward a clump of bushes, with the youth and the tattered soldier in pursuit. As they overtook him, the tall soldier pleaded to be left alone and lurched ahead with "ritelike" movements. He resembled "a devotee of a mad religion," and they stood off in awe of him. Finally he became motionless, and with figure erect and bloody hands at his side he waited for the thing he had come to meet. "He was at the rendezvous."

COMMENT: It has been suggested that Alan Seeger's fine poem of World War I, "I have a rendezvous with Death," owes its title (and perhaps its basic conception) to this passage of Crane's. The poem concludes:

. . . I've a rendezvous with Death
At midnight in some flaming town,
When Spring trips north again this year,
And I to my pledged word am true,
I shall not fail that rendezvous.

After a brief silence, Conklin's chest began to heave, with increasing violence "as if an animal was within and was kicking and tumbling furiously to be free."

COMMENT: Crane's technique of inversion (such as the imputation of will and purpose to nature at the same time that he practically denies it to human beings) reaches its extreme form in this image, in which the traditional figure of the spiritual soul striving for release from the animal body becomes an animal struggling to be free of a cage or trap. Even the non-Christian twentieth-century Irish poet W. B. Yeats (in "Sailing to Byzantium") speaks of his heart as "sick with desire / And fastened to a dying animal."

The youth writhed at the sight and fell to the ground, wailing. Conklin's form suddenly stiffened; a "creeping strangeness" came over him and he danced a sort of "hideous hornpipe," with his arms flailing about in "imp-like enthusiasm." He fell forward like a tree, and his left shoulder struck the ground after which the body "seemed to bounce a little way from the earth." The face was pastelike, the mouth open and the teeth showing in a laugh. His side looked as though it had been chewed by wolves. The youth shook his fist at the battlefield, and (the famous ending) "the red sun was pasted in the sky like a wafer."

COMMENT: This line has provoked a good deal of discussion and controversy, mainly centering on the question of whether the word "wafer" is to be taken merely as "sealing wafer" (the wax seal for an envelope) or "communion wafer" (the sacramental form of Christ's body), and, consequently, whether the image should be regarded simply as a bit of naturalistic description or as a symbolic allusion to the death of Conklin as a Christ figure through whose "sacrifice" Henry Fleming achieves his "redemption." In support of the symbolic interpretation, notice should of course be taken of the continuing religious metaphor appearing in all the earlier chapters, as well as the references to Conklin's bloody hands, his wounded side, and the "passion of his wounds." Somewhat less impressive details for purposes of argument are his initials (J. C., for Jesus Christ?) and the description of his body as seeming "to bounce a little way from the earth" (the Resurrection?). Against the symbolic reading—at least in its form of a consistent and absolute analogy between Christ and Conklin—are any number of other details, such as his identification as a "devotee of a mad religion" (which hardly squares with the relationship of Christ to Christianity).

CHAPTER 10

This chapter opens with a sharp contrast of attitudes toward Conklin's death. The tattered man muses thoughtfully, and can only remark, "Well, he was a reg'lar jim-dandy," while the youth throws himself on the ground in an agony of grief. But looking up suddenly he observed that the tattered soldier was himself swaying uncertainly on his legs and had grown pale. To Henry's apprehensive words, however, he replied merely that all he needed was some pea soup and a good bed. As they gazed together at the corpse, the youth "murmured something," and his companion simply repeated his earlier comment, "Well, he was a jim-dandy, wa'nt'e?"

COMMENT: The youth's "murmur" is either one of Crane's not infrequent exasperatingly vague declarations, or else is meant to suggest, perhaps, that his response to Conklin's "ritual" death is an automatic, nonverbal murmur akin to the "chanted chorus" of insects and birds in the cathedral of the forest—another sign of his gradual assimilation into the *pattern* of nature.

As they stole away from the fallen body, the tattered soldier groaned once more, and the youth wondered if he was to be the "tortured witness" of another death. But his friend reassured him with lighthearted words that he was not about to die.

The tattered soldier then thinks of his own wound and how he received it. He was fighting when all of a sudden a fellow alongside (Tom Jamison) began to swear at him for not noticing that he had been shot. He had put his hand up to his head and discovered a wound, "hollered" and ran, and then felt another hit in the arm. He would be fighting yet, he mused, if it hadn't been for Tom Jamison. (Another instance of the part played by *chance* in the matter of courage.) Quickly, the tattered man leaves the subject of his own wounds, and turns to the youth, asking him where *his* wound is "located." It might be inside, he goes on, "an' them plays thunder." It might be some "queer kind' a hurt," he decides, and asks again where it is "located."

COMMENT: The tattered man's insistence here, particularly his desire to know where Henry's wound is "located" (as if it were some precise point, to be graphed with coordinates) underscores the youth's own problem of finding the locus of courage (in heart? head? legs and arms?).

In rage and exasperation, the youth dismisses the tattered man's questions. His companion's curiosity was always "upraising the ghost of shame." With a glance of hatred and contempt he said good-bye to the other, who thereupon floundered in a spate of half-formed statements and questions, finally giving in to hallucinations in which he saw the youth as Tom Jamison, and chided him for going away while his wound needed caring for. As the youth climbed a fence he looked back to see the tattered man wandering about helplessly in a field. The narrator declares that the youth "thought that he wished he was dead" and "believed that he envied" the dead men whose bodies lay strewn over the battlefield. The tattered man's questions were a sign of a pitilessly probing society, sure to reveal the crime in his bosom. He could not "defend himself against this agency."

COMMENT: The youth's identification of his own fraternity—his fellow soldiers—as an "enemy" against which he must "defend" himself breaks down even further the easy categories of "friend" and "enemy" and thus contributes to his growing sense that "courage," whatever it might be, is not to be achieved through any sort of analytical formula.

SUMMARY: This chapter clearly belongs to the "tattered man," and raises important questions about his significance for the total meaning of the book. The following are some of the contributions this chapter makes:

1. Aside from its conformity to Crane's general method of identification through an epitomizing phrase ("tall soldier," etc.) the description "tattered man" provokes certain ambiguous responses in the reader. Like a baggy-pants clown, he combines humor and pathos, in a vague gamut of echoes between such extremes as the nursery-rhyme "man all tattered and torn" and the motley-garbed fool in *King Lear.*

2. Not only is the "tattered man" an objectively ambiguous figure, but his own responses to the horror of wounds and death ("fun," "funny," "queer," "the funniest thing," "a reg'lar jim-dandy," etc.) symbolize the bizarre warping of emotions that the nightmare of battle can produce. Even the friend, Tom Jamison, who sympathetically calls attention to this wound does so with a bellowed curse—"yeh blamed infernal."

3. In realistic terms the "tattered soldier's persistent questioning leads the youth to the realization that he can not possibly hope to keep his crime concealed; in metaphoric terms the ambiguity which radiates from the "tattered soldier's" action is matched by the youth's imaginative embodiment of his own army as an "enemy" against which he must defend himself.

CHAPTER 11

Henry becomes aware of the increasing "furnace roar" of the battle; brown clouds floated to the heights, the noise approached, and the woods "filtered men."

COMMENT: The naturalistic (and traditional) description of battle noise as a roar is significantly qualified here. "Furnace roar" and "filtering" woods suggest that battle is a kind of chemical process in which things are purified by fire, an image which looks back to Chapter 2 in which the youth had compared his own desire for blaze, blood, and danger, to the chemist's requirements for ingredients to be employed in an analytical process.

The roadway was a confused jumble of retreating men, wagons, and horses. It was comforting to the youth, who was able to use the uproar to magnify in his mind the horrors of the battle, and thus to vindicate his own desertion. Presently an advancing column of infantry appeared, like a sinuous serpent, pushing forward by main force and swearing "many strange oaths." They were eager to confront the enemy, proud of their forward rush, filled with a "fine feeling" of importance. They were a reproach to the youth, just as the retreating hordes were a vindication. He wondered what they could have eaten, that they could be in such a hurry to meet their doom. They inspired in him once more romantic visions of himself as a dashing figure "leading lurid charges" and standing calmly in the face of danger. Uplifted by these thoughts he felt a quiver of war desire, knew the frenzy of a successful charge. "For a few moments he was sublime." Then, as he reflected on the difficulties of the thing, he hesitated. Each doubt, for a time, was easily resolved. He had no rifle—yet rifles abounded on the field. He could not find his regiment—yet he could fight with any regiment. He might be observed skulking back by some of his comrades—yet in the fight his face would be hidden. Finally, however, his "courage expended itself on these objection." And in any case various physical ailments had begun to cry out. He had a scorching thirst; his skin was dry; his bones ached; his feet were sore. Hunger was causing him to sway; it blurred his sight. It was impossible, he now thought, that he should ever be a hero. "He was a craven loon." Yet a certain "mothlike quality" within him kept him near the battle.

COMMENT: This is a reference of course to the fable of the moth and the flame (instinctively it seeks the flame and is consumed by it). In this image the human-as-animal figure and the battle-as-fire figure merge. It is a reminder that instinct continually operates in the youth to offset the decisions arrived at speculatively.

The youth wished to discover who was winning, and had to admit (apologetically) to his conscience that a defeat would be a favorable thing for him; in the general rout he could easily convince others that he had not run faster or farther then they. He began to construct an elaborate justification for his welcoming to defeat. Other defeats had been mourned for a while but were in time forgotten. And after all it was the generals, not the men, who had to bear the brunt of public criticism. Indeed, public opinion would probably hit upon the wrong general anyway, and he would then be forced to spend his remaining days composing replies to the allegations of his failure—unfortunate, but hardly of any consequence to Henry Fleming. He himself would be vindicated. A prophet who predicts a flood should be the first man to climb a tree. Moral vindication seemed very necessary to him. Unaccountably, these self-glorifying thoughts gave way to self denunciation. He saw himself now as a villain, and imagined his comrades' dripping corpses tacitly rebuking him as their murderer. Once more he envied the corpses. Many of them no doubt would receive their laurels from tradition without having really been tested. Theirs would be stolen crowns and robes of sham.

But defeat of the blue army quickly appeared to him as unthinkable. The mighty blue machine would turn out victories "as a contrivance turns out buttons." He tried to think of a "fine tale" with which he could turn back the jeers which were certain to come his way, but he found that it was impossible. They were all vulnerable. He would be able to meet sneers and laughter only with stammering hesitation. He would become an object of insolence and scorn —a "slang phrase."

SUMMARY: This chapter is notable for its pattern of quick alternation between optimism and despair, self-scorn and self-glorification, romantic visions and realistic descriptions. In this respect, it conveys well the turmoil of the mind lost in the agony of rationalization continually punctured by true perceptions. In addition:

1. The figure of battle as furnace (roaring and flaming), which in any case carries almost mythic connotations of "purification by fire," catches up earlier suggestions of the "chemistry of battle" and looks ahead to a comparison of the youth to the moth which seeks the flame. In general, the effect is to keep in the offing a strong hint that the youth will achieve redemption in battle, and that this will be attained through the domination of feeling over speculation.

2. The religious metaphor continues to provide an ironic undercurrent to the narrator's descriptions:

a. The advancing regiment appears as a "procession of chosen beings" (hence "chosen people").
b. The youth "could have wept in his longings" ("by the waters of Babylon we sat down and wept"—Psalm 137).
c. The youth refers to himself at different moments as "prophet," "seer," and "cowled man."
d. The slain are said to wear "stolen crowns" and "sham robes" (possibly merely the classical laurel and toga, but perhaps suggesting also the crown of martyrdom and the robes of the elect).

The effect of the "religious" imagery is still one of wry insinuation that the parallel between religious and military "zeal," "ardency," "ceremony," "worship," and so forth is sound enough, but that it has to be applied consistently, so as to include such things as "bloody sacrifice," "spiritual desolation," and "martyrdom."

CHAPTER 12

As the chapter opens, the same column of men which had moments before advanced so stoutly and gestured so heroically came flooding out of the woods in retreat. The youth was struck dumb in agony and amazement, and threw aside his "mental pamphlets on the philosophy of the retreated and rules for the guidance of the damned."

COMMENT: This is perhaps a reference to the unwitting pretentiousness of the titles of philosophical works which promise to teach codes of action from a purely theoretical standpoint (perhaps even specifically to such a title as the twelfth-century Jewish theologian Moses Maimonides' *Guide for the Perplexed*). If so, the irony is twofold, in that no "mental pamphlets" are of any avail in the heat of battle, and also in the fact that the youth has come to see his position not as of one "perplexed," but of one "retreated . . . and damned."

The fight, he saw, was lost. The blood-swollen god of war intended to glut itself further. He wanted to cry out, to make a rallying speech, but he could not. Without thinking, he plunged into the midst of them, firing incoherent, unheeded questions at them as they galloped along. Finally he clutched a man by the arm, a man with livid face and rolling eyes, who screamed "Let go me!" and promptly brought his rifle butt down on the youth's head and ran on.

The youth's fingers "turned to paste," and his muscles relaxed. ". . . He saw the flaming wings of lightning flash before his vision. Suddenly his legs seemed to die. He sank writhing to the ground. He tried to arise. In his efforts against the numbing pain he was like a man wrestling with a creature of the air."

COMMENT: This passage is rich with significance. First of all, we note that this is Henry's "wound"—what will become his "red badge of courage," and it is inflicted upon him not by the enemy but by one of his own comrades, and a fleeing man at that. Furthermore, the realistic description of the shock and pain (the flash before the eyes, and the rumble in the head) is couched in terms which suggest the suddenness as well as the celestial portentousness of a visionary experience leading to a conversion. Quite specifically, it suggests an analogy with the experience of Saul on the road to Damascus, who fell at a lightning flash to the ground, trembling and astonished, and who, after three days of blindness, was restored to himself as a servant of the Lord. Similarly, the youth's failure to submit to the "religion" of war identifies him as a pagan; after the "lightning flash" and the "rumble of thunder" he falls writhing to the ground, senses dulled, and finally arises and walks "tall soldier fashion" in search of a secluded place to rest.

As he recovers from his swoon, the first thing he notices is a number of officers who are in fact behaving in a most valorous fashion. One, on a "besplashed charger," was making excited motions "with a gauntleted hand." A squadron of cavalry rode up and there was a mighty altercation. The guns suddenly roared out, belching and howling "like brass devils guarding a gate." As he walked on, the "purple darkness was filled with men who lectured and jabbered," with overturned wagons, bodies of horses, and parts of war machines. "It had come to pass" (notice the biblical phrasing) that his wound pained him but little. It had a cool, liquid feeling about it, though his head felt greatly swollen. He was worried, in fact, by his wound's new silence, yet he found opportunity to think about his home, and call up memories of his mother's dishes, the glowing walls of the kitchen, and swimming expeditions with his school chums. Soon, however, he was overtaken by weariness, and slumped along with head bowed until a man with a cheery voice fell in with him, and began to question him, and to talk about his own experiences in battle, concluding that "it was the most mixed up dern thing I ever see." As they passed a wounded officer, the cheery man observed wryly that he would not be so concerned with thoughts of glory when they began to saw off his leg, but added sympathetically, "Poor feller! My brother's got whiskers jest like that." He then embarked on a detailed and matter-of-fact account of the manner in which a friend of his (named "Jack") had met his death that day. All the while that he talked, the man of the cheery voice threaded his way through the mazes of the forest with great keenness until he had found the youth's regiment. With a warm hand clasp, he took his leave, and only then did the youth realize that he had not once caught a glimpse of his face.

SUMMARY: There are two events of central importance in this chapter—the youth receives a head wound from a fleeing comrade; he falls in with a soldier with a "cheery voice," who guides him back to his regiment:

1. The wounding has three main aspects.

a. The basic tone of irony in the *Red Badge* finds, in this central incident, a strong emphasis since the youth is wounded by a "friend," by the *butt* of a rifle, and by a fleeing (hence "cowardly") man, while he himself is trying to move toward the front.
b. In terms of the religious metaphor this becomes a "visionary" experience for the youth, attended by lightning (before his eyes) and thunder (within his head), out of which springs his "conversion."
c. His fall to the ground and consequent efforts to rise "like a babe trying to walk, to his feet" suggests his reduction to a condition of psychological and emotional "infancy" (like King Lear on the health) from which point his re-education may begin.

2. The encounter with the "cheery-voiced" man (just after his wound) stands in contrast to his encounter with the "tattered soldier" (just before it). Since he is now "wounded" the cheery soldier accepts him without quizzing him about his wounds and parts with a warm handshake. This anticipates the welcome Henry receives (to his surprise) from his comrades in the 304th.

CHAPTER 13

As the youth approached the campfire tended by members of the 304th he thought of hiding in the darkness, but hunger and exhaustion drove him on. Suddenly he was challenged by a shadowy figure with a rifle. It was Wilson (the "loud soldier"), who promptly welcomed Henry with affectionate remarks. The youth thought he had to produce a tale to defend himself against the barbs of his comrades, so he spoke of the terrible fighting he had been in, his separation from the regiment, and his having been "shot" in the head. At this, the corporal (Simpson) stepped up and, recognizing Henry, joined Wilson in exclamations of concern. As Simpson walked off with the youth, Wilson offered him his blanket and his canteen full of coffee.

Once back in the glare of the fire, the corporal had a look at the youth's head, and whistled through his teeth as he probed the "splashed blood and the rare wound." He concluded that the youth had been grazed by a ball, just a "damn' good belt on the head an' nothin' more." Promising to send Wilson to care for him, the corporal went off. As the youth looked around in the dim light, he saw sprawling bodies, and pallid and ghostly visages, looking like men drunk with wine—the "result of some frightful debauch." On the other side of the fire an officer was sleeping, his back against a tree. His body swayed and his jaw hung down; he was the "picture of an exhausted soldier after a feast of war." He had obviously gone to sleep with his sword in his arms, but it had fallen and the brass hilt was in contact with the fire. In the gleam of rose and orange light other sleeping forms could be discerned. "The fire crackled musically." Leaves, silver in color and edged with red, moved softly. Occasionally, in this "low-arched hall," soldiers shifted their positions, sat, blinked at the fire, and lay down once more.

COMMENT: This scene is clearly meant to parallel that earlier scene (Chapter 7) in which the forest is viewed as a chapel formed by arching boughs, in which the youth comes across the dead soldier, his back propped against a tree. Here, the forest is no longer a "chapel" but a "low-arched hall" (perhaps suggesting the mead hall of Anglo-Saxon warriors).

The youth's reverie was interrupted by the arrival of the loud soldier, who moved about "with the bustling ways of an amateur nurse." ". . . He fussed around the fire and stirred the sticks to brilliant exertions. He made his patient drink largely from the canteen that contained the coffee. It was to the youth a delicious draught. He tilted his head afar back and held the canteen long to his lips. The cool mixture went caressingly down his blistered throat. Having finished, he sighed with comfortable delight."

COMMENT: This certainly is one of the most contrived "poetic" passages in the entire book. One notices the continued alliteration of *f* and *c*, as well as such strained effects as "stirred the sticks" and "long to his lips." The result is a half-ironic, somewhat mocking tone, serving to counterpoint the serious theme of "heroic comradeship" which the imagery of the chapter (the "low-arched hall," epic-warrior motif) suggests.

Wilson then made a bandage out of a handkerchief and placed it on the youth's head, tying it in a "queer knot" at the back of his neck. To Henry, the cold cloth felt like a woman's tender hand. Wilson's solicitousness, however, began to make him uneasy, and he fumbled with his buttons. The loud soldier then prepared his own blanket as a bed for the youth, who gratefully stretched out on the ground. "He gave a long sigh, snuggled down into his blanket, and in a moment was like his comrades."

COMMENT: The narrator's final statement is deliberately ambiguous. Henry *is* like his comrades in the literal sense that he is now wrapped in a blanket and sleeping just as they are. But in another sense the statement is merely a question: Is his "wound" simply a fortuitous occurrence, which has made it possible for him to rejoin his comrades, from whom he does not actually differ with respect to "courage" by any perceptible degree?

SUMMARY: The youth's apprehensions about being jeered at turn out to be groundless. He is received affectionately by Wilson and Simpson, and given the food and rest he needs. Other significant developments:

1. The youth's earlier vision of the forest as a chapel is transformed into one of the forest as a warriors' hall—with a striking parallel between the dead soldier of Chapter 7 and the sleeping officer of Chapter 13.
2. A change has come over Wilson. Not boisterousness but a gentle solicitude seems to be his main characteristic.
3. Style—particularly the overly "poetic" touches which are used to describe Wilson's actions—continues to act as a qualification of meaning, giving a touch of irony to the narrator's vision of "comradeship."

CHAPTER 14

As the youth awakened from what seemed like a thousand-year sleep, the "quaint light" imparted a corpselike hue to the tangled limbs about him. "His disordered mind interpreted the hall of the forest as a charnel place," but he quickly recognized that this thought was not a fact but a prophecy. In the "heraldic wind of the day," and amidst distant bugles and the rumble of drums the regiment arose. The youth's head felt like a melon, and as Wilson tinkered clumsily at the bandage Henry rebuked him with angry words. Wilson responded in a mollifying tone of voice, and continued to care for Henry's wants; his manner, as the youth began to note, was changed remarkably. He had a "quiet belief in his purposes and abilities. . . . The youth wondered where had been born these new eyes." Wilson seemed to have "climbed a peak of wisdom" from which he could see his own insignificance.

COMMENT: The change in Wilson's character is much too abrupt to be realistic, and it proves that *The Red Badge* is not a psychological novel in any ordinary sense. Wilson's change may well be related to the "religious" metaphor also, in the sense that he has miraculously conformed to a martial equivalent of the command, "Know thyself"; has "put off the old man and put on the new"; and is no longer "wise in his own conceits."

With some embarrassment Henry pointed out to Wilson the change that had come over him, but Wilson replied casually that he had been a big fool "in those days." Then, after some perfunctory comments about yesterday's battle, the youth reported the fact that Jim Conklin had died, receiving in reply only the noncommittal remark, "Yeh don't say so. Jim Conklin . . . poor cuss!" Just then a fracas erupted among some soldiers nearby, and Wilson's efforts to restore only peace achieved for him a challenged to a fight with "a huge soldier" (named Jimmie Rogers). The youth continued to comment on the striking change in his nature, but Wilson shunted aside his remarks, preferring to talk about the dispersion of the regiment on the previous day. "They'd been scattered all over, wanderin' around in th' woods, fightin' with other reg'ments, an' everything. Jest like you done." "So?" said the youth (on which noncommittal reply the chapter ends).

SUMMARY: This brief chapter

1. confirms the change in Wilson's character, and interprets it in terms of the religious metaphor

2. establishes beyond question the youth's acceptance by the regiment

CHAPTER 15

The regiment was just about to march when the youth suddenly remembered the little packet of letters which Wilson (henceforth called usually "his friend") had entrusted to him. He rejoiced in the fact that he possessed a weapon which he could use against Wilson if he should begin to question him about the previous day's battle. He adopted an air of condescension. *His* mistakes had been performed in the dark, so he was still a man. Past sufferings were put aside; he had a full stomach and the respect of his fellows. He triumphed in his escape from retribution. He had confidence in himself as a man of experience. In his elation he saw himself as the "chosen of the gods." Even his escape was conducted with dignity, and he felt only scorn for the terror-struck faces of the other fleeing men.

This reverie was interrupted by the voice of Wilson, who sheepishly asked him for the packet of letters. Unable to invent a sufficiently apt comment on the affair he returned the letters silently, taking credit for his great generosity. The more Wilson blushed in shame, the more Henry felt full of virtues. He became certain that he could entertain audiences at home with romantic tales of his martial accomplishments.

SUMMARY: The youth's satisfaction over his unchallenged return to the regiment turns to a feeling of superiority and condescension towards Wilson, who has made himself vulnerable with his maudlin speech and the packet of letters. Henry so far forgets his own former acts as to credit himself with a heart that is "strong and stout."

PART IV: THE FIRST CHARGE

CHAPTER 16

This chapter opens with a style and imagery suggestive of the tedium of battle. "A sputtering of musketry was always to be heard. Later, the cannon had entered the dispute. In the fog-filled air their voices made a thudding sound . . ."

COMMENT: Rhythm is occasionally used by Crane to suggest an attitude—at times one of sarcastic exaggeration. Here, the onomatopoeia in the word "sputtering" (indicating in its very sound its meaning of "ineffectual, sporadic noise") reinforces the jingling ineffectuality of the rhythm (the opening sentence is also a perfect "fourteener").

x / x / x / x /
"A sputtering of musketry / /
x / x / x /
was always to be heard."

The curving line of rifle pits looked like a large furrow. In front was a field filled with deformed stumps. From the woods came a "dull popping" noise, and from the right the sounds of a "terrific fracas." Men "cuddled" behind the embankment; "idle flags were perched" on the hills; the guns were engaged in a "stupendous wrangle." The sound of musketry "growing like a released genie of sound," emphasized the generally disheartened condition of the men. They could not comprehend the idea of defeat. Before the sun had completely obliterated the morning mists, they were retiring through the woods, pursued by the shrill yells of the enemy. The youth, though he realized it might sound unhandsome for him to criticize other men, embarked upon a long denunciation of the commander of his forces. His friend (Wilson) charitably defended the commander, but the youth persisted, demanding loudly, "Don't we do all that men can?" He was dumbfounded at this sentiment as soon as it broke from his lips, but, remaining unchallenged, he recovered his "air of courage," and continued to castigate the mistakes made by "some derned old lunkhead of a general." A sarcastic man asked Fleming if he thought that perhaps he had fought the whole battle himself, and he felt himself pierced by this speech, reduced to an "abject pulp," with quaking legs and a frightened glance. He became more conciliatory and modest.

The rest of the troops were sullen and testy, cursing and muttering as they were pursued by a noise like "the yellings of eager, metallic hounds." As they halted in a clear space, it became apparent that the enemy was about to attack, and there was much growling and swearing. Henry continued his critical murmurings, sharply rebuking an optimistic comment offered by Wilson. A "savage-minded lieutenant" vented his own dissatisfaction by telling them both to shut up. Just as the sun shed its full radiance on the thronged forest a rifle and was followed by a "mighty song of clashes and crashes" which became in turn the rolling thunder of a battle roar. The men, exhausted and hesitant, awaited the shock. Though some flinched and shrank, "they stood as men tied to stakes."

SUMMARY: This chapter is mainly important as showing the youth involved in another kind of mental and emotional turmoil. Formerly introspective, cautious, self doubting, he has now gone to the other extreme, and, with excessive zeal of the new convert (ironically, since even he is continually aware of his small claim to "courage") criticizes what he conceives to be the shortcomings of those about him.

1. Imagery: in their exhaustion the blue soldiers are represented as the object of a "hunt," pursued by "barks" and "hounds."

2. In the jibe of the "sarcastic man" the youth has actually received a second "wound" (it pierces him, weakens his legs, and so forth). This too changes him, making him henceforth a "modest person."

CHAPTER 17

The opening paragraph of this chapter describes the youth as fuming with exasperation at the enemy's refusal to give him time to think—to compose himself. He felt that he had earned the right for "contemplative repose."

COMMENT: We are here reminded that "courage" and "cowardice" have a great deal to do with the opportunity for reflection; Crane is perhaps suggesting that Henry's long period of training and anticipation had conditioned him toward the act of flight.

Yesterday he had hated the universe; today he had "a wild hate for the relentless foe." If they chased him like a kitten he too might develop teeth and claws. At Wilson's calm observation that it seemed they would be driven into the river, the youth cried out savagely. His eyes burned and his teeth were set in a "curlike snarl." The "awkward bandage was still about his head, and upon it, over his wound, there was a spot of dry blood."

COMMENT: This spot of blood is, in the most literal sense, his "red badge of courage." We are somehow made to imagine that the youth's feeling of terrible hate, his "curlike" rage, and even his very *sense* of himself as a wounded, tormented, picturesquely desperate figure, are translated directly into the *actions* Fleming takes, which will later add up to the abstraction of *courage.*

His fingers twined nervously about his rifle. His rage became a "dark and stormy specter." Suddenly he was again in the midst of a dense wall of smoke, pierced by knifelike fire from the rifles. As in a dream, he sensed that he was pushing back fierce onslaughts of slippery creatures, who skillfully evaded their "beams of crimson." His rifle became an "impotent stick"; losing the habit of balance, he fell heavily; his brain was in chaos. Mechanically he stuffed cartridges into his rifle, aimed, and pulled the trigger. Each time the enemy fell back he went forward, insolently inviting pursuit. "He was so engrossed in his occupation that he was not aware of a lull." He had become such a demon of battle that he kept firing when the enemy was no longer in sight. His astonished comrades had to stop him. As he sprawled on the ground his flesh seemed on fire, and the battle sounds rang in his ears. He seemed drunk with fighting. The lieutenant paid him a magnificent compliment, while others regarded him with awe-struck looks. The friend asked if anything was the matter with him. These things caused the youth to understand that he had become "a barbarian, a beast." He fought "like a pagan who defends his religion." His obstacles had "fallen like paper peaks, and he was now what he called a hero. And he had not been aware of the process. He had slept and, awakening, found himself a knight."

COMMENT: Instinct, reflexes, compulsive motions—these have been as responsible for the youth's courageous actions as they were for his earlier flight. The only differences have been in external circumstances, in physiological condition, and in the role which accident had thrust on him—that of the "wounded hero."

The lieutenant cried out deliriously in wild, incomprehensible laughter, unconsciously addressing all martial comments to the youth, while the clamor of musketry still came from the forest. Smoke, arising from it "as from smoldering ruins, went up toward the sun now bright and gay in the blue, enameled sky."

COMMENT: The forest is no longer cathedral or chapel, the sun no longer blood-red but bright and gay. These impressionistic touches signalize the youth's changed attitude toward war.

SUMMARY:

1. The enemy charge, begun in the last chapter, is turned back.

2. The youth becomes a "hero," as a result of

a. lack of time to speculate and ponder
b. sheer exasperation which, coupled with exhaustion, is metamorphosed into blind hatred for the enemy
c. the same intense imaginative power that worked towards his earlier flight—except that it now causes him to see himself as a "hunted animal" making a desperate last stand

CHAPTER 18

Though the struggle in the forest increased its din, the "ragged line" of the 304th enjoyed a short lull. A man who had been shot through the body (Jimmie Rogers) cried out bitterly, thrashing about in the grass, and twisting his body into strange positions. The youth's friend, thinking he had seen a stream, went to fetch water. Henry accompanied him, and after a vain search for the stream, during which they spied a burning house, crowds of retreating infantry, and other evidences of the continuing battle, they came upon a mounted general and his staff, who were maneuvering their horses around a wounded man who was crawling on his hands and knees.

COMMENT: This chapter contains a number of sharp parallels with earlier scenes. Rogers' pained contortions resemble the "hideous hornpipe" danced by Conklin in his death throes; the encounter with the "jangling general and his staff," is like the youth's first encounter with the "jingling general" (in both of which a strategic maneuver is overheard). In this chapter the description is less impressionistic, perhaps suggestive of the youth's growing realism.

Fleming and Wilson lingered nearby, hoping to hear "some great inner historical things," but discovering only that the 304th, which one of the officers compared to "a lot 'a mule drivers," was going to be thrown into the breach to stop the attack—with the likelihood that few of them would get back alive. The youth felt suddenly aged. He was given "new eyes," and the most startling thing to learn was that he was very insignificant. They returned only to meet with a wrathful outburst by the lieutenant for their delay—an outburst which was quickly quelled, however, by the news they brought. Upon hearing it many tightened their belts and hitched up their trousers. The officers, like "critical shepherds," tried to form orderly ranks. None of the others seemed occupied by large thoughts, and Wilson and Fleming mutually nursed their "ironical secret."

SUMMARY: During a lull in the fighting the 304th rests. Wilson and Fleming look for water, and overhear the commanding general's order to send them into the breach. Significant points:

1. Parallels with earlier episodes (contortions of wounded soldier, wounded man crawling out of roadway, youth overhearing general's command) underscore Henry's altered imaginative tendencies.

2. The overheard reference to the 304th as "mule drivers" is the ultimate step in the process of de-romanticizing war.

3. The youth for the first time becomes aware of his own insignificance. Couched as it is in terms of his being given "new eyes," this awareness enters into the pattern of religious metaphor ("putting off the old man," "dying to self").

CHAPTER 19

An officer rode up, waving his hat, and the line toppled forward. The youth lunged ahead, his face drawn hard, his eyes "fixed in a lurid glare, and his features red and inflamed." The bandage was now a "dingy rag with a spot of blood." Henry headed for a clump of trees, as the regiment, leaving behind a "coherent trail of bodies," seemed to pass into a clearer atmosphere. His senses were heightened; he saw every blade of grass, every curlicue of cloud. The furious rush turned into a frenzy, barbaric cheerings "tuned in strange keys that can arouse the dullard and the stoic." It was a "mad enthusiasm," a "delirium . . . heedless and blind to the odds."

COMMENT: The description of the charge as "frenzy," "delirium," and "enthusiasm"—all terms with connotations of religious zeal—leads to one of the rare statements made by the narrator in explanation of courageous actions: "It is a temporary but sublime absence of selfishness. And because it was of this order was the reason, perhaps, why the youth wondered, afterward, what reasons he could have had for being there." That is, the youth does not realize, when he has time to reflect, that he too was possessed by a frenzy. Finally, their energies slackened and they faltered and hesitated. They were become men again.

Vaguely, the youth felt that he was in some "new and unknown land." Scattered sounds of musketry became a steady roar, and bodies dropped all around. As the regiment dwindled the men appeared dazed—overcome with a "fatal fascination." (This is the crucial moment, which might result either in a charge or a retreat.)

Suddenly, above the sounds of battle, was heard the roar of the young lieutenant. "He strode suddenly forth, his infantile features black with rage." Cursing mightily, he urged them on. Wilson fired a shot at the woods ahead and the men seemed roused to action by it. As they moved ahead jerkily, many could be seen to cower behind trees, as if amazed at the disturbance they had created. "It was the dominant animal failing" (says the narrator, in what is apparently an attempt to define "cowardice") "to remember in the supreme moments the forceful causes of various superficial qualities." The lieutenant continued to bellow profanely, and grabbed the youth by the arm as if he intended to drag him to the fray. With a feeling of "indignation" Henry wrenched free, and followed by Wilson and the lieutenant, galloped ahead. Looking like a "tortured savage" and running like a "madman," the youth closed the gap. "Pulsating saliva stood at the corners of his mouth."

COMMENT: Objectively regarded, the youth seems in this moment of "courage" most like an animal. Inwardly (and Crane appears to be suggesting an ironic contrast between inner and outer states) he is gripped by the delusion that the flag he was urging on was a "radiant goddess . . . a woman, red and white, hating and loving, that called him with the voice of his hopes."

In an instant, the color sergeant flinched and faltered. Henry and his friend together seized the staff from the dead man's hands, and as the corpse swayed one arm swung high "and the curved hand fell with heavy protest on the friend's unheeding shoulder."

SUMMARY: This chapter covers the charge made by the 304th, from the waving of the officer's hat which begins it, through the moment of wavering intentions, to the renewed burst of speed during which Fleming and Wilson seize the flag from the dead color-bearer.

1. From the standpoint of the main theme, we find here that much attention is given to the "psychology" of "courage." It is shown variously as

a. an enthusiasm producing "a temporary and sublime absence of selfishness," (an "ethical" aspect)
b. a reversion to savagery and animalism (a "naturalistic" aspect)
c. an ennobling, empowering love centered on the flag as "goddess," (a "religious" aspect)

2. Parallels with previous motifs and images:

a. In the vision of the lieutenant's "infantile features black with rage" as he urges them on, the "infancy" figure and the "religious" metaphor merge in an ironic version of the biblical text: "A little child shall lead them."
b. The youth's acquisition of "courage" in succumbing to the romantic symbolism of the flag parallels (also ironically) the part played by the disappointment of romantic expectations in his earlier flight.

CHAPTER 20

In "projectile fashion" the charge spent itself, and the men slowly retreated, contrary to the anguished commands of the officers. One red bearded officer with a "voice of triple brass" was ordering, "Shoot into 'em, Gawd damn their souls!"

COMMENT: There is a bit of subtle irony in the phrase "triple brass." It is taken from the *Odes* of Horace: "Heart of oak and triple brass lay round the breast of him who first to the savage sea entrusted his frail bark." It is the red-bearded officer's *voice*, not his heart, which is of "triple brass."

In the melee Wilson and Fleming scuffled briefly over the flag, until the youth roughly pushed his friend away. The regiment continued to retreat under the merciless pelting of bullets, glowering at the officers who harangued them. Stragglers shot irritably at the advancing foes. Among them was the youthful lieutenant, whose wounded arm hung rigidly at his side. The "multiplied pain" seemed only to increase his abilities in swearing. The youth plodded along scowling, wishing he might avenge himself on the officer who had called them "mule drivers." He was possessed by the "rage of the baffled," unable by any amount of cajoling to turn the direction of march. The regiment was a machine run down.

In the smoke and haze the regiment frequently lost its way, and became panic stricken, giving way to hysterical cries, and runnings hither and thither. Amidst the panic the youth stolidly carried the colors, while the officers labored to form the men into a defensive group. The wounded lieutenant stood mutely, his sword held like a cane. He was "like a babe which, having wept its fill, raises its eyes and fixes them upon a distant toy." The youth could see that he was gazing at a body of enemy soldiery, and it seemed to him, too, that their uniforms were "rather gay in effect" and accented with brilliant hues. The clothes seemed new. At the lieutenant's discovery of them, the blue regiment let loose a volley from their "energetic rifles."

COMMENT: Even the "infancy" figure is employed here to comment on the instinctive, compulsive nature of actions which later appear to have been "courageous." The lieutenant's brave and self-neglectful stand is interpreted by the narrator as a child's fascination with a colorful bauble, once it has cried its fill.

Angry firings passed back and forth, while the enemy pushed on relentlessly and the youth sat gloomily on the ground, the flag resting between his knees. But the enemy's blows finally weakened, and when the smoke cleared the ground would have been an "empty stage" were it not for a few fantastically twisted corpses on the green. The blue ranks cheered in elation. Events proved that they were not hopelessly outnumbered. They felt a new enthusiasm, new pride, new trust. "And they were men."

SUMMARY: The uncertainty, the vacillation, and the motiveless actions of individuals are here mirrored in the adventitious changes of fortune which the enemy forces undergo. The blue charge spends itself; they retreat in discouragement, a "machine run down"; the gray line then charges, is discovered by an accidental lifting of the smoke (partly because of the newness of their uniforms), and is driven back. (There is some irony in the fact that the 304th, without being aware of it, is becoming a "veteran" regiment turning back the charge of an "untried" enemy force.) Various images appear in new and suggestive forms, some of which are

1. the "epic" theme—here in the "red-bearded officer with the *voice* of triple brass"

2. the "automation" figure—the 304th now a "machine run down"

3. the "infancy" figure—the lieutenant's child-like fascination with "newness" actually helps to turn the charge

4. the "regiment as a broom" metaphor, by virtue of the forward pointing flagstaff, enables the youth to see their possible capture as a broom being swallowed "with bristles forward"

CHAPTER 21

Seeing that they were now free of menacing enemies, the regiment, with anxious backward glances, continued its return to the blue entrenchment. As they approached, they were met by jeers and sarcastic questions, and challenges to fist fights filled the air. The youth "glowered with hate at the mockers," while many of his comrades marched along with heads bowed in shame. Gradually he came to realize the absurdly little distance over which they had traveled, and felt that there was a kind of bitter justice in the taunts of the bronzed veterans, and began to look with disdain on his choking, misty eyed fellows who strewed the ground. He managed to take some joy, however, in reflecting on his own actions.

His reverie was sharply punctured by the arrival of the officer who had called them "mule drivers," who now rode up savagely to criticize their colonel (MacChesnay) for the awful mess he had made of things. The colonel defended himself lamely, and the irate general rode off. Along the line men reacted with astonishment at the news that they had been reproached, and lapsed into rebellious silence. The youth reacted with a "tranquil philosophy" he had developed, and his friend wore an air of grievance before injustice. They were soothing each other's feelings when several men hurried up to inform them that the colonel had singled Fleming and Wilson out for great praise, saying, "they deserve t' be major generals." With outward modesty, but ill concealed pleasure, they received these remarks with mutual glances of joy and congratulation. They had a "grateful affection" for the colonel and the lieutenant.

SUMMARY: The 304th returns to their own line, amid jeers and catcalls. The colonel is sharply rebuked by the general for failing to go the extra hundred feet that would have made it a successful charge. Fleming and Wilson, however, are singled out for bravery, and become suffused with joy and affection for their officer. The chapter is mainly straight narrative, with very little impressionistic description. (The youth has been almost as unaware of the intrepidity of his actions as he was of the timidity which had caused him to flee, and the recognition he receives is almost as accidental as his earlier "wound" in the head.)

CHAPTER 22

At the enemy's next charge the youth felt a supreme self-confidence, which cast its spell over his imaginative grasp of the events before him. Two regiments, a short way off, fought a "blazing" encounter with two of the enemy. A "magnificent brigade" entered a wood, fought, and emerged once more with a jaunty air. "Gruff and maddened" guns "denounced" the enemy. When the four regiments parted the youth could see the two flags "shaking with laughter" amid the remnants of battle. Presently, a solemn but irritating stillness occurred, only to be followed quickly by the renewed din of guns. Desperate rushes of men swelled to and fro. A group of gray forms went forward in "houndlike leaps" and swallowed a mouthful of prisoners, after which a blue wave crashed with thunderous force against a gray obstruction. Vantage points were exchanged like "light toys."

When its time came the 304th charged furiously, ramrods clanging, and arms pounding cartridges into guns. In a brief moment they were smudged with battle dirt once more. The lieutenant was stirred to new exertions in the composition of oaths. The youth, since he bore the colors, remained a spectator of the great drama which confronted him. He was practically oblivious to the exclamations and forced breathings which the scene drew from him. So too with his comrades, for when a gray line came within range they threw up their rifles and fired automatically, without waiting for a command. They fought swiftly and savagely. The youth had resolved not to budge—the "arrows of scorn" which had been loosed at him had generated a fierce hatred within. He conceived of his ultimate revenge taking the form of his torn body lying on the battlefield as a mute reproach to the officer who (in calling them "mule drivers" and "mud diggers") had "dubbed him wrongly." As he watched, the orderly sergeant of the company was shot through the cheeks and ran screaming to the rear, his mouth a "pulsing mass of blood and teeth." Others, too, fell, their bodies twisted into fantastic shapes. He saw Wilson, who now appeared as a "vehement young man, powder-smeared and frowzled." The lieutenant was still cursing, but with the air of a man who was "using up his last box of oaths." The fire of the regiment was beginning to wane.

SUMMARY: Here we see the youth lost in a kind of euphoria, looking at the battle as a spectator. The main line of the enemy makes occasional forays out from behind the protection of a fence, but finally settles down behind it.

1. From the standpoint of the youth's psychological state, this is a lull before the stormy charge he will make in the following chapter.

2. As for his comrades, their status as "veteran troops" becomes increasingly clear, with the growing automatism they gain.

CHAPTER 23

The colonel appeared on the run, and calling for a charge. The youth saw, too, that to remain where they were was certain death. He expected that his comrades would have to be driven to the attack, but was surprised to see that they were eager for the rush. There follows one of the most memorable passages in the book: ". . . At the yelled word of command the soldiers sprang forward in eager leaps. There was new and unexpected force in the movement of the regiment. A knowledge of its faded and jaded condition made the charge appear like a paroxysm, a display of the strength that comes before a final feebleness. The men scampered in insane fever of haste, racing as if to achieve a sudden success before an exhilarating fluid should leave them."

COMMENT: It is significant that the regiment, collectively at their most "courageous" moment, should be depicted as being in the grip of paroxysm—an involuntary, reflexive action. The narrator also refers to it shortly as "an enthusiasm of unselfishness," a "state of frenzy," and a "sublime recklessness," and notes that the youth himself "felt the daring spirit of a savage religion-mad," and was "shaken and dazzled by the tension of thought and muscle." Clearly, this is Crane's way of equating bravery with the compulsive responses of an orgiastic frenzy, and he emphasizes its sublogical character by remarking that in all of this "there was no obvious questioning, nor figurings, nor diagrams."

As the blue wave rolled on many of the enemy turned and ran, except for one "obdurate group" entrenched behind a fence. Suddenly, they clashed, the cheers of the men in blue turning to yells of wrath as they sought the foe. The youth regarded the enemy flag as a "craved treasure of mythology" and leaped at the rival color bearer, who was mortally wounded. Wilson preceded him, however, and wrenched the flag free, amid wild clamorings of cheers.

When the smoke cleared, four of the enemy were seen to have been captured. One, with a superficial foot wound, was cursing heartily; another—a boy in years—took his plight calmly and good-naturedly; a third reacted with a morose stoicism; and the fourth seemed lost in an abject and profound shame over his captivity. Amid celebration, the youth and his friend sat congratulating each other.

SUMMARY:

1. This chapter contains the climax of the novel, both from the standpoint of *action* (the enemy position is finally overwhelmed, and prisoners are taken) and of *theme* (the regiment and the youth resolve the problem of "courage" in an orgiastic plunge into the midst of the enemy).

2. In addition, a number of image patterns achieve their final statement. Two examples:

a. "Religious" metaphor—the youth finally feels himself "capable of profound sacrifices, a tremendous death."
b. The pagan "epic" motif—the enemy flag, now viewed as a "craved treasure of mythology" (like the Golden Fleece) is seized by Wilson and Fleming.

3. There is a fine irony in the fact that the prisoners are mirrors of the very attitudes displayed by the soldiers in blue.

CHAPTER 24

As the roarings ceased, the youth felt almost a regret at their passing. In a short time the regiment received orders to move, and trampled slowly back over the same ground. Finally, the youth understood that it was all over, though it took some time for his mind to cast off its "battleful ways." Like a spectator watching a procession of memory he reviewed his performances, and was gleeful at the fact that his public deeds "were paraded in great and shining memory." Taking great pleasure in his reflections, "he saw that he was good."

COMMENT: This clearly echoes Genesis (1:31): "And God saw every thing that he had made, and, behold, it was very good." It is the youth's moment of supreme inflation, during which he contemplates his accomplishments from a godlike eminence, ignoring entirely both their insubstantiality and his own passive role.

This reverie was marred only by the ghost of his first flight, and the image of the tattered soldier whom he had deserted in the field (and the possibility that he might have been detected). Giving vent to a small outcry, he was accosted by his friend Wilson, but replied merely with a string of crimson oaths. For a time all elation was gone from him, yet he gradually found the strength to put his sin at a distance. He could now "look back upon the brass and bombast of his earlier gospels and see them truly." In despising them, he gained assurance, and felt that, after all, he was a man.

Though others muttered as they slogged along in the rain, the youth smiled, having rid himself of the "red sickness of battle." The sun's golden rays pierced through the leaden rain clouds.

SUMMARY: The final chapter shows the blue soldiers turning, after their success, back to the rear. The youth is first seen to be elated with his performance, then wretchedly fearful of exposure, and finally calm and optimistic in the assurance of his achieved manhood.

Other details:

1. The "religious metaphor" appears once in an ironic version (the youth's "godlike" surveyal of his accomplishments), and once in a serious version (Henry's rejection of his "earlier gospels" of vanity).

2. This final use of the religious motif, which amounts to a Pauline "putting on of the new man," merges with the pattern of primitive anthropological imagery in the suggestion that battle has also been for the youth his *rite de passage* (passage from youth to manhood).

3. The final element of nature imagery supports both of the above details. The wretched sky, filled with rain clouds, and the muddy trough of the road, give way to a vision of fresh meadows and cool brooks dominated by the golden sun.

Character Analyses

"THE YOUTH" (HENRY FLEMING): In one sense the entire book is a character analysis of Henry Fleming, and it seems pointless to try to condense Crane's own elaborately conceived fiction. But we do learn a number of things about the youth initially. He is sensitive, introspective, and romantic, and above all eager to test his own inner depths. From one point of view Henry's progress through the book amounts to a series of shocking contrasts between the glorified images of heroic deeds his imagination conjures up and the grim realities of battle, death, and decay. His initial ignorance of his own limits causes Fleming to vacillate between diffidence and braggadocio, as he speculates about his possible reactions under fire; at first, of course, he flees, but ultimately he comes to terms with himself and evolves into a normal (perhaps even a heroic) "veteran." With an extraordinarily complicated narrative irony, Crane, by shifting back and forth from the viewpoint of the youth himself to that of a critical and omniscient observer, presents a parade of persons and events which objectify in a more or less impressionistic fashion the youth's quest for self-knowledge and a more perfect integration of thought, feeling, and action. Jim Conklin's example, the tattered man's exhortations, the cheery man's firm guidance, the kindly ministrations of Wilson—all mark periods in Fleming's psychological growth. As Crane presents it, the climax of the process is the charge, in the course of which Henry's acquired ethical feeling of brotherhood, the surge of natural impulse, and a quasi-religious spark of enthusiasm blend to produce what the world calls "heroism."

THE "TALL SOLDIER" (JIM CONKLIN): We encounter Conklin three times. He first appears as a somewhat opinionated—almost overbearing—individual, one whom the very prospect of war has transformed from an unimpressive plodder into a self-assured warrior. On his second appearance the near approach to battle seems to have infused into him a professional coolness and proficiency. Conklin's third (and last) appearance is as the "spectral soldier" in the line of wounded men retreating to the rear. Here he has become a symbol of an absolute yielding to the pressures of combat—a sacrifice to the gods of war (with a possible resemblance of some sort to Christ, the sacrificial Victim).

THE "LOUD SOLDIER" (WILSON): Wilson is a very simple character, but one who undergoes a remarkable transformation. Only in the beginning, before combat, is he the "loud soldier," a querulous, argumentative fellow, given to peremptory challenges and sarcastic comments. As the 304th approaches the line of fire, however, he comes to Henry with the lugubrious prediction that this is to be his first and last battle. When they next meet, after Fleming's retreat and the blow on the head, he has been utterly changed from his former attitudes, and is a gentle and humble companion. Thereafter he is referred to by Crane as "the friend," and seems to stand as an emblem of the kind of personal "reformation" war is capable of bringing about.

THE "YOUNG LIEUTENANT" (HASBROUCK): Hasbrouck is an example of the man who can perform heroically without the agony of self-questioning. He is a natural leader—brave, blunt, and harsh when necessary, but respected for his abilities and accomplishments. His youth and his uncomplicated approach to the question of "bravery" make him a foil to Fleming.

THE "TATTERED MAN": This unnamed soldier is one of Crane's most mysterious creations. He exemplifies an attitude—one of absolute, naive simplicity—which, by being the very epitome of ingenuousness, represents an unwitting threat to the dissembler.

THE "CHEERY MAN": Like the "tattered man" he is without a name, and, for the youth, without a face. He seems to Henry to possess a "magic wand" by which he threads his way through the mysterious darkness, and yet his conversation is most prosaic and his achievements most practical—he returns the youth to his comrades.

"HE OF THE INJURED FINGERS" (BILL SMITHERS): Smithers is by no means a major character but he stands as a curious antithesis to Henry. He too has a spurious wound, but it enables him to malinger his way through the battle, while a strain of inventive comedy helps him to save face.

Sample Essay Questions and Answers

1. In what respects may Crane's style be said to be "poetic"?

ANSWER: One might make a very rough distinction between narrative fiction and poetry by indicating that the former emphasizes the larger elements of plot, characterization, and action whereas the latter presents its meaning through patterns for imagery, rhythm, diction, and figurative language. In poetry the emphasis is on the word and the image—in the novel it is on episode and character relationship and development. It seems clear, however, that Crane relies heavily on poetic techniques to achieve his meaning. The personification of the forces and the engines of war, and the tendency to represent human intentions and manmade objects as parts of an organismal process are basic features of Crane's style, helping to express his ironic and skeptical viewpoint. He uses color to symbolizes attitudes and moods, and rhythm to suggest psychological states or the pace of action. Crane's diction (at times markedly

Biblical) amounts to a general pattern of allusion, defining war as a kind of sacrilege. All these factors indicate that any definition of *The Red Badge* as a novel should be broad enough to include its use of poetic techniques.

2. How is the narrator's point of view related to the total meaning of the book?

ANSWER: The narrator's point of view consists of a complicated sort of irony towards his chief character, Henry Fleming, and his subject, war. He allows himself a limited access into the youth's mind, sufficient to make clear Henry's initial and continuing tendency to romanticize sordid realities, but he continually retreats to a more objective and external ground when, for example, he wishes to comment ironically on the indifference which Nature displays towards man's pretentious efforts to outstrip her limitations. The narrator is simultaneously critical of society's stupid blasphemies against the order of nature, and of nature itself, which places such unreasonable obstacles in its way. The individual too, to the extent that he strives in isolation towards ego fulfillment, appears in an ironic light. In short, the point of view is fundamentally ambiguous, critical and sympathetic in an imponderable blend.

3. What is the significance of the description of the four prisoners taken by the soldiers in blue?

ANSWER: For one thing, the very fact that "the enemy" is now visualized as a mere group of men—very prosaic and practically indistinguishable from their captors—signalizes the end of any possibility of conceiving of the enemy as "dragons" or "monsters." More profoundly, perhaps, the capture of these men suggests that Fleming has even gone beyond identification with the members of his own regiment to identification with the "enemy," hence achieving status in a human totality. For their individualizing traits, while they repeat characteristics formerly noted in Henry's comrades, also serve as emblems of his own questing personality. One nurses a "superficial wound"; another is a boy with "bright and keen eyes"; a third is morose and stoical; the fourth is lost in abject shame. In capturing and comprehending them, Henry comes to further knowledge of himself.

4. Explain the symbolic interpretation which may be placed upon the youth's encounter with the corpse in Chapter 7.

ANSWER: The following three points may suggest the way to a more complete analysis:

a. In the "religious half light" of the "chapel" made by arching boughs, the corpse with its back against a "columnlike tree" becomes a sacrifice to the gods of war (who must also be identified to some extent with nature herself).

b. The corpse's change of colors—to a "melancholy green," a "dull hue," and "appalling yellow," and "gray"—points almost to an autumnal decline, suggesting that the victims of war blend inevitably into the cyclical progress of the seasons.

c. The look which the youth exchanges with the corpse indicates their essential kinship. He may flee from a particular occasion of battle, but the process of nature identified in this scene is a heritage that he cannot escape.

5. Discuss the "realistic" aspects of Crane's method of introducing his readers to new characters and new scenes.

ANSWER: Like Conrad, particularly in *Lord Jim*, Crane wants to provide his reader with a sense of the rush and flux of events—to re-create for him the air of confusion and disconnectedness which surround our apprehension of violent affairs in real life. In *The Red Badge* we do not find, as we do in *Lord Jim*, confusing shifts of time attributable to the idiosyncrasies of memory of a narrator whose own evaluation of events controls his selection and ordering of them, but we do notice on the part of the narrator a refusal to make clear expository comments on the action. For example, we learn in Chapter 2 that a man who has fallen down during the march has had his fingers stepped on, but he is identified only as "he of the injured fingers." At the beginning of Chapter 4 we overhear a snatch of conversation about the same incident, in which we learn that the soldier's name is Bill, and that he is believed to have shown considerable pluck in refusing to allow a doctor to amputate his three crushed fingers. In Chapter 6 another bit of conversation introduces a man who complains about the fighting and wishes that "Bill Smithers had trod on my hand insteader me treddin' on his'n," and we are made aware of the possibility that Smithers' minor injury may have given him a fortunate excuse for malingering and avoiding real danger (a possibility that receives further confirmation in Chapter 24). The reader only gradually learns the identity of Bill Smithers, even while he is made to modify in succession his attitudes toward Bill, just as this experience comes to us in real life. Withal, there is a sense of connectedness and continuity underlying the effect of confusion and of groping efforts to learn the details of the surrounding situation.

6. *Does* Henry Fleming undergo a change of character in the course of the novel?

ANSWER: There are basically three points of view on this question.

a. Some critics believe that Henry is "redeemed" from his cowardice, perhaps by the example of the "sacrificial" death of Jim Conklin and the new humility of Wilson—that he not only becomes heroic in battle but undergoes a complete reversal of personality, putting aside his youthful vanity and braggadocio and achieving the reasoned assurance of manhood.

b. Others believe that Fleming's "reform" is merely specious, and his self-knowledge a delusion—that once removed from the excitement and glamor of the battlefield he will return to his shallow attitudes. This, so it is argued, is indicated by the youth's sanguine expectations of a long life of peace as he marches away from the battle at the book's end.

c. A third group rejects both the "religious reformation" notion as well as the theory that Henry has not developed at all, and suggest instead that there is indeed a growth in Henry's attitude and insight, but that it occurs purely on the natural level of a deepening psychological awareness and ability to evaluate experience. This view in its general form rejects any symbolic reading of *The Red Badge*.

Actually, Crane's complicated irony and the lack of an unambiguous narrative and expository voice make it extremely difficult to deduce Crane's meaning. Growth there seems to be—though our interpretation of the form it takes may have to await further critical evaluation.

Nathaniel Hawthorne's The Scarlet Letter

Plot Summary and Comment

CHAPTER I: "THE PRISON-DOOR"

Hester Prynne has committed adultery. Two years ago her husband in Europe sent her on ahead to America while he settled some business affairs. Alone in the small town of Boston, Hester has shocked and angered her neighbors by secretly taking a lover and bringing forth a girl child. The Puritans of Boston are shocked that she has done this thing. They are angry because she will not reveal the name of the father of the child. Although the usual penalty for adultery is death, the Puritan judges (called magistrates) have decided to be merciful to her, declaring that Hester's punishment will be to stand for several hours on the scaffold (a high platform near the marketplace) in full view of everyone. She will hold her infant in her arms and will be wearing on the breast of her dress a piece of scarlet cloth formed into the letter "A." Part of her punishment is that she will continue to wear this letter on her breast for the rest of her life.

As the story opens in the month of June, in 1642, a group of Puritan men and women gather in front of the door of the prison waiting for Hester to make her appearance. The early settlers felt it necessary to build a prison and to set aside a cemetery as stern reminders of life and death. The gloomy building looks out on a grass plot covered with "unsightly vegetation" except for one, wild rosebush which blossoms near the threshold of the prison. The "fragrance and fragile beauty" of this one simple flower is a "token" (a symbol) that Nature may pity man, even though men may be inhuman to other men. The author wonders about the origin of the rosebush—as to whether it has perhaps survived the wilderness in which it originally grew, or whether it had "sprung up" in the footsteps of another rebellious woman, who, a few years before, had entered the same prison door. At the "Threshold" of the story the author picks one of the roses and presents it to the reader "to symbolize" the "moral blossom" (in other words—the happy ending) of this tale of human weakness and sorrow.

COMMENT: The first sentence of the romance introduces a major character, that is, the community. The predominant mood of the tale is established by the words "sad-colored" and "grey." The word "hoods" suggests the secrecy and hyprocrisy of a leading male character, Arthur Dimmesdale; in contrast, "bareheaded" represents the open repentance of Hester, the main female character who wears the scarlet letter. The setting is Puritan Boston, near the present site of King's Chapel on Tremont Street. Following the literary principle of "associational psychology" (which connects certain places and historic scenes with current problems and tensions of characters), the introduction of the words "Boston," "Cornhill," "King's Chapel," and "Anne Hutchinson " brings to the mind of the reader a picture of historic Boston and early American Puritanism. The title, *The Scarlet Letter*, has a symbolic word in it. Thus it is suitable that the first chapter should refer to a symbol (a "token"), the red blossom of the "wild rose-bush." Whereas the scarlet letter is the symbol of Hester's adultery (the reason why she is wearing the letter "A" on her breast), the rosebush is symbolic of the sympathetic heart of nature, contrasted with the "unsightly vegetation" of the prisonyard, which represents the hard-hearted Puritans about to stare at and denounce Hester. (She is to stand on a high platform, called a scaffold, in full view of everyone, as a public penance for committing adultery.) Near the end of the chapter, the mention of the name Anne Hutchinson is very interesting, for she was an early feminist (a fighter for women's rights). Hester Prynne, later on in the story, is in her own way a sort of feminist. There is, in the same sentence mentioning Anne Hutchinson, a fine example of Hawthorne's use of the indirect method. Using the word "whether" several times in a row, he presents a number of possibilities as to what the answer to a question might be. He allows the thinking reader to make up his own mind about the suitable answer to the question. The theatrical technique of indicating that the reader is at the "threshold" of the tale (in this instance, Hester's prison door sill) is a typical Hawthorne device. (This same idea is also used at the beginning of *The House of the Seven Gables*).

SUMMARY: The opening chapter establishes the following important points about the story:

1. The tale begins in Puritan Boston in June, 1642.

2. Hester Prynne has committed adultery. Wearing the scarlet letter "A," she is soon to leave the prison with her child. Then she will stand for a few hours on the scaffold for all to see.

3. The Puritans are a very critical group, always ready to punish wrongdoing.

4. Nature, symbolized by a "token" rosebush, is kind to man, in contrast to man's inhumanity to man.

CHAPTER II: "THE MARKET-PLACE"

Hester Prynne, wearing a scarlet piece of cloth formed into the letter "A," walks from the prison to the marketplace. She carries in her arms a tiny, baby girl—the result of her adultery. She is severely criticized by members of the crowd. When she is on the scaffold platform, she tries to forget the present by remembering the past.

The scene begins in front of the jail in Prison Lane. The Puritans of Boston stare at the door which Hester Prynne will come through. The author mentions the people who may possibly come out of the prison door on the way to punishment in the marketplace. Perhaps a "sluggish bond servant" or an "undutiful child" is to be whipped. Perhaps one of another religious group (or even an Indian) is to be driven out of town. Perhaps there is to be death at the gallows for a witch, like Mistress Hibbins, Governor Bellingham's sister. Little sympathy is given anyone on the way to the town scaffold. The watchers are very solemn, which is suitable for people for whom religion and law mean practically the same thing. From a group of five women comes the first dialogue in the story. One "hard-featured dame of fifty" feels that Hester Prynne's sentence is much too slight. Another joins in to suggest that the Reverend Arthur Dimmesdale, Hester's minister, is disturbed at the "scandal" in his congregation. A third adds that she believes the magistrates (the judges) should brand Hester's forehead, for she suspects the guilty woman capable of covering up the scarlet letter "A" on her breast with a pin. A fourth woman, a young mother, gently remarks that Hester might cover up the letter, but the pain of it will remain "always in her heart." The fifth and most cruel of these self-appointed "judges" strongly declares that the laws of both the Bible and the colony demand Hester's death for adultery. A nearby man finds fault with the small group of women; he points out that the door of the prison is about to be opened. First, there appears an official whose appearance suggests the "whole dismal severity of the Puritan code of law." Then, he pulls along Hester Prynne, who bears in her arms little Pearl, an infant about three months old. (Even at this moment when she comes through the prison door, Hester walks with "natural grace and force of character." This emphasizes her independent spirit.) Blinking, the infant tries to turn its face away from the strong sun. At first, Hester wants to cover her scarlet letter by holding the baby close to her bosom. Deciding that "one token of her shame" (the child) will "poorly hide another" (the scarlet letter "A"), she places the child on her arm and looks around at the townspeople. For the first time, the observers get a good look at Hester's symbol of adultery. It is the letter "A" on "fine red cloth, surrounded with an elaborate embroidery and fantastic flourishes of gold-thread," attached to the bodice of her gown. Hester is a woman of large build with an elegant figure. She has very glossy, "dark and abundant hair," a beautiful face with regular features, a rich complexion, and distinct brows and dark eyes. Her womanly qualities, emphasizing "state and dignity," shine even at the moment when she leaves the jail. Her dress, made when she was in the prison, appears to express the spirit and the "desperate recklessness of her mood." (She dares to express her independence only in the matter of her clothing.) The scarlet token awes the townspeople. Again, three of the women criticize Hester, this time pointing out her dress. The third of the trio asks for charity toward the fallen woman. The official announces that Hester is to show her letter on the scaffold in the marketplace until one hour past noon. Then he cries out a blessing that in the "righteous" Massachusetts Bay Colony sin is "dragged out into the sunshine." Hester, followed by a crowd of "stern-browed men," "unkindly visaged women," and "curious school-boys," begins the walk from the jail to the marketplace. Through her manner seems proud, she is in agony, as if her heart were being tramped on by the accusing Puritans. She finally arrives at a scaffold erected almost beneath the eaves of a church. This scaffold is the platform of a pillory (a device used to hold tightly the neck and wrists of a victim). Hester is not to be placed in this machine, but she is to stand for a certain length of time on the platform (which is "about the height of a man's shoulder above the street"), displaying two tokens of her adultery—the scarlet letter and her child. A Papist (Roman Catholic) would perhaps be reminded of "the image of Divine Maternity" (the Virgin Mary) by this picture of Hester and her infant. However, the unhappy Puritan mother does not represent "the sacred image of sinless motherhood." On a balcony of the meetinghouse, overlooking the pillory platform, are seen standing the most important personages of the colony: the Governor, several of his counsellors, a judge, a general, and the ministers of the town. To lessen her intense mental suffering, Hester's mind and memory turn back to her past in Europe, as she pictures "scenes" and faces much contrasted with the rough town streets and inhabitants of the Boston colony. She reviews happenings from her infancy, as well as from her school days. Also, recollections of things of more recent years fly through her mind like events in a "play." Because she tries to lose herself in memories of the past, she is able to endure the humiliation of the moment. From the "point of view" of the scaffold, Hester summarizes the important places and people in her life since the days of her infancy. She visualizes her native village in Old England and her parents' poor home. She thinks again of her father and mother, recalling their love and concern for her welfare. She remembers her own youthful face. She examines a face, "well stricken in years, a pale, thin scholar-like visage." Her reminiscence stays with this elderly scholar: she recalls that his eyes, dim and weary from reading books, once in a while would attempt to analyze the "human soul." She further pictures his figure, "slightly deformed, with the left shoulder a trifle higher than the right." Next, Hester's mind wanders to the scene of a continental European city to which she went as the wife of this "misshapen scholar." She in her youth was "like a tuft of green moss;" he in his old age resembled the "crumbling wall" to which she in her poverty-stricken "green" youth had to cling. Hester's mind then jumps ahead several years. She is rudely brought back to where she is on the scaffold. In amazement, she clutches the child to her breast and looks down. Then, having difficulty in believing that she is standing where she is, she places her finger on the scarlet letter.

COMMENT: The Puritans believed in a theocratic state (a situation where the Church and

State share authority). This is based on the social order pictured in the Old Testament, and it is explained by scholarly clergymen (such as John Wilson and Arthur Dimmesdale, English university graduates). Emphasis is placed on the Biblical Covenant which promises obedience to elected leaders ("magistrates" in the Puritan colony) who may easily be replaced because of poor leadership. The Puritan theocracy, with the Church and State having equal responsibility for keeping law and order in the colony, is always in the background of the story, *The Scarlet Letter.* It helps explain the different professions represented by the characters assembled on the balcony overlooking the scaffold (the Governor, a military man, and the ministers). The Scriptures demand death for adultery, and the Puritan laws closely follow the Biblical pattern. The Puritan "fathers" stress fidelity in marriage and the sacredness of the family. Thus, Hester's crime of adultery is punishable by death. Since her husband (Dr. Prynne) is reported to be dead, the magistrates extend to her what they consider to be "great mercy." Hester is a typical nineteenth-century woman of ill repute (as far as literature goes), for she has dark hair, and is of a passionate nature. Hawthorne describes many of the scenes as if they were seen by a spectator from a theatre seat: that is, as if the setting, the characters, and the action were all viewed on the picture frame stage of the movies or the Broadway theatre. The "dusky mirror" is the first of Hawthorne's many shiny surfaces used for literary purposes in this story. In this case, Hester is rapidly reviewing her past life in the gloomy "mirror" of introspection, that is, she analyzes her own previous life before coming to Boston. (Most of the other mirrors in this book have physical surfaces; they are not reflections of the imagination. See later comments.) Hester remembers that the prying eyes of her husband, Dr. Prynne, were once capable of analyzing people. This is a subtle foreshadowing (looking ahead toward) the horrors to come later in the tale, when the scientist Chillingworth (actually Dr. Prynne) attempts in revenge to examine the soul of the guilty and hypocritical Dimmesdale.

SUMMARY: In this chapter the following things happen:

1. Female spectators severely criticize Hester for her adultery. The harsh, Puritanical point of view is noted in the unfriendly attitude of the townspeople toward Hester.

2. Hester leaves the jail with her child. She is unhappy, but she is not a broken woman. She is very attractive. On the breast of her unusual dress, she wears a scarlet letter "A."

3. The scaffold and the pillory are described. (It is important to have a good picture in one's mind of this setting, for many of the key scenes of the tale take place on this spot.)

4. Members of the Boston Theocracy (the Governor, his staff, and the ministers) stand on the balcony overlooking the scaffold.

5. Hester remembers places and people from her past in the "dusky mirror" of her imagination.

CHAPTER III: "THE RECOGNITION"

Hester Prynne is observed on the scaffold by a man who recognizes her. The "stranger" learns her story from a townsman. Reverend Wilson, Governor Bellingham, and Reverend Dimmesdale all speak to Hester, each concerned that she should tell the name of her lover. When Dimmesdale asks her and she refuses to tell, the minister is greatly relieved.

Hester sees an Indian at the edge of the crowd watching her. Beside him is the "figure" of a "white man, clad in a strange disarray of civilized and savage costume." He is short, has a wrinkled face, and reveals "a remarkable intelligence in his features." When she notes that one of his shoulders is higher than the other, she instinctively presses the infant to her bosom. At first, "the stranger" casually observes Hester. Suddenly, he recognizes her. Noting that Hester is staring at him, also in recognition, he deliberately raises his finger to his lips in a gesture of secrecy. Casually questioning a townsman in general terms as to Hester's identity and the nature of her crime, he responds to this information with an account of his own "grievous mishaps by sea and land," and of his being held in captivity by Indians in the south. He has been brought to Boston to be ransomed. The "stranger" is given a detailed description by the townsman of Hester Prynne's husband (whom the reader suspects to be the questioner himself). He finds himself pictured as a "learned man, English by birth," who, after living for a long time in Amsterdam, had decided to come to the New World to join the Massachusetts Bay Colony. Remaining in Holland to settle some "necessary affairs," he had sent his wife (Hester Prynne) ahead. Over a period of two years, nothing has been heard of him, and his wife has brought forth a child. Smiling bitterly, "the stranger" asks the name of the father of the child. He is told that "Madam Hester absolutely refuseth to speak" and that "the guilty one" may be watching her at this very moment. Because Hester is "youthful and fair," because she was probably "strongly tempted to her fall," and also because "her husband may be at the bottom of the sea," the magistrates have not given her the penalty of death. She has been sentenced to stand for "three hours on the platform of the pillory" and then, for the rest of her life, to wear on her bosom the scarlet letter "A," signifying adultery or adultress. Considering this a "wise sentence," "the stranger" regrets that the name is not known of the father of the child. Three times he says: ". . . he will be known!" Then he leaves. Hester has been almost overwhelmed at the sight of Roger Prynne and is glad to see him in the presence of the "thousand witnesses," rather than "to greet him, face to face, they two alone." She dreads the moment when the two of them will be together alone. All at once, she hears a voice behind her, coming from the balcony attached to the meetinghouse. She looks up to see Governor Bellingham, surrounded by four sergeants and some very dignified members of the Puritan community. The speaker, "a man of kind and genial spirit," is the famous scholar John Wilson, the oldest clergyman in Boston. Familiar with "the shaded light of his study," he seems unsuitable to be one dealing "with a question of human guilt, passion, and anguish." He tells Hester that his youthful fellow clergyman, her own pastor (the Reverend Arthur Dimmesdale), should force her to tell the name of the father of the child. He explains Dimmesdale's point of view that it is "wronging the very nature of woman to force her to lay open her heart's secrets in such broad daylight, and in presence of so great a multitude." At this point, Governor Bellingham declares Dimmesdale responsible for obtaining Hester's "repentance" and "confession." All eyes turn to observe the young minister. He has a "very striking aspect," with a high forehead, large, brown eyes, and a "tremulous" mouth. He has a "half-frightened look" and is evidently a person who likes to be alone. Reverend Wilson pleads with him to speak. Dimmesdale begins by looking steadily into her eyes and telling her that she must understand that he, as her pastor, is accountable for her behavior. If she feels that for her "soul's peace" she should confess the name of her "fellow-sinner and fellow-sufferer," then she should "speak out the name." Her sin has been revealed, and she will "work out an open triumph over the evil" within herself. But, he continues, the father of the child may not have the "courage" to confess and must therefore "add hypocrisy to sin." All of the listeners think the young minister's touching speech will cause Hester to confess. Even the infant looks toward the speaker. But, Hester will not speak the name. Reverend Wilson suggests that confession would help remove the scarlet letter from her bosom. Hester refuses again, saying that she wishes she might endure the "agony" of the father of the child. A cold and stern voice from the crowd (Dr. Prynne's voice) demands she speak. Again she refuses. Arthur Dimmesdale, in a dramatic aside, murmurs: "She will not speak!" Then, for over an hour, Reverend Wilson speaks to the crowd about various kinds of sin, making many references to the scarlet letter on Hester's breast. Exhausted, Hester stands on the scaffold, occasionally and mechanically attempting to hush the wails and screams of the infant in her arms. Finally, she is returned to the darkness of the prison.

COMMENT: Note that over and over again, both in the dialogue and in Hawthorne's descriptive passages, the white man who stands on the edge of the crowd is called the "stranger." This is Hawthorne's bow to a literary convention of his day, that is, the introduction of an "unknown" character, often called the "stranger." (Both Hawthorne and his literary contemporary, James Fenimore Cooper, borrow this artistic device from the English novelist Sir Walter Scott.) Each of Hawthorne's romances features an "unknown" character, as well as many of the tales. It is ironical that the "stranger" (actually Dr. Prynne in disguise) must hear his own story retold by a townsman, but this is a fine device for allowing the reader to gain more knowledge of Hester's past. The placing of the clergy and the magistrates together on the balcony points to the fact that in a theocracy (a state ruled by God) the state is the arm of the church, charged with enforcing its edicts.) Reverend Wilson's comments about his fellow clergyman, Dimmesdale, allows the reader to have a good picture in his mind of the young minister before he speaks. (Compare the effect of this speech by Dimmesdale with that of his Election Day Sermon in Chapter XXII, "The Procession.") Dimmesdale describes how he feels about his own involvement in Hester's sin, but the members of the audience, of course, do not realize that he is telling of his own suffering. When he urges Hester to speak and she still refuses, the young clergyman murmurs an "aside": "Wondrous strength and generosity of a woman's heart! She will not speak!" (An aside is made up of lines spoken privately by an actor and supposed to be heard by the audience but not by the other actors.) This use of the "aside" shows the influence of the theatre on Hawthorne, as well as his use of melodramatic, Gothic writing techniques of his own day, emphasizing artificial, theatrical devices.

SUMMARY: In this chapter the following things happen:

1. Hester's husband, Dr. Prynne, appears on the edge of the crowd observing her. He signals that she is not to publicly recognize him. Through a conversation between a townsman and him (he is called the "stranger"), we learn that he has been detained in the wilderness by the Indians, and we get his displeased reaction to the fact that Hester will not name the father of her child.

2. The power of the Boston Puritan theocracy is emphasized, as Governor Bellingham, his military aides, and the Reverends Wilson and Dimmesdale are seen sitting on the balcony high above Hester's scaffold of penance.

3. One after another, Reverend Wilson, Governor Bellingham, and Reverend Dimmesdale speak to Hester, urging her to name the father of her child. Dimmesdale's speech mentioning her "fellow-sinner and fellow-sufferer" is filled with irony (saying one thing and meaning another). In speaking of Hester's lover, he is referring to himself— but only Hester and he know this fact. (Hawthorne has not named him as the father of the child, but the reader begins to suspect this to be so.) Hester establishes her love for Arthur Dimmesdale when she says that she wishes she "might endure his agony" as well as her own.

CHAPTER IV: "THE INTERVIEW"

Hester and her baby, Pearl, both need medical attention, so a physician named Roger Chillingworth is brought to them in the prison. He is the "stranger" (actually, Dr. Prynne, her husband). After giving them medical care, Chillingworth discusses Hester's situation, demanding to know the name of her lover. She refuses to tell him. Back in the prison, Hester Prynne is found to be "in a state of nervous excitement," so much so that the jailer, Master Brackett, thinks it best to bring in a doctor. The infant also seems to be in deep distress. Master

Brackett brings into Hester's cell "the stranger" who earlier that day was so very much interested in her case. (For the purpose of convenience, he is living in the prison until his ransom has been arranged with the Indians.) The physician is introduced as Roger Chillingworth. He asks to see Hester alone, claiming that he will cause her to be more ready to accept "just authority" than she has been thus far. First, he cares for the child, by preparing some simple remedy. Hester thinks he wishes to poison the baby, but he assures her that the medicine will be good for it. Shortly, the infant sleeps. After looking intently for a while at Hester, he mixes a drink to help calm her. She questions him as to whether or not the medicine will kill her. He explains that he wishes for her to live, so that the "burning shame" (the scarlet letter "A") will continue to "blaze" upon her bosom. At this point, he touches the letter, and it seems to "scorch into Hester's breast," as if it were "red-hot." She drinks the medicine and seats herself on the bed, with him in a chair beside her. He begins to talk, blaming himself for marrying a girl of her youth and beauty. He says that he should have known from the beginning that she would someday be wearing a scarlet letter. Hester quietly replies: "I was frank with you. I felt no love." He admits that she had not deceived him in this respect. He remarks that his life had been lonely and "cheerless" before he had married her. She had brought "warmth" into his existence. At this time, Hester murmurs that she has "wronged" him. He answers that they "have wronged each other" and that *his* was "the first wrong" because he, an old man, should never have married a "budding youth." Thus, Chillingworth says: "I seek no vengeance, plot no evil against thee. Between thee and me the scale hangs fairly balanced." Then, he demands to know the name of Hester's lover. She replies: "Ask me not! That thou shalt never know!" He tells her that few things remain "hidden from the man who devotes himself" to the "solution of a mystery." All others may be deceived as to the man's name, but he will not be. He declares: "I shall seek this man." He feels that he will find him, for there will exist a certain bond of sympathy between the lover and himself when he comes near him. Hester's lover will "tremble," and Chillingworth will "shudder" in response. Then, Hester's husband cries out: "Sooner or later, he must needs be mine!" Chillingworth realizes that Hester's lover will wear "no letter of infamy wrought into his garment," but he claims he will be able to read the letter on the guilty man's heart. He will not betray him to the law, threaten his life, or even damage his reputation. Also, the unknown lover may even "hide himself in outward honor." Chillingworth then asks Hester to do but one thing, and that is to keep secret the fact that he, himself, is Dr. Prynne, her husband. Even though she is not to be known as his wife, he still feels a closeness of connection with her and intends to stay in the town where she, her child, and her lover live. Hester asks why he does not publicly reveal her identity as his wife and cast her off. He explains that it might be that he does not care to be known as the husband of a "faithless woman." Then Hester swears an oath that as far as the rest of the world is concerned her husband (Dr. Prynne) is dead. Above all, she is not to tell the secret of her husband's identity to her lover. Chillingworth smiles as he leaves Hester. She asks if he is "like the Black Man that haunts the forest." She wonders if he has led her into a "bond that will prove the ruin "of her soul. He says: "Not thy soul, no not thine!" Thus Chillingworth's cold and devilish revenge begins.

COMMENT: Throughout the romance, Pearl is seen as a token, a living representation, of her mother's sin of adultery. In this chapter the child's "convulsions of pain" physically parallel the "moral agony" endured during the day by the unhappy mother. When the doctor, Roger Chillingworth, prepares to sooth the child by some medicine, Hester is afraid that he wishes to kill her; but he has no such object in mind. When Hester asks him whether he is giving her a poisonous drink, he explains to her that he does not desire her death, for he wishes her to live, and seeks "no vengeance" against her. But he establishes here the point that he does seek revenge on Hester's lover. Thus, one of the main threads of the plot begins here: Chillingworth's search for, and revenge upon, the father of Pearl. He indicates that he intends to "ruin" the soul of his victim. Often, Hawthorne tells us about his characters through elaborate descriptions of their actions and thoughts. Note that in this chapter the intimate conversation between Hester and her husband reveals much about their past actions, and helps us anticipate their future patterns of action.

SUMMARY: The developments in this chapter are as follows:

1. Hester, alone except for her child, finally meets face to face her husband, Dr. Prynne, when he comes to the jail to give them medical attention. He has adopted the pseudonym (fictitious name) Roger Chillingworth. At first, she fears that he wishes them bodily harm, but he assures her that he wishes her to live—to live in shame. His object is to have revenge on her lover, whose name he expects her to reveal to him. When she refuses to tell him the identity of the father of the child, he explains that he will persist until he eventually learns the man's name.

2. Hester promises not to make known to the Boston citizens that Roger Chillingworth is actually her husband, Dr. Prynne.

CHAPTER V: "HESTER AT HER NEEDLE"

Hester leaves the prison and establishes herself and the child in a small cottage near the seashore. She is alone most of the time. She earns her living by fine sewing and embroidering. She gives much of her time to doing good works among the poor and the unfortunate. Her sin causes her to be able to recognize hidden sin in others.

Hester leaves the prison alone, trying to accustom herself to the "daily custom" of always being "the general symbol at which the preacher and moralist might point." She knows that pure, young people will "be taught to look at her . . . as the figure, the body, the reality of sin." She has nothing to look forward to but an endless series of burdensome days, "each of its own trial." She is not restricted by judgment handed down to her by the magistrates to stay in Boston. She may leave and return to Europe; it would even be possible to disappear into the forest and live among the Indians. But she seems compelled to stay in the place where a "great and marked event has given . . . color" to her life. Her "sin" is the root "she has struck into the soil." She is held by a "chain" made "of iron links." It is possible that she stays in Boston because her former lover is near her. She tells herself that "the scene of her guilt" has been here, and "the torture of her daily shame" will eventually cleanse her soul. Hester settles herself and her infant child on the edge of the town in a small, abandoned, thatched cottage, not near any other settler's home. Her "lonesome dwelling" is near the sea. People begin to look at her house with questioning eyes. Small children find their way there and peep through the window to watch her sew. They might observe her standing in the doorway of her house, working in her garden, or walking along the path from town. Catching sight of the scarlet letter, they fearfully run away. Meanwhile, Hester earns her living by sewing. The "curiously embroidered letter" on her breast is a "specimen of her delicate and imaginative skill." Although most of the Puritans are required to wear dark and simple clothing, public ceremonies (such as "the installation of magistrates") are occasions when the officials wear "ruffs, painfully wrought bands, and gorgeously embroidered gloves." At funerals, both corpses and mourners are elaborately dressed. Baby linen is also very decorative. Hester's "handiwork" becomes "the fashion," for a variety of reasons, such as pity or curiosity. Possibly she sews better than anyone else at the time. At any rate, she is satisfactorily paid for as much sewing as she cares to do. Prominent people in Boston choose to wear the garments she makes. She sews the ruffs of the Governor, military men's scarfs, the minister's "band" (a high collar), little caps for babies, and coffin clothes for the dead. The one thing she does not embroider is "the white veil . . . of a bride." This shows that "society" still frowns "upon her sin." For her labor, Hester asks in payment only enough for the simple needs of life for herself and some extras for Pearl. She dresses herself in dark, coarse material, which causes the scarlet letter to blaze out at the world in contrast. Pearl's dresses are seen to be "fanciful," accenting the "airy charm" of the child. The rest of her money Hester spends on charity, which is not always appreciated. She spends much time "making coarse garments for the poor." Hester's "taste for the gorgeously beautiful" finds expression in "the delicate toil of the needle." She feels separated from society, even from those for whom she sews. Criticized severely at times by women "of elevated rank" and by the "poor" whom she often aids, Hester remains a patient martyr. One thing she will not do: she will not pray for her enemies, for she is fearful that "the words of the blessing" might "twist themselves into a curse." Day after day, Hester suffers as a result of her sin. Ministers attract crowds in the street by giving her words of moral advice, and choose her as the subject of sermons. Children run after her condemning her with a fearful name. Strangers curiously regard the letter. And yet, Hester never covers the token of her adultery with her hand, as she is sorely tempted to do at times. Once in a while someone (very likely Dimmesdale) looks at the letter, and for a moment she feels relief, "as if half of her agony" is being shared. Being alone much of the time, Hester's "imagination" is "somewhat affected." She begins to believe that the scarlet letter has furnished her "with a new sense," that is, it gives her a "sympathetic knowledge of the hidden sin in other hearts." Her instinct tells her that "if truth were everywhere to be shown, a scarlet letter would blaze forth on many a bosom beside Hester Prynne's." Sometimes, she senses an "evil thing . . . at hand" when she passes a highly respected "minister or magistrate, the model of piety and justice." She feels a bond of "sisterhood" as she catches the "sanctified frown of some matron" of the highest reputation. At times, she is aware that a "companion" in sin is near her; looking up, she notes the eyes of a young maiden quickly withdrawn from the scarlet token of adultery. And yet, in the face of all these instances, Hester continues "to believe that no fellow-mortal" is "guilty like herself." Some idle gossips declare that the letter is not made of scarlet cloth, but that it is "red-hot with infernal fire, lighting Hester Prynne's path at night-time."

COMMENT: This chapter fills in necessary background to the romance, beginning with the time when Hester comes from the prison for the first time to start life all over again, and continues through the first years of young Pearl's existence. Deciding not to leave the colony, Hester finds a small cottage, physically isolated from the other members of the community, as she is spiritually separated from them. She earns her daily bread by expert sewing and embroidering of magnificent garments for public ceremonies. Of course, public prejudice does not allow her to make the white veil of a new bride. Note that Hester, dressed in humble and somber clothes, must create for others beautiful clothing representative of worldly pomp and splendor. Hester begins the first of her many and continuing acts of charity toward others-some of whom only cruelly insult her, reminding her of her past sin. (Compare this with the ending of Chapter XXIV, "Conclusion," where her "A" becomes a symbol for "Angel" because of her repeated good works.) Hester's experience with sin has made her able to recognize sin in others in Boston.

SUMMARY: The following points are made in this chapter:

1. The end of the first part of the romance is reached as Hester leaves the prison with her infant child. She decides to stay in Boston, suffering daily penance as people stare at her scarlet letter.

2. The unhappy mother settles down in a small isolated cottage, and time passes slowly as her child begins to grow, and people—especially children—watch her daily activities.

3. Sewing for her living, Hester is in great demand for her fine embroidery on garments of state, for funeral clothing, and for baby linen. She is not allowed to touch the pure white veil of a new bride.

4. She dresses Pearl extravagantly in vivid colors, while she, herself, is clad in somber garments, decorated only by the brilliant scarlet "A."

5. Her experience with sin has given her the power to recognize sin in others—even those of high reputation in the community.

CHAPTER VI: "PEARL"

Pearl, a beautiful child dressed in bright colors, is difficult to manage. Her mother must often allow her to have her own way. Hester's scarlet letter attracts the little girl's attention. Once in a while, Hester is worried because a "fiend" appears to peep out of Pearl's eyes.

The infant Pearl, "a lovely and immortal flower," has sprung from "a guilty passion." As the child grows, the mother sees intelligence and beauty before her. Hester has named her baby "Pearl" because she represents a purchase of "great price." Man has given Hester a scarlet letter to remove her from "human sympathy," whereas God has given her a "lovely child,' placed "on that same dishonored bosom." Hester is apprehensive that her own sin will be reflected in the child's nature by some "dark and wild peculiarity." Pearl has "no physical defect," having "perfect shape," "vigor," and easy use of all her limbs. Her "native grace" and beauty are beautifully dressed by Hester in the "richest" cloth sold in Boston. The child's manner varies from that of a "peasant-baby" to that of "an infant princess." And yet with it all, she has her mother's passionate nature. She does not find it easy to obey rules. Hester recognizes in Pearl her own "wild, desperate, defiant mood, the flightiness of her temper," and the gloom which broods in her own heart. As to disciplining the child, Hester is not oversevere with her. At first, she tries to have a "tender, but strict control" over her, but eventually she finds out that both "smiles and frowns" prove of little help. Hester allows "the child to be swayed by her own impulses," according to the "caprice" of the moment. Sometimes the mother wonders if instead of a "human child" Pearl might be "an airy sprite," a creature from another world. In her "wild, bright, deeply-black eyes," there is a strange otherworldly look. Disturbed by the behavior of her unusual child, Hester sometimes bursts into "passionate tears." Pearl responds by frowns and an unsympathetic "look of discontent," or else she breaks out into "a rage of grief" as she tells her mother how much she loves her. Hester's "only real comfort" is when Pearl is asleep. Soon the child grows old enough to talk with others, but she speaks to none but her mother, who is never without her on her walks about the town. Pearl sees other children, but she will not answer their greetings. If they group around her, she gathers up stones to throw at them and cries out in shrill tones. The "little Puritans" are very "intolerant" of the mother and child and often "scorn" them in their hearts and say unkind things to them. Both Hester and Pearl stand "together in the same circle of seclusion from human society." At home, the child makes companions of everyday objects. She talks with ancient pine trees, imagining them to be "Puritan elders." She sees the "ugliest weeds of the garden" as their children, and she steps on them or uproots them. Her rapid, darting activity resembles the "play of the northern lights." Among all of the varied "offspring of her own heart and mind," she never once creates a friend. Always she recognizes and attacks a world which is against her. Sometimes, Hester groans out: ". . . what is this being which I have brought into the world!" Pearl only answers with a smile. The "first object" of which Pearl seems to become aware is Hester's scarlet letter. When she is only an infant in the cradle, she reaches up her little hand and grasps it, attracted by "the glimmering of the gold embroidery about the letter." Gasping, Hester clutches the "token" and Pearl looks into her mother's eyes and smiles.

After this time, Hester dreads when the child will look at the letter "with that peculiar smile" and the "odd expression of the eyes." Once, Hester looks at herself in "the small black mirror of Pearl's eyes," and she sees another face look out at her, "a face, fiend-like, full of smiling malice." On another day, Pearl picks "handfuls of wildflowers" and throws them, one by one at her mother's bosom. When she hits the scarlet letter, she excitedly dances up and down, much to the pain of her mother. Having thrown all of the flowers, she stands still and gazes at Hester. The mother imagines that a "little, laughing image of a fiend" is peeping out at her. Hester tells the child that their "Heavenly Father" sent her to earth. Pearl positively answers: "I have no Heavenly Father!" Hester then recalls "the talk of the neighboring townspeople" which suggests that little Pearl is the "offspring" of a devil.

COMMENT: Pearl represents to Hester great sorrow (her adultery) and great joy (her child). Although the mother is not permitted to clothe herself in bright colors, she finds a sense of relief in dressing her child in gleaming colors, imaginatively arranged. Even as Hester's somber garments represent her restraint in dealing with the world around her, so, too, do Pearl's clothes reflect the child's spirited attitude toward everything about her. The unkind behavior of the Puritan children toward Pearl is parallel to the conduct of their parents towards Hester. Pearl has an aggressive attitude toward her mother, as well as her make-believe playmates and other children. She pains her mother by throwing flowers at the scarlet letter. Then she further disturbs Hester by asking where she (Pearl) came from. She rejects her mother's answer—her "Heavenly Father." This causes Hester to remember the talk of the townspeople regarding a theory that Pearl is descended from the devil. (This might be compared later on with Mistress Hibbins's attempts to connect Hester and Dimmesdale with the "Black Man of the Forest.")

SUMMARY: The following points are made in this chapter:

1. Man has marked Hester's sin by a scarlet letter, whereas God has given her a beautiful child.

2. Pearl is a beautifully dressed little girl who is not easy to govern by rules. Seeming like an "airy sprite," she greatly troubles her mother.

3. By resenting and reacting against the Puritan children, Pearl joins her mother "in the same circle of seclusion from human society."

4. Hester is frightened and made very thoughtful by seeing a "face, fiend-like, full of smiling malice" shine out of the mirror of Pearl's eyes.

5. Pearl denies having a "Heavenly Father," causing Hester to remember village gossip about Pearl being fathered by the devil.

CHAPTER VII: "THE GOVERNOR'S HALL"

Because townspeople speak of taking Pearl from her, Hester goes to Governor Bellingham's mansion to ask him to help her. In the highly polished breastplate and headpiece of a suit of armor, Pearl sees the reflection of her mother's scarlet letter greatly exaggerated. Hester notes that the child's appearance (reflected in the unusual mirror) is that of an "imp."

One day Hester goes to Governor Bellingham's mansion to deliver a pair of "fringed and embroidered" gloves for him to wear on "some great occasion of state." At the moment, Governor Bellingham is not the chief magistrate of the colony, yet he is in an influential position. Besides delivering the gloves, Hester has another more important reason for her trip: some people of Boston suggest that, for the good of her soul, little Pearl should be removed from her mother's care. Governor Bellingham, himself, is one of the important people promoting this idea. Hester is accompanied on her way to the governor's mansion by Pearl. Pearl is seen as a child of "rich and luxuriant beauty" with deep glowing eyes and dark "glossy brown" hair. There is "fire in her and throughout her." She is dressed in a crimson velvet gown highly embroidered with gold thread. She seems a token of Hester's adultery, as much as the scarlet letter which her mother is "doomed to wear upon her bosom." As they walk along Puritan children observe them, and decide to throw mud at them. To their surprise Pearl frowns, stamps her feet, shakes her hand in a threatening gesture and, screaming, rushes at them. They flee. They soon arrive at Governor Bellingham's large wooden mansion house. The outside is covered "with a kind of stucco, in which fragments of broken glass, are intermixed." Pearl, pleased with the house, dances up and down in admiration, demanding that the sunshine which reflects from the broken bits of glass be "stripped off its front, and given her to play with." Her mother explains that this is impossible. They are greeted at the door by one of the governor's bond-servants, wearing the customary blue coat of serving-men of the period. They are told the governor is busy with several ministers and a "leech" (doctor). Hester grandly says she will enter. The servant, misinterpreting the "glittering symbol" on her bosom as an elaborate status symbol, admits her. Hester and Pearl walk around the hall of the mansion and inspect it. They see a wide and quite high room with hall windows at one end. The chairs are large and elaborately carved according to the style of the Elizabethan age. On a table stands a "large pewter tankard" with a tiny bit of ale left in it. A row of portraits hang on the wall. The people represented in the pictures look like the "ghosts, rather than the pictures" of actual people. Featured in the center of the hall is a suit of mail of contemporary era. There is a particularly well-burnished helmet and breastplate—so highly polished, in fact, that they "glow with white radiance, and scatter an illumination everywhere about upon the floor." Pearl stands admiring "the polished mirror of the breastplate." To Hester's surprise the child says: "Mother, I see you here. Look! Look!" Hester sees that the shining breastplate has formed a peculiarly effective "convex mirror" exaggerating whatever is in the middle of the mirror. As she stands directly in front of the mirror the scarlet letter becomes the most prominent feature of her appearance. She seems absolutely hidden behind it. To increase her mother's discomfort, Pearl points upward "at a similar picture in the head piece" which also exaggerates the scarlet letter. Hester's agony is increased as she sees reflected in the mirror Pearl's "look of naughty merriment." She draws Pearl aside to look at the garden. They see that attempts to create a formal English garden have failed, for cabbages and pumpkins are evident "in plain sight." They see rosebushes and apple trees. Pearl begins to cry for a red rose. Her mother hushes her as she hears the voices of the governor and his guests approach them. Just before the governor appears, Pearl gives a childish scream—for her curiosity is aroused by the coming of the gentlemen.

COMMENT: Much of this chapter is concerned with how the Puritans react to little Pearl, whose "rich and luxuriant beauty," splendidly dressed by her mother, reminds everyone of Hester's adultery. Actually, Hester has spent many hours building up this likeness between Pearl and the scarlet letter. Even small Puritan children reject Pearl; who is quite capable of frightening them by screaming and rushing at them. The Governor's mansion, with the sunshine reflecting from the tiny fragments of glass stuck into the stucco on the outside, is greatly admired by Pearl. Sunshine always appeals to Pearl. She even considers it a plaything. (The sun always seems to disappear when Hester appears. As the story unfolds, notice how the sun shines near Pearl and then is blotted out by a cloud at any time that Hester comes on the scene.) The breastplate of the suit of armor is convex (rounded outward, like the exterior of a globe). Any object reflected in the highly polished surface of this mirror-like breastplate will be exaggerated in the middle; in fact, the center part, being nearer to what is being reflected, will present a larger picture than that seen on the edge of the "mirror." (This is what happens in highly exaggerated carnival mirrors.) When Hester stands exactly in front of this "convex mirror," the scarlet letter "A" is greatly exaggerated. The unusual largeness of the "A" is what Pearl so very gleefully calls to her mother's attention. (A literary term for the ridiculous increase in size of this letter is "giantism.") There are double images in the headpiece of the suit of armor: first, Hester's scarlet letter "A"; second, little Pearl's "look of naughty merriment." Thus, the two main symbols of the romance come together here.

SUMMARY: The high points of the action in this chapter are as follows:

1. Hester goes to Governor Bellingham's mansion to enlist his help against those (including himself) who wish to remove Pearl from her care.

2. On the way to the Governor's house, Pearl attacks and scatters a group of little Puritans who are planning to throw mud at the child and her mother.

3. Pearl is fascinated by the decorations on the outside of the mansion. The main hall of the building is pictured in detail. Among the wall ornaments is a suit of mail (armor), featuring a highly polished breastplate and helmet. Pearl sees her mother's scarlet letter "A" grotesquely (horribly) exaggerated in the "convex mirror" formed by the front of the breast plate. She also points to the same image reflected in the helmet. Hester is especially disturbed, for she sees reflected in the same mirror the "elfish" look on Pearl's face.

4. Mother and daughter explore Governor Bellingham's garden, where Pearl cries for a red rose.

CHAPTER VIII: "THE ELF-CHILD AND THE MINISTER"

Governor Bellingham is surprised to see Pearl in his house. He examines the child concerning her Christian upbringing. He is displeased with what she says. Hester then makes a passionate plea to Reverend Arthur Dimmesdale to help her. The minister convinces the Governor that Hester and the child should remain together.

Governor Bellingham appears, accompanied by three men—John Wilson, Arthur Dimmesdale, and Roger Chillingworth. The Governor has been pointing out the beauties of his estate. He looks more stern than he actually is. He is accustomed to living in luxury. Even such a venerable minister as the Reverend John Wilson approves of "good and comfortable things." But, of course, Reverend Wilson must disapprove "of such transgressions as that of Hester Prynne." Arthur Dimmesdale appears ill. Arriving suddenly at the door of his mansion, the Governor almost stumbles over little Pearl. She reminds him of the "children of the Lord of Misrule," tiny, fantastically dressed children participating in masques at the court of King James I. Pearl identifies herself and her mother, and the Governor speaks in an uncomplimentary manner of Hester as a "scarlet woman." At this point, Governor Bellingham assumes an official air and sternly explains to Hester that Boston officials question whether or not Pearl should be left to the "guidance" of one who has "stumbled and fallen." Frantically, Hester replies that she is capable of teaching her child. She says that she has learned from her experience. At this time, Reverend Wilson questions Pearl in religious matters. Obstinately, Pearl closes her lips and opens them only to mumble odd assortments of words. Finally, she announces that she has "been plucked by her mother off the bush of wild roses that grow by the prison door." The Governor is astonished and immediately declares that Pearl is "in the dark as to her soul, its present depravity, and future destiny." With great excitement Hester reacts, exclaiming that the child is her "happiness" as well as her "torture." She cries out: "Pearl keeps me here in life! Pearl punishes me too!" Reverend Wilson assures her that the child will be "well cared for." Hester firmly declares, "I will not give her up!" Impulsively, she turns to Reverend Dimmesdale, saying "speak for me. . . Look thou to it! I will not lose the child! Look to it!" Reverend Dimmesdale gently begins to discuss what he calls the "awful sacredness in the relation between this mother and this child." He points out that the child reminds our people of the scarlet letter which "sears" Hester's bosom. He furthers his argument by claiming that Hester needs Pearl as a reminder of her past sin in order to "preserve her from blacker depths of sin into which Satan" might still plan to plunge her. The Governor is satisfied. The child will remain with its mother. Dimmesdale quietly withdraws to a nearby window. Pearl softly steals towards him and "taking his hand in the grasp of both her own" leans her cheek against it. The minister responds by placing his hand on the child's head, and then after a brief hesitation kisses her brow. Roger Chillingworth, looking much uglier and even more misshapen than he was three years ago, suggests that an observer might "analyze" Pearl's "nature" and "give a shrewd guess" at her father. As Hester leaves the Governor's mansion, his "bitter-tempered sister," Mistress Hibbins, invites Hester to join a "merry company" which meets in the forest this very night under the guidance of "the Black Man." Hester smilingly refuses, saying that if Pearl had been taken from her, she would very likely have been in the party.

COMMENT: Dimmesdale seems to be suffering from poor health. One reason might be that he labors long and hard at his religious duties, but another—more important—reason is probably that he is plagued by his conscience, the knowledge of his hypocrisy. This is the first time in the romance that he seems to have changed to any extent, or to have developed as a character. Governor Bellingham's reference to the "court mask" of King James I's time suggests that the Governor has known a more sophisticated life in the past than that which Boston provides for him at the moment. (The masks—sometimes called "masques"—of the English court were highly elaborate affairs, with symbolic characters wearing fantastic costumes.) Pearl reminds the Governor of his past days when he sees her bright dress. Hester sees that Chillingworth's features have changed. He seems much more like a devil than before. He reacts to Dimmesdale's plea for Hester with the words: "You speak, my friend, with a strange earnestness." Perhaps he is beginning to suspect that Dimmesdale is the man he is seeking. Mistress Hibbins, who speaks to Hester when she leaves the mansion, is a caricature character (one whose personality, speech, and dress are extremely exaggerated, so as to produce an absurd effect).

SUMMARY: In this chapter, the plot moves forward, emphasizing the following points:

1. Governor Bellingham, accompanied by the Reverend John Wilson and Arthur Dimmesdale, is surprised to discover the elaborately dressed Pearl in his hall.

2. The Governor sternly tells Hester that many people doubt that she should have the care of little Pearl. Hester vigorously defends her position against both the Governor and Reverend Wilson. The two men are disturbed at the child's lack of religious knowledge. Then, Hester makes a direct appeal to Arthur Dimmesdale, demanding that he speak in her behalf. Dimmesdale explains his point of view to the other two men. He says that Hester, as a fallen woman, needs Pearl as a living symbol to help protect her from further sin. They agree. Hester is to be allowed to keep the child.

3. Pearl tenderly caresses Dimmesdale's hand, and he kisses her brow.

4. Mistress Hibbins, Governor Bellingham's sister, makes her first appearance in the romance, as she invites Hester to a festivity in the forest that night. Hester refuses the invitation to join the Governor's sister when she goes to see the Black Man of the Forest.

CHAPTER IX: "THE LEECH"

Hester Prynne's husband, Dr. Prynne, is surprised to see his young bride on a scaffold wearing the scarlet letter of an adultress. Deciding to practice medicine in the new world, he chooses to settle in Boston under the assumed name of Roger Chillingworth. His plan is to find out the name of his wife's lover. He suspects the guilty man to be the Reverend Arthur Dimmesdale. Becoming a constant companion to the young minister, he eventually moves into the same house with him.

Roger Chillingworth (the name we shall give to him from now on) came out of the wilderness as an elderly, travel-worn man. When he found his wife on the scaffold, he decided he wanted no public connection with her. He further decided that his life had taken on a "new purpose." He was determined to name his wife's lover. He finds that establishing himself as a doctor (sometimes called a "leech") is an easy thing to do since Boston has no trained physician at the moment. People are delighted to have him become a member of the colony, not only because of their need for him, but because their beloved Mr. Dimmesdale is beginning to show signs of failing health. The young minister, himself, claims that Providence might see fit to remove him "because of his . . . unworthiness." As he says this, he places his hand over his heart, first growing red and then white, as if he were in pain. (This is the first time that Dimmesdale is noticed placing his hand over his heart. This action takes place many times as the story unfolds.) Chillingworth wanders about the edges of the settlement gathering herbs, blossoms of wild flowers, roots, and tree twigs. In captivity to the Indians he had learned how to use these simple objects of nature for medical purposes. Chillingworth expresses great concern over Dimmesdale's health. No longer does Dimmesdale put his hand over his heart as an occasional, "casual gesture," but rather this gesture has become a "constant habit." Finally, the young minister agrees to consult with Chillingworth. The two men take long walks while Dimmesdale unburdens his mind to the physician, but at no time does he mention what might be troubling his heart. Chillingworth attempts to probe. A great intimacy grows up between the two men, but still their companionship is based on their discussions of philosophy, of religion—of those things they both see in the world about them. Finally, Chillingworth moves into the house occupied by Dimmesdale. The young minister's rooms are hung with tapestry. The physician-scientist's rooms are arranged as a study and laboratory. Some people are delighted that Dimmesdale has the constant companionship of the physician, but many people, by instinct, begin to distrust Roger Chillingworth. They remember that when he came to town, his face was calm. Now, there is "something ugly and evil" in his expression. Some people even go so far as to suggest that Roger Chillingworth might be haunting the young minister as a representative of the devil.

COMMENT: What a strong personality Roger Chillingworth is! He comes to Boston to claim his bride and to live happily forever after with her. He discovers her shame (adultery), and then he promptly and privately disowns her. He substitutes a new goal—this time it is a search for the identity of his wife's lover. How carefully he plans his campaign. He fits beautifully into the scheme of things in Boston, for there is great need for a "leech" (a doctor). He soon becomes the close friend of Reverend Arthur Dimmesdale, who seems in need of medical attention. However, even after Chillingworth moves into the same house with Dimmesdale, the young minister does not completely unburden his heart to his companion and friend. Dimmesdale begins the habit of placing his hand over his heart, as if he feels a pain there. (See the beginning of Chapter XXIV, "Conclusion," where the discussion centers around the possibility that Dimmesdale has a self inflicted wound over his heart.) The tapestry hangings in Dimmesdale's apartment are symbolic, for the characters shown in the tapestry parallel those in our story: David resembles Dimmesdale, Bathsheba resembles Hester, and Nathan the Prophet is quite similar to Chillingworth.

SUMMARY: The following points are brought forward in this chapter:

1. Roger Chillingworth rejects his wife, Hester, and takes up residence in Boston as a doctor, with one aim in mind—to find the name of Hester's lover. He becomes a familiar figure to the Puritans as he walks around gathering such things as herbs and tree bark for his medical practice.

2. Dimmesdale and Chillingworth become closely associated with each other, enjoying pleasant walks together, as well as long discussions of matters of philosophy and religion. Finally Chillingworth moves into the same house as Dimmesdale. Some people are pleased to have a physician-friend attend their beloved minister, Reverend Dimmesdale. Some, however, suggest that Chillingworth might be haunting the sick minister. (During the few years that the "leech," Chillingworth, has been living in Boston, his face has begun to take on an "ugly and evil" look. The pursuit of revenge is making him into a fiendish sort of person.)

CHAPTER X: "THE LEECH AND HIS PATIENT"

Roger Chillingworth, the physician, and Arthur Dimmesdale, the patient, have a long talk in Roger's laboratory about Arthur's poor health. The doctor questions Arthur as to whether or not everything has been told him about the case—whether or not Arthur has omitted something of importance about himself. The minister grows angry and leaves. Eventually the two become friends again.

This chapter is a continuation of the preceding chapter, with the exception that both the minister and his physician engage in dialogue, whereas in the preceding chapter there was almost no dialogue. Chillingworth digs into Dimmesdale's heart "like a miner searching for gold." During the conversation between the two he learns of many things concerning Dimmesdale's thoughts: his hopes for mankind; his love of souls; his pureness of sentiment; and his natural holiness. And yet with all this, Chillingworth feels intuitively that Dimmesdale is hiding something from him. It is strange that the minister does not suspect his doctor of being more curious than he should be. One day, in Chillingworth's laboratory, the two men fall into a casual conversation about some dark, flabby herbs which Dimmesdale has recently gathered. Very pointedly the physician says that the herbs were found growing on a grave—in fact, they probably have grown "out of" the heart of a dead man, representing "some hideous secret that was buried with him, and which he had done better to confess during his lifetime." (The physician is casting out a strong hint, encouraging the minister to talk about himself.) Dimmesdale replies that possibly the dead man desired "to confess," but he could not do so. He continues by saying that at the Judgment Day the man will confess "with a joy unutterable." Chillingworth says that the guilty one might achieve "solace," or relief, now. Why should he wait? Dimmesdale agrees in theory with the "leech," as he remembers watching "relief" on the faces of many people who had confessed their sins to him before their deaths. He goes on to explain (in one of the key passages of the book) that some sinners "shrink from displaying themselves black and filthy in the view of man." He explains that confession of past evil might make it impossible for them to continue serving "their fellow-creatures." Thus, these unhappy sinners daily walk around "looking pure as new-fallen snow while their hearts are all speckled and spotted" with sin. Chillingworth vigorously answers that a "false show" cannot be better "than God's own truth." Dimmesdale says that this is possibly very true, and then he changes the subject to his own state of health. At this time the two men hear the "clear, wild laughter" of a young child's voice, coming from the burial-ground next door. They see Pearl dancing from one grave to another. In answer to her mother's demand that she behave, Pearl takes some prickly burrs from a burdock and then arranges them "along the lines of the scarlet letter" on her mother's bosom. Chillingworth remarks that there is "no law. . . mixed up with that child's composition." Dimmesdale thoughtfully answers that the child enjoys "the freedom of a broken law." Overhearing the conversation, Pearl throws one of the prickly burrs at Dimmesdale. He shrinks back. Pearl claps her hands in childish ecstasy. (This is a dramatic moment, for the four main characters of the book look at each other in silence. Seldom are all four characters on the scene at the same time.) Pearl breaks the spell by urging her mother to come away, or else "yonder old Black Man" might catch her. The child adds that the Black Man has "got hold of the minister already." (Note how the intuition of the small child allows her to sense the true situation existing between the two men.) The mother and child leave, as Chillingworth questions whether or not Hester Prynne is "less miserable" because she wears the scarlet letter for all to see. Speaking of himself, Chillingworth says that to show one's pain is better "than to cover it all up in his heart." At this point Chillingworth bluntly asks Dimmesdale if the sick minister has told his physician everything that might concern his case. Dimmesdale says all has been told. Chillingworth declares that sometimes a "bodily disease" may be only a "symptom" of a spiritual ailment. He then asks if the minister cares to "lay open to him the wound or trouble" in his soul. Dramatically Dimmesdale cries out: "No!—not to thee!—not to an earthly physician!" He says he will assign himself to his God. Then he leaves, angry. Chillingworth watches his friend leave, remarking to himself that Dimmesdale is capable of sudden and unusual "passion." He then speculates that very likely the minister has before this time "done a wild thing . . . in the passion of his heart." Eventually, the two men become friends again. One day, Chillingworth walks quietly into his friend's apartment. He finds Dimmesdale fast asleep. Advancing to his patient, the doctor removes the "vestment" that covers the top of the sleeping man's chest. Chillingworth stares and stares—then he turns away. The doctor's face reflects "wonder, joy, and horror . . . rapture." He throws his arms into the air; he stamps his feet on the floor. In his ecstasy, he resembles Satan.

COMMENT: Note that Chillingworth begins his search for Hester's lover with the feeling that he only wants to reveal the "truth." Before he knows it, he is overcome by a "terrible fascination," which forces him to probe and dig into the heart of his suspected victim (Dimmesdale). Finally, he is a man seeking a devilish revenge. He wishes the minister to suffer pangs of conscience, to be aware of his own (Dimmesdale's) hypocrisy. This chapter contains much dialogue between the two men, as they fence with each other—Chillingworth constantly attempting to corner Dimmesdale, and Dimmesdale always offering vague and general explanations for the leech's probing, personal questions. Very often in the dialogue, when the minister is speaking of the "relief" which comes after the "outpouring" of confession, he shows how very much he would like to have that same "relief" (that "joy unutterable") through confession of his sins. In a key speech, Dimmesdale does explain why a sinner (of spotless reputation) might not confess: it is because such a person would lose his "pure" reputation and would no longer be able to serve others. He would be held in general contempt. (One wonders how much of Dimmesdale's point of view is due to his wish for service, and how much is determined by his unwillingness to be disgraced.) How very cleverly Hawthorne breaks into the dialogue with the brief scene showing Pearl dancing in the graveyard. The presence of Pearl (who is indirectly being discussed) adds to, or heightens, the dramatic effect of the conversation. At the end of the chapter, Chillingworth looks at Dimmesdale's chest and sees something there which brings him "ecstasy." At last, he has some definite proof that the unhappy clergyman should be the victim of his revenge.

SUMMARY: This chapter, filled with dialogue, contains the following points:

1. Chillingworth has been digging into Dimmesdale's heart through conversation, much as a miner digs into the earth. He finds many wonderful thoughts, but he does not uncover anything that positively states that the young minister is Hester's lover.

2. Chillingworth tries to get Dimmesdale to confess, by drawing a parallel with the case of a man who did not confess his earthly sins and who had "ugly weeds' growing from his heart "in remembrance" of his sins.

3. Dimmesdale discusses how wonderful confession is, for it relieves a sinner's conscience. He adds that some men cannot confess their sins, for then they might lose their chances for doing good for man in the future, because of their public disgrace.

4. Hester and Pearl walk in the neighboring graveyard. Pearl skips from grave to grave, throws a prickly burdock burr at Dimmesdale, and tells her mother to come away from the "Black Man" (Chillingworth), for she says her mother might be caught by Chillingworth as the minister is already.

5. Chillingworth tells Dimmesdale to relieve his soul by telling him (the "leech") of his inner troubles. The minister says "No!" Then he rushes away.

6. Chillingworth walks quietly into Dimmesdale's room when the minister is asleep in a chair. The doctor pushes aside the covering of the sleeping minister's chest and feasts his eyes on what might be a self-inflicted wound—a letter "A"!

CHAPTER XI: "THE INTERIOR OF A HEART"

Roger Chillingworth becomes the source of much torture to Arthur Dimmesdale, although the sickly minister does not quite realize he is being persecuted by his companion. Dimmesdale is very much aware of his hypocrisy, and he wishes (so he tells himself) to confess his sin. He cannot do so. His congregation feels him to be the holiest of the holies. Throughout long dark nights he tortures himself physically and mentally.

Chillingworth, now convinced that Dimmesdale is the guilty party, decides to have a terrible revenge on the minister. His plan is to "make himself the one trusted friend" of Dimmesdale, the one who will receive in confidence the minister's fears, remorse, agony, and repentance. The physician gloats over the idea that he "the Unforgiving" will listen to the cries of the "Pitiless." Yet one thing does upset this plan a bit, and that is Dimmesdale's "shy and sensitive reserve." But to overcome this, the watchful doctor chooses his time carefully to subtly suggest some idea that will fill the minister with fear. For the most part Dimmesdale does not realize that he is being manipulated by the "leech" much as a mouse is played with by a cat. Once in a while his instinct tells him everything is not right, and for a moment he looks with "horror" at the deformed Chillingworth. However, on the surface seeing nothing wrong with the old man, Dimmesdale blames himself for not truly appreciating his physician friend. The sense of hypocrisy in Dimmesdale has had an unusual effect upon his preaching. His daily agony has made him sensitive to the needs, trials, and distress of others. He becomes increasingly famed among the Boston clergy. Some of his fellow ministers are greater scholars than he. Some have sturdier minds than his. Some have a greater spiritual presence. But Dimmesdale surpasses them all in one way: he possesses the "Tongue of Flame," for he is able to interpret humble, commonplace, familiar things of the ordinary world as having spiritual significance. Dimmesdale's congregation believe him to be "a miracle of holiness." The ground on which he walks they believe to be "sanctified."

Young maidens of his church find him irresistible. The aged members of the congregation greatly admire him. In the face of all this admiration Dimmesdale longs "to speak out, from his own pulpit, at the full height of his voice," telling the people the truth about himself: "I . . . am utterly a pollution and a lie!" Several times Dimmesdale draws a long breath in his pulpit ready to tell his hearers that he is "altogether vile."

He does tell them that he is vile, but he never gets to the place in the sermon when he explains why he is unworthy. (This is a form of hypocrisy, for he realizes he has no true intention of telling the complete truth.) His conscience does bother him, however, and he spends long nights in agony considering his sin. Sometimes he takes from a secret closet a "bloody scourge" (a whip with sharp particles attached to it). As he whips himself, he laughs bitterly. He fasts, going without food for long periods of time. He sits alone in total darkness through long nights. He varies this last activity by sometimes "viewing his own face in a looking-glass" with the aid of a powerful light. This "constant introspection" (looking inwardly at himself) tortures him but does not purify him. At times, his brain becomes weary and "visions" flit across the surface of the looking-glass: sometimes he sees demons who beckon to him; at other times he sees angels who look sorrowfully at him; and then he views "dead friends of his youth," his father and his mother; finally, he sees Hester Prynne leading little Pearl by the hand. Everything has a bitterness about it to Dimmesdale. He realizes that he is an "untrue man," for as far as he is concerned "the whole universe is false." One night when he is particularly unhappy, Dimmesdale gets up from his chair and prepares himself to leave the house.

COMMENT: This is one of the key chapters of the entire book. We see Arthur Dimmesdale egged on by Chillingworth. We are given the generalization that the guilty minister suffers many tortures as the result of his hypocrisy. Then we are given the specific details concerning his torment. He uses the "scourge" (whip) to satisfy himself that not only Hester, but he, too, is suffering because of his sin with Hester. This active, physical torture is followed by another type of agony, this time a slower sort of punishment—the fast. He goes without eating until his body trembles with weakness. Keeping midnight "vigils" (watches), he sometimes suffers in darkness. At other times, he studies his face in a mirror with the help of a powerful light. This act, of carefully looking at himself in a mirror, is parallel to what happens daily in his life: his conscience looks at him and declares him a sinful hypocrite. Hester is able to externalize (put on the outside) her sin (adultery) by openly wearing the scarlet letter. But he feels he must always hide his guilt, and so he suffers from introspection (looking at and analyzing his own emotions).

SUMMARY: This chapter makes the following main points:

1. Chillingworth has come to the point where he is certain Dimmesdale is the guilty man he has been searching for. By subtle means, he vengefully tortures the hypocritical minister.

2. Dimmesdale's knowledge of sin has made him sympathetic to the sins of his fellow men. His reputation grows as his sermons become more and more inspired. He tries to confess his sin, but his unfinished confessions lead the members of his congregation to believe that he is a "saint on earth." They say that if *he* is sinful, how much more sinful they must be!

3. Dimmesdale punishes himself by the whip, by denying himself food, and by keeping lonely watches through the night. At times, he studies his own face in a mirror.

CHAPTER XII: "THE MINISTER'S VIGIL"

Dimmesdale stands on top of the scaffold and shrieks. He is joined on the scaffold by Hester and little Pearl, and the three hold hands together. Chillingworth comes along and finally conducts the weary Dimmesdale home.

Dimmesdale mounts the scaffold seven years after Hester had stood on it for penance. It is Saturday, on a dark night in early May. It is about midnight. He is drawn to Hester's scaffold of penance by "remorse." The fact that it is at night is representative of his "cowardice." Suddenly he shrieks aloud. He thinks he will awaken the whole town, but he does not do so. Only two people respond to his cry—the old magistrate, Governor Bellingham, and his sour-faced sister, Mistress Hibbins. The two people awakened by his cry finally go back to bed. Reverend Wilson is seen walking along carrying a dim lantern. This worthy minister has just come from the "death chamber" of Governor Winthrop. Dimmesdale imagines that he speaks to the Reverend John Wilson, but he does not, for his mind is now playing tricks on him. He begins to think that he might not be able to leave the scaffold (because his limbs are beginning to grow stiff with the cold), and he imagines many early risers finding him crouched on the platform in the morning. He pictures elderly leaders of the community, as well as Governor Bellingham and Mistress Hibbins, all staring at him on the platform. He imagines "Father Wilson," the elders and deacons of his church, and Boston's purest young maidens turning their amazed faces up towards him. Almost hysterically, he laughs. His laugh is answered by a "light, airy, childish laugh," belonging to Pearl. Hester and Pearl are just returning from Governor Winthrop's deathbed where Hester has "taken his measure for a robe." At Dimmesdale's invitation the two newcomers climb the steps of the platform. Quietly the minister takes one of Pearl's hands; Hester takes the child's other hand. It is a still moment. Pearl inquires if the minister will join them tomorrow noon in the same place. The minister says he cannot, but that he will join hands with the two at "the great judgment." (Dimmesdale soothes his own conscience by such a plan, that is, to confess his sins when all sins of the world are to be accounted for, according to his Puritan doctrine.) All at once, a meteor flashes through the sky, lighting all about them. To the guilty Dimmesdale the meteor has the "appearance of an immense letter—the letter 'A.'" (Dimmesdale has adultery on his mind and his "guilty imagination" makes him connect this sin with all those around him.) Not only does this sudden flash of light reveal Pearl holding by each hand one of her parents, but it also reveals (especially to Pearl) the figure of Roger Chillingworth standing near the scaffold scowling at them like an "arch-fiend." Instinctively, Dimmesdale gasps, "Who is that man, Hester?" A moment later, he says, "I have nameless horror of the man!" He appeals to Hester to help him. Pearl mumbles into the minister's ear some childish "gibberish," in an attempt to identify Chillingworth. When Dimmesdale asks if she mocks him, she replies that he did not promise to take her mother's hand and her own hand in the noonday sun in front of other people. At this point, Chillingworth explains that he has spent the "better part of the night" at the bedside of the dying Governor Winthrop. He then demands that Dimmesdale accompany him home. The two leave together. On the next day, the Sabbath, Dimmesdale preaches his finest sermon to date. As he leaves his pulpit, the church sexton holds up to him his own black glove as he explains that it had been found on the scaffold where it was probably dropped by Satan. The sexton also provides an interpretation of the meteor. He believes the letter "A" stood for "Angel," because Governor Winthrop became an angel when he died.

COMMENT: Driven by remorse and conscience, Dimmesdale goes to the marketplace and climbs the steps of the scaffold. He feels that he must stand in the very place where Hester humiliated herself by being stared at and abused by the townspeople. Being here will perhaps help relieve his pain—salve his conscience. Since he has dressed himself as he dresses when he preaches, he might possibly have in the back of his mind that he will be discovered by indignant members of his congregation who will publicly accuse him of sin and end his torture. His cry into the night only awakens Governor Bellingham and his sister, Mistress Hibbins. This attempt to draw attention to himself as a sinner is as ineffective as his previous unsuccessful efforts have been when he has tried to confess in the pulpit. In this key scene (that is, scene which is important in the development of the plot and the characters), the four main characters are brought face to face in a dramatic situation. Hester, Pearl, and Dimmesdale, when they hold hands on the scaffold, form a dramatic tableau (a picture which has some special significance, appearing as if it were posed, as people pose to have a picture taken). In this case the family relationship is emphasized, as Pearl stands between her parents, holding a hand of each. Dimmesdale refuses Pearl's request that on the following day in public he repeat this tableau (the symbolic holding of hands). Chillingworth, the fourth important character, stands watching them near the scaffold. By pointing her finger at the villain (Chillingworth), Pearl makes him an important part of the scene. How dramatic the moment is when the meteor (perhaps a shooting star) makes the night as bright as day to reveal four characters together! History tells us that Governor Winthrop died in 1649. We know Pearl is seven years old at this time. Thus, we can date the beginning of the story as 1642.

SUMMARY: The following things happen in this important chapter:

1. Dimmesdale stands on the scaffold at midnight and cries out, hoping to relieve his conscience.

2. Hester and little Pearl join the saddened minister on the scaffold, where they clasp hands.

3. Chillingworth watches the three of them, as a meteor streaks by in the sky lighting up the landscape. The hypocritical minister thinks the meteor takes the shape of a letter "A," which his guilty imagination imagines to stand for adultery. (The members of his congregation, the next day, feel the "A" stands for "Angel," which they believe Governor Winthrop became the previous night when he died.)

CHAPTER XIII: "ANOTHER VIEW OF HESTER"

Upset at Dimmesdale's sad physical condition, Hester Prynne decides that she must help him. Over the period of seven years of wearing the scarlet letter, she has become an accepted, relatively respected, member of the community.

Hester realizes that there is a force damaging Dimmesdale's sense of peace other than his conscience alone. She realizes that Chillingworth is that evil force. Over a period of seven years her scarlet letter had become a "familiar object to the townspeople." To her credit she had never fought the public—she has always submitted "to its worst usage." For seven years her life has been "blameless." She has given generously to the poor; she has nursed the sick. Many people begin to consider her a "Sister of Mercy." The letter "A" begins to become the symbol of her "helpfulness," meaning to some people not adultery, but "Able." Hester never demands public approval. Where there is darkness, sickness and poverty, there she is, too. Hers is not an existence filled with sunshine; hers is a dark world. The magistrates (judges) gradually begin to recognize her helpfulness. One sacrifice has been made by Hester through the wearing of the scarlet symbol—she has lost much of her femininity. Her somber looks, her hair hidden under a cap, and her reserved manner cause her to seem very stern. Of course, the fact that she once had allowed herself to be tender and has suffered considerably because of that influences her behavior now. She must not seem a loose woman in any way. If she were alone she might have difficulty in keeping her solitary, stern position. But little Pearl has caused her to carefully regulate her behavior. (If Hester were to live at a later period in history, she would probably be known as a feminist, a champion of women's rights.) Although Hester presents a submissive appearance to the great satisfaction of her fellow Puritans, inwardly she lives in darkness and receives no comfort. Evidently, the scarlet letter represents a certain form of public penance, but it has not truly purified. Her knowledge of sorrow helps her understand the great sadness in Dimmesdale's heart. She decides to help him. She knows that Chillingworth, Dimmesdale's "secret enemy," has falsely been pretending to be a "friend and helper" to the unhappy minister. Until this time she has had her lips sealed regarding her association with Chillingworth, for the vengeful old man had demanded this of her when he visited her seven long years ago in the prison. Hester makes up her mind to meet Chillingworth and talk the matter over with him. One afternoon, she finds him as he is walking, gathering roots and herbs for medical supplies.

COMMENT: Over a period of seven years since the birth of Pearl, Hester's reputation in the community has improved greatly. Her good deeds have caused many of the Puritans to change their original interpretation of the scarlet letter "A" for adultery. Now some speak of it as meaning "Able," representing her willingness to help others and her strength. (The Puritans believed in faith in religion, emphasizing belief in the Bible more than good works. Hester gets their admiration for her good works.) Since Hester is not allowed to feel emotional about problems of the day, she spends her time thinking. She thinks much about the suffering of Dimmesdale. She finally decides that she must try to help him.

SUMMARY: The following points are made in this chapter:

1. Hester's reputation in the community has improved remarkably. Many people now admire her for her good deeds.

2. Hester covers up most of the softening signs of her feminine nature. She thinks about the place of woman in the world.

3. She plans to help Dimmesdale in his sorrow.

CHAPTER XIV: "HESTER AND THE PHYSICIAN"

Hester speaks to Roger Chillingworth and tells him that she must tell Dimmesdale the old man's true name.

First, Hester tells Pearl to run to the edge of the shore and play. The child stops at a pool of water left by the "retiring tide," and peeps in at the water-mirror. Pearl finds herself looking at an elfish playmate, mirrored back at her from the water. She beckons to the playmate to join her, but the elfish maiden in the water beckons back to Pearl. Chillingworth tells Hester that one of the magistrates has been discussing the question of her removing the scarlet letter from her breast. Hester tells the old man that it is not the place of the magistrates "to take off this badge." She also says that if she were worthy of having it removed, "it would fall away of its own nature." Hester is shocked to see how much Chillingworth has changed in several years. Once he was quiet and studious; now his expression is "almost fierce," and he has a false smile. At times, a red light seems to gleam out of his eyes. He has enjoyed his seven years of torturing Dimmesdale. Hester tells him that she feels a duty towards Dimmesdale to tell him of Chillingworth's true identity— that he is her husband. She further tells the old physician that he has caused Dimmesdale "to die daily a living death." She adds that she "acted a false part" when she agreed to hide Chillingworth's identity. The old man says: "What choice had you?" Chillingworth tells of the great effort he has put forth in caring for the ill minister's health. Then he gloats as he says that he has "grown to exist only by this perpetual poison of the direst revenge!" Suddenly the old man realizes the depths of evil to which he has sunk—it is as if he were truly seeing himself in a mirror for the first time. Hester asks if Dimmesdale has not been punished enough. The physician cries out: "No!" Gloomily he tells of his own happy days in the past when he worked "faithfully for the advancement of human welfare." He says that he is a "fiend." Hester remarks that she did this to him, and she wonders why he has not revenged himself on her. He says to her: "I have left thee to the scarlet letter." Hester then firmly tells Chillingworth that she intends to reveal his true identity to the suffering Dimmesdale. She asks the physician if he would not like "to pardon" the man who has wronged him—Dimmesdale. He answers that it is not in his power to do this, explaining that it is his fate to hate and torture Dimmesdale.

COMMENT: Notice in the first paragraph another one of Hawthorne's mirrors—this time a water-mirror. Pearl looks at a pool of water and sees her own "elf smile" peep back at herself. At this point in the story, we see Chillingworth completely changed from the kindly scholar pictured in Chapter II. An evil-faced man with a false smile, he welcomes the opportunity to openly discuss Dimmesdale with Hester. He claims to have preserved Dimmesdale's life by his medical attentions—all for the purpose of continuing to have a victim for his (Chillingworth's) revenge. (Compare this with one of his comments in Chapter IV, when he tells Hester that he wishes her to live so that she might still be shamed by wearing the scarlet letter.) This chapter contains one of the turning points of the book, for Hester makes the decision that she must tell Dimmesdale who his enemy is. Then she informs the "enemy" (Chillingworth) of what she plans to do.

SUMMARY: This chapter brings out the following important points:

1. Hester talks with Chillingworth. He tells her that some of the Puritans are discussing the possibility of permitting her to remove the scarlet letter from her breast.

2. Hester notes how evil Chillingworth has grown to look. (His desire for revenge on Dimmesdale has done this to him.) The "leech" admits he has become a "fiend."

3. Because she feels she still has a "duty" toward Dimmesdale, Hester tells Chillingworth that she must tell the unhappy minister that the physician is the one who is torturing him, and why.

CHAPTER XV: "HESTER AND PEARL"

Hester declares that she hates Chillingworth, for he has done her more wrong than she has done him. She calls Pearl to her, noting that Pearl has made a green letter "A" very much like her mother's scarlet letter. For the rest of the day and part of the following morning Hester is pestered by the questions of Pearl concerning the meaning of the scarlet letter. The child also asks why the minister keeps his hand over his heart. As Chillingworth leaves Hester at the edge of the sea, she has unhappy and evil thoughts about him.

She wonders if a circle of shadow moves along around him as he gathers his herbs. She says bitterly: "I hate the man!" She tries to stop herself from thinking further about her dislike of Chillingworth. She remembers her life with him nine years ago in Europe. Yet every memory that at one time might have been happy now seems to be ugly and sad. She wonders how she could have been persuaded to marry him. Then she declares aloud: "He betrayed me! He has done me worse wrong than I did him!" She is thinking of the fact that she, an innocent young woman, married an elderly scholar with whom she had very little in common. Hester herself feels no sorrow for Chillingworth's misery. All this time, little Pearl is keeping herself busy at the edge of the water. She flirts with herself in the water-mirror. She makes boats out of birch bark. She captures tiny sea creatures stranded on the shore. She throws up white foam into the air, chasing after it as the breeze blows it here and there. Finally, she picks up tiny pebbles and throws them at beach birds. She believes she has broken the wing of one of the creatures. Then she settles down to gather seaweed to make herself look like a mermaid. Using eel-grass she forms a bright green "A." Hester comes on the scene and sees her child with a green "A" on her breast. She asks the child if she has any idea why her mother is wearing the scarlet letter. Pearl replies: "It's for the same reason that the minister keeps his hand over his heart!" She adds that the old man Hester has been talking with (Chillingworth) will know why the minister does this. For a moment Hester thinks she may be able to tell Pearl why she does wear the letter on her bosom, but she finally decides she cannot inform the child. She says that she knows little of the minister's heart and that she wears the scarlet letter "for the sake of its gold-thread." This is the first time in seven years that Hester has suggested that the scarlet letter does not represent adultery. As a part of her penance, she has accepted freely the meaning given to the letter by the authorities. During the evening, and just before Pearl goes to bed, Pearl questions her mother about the meaning of the scarlet letter. In the morning she repeats the question—"Why does the minister keep his hand over his heart?"

COMMENT: Notice that now Hester has very unpleasant memories of her past life with Chillingworth. She blames him for marrying her. Pearl, the elf-like child, all this time has been very much enjoying the sight of her own reflection in the pool of water. Then she takes eel-grass and forms it into a green letter "A" on her childish breast. Much of the conversation in this chapter between the mother and child takes place because of this green letter. Pearl, for some unknown reason, connects her mother's scarlet letter "A" with the minister's putting his hand over his heart. Hester wonders, at this point, if she might make a confidant of Pearl. Perhaps she can tell her of some part of her sorrow. Then she realizes that she cannot do this. When she says to the child that she wears the symbol "for the sake of its gold thread," it is the first time she has ever denied the meaning of her scarlet letter. In the manner of a child, Pearl continues to question her mother about the meaning of the letter and, also, of the minister's keeping his hand over his heart. Hester brushes aside the questions.

SUMMARY: The following things take place in this chapter:

1. Hester sees Chillingworth as an evil old man. She feels he has "betrayed" her.

2. Pearl flirts with her reflection in the water and then makes a green letter "A" out of eel-grass and puts it on her own breast.

3. Hester and Pearl discuss the scarlet letter and where it came from. The child, for no apparent reason, connects it with Dimmesdale's putting his hand over his heart. Hester almost decides to share with Pearl some of her sorrow. Then she decides against telling the little girl the truth about the letter. She answers Pearl's question by saying that she wears it because of goldthread.

CHAPTER XVI: "A FOREST WALK"

Hester prepares to meet Dimmesdale. Accompanied by Pearl, she walks in the forest and discusses with the child the Black Man. Pearl stays near the edge of a brook and plays in the water, while Hester gazes at Dimmesdale walking along with his hand over his heart.

For a few days after her talk with Chillingworth Hester tries to meet Dimmesdale accidentally on one of his solitary walks. Never do their paths seem to cross. Finally she hears that he has gone to visit the Apostle Eliot, who is in the forest among the Indians whom he had converted to Christianity. Hester takes this opportunity to meet him. She and Pearl walk to the forest. The sunlight dances to and fro among the trees, once in a while shining on little Pearl—but never shining on Hester. Pearl tells her mother that the sunlight "will not flee" from her because she wears nothing on her bosom yet. Hester tells her that she hopes the child will never wear such an ornament on her breast. Innocently, Pearl asks if the letter will not "come of its own accord" when she is a grown woman. Her mother answers her by sending her to play in the sunshine. Hester approaches the child, and as she nears the circle of light the sunshine vanishes. Pearl then asks her mother to tell her a story about the Black Man. She inquires whether or not her mother had ever met the famous Black Man. Hester inquires how the child knows about the Black Man. It seems that, when Hester was watching near a sickbed in a neighboring house the previous evening, an old woman talked about the Black Man and mentioned that many people had "written in his book." Mistress Hibbins was one of the persons said to have written in the Black Man's evil volume. The old woman the previous night also said (reports the child) that the scarlet letter is the Black Man's mark on Hester. The child also reports that Hester is said to meet the evil one in the forest at night. Hester denies having left the child alone and tells her that she had met the Black Man once in her lifetime. She quietly says: "This scarlet letter is his mark!" All this time the mother and child have been following the bank of a stream. Pearl speaks to the stream, asking why its voice is so very sad. The mother tells Pearl she hears a footstep on the path. She wishes Pearl to play in that place while she goes to speak with the new arrival. Pearl again asks her mother about the Black Man and suggests that the evil one has placed a mark on the minister's chest. She asks why the Reverend Dimmesdale does not wear "his mark" on the outside (on his clothing), as Hester does. Pearl wanders along listening to the babbling of the stream. Hester, remaining in the shadows cast by the trees, watches Dimmesdale come toward her along the forest path. She notes his feeble appearance. He looks aimless, as if he were truly ready to die and be finished with life. He keeps his hand over his heart.

COMMENT: This brief chapter helps set the stage for Hester's interview with Dimmesdale (which is the topic of the following two chapters). Hester has chosen the forest as a place where she might best meet the minister, for they will be less disturbed in the freedom of the forest than they might be in the town. Chillingworth's "interference" must be avoided. The minister has been on a visit to the Apostle Eliot, who has spent much of his life preaching to the Indians and making Christian converts. (John Eliot, Apostle to the Indians, is an historical personage, described in Cotton Mather's *Magnalia Christi Americana.*) The use of the sun as a symbol is noted here: Pearl plays in the sunshine, for she has not sinned; the sunlight disappears when Hester enters the scene, for she has sinned. The little brook is not only a part of the forest setting; it is used as a parallel to little Pearl and her life. For instance, the brook comes from a "mysterious" well-spring and travels through "scenes" shadowed by the gloomy forest. As for Pearl, her origin is partly mysterious (in so far as the identity of her father is concerned), and her life with her mother has gloomy moments (when the Puritan children and their parents are not pleasant toward them). At the end of the chapter when Hester sees Dimmesdale approach through the forest, the minister looks as if he were ready to die. Hester has decided to come to his rescue at the right time.

SUMMARY: In this connecting chapter the following things happen:

1. Hester prepares to meet Arthur Dimmesdale in the forest, when he returns from seeing his friend, the Apostle Eliot.

2. The sunshine is all around Pearl, but it disappears when Hester comes near it.

3. Hester and Pearl discuss the Black Man. The mother tells her daughter that the scarlet letter is "his mark."

4. Pearl begins to connect the Black Man with Hester's scarlet letter, and with the minister's placing his hand over his heart.

5. Dimmesdale comes down the forest path. He looks as if he would be very glad to die at any moment. He keeps his hand over his heart.

CHAPTER XVII: "THE PASTOR AND HIS PARISHIONER"

Hester Prynne and Arthur Dimmesdale meet in the forest and discuss some of the things that have been bothering them for the last seven years. This is the first time in the book that these main characters frankly discuss their situation. They decide to leave the colony together.

When Hester first speaks to Dimmesdale in the forest he is very surprised, for he is not quite sure that a human being is talking to him. Hester's somber clothing and the heavy foliage cause her to be seen with difficulty. The two lovers address each other wonderingly—almost as if each doubted that the other lived. In one way, each seems to be a "ghost" to the other. As one looks into the face of the other, he sees mirrored some of his own sorrow. Arthur touches Hester's hand. This, at least, makes them feel they are living creatures in the same world. They sit on a heap of moss and talk in general terms about the weather and each other's health. Gradually, they approach the topic on the mind of each, that is, the effect of their sin on their present happiness. He tells her that he has no peace—he has "nothing but despair." He explains that if he were a man without conscience, filled with "coarse and brutal instincts," he would have peace at the moment. He summarizes his position by pitifully saying: "Hester, I am most miserable!" Hester points out to him that the people "reverence" him and that he does much good among the members of his congregation. He answers that he looks inward at himself and sees the "black reality" which the people are admiring. He says there is great "contrast" between what he seems and what he is. Hester tells him that his "good works" have helped prove his repentance—that he should have peace because of them. He says this is not so. He tells Hester that she wears the scarlet letter "openly" upon her bosom. His letter "burns in secret." He admits that he is greatly relieved to be able to look into the eyes of a person (Hester) who sees him for what he is. He wishes he had one friend (or one enemy) to whom he could daily reveal himself as a sinner. Hester tells him she could be the friend: then, she tells him that he has an enemy who lives under the same roof as he. The minister clutches at his heart and is speechless for awhile. Now Hester realizes how much harm she is responsible for, because she has not told him of the constant presence of his enemy. She suddenly realizes that Chillingworth's prodding could very easily push the suffering minister toward insanity. Hester realizes that she still loves Arthur. The truth dawns upon her. The loss of Dimmesdale's reputation—even death itself—would be better than the living torment that the unhappy minister is in at the moment. She tells him that she has been truthful about all things, except for revealing Chillingworth's identity to him. Then she says: "That old man—the physician . . . he was my husband!" Dimmesdale throws Hester a black, fierce frown. Then he sinks to the ground and buries his face in his hands. He says that he should have known this, for he has found the sight of Chillingworth distasteful. He says: "Woman . . . I cannot forgive thee!" Hester cries: "Thou shalt forgive me!" Then tenderly she throws her arms about him and caresses him. Finally, he says that he forgives her. Dimmesdale then says that there is one sin worse than his sin (of hypocrisy). That sin is the vengefulness of Chillingworth. Then the unhappy minister explains why Chillingworth is a very great sinner. It is because "he has violated, in cold blood, the sanctity of a human heart." He refers to the old physician's probing into his own heart. The two sit side by side, hand in hand, gazing at each other. All at once a thought crosses his mind. He realizes that Chillingworth knows Hester's "purpose to reveal" his real identity. (Chillingworth will know that Dimmesdale distrusts him.) The minister wonders if the fiendish old man will keep this a secret. Hester says that she thinks he will but that he will find other means of annoying Dimmesdale. Dimmesdale is completely frustrated and just about decides to give up hope completely. He asks Hester to help him. Hester tells him that he does not need to stay in Boston. He can go into the wilderness, or he can go back to England—or perhaps some other part of Europe. Dimmesdale says that he is "powerless to go." Hester says he must "begin all anew!" She even suggests that he might change his name and build a proud reputation under some other name. He answers that he has "not the strength of courage left" to go into the "wide, strange, difficult world, alone." She whispers "Thou shalt not go alone."

COMMENT: This is the first time that Hester Prynne and Arthur Dimmesdale have been together since the midnight watch on the scaffold. At that time they had been observed by Pearl and

Chillingworth. Now they are alone, for Pearl is playing at some distance in the forest. It is a relief for Dimmesdale to admit to Hester that he is a hypocrite. She comforts him. But then she startles him by informing him that his friend Chillingworth is his enemy. He is angry with her for not telling him sooner. Finally, he forgives her. He begins to feel sad, for he has the idea that there is no hope for him in the future. Hester again comforts him, explaining that he need not flee alone. The whole chapter is a series of emotional shifts for Dimmesdale. He is sad; he is angered; he is depressed. In each case, he is given comfort by Hester. They both agree Chillingworth's sin of vengeance is worse than any of their sins.

SUMMARY: The following things happen in this chapter:

1. Hester and Arthur meet in the forest. He reveals to her that he is filled with despair. He recognizes that *she* has had some relief by wearing her scarlet letter on her bosom. He has hidden his sin and suffers the pangs of conscience alone.

2. Hester tells Arthur that Chillingworth is his enemy and that the old physician is her husband (Dr. Prynne). Dimmesdale is crushed and angry. Finally, he forgives her.

3. Arthur is too weak to leave Boston alone. They start to plan to leave the colony together.

CHAPTER XVIII: "A FLOOD OF SUNSHINE"

Hester convinces Arthur that they should leave Boston together. Pearl is called over to meet the minister.

Hester for seven long years had been looking at life around her from the point of view of a spectator. Dimmesdale, as a leading clergyman of Boston, looks at the same life that Hester views, but he is forced by the prejudices of the church to evaluate situations according to standard patterns of behavior. Hester, in a way, has freed herself by being solitary. On the other hand, Dimmesdale has become a prisoner of society. At first, Dimmesdale feels he should not go away from Boston, but finally he changes his mind and decides that he might enjoy a "better life" with Hester somewhere else. To his own surprise he feels a sudden joy. He wonders why this decision has not been arrived at sooner. Hester tells him not to look back. Then she undoes the clasp fastening the scarlet letter to her bosom, and throws the symbol of shame on top of a pile of withered leaves. The letter almost falls into a small stream. Just as Dimmesdale immediately found happiness when he made the decision to go away with Hester, so does Hester find great relief by removing from her bosom the symbol of adultery. Impulsively, she takes off her cap and lets her long, dark hair fall around her shoulders. She smiles tenderly. Her beauty reappears. Then, the sunshine starts to fill the forest around the two happy people. It would seem as if these two have the sympathy and approval of nature. At this point, Hester is reminded of little Pearl and tells Arthur that he must see her now with his new outlook. The minister is afraid that she will shrink away from him. Hester calls to Pearl, who is standing some distance away in the forest. The child starts slowly toward the mother. The little creatures of the forest do not seem to fear her. A partridge, a pigeon, a squirrel, a fox—and even a wolf: all look at her and show no fear. Possibly these wild creatures recognize a "wildness in the human child" very much like their own. Pearl has gathered flowers. She walks very slowly towards her mother, for she sees Arthur Dimmesdale.

COMMENT: How Hester changes when she throws aside her scarlet letter! She frees her long hair from under her close cap. She smiles. She looks tender and womanly. The sun, which always before stayed away from her, now shines all about her. She is eager to have Pearl and Arthur meet and love each other. On the other hand, Pearl is not anxious to join her mother and the minister, for she is not altogether comfortable in the minister's presence. Also, her mother somehow seems changed. This chapter is a logical introduction to the following one because it ends as Hester and Arthur discuss Pearl. The next chapter pictures the three people together.

SUMMARY: The following things happen in this chapter:

1. Hester shows that she is a woman of strong character. She persuades Dimmesdale that he can still be happy, if he will leave Boston with Pearl and her. He is filled with hope and joy at this idea.

2. Hester removes the scarlet letter from her bosom. Then she lets her hair go free from under her cap. She smiles and is very feminine—a great contrast to her previous drab look. Nature is sympathetic to her, for the sunshine suddenly surrounds her.

3. The mother calls Pearl to join them. As she walks slowly toward the waiting pair, the little girl is casually noticed by several wild animals in the woods. She decorates herself with wild flowers.

CHAPTER XIX: "THE CHILD AT THE BROOK-SIDE"

Hester calls to Pearl, telling the child to join the minister and her. Pearl hesitates for a long time, staring curiously at her mother. Finally, Hester realizes that Pearl is upset because the scarlet letter has been removed from her mother's bosom. The child grows angry, Hester replaces the scarlet letter, and the child joins her parents.

As Hester and Arthur watch Pearl while she is approaching, Hester mentions the fact that Pearl has inherited from Dimmesdale his "brow." Dimmesdale claims that he sees his own features in her face—in fact, he has been afraid that "the world might see them." Hester and Dimmesdale are united in Pearl. She is a "symbol" of their love. The mother asks the father not to excite the child when he greets her. Hester feels that finally the child will love its father. Dimmesdale reminds Hester that he is not at his best with children. He does remember, however, Pearl's caressing his hand in Governor Bellingham's hall. Pearl stands at the edge of a brook, silently gazing at the waiting pair, and her reflection in the water is a thing of beauty. In some ways, Hester feels herself separated from the child. The mother encourages the child to come to her, but the child does not respond to her. All at once, Dimmesdale places his hand over his heart. Then, Pearl stretches out her hand and points with her small forefinger at her mother's breast. (The water-mirror exactly reproduces this scene—a young child, decorated by flowers, standing in a ray of sunlight and pointing her forefinger toward some distant object.) Hester again invites the child to come nearer. Pearl points. She frowns. She stamps her foot. She screams. All this time, Pearl's reflection is seen in the brook. (It is almost as if there were two children excited about something.) Then, Hester realizes what is the matter. She says: "Pearl misses something which she has always seen me wear." Upset, the minister asks Hester to do something to quiet the child. He adds, "if thou lovest me." (Seldom has Dimmesdale allowed himself to be so affectionate in speech.) Hester tells the child to bring the scarlet letter to her. The child refuses. Then Hester takes up the letter and fastens it again to her bosom. She follows this by confining all of her hair beneath her cap. All at once her feminine warmness disappears. She is again the same somber Hester that she was earlier in the day. Then, the child comes to her mother, kisses her and even kisses the scarlet letter. The mother and child discuss the minister. Pearl wondersif Dimmesdale will return with them to the town, "hand in hand." Hester says he will not at this time but eventually the three of them will have a "home and fireside" of their own. Pearl asks the inevitable question: "And will he always keep his hand over his heart?" Mother and daughter join the clergyman. He kisses Pearl on the brow. The child runs to the brook and scrubs the kiss from her forehead.

Then, she stays apart from them while they make arrangements for their future.

COMMENT: How very deep must be Dimmesdale's sense of guilt and hypocrisy if he thinks that people might recognize his features in little Pearl's face! The minister is almost afraid of Pearl (as he is of most children), but he does remember her moment of gentleness when she caressed his hand in Governor Bellingham's hall. Pearl lingers at the edge of a brook where her reflection is mirrored in a small pool. The child looks almost like another being, as she hesitates in the sun at the edge of the pool. With childish directness she points toward what is causing her to be so slow in approaching her mother: it is the absence of the scarlet letter on Hester's breast. All of this scene is mirrored in the brook as Pearl has a tantrum—screaming, shrieking, pointing, and stamping. The mirroring of the scene makes it seem even twice as disturbing as it is. When Hester picks up the letter and pins it again on her dress, Pearl's anger disappears. But the happiness which has briefly been Hester's (with the removal of the scarlet letter) is also ended—Hester is once again a captive to shame and the scorn that society has prescribed for her. (Notice the pattern of emotional rhythm in this story. Whenever one character is happy, it is more than likely that there is someone near (or involved with him) who is unhappy. Hawthorne often writes of contrasts in emotions.)

SUMMARY: Notice the following points in this chapter:

1. Hester and Arthur discuss little Pearl's strong affections. The minister is uncertain how the child will respond to him.

2. Pearl will not approach her mother and Dimmesdale, because Hester has removed the scarlet letter from her bosom. The child goes into a tantrum, all of which is mirrored in a pool at the edge of a brook.

3. Hester replaces the letter on her bosom and Pearl rejoins her mother for a while. Then, the child retreats to a distance while her mother and the minister plan their escape from Boston.

CHAPTER XX: "THE MINISTER IN A MAZE"

Hester and Dimmesdale plan to leave the colony on the fourth day following their conversation in the forest. When Dimmesdale returns to the town after talking with Hester, he meets five people (one at a time) and one group of people. He is tempted to say shocking things to them. When he arrives at his dwelling, he chats with Chillingworth, informing him that he will need no more of his medicine. Then, he spends the entire night writing an inspired Election Day Sermon.

At first, when Dimmesdale leaves Hester and Pearl in the forest, he cannot be sure that what has recently happened is really true. He thinks that perhaps he has been dreaming, but the sight of Hester and Pearl reminds him that he can take hope for the future. Arthur and Hester plan to go to the Old World. They plan to set sail on a vessel which has recently arrived from the Spanish Main. Their first destination will be Bristol, England. Through her nursing Hester has come to know the captain and some of the crew. Dimmesdale is happy that they will leave on the fourth day, for on the third day he is "to preach the Election Sermon." Excited, and filled with energy, Dimmesdale hurries back to town. Everything he sees looks different to him now, after his talk with Hester. This is because he himself has changed. Suddenly he has impulses to do strange or wicked things. First, he meets one of the oldest deacons of his own church. He has to restrain himself from saying some vile things about the Communion Supper (the taking of the bread and the wine, one of the most sacred parts of the Puritan church services). Second, as he walks along he catches up with the "Eldest female member of his church." He finds that he must stop himself from breathing into her ear an "unanswerable argument against the immortality of the human soul." He mumbles something to her and she throws him a look of "divine gratitude and ecstasy." Third, he meets the youngest female member of his congregation. He is tempted to whisper to her some evil thought that might eventually mislead her. He acts as if he does not recognize her, and he hurries onward. Fourth, Dimmesdale meets a group of "little Puritan children." He is tempted to stop and teach the little ones "wicked words." He restrains himself. Fifth, he meets a "drunken seaman" from the ship in the harbor. He wants to shake hands with the sailor and to throw a few oaths back and forth with him. He again succeeds in restraining himself. Sixth and finally, he meets Mistress Hibbins who looks very grand, being richly decked out in a gown of velvet. The old woman speaks to him with great familiarity, suggesting that he has been in the forest to talk with the "Black Man." Dimmesdale tells her he has been to see his friend, the Apostle Eliot, who has been converting the Indians to Christianity. Mistress Hibbins does not believe him. When Dimmesdale reaches his apartment, he looks around the walls. All at once he realizes that his customary surroundings look strange to him. Again he knows that he is a different man from the one who left this chamber earlier. A knock comes at the door and Roger Chillingworth enters. The physician asks about Dimmesdale's health. The minister then tells him that there will be no more need for Chillingworth's drugs. (He adds ironically to this the words: "good though they be, and administered by a friendly hand.") There is something is his tone that tells the old man that the young minister no longer considers him a "trusted friend," but that he now thinks of the physician as "his bitterest enemy." However, nothing is said on the surface of the conversation to indicate that the men are enemies. Chillingworth asks if he might use his medical powers to help make Dimmesdale "strong and vigorous" in preparation for the delivery of the Election Sermon on the next day. He adds that the people are afraid that with the arrival of another year they may find their minister gone. With double meaning again the minister says, "yea, to another world." (Chillingworth does not realize at this time that Dimmesdale plans to go to "another world"—the Old World.) After Chillingworth leaves, Dimmesdale eats a hearty meal. Then he flings into the fire the Election Sermon he had already begun. With great "thought and emotion," he composes an inspired sermon. When dawn arrives, he is still writing.

COMMENT: Arthur Dimmesdale has suffered from so many unhappy dreams and visions that it seems quite natural when he doubts at first that he has just talked with Hester and Pearl in the forest. He is very pleased that he will be able to deliver the Election Sermon on the day before they expect to leave for Europe. To be chosen to give this sermon is the highest honor any minister can have in 17th century Boston. He convinces himself that he is glad to be able to fulfill his public duty by preaching on this very special occasion. Actually, he is very proud of himself and is overcome by false humility.(He resembles men who want to run for high political office, but who tell people that they campaign because their friends insist on it.) Note how changed everything looks to Dimmesdale when he returns from the forest, all excited with his plans to leave Boston—his place of torture. The six encounters he has on the way home are with people who are representative of different groups in the story. (This is somewhat like a review of many of the main characters near the end of the story.) The old deacon might stand for the ritual and ceremony of the church Dimmesdale has been connected with. The old woman is one of those who have considered him an earthly angel, as he has preached hope to her. The young maiden (a member of his church, too) might resemble Hester Prynne who also was once young and innocent—and a member of Dimmesdale's parish. The Puritan children have been seen several times before when they irritated

Hester and Pearl. The drunken seaman is one of the last to be added to the tale, representing Arthur and Hester's plan for escape. Mistress Hibbins, with her knowing remarks about the Black Man, makes one think of little Pearl's often-repeated comment about Hester's scarlet letter and the Black Man of the forest. When Dimmesdale arrives home, he is ironic (saying one thing, and meaning another): he refers to Chillingworth's giving him drugs with a "friendly hand."

SUMMARY: The following things happen in this chapter:

1. Hester Prynne and Arthur Dimmesdale have determined to flee Boston on a vessel which will sail to Bristol, England, in three days. Dimmesdale is pleased and proud that he will be able to preach the Election Sermon on the day before their departure.

2. Dimmesdale's decision to leave fills him with a sense of freedom. He sees everything in a different light. He meets several people on his way home from the forest. (They are an old deacon of his church, the oldest woman of his congregation, the newest female member of his parish, a group of Puritan children, a sailor from the ship on which he will sail, and Mistress Hibbins.) Governor Bellingham's sister tells him she knows of his dealings with the Black Man of the forest.

3. Arriving home, Dimmesdale informs the physician (Chillingworth) that he will no longer need his medical aid. Then, Dimmesdale spends the entire night rewriting his Election Sermon.

CHAPTER XXI: "THE NEW ENGLAND HOLIDAY"

The people of Boston have elected a new governor for the coming year. Each year when the new official is to take office, there is a public holiday. Everyone gathers in his best clothing in the marketplace, and there are games played in the midst of a carnival atmosphere. The high point of the day is the Election Sermon, to be delivered this year by Arthur Dimmesdale. Hester and Pearl are the objects of the curiosity of the townspeople, Indians, and the crew of a vessel which has recently put into port.

Hester and Pearl arrive in the marketplace on the day of the holiday. Everywhere people are walking about. Even the settlers who live on the outskirts of the town have come to participate in the festivities. Hester is dressed quietly in coarse grey cloth. Her face is "like a mask." A keen observer might notice a small light in her face. Inside, she can whisper, "look your last on the scarlet letter and its wearer!" Hester thinks of herself as being on the high seas in a few hours, leaving Boston forever. Pearl is brightly dressed. She moves about "with a bird-like movement." Sometimes she bursts into wild shouts. She comments on all the workmen she sees in their best clothes. She wonders why Master Brackett, the old jailer, nods and smiles at her. Her mother tells her the old man remembers her as a child. Pearl notices the Indians and the sailors, and she wonders why they are there in the marketplace. Her mother explains to her that all of these people are waiting to see the procession pass by. Pearl wonders if the minister will hold out his hands to her. Her mother tells her that he will not do this today. Almost to herself, the child comments that the minister is a "strange, sad man . . . with his hand always over his heart!" Everybody seems to be filled with joy. The men are participating in sports. Some are wrestling; some are in friendly matches with the quarter-staff; some are opponents with swords. A party of Indians and some of the crew of the vessel stand watching the Puritans. The sailors are rough-looking men, dressed in colorful costumes. The captain of the vessel soon enters the marketplace in conversation with Roger Chillingworth, the physician. The captain is dressed in a suit covered with ribbons. He has gold lace on his hat, which is also encircled by a gold chain. The captain sees Hester Prynne, and, recognizing her, speaks to her. Hester is near no one at the time, for people generally stand away from her. The commander of the vessel explains to her that one more passenger is to take ship with them. He feels that he is very fortunate that a doctor will be traveling with them. Hester is startled. The captain continues his conversation, saying that Chillingworth will take ship with them. (Evidently Chillingworth has suggested that he is a close friend of Dimmesdale, and so the captain thinks everything will be all right if the physician accompanies his "friend.") Hester looks up, to see Roger Chillingworth smiling at her from a distant part of the marketplace. His smile fills her with fear.

COMMENT: This chapter contrasts in several ways with the few before it. For instance, the last chapters have been concerned with the feelings, thoughts, and actions of small groups of people—often only one or two at a time, such as Hester and Arthur. This chapter is filled wtth people—not only members of the Puritan community, but also Indians from the forest and sailors from the distant seas. By introducing outside elements, such as the sailors, one is more aware of the world outside Boston; therefore, Héster's "A" seems a bit less significant. Her trouble seems more like one happening among all the many happenings in a big world. (Before this, most of the dialogue and action have centered around Hester's symbol of adultery.) The seamen are described as being lawless in every way, and Hester's sin seems somewhat mild compared to acts the sailors might daily commit. This chapter portrays a picture of Puritan times, and it shows how settlers in the New World enjoy some of the same physical activities as their relatives in the Old. For example, the people relax by participating in (or watching) sports, such as wrestling, duels with the quarter staff (long, heavy, iron-tipped poles), and exhibitions with the sword. After all the varied activity in the marketplace is pictured, the action simmers down again at the end of the chapter, when Hester is horrified to learn that Chillingworth knows of the planned escape by Arthur, Pearl, and herself. She is visibly distraught at the idea that he will sail with them.

SUMMARY: This chapter contains the following important points:

1. Hester and Pearl come into the marketplace where many people have gathered to celebrate the election of the new governor. There are many people there, including the townspeople, Indians, and sailors from a vessel in the harbor. All are waiting to see the procession pass. Hester is quietly dressed; Pearl is brightly clothed.

2. The Puritans enjoy their holiday by watching or playing at sports. They look forward to the parade of the important members of the community and the soldiers—all of whom (dressed in their best) will be marching to music.

3. The sailors from the Spanish Main (probably the Caribbean Sea) are pictured in their bright costumes, as they wander around smoking and drinking. The captain of the vessel is elaborately dressed, with much decoration.

4. Hester is horrified to learn from the commander of the ship that Chillingworth is to set sail on the same vessel which she and her two loved ones plan to use to escape from Boston.

CHAPTER XXII: "THE PROCESSION"

This important chapter is concerned with a description of the procession; a conversation between Hester and Pearl about the minister; a series of unpleasant remarks about Dimmesdale by Mistress Hibbins; and the appreciation by Hester and the other members of the congregation of Dimmesdale's Election Sermon.

Before Hester can gather her wits about her (after being shocked by the news that Chillingworth will accompany them on the ship), the procession is heard approaching. First comes the music, played by the drum and some light woodwind instruments. Pearl is thrilled at the sound. Next in the procession come the soldiers, most of whom are gentlemen dressed in soldiers' uniforms. (They resemble the modern National Guard.) They, too, are brilliantly dressed. Then are seen the magistrates (rulers) of the colony: Bradstreet, Endicott, Dudley, and Bellingham. The magistrates are followed by the minister who is to deliver the Election Sermon—Arthur Dimmesdale. He is a different Dimmesdale. His steps are not feeble; his body is not bent; his hand does not rest upon his heart. There is a spiritual look upon his face. He looks deep in thought. Hester watches him closely. She remembers some of their past moments together. He does not seem to be the same man that she has been encouraging with the thought of escaping Boston. Even little Pearl does not quite recognize him. She says that, if she had been sure who he was, she would have run to him and kissed him before all the people. Another observer of the procession is Mistress Hibbins, who is magnificently dressed with three ruffs around her neck, a gown of costly velvet, and a gold-headed cane. Mistress Hibbins whispers confidentially, to Hester. She declares to Hester that Dimmesdale has been a part of the Black Man's group in the forest. Mistress Hibbins says that Hester wears her token of sin openly. She further declares that the minister hides his sin "with his hand always over his heart." With a shrill laugh the old gentlewoman leaves. Hester does not enter the church. She stands near the scaffold, within listening distance of Dimmesdale who is delivering the sermon in the church. Although she cannot catch every word Dimmesdale speaks, Hester is aware of the general tone and spirit of what the minister is saying. She recognizes that a human heart is trying to reveal its secret, without specifically explaining all the details. While Hester listens. Pearl wanders about. The ship's master takes from his hat the gold chain that is twisted about it and throws it to the child. The captain sends a message to Hester by the child Pearl. It is that Chillingworth says he will bring Dimmesdale on board the ship with him, and that Hester only need be concerned with Pearl and herself. Hester is surrounded by people from the country roundabout who had heard about the scarlet letter, but who had never seen it. These spectators are joined by the sailors and the Indians and even some of the townspeople. The chapter ends as two of the most important people of the romance are both being observed—Hester by curious people who are staring at her scarlet letter, and Dimmesdale by an audience which has been greatly, emotionally effected by his passionate sermon.

COMMENT: The procession is one of Hawthorne's ways of bringing many of his characters together. The procession organized for the festivities before the Election Sermon is of this type. The music comes first, followed by soldiers (who maintain law and order). The group of Governors and magistrates then makes its way along. In an honored position follows the representative of the church (in this case, Arthur Dimmesdale). Hester has helped give Arthur new courage. He has used this new courage to become more spiritual than ever before. Thus, he does not see Hester (his inspiration and hope) as he marches in the procession. One sympathizes with Hester when she faintly resents his not noticing her. Yet Hester defends Dimmesdale when Mistress Hibbins criticizes him. The old "witch" has noted the same thing that has often been on little Pearl's mind, that is, the minister keeps putting his hand over his heart. Dimmesdale's sermon is not summarized for us, but the general import of it is known as Hester reacts to what she faintly hears. She is aware of the agony in the minister's voice. The pain in Dimmesdale's heart and soul is evident in his tones. The minister's anguish is matched by Hester when the ship captain sends a message to her through Pearl. Chillingworth plans to help Dimmesdale to board the ship. There seems to be little hope for Hester and Dimmesdale. They are to be followed by the fiend—Chillingworth. There seems to be no escape.

SUMMARY: This dramatic chapter emphasizes the following points:

1. To celebrate the annual holiday for the election of a new governor, there is a procession of the most important people in Boston. The parade begins with music, which is followed by soldiers in shining metal uniforms. Next come the political leaders of the colony (the governor and chief magistrates). At the end of the parade—in the place of honor—is the Reverend Arthur Dimmesdale, who is to preach the Election Sermon.

2. Hester notices that Arthur seems to have changed in appearance, since their talk in the forest. He has energy and seems to be concentrating his thoughts on something. He looks like a man filled with a purpose. Even Pearl sees that he has changed in some way. Mistress Hibbins talks to Hester and disparages Dimmesdale's sincerity. The old woman is convinced that the minister puts on a pious front for the public—but that, in reality, he is a follower of the Black Man in the forest.

3. Dimmesdale delivers the sermon in the meetinghouse. Hester leans on the scaffold and listens to his tones and accents as they faintly come to her muffled by the walls of the church. Although she cannot clearly hear the words, she recognizes a great depth of sorrow in the gushing of Dimmesdale's voice.

4. While Hester stands listening, Pearl darts around the marketplace. The captain of the ship in the harbor sends a message to Hester through the child. The message is that Chillingworth assures the captain that he (Chillingworth) will see that his "friend" (Dimmesdale) gets on the vessel and that Hester need have no concern for him. She is horrified.

5. The chapter ends as Hester is surrounded by an unsympathetic circle of curious people inspecting her scarlet letter. At the same time, Dimmesdale is viewed by an audience whom he has just fascinated and thrilled with a magnificent Election Sermon. (What a contrast there is in the ways people are looking at the two people involved in the same sin!)

CHAPTER XXIII: "THE REVELATION OF THE SCARLET LETTER"

In this dramatic chapter, the procession of officials is seen leaving the meetinghouse. Dimmesdale, no longer charged with energy, shuffles along. As the procession passes the scaffold, Dimmesdale calls to Hester and Pearl. Although Chillingworth tries to stop the determined minister, Arthur Dimmesdale climbs to the platform of the scaffold with Hester and her child. And, in a very straightforward manner, he confesses to the crowd that he is Pearl's father. Then, he tears away the upper part of his ministerial garment, revealing a "red stigma." Exhausted and crushed, he dies. The crowd murmurs in wonder—the revelation (true meaning of) of the scarlet letter has stunned them.

As the chapter opens. Dimmesdale has just brought his sermon to a close. The audience is still. Then, it pours out into the marketplace. In the open air the excited listeners begin to explain to each other how wonderful this Election Sermon has been. The subject of the sermon was the relationship between God and man, with special reference to mankind in New England. At the end of the sermon Dimmesdale prophesied a glorious future for the people of the Boston colony. The whole sermon had an undertone of sadness—almost as if their beloved minister were bidding good-by to them before starting out on a journey. (This journey might well be death.) At this time, Arthur Dimmesdale stands at the most triumphant moment of his existence. This is the high point of his career as a minister. He bows his head on the cushions of the pulpit, as the members of his congregation look at him idolatrously. (Meanwhile, Hester Prynne is outside the meetinghouse, and is circled by a curious group of spectators staring at the scarlet letter.) Now the music begins again, and the "military escort" falls into place. The procession has started. The magistrates and the governor, as well as the Boston ministers, are on their way to the town hall, where they will enjoy a "solemn banquet" to round out the ceremonies of the day. In the middle of the marketplace the parade is greeted by a loud roar of approval. The man who is being cheered most enthusiastically by the townspeople is Arthur Dimmesdale. All eyes turn toward him. The shouting dies into a murmur. He has changed within the last few minutes. His energy seems gone. His cheeks are pale. He walks as if he might fall at any moment. Reverend John Wilson offers to help him, but Dimmesdale refuses aid. Now he is opposite the scaffold. Dimmesdale pauses. The music being played for the procession urges him to continue "onward to the festival." But he stops. Governor Bellingham, upset, leaves his place in the procession, in order to offer aid to Dimmesdale. The minister gives the magistrate a look that causes him to return to his original position among the other magistrates. Then Arthur Dimmesdale turns toward the scaffold, stretches forth his arms and says: "Hester, come hither! Come, come, my little Pearl!" He gives them a look full of terderness. Pearl runs to him and clasps her arms about his knees. Hester draws near him, but pauses before she reaches him. Suddenly, Roger Chillingworth pushes through the crowd and catches Dimmesdale by the arm, whispering: "Madman, hold! What is your purpose? Wave back that woman! Cast off this child! All shall be well!" Dimmensdale says: "Thou art too late!" He continues: "With God's help I shall escape thee now!" Then Dimmesdale calls on Hester to give him her "strength." He wants not only her spiritual strength, but he wishes her physical strength, so that she might help him climb to the platform of the scaffold. The crowd goes wild. They do not want to recognize the solution to this puzzle: they cannot allow themselves to believe that Dimmesdale has a close relationship to Hester and Pearl. There are four people now standing on the scaffold—Hester, Arthur, Pearl and Roger Chillingworth. (Chillingworth finds he must be with the people he has been so closely associated with.) Dimmesdale tells Hester that he is about to die. He wishes to share her "shame." Then, he passionately denounces himself to the spectators, as he reveals that he is Pearl's father. He explains that he has his own "red stigma" very much like Hester's scarlet letter. With a violent motion he tears away the "ministerial band" at the top of his garment. The audience is shocked. (Evidently, Dimmesdale has been punishing himself by mutilating the flesh of his breast, sketching out a letter very much like Hester's scarlet letter "A.") Dimmesdale sinks to the platform of the scaffold. Hester helps prevent him from falling. Chillingworth kneels beside him, saying, "Thou hast escaped me!" Dimmesdale asks God's forgiveness for the physician, adding that Chillingworth has also "deeply sinned." (This, of course, is a reference to Chillingworth's desire for revenge.) Dimmesdale invites Pearl to kiss him. She does. Then the child cries, the tears flowing "upon her father's cheek." Hester wonders if she and Arthur will meet again in another life. Dimmesdale fears that they may not. He is grateful that God has been merciful to him by giving him the "burning torture to bear" upon his breast, by sending Chillingworth to torment him, and by encouraging him to confess on the scaffold. Then Arthur Dimmesdale dies.

COMMENT: This is probably the most dramatic chapter of the entire book. It is filled with high points. Dimmesdale finishes his sermon, and the people are almost stunned into silence with admiration at his brilliant, inspired thoughts. Then, they outdo each other, loudly declaring that never before has man spoken so well. The procession of prominent people threads its way through the excited people. The townspeople cheer. Suddenly, in great contrast, is seen the changed figure of the minister. He no longer is strong and hearty. He almost staggers. How he has changed from what he was a few minutes ago—at the end of his triumphant sermon. He totters on his feet. Evidently, he is gathering his courage to do the thing which has represented horror and disgrace to him: he is about to confess. How dramatic is his beckoning to Hester and Pearl to join him! Even more dramatic is Roger Chillingworth's attempt to stop Dimmesdale from confessing. When the feeble minister calls upon Hester to help him climb the steps of the scaffold, the crowd is very curious. Chillingworth instinctively follows them up the stairs to the platform of the scaffold, for he has been one of the "actors" in this "drama of guilt and sorrow." Dimmesdale refers to his "own red stigma," and then he pushes aside his clerical neckpiece and reveals it to the "horror-stricken multitude." (One never knows exactly what Dimmesdale's "stigma" is, but it might resemble the marke of a branding iron formed into the letter "A." The minister refers to it as being the "type" of what has "seared" his own heart.) Arthur Dimmesdale has thus gained a strange sort of humility. He has faced up to the situation—that is, he has freely admitted his part in Hester's sin. He believes that he and Hester may never meet in a life after death. He is even grateful for the torture he has been through, for he feels that he has been saved (and forgiven) through his torment. Thus, he dies, believing he has paid the price for his sin through his suffering.

SUMMARY: This chapter contains the following dramatic happenings:

1. Dimmesdale concludes his Election Sermon which is cheered by the townspeople in the marketplace.

2. The procession starts to leave for the town hall where a banquet is to close the ceremonies of the day. People suddenly notice that Dimmesdale no longer is filled with great energy; he seems weak and tottering.

3. Dimmesdale stops opposite the scaffold and calls Hester and Pearl to his side. Chillingworth tries to stop him, but he pays no attention to the old physician. Then they all mount the steps of the scaffold, Hester helping Arthur (who has Pearl's hand clasped in his), with Chillingworth irresistibly drawn along behind them. Dimmesdale informs the amazed townspeople that he is Pearl's father. He stuns them by tearing away the clerical cloth around his neck and revealing his "red stigma" (an unhealed wound probably formed in the shape of the letter "A"). Then, solemnly saying farewell, Arthur Dimmesdale dies.

CHAPTER XXIV: "CONCLUSION"

The story is brought to a close as Hawthorne explains different points of view about what happened on the scaffold after the Election Sermon. Chillingworth dies, leaving a great deal of property to Pearl. Hester and Pearl leave Boston. Later Hester returns alone. She lives in the same house in which she had lived previously. Unhappy women in Boston come to her for advice. It is believed that Pearl has been married in Europe. Hester dies and is buried beside Dimmesdale.

Most of the spectators who watch and listen to Dimmesdale on the scaffold later agree that they had seen a scarlet letter on his breast. There is a variety of opinion as to how the letter came to be there. Some people believe Dimmesdale inflicted it on himself, as he daily endured torture with the knife. Others feel that the avenger, Chillingworth, had caused the letter to appear through the use of magic and drugs. Still others feel that remorse, "gnawing" from Dimmesdale's heart outward, finally appeared on the surface of his breast in the form of a scarlet letter. A few people insist that Dimmesdale had no mark on his breast and that he spoke with Hester on the scaffold, to point out to the spectators that he humbly considered himself a sinner. The moral of the story is taken from Dimmesdale's experience. It is: "Be true! Show freely to the world, if not your worst, yet some trait whereby the worst may be inferred!" After Dimmesdale's death Chillingworth loses his sense of direction. He has concentrated on revenge, and now that there can be no more revenge he loses his purpose in life. He has nothing to do. Within the year he dies, leaving Pearl a large amount of property both in America and in England. Pearl becomes "the richest heiress of her day in the New World." (Hawthorne suggests that now the child might marry into any devout Puritan family, for her money makes her very attractive.) Hester and Pearl soon leave the colony and are not heard of for a number of years. Finally, Hester reappears in Boston and takes up residence in the same little cottage she had occupied before. She even wears a scarlet letter on her breast. Pearl is not with her. People are not sure if she is alive or not, but gifts and letters come from Europe for Hester, indicating that someone of wealth has affection for her. Hester occupies a respected position in the Boston community. People bring their problems to her, particularly women unhappy in love. Hester soothes them. After many years Hester Prynne dies and is placed beside Arthur Dimmesdale in the burial ground. One tombstone serves both the lovers. How very suitable it is that the inscription (concerning a scarlet letter on a black background) should at last bring the two lovers together.

COMMENT: And so Hawthorne draws the threads of his story together, making sure that most of the reader's questions are answered. The spectators who witnessed Dimmesdale's confession on the scaffold do not all later agree as to what they have seen. Most of them agree that there was on Dimmesdale's breast a scarlet letter very much like Hester Prynne's. However, his was "imprinted in the flesh." Since people often see only what they want to see—and also believe only what they want to believe—there are different versions of this part of the tale. Some clearly saw; others definitely did not. Among those who saw, opinion is divided as to how the "red stigma" happened to appear on the minister's breast. Chillingworth has fed his whole soul on revenge. When Dimmesdale passes away, there is no longer anyone to have revenge on, so he dies within the year. He has much wealth (in property) which he wills to Pearl. Hester and Pearl disappear from Boston. In later years, Hester returns alone to her small cottage by the seashore where she again wears her scarlet letter "A" and does many good deeds and gives good advice, especially to the women who suffer in love affairs—or for lack of them. Letters and fine gifts from Europe indicate that someone there cares for Hester. On Hester's death, she is buried near Dimmesdale. The same tombstone serves both lovers.

SUMMARY: The following points are made in this concluding chapter:

1. Opinions vary as to what happened on the scaffold. Most people later agree there was some sort of a scarlet letter imprinted in Dimmesdale's flesh. People have different ideas as to how the letter arrived there. Some insist that Dimmesdale inflicted the wound upon himself. Others believe that Chillingworth "caused it to appear," by the use of magic and poisonous drugs. Still others feel that the "tooth of remorse" gnawed from Dimmesdale's guilty heart outward until it could be seen on the minister's breast. Then there are others who (due to a certain sense of loyalty toward Dimmesdale) deny "that there was any mark whatever on his breast." This group also refuses to admit that the minister had any connection with Hester Prynne's scarlet letter. (They explain that his calling Hester and Pearl to the scaffold with him was due to his great humility; he wished to point out to people that "we are sinners all alike.")

2. Hawthorne indicates that the moral of the story is based upon Arthur Dimmesdale's experience with sin and hypocrisy. The point of it is that one should be truthful about oneself and show the world at least some typical part of his sin.

3. When Dimmesdale dies, Chillingworth loses his purpose in life—revenge. Within the year, he dies, leaving much property in America and Europe to Pearl.

4. Hester and Pearl shortly disappear from the colony. Years later, Hester returns to Boston to live alone in her small cottage by the seashore. She always wears the scarlet letter "A." It is thought that Pearl has married in Europe. Hester often receives costly gifts from abroad. Hester becomes a gentle comforter to women who come to her for help, especially for advice about unhappy love affairs. Finally, Hester Prynne dies and is buried beside Arthur Dimmesdale in the burial ground near King's Chapel. Their tombstone reads: "On a field, black, the letter A, red."

Character Analyses

HESTER PRYNNE: Hester Prynne, Boston adultress, is first seen (in Chapter II) as she comes from prison. The picture we have of her is almost as if it were in the words of one of the spectators who explains what he saw to someone who had to stay at home. The reporting spectator might say: "The young woman was tall, with a figure of perfect elegance on a large scale. She had dark and abundant hair, so glossy that it threw off the sunshine with a gleam, and a face which, besides being beautiful from regularity of feature and richness of complexion, had the impressiveness belonging to a marked brow and deep black eyes. She was ladylike, too, after the manner of the feminine gentility . . . characterized by a certain state and dignity . . . And never had Hester Prynne appeared more ladylike . . . than as she issued from the prison . . . her beauty shone out. . . ." The reporter continues about her clothing, saying that it "seemed to express the attitude of her spirit, the desperate recklessness of her mood, by its wild . . . peculiarity. But the point which drew all eyes . . . was that SCARLET LETTER, so fantastically embroidered . . . upon her bosom." The excited spectator finishes off his report by explaining that Hester Prynne seemed separated from everyone by the scarlet letter "A" on her bosom. She is separated from mankind. She appears dignified—almost pridefully so—but her spirit inside droops, and her heart is filled with agony. Finding no relief from the outside world, Hester has to seek help from the inside world—the world of her memories and her imagination. Thus, depending on her thoughts, she bears up under the public indignation at her adultery.

Throughout the story, Hester generally remains silent, accepting the abuse of Puritan parent and child alike. Only when public criticism threatens her two loved ones (Pearl and Dimmesdale) does she speak up to the Boston townspeople. She defends her capability to care for Pearl when she talks with Governor Bellingham, one of the people planning to take the child from her. She speaks strongly to Chillingworth about his torturing Dimmesdale. She encourages Dimmesdale to flee the colony. She is well-known for her submissiveness, for she never complains. She nurses and aids the poor; in return, they say bitter things to her; yet she accepts it all. She sews gorgeous garments for the Boston magistrates, and she wears very plain, coarse clothing. She submits to everything—on the outside. But inside, she is a different person. She feels that she is paying for her sin of adultery by accepting the unpleasant criticism of the townspeople, as well as by wearing the scarlet letter "A" on her breast. She submits every day; but inwardly, she is not truly sorry for her sin. She is isolated from her fellow human beings; she has little left to do but to think. Think, she does. She speculates about woman's place in the world. If she were not a sinner (having lost her good name through adultery), she would very likely be a leading fighter for women's rights (feminism). She has few fears, for she has reached the bottom of the social ladder. Her one proud possession is her daughter, little Pearl, whom she dresses in brilliant colors representing her own spirit of inward resistance, although the child is the living symbol of her adultery. Since Hester is open to criticism from anyone in town, she finds she must appear unemotional. She wears her hair under a tight-fitting cap. Her natural womanly manner is completely covered. Only when she is with Pearl does she seem impulsive and warm. Otherwise, the public views her as a cold, bloodless statue. Since Hester speaks relatively little, her few remarks are well chosen and well phrased. She speaks with calm detachment when she discusses Arthur Dimmesdale with Roger Chillingworth. After the physician has left her, she does break out with one bitter remark: "I hate the man!" When Hester feels the freedom of the forest, she relaxes to some extent. Prying eyes do not observe her there. As she removes her scarlet letter "A" and lets down her long, dark hair from under her cap, she is immediately changed. Her feminine qualities, her youth, her beauty—all return to her. Then, at last, the sunshine pours down upon Hester. (The sun has always lingered around little Pearl, but it always has disappeared with the approach of Hester and her scarlet letter.) The story has a fitting ending, as one pictures Hester Prynne living to a ripe old age, always being helpful to those less fortunate than she, always consoling women whose hearts are filled with grief from unhappy love affairs—and always wearing her symbol (for "adultress" turned to "able"): the scarlet letter.

ARTHUR DIMMESDALE: Hester Prynne's guilty partner in sin, Arthur Dimmesdale, does not make his appearance in the story until well into Chapter III. He is first seen through the eyes of the crowd viewing Hester Prynne's penance on the scaffold. He is pictured as if he were being described by one of the spectators for the benefit of a watcher of short stature—one who is not tall enough to be able to see easily the impressive young minister. The running account goes something like this: The Reverend Arthur Dimmesdale is a "young clergyman . . . from one of the great English universities, bringing all of the learning of the age into our wild forest-land. . . . A person of very striking aspect, with a while, lofty . . . brow, large, brown, melancholy eyes, and a mouth . . . expressing . . . a vast power of self-restraint. . . . An air about this young minister—an apprehensive, a startled, a half-frightened look—as of a being . . . quite astray and at a loss in the pathway of human existence . . . only . . . at ease in some seclusion of his own." Arthur Dimmesdale often speaks in a voice which is "sweet, rich, deep, and broken." His message comes out through the sound of his voice, rather than through his voice. As the story progresses, Dimmesdale is very often found holding his hand over his heart. (It is very likely that he has a physical pain in the region of his heart, for in Chapter XXIII he reveals to the audience a red stigma—an unhealed wound in the form of a scarlet letter—over his heart). Gradually he becomes more careworn, and his eyes have "a world of pain in their troubled and melancholy depths." In a conversation in Chillingworth's laboratory, Dimmesdale explains (in a veiled manner) why he cannot confess his part in Hester's sin. It is because he cannot reveal his sinfulness and then be allowed to keep on doing good works for men. People would be repulsed by him; they would have no more to do with him. (This explanation is made, of course, as a reason why men—in general—do not confess their sins. Chillingworth suspects that the minister is the man he is looking for; but it is only later in the same chapter that he knows for sure, when he examines the wounded breast of the sleeping Dimmesdale.) Arthur Dimmesdale begins to feel distrustful of Roger Chillingworth, although he can find no definite reason for this feeling. Dimmesdale is very popular as a minister. One strong reason for this is his sympathy for mankind. His own sinful act has made him aware of the state of mind of the ordinary sinner. He communicates this sense of deep sympathy so that people begin to idolize him. Over and over again, he starts to confess his sin as he faces his Sunday congregation. In general terms, he speaks of his own great sin—but he always takes the coward's way out at the end of the sermon; and thus he finishes without really confessing anything. Members of his parish return home from church declaring to each other how great their own sins must be—if their sainted

Reverend Dimmesdale considers himself a sinner. Dimmesdale, the hyprocrite, eases his conscience by his midnight watches, alone in his chamber. Sometimes he scourges himself; sometimes he goes without food; and sometimes he closely examines his face in a well-lighted mirror. Since he knows himself to be a hypocrite, he is often quietly suspicious of the motives of people about him. Unable to endure his solitary guilt, in the middle of one May night he climbs the scaffold (where Hester stood in penance) and shrieks aloud—almost hoping he might be heard and discovered, and thus end his misery. He does make some progress toward his later confession, however, for he and Hester together hold little Pearl's hands, and he feels closer to the two than he has felt for some time. Later in the forest, Arthur tells Hester of his great suffering—of his remorse and the pangs of conscience which torment him. When Hester informs him that Chillingworth is his enemy, he rouses himself enough to be angry at her for not telling him sooner. Using her womanly tenderness, she gains his forgiveness. Then, the weak Dimmesdale begins to depend on the strong Hester for moral support. She persuades him that he and she (and Pearl) can flee the colony. He takes heart. Here Dimmesdale begins to make some rapid changes in his point of view. On his way home from the forest, he is tempted to speak shocking words to Puritan men, women, and children as well as to the sailors of the vessel he plans to sail on. His experience with Hester has started to free him. He is actually exhilarated. After eating a hearty meal, he writes an "inspirational sermon. Then a curious thing happens. He has received hope from Hester. He transfers this hope for the future into religious terms. On the way to deliver the Election Sermon he is so spiritually exalted that he does not even notice Hester as he passes her. (He is an important part of the procession.) Hester knows that she has helped place him in this inspirational mood. She somewhat resents his inability to acknowledge her. On the day before his departure for the Old World and a new life, Dimmesdale arrives at the high point of his religious career—the delivery of the Election Sermon. His pride causes him to want this highest of honors accorded to Puritan ministers. Very likely, his preparation for the sermon has so inspired him that he then finds the courage to confess his share of Hester Prynne's sin. After his confession he dies a happy man, in that he feels he is now acceptable in God's eyes. His hypocrisy should be forgiven (according to Puritan doctrines) because he has humbled himself and revealed his sin. Hester Prynne has won her peace of mind by being forced to submit publicly to people's harsh criticism. Dimmesdale wins his peace finally by a comparable revelation of his part in the sin.

ROGER CHILLINGWORTH: The villain of the story, Roger Chillingworth, makes his first appearance in Chapter III. He is seen by Hester Prynne when she is on the scaffold fulfilling her penance. He is described as if she were talking to herself in a hurried manner. First, she notes a "white man, clad in a strange disarray of civilized and savage costume," standing on the edge of the crowd. He is short and has a wrinkled brow. There is a "remarkable intelligence in his features." One of his shoulders rises higher than the other. He is not yet old enough to be termed "aged." For some time in the story, he is called the "stranger." Later, he takes the name "Roger Chillingworth," though he actually is Dr. Prynne (Hester's husband). In Europe he studied alchemy; in the American wilderness he has experimented with herbs used by the Indians. Thus, he is able to fit nicely into the Puritan community as a doctor. (He is sometimes referred to as the "leech.") In the prison, he tries to force Hester to tell him the name of her lover. This she will not do. He then promises vengeance on the soul of the unknown man, the father of Pearl. He says he will not prosecute Hester—he will let the scarlet letter "A" on her bosom do that for him. As time passes, Roger Chillingworth's physical appearance changes for the worse. Hester sees him at Governor Bellingham's mansion. His features have become "uglier"; his dark complexion has become "duskier"; and his figure has become even more "misshapen." After Dimmesdale offers his series of logical reasons why Pearl should not be removed from Hester's care, Chillingworth throws out his first remark to the minister, which suggests that the physician begins to suspect that the minister is the guilty man he is searching for. He says that Dimmesdale speaks "with a strange earnestness." Chapter IX, "The Leech," explains much about Chillingworth. He becomes the minister's physician. The two men spend much time together walking and talking. Chillingworth moves into the same house with Dimmesdale, and the "leech" sets up a laboratory.

In Chapter X, entitled "The Leech and His Patient," the two men are in conversation about sin and the value of confession. Subtly, the physician points out to Dimmesdale that a "false show" (hiding sin) must not be preferred to "God's own truth" (confession). At this time, little Pearl sees Chillingworth and calls him the "old Black Man." (This expression is often used for Chillingworth when Pearl speaks of him later in the tale.) When the "leech" sees Dimmesdale's breast (with the red, unhealed wound in the flesh), he resembles Satan in great joy looking at a lost soul entering his kingdom of hell. This same look of the "arch-fiend" is repeated when Chillingworth stands in the marketplace in the middle of the night, observing Pearl with her mother and father. The light of the meteor reveals Chillingworth's expression—first with a smile, then with a scowl. The physician guesses at the state of mind which sends Dimmesdale out into the night. Hypocritically, he cautions Dimmesdale about studying too many books that trouble his brain—causing him to wander about in the night. When Hester Prynne decides that she must talk with Chillingworth about Dimmesdale, she goes to meet him by the seashore. She notes that in seven years he has lost his "studious" appearance and has taken on an "eager, searching, almost fierce, yet carefully guarded look." He covers this expression "with a smile." Sometimes a "glare of red light" gleams out of his eyes. He has changed himself "into a devil" by "devoting himself to the constant analysis of a heart full of torture." He has enjoyed this analysis, gloating all the while. Telling Hester how he feels about Dimmesdale, he describes himself as a "fiend." He feels it is his "fate" to torment the minister. After he leaves Hester, she looks after him and declares aloud how she hates him, for he has done her "worse wrong" than she had done him. (She believes that he, an older man, should never have married her, a young woman.) Hester reveals to Arthur the identity of his false "friend." Then, Dimmesdale makes a dramatic statement about the fiendish Chillingworth: "That old man's revenge has been blacker than my sin. He has violated, in cold blood, the sanctity of a human heart." (Most readers agree with the minister that the sin of revenge, an act of intellectual pride, is worse than the sin of hypocrisy.) Chillingworth is last seen when, at the edge of the scaffold, he tries to prevent Dimmesdale from making a public confession. Dimmesdale calls him "tempter," declaring that he will "escape" him. When the determined minister mounts the steps of the scaffold, he is followed by Chillingworth who has been so closely "connected with the drama of guilt and sorrow" that he seems "entitled . . . to be present at its closing scene." After Dimmesdale confesses and dies, Roger Chillingworth loses his purpose in life. Within the year, Chillingworth—the avenger, the "fiend"—dies, leaving considerable property in Europe and America to Pearl. Dimmesdale, dying on the scaffold, cries out that God has shown mercy toward him, by sending Chillingworth, that "dark and terrible old man, to keep the torture always at red-heat!"

PEARL: Descriptions of little Pearl, Hester Prynne's child of sin, form a rich part of the story. With rare exception, wherever the mother is found, the child is also there. (The very first picture one has of Hester is in Chapter II, when the town official escorts her from the prison so that the townspeople might see her. Pearl is there also—"a baby of some three months old," winking and turning her little face from the bright sun.) As Pearl grows older, her mother dresses her in "fanciful" clothing of bright colors, adding to the strange charm the child already possesses. In Chapter VI, entitled "Pearl," there is a full-length picture of young Pearl. She is described as a "lovely . . . flower," having sprung from a "guilty passion." Little Pearl has beauty; she has intelligence; she has physical gracefulness. Her mother has named her Pearl, "as being of great price. . . her mother's only treasure!" If she is crossed in any way, the child flies into a passion. She obeys no rules unless she wishes to do so. Her moods change quickly. At one moment, she is wild, desperate, defiant, and filled with bad temper and gloom; then, suddenly, she can change into the sunny, happy child who wants to assure her mother of her love by kissing and caressing her. Pearl seems to have no set standard to govern her own behavior—she reacts according to her particular feeling of the moment. She has a "certain peculiar look" on her face which sometimes causes Hester to question whether or not Pearl is a "human child" or a being from another world (like a "little elf"). Her eyes are "wild, bright, deeply-black." She is described as an "imp of evil, emblem and product of sin." The Puritan children flee in fear when resentful Pearl chases after them, flinging stones and shrill words at them. (She is in as much social isolation as that in which her mother finds herself.) Once, Hester is frightened when she looks into the "mirror of Pearl's eyes." She sees a "freakish, elfish" look there; then, she believes she sees a "face, fiend-like, full of smiling malice," peeping out at her. In the headpiece of the armor in Governor Bellingham's hall, Hester is disturbed to see Pearl's expression, as it is reflected in the metal mirror. The child has an "elfish" look of "naughty merriment," as if an "imp" were "seeking to mould itself into Pearl's shape." Attracted by the brightness of her mother's scarlet letter, the three-year-old Pearl plays games, flinging wildflowers at her mother's symbol of sin. When Pearl playfully declares that she has "no Heavenly Father," Hester remembers that some of the townspeople regard Pearl as an offspring of the devil. When Pearl is seven years old, she joins hands with her mother and father on the scaffold in the middle of the night. At this time, she asks the minister if he will join hands with her mother and her in the daylight of the next day. It is Pearl who points her finger toward Roger Chillingworth, making him a part of the dramatic scene, when the meteor reveals his presence nearby. (She often acts as a linking character, connecting different combinations of people through her childlike, penetrating comments—such as her comment that her mother wears the scarlet letter for the same reason that the "minister keeps his hand over his heart.") Consider Pearl as an influence on her mother's conduct; for example, Hester without a helpless child to protect and guide might not accept her punishment quite so passively as she seems to. Sometimes Pearl is fanciful to the point that she is almost amusing. For instance, while her mother talks with Roger Chillingworth near the seashore, the imaginative child makes herself a mermaid's costume out of seaweed. Then, as a crowning touch, she gathers some eel-grass and makes for herself a green letter "A," imitating as closely as possible her mother's scarlet letter. Pearl often plays in the sunshine; whereas, in contrast to this, the sunshine will not shine directly on Hester The child is so close to nature that the little animals (in the forest scene), such as partridges, pigeons, and squirrels, almost completely ignore her when she is passing by them. They recognize a "wildness in the human child" comparable to their own. During the interview in the forest between Hester and Arthur, the mother calls Pearl to her side. The child refuses to come near her mother, because she misses the sight of the scarlet letter which Hester has cast off. Hester replaces the letter and the child joins her. (How interesting this scene is, for the child and the letter parallel each other; both represent the mother's sin—the child being a physical representation and the scarlet letter being a symbol.) During the festivities of the New England Holiday, it is Pearl who describes Dimmesdale. She remarks that in the dark nighttime and in the forest he is one type of person (friendly and loving); in the "sunny day," he is a different sort of man, for he does not know them. She remarks: "A strange, sad man is he, with his hand always over his heart!" (Pearl is a very sympathetic person in that she does sense unusual aspects of situations, such as Dimmesdale's different behavior in different places.) As the story nears its conclusion, there is little dialogue from Pearl who senses situations through intuition (that is, knowledge without reasoning). At the end of the tale, most of the threads of the plot are unraveled (Dimmesdale learns Chillingworth's true identity; Hester plans to escape with her lover and her child; Dimmesdale confesses his sin). Pearl, by instinct, has supposed some things to be true which are true. At the end of the story, the duties of Pearl, Hester's "messenger of anguish," seem to be at an end. Chillingworth has left Pearl a considerable amount of property in England and in America. She is wealthy. The close of the tale finds Pearl far from Boston (no longer with her mother), very likely happily married with a child of her own.

MINOR CHARACTERS: All of Hawthorne's works of long fiction feature four main characters—two men and two women. Although the reader often has the feeling that the story involves many people, when a list of characters is made there are found to be very few characters except the main four. (Hawthorne gives the impression of large numbers by including people in crowd scenes, such as in processions and groups of town people.) Mistress Hibbins is perhaps one of the most interesting of the minor characters in *The Scarlet Letter.* She is Governor Bellingham's "bitter-tempered sister," who a few years after the main action of the story is "executed as a witch." The "witch-lady," Mistress Hibbins, often talks of a "merry company in the forest" which meets at night with the "Black Man." Mistress Hibbins is a very specialized type of character, for she is a caricature type. (A caricature is a picture or description in which physical features, personality, or dress are so exaggerated that an absurd effect is produced.) In the matter of physical appearance, Governor Bellingham's sister looks like many other people. It is in the matter of her dress and personality (revealed through her actions) that she differs. Whenever she meets Hester Prynne, she feels called upon to invite Hester to join the Black Man and his company in the forest. Her repeated invitation forms sort of a "tag line," that is, a speech that the reader begins to associate with her. (Compare this with "tag lines" used by theatre and television actors, who identify themselves for an audience by having their own special catch-words or phrases.) Each character in the story views what he sees or hears, in the light of his own experience. In Chapter XII, when Mistress Hibbins hears Dimmesdale's cry in the night (from the scaffold), she thinks she is hearing the cries of "fiends and night-hags," with whom she is said to associate during her midnight excursions into the forest. One of the most dramatic scenes, in which the "sour and discontented" Mistress Hibbins takes part, occurs at the time when Dimmesdale returns from his forest interview with Hester (in Chapter XX). She accuses the minister of returning from a meeting with the Black Man of the forest. He explains that he has been visiting his pious friend, John Eliot (which is, to some extent, true). She answers to the effect that he lies very well. Mistress Hibbins sees Dimmesdale in the procession and confides to Hester that the pious minister in the procession is very much of a contrast with the Arthur Dimmesdale she knows who dances during the forest festivities of the Black Man. The Governor's sister points out to Hester that she (Hester) wears her scarlet letter "openly," but that Dimmesdale "seeks to hide" something, "with his hand over his heart." Another aspect of Mistress Hibbins as a caricature character is the matter of her dress—her choice of clothing. She lives among Puritan folk who by law are required to wear somber clothing. (Even the magistrates wear their rich garments only at important ceremonial occasions.) At least twice, Mistress Hibbins is seen gorgeously dressed. First, she is seen by Dimmesdale on his return from the forest. She makes a "very grand appearance; having on a high head-dress, a rich gown of velvet, and a ruff done up with . . . yellow starch." During the New England Holiday festivities, she is seen "arrayed in great magnificence, with a triple ruff, a broidered stomacher, a gown of rich velvet, and a gold-headed cane." (A "ruff" is a wheel-shaped stiff collar, worn by men and women in Puritan times; a "stomacher" is the heavily embroidered or jeweled front part of a garment worn by elaborately dressed women of Mistress Hibbins' day.) Both through her actions and her speech, Governor Bellingham's sister, Mistress Hibbins, is a caricature. She adds variety and color to the story; because her comments do not necessarily need to be logical in their content, she is allowed to react instinctively (and sometimes correctly) to the other characters.

Governor Bellingham is a minor character who represents the law. A chief magistrate, he is seen first when Hester is brought to the scaffold for her penance. He is on the balcony, surrounded by representatives of the state and church. He wears a "dark feather in his hat, a border of embroidery on his cloak, and a black velvet tunic beneath." He is a man "advanced in years, with . . . hard experience written in his wrinkles"—a man well suited to be the "head and representative" of the Boston community. (Because he is the Governor, and because he represents the authority of the community on special occasions, he is particularly elaborately dressed.) The Governor's mansion, which Hester and Pearl visit, is a spacious, stucco-covered building. The furnishings in the main hall resemble those found in houses of wealthy gentlemen in England. The suit of armor on the wall was made for Governor Bellingham the same year that he left London to come to New England. He is proud of his garden and takes pleasure in showing it off to visitors, as he does when the Reverends John Wilson and Arthur Dimmesdale and Roger Chillingworth visit him. The Governor is very interested in religious matters and feels it his duty to instruct Reverend Wilson to question Pearl closely regarding her home training in religion. When Pearl refuses to answer his questions, the Governor is greatly disturbed; he is finally satisfied when Reverend Dimmesdale explains to him that the child will be a great help in saving Hester from more sin. At the end of the story, Governor Bellingham is seen in the procession with the other magistrates. He and his fellow magistrates are described as being men of good size, physically, as well as men of "self-reliance." Governor Bellingham is a relatively kindly man of authority who represents the authority of the state, as compared with Reverends Dimmesdale and Wilson who represent the authority of the church.

The Reverend John Wilson is the oldest of the group of ministers in Boston. He is a "great scholar" and a "man of kind and genial spirit." Beneath the edge of his skullcap peeps out a "border of grizzled locks." An intelligent man, he is more used to the "shaded light of his study" than the bright sunshine of the day. His fame as a scholar has not prepared him for the problems connected with "human guilt, passion, and anguish." Reverend Wilson persuades Dimmesdale to speak to Hester on the scaffold to see if she will reveal the name of her lover. The next time Reverend Wilson is seen is when Hester goes to Governor Bellingham's mansion to protest the possibility of Pearl's being taken from her. Mr. Wilson is being shown the Governor's garden along with Dimmesdale and Chillingworth. When Pearl resists the Governor's attempts to question her, Wilson tries. He is a "grandfatherly" sort of person, being "usually a vast favorite with children." But Pearl does not respond to him. Dimmesdale saves the day (at Hester's urgent request), when he explains the role that Pearl might play in helping Hester keep free from more sin. In Chapter XII, there is a brief picture of Wilson as he walks alone in the middle of the night, lighting himself home by the rays from a "glimmering lantern." He is returning from Governor Winthrop's death bed. The last view of John Wilson is after the Election Sermon, when he offers his arm to Dimmesdale as the procession is on its way from the meetinghouse to the town hall. Dimmesdale repels the "old man's arm" and totters on alone. This last action of the "venerable" pastor is typical of him. He has always been essentially kindly and often has put out his hand to help people. In contrast to the meanness, severity, and hypocrisy of many of the Puritans, the Reverend John Wilson is a man of great mercy and kindness.

Sample Essay Questions and Answers

1. Name a few of the themes (basic ideas) Hawthorne introduces in *The Scarlet Letter* and show how he develops them.

ANSWER: (1) Basic to an understanding of this work is the knowledge that Hawthorne is not exalting and praising Puritanism and that his romance is a *detailed criticism of the Puritan way of life.* He is building up an elaborate picture to show his contempt of a society which could be so intensely intolerant of individuals and their slips from the path of virtue. The women in Chapter II (to the best of our knowledge, representative of Boston womanhood) are vicious in their criticism of Hester. They regret she is not to die—or, at least, to be branded on the forehead with a hot iron. (These women match the three witches in Shakespeare's *Macbeth* in unattractiveness of personality.) Consider Hester's good deeds to the poor (nursing and sewing); the very ones she helps generally throw bitter words in her face. (Later in her life, Hester is a respected member of the community, for the passage of time and her continued good deeds help many people to forget her sin of adultery.)

(2) To an extent, Chillingworth represents *pride of intellect.* He is a scientist-physician, proud of his achievements. When he finds Hester in her distressed condition on the scaffold, he rejects her. His pride is hurt. Here is a struggle between the head (study, reflection, and speculation) and the heart (his former affection for Hester). If he were to allow his heart to win the struggle, he might still be capable of future happiness. But, as is often the case with the scientist (says Hawthorne), he brings suffering on himself because of his disregard of the basic laws of human affection and brotherhood.

(3) A major theme in Hawthorne's works is *the evil of isolation,* that is, one's being separated from others (physically, socially, mentally or morally). Because of her sin of adultery, Hester Prynne is isolated from Boston society. She lives in a cottage separated from others in the community. She is not allowed to sew certain objects (such as new bride's veils), for her tainted hands would soil them. She has no idle chatter with others. She is either ignored or taunted by parents and children alike. But through her admission of her sin, and by her good works, she is partially redeemed and is readmitted into society. Many examples could be cited to point out the isolation of Dimmesdale (secretly suffering with remorse and a bad conscience) and Chillingworth (eagerly pursuing the victim of his revenge). Even little Pearl (the product of the sin which has caused the various types of isolation) is isolated, not only from other children, but also from her mother (to a great extent) and from her father (until near the end of the story).

(4) Guilt which is admitted openly, such as Hester's daily wearing of her scarlet symbol, eventually is cleansed out of the system. *Guilt which is hidden* (such as Dimmesdale's) succeeds only in exciting remorse, a bad case of conscience, and eventual hypocrisy. The Puritan belief in confession as a means of purifying the soul applies here. Hester's wearing of the letter is a daily confession. She suffers less and less as time goes on. People begin to forget her past difficulties. In contrast to this, Dimmesdale has not confessed, and his troubled conscience bothers him almost as much as the "red stigma" (unhealed wound on his breast) over which he often places his hand. Actually, Hester's wearing the scarlet letter does not make her truly regretful of her sin (as it is supposed to do). It only makes her submissive, and the Puritan community is happy and contented that it has the upper hand over her. In like fashion, Dimmesdale's "red stigma" represents his deep regret for the sin, but it is not a proper substitute for public confession.

2. Show how Hawthorne in *The Scarlet Letter* uses names of people who actually live to give added meaning to his story.

ANSWER: Two of the characters who appear in the story did live in Boston in the 1640s and 1650s. They are the Reverend John Wilson and Governor Bellingham. Hawthorne identifies John Wilson as "the eldest clergyman of Boston, a great scholar . . . and withal a man of kind and genial spirit." Colonial histories help support this complimentary picture of the famous clergyman. He and Arthur Dimmesdale are fellow workers in the area of religion. Hawthorne's romance, half-way between the worlds of reality and imagination, thus has one fine example of reality (Wilson) placed beside an unusual creation of the imagination (Dimmesdale). The other character who actually lived in Boston is Governor Bellingham. The Boston community is ruled by a combination of the church (Wilson, Dimmesdale, and the other ministers) and the state (the magistrates, especially Governors Bellingham and Winthrop). (This is called a theocratic state.)

Five individuals are merely mentioned in the story, but each adds a special flavor of his own to the tale. They are Anne Hutchinson, Governor Winthrop, John Eliot, and Sir Thomas Overbury and his contemporary, Ann Turner. The use of Anne Hutchinson's name at the end of the first chapter foreshadows (looks forward toward) certain aspects of Hester Prynne later in the novel. Anne Hutchinson, who disturbed the Puritan authorities a few years before Hester Prynne's time, was an early feminist—a fighter for women's rights. Hester, occupying the same prison which had once confined Anne Hutchinson, throughout the story—and especially in the next to last paragraph of the work—is concerned with a "new truth" about the "relation between man and woman." The early mention of Anne Hutchinson prepares our minds for the kind of woman Hester might have developed into—if she had not been forced to wear the scarlet letter. Governor Winthrop is not seen in the story, but the fact that the seven-year-old Pearl has been with her mother at his deathbed helps us decide the definite date of the beginning of the novel. He died in 1649. Hester first stands on the scaffold in 1642. Hester came to America in 1640, two years before this time.

Actually the Apostle Eliot also lived at this time. Dimmesdale told Mistress Hibbins he had been to see him in the forest. (Hawthorne admired some of Cotton Mather's writings concerning Puritan days. Mather wrote a fine biographical sketch of John Eliot, Apostle to the Indians, in his *Magnalia Christi Americana.*) Anne Turner, the "especial friend" of Mistress Hibbins (mentioned in Chapter XX), had taught the witch-lady the secret of doing up the ruff around her neck with yellow starch. Ann was hanged "for Sir Thomas Overbury's murder." (There was a famous trial in England over the death of Overbury in 1613.) Following the old maxim that "birds of a feather flock together," one sees another aspect of Mistress Hibbins' already darkened personality-she is the "especial friend" of a murderess.

3. Hawthorne probably used more mirrors for literary purposes than anyone else in American literature. Point out the mirrors in "The Custom House" and *The Scarlet Letter* and suggest briefly how several of them are used.

ANSWER: (1) "*The Custom House*": Hawthorne remembers his dreary days in the Salem Custom House: "My imagination was a tarnished mirror." The "fire" produces a "*reflected gleam* from the polish of the furniture." "Glancing at the *looking-glass*, we behold . . . the smouldering glow of the half-extinguished anthracite, the white moonbeams on the floor . . . with one remove further from the actual, and nearer to the imagination." (The last sentence is a part of Hawthorne's theory of romance.) *Chapter II*: Hester, on the scaffold, remembers "her own face . . . illuminating all the interior of the *dusky mirror* in which she had been wont to gaze at it." *Chapter VI*: Hester sees in little Pearl a "shadowy *reflection* of the evil . . . in herself." Hester looks at "*her own image*" in the eyes of Pearl; then she sees "another face, in the *small black mirror* of Pearl's eye." *Chapter VII:* Pearl looks into the "*polished mirror of the breastplate*" of the suit of armor in Governor Bellingham's hall.

Hester looks, and she sees that, "owing to the peculiar effect of this *convex mirror,* the scarlet letter" is "represented in exaggerated and gigantic proportions. . . ." (The rounded-out mirrored surface creates a strange, exaggerated effect.) Pearl's "look of naughty merriment" is "likewise *in the mirror*" of the headpiece of the suit of armor. *Chapter XI*: Often at night, Dimmesdale views "his own face in a *looking glass,*" by the "most powerful light" that he can throw upon it. (This is suggestive of his constant searching within himself—examining his bad conscience.) Sometimes "visions" would "flit before him . . . within the *looking glass.*" *Chapter XIV*: Pearl peeps "curiously into a pool, left by the retiring tide as a *mirror* . . . to see her face in." There peeps at her "out of the pool . . . the image of a little maid," whom Pearl invites "to take her hand, and run a race with her." This scene helps further accent Pearl's "elfish" personality. Beside the seashore, Chillingworth describes to Hester how he has tortured Dimmesdale. "The unfortunate physician, while uttering these words," lifts "his hands with a look of horror," as if he is viewing "some frightful shape," that he cannot recognize, "usurping the place of his own *image in a glass.*" (This is an instance of self-revelation through the mirror image.) *Chapter XV*: At the edge of the seashore, Pearl flirts "fancifully with her own *image in a pool of water,* beckoning the phantom forth." Finding that "either she or the image" is unreal," she turns to other activities. *Chapter XVI*: In the forest, Hester and Pearl watch the "*reflected light*" on the surface of the water. They wonder if the "old forest" might "*mirror*" its strange tales "on the smooth surface of a pool." *Chapter XIX*: While Pearl waits for her mother and Dimmesdale to talk in the forest, she stands by the brook which chances "to form a pool, so smooth and quiet" that "*reflected*" in the still water is a "*perfect image of her figure* . . . but more refined and spiritualized than the reality." The "*image*" seems "to communicate somewhat of its own shadowy and intangible quality to the child itself." When Pearl points her finger toward Hester's breast, where the scarlet letter has been, there, "beneath, in the *mirror of the brook,*" is the "*image* of little Pearl, pointing her small forefinger too." Pearl becomes angry. "In the brook, . . . is the fantastic beauty of the *image,* with *its reflected frown, its pointed finger, and imperious gesture,* giving emphasis to the aspect of little Pearl." Then Pearl bursts into a "fit of passion," and "in the brook, once more," is the "shadowy wrath of Pearl's *image.*" (Hester, disturbed at Pearl's behavior, is upset at seeing both the child and her fantastic reflection.) *Chapter XXI*: The festivities of the "New England Holiday" are a "*dim reflection of a remembered splendor.*" The activities centering around "the annual installation of magistrates" do not really compare with the magnificent displays in London at a "Lord Mayor's show."

4. Describe various aspects of Puritanism pictured in *The Scarlet Letter.*

ANSWER: Hawthorne is very much concerned with the intolerance and bigotry of his Puritan ancestors. In *The Scarlet Letter,* he creates characters and situations to help project his complex and ambiguous point of view about Puritan Boston. The story is set in the 1640s and 1650s during the relatively early years of the Boston colony. The early Puritans believe in a Trinity with absolute power, controlling everything. Man has no real decisions to make concerning the world around him, for God—at His whim—will completely decide for him. There is hope through the sacrifice of the Christ. But not all people are to be saved. The Doctrine of the Elect states that God chooses some for heaven—and, in the same manner, allows others to go to hell. One does not exactly know if he is destined for heaven, but generally—as in the case of Dimmesdale, the highly reputable Boston minister—there is a strong feeling that some sainted individuals are certainly fated to go heavenward. In *The Scarlet Letter,* part of Dimmesdale's torture is his knowledge of his own sin, which, unconfessed, will keep him from heaven. Faithfulness between husband and wife is important. Certainly a woman destined for heaven would never commit adultery (as Hester Prynne does). She could not do so if she wished to, because her conduct is determined ahead of time. Then too, Hester and Arthur's actions are affected by predestination. Since Adam and Eve, man has lost the power to make decisions for himself, for, through "original sin" (disobedience to God's will in the Garden of Eden), man has lost the power of free will. God the Absolute makes all the decisions. Near the end of Chapter XIV, Chillingworth says to Hester that, since her "first step" in the wrong direction, "it has all been a dark necessity. . . . It has been our fate." He refers to the consequences of her action. Hester's disobedience to God's will is her act of adultery, a fearful word in Puritan days, for this act (against fidelity in marriage) endangers the very basis and strength of Puritan life. The Puritans are intolerant of anything they consider to be evil. Their community, Boston, is an experiment which the Christian world is watching with interest—so intolerance of evil must be their watchword. Hester is forced to openly accept her shame. Dimmesdale, her lover, is able to avoid public shame, but he cannot avoid great suffering, due to the awareness he has of his own hypocrisy—his own unworthiness. Another aspect of Puritan thought is the source of God's will. It is in the Bible (the Scriptures). The Puritans distrust nature as a guide for behavior. (Hester and Dimmesdale feel free in the forest during their talk.) University trained clergymen (such as Dimmesdale and Wilson from Cambridge, England) are highly respected, for they are well able to interpret the meaning of the Bible. (Note the contrasting effect of the Biblical scenes in the tapestry in Dimmesdale's apartment. David, Bathsheba, and Nathan the Prophet are not exactly representative of the Chrisitan virtues of fidelity emphasized by the Puritans.) The Puritan belief that man is saved by faith, rather than by works, is seen in *The Scarlet Letter*. Over and over again, Hester aids those around her who need help. She especially makes great efforts to nurse and sew for the poor. Often this group repays her by taunting her with bitter words. In the official estimation of the Puritans, Hester has not advanced her standing any by helping others. Actually, over a period of time, she has been able to reclaim much of her good name, for people finally begin to interpret her scarlet letter "A" as meaning "A" for "Able" (or even "Angel"). The Puritans believe in the value of confession. The first members of the Boston Puritan church are required to make a public acknowledgment of their sins. (Later, the new members of the Puritan group are allowed to confess their sins in the privacy of the minister's study.) How Hester's scarlet symbol must delight her viewers, for she is constantly confessing to the world by displaying her letter of adultery! How unattractive to Dimmesdale must confession be! He can work himself into an emotional state in which he feels that at any moment he may confess (such as his humiliation in the pulpit, or his scream for attention on the scaffold in the middle of the night). But, having relieved his conscience to some extent by these long preparations, he then retreats from actually telling his sin. His hidden sin burns inside his breast. This remorse is intensified by the goading of Chillingworth, who has no real wish to reveal Dimmesdale as a sinner to his congregation. His wish is to torture him with thoughts of public shame if the sin is discovered. Another angle of importance is the strong Puritan distrust in decisions reached only by the head; the Puritans feel the necessity of understanding being a result of spontaneous decision coming from the heart. Notice that Dimmesdale's great popularity as a speaker stems form his wonderful ability to excite the imagination, to fire the enthusiasm, of his hearers. Dimmesdale does not appeal solely to the mind—his greatest sermons speak to the heart. One sin strongly condemned by the Puritans is intellectual pride, the cause of Adam's fall and all our woe. How they admire the humility of Dimmesdale when from his pulpit he begins to paint a picture of himself as a miserable sinner! His unfinished confession causes them to exalt him and to examine over again their own many failings. One very important aspect of Puritan society is its form of government—the theocratic state. In Boston, the church is so very important that it shares authority with the state in governing the colony. This procedure is based upon the social order described in the Old Testament. Scholarly, university trained ministers (such as the Reverend John Wilson and the Reverend Arthur Dimmesdale) interpret the Scriptures. The principle is the same as that established for the ancient Biblical Covenant which assured obedience to properly elected leaders. These leaders could be displaced if they were unworthy. In the procession before the Election Sermon, Reverend Arthur Dimmesdale walks in the place of honor. His sermon is the high point of the entire "New England Holiday." Hawthorne chooses a wonderful method of showing his distrust of the Puritan way of life. He creates one of his major characters (Dimmesdale) as not only a highly respected member of the Puritan community, but as a weak and suffering hypocrite.

(Continued)

(Continued)

MACHIAVELLI - The Prince
MARLOWE - Dr. Faustus
Marxist & Utopian Socialists
MELVILLE - Billy Budd
MELVILLE - Moby Dick
MILLER - The Crucible/A View from the Bridge
MILLER - Death of a Salesman
MILTON - Paradise Lost
MORE - Utopia
MORRISON - Beloved
Mythology
The New Testament
NIETZSCHE - The Philosophy
The Old Testament as Living Literature
O'NEILL - Long Day's Journey into Night
O'NEILL - The Plays
ORWELL - Animal Farm
ORWELL - 1984
PATON - Cry the Beloved Country
PLATO - The Republic and Selected Dialogues
POE - Tales and Poems
POPE - Rape of the Lock & Poems
RAWLINGS - The Yearling
REMARQUE - All Quiet on the Western Front
Rousseau & the 18th Century Philosophers
SALINGER - Catcher in the Rye
SALINGER - Franny & Zooey
SARTRE - No Exit/The Flies
SCOTT - Ivanhoe

SHAKESPEARE - Antony and Cleopatra
SHAKESPEARE - As You Like It
SHAKESPEARE - Hamlet
SHAKESPEARE - Henry IV, Part 1
SHAKESPEARE - Henry IV, Part 2
SHAKESPEARE - Henry V
SHAKESPEARE - Julius Caesar
SHAKESPEARE - King Lear
SHAKESPEARE - Macbeth
SHAKESPEARE - The Merchant of Venice
SHAKESPEARE - A Midsummer Night's Dream
SHAKESPEARE - Othello
SHAKESPEARE - Richard II
SHAKESPEARE - Richard III
SHAKESPEARE - Romeo and Juliet
SHAKESPEARE - Selected Comedies
SHAKESPEARE - Sonnets
SHAKESPEARE - The Taming of the Shrew
SHAKESPEARE - The Tempest
SHAKESPEARE - A Winter's Tale
SHAKESPEARE - Twelfth Night

SHAW - Major Plays
SHAW - Pygmalion
SHAW- Saint Joan
SINCLAIR - The Jungle
Sir Gawain and the Green Knight
SKINNER - Walden Two
SOLZHENITSYN - One Day in the Life of Ivan Denisovich
SOPHOCLES - The Plays
SPENSER - The Faerie Queene
STEINBECK - The Grapes of Wrath
STEINBECK - Major Works
STEINBECK - Of Mice and Men
STEINBECK - The Pearl/Red Pony
SWIFT - Gulliver's Travels
THACKERAY - Vanity Fair/Henry Esmond
THOREAU - Walden
TOLKEIN - Fellowship of the Ring
TOLSTOY - War and Peace
TURGENEV - Fathers and Sons
TWAIN - Huckleberry Finn
TWAIN - Tom Sawyer
UPDIKE - Rabbit Run/Rabbit Redux
VIRGIL - The Aeneid
VOLTAIRE - Candide/The Philosophies
VONNEGUT - Slaughterhouse Five
WALKER - The Color Purple
WAUGH - Major Works
WELLS - Invisible Man/War of the Worlds
WHARTON - Ethan Frome
WHITMAN - Leaves of Grass
WILDE - The Plays
WILDER - Our Town/Bridge of San Luis Rey
WILLIAMS - The Glass Menagerie
WILLIAMS - Major Plays
WILLIAMS - A Streetcar Named Desire
WOLFE - Look Homeward, Angel/Of Time and the River
WOOLF - Mrs. Dalloway/To the Lighthouse
WORDSWORTH - The Poetry
WRIGHT - Native Son
YEATS - The Poetry
ZOLA - Germinal